MARKETING MANA

MARKETING MANAGEMENT

S. Ramesh

Professor & Dean
Faculty of Commerce & Management Studies
Post Graduate Centre, Mount Carmel Autonomous College
Bangalore, Karnataka

C.S. Jayanthi Prasad

Associate Professor
School of Management Studies
Jaya Prakash Narayan College of Engineering
Dharmapur - Mahabubnagar (Dist.) - 509 001
Andhra Pradesh

I.K. International Publishing House Pvt. Ltd.

NEW DELHI • BANGALORE

Published by

I.K. International Publishing House Pvt. Ltd.
S-25, Green Park Extension
Uphaar Cinema Market
New Delhi – 110 016 (India)
E-mail: info@ikinternational.com
Website: www.ikbooks.com

ISBN 978-93-81141-86-1

© 2012 I.K. International Publishing House Pvt. Ltd.

10 9 8 7 6 5 4 3 2 1

Published by Krishan Makhijani for I.K. International Publishing House Pvt. Ltd., S-25, Green
Park Extension, Uphaar Cinema Market, New Delhi – 110 016 and Printed by Rekha Printers
Pvt. Ltd., Okhla Industrial Area, Phase II, New Delhi – 110 020.

Preface

The significance of Marketing hardly needs any emphasis today as we march towards virtually a global economy. Marketing function is undergoing a transformational change from segmentation to consolidation, new products to new markets, service extension to service precision, customer advantage to competitive advantage, competition to cooperation, product life cycle to customer life cycle, consumerisation to consumer education, brand extension to brand equity, selling products to selling concepts, monologue to dialogue, consumer extension to consumer retention, product innovation to product redefinition which is unprecedented in the heart of a revolution that questions the very foundation of Marketing.

This revolution which is long overdue challenges the definition, direction and future of the marketing function and offers an exciting opportunity to restore marketing to the art of driving business results based on the science of understanding and adding value to current, future, felt and latent needs of customers. The need of the hour is building customer loyalty as more companies look to capture and maintain strong relationships with not only high-value customers but also with each and every segment, to derive the long-term strategic benefits which far exceed the costs.

These developments have compelled marketers to think of new techniques, methods, practices and strategies to not only find new markets and new consumers but also in engaging and retaining the existing markets and existing consumers. It is in fulfilling this felt need that we introduce this book which is presented in a simple language, lucid style easy and logical flow in different chapters beginning with basic marketing followed by all the ingredients of the marketing mix and latest concepts and developments. At the end of every chapter summary, cases and review questions have been provided. We are sure that this book will fulfill the needs of commerce and management students preparing for university and professional courses, teachers, practising marketing professionals and researchers.

We thank Sri. C.S. Rama Kanth, Sri. K.S. Ravikumar, Sri. V. Venkat Rama Rao, Smt. Vijaya Laxmi, Mrs. Ragini, Ms. Anu Sri, Mr. Abhiram and family members, Dr. H. Muralidharan, Mr. Jayaprakash, Sri. Govinda Gowda, Sri. K.S. Ravi Kumar, Dr. Subhash Kulkarni and all others who directly or indirectly helped us in our endeavour. Our sincere thanks to I.K. International Publishing House Specially the Chairman Sri. Krishan Makhijani, Director Sri. Vrajesh Makhijani and Deputy General Manager Sri. V.R. Babu, for Motivating us and Publishing this Book. Finally we thank our colleagues and students for their encouragement and support.

Authors

MARKETING

MARKETING	:	Activity
MARKETIN	:	Every Market say Welcome
MARKETI	:	Every Market say I the Leader
MARKE	:	Representation of a Concern
MARK	:	Trademark, Symbol
MAR	:	To Improve the Things
MA	:	All together
M	:	Money, Materials, Men & Women, Machines so on........

CONTENTS

7. Marketing Communication and Promotional Strategies   399

MARKETING AND ITS ENVIRONMENT

STRUCTURE

1.1   INTRODUCTION

Different people with different objectives would like to learn marketing. However, marketing, as you will soon see, is important whether you are in marketing function or any other function of a business. Besides, marketing is a very exciting and competitive field. It requires more and more intellectual creativity process to make it success. Thus, you have embarked on the study of an exciting subject which can also increase your innovative thinking. It is presumed that such knowledge about marketing decisions and processes will not only improve your personal competence but will also help in attaining your organisational objectives.

1.2   MEANING OF MARKETING

In USA, so many administrators were asked about the meaning of marketing. As many of them said that marketing is selling, advertising and public relations. It is no wonder that the Americans are bombarded with TV commercials, newspaper advertising, sales calls, etc.

Even in India when you ask any manager this kind of question, the majority of them give similar reply. It is important to understand that marketing is much more than selling or advertising, although these do form part of the marketing functions.

1.2.1   Social Definition

Marketing is a societal process by which individuals and groups obtain what they need and want through creating, offering and freely exchanging products and services of value with others.

1.2.2   Management Definition

It is the process of planning and executing the conception, pricing, promotion and distribution of ideas, goods and services to create exchanges that satisfy individual and organisational goals. So many eminent scholars have quoted the marketing term as:

> *"Marketing is a societal process by which individuals and groups obtain what they need and want through creating, offering and freely exchanging products and services of value with others."*
>
> — *Philip Kotler*

> *"Marketing is the preference of business activities that directs the flow of goods and services from producer to consumer or user."*   —*American Marketing Association*

"Marketing consists of all activities by which a company adapts itself to its environment creatively and profitably."

— *Ray Corey*

"Marketing is so basic that it cannot be considered a separate function. It is the whole business seen from the point of view of its final result, that is, from the customer's point of view... Business success is not determined by the producer but by the customer."

— *Peter Drucker*

1.3 SCOPE OF MARKETING

The scope of marketing, i.e., modern marketing, is very wide. It includes all those activities which are involved in discovering the present and potential requirements of consumers for goods and services and in ensuring the flow of those goods and services from the producers to the final consumers.

Marketing covers a number of activities. They are:

   (a) Buying and assembling
   (b) Selling
   (c) Transportation
   (d) Storage and warehousing
   (e) Standardisation and grading
   (f) Financing or supply of capital
   (g) Risk-bearing
   (h) Market research
   (i) Advertising
   (j) Personal selling and
   (k) Sales promotion

1.4 IMPORTANCE AND CORE CONCEPTS OF MARKETING

1.4.1 Importance of Marketing

Marketing is a very important aspect in business since it contributes greatly to the success of the organization. Production and distribution depend largely on marketing. Many people think that sales and marketing are basically the same. These two concepts are different in many aspects. Marketing covers advertising, promotions, public relations, and sales. It is the process of introducing and promoting the product or service into the market and encourages sales from the buying public. Sales refer to the act of buying or the actual transaction of customers purchasing the product or service. Since the goal of marketing is to make the product or service widely known and recognised to the market, marketers must be creative in their marketing activities. In this competitive nature of many businesses, getting the product noticed is not that easy. Strategically, the business must be centred on the customers more than the products.

Although good and quality products are also essential, the buying public still has its personal preferences. If you target more of their needs, they will come back again and again and even bring along recruits. If you push more on the product and disregard their wants and the benefits they can get, you will lose your customers in no time. The sad thing is that getting them back is the hardest part.

Marketing Promotes Product Awareness to the Public

It has already been mentioned in the previous paragraph that getting the product or service recognised by the market is the primary goal of marketing. No business possibly ever thought of just letting the people find out about the business themselves, unless you have already established a reputation in the industry. But if you are a start-out company, the only means to be made known is to advertise and promote. Your business may be spending on the advertising and promotional programmes but the important thing is that product and company information is disseminated to the buying public. Various types of marketing approaches can be utilised by an organization. All forms of marketing promote product awareness to the market at large. Offline and online marketing make it possible for the people to be educated with the various products and services that they can take advantage. A company must invest in marketing so as not to miss the opportunity of being discovered. If expense is to be considered, there are cost-effective marketing techniques a company can embark on such as pay-per-click ads and blogging.

Marketing Helps Boost Product Sales

Apart from public awareness about a company's products and services, marketing helps boost sales and revenue growth. Whatever your business is selling, it will generate sales once the public learns about your product through TV advertisements, radio commercials, newspaper ads, online ads, and other forms of marketing. The more people hear and see more of your advertisements, the more they will be interested to buy. If your company aims to increase the sales percentage and double the production, the marketing department must be able to come up with effective and strategic marketing plans.

Marketing Builds Company Reputation

In order to conquer the general market, marketers aim to create a brand name recognition or product recall. This is a technique for the consumers to easily associate the brand name with the images, logo, or caption that they hear and see in the advertisements. For example, McDonalds is known for its arch design which attracts people and identifies the image as McDonalds. For some companies, building a reputation to the public may take time but there are those who easily attract the people. With an established name in the industry, a business continues to grow and expand because more and more customers will purchase the products or take advantage of the services from a reputable company.

Marketing plays an essential role in the success of a company. It educates people on the latest market trends, helps boost a company's sales and profit, and develops company reputation. But marketers must be creative and wise enough to promote their products with the proper marketing tactics. Although marketing is important, if it is not conducted and researched well, the company might just be wasting on expenses and time on a failed marketing approach.

Marketing has been defined in various ways, which are expressed above. We like the following definition of marketing.

Marketing is a social and managerial process by which individuals and groups obtain what they need and want through creating, offering, and exchange products of value with others.

This definition of marketing rests on the following core concepts: needs, wants, and demands; products; value, cost, and satisfaction; exchange, transactions, and relationships; markets; and marketing and marketers. This is illustrated in Fig. 1.1:

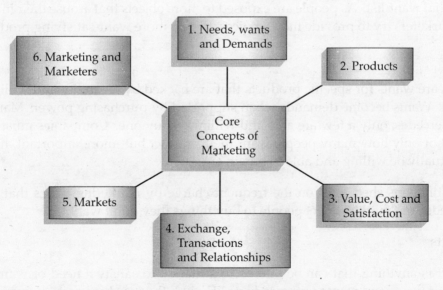

Fig. 1.1 Core concepts of marketing.

1.4.2   Core Concepts of Marketing

1. Needs, Wants and Demands

Marketing thinking starts with the fact of human needs and wants. People need food, air, water, clothing, and shelter to survive. Beyond this, people have a strong desire for education, and other services. They have strong preferences for particular versions and brands of basic goods and services.

A useful distinction can be drawn between needs, wants and demands.

Need

The most basic concept underlying marketing is that of human needs. A need is a state of felt deprivation. It is a part of the human makeup. Humans have many needs, viz., physical needs, social needs, spiritual needs, and so on.

Wants

Wants are the form taken by needs as they are shaped by the one's culture and personality. Wants are thus shaped by both the internal and external factors. Wants are described in terms of objects that will satisfy needs. For example, thirst is a need. To quench this thirst, a person may consider a number of options–drink water or a soft drink or a fruit juice. These objects (which represent the different choices for a person to fulfil his/her need) comprise the potential want-list. As people are exposed to more objects that arouse their interest and desire, marketers try to provide more choices, that is, more want-satisfying products.

Demands

Demands are wants for specific products that are backed by an ability and willingness to buy them. Wants become demands when supported by purchasing power. Many people want a Mercedes; only a few are able and willing to buy one. Companies must therefore measure not only how many people want their product but, more important, how many would actually be willing and able to buy it.

These distinctions shed light on the frequent charge by marketing critics that "markets create needs" or "marketers get people to buy things they don't want."

2. Products

A product is anything that can be offered to a market to satisfy a need or want. People satisfy their needs and wants with products. Though the word suggests a physical object, the concept of product is not limited to physical objects. Marketers often use the expressions goods and services to distinguish between physical products and intangible ones. These goods and services can represent cars, groceries, computers, places, persons and even ideas. Customers decide which entertainers to watch on television, which places to visit for a holiday, which ideas to adopt for their problems, and so on. Thus, the term 'product' covers physical goods, services and a variety of other vehicles that can satisfy customers needs and wants. If at times the term 'product' does not seem to be appropriate, other terms such as market offering, satisfier are used.

3. Value, Cost and Satisfaction

When the customers have so many choices to choose from to satisfy a particular need, how do they choose from among these many products? They make their buying choices based on their perceptions of a product's value. The guiding concept is customer value. A customer will estimate the capacity of each product to satisfy his need. He/she might rank the products from the most need-satisfying to the least need-satisfying. Of course, the ideal product is the one which gives all the benefits at zero cost, but no such product exists. Still, the customer will value each existing product according to how close it comes to his/her ideal product and end up choosing the product that gives the most benefit for the rupee–the greatest value.

$$\text{Value} = \frac{\text{Benefits}}{\text{Costs}}$$

$$\text{Benefits} = \text{Functional benefits} + \text{Emotional benefits}$$

$$\text{Costs} = \text{Monetary costs} + \text{Time} + \text{Energy} + \text{Psychic costs}$$

4. Exchange, Transactions and Relationships

The fact that people have needs and wants and can place value on products does not fully define marketing. Exchange is one of the four ways people can obtain products.

1. **The first way is self-production:** People can relieve hunger through hunting, fishing, or fruit gathering. They need not interact with anyone else. In this case, there is no market and no marketing.
2. **The second way is coercion:** Hungry people can wrest or steal food from others. No benefit is offered to others except that of not being harmed.
3. **The third way is begging:** Hungry people can approach others and beg for food. They have nothing tangible to offer except gratitude.
4. **The fourth way is exchange:** Hungry people can approach others and offer a resource in exchange, such as money, other goods, or a service.

Marketing arises from this last approach to acquiring products. Exchange is the act of obtaining a desired product from someone by offering something in return. Exchange is defined concept underlying marketing.

For exchange to take place, five conditions must be satisfied.

1. **There should be at least two parties.**
2. **Each party has something be of value to the other party.**
3. **Each party is capable of communication and delivery.**
4. **Each party is free to accept or reject the offer.**
5. **Each party believes it is appropriate or desirable to deal with the other party.**

If these conditions exist, there is a potential for exchange. Whether exchange actually takes place depends upon whether the two parties can agree on terms of exchange that will leave them both better off (or at least not worse off) than before the exchange.

Exchange must be seen as a process rather than as an event. Two parties are said to be engaged in exchange if they are negotiating and moving toward an agreement. If an agreement is reached, we say that a transaction takes place.

A **transaction** consists of a trade of values between two parties. We must be able to say A gave X to B and received Y in return. Jones gave $400 to Smith and obtained a television set. This is a classic monetary transaction.

A transaction involves several dimensions: at least two things of value, agreed-upon conditions, a time of agreement, and a place of agreement.

A transaction differs from a transfer. In a transfer, A gives X to B but does not receive anything tangible in return. When A gives B a gift, subsidy, or a charitable contribution, we call this a transfer, not a transaction. Marketers have recently broadened the concept of marketing to include the study of transfer behaviour as well as transaction behaviour. In the most generic sense, the marketer is seeking to elicit a behavioural response from another party. A business firm wants a response called a joining; (a social-action group wants a response to some object from target audience).

Relationship is building long-term mutually satisfying relations with customers, suppliers, distributors in order to retain their long-term preference and business.

5. Markets

A market consists of all the potential customers sharing a particular need or want who might be willing and able to engage in exchange to satisfy that need or want.

Originally, the term market stood for the place where buyers and sellers gathered to exchange their goods, such as a village square. In economics, the term market to refers to a collection of buyers and sellers who transact over a particular product or product class, hence housing market, the grain market, and so on. The relationship between the industry and market are shown below in the Fig. 1.2.

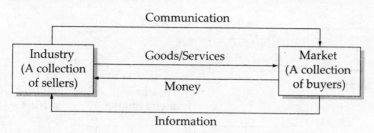

Fig. 1.2 A simple marketing systems.

The sellers and the buyers are connected by flows. The seller sends goods and services and communications to the market; in return they receive money and information. The inner loop shows an exchange of money for goods; the outer loop shows an exchange of information. Business people use the term markets colloquially to cover various groupings of customers. They talk about need market (such as the diet seeking market); product market (such as the shoe market); demographic market (such as the youth market); and geographic market (such as French market). Or they extend the concept to cover non-customer groupings as well, such as voter market, labour market and donor market.

6. Marketing and Marketers

The concept of markets brings us full circle to the concept of marketing means human activity taking place in relation to markets. Marketing means working with market to actualise potential exchanges for the purpose of satisfying human needs and wants.

If one party is more actively seeking an exchange than the other party, we call the first party a marketer and the second party as a prospect. A marketer is someone seeking a resource from someone else and willing to offer something of value in exchange.

The marketer, in other words, can be a seller or a buyer. Suppose several persons want to buy an attractive house that has just become available. Each prospective buyer will try to market himself or herself to be the one the seller selects. These buyers are doing marketing! In the event that both parties actively seek an exchange, we say that both of them are marketers and call the situation one of reciprocal marketing.

The company and the competitors send their respective products and messages directly and or through marketing intermediaries to the end-users. Their relative effectiveness is influenced by their respective suppliers as well as major environmental factors. Fig. 1.3 represents the main elements in a modern marketing system.

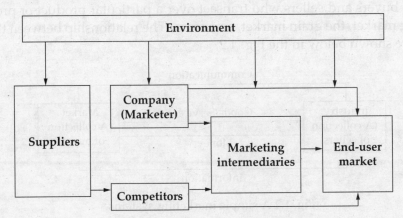

Fig. 1.3 Modern marketing system.

Marketing Management

According to American Marketing Association.

Marketing (Management) is the process of planning and executing the conception, pricing, promotion, and distribution of goods, services, and ideas to create exchange with target groups that satisfy customer and organisational objectives.

Marketing management involves all the key functions such as planning, analysing, implementation, and control. And the goal is to produce satisfaction for the parties involved.

Marketing management can occur in an organisation in connection with any of its markets. Consider an automobile manufacturer. The vice-president of personnel deals with labour market. The vice-president of purchasing deals with the raw materials market, and the vice-president of finance deals with the money market. They must set the objectives and develop strategies for achieving satisfactory results in these markets. Marketing work in the customer market is formally carried out by sales managers, salespeople, advertising and promotion managers, marketing researchers, customer service managers, product and brand managers, and the marketing vice-president. Each job carries well-defined tasks and responsibilities. On the other hand, product managers, market managers, and the marketing vice president manage programmes. Their job is to analyse, plan, and implement programmes that will produce a desired level and mix of transactions with target markets.

Marketing managers cope with these tasks by carrying out marketing research, planning, implementation, and control. Within marketing planning, marketers must make a decision on target markets, market positioning, product development, pricing, distribution channels, physical distribution, communication, and promotion.

Evolution of Marketing

As noted earlier, exchange is the origin of marketing activity. When people need to exchange goods, they naturally begin a marketing effort. **Wroe Alderson**, a leading marketing theorist has pointed out, 'It seems altogether reasonable to describe the development of exchange as a great invention which helped to start primitive man on the road to civilisations. Production is not meaningful until a system of marketing has been established. An adage goes as: Nothing happens until somebody sells something. Although marketing has always been a part of business, its importance has varied greatly over the years. Table 1.1 identifies five eras in the history of marketing: the production era, the product era, the sales era, the marketing era and the relationship marketing era.

In the production era, the production orientation dominated business philosophy. Indeed business success was often defined solely in terms of production victories. The focus was on production and distribution efficiency. The drive to achieve economies of scale was dominant. The goal was to make the product affordable and available to the buyers.

Table 1.1 Evaluation of marketing

Era	Prevailing attitude and approach
Production	Consumers favour products that are available and highly affordable
	☞ Improve production and distribution
	☞ Availability and affordability is what the customer wants
Product	Consumers favour products that offer the most quality, performance and innovative features
	☞ A good product will sell itself
Sales	Consumers will buy products only if the company promotes/sells these products
	☞ Creative advertising and selling will overcome consumers resistance and convince them to buy
Marketing	Focuses on needs/wants of target markets and delivering satisfaction better than competitors
	☞ The consumer is king! Find a need and fill it
Relationship marketing	Focuses on needs/wants of target markets and delivering superior value
	☞ Long-term relationships with customers and other partners lead to success

In the product era, the goal was to build a better mouse trap and it was assumed that buyers will flock the seller who does it. However, a better mouse trap is no guarantee of success and marketing history is full of miserable failures despite better mouse trap designs. Inventing the greatest new product is not enough. That product must also solve a perceived marketplace need. Otherwise, even the best-engineered, highest quality product will fail. In the sales era, firms attempted to match their output to the potential number of customers who would want it. Firms assumed that customers will resist purchasing goods and services not deemed essential and that the task of selling and advertising is to convince them to buy. But selling is only one component of marketing. Next came the marketing era during which the company focus shifted from products and sales to customer's needs. The marketing concept, a crucial change in management philosophy, can be explained best by the shift from a seller's market–one with a shortage of goods and services–to a buyer's market–one with an abundance of goods and services. The advent of a strong buyer's market created the need for a customer orientation. Companies had to market goods and services, not just produce them. This realisation has been identified as the emergence of the marketing concept. The keyword is *customer orientation*. All facets of the organisation must contribute first to assessing and then to satisfying customer's needs and wants. The relationship marketing era is a more recent one. Organisations carried the marketing era's customer orientation one step further by focusing on establishing and maintaining relationships with both customers and suppliers. This effort represented a major shift from the traditional concept of marketing as a simple exchange between buyer and seller. Relationship marketing, by contrast, involves long-term, value-added relationships developed over time with customers and suppliers.   Table 1.2 summarises

Table 1.2 Comparison between transaction-based marketing and relationship marketing

Characteristic	Transaction-Based Marketing	Relationship Marketing
Time orientation	Short term	Long term
Organisational goal	Make the sale	Emphasis on customer retention & satisfaction/ delight
Customer service priority	Relatively low	Key component
Customer contact	Low to moderate	Frequent
Degree of customer commitment	Low	High
Basis for seller customer interactions	Conflict manipulation	Cooperation; trust
Source of quality	Primarily from production	Company-wide commitment

the differences between transaction marketing (i.e., exchanges characterised by limited communications and little or no ongoing relationship between the parties) and relationship marketing.

Functions of Marketing

Firms must spend money to create time, place and ownership utilities as discussed earlier. Several studies have been made to measure marketing costs in relation to overall product costs and service costs and most estimates have ranged between 40-60 per cent. These costs are not associated with raw materials or any of the other production functions necessary for creating form utility. What then does the consumer receive in return for this proportion of marketing cost? This question is answered by understanding the functions performed by marketing. Marketing is responsible for the performance of 8 universal functions (Table 1.3):

Table 1.3 Functions of marketing

Marketing function	Description
A. Exchange functions	
1. Buying	Ensuring that product offerings are available in sufficient quantities to meet customer demands.
2. Selling	Using advertising, personal selling and sales promotion to match goods and services to customer needs.
B. Physical distribution functions	
3. Transportation	Moving products from their points of production to locations convenient for purchasers.
4. Storing	Warehousing products until needed for sale
C. Facilitating functions	
5. Standardising and grading	Ensuring that product offerings meet established quality and quantity control standards of size, weight and so on.
6. Financing	Providing credit for channel members or consumers
7. Risk taking	Dealing with uncertainty about consumer purchases resulting from creation and marketing of goods and services that consumers may purchase in the future.
8. Securing marketing information	Collecting information about consumers, competitors and channel members for use in marketing decision-making.

buying, selling, transporting, storing, standardising and grading, financing, risk taking and securing marketing information. Some functions are performed by manufacturers, others by marketing intermediaries like wholesalers and retailers. Buying and selling, the first two functions represent exchange functions. Transporting and storing are physical distribution functions. The final four marketing functions–standardising and grading, financing, risk taking and securing market information–are often called facilitating functions because they assist the marketer in performing the exchange and physical distribution functions.

1.5   APPROACHES TO THE STUDY OF MARKETING

There are many approaches to the study of marketing. The most important approaches are:

- ☞ Commodity or Product Approach
- ☞ Institutional Approach
- ☞ Functional Approach
- ☞ Decision–making Approach or Managerial Approach
- ☞ Societal Approach
- ☞ Systems Approach.

1.5.1   Commodity or Product Approach

Marketing is concerned with the flow of products or commodities from the places of production to the places of consumption. So, this approach is adopted by some. This approach centres around the products. Under this approach, a detailed study of the different aspects of the marketing of a specific product, from product planning and development to its sale and consumption, is undertaken. The detailed study of a product covers the study of the class or kind of the product, its characteristics, the sources and conditions of its supply, the nature and the volume of demand for the product, the means of the transport used for its movement. The channels adopted for its distribution, standardisation and grading, branding, packaging and advertising policies adopted in the marketing of the product, its price, etc. For example, when a study of the marketing of soaps is undertaken, a detailed study of the various aspects of the marketing of soaps is undertaken.

The main advantage of this approach is that one gets the full picture of the marketing of individual products. The chief drawbacks of its approach are:

1. This approach is time-consuming.
2. As the study of every selected product is undertaken, under the same heads, the study becomes repetitive, laborious and tedious.

3. This approach helps us to understand the features of the selected commodities only. It does not help us to acquire a comprehensive knowledge of the broad field of marketing.
4. The classification of the products also creates the problems.

1.5.2 Institutional Approach

Marketing involves a number of institutions and agencies at every stage from product planning to sale and consumption.

Institutional approach centres around the various institutions or agencies that take part in the distribution of goods from the producers or manufacturers to the final consumers or users. Under this approach, a detailed study of the functions and the problems of the various institutions or agencies engaged in marketing of goods are undertaken. Here, we study the functions and the problems of producers or manufacturers, merchant middlemen like wholesalers and retailers, agent middlemen like brokers, commission agents, manufacturer's agents and selling agents and facilitating institutions, such as banks, insurance, companies, advertising agencies, marketing consultants, licensed graders and inspectors, etc. connected with the marketing of goods. We also study here, the functions and problems of regulated markets, produce or commodity exchanges, stock exchanges and government institutions connected with marketing.

The chief merit of this approach is that one will be able to understand the important functions performed and the problems faced by each institution or agency engaged in the process of marketing.

The chief drawback of this approach is that it leaves one with inadequate knowledge of marketing.

Another drawback of this approach is that it fails to indicate effectively the interrelations of all the institutions connected with marketing.

1.5.3 Functional Approach

Marketing is a sum of several functions. As such this approach is followed by many.

This approach centres around the functions of marketing. Under this approach, a detailed study of the major functions of marketing, such as buying, selling, transportation, storage, standardisation and grading, financing, risk bearing, collection of market information, etc. is undertaken.

The chief merit of this approach is that it helps us to understand the various functions of marketing and their relative importance in marketing in detail.

Further, this approach helps us to have a much comprehensive understanding of marketing.

Again, it is a time saving approach, as it avoids much repetition.

However, this method suffers from some drawbacks. They are:

(a) The main drawback of this approach is that it lays too much emphasis on the functions of marketing rather than showing how they are applied to specific business operations.
(b) Further this approach is repetitive to some extent.
(c) Again, this approach is the problem of elimination of the unnecessary marketing functions from the necessary functions. The problem of elimination of unnecessary functions from necessary functions is really difficult, as the marketing functions are numerous.

1.5.4   Decision-Making Approach or Managerial Approach

This approach is of very recent development. This approach is based on the fact that marketing is a management function and every stage of marketing, decision-making by the management is involved. So there should be decision-making approach.

This approach centres around the managerial decisions. At every stage of marketing process, decision-making is involved. Managerial decisions are taken, taking into consideration the two types of variables or factors, viz., (1) the controllable variable and (2) the uncontrollable variables. The controllable variables refers to the individuals firm's adjustments in prices, products, publicity, personal selling, etc. Which are under the control of the firm. The uncontrollable variables refer to the interaction of economic, psychological, political and social factors which are beyond the control of the firm. A detailed study of how the managerial decisions are taken on the management tasks, such as the selection of the channels of distribution, advertising campaign, pricing, etc. is undertaken.

The chief merit of this approach is that it is of immense help to the marketing management.

The main drawbacks of this approach are:

(i) This approach lays emphasis on the application side (i.e., practical side) of the marketing problems. It does not give an overall idea about marketing theoretically.
(ii) This approach cannot be adopted independently. It has to be undertaken along with functional approach, as functional study (i.e., study of the functions of marketing) is quite necessary for managerial decisions.

1.5.5   Societal Approach

The societal approach is a recent development. It has gained momentum since 1980.

In the societal approach to the study of marketing, marketing is regarded as a means to determine the needs, wants and interests of the society and to deliver the desired satisfaction more effectively and efficiently than competitors in a way that preserves and enhances the society's well-being.

Under the societal approach, the focus of study is the interactions between the various environmental factors and the marketing decisions and their impact on the well-being of the society.

The advantage of societal approach is that it is helpful in creating an intelligent consumption pattern, serving the ecological needs and helping the industry to grow and prosper.

1.5.6   Systems Approach

The systems approach also is a recent development.

Under the systems approach to the study of marketing, marketing process is regarded as a system, i.e., a set of interdependent functional components or parts, called subsystems, coordinated to form an integrated or unified whole, to accomplish a set of objectives.

The systems approach recognises the interrelations and the interconnections of the various components or parts of the marketing system, such as product planning, pricing, promotion, distribution, etc.

The systems approach is helpful for logical and orderly analysis of marketing activities. Further, it emphasises the marketing linkage inside and outside the changing environment. It also stresses the changing environment.

1.6   COMPANY ORIENTATIONS TOWARDS MARKETPLACE

There are five competing concepts under which organisations conduct their marketing activity.

1.6.1   Production Concept

The production concept is one of the oldest concepts guiding sellers. The production concept holds that consumers will favour those products that are widely available and in low cost. Managers of production-oriented organisations concentrate on achieving high production efficiency and wide distribution coverage.

The first is where the demand for a product exceeds supply, as in many third world countries. Here consumers are more interested in obtaining the product than in its fine points. The suppliers will concentrate on finding ways to increase production. The second situation is where the product's cost is high and has to be brought down through increased productivity to expand market. Texas Instruments provides a contemporary example of the production concept.

Texas Instruments is the leading American exponent of the "get-out-production", "cut-the-price" philosophy that Henry Ford pioneered in the early 1900s to expand the automobile market. Ford put all of his talent into perfecting the mass production of automobiles to bring down their cost so that America could afford them. Texas Instruments put all of its efforts in building production volume and improving technology in order to bring down costs. It uses its lower costs to cut prices and expand the market size. It strives to achieve the dominant position in its markets. To Texas Instruments, marketing primarily means one thing—bringing down the price to buyers. This orientation has also been a key strategy of many Japanese companies.

Some service oriented organisations also follow the production concept.

1.6.2   Product Concept

The term 'product' is widely used to refer a market offering of any kind. In its broadest sense, this may be anything from the physical to the abstract–an idea or a moral issue. Generally, however, most products are made up of a combination of physical elements and services. This is true in services marketing, where the service offering can include tangible features, such as food in a restaurant, or be a 'pure' service, intangible in nature.

A service product refers to an activity or activities that a marketer offers to perform, which results in satisfaction of a need or want of predetermined target customers. It is the offering of a firm in the form of activities that satisfies needs such as hairstyling done by a barber.

Consumers will buy only what suits them. As customers, we buy different kinds of products and services to satisfy our various needs. We buy toothpaste, butter, shaving cream, pen, scooter, and ticket for the U.S.A. and many other such items in our daily life. As we understand, our decision to buy an item is based not only on its tangible attributes but also on psychological attributes such as services, brand, package, warranty, image, and other discussions about the marketing of goods apply to services as well. Services have special characteristics that make them different than products.

According to Alderson, W., "Product is a bundle of utilities consisting of various product features and accompanying services."

According to Schwarte, D.J., "A product is something a firm markets that will satisfy a personal want or fill a business or commercial need".

Product concept will also lead to marketing myopia. Every major industry was once a growth industry. But some that are now riding a wave of growth enthusiasm are very much in the shadow of decline. Others which are thought of as seasoned growth industries have stopped growing. In every case the reason growth is threatened, slowed, or stopped is not because the market is saturated. It is because there has been a failure of management.

Today TV is a bigger business than the old narrowly defined movie business ever was. Had Hollywood been customer-oriented (providing entertainment), rather than product-oriented (making movies), would it have gone through the fiscal purgatory that it did? I doubt it. What ultimately saved Hollywood and accounted for its recent resurgence was the wave of new young writers, producers, and directors whose previous success in television had decimated the old movie companies and toppled the big movie moguls.

1.6.3   Selling Concept

The selling concept is another common approach many firms take to the market.

"The selling concept holds that consumers, if left alone, will ordinarily not buy enough of the organisations products. The organisation must therefore undertake an aggregate selling and promotion effort."

The selling concept is practised most aggressively with "unsought goods", those goods that buyers normally do not think of buying, such as insurance, encyclopedias, and funeral plots. These industries have perfect various sales techniques to locate prospects and hard-sell them on the product benefits. Hard selling also occurs with sought goods, such as automobiles.

From the moment, the customer walks into the showroom, the auto salesperson "psyches him out." If the customer likes the floor model, he may be told that there are balks at the price, the salesperson offers to talk to the manager to get a special concession. The customer waits ten minutes and the salesperson returns with "the boss doesn't like it but I got him to agree." The aim is to "work up the customer" and "close the sale".

The selling concept is also practised in the non-profit area by fund raisers, college admissions offices, and political parties. A political party will vigorously sell its candidate to the voters as being a fantastic person for the job. The candidate stomps through voting precincts from early morning to the late evening shaking hands, kissing babies, meeting donors, and making breezy speeches. Countless dollars are spent on radio and television advertising, posters, and mailing. Any flaws in the candidate are concealed from the public because the aim is to make the sale, not the candidates are concealed from the public because the aim is to make the sale, not worry about post-purchase satisfaction. After the election, the new official continues to take a sales-oriented view toward the citizens. There is little research into what the public wants and a lot of selling to get the public to accept policies that the politician or party wants.

1.6.4   Marketing Concept

The marketing concept is a business philosophy that challenges the previous concepts. Its central tenets crystallised in the mid 1950's.

The marketing concept holds that the key to achieving organisational goals consists of determining the needs and wants of target markets and delivering the desired satisfactions more effectively and efficiently than competitors.

The marketing concept has been expressed in many colourful ways:

"Meeting needs profitably."
"Find wants and fill them."
"Love the customer, not the product."
"Have it your way." (*Burger King*).
"You're the boss." (*United Airlines*)
"To do all in our power to pack the customer's dollar full of value, quality and satisfaction." (*J.C. Penney*).

Theodore Leavitt drew a perceptive contrast between the selling and marketing concepts.

Selling focuses on the needs of the seller, marketing on the needs of the buyer. Selling is preoccupied with the seller's need to convert his product into cash; marketing with the idea of satisfying the needs of the customer by means for the product and the whole cluster of things associated with creating, delivering and finally consuming it.

The marketing concept rests on four main pillars, namely, target market, customer needs, coordinated marketing, and profitability. In Fig. 1.4, where they are contrasted with a selling orientation, the selling concept takes an inside-out perspective. It starts with the factory, focuses on the company's existing products and calls for heavy selling and promoting to produce profitable sales. The marketing concept takens an outside-in perspective. It starts with a well-defined market, focuses on customer needs, coordinates all the activities that will affect customers, and produces profits through creating customer satisfaction. Here we are examining how each pillar of the marketing concept contributes to more effective marketing. Both the concepts are shown in Fig. 1.4.

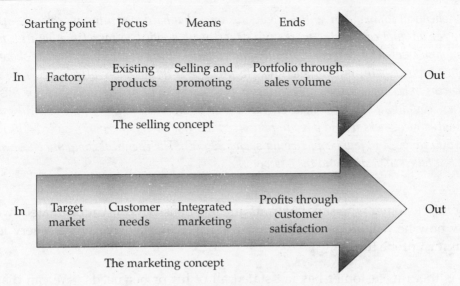

Fig. 1.4 Marketing and selling concept.

1.6.4.1   Target Market

No company can operate in every market and satisfy every need. Nor can it even do a good job within one broad market; even mighty IBM cannot offer the best solution for every information processing need. Companies do best when they define their target market(s) carefully and prepare a tailored marketing programme:

An auto manufacturer can think of designing passenger cars, station wagons, sports cars, and luxury cars. But this thinking is less precise than defining a customer target group. One Japanese car maker is designing a car for the career woman, and it will have many features that male dominated cars don't have. Another Japanese car maker is designing car for the "town man," the young person who needs to get about town and park easily. In each case, the company has clarified a target market, and this will greatly influence the car design.

1.6.4.2   Customer Needs

A company can define its target market but fail to fully understand the customer's needs. Consider the following example.

A major chemical company invented a new substance that hardened into a marble-like material. Looking for an application, the marketing department decided to target the bathtub market. The company created a few model bathtubs and exhibited them at a bathroom trade show. They hoped to convince bathtub manufacturers to produce bathtubs more attractive, none signed up. The reason became obvious. The bathtub would have to be priced at $2,000; for this price, consumers could buy bathtubs made of real marble or onyx. In addition, the bathtubs were so heavy that homeowners would have to reinforce their floors. Furthermore, most bathtubs sold in the $500 range, and few people would spend $2,000. The chemical company chose a target market but failed to understand the customers.

Consider the customer who says he wants an "inexpensive" car. Unfortunately, we would not know how he will judge whether a car is really inexpensive. At the very least, the marketer must probe further.

The fact is that the customer has not stated all of his or her needs. We can distinguish among five types of needs.

1. **Stated needs:** The customer wants an inexpensive car.

2. **Real needs:** The customer wants a car whose operating cost, not its initial price, is low.

3. **Unstated needs:** The customer buys the car and receives a complimentary U.S. road atlas.

4. **Secret needs:** The customer wants to be seen by friends as a value-oriented savvy consumer.

Responding to the customer's stated need often shortchanges the customer. Consider a carpenter who enters a hardware store and asks for a sealant to seal windows to frames. This carpenter is stating a solution, not a need. The need is to fix glass to a wooden frame. The hardware store salesperson might suggest a better solution than a sealant, namely, using a tape. The tape has the additional advantage of zero curing time. In this case, the salesperson has aimed at to meet the customer's real need not the stated need.

Customer-oriented thinking requires the company to define customer needs from the customer point of view.

Why is it supremely important to satisfy the target customer? Basically because a company's sales period comes from two groups: new customers and repeat customers. It always costs more to attract new customers than to retain current customers. Therefore, customer retention is more critical than customer attraction. The key to customer retention is customer satisfaction. A satisfied customer.

1. Buys more and stays "loyal" longer.
2. Buys additional products as the company introduces and upgrades its products.
3. Talks favourably about the company and its products and services.
4. Pays less attention to competing brands and advertising and is less price sensitive.
5. Offers product/service ideas to the company.
6. Costs less to serve than new customers because transactions are routine.

Thus, a company would be wise to regularly measure customer satisfaction. The company would phone a sample of recent buyers and inquire how many are highly satisfied, somewhat satisfied. Indifferent, somewhat dissatisfied, and highly dissatisfied. It would also find out the major factors in customer satisfaction and dissatisfaction. The company would use this information to improve its performance in the next period.

Listening is not enough. The company must respond constructively to the complaints.

Of the customers who register a complaint, between 54 and 70% will do business again with the organisation if their complaint is resolved. The figure goes up to a staggering 95% if the customer feels that the complaint was resolved quickly. Customers who have complained to an organisation and had their complaints satisfactorily resolved tell an average of five people about the treatment they received.

A customer-oriented company would track its customer-satisfaction level each period and set improvement goals. For example, Citibank aims to achieve a 90% customer satisfaction level. If Citibank continues to increase its customer satisfaction level, it is on the right track. And the concern will be in growth level in the competitive environment.

1.6.4.3 Coordinated Marketing

Unfortunately, not all company employees are trained and motivated to work for the customer. An engineer complained that the sales people were "always protecting the customer and not thinking of the company's interest." He went on to blast customers for "asking for too much." The following situation highlights the coordination problem.

"The marketing vice-president of a major airline wants to increase the airline's traffic share. His/her strategy is to build up customer satisfaction through providing better food, cleaner cabins, and better-trained cabin crews. Yet he/she has no authority in these matters. The catering department chooses food that keeps food costs down; the maintenance department uses cleaning services that keep cleaning costs down; and the personnel department hires people without regard to whether they are friendly and inclined to serve other people. Since these departments generally take a cost or production point of view, he/she is stymied in creating a high level of customer satisfaction."

1.6.4.4   Profitability

The purpose of the marketing concept is to help organisations achieve their goals. In the case of private firms, the major goal is profit; in the case of non-profit and public organisations, it is surveying and attracting enough funds to perform their work. Now the key is not to aim for profits as such but to achieve them as a by-product of doing the job well. The General Motors executive who said, "We are in the business of making money, not cars," is misplacing the emphasis. A company makes money by satisfying customer needs better than competitors can.

Nevertheless, marketers must be involved in analysing the profit potential of different marketing opportunities. The following story illustrates this.

An American shoe company sent its financial officer to a Pacific island to see if the company could sell its shoes there. In a few days, the officer wired back; "The people here don't wear shoes. There is no market." The shoe company decided to send its best and oustanding sales person to that particular country to check this problem. After a week, the sales person also wired back: "The people here don't wear shoes. There is a fabulous market!"

The shoe company next sent the marketing vice-president to assess the situation. After two weeks, the marketing vice-president wired back. "The people here don't wear shoes, however, they have bad feet and could benefit from wearing shoes. We would need to gain the tribal chief's cooperation. The people don't have any money, but they grow great pineapples. I have estimated the sales potential over a three-year period and all of our costs, including selling the pineapples to a European supermarket chain, and concluded that we could make a 30% return on our money. I say that we should go ahead.

1.6.4.5   Organised Resistance

Some company departments, often manufacturing, finance, and R&D, do not like to see marketing built up because it threatens their power in the organisation. The nature of the treat is illustrated in the Fig. 1.5.

Initially, the marketing function is seen as one of several equally important business functions in a check balance relationship. Figure 1.5(a).

Figure 1.5(b) represents a dearth of demand then leads marketers to argue that their function is somewhat more important than the others.

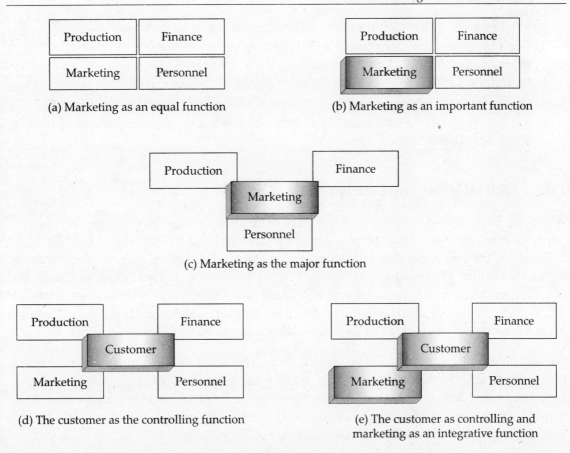

Fig. 1.5 Evolving views of marketing's role in the company.

Figure 1.5(c) represents a few marketing enthusiasts go further and say marketing is the major function of the enterprise, for without customers, there would be no company. They put marketing at the centre, with other business functions serving as support functions.

Figure 1.5(d) this view incenses the other managers, who do not want to think of themselves as working for marketing. Enlightened marketers clarify the issue by putting the customer rather than marketing at the centre of the company.

They argue for a customer orientation in which all functions work together to sense, serve, and satisfy the customer. Finally, some marketers say that marketing still needs to command a central company position if customer's needs are to be correctly interpreted and efficiency satisfied. Figure 1.5(e).

The marketer's argument for the business concept shown in Fig. 1.5 is as follows:

1. The company's assets have little value without the existence of customers.

2. The key company task is therefore to attract and retain customers.
3. Customers are attracted through competitive superior offers and retained through satisfaction.
4. Marketing's task is to develop a superior offer and deliver customer satisfaction.
5. Customer satisfaction is affected by the performance of the other departments.
6. Marketing needs to influence these other departments to cooperate in delivering customer satisfaction.

1.6.5   Societal Marketing Concept

A number of present-day social problems like drug abuse, pollution control, safer driving, immunisation, non-smoking, birth control, etc. are in need of innovative solutions and approaches for gaining public attention and support. Marketing men by their training are finely attuned to market needs, product development, pricing and channel issues, and mass communication and promotional techniques, all of which are critical in the social area. Remember, social marketing is sufficiently distinct from business marketing and requires fresh thinking and new approaches to the solution of social problems.

Societal marketing typically has to deal with market's core beliefs and values, whereas business marketing often deals with superficial preferences and opinions. Societal marketing has to work with channel systems that are less well defined and less motivated. Only through applying concepts and tools to a large number of social cases one would be able to learn the power and limits of the societal marketing concept.

1.7   MARKETING PLANNING PROCESS

Strategies

The development of the marketing strategy and selection of a target markets(s) tell the marketing department which customers to focus on and what needs to attempt to satisfy. The next stage of the marketing process involves combining the various elements of marketing mix into a cohesive, effective marketing programme.

How are the marketing objectives going to be achieved? This is the burden of marketing strategy. In fact, marketing strategy formulation is the core of marketing planning after all, it is strategy that renders a firm distinct from another and makes its offering unique compared to those of its competitors. Again, it is strategy that brings home the income and profits expected from the business. Different organisations seek their objectives in some manner so for this concept, two organisations were been taken as examples (a) P&G (Procter & Gamble Co.) (b) HLL (Hindustan Lever Limited).

P&G

Procter & Gamble Co. (P&G) is an American company based in Cincinnati, Ohio that manufactures a wide range of consumer goods. In India Procter & Gamble has two subsidiaries: P&G Hygiene and Health Care Ltd. and P&G Home Products Ltd. P&G Hygiene and Health Care Limited is one of India's fastest growing Fast Moving Consumer Goods Companies with a turnover of more than ₹500 crore. It has in its portfolio famous brands like Vicks & Whisper. P&G Home Products Limited deals in fabric care segment and hair care segment. It has in its kitty global brands such as Ariel and Tide in the fabric care segment, and Head & Shoulders, Pantene, and Rejoice in the hair care segment.

We have made three strategic "how-to-win" choices to capture these growth opportunities.

First, we will leverage our core strengths–consumer understanding, brand-building, innovation, go-to-market capability and scale–to execute the company's growth strategies. These strengths create significant competitive advantage for P&G, particularly when we leverage them together as interdependent capabilities to win. We see opportunities to apply P&G's strengths in several areas–from expanding category, country and channel portfolios globally to extending distribution and store coverage in developing markets. This will continue to be a primary how-to-win focus area for P&G.

Second, we are elevating simplification, scale and execution to how-to-win strategies. These are key improvement areas where we believe we can create the greatest value and competitive advantage.

Our simplification efforts have one goal: to make it easier for each P&G employee and business partner to improve more lives in more parts of the world more completely. As P&G has grown larger, we've naturally become more complex. We are removing complexity so our brands are more affordable and to make the company more innovative and agile. We're reducing senior management positions and layers, and improving decision-making, by simplifying our organisation structure. We're also making other important interventions to simplify business processes such as business planning, product launch, and product formulation. We want to become a $100 billion company with the speed and agility of a $10 billion company. We consider scale to be a tremendous growth opportunity. We're leveraging scale efficiencies to deliver best-in-class cost structures throughout our business. We're using our R&D and supply chain scale to create alternative materials that minimise exposure to volatile commodity markets. We're creating the technology infrastructure to rapidly transfer best-in-class knowledge across our global organisation. And more. I'm confident this focus will yield dramatic benefits for the company over time.

Execution is, of course, the only strategy our customers and consumers ever see, so we must do it with excellence, always. We are placing even sharper emphasis on consistent, quality execution in every part of our business. Third, we are leading change to win with consumers and customers. We are becoming an even more collaborative organisation, inside and outside our company. We're getting flatter, faster and simpler. We're changing how we compensate people to reinforce and reward behaviours that allow us to meet our simplification, scale and disciplined execution objectives. We're making the investments to be networked globally and digitised from end to end. And we're building the capability to operate on a demand-driven, real-time, future-focused basis everyday. In today's economic environment, many companies are cutting back on investments in their people. P&G is increasing its investment. We know without doubt that P&G people are our most important asset, and we will continue to invest in their growth, capability, and productivity.

Our Purpose

We will provide branded products and services of superior quality and value that improve the lives of the world's consumers, now and for generations to come. As a result, consumers will reward us with leadership sales, profit and value creation, allowing our people, our shareholders and the communities in which we live and work to prosper.

A mission statement is a formal short written statement of the purpose of a company or organisation. The mission statement should guide the actions of the organisation, spell out its overall goal, provide a sense of direction, and guide decision-making. It provides "the framework or context within which the company's strategies are formulated."

Mission statements often contain the following:

1. Purpose and aim of the organisation.
2. The organisation's primary stakeholders: clients, stockholders, congregation, etc.
3. Responsibilities of the organisation toward these stakeholders.
4. Products and services offered.

Some mission statements are complex, long, and very broad, for example:

Since its inception in 1982, La Unidad Latina has remained on the vanguard of political and community empowerment by developing influential leaders that strive to exert knowledge and power into its peers in order to attain mutual success. LUL is committed to academic excellence, leadership development and cultural enlightenment, enhanced by a diverse cognizant membership. LUL strives to preserve and promote an inclusive intellectual environment for its members, in addition to the general community.

In contrast, some mission statements are simple and direct, for example:

To protect and promote the interests of motorcyclists while serving the needs of its members.

The classic example of the mission statement is the Preamble to the Constitution of the United States:

We the People of the United States, in order to form a more perfect Union, establish Justice, insure domestic Tranquility, provide for the common defence, promote the general Welfare, and secure the Blessings of Liberty to ourselves and our Posterity, do ordain and establish this Constitution for the United States of America.

HLL

HLL Lifecare Limited (HLL) commenced its journey to serve the nation in the area of healthcare, on 1st March 1966, with its incorporation as a corporate entity under the Ministry of Health and Family Welfare of the Government of India. HLL was set up in the natural rubber rich state of Kerala, for the production of male contraceptive sheaths for the National Family Welfare Programme.

The company commenced its commercial operations on 5th April 1969 at Peroorkada in Thiruvananthapuram (formerly Trivandrum). The plant was established in technical collaboration with M/s Okamoto Industries Inc. Japan. Two most modern plants were added, one at Thiruvananthapuram and the other at Belgaum in 1985. Another plant was added in the early nineties at Aakkulam in Thiruvananthapuram for the production of Blood Transfusion Bags, Copper T IUDs, Surgical Sutures and Hydrocephalus Shunt.

HLL has grown today into a multi-product, multi-unit organisation addressing various public health challenges facing humanity.

On the path of rapid growth, HLL has set its sights to be a ₹1000 crore company by the year 2010. HLL has been declared a Mini Ratna Company by the Government of India and upgraded as a Schedule B PSU.

HLL Lifecare Limited is the only company in the world manufacturing and marketing the widest range of contraceptives. It is unique in providing a range of condoms, including female condoms, intrauterine devices, oral contraceptive pills, steroidal, non-steroidal and emergency contraceptive pills; and tubal rings. HLL today produces 1.316 billion condoms making it one of the world's leading manufacturers of condoms, accounting for nearly 10 per cent of the global production capacity.

Marketing

Over the past two decades, HLL has steadily set up a strong and sound infrastructure for direct marketing. HLL has put in place a vast distribution network covering the length and breadth of the country. HLL's products today reach over 200000 retail outlets, covering

3500 hospitals, reaching over 30000 medical professionals, with over 2800 stock points, has over 700 frontline team members placed in every town, with offices in all metros and mini metros, and reaching over one lakh villages in the remotest corners of the nation.

It is the leading social marketing organisation in the country in the area of contraceptives–with a market share of over 65 per cent in the rural and semi-urban markets, including in the highly populated states of UP, Madhya Pradesh, Bihar, etc.

HLL has made vast inroads in the commercial segment too, with the growth in its market share from 0.1 per cent in the nineties to 15 per cent at present. HLL's products are today exported to over 115 countries.

Corporate Vision and Plans Ahead

HLL has drawn up a comprehensive plan to expand its portfolio in the area of health care and contraceptives–its core areas, to achieve rapid growth. The objective is to achieve through this process a turnover of ₹1000 crores by 2010. With nearly 1900 highly skilled and learned manpower, and several world leaders as partners, HLL has over the past four decades stood to uphold its mission to achieve and sustain a high growth path, and focus on five key thrust areas to achieve its vision. These are customers, employees, business, innovation and social initiatives.

In the future, through technical collaborations, marketing alliances and joint ventures, HLL wishes to keep alive the dream of all humanity - of a healthier, happier world.

Motto

Innovating for Healthy Generations.

Vision

HLL will establish itself as the leader in its core activities, through a process of continuous innovation and participatory approach in order to

- Provide best value to the customer.
- Be an employer of choice.
- Promote the cause of family health in general, and women's health in particular.

Mission

To accomplish the Corporate Vision, HLL outlined a mission to be a world-class health care company by the year 2010, with focus on five key areas, namely

1. Business

2. Customer
3. Innovation
4. Employee
5. Social sector initiatives.

Business Leadership

- Attain rapid growth and global levels of operations with cost competitiveness.
- Be among the top three players in each main product category.
- Become the organisation to be benchmarked with.
- Become an acknowledged and admired leader at industry forums.

Obviously, all firms in an industry cannot and do not seek the No. 1 position. Many are content with a follower's position while a few prefer to the niche players. Whatever be the case, marketing strategy will clearly specify the position that a unit seeks in the industry.

Developing the detailed marketing plans and programmes

Marketing strategy which is essentially a broad game plan, has to be elaborated into detailed functional plans and programmes. Obviously, detailed functional plans will emanate from and be in tune with the marketing objectives and marketing strategy of a firm.

Sometimes managers fail to understand the importance of detailed functional plans, they readily blame the strategy if the expected results do not materialise, they fail to analyse whether the failure was on account of the ineffectiveness of the strategy or the ineffectiveness of detailed functional plans.

There are some core functional plans:

1. Product plan/production plan
2. Sales forecasts/sales plan
3. Physical distribution plan
4. Channel plan
5. Advertising and sales promotional plan
6. Sales force plan
7. Sales organisation plans

The marketing planning process can be accompanied with the above concepts and also marketing planning process is in need of budgets and financial versions with physical plans. Marketing planning will not be complete until the various marketing activities that are planned are accounted for in financial terms. The following table represents the component tasks in the marketing process.

The Marketing Planning Process

1. Environment Appraisal

1. Analysing the environment and spotting the opportunities and threats.
2. Pinpointing and shorting the opportunities actually available to a unit and which can be tapped by the unit.
3. Analysing the market/customer.
4. Analysing industry and competition.

2. Internal Appraisal of the Unit

1. Analyse the strengths and weaknesses of the unit.
2. Assessing the health and status of the different product lines/products/brands.
3. Assessing the competitive advantages and core competencies of the firm and examining the ones that are useful to the unit.

3. Setting the Marketing Objectives of the Unit

1. Deciding which of the spotted opportunities should be pursued considering the unit's capabilities and limitations.
2. Pinpointing the areas in which marketing objectives have to be set, (e.g., sales volume, profits, market share, service and marketing innovation).
3. Assessing the current performance in the key areas.
4. Setting measurable, clear-cut, and explicit objectives in each key area.

5. Setting the objectives as above for each product/market.

4. Developing the Marketing Strategy
Selecting the target market

1. Studying the customer, his buying motives and buying behaviour.
2. Segmentation of the market using relevant bases.
3. Evaluating each of the segments.
4. Selecting the appropriate segments as the target market.

Deciding the positioning strategy
Developing the marketing mix

1. Deciding the approach in respect of each of the four Ps.
2. Deciding the relative weightage to be assigned to each of them.
3. Providing for the impact of the uncontrollable, environmental variables.

5. Developing the Detailed Functional Plans of Marketing

1. Product plan/production plan
2. Sales forecast/sales plan
3. Physical distribution plan
4. Channel plan
5. Advertising and sales promotion plan
6. Sales force plan
7. Sales organisation plan.

Formulating marketing strategies

There are three main tasks which formulate the marketing strategies:

1. Selecting the target market
2. Positioning the offer
3. Assembling the marketing mix

This implies that the essence of the marketing strategy of a firm for a given product/brand can be grasped from the target market chosen, the way it is positioned and how the marketing mix is organised.

1. Selecting the Target Market

To say that target market selection is a part of marketing strategy development is just stating the obvious. It does not fully bring out the import of the inseparable linkage between the two when selection of target market is over an important part of the marketing strategy of the product is determined, defined and expressed. Market segmentation and target process focuses on several other factors we shall glance this concept in more detail in market segmentation chapter.

Hero Honda focus towards target market and a message by Atul Sobti, Executive Director

Encouraged by impressive sales volume in the first eight months of this financial year, two-wheeler market leader Hero Honda Motor Ltd. (HHML) has revised its annual sales volume growth to 20 per cent from 15 per cent set at the beginning of the year. HHML expects to close the current financial year with sales of nearly 2.5 million units and lap up half the market by March 2005. HHML's total sales of two-wheelers in the first eight months stood at 17,05,230 units, recording a growth of 29.45 per cent over the same period last year (13,17,248). Exports during the period grew by 63.82 per cent to touch 38,000 units, while domestic sales grew by 28.83 per cent to 16,67,238 units. Though the average growth in sales for the first eight months was almost 30 per cent, the overall growth for the year is pegged at 20 per cent only. "This is more due to the 'lower-base' factor in the first half of the previous financial year. Even a 20 per cent overall growth for this financial year would be an impressive one," HHML's executive director (business operations), Atul Sobti, said. The company's growth in this year is still far ahead of the market average. According to the monthly flash report from Society of Indian Automobile Manufacturers released today motorcycle sales in the eight months of the fiscal were up 15.39 per cent to 3,207,515 units against 2,779,806 units sold in April-November 2003.

Discussing the company's short-term and medium-term plans, Sobti said that the company's plans to enter the scooter market was 'on course' and is its products will hit the roads in the next two years. "Our plans to enter the scooters market is to ensure that we get new customers (for scooters) who are not visiting our showrooms at all. We plan to add more (new) customers, through these products, under the Hero Honda fold," he said. He added that HHML will be present in both scooters and scooterette market. He said that the new dynamics drive the two-wheeler market every year. In the last two years, two-wheeler sales recorded impressive growth with a slew of new products launched by major manufacturers at very competitive prices. "The markets also grew despite the fact that these two years did witness any extraordinary monsoon," Sobti said. He added that growth in the current financial year, that has exceeded the most bullish prediction made in the beginning of the year was possibly due to high replacements happening in the market.

2. Positioning

The next major aspect of marketing strategy relates to positioning of the offer. The firm has already selected the target market and decided its basic offer. Now, what is the conjunction between these two factors? How do they get connected? What is the interface?

In other manner

— What is the locus the firm seeks among the customers in the chosen target market with its offering?

— How would the firm want the consumer to view and receive the offer?

For example: Does the firm want to lodge the product as the most distinctive offer in the market?

Or as the most prestigious offer?

Or as the most competitive offer in the market?

Or is the firm seeking the leader position with its product offer?

There are so many issues that the firm has to grapple within positioning. While framing marketing mix also, the firm will agitate over these issues.

3. Assembling the Marketing Mix

Marketing mix itself means assembling the four Ps (Product, Price, Place and Promotion). Marketing in excellent combination always the firm has to seek target-oriented sales and with a optimum level of profits. It considers different marketing mixes with varying levels of expenditure on each marketing activity in terms of its sales and profits. It then focuses on the combination mix of product, price, place and promotion that is according to the judgement.

Mix has to be worked out for every brand

Marketing mix has to be worked out for every brand because the market fight is finally at the brand level. And it is the marketing mix that decides how much leeway and resources the brand has at its disposal.

Deciding the Weightage of each 'P'

Always marketing mix orientation goes towards weightage to be assigned to each of the Ps is the core of marketing mix formulation. One firm may assign maximum weightage to the product, and build up its technological superiority and functional benefit. Anatomy firm in the same industry may assign maximum weightage to distribution, yet attaining to promotion.

4. Marketing Mix Serves Customers

Ultimately, the marketing mix of a firm corresponds to its total product offering. And, this total product offering is supposed to serve few customer.

So, it follows that marketing mix formulation has to takes its cue directing and totally from customers/market.

5. Marketing Mix is not fixed

The marketing mix is a core and dynamic entity. It needs innovation, upgradation depending on the situations.

Marketing Strategies Fall Under Two Categories

1. The price oriented strategies.
2. The differentiation oriented strategies.

In other words, they are only two broad routes available for forgoing marketing strategies, any strategy has to be ultimately either a price oriented or differentiation oriented strategy.

1. Price Oriented Marketing Strategy

Firms taking to the price route in marketing strategy compete on the strength or pricing. They use price as their competition level.

And they can afford to offer lower prices and still make the targeted profits. They elbow out competition with the cushion. They enjoy in the matter of pricing.

2. Differentiation Based Marketing Strategy

The differentiation route to strategy resolves around aspects other than price. It works on the principle that a firm can make its offer distinctive from all competitors' offers and win through the distinctiveness. And a firm adopting such route can price its product on the perceived value of that attributes of the offer and root necessarily on competition parity basis.

Differentiation can be based on Multitude Attitudes of the Offer

The interesting point is that the offer can be differentiated on any of the multitude of attributes that normally form part of any offer. The product with its innumerable features, the service and other functions performed by the firm or all possible sources of differentiation.

Examples of Differentiations

Modi Xerox uses its service strength and its collaboration with Rank Xerox as its differentiation themes.

Garden Silks uses its strength in design as the differentiation plank.

Eureka Forbes has successfully used home selling as its distinctiveness.

Citibank differentiates on its personalised service. IT (information technology) claims that it employs only professionally qualified people and the person who answers a customer's phone call will be competent to solve all the problems raised by the customer.

To cite some more examples, IBM uses technology and service as its differentiation planks, Caterpillar Tractor uses its service strength/global dealer network and Rolls Royce, its quality.

Differentiation helps a Firm Move Away from Competition

Most of the business sectors are facing cold wars regarding product differentiation rather than price. The major temptation as well as advantage with differentiation strategy allows a business firm from the disadvantages of a wholly price based fight. In other sense, differentiation allows flexibility in non-price front, and speciality of its offer.

To Resort to Differentiation, a firm should possess Relevant Competitive advantages

In the present scenario, differentiation is one common route that every firm wants to be in competitive advantage as niche. Brand image, unique process, strong collaboration, advance facilities, R & D facilities and others with competitive environment.

Specimen Marketing Strategy: HMT Tractors

HMT produces items like watches, tractors, dairy and printing machinery, dye casting and plastic injection moulding machines. Other items which are being produced are lamps, etc. tractors were allotted in the natural market zone for tractors.

To supplement HMT tractor production a second tractor assembly line for 45 HP (Horse Power) and 59 HP tractors has been in operation since 1985 at SAS Nagar (Mohali) to meet the requirements of tractors in Punjab.

Overall Marketing Objectives and Strategy

(A) Marketing Objectives
1. Directional Mission: Diversification of its product range to provide cushion for the cyclical variations in the machine tool market.

2. Goals: Specific goals in the next $(1, 2, \ldots 5)$ years for tractors are
   - (a) Sales in terms of number and value of tractors
   - (b) Sustained growth in volume of (say 5%) per annum

(B) Product Strategy

From assembling tractors from CKD (completely knocked down) packs with 100 per cent improved components, to fully indigenizing its manufacturer over a span of five to seven years through planned and systematic reduction of improved content. Later to acquire design capabilities for developing tractors of different HP, the production of tractors began at Pinjore in June 1971, and model 2511 was fully indigenized in a short span of five years. Later, design capabilities were acquired and 35 HP and 45 HP tractors were developed. The 59 HP tractors is in advanced stage of indigenization.

To develop research and development centre for prototype assembly, engine testing, sub-systems testing, test farms and tracks to stimulate field conditions.

(C) Competitive Strategy

1. To have the widest range of tractors and variants on its regular production schedule as a differential advantage vis-a-vis its competitors.
2. Anticipation about sales of HMT will take away from different well-established manufacturers in the field including increase in market share. Since the competitors are expected to respond through appropriate competitive strategies, the company plans to develop and maintain its technological and widest range superiority.

(D) Segmentation Strategy

(i) Customer Target

1. Marketing effort will be directed at Haryana, Punjab, U.P., Bihar, Rajasthan, M.P., and other states in the western and southern parts of the country.
2. Variants like Rice Special, Paddy Pedlar, Forest Special and Hauler will be developed and marketed to suit different types of needs of farmers.
3. Front and rear loaders, mini skidders and hydro dozers will be some of the attachments that will be mounted on HMT tractors not only to cater to find operations but also for use in variety operations.

(E) Supporting Strategies

The key elements of HMT's marketing support programmes are as follows:

1. Participation in exhibition is one important method that will be used in promotion of the sale of HMT tractors. (For example, HMT participated in IMTEX' 86 held in Bombay in 1986).
2. Price strategies.
3. Distribution and service.

1.8 MARKETING MIX

Marketing is performed within a certain environment which itself is always changing. The marketing activities have, therefore, to change in consonance with the environment to be continuously effective. In order to appreciate this process it is easier to divide the marketing activities into four basic elements which are together referred to as the marketing mix. These four elements are:

Product: As all these four start with the letter "P", they are referred as four "Ps" of the marketing mix.

The word product stands for the goods or services offered by the organisation. Once the needs are identified, it is necessary to plan the product and after that keep on analysing whether the product still satisfies the needs which were originally planned for, and if not, determine the necessary changes. Product models represented in Fig. 1.6.

Fig. 1.6 Product.

Price refers to the money value that the customer has to pay. The product has to be adequately priced. This involves consideration of the profit margin, the cost, the possibility of sales at different prices and the concept of the right price. Fig. 1.7 represents price quote.

Fig. 1.7 Price.

Physical distribution or place refers to the aspect of the channels of distribution through which the product has to move before it reaches the consumer, it also includes the logistics aspects of distribution such as warehousing, transportation, etc., the organisation must decided whether it should sell through wholesalers and then to retailers, who ultimately sell to consumer. Fig. 1.8 shows process of physical distribution.

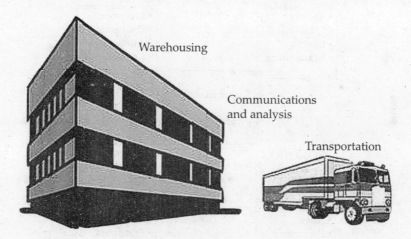

Fig. 1.8 Physical distribution.

Promotion is the aspect of selling and advertising, or communicating the benefits of the product or service, to the target customers of the market segment involved in order to persuade them to purchase such products or services as shown in Fig. 1.9.

Fig. 1.9 Promotion.

The marketing manager is a mixer of ingredients, according to James Culliton, a noted marketing expert, who coined the expression, "**Marketing Mix**".

*The marketing mix is the set of controllable, tactical, marketing tools that the firm blends to produce the response it wants in the target market—**Philip Kotler**. The marketing mix consists of the variables, product, price, place and promotion, well known as the four Ps of marketing as classified by McCarthy as shown in Fig. 1.10 different tools under marketing mix.*

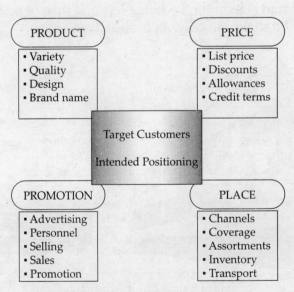

Fig. 1.10 Tools under marketing mix.

To be effective, marketing people have to consider the four Cs first and then build the four Ps based on the requirements as mentioned below and also represented in Fig. 1.10:

Four P's		Four C's
1. Product	$\longrightarrow$	Customer solution
2. Price	$\longrightarrow$	Customer cost
3. Place	$\longrightarrow$	Convenience
4. Promotion	$\longrightarrow$	Communication

The Role of Marketing Mix in Marketing Planning and Marketing

Marketing mix has an important role to play in marketing planning and marketing strategy. Planning is an important managerial activity. Which is a basic requirement for all organisations? Any organisation will need general and specific plans to fulfil its objectives.

The primary concern of marketing planning is marketing strategy formulation, marketing planning, involves preparing action plans to shape the future growth of an organisation. Achieving profitability, meeting competition, protecting and improving market share, and promoting brand image are its concerns.

Market planning and strategy formulation is to be done reckoning the environmental variables of marketing like competition, the consumer, the government, and legal, political and natural forces. While the organisation can choose, alter and control its marketing mix variables, it cannot choose or alter the environmental variables against which the products are marketed.

The four Ps of marketing have to be assembled in the best possible combination. This process involves choosing the appropriate marketing activities and the allocation of the appropriate marketing effort and the resources to each one of them. The organisation has to consider how to generate targeted sales and profitability. It is necessary to work out marketing mix for every brand because the competition in the market is ultimately at the brand level. And it is the marketing mix that decides how much strength the brand has at its disposal to fight competition.

Choosing the Optimum Marketing Mix

In theory as well as in practice the marketing mix elements can be combined in any number of ways. The marketing mix elements are substitutable by one another to a certain extent. Resources can be taken away from one element and assigned to another, to achieve balance as per the marketing objective of the firm. The organisation can achieve its marketing objective using different combination of the marketing mix.

This is done by assigning relevant weightage to each element depending on the objectives and the context. Even within an element, weightage may have to be given to various sub-elements.

For example, within promotion, advertising and brand building activities may get a higher weightage of the objective is higher market share in the long run. Personnel selling and sales promotion may get a higher weightage, if the objective is higher sales in the short run.

The marketing mix is the most visible part of the marketing strategy of an organisation. The strategy manifests through the marketing mix of the organisation–through what the organisations does with product, price, distribution and promotion.

1.9   ENVIRONMENTAL SCANNING AND ENVIRONMENTAL MANAGEMENT

Marketers must carefully and continually monitor crucial trends and developments in the business environment. Environmental scanning is the process of collecting information about the external marketing environment to identify and interpret potential trends. This activity then seeks to analyse the collected information and determine whether identified trends represent opportunities or threats to the company. This judgment, in turn, allows a firm to determine the best response to a particular environmental change. Environmental scanning is a vital component of effective environmental management.

Environmental management is the effort to attain organisational objectives by predicting and influencing the firm's competitive, political-legal, economic, technological and social-cultural environments. The development of a global marketplace has complicated environmental scanning and environmental management. These processes may now need to track political developments, economic trends and cultural influences anywhere in the world.

While the marketing environment may exceed the confines of the firm and its marketing mix components, effective marketers continually seek to predict its impact on marketing decisions and to modify its conditions whenever possible.

The environment may be grouped into two parts. They are:

1. Micro environment
2. Macro environment

1.9.1   Micro Environment

Micro environment refers to the company's immediate environment, i.e., those environmental factors that are in its proximity. These factors influence the company's non-capability to produce and serve in the market. These are also the groups of people who affect the company's prospectus directly. These factors are:

- Organisation internal environment

- Suppliers
- Market intermediaries
- Customers
- Competitors
- Company resources
- Management philosophy
- Public

❊ Organisational Internal Environment

The internal environment of an organisation consists of such factors such as the financial and non-financial factors. Production and human resource capabilities influence its marketing decisions to a great extent. In the organisation marketing managers, in formulating plans, must take into account the other groups such as top management, R&D, purchase and sales and development should make decisions regarding their market proposals.

❊ Suppliers

Even regarding the suppliers the organisation can think of availing the required material or labour according to its manufacturing programme. It can adopt a purchase policy which gives bargaining power to the organisation.

❊ Market Intermediaries

Normally, every producer has to appoint a number of intermediaries in assisting him in promoting, selling, and distributing the goods and services to ultimate consumers. The intermediaries are middlemen (wholesalers, retailers, and agents, etc.), distributing agencies, market service agencies and financial institutions.

❊ Customers

The customers of a company may be of five kinds—ultimate consumers, industrial consumers, resellers, government and other non-profit consumers, international consumers. It must not be forgotten that the satisfaction of customer and consumer is the main motto of every business firm. The population also contains the prospective consumers of company's products and the company has to identify them which are not easy. Goodwill built up by the company sometimes influences the consumers to become the customer of the company.

❊ Competitors

Competitors are those who sell the goods and service of the same and similar description, in the same market. Apart from this competition there are other forms of competition like product differentiation. It is therefore necessary to build an efficient system of marketing. This will arouse confidence and better results. For this purpose, first of all, competitors are to be identified and closely monitored.

❉ Company Resources

Companies are not alike in terms of their mix of resources, namely, people, finances and facilities. Many executives believe that a firm's most important asset is its employees and that success is highly influenced by the quality of the company management and the skills of its marketing, R&D and production personnel. For some types of industries, success is heavily dependent on the competence of the people in particular functional areas—engineering for capital goods industries such as tooling and production machinery, finance for capital intensive industries such as steel and petroleum, and marketing for consumer packaged goods companies.

❉ Management Philosophy

Marketing strategies that differ greatly from top management's philosophy have little chance of being approved or of receiving enthusiastic support if they are accepted. Management with a more conservative philosophy feel more comfortable with steady but unspectacular growth, maximisation of cash flow from current business, high dividends, and investments.

❉ Public

It is the duty of the company to satisfy the people at large along with its competitors and the consumers. It is necessary for future stay and growth. The actors of the company do influence the other groups forming the general public for the company. A public is defined as "Any group that has an actual or potential interest in or impart on a company's ability to achieve its objectives".

1.9.2 Macro Environment

Macro environment refers to those factors which are not concerned with the immediate environment. These factors are external to the company and are quite uncontrollable. These factors do not affect the marketing ability of the concern directly but it indirectly influences the marketing decision of the company. As against this macro environmental factors directly affect the company's marketing activities and these forces are internal and controllable to some extent. The following are the factors that affect the company's marketing decisions.

The Competitive Environment

The interactive exchange in the marketplace as organisations vie with one another to satisfy customers creates the competitive environment. Marketing decisions by each individual firm influence consumer responses in the marketplace. They also affect the marketing strategies of competitors. As a consequence, decision-makers must continually monitor competitors' marketing activities–their products, channels, prices and promotions.

Few organisations enjoy monopoly positions in the marketplace. Utilities such as electricity, water and cooking gas accept considerable regulation from local authorities. Other firms, such as manufacturers of pharmaceutical products, sometimes achieve temporary monopolies as a result of patents. Marketers actually face three types of competition. Their most direct competition occurs among marketers of similar products, as when an insurance firm competes with other insurance firms. The second type of competition involves products that users can substitute for one another. In the transportation industry, the no-frills, low-cost airliners compete with train and luxury bus services. A change such as a price increase or an improvement in a product's capabilities can directly affect demand for substitute products. The final type of competition occurs among all other organisations that compete for consumers' purchases. Traditional economic analysis views competition as a battle among companies in a single industry or among firms that product substitute goods and services. Marketers must, however, accept the argument that all firms compete for a limited pool of discretionary buying power.

Because the competitive environment often determines the success or failure of a product, marketers must continually assess competitors' marketing strategies. A firm must carefully monitor new product offerings with technological advances, price reductions, special promotions or other competitive variations, and the firm's marketing mix may require adjustments to counter these changes.

Every firm's marketers must develop an effective strategy for dealing with its competitive environment. One company may compete in a broad range of markets in many areas of the world. Another may specialise in particular market segments, such as those determined by customers' geographic, age or income characteristics. Determining a competitive strategy involves answering three questions:

(a) Should we compete?

The answer to this question depends on the firm's resources, objectives and expectations for the market's profit potential. A firm may decide not to pursue or continue operating a potentially successful venture that does not mesh with its resources, objectives or profit expectations.

(b) If so, in what markets should we compete?

The answer requires marketers to acknowledge their limited resources (sales personnel, advertising budgets, product development capabilities, and so on). They must accept responsibility for allocating these resources to the areas of greatest opportunity.

(c) How should we compete?

This requires marketers to make product, pricing, distribution and promotional decisions that give their firm a competitive advantage in the marketplace. Firms can compete on a wide variety of claims, including product quality, price and customer service. For example, a retailer may gain competitive advantage by providing superior customer service, while another retailer competes by providing low prices.

With increased international competition and rapid changes in technology, many firms are using time as a strategic competitive weapon. A time-based competition strategy seeks to develop and distribute goods and services more quickly than competitors. The flexibility and responsiveness of a time-based strategy enables the firm to improve product quality, reduce costs, respond to competition and expand the variety of its products to cover new market segments and enhance customer satisfaction.

The Political-Legal Environment

No one should start playing a new game without first understanding the rules, yet some businesses exhibit remarkably limited knowledge about marketing's political-legal environment–the laws and their interpretations that require firms to operate under certain competitive conditions and to protect consumer rights. Ignorance of laws, ordinances and regulations or failure to comply with them can result in fines, embarrassing negative publicity and possibly expensive civil damage suits.

Businesses need considerable diligence to understand the legal framework for their marketing decisions. Numerous laws and regulations affect those decisions, many of them vaguely stated and inconsistently enforced by a multitude of different authorities. Regulations affect marketing practices, as do the actions of independent regulatory agencies. These requirements and prohibitions touch on all aspects of marketing decision-making—designing, labelling, packaging, distributing, advertising and promoting goods and services. To cope with the vast, complex and changing political-legal environment, many large firms have in-house legal department; small firms often seek professional advice from legal experts. All marketers, however, should be aware of the major regulations that affect their activities.

Some of potential issues from the political-legal environment to affect businesses include:

1. The national foreign policy can dominate the international business decisions of the local firms.
2. The political ideology of the government can affect the international brands wanting to enter a market.

3. The competitors who work closely with the government can help erect trade barriers for a firm.
4. Global trade organisations can enforce trade barriers when their regulations and guidelines are not observed.
5. A host nation may levy anti-dumping duties on a foreign firm and such a decision may be dominated by the local businesses lobbying with the government.
6. Copyright infringements, trademark and intellectual property rights violations.
7. Price regulations preempt any pricing strategy.
8. Direct comparative advertisements may not be allowed in few countries.

Each one of the above issues has serious implications for the marketer in his marketing decision-making. Ignorance of the law is no excuse and breaking of the law is an offence.

The Economic Environment

The overall health of the economy influences how much consumers spend and what they buy. This relationship also works the other way. Consumer plays an important role in the economy's health. Indeed, consumer outlays perennially make up around two-thirds of overall economic activity. Since all marketing activity is directed toward satisfying consumer wants and needs, marketers must understand how economic conditions influence consumer buying decisions.

Marketing's economic environment consists of forces that influence consumer buying power and marketing strategies. They include the stage of the business cycle, inflation, unemployment, resource availability and income.

Inflation devalues money by reducing the products it can buy through persistent price increases. It would restrict purchases less severely if income were to keep pace with rising prices, but often it does not. Inflation increases marketers' costs such as expenditures for wages and raw materials and the resultant higher prices may therefore negatively affect sales. Inflation makes consumers conscious of prices, especially during periods of high inflation. This influence can lead to three possible outcomes, all of them are important to marketers. (1) Consumers can elect to buy now, in the belief that prices will rise later, (2) They can decide to alter their purchasing patterns and (3) They can postpone certain purchases.

Unemployment is defined as the proportion of people in the economy who do not have jobs and are actively looking for work. It rises during recessions and declines in the recovery and prosperity stages of the business cycle. Like inflation, unemployment affects marketing by modifying consumer behaviour. Instead of buying, consumers may choose to build their savings.

Income is another important determinant of marketing's economic environment, because it influences consumer buying power. By studying income statistics and trends, marketers can estimate market potential and develop plans for targeting specific market segments. For marketers, a rise in income represents a potential for increasing overall sales. But they are most interested in the disposable income, which is the amount of money that people have to spend after they have paid for necessities. Consumers' disposable income varies greatly by demographic variables such as age group and educational levels.

The Technological Environment

The technological environment represents the application of marketing to discoveries in science, inventions and innovations. New technology results in new goods and services for consumers; it also improves existing products, strengthens customer service and often reduces prices through new, cost-efficient production and distribution methods. Technology can quickly make products obsolete, but it can just as quickly open up new marketing opportunities. Technology is revolutionising the marketing environment. Technological innovations not just create new products but also whole new industries. Recently, the Internet has been transforming the way companies collaborate with different stakeholders to create more value for the customers. Technology can sometimes address social and environmental concerns by offering a cheap, non-polluting, energy-conserving, safe product and also create parity among consumers by providing equal access and opportunity. Marketers who monitor new technology and successfully apply it may also enhance customer service.

The Sociocultural Environment

The sociocultural environment of marketing describes the relationship between marketing and society and its culture. Marketers must cultivate sensitivity to society's changing values and to demographic shifts such as population growth and age distribution changes. These changing variables affect consumers' reactions to different products and marketing practices. The sociocultural context often exerts a more pronounced influence on marketing decision-making in the international arena than in the domestic arena. Learning about cultural and social differences among countries proves a paramount condition for a firm's success abroad. Marketing strategies that work in one country often fail when directly applied in other countries. In many cases, marketers must redesign packages and modify products and advertising messages to suit the tastes and preferences of different cultures.

Changing social values have led to the consumerism movement which is a social force within the environment designed to aid and protect buyers by exerting legal, moral and economic pressures on business.

Consumerism also advocates the rights of the consumers such as:

1. The right to choose freely–Consumers should be able to choose among a range of goods and services
2. The right to be informed–Consumers should have access to enough education and product information to make responsible buying decisions
3. The right to be heard–Consumers should be able to express legitimate complaints to appropriate parties–be it manufacturers, sellers, consumer assistance groups and consumer courts
4. The right to be safe–Consumers should feel assured that the goods and services they purchase will not cause injuries in normal use. Product designs should allow average consumers to use them safely.

The sociocultural environment for marketing decisions at home and abroad is expanding in scope and importance. Today, no marketer can initiate a strategic decision without taking into account the society's norms, values, culture and demographics. Marketers must understand how these variables affect their decisions. The constant influx of social input requires that marketing managers focus on addressing these questions instead of concerning themselves only with the standard marketing tools.

1.10   GREEN MARKETING

According to the American Marketing Association, "Green Marketing" is the marketing of products that are presumed to be environmentally safe. Thus, green marketing incorporates a broad range of activities, including product modification, changes to the production process, packaging changes, as well as modifying advertising. Yet defining green marketing

is not a simple task where several meanings intersect and contradict each other; an example of this will be the existence of varying social, environmental and retail definitions attached to this term. Other similar terms used are Environmental Marketing and Ecological Marketing.

The term Green Marketing came into prominence in the late 1980s and early 1990s. The American Marketing Association (AMA) held the first workshop on "Ecological Marketing" in 1975. The proceedings of this workshop resulted in one of the first books on green marketing entitled "Ecological Marketing".

The first wave of Green Marketing occurred in the 1980s. Corporate Social Responsibility (CSR) Reports started with the ice cream seller Ben & Jerry's where the financial report was supplemented by a greater view on the company's environmental impact. In 1987, a document prepared by the World Commission on Environment and Development defined sustainable development as meeting "the needs of the present without compromising the ability of future generations to meet their own need", this became known as the Brundtland Report and was another step towards widespread thinking on sustainability in everyday activity. Two tangible milestones for wave 1 of green marketing came in the form of published books, both of which were called Green.

Who is doing Green Marketing?

Companies large and small are realising the benefits of going green, and integrating that into their marketing messages. According to a 2009 January/February study by the American Marketing Association, more than half of corporate marketers believe that their organisations will increase their involvement in environmental sustainability over the next two to three years, and 43% say their companies will increase marketing of these programmes. As further proof of the growing popularity of green marketing, Datamonitor Product Launch Analytics shows 458 product launches so far in 2009 of package-goods products that claim to be sustainable, environment-friendly, or "eco-friendly." If that pace holds all year, it will triple the number of green launches last year, which in turn was more than double the number in 2007.

Effectiveness

Successful marketing is customer-centric, so if sustainability and eco-friendly products are important to customers, green marketing may be effective. Green is becoming more and more mainstream—becoming more important to increasing numbers of people. An excellent example of a large company embracing green marketing is Scott, a $2 billion global value brand that reaches one in three U.S. households—a very mainstream customer base. Scott is launching a new line of toilet paper, paper towels, napkins, and wipes made from 40%-50% recycled content. The decision was based on research conducted on Scott's value-minded customers: the research found that 86% are interested and 41% are very interested in products with recycled content.

Companies can determine if environmental concerns are important to customers by simply asking them. Set up interviews, post a survey on the corporate Website, or send emails requesting customers' feedback. At the very least, customers will appreciate the interest in their opinion, and a great new opportunity to meet customer needs may be uncovered.

Companies have been touting the green benefits of their products and initiatives for quite some time. Following the initial wave of green marketing messages, consumers became turned off by green marketing due to a number of claims that were fraudulent or misleading, and due to the saturation of green marketing. However, Nielson's concept-testing service BASES found that now, more than 80% of consumers in all categories–including 89% of those most inclined to buy green but also 80% of those unconcerned about green claims– found green claims completely or somewhat believable. Only 9%–16% of consumers said they believe green products aren't as green as claimed.

Before launching a green marketing campaign, companies should be able to substantiate the environmental claims they plan to make. Though the FTC (Federal Trade Commission) does not set definitive standards for the use of specific environmental claims, its policy states that "any party making an express or implied claim that presents an objective assertion about the environmental attribute of a product, package, or service must, at the time the claim is made, possess and rely upon a reasonable basis substantiating the claim."

Companies also need to ensure claims aren't too broad. According to the FTC's green guide, an environmental marketing claim should make clear whether the environmental attribute or benefit being asserted refers to the product, the product's packaging, or a service; or to a portion or component of the product, the product's packaging, or service. Companies should be careful to tailor their claims so as not to overstate the environmental benefit or attribute.

Green Marketing Basics

For green marketing to be effective, consider the following:

1. Balance environmental issues with primary customer needs. If customers aren't going to use environmental issues to gauge products and companies, and if environmental initiatives are not going to drive a purchasing decision or brand loyalty, green marketing isn't going to be an effective use of the marketing budget.
2. The green marketing claims must be credible. Companies need to provide a level of detail about the claims that make them meaningful, and be able to substantiate those claims. Customers need to believe the claims for green marketing to be effective.
3. Green marketing must empower the customers. The green marketing message must make customers feel that by using the product or service they will make a difference.
4. Overcome customers' concerns about price and product performance. Educate customers about the benefits the product or service provides, and provide testimonials, case studies, or research reinforcing the performance and value claims.

Green marketing can be an effective and useful tool, but it must align with customers' needs. If environmental concerns aren't important to customers, green marketing will not be effective. However, if customers do place high importance on green products and sustainability issues, green marketing can be a powerful way to positively position the company and its products and services.

Green Products

There is no widespread agreement on what exactly makes a product green. Some general guidelines include that a green product

1. does not present a health hazard to people or animals;
2. is relatively efficient in its use of resources during manufacture, use, and disposal;
3. does not incorporate materials derived from endangered species or threatened environments;
4. does not contribute to excessive waste in its use or packaging; and
5. does not rely on unnecessary use of or cruelty to animals.

Other favourable attributes from the green point of view are the incorporation of recycled materials into the product and the product's own recyclability. A great deal of work in the determination of these factors is concerned with a product's environmental impact at various stages of its useful life. Life cycle analysis (LCA) and product line analysis (PLA) studies measure the environmental impact of products over their entire life cycle, that is, from the "cradle to the grave." Such studies track resource use, energy requirements, and waste generation in order to provide comparative benchmarks enabling manufacturers and consumers to select products involving the least impact upon the natural environment. Though useful, LCA studies have been criticised for their subjectivity in setting analysis boundaries and for difficulties in establishing comparable impacts across environmental media, e.g., "How many tons of carbon dioxide emissions equal the release of one picogram of dioxin?"

Information from these studies and additional consumer research is being used to develop new products and to redesign existing products and services in order to reduce environmental impact. The U.S. Office of Technology Assessment (OTA, a congressional research department that was closed in 1994) advocated green design: "a design process in which environmental attributes are treated as design objectives, rather than as constraints... green design incorporates environmental objectives with minimum loss to product performance, useful life or functionality." "Design for the environment," "design for durability" and "design for disassembly" have become popular phrases at companies seeking to prevent waste and manage material flows more efficiently. Products and packaging are being redesigned to use less materials or to be easily disassembled so high-value components can be recycled or refurbished more readily. Of course, numerous trade-offs must be made weighing health and safety attributes and consumer desires for convenience against packaging, energy use, and recycling requirements.

Some drawbacks of green marketing are thus:

1. The perception of "green washing".
2. Disputes and contention surrounding the exact meaning of a green product.

Green washing pertains to when a firm misleadingly produces a product, with ostensible green characteristics, which is not actually environmentally sound. In addition to evident ethical issues concerning deceit, such conduct can undermine an organisation's drive to be deemed a "green" company. Accordingly, a firm must be sincere in its efforts to be environmentally sound, regarding its environmental practices and policies.

Moreover, the extent and nature of a green product can be a moot point. To some, a product must be wholly green to be viewed as green. To others, a product may only possess a reduction in environmentally harmful inputs to be worthy of being labelled green. Nonetheless, a firm can enhance its green marketing efforts if it persuades consumers that the purchase of green products can enhance environmental protection.

1.11   THE ROLE OF MARKETING IN RELATION TO SOME SELECTED SECTORS

Agricultural Development and Farm Productivity

Many of you probably know that in many developing countries agriculture still occupies a high degree of importance and the nation's economic development is closely tied to agricultural development.

There are millions of small farmers who cultivate ten or fewer acres of land, and these account more than 60 per cent of population in the third world. However, many of these farmers do not have access to the market system prevailing in these developing countries. Fortunately in India though we have been successful in improving out farm productivity to a significant level but did not envisage the magnitude of distribution tasks entitled in the marketing of essential foodgrains and agricultural raw materials. The drought of 1966-67 was an eye-opener for the government and made everyone in the administration realise the urgency of a planned programme for foodgrains distribution. And it has been found that marketing techniques, like product demonstration, word-of-mouth publicity and point-of-sale display play an effective role in the adoption of new ideas.

Industrial and Entrepreneurial Growth

We shall now introduce you some of the important issues in this area which the developing countries are facing and how these need to be approached. One of the issues relates to technology transfer and development. Many developing nations in their quest for industrial growth have imported sophisticated intensive technology from the west. This has put an enormous burden on the nation's resources of foreign exchange. In the process, the technological and capital needs of small industries have been largely neglected. The plight of small industries is parallel to the plight of small farmers mentioned earlier. If Japan's experience teaches any single lesson regarding the process of economic development in Asia, it is the cumulative importance of a myriad of simple improvement in technology which do not depart radically from tradition of requiring large units of new investment. The growth and productivity of small industries scattered throughout the nation help in a number of ways. Some of these are:

1. Provide the basic infrastructure that is needed to industrialise a developing nation.
2. Create more and more new jobs because they are labour intensive.
3. Suffer less from the scarce resources of managerial talents because the running on small business is relatively less complicated.
4. Provides the nation with a vast pool of individual entrepreneur with management skills learned on the job.

And so far as the infusion of marketing philosophy to small industries is concerned, organisationally speaking it is relatively a small task. Further, such a growth of local economics through the spreading of small industries could prove to be further points of distribution for products that need to be mass marketed.

Export Promotion and Tourism

Export trade and tourism represent sectors which are extremely crucial to the growth of developing economy insofar as the building up of foreign exchange reserves is concerned. These are areas where the government should try to attain the least bureaucracy, but ensure the strictest form of quality control on products leaving the nation's shores and services provided to the visiting tourist.

One of the important shortcomings of India's drive for export promotion is its inability to view export trade as a marketing problem. Export promotion measures had for a long time neglected the need for dynamic market information and product adaptation.

Generally, promotion of tourism calls for a comprehensive marketing strategy designed to provide a well-knit package of services such as hotel, foreign exchange, transportation and sightseeing.

1.12   INDIAN MARKETING ENVIRONMENT

For global marketers India is not just a single country, it is further divided into two different countries: India and Bharat. India is looked and appreciated by the whole world. It is growing at the second fastest rate. Its a outsourcing hub, skilled workforce, nuclear and space power and everything to become a world power. On the other hand, Bharat involves poverty, illiteracy at high levels, corruption, mismanagement, violence between religions and like that. So in this way whosoever desires to enter in the Indian market must realise both the faces of this country. They should realise the serious challenges of doing business here like segmenting the market properly, Understanding country's social and cultural issues, getting through government bureaucracy and understanding economic and political situation. There have been bunch of examples of companies who have tried to enter in Indian markets without taking care of these issues and have failed badly

Now before understanding Indian marketing environment, it is important to understand what is marketing environment. The marketing environment consists of factors and forces outside or inside the organization that affect its business in the market. The marketing environment is divided into tow different environments.

- **Micro Environment:** It consists of factors close to the companies that have a direct impact on the organization strategy. This includes company's suppliers, distributors, customers and competitors.

- **Macro Environment:** It consists of larger societal forces. And these are beyond the control of the organization. These shape the characteristics of the opportunities and threats facing accompany. For example, economic, cultural, political, demographic and technological.

The firm has to know where the environment is heading, what trends are emerging therein and what should be its response to the environment changes. Only by analysing the environment, can the firm grapple with these issues.

1. Purpose of marketing environment analysis.
2. To know where the environment is heading.
3. To discern which events and trends are favourable from the standpoint of the firm.
4. To project how the environment–each factor of the environment–will be at the future point of time.
5. To assess the scope of various opportunities and shortlist those that can favourably impact the business.

The framework of marketing environment is expressed in the following ways:

The Demographic Scene

If we follow the adage 'market means people', India with a population of over 100 million is the second largest market in the world. And the population is growing at the rate of over 2 percent per annum. The life expectancy of the people of India are widely distributed over the length and covers 3.3 million sq. km. India has a large pool of highly qualified manpower including over two and a half million engineers and scientists. The people of India profess groups - Hindus, Muslims, Sikhs, Christians, Zoroastrians, Buddhists and Janis are there in India. Languages are different spoken by the different segments of people.

It is the study of the people in terms of their age, gender, race, ethnicity, and location. Demographic characteristics strongly affect buying behaviour. The current population of India is 1.18 billion and it is the second most populous country in the world next to China. And it was projected that by 2010, it will overtake China with 1.53 billion. Obviously that's not a good news but for marketers there lies lots of opportunities. Fast growth of population accompanied with rising income means expanding markets. And among this 1.18 billion population, more than 50% are below 25 years of age. And that is the reason why there is tough competition in the area of soft drinks, networking sites, stylish mobile handsets, job portals and all. Estimated in 2008, around 71% population lives in rural areas even after so much migration to urban cities and that is the reason why low cost brands have started targeting rural communities. They put Camps, Hut in melas to promote their products. Literacy rate, as estimated in 2009, for men it was 76.9% and for women it was 54.5%, though there is still wide gender disparity, but it has been observed that growth in women literacy rate is more than men's. So women are another big target for marketers. Especially for home based products, as we know women are the chief person to select them for her home.

The General Economic Scene

The Indian economy has moved decisively to a higher growth phase in comparison to the previous years. The projected economic growth rate for the current year is nearly around 8.7% which is a significant achievement. In order to meet the targeted growth rate of 9% for the 11th Five year Plan there was acceleration in domestic investment and savings rate. But there are also certain shortcomings with respect to this phenomenal increase in growth rate as the economy was not prepared to face the challenge of inflation in the economy. The world prices of crude oil, commodities and food grains have risen sharply since the last year. Among the commodities the price of copper, iron ore, tin are elevated. So the basic challenge for the government is to keep the inflation under check and manage the capital flows more effectively. Especially now since the rupee has appreciated, the export sector is affected to a great extent and there has been a slowdown in the consumer goods segment. Though this is a boom for the Indian economy it has affected the employment status of those working in the multinational companies as the dollar value has depreciated and they are unable to meet the expectations of the employees with regard to the pay packages. But on the other hand the companies importing goods from other countries will benefit greatly. Now our great concern is that in order to increase the growth rate according to our set target as per the 11th Five year Plan we need to have certain additional reforms. Experts estimate that by 2025, India's share in world GDP is expected to rise from 6% to 11% wherein that of US will witness a fall from 21% to 18%. India is expected to be the 3rd largest economy in the world by 2025. The country has seen a growth of 9.0 percent during 2005-2006, 9.4 percent during 2006-2007 and 8.7 percent in 2007-2008.

Agriculture, forestry and allied activities constituted around 32 percent of the GDP at factor cost, industry constituted 43%, and services 25%. Throughout the seventies, India was among the slow growth countries within the developing world and her unspectacular average annual growth of 3 to 3.5% was dubbed the 'Hindu rate of growth'. In the eighties India's economic growth averaged five percent per annum. In the nineties an environment for faster economic growth was created through the new economic policies.

The economy is expected to move on to a higher growth curve in the coming years. It is estimated that over the medium term, Indian economy can achieve a growth rate of 7.5% or more on a stable basis. Growth of corporate sector and stock markets is usually an important indicator of the sophistication and growth of an economy. During the last two decades, India's corporate sector has grown substantially. The growth in the eighties has been particularly striking, and the growth in the nineties has been spectacular following the liberalisation, by the above figures expansion of the stock market is a clear indicator of the expansion of the economy.

The Agricultural Scene

Agriculture is a prominent sector of the economy of India. It has always been the backbone of the national economy. It has maintained its pre-eminent place, even after the country went through a good measure of industrialisation, nearly 3/4th of the total population of the country depends directly on it. Agriculture also supplies the raw materials to a large section of Indian industry. Several of the consumer goods industries which all these years were depending on the urban markets for their business have now come to depend on the vast rural markets of the country. It means that growth in agriculture would be one main indicator of the level of the nation's market. The favourable developments on the agricultural scene have been largely the result of the remarkable agricultural breakthrough achieved by India in the last sixties through the technical group, referred to as 'Green Revolution'. Prior to the green revolution, increase in farm production in India came mainly through enlargement of the area under the plough and the area under irrigation and changes in the cropping pattern. As a contrast, the green revolution was a great turning point in Indian agriculture that of his total traditionality and exchangeability; it laid to rest the vision of the Indian farmer as a stubborn, changeless, robot, slavishly following his inherited agricultural traditions. Indian agriculture has successfully crossed the stage of transition, from a home need-based land use system to a market-oriented land use system. The markets that we can see in the rural areas of India today are the direct outcome of the prosperity brought in by the revolution on the farm front.

Agricultural sector in particular has seen the most dismal performance for the Indian economy in spite of the fact that more than 58% of the country depends on agriculture, directly or indirectly and there are more than 115 million farming families in the country. From strong roots of a growth of 9.1% in 2003-2004, it has fallen down to 2.7% during 2007-2008. India is the largest producer of jute, tea and jute like fibre. At the same time, the country is the largest consumer of tea in world as well. India exports tea to more than 80 countries and accounts for 14% of world tea trade. India's milk production is also the highest in the world. In terms of area, India has the 1st rank in total irrigated land in the world. The country is placed 3rd among cereal production, having the 2nd largest position when it comes to wheat and rice and the largest in the world for production of pulses.

Agricultural sector though heavily subsidised and funded by the government lacks the technological upliftment and the practices in the sector even today are mostly third world.

The Industrial Scene

Over the past forty years or so, India has achieved substantial industrial advancement. A solid industrial base has been created and a considerable degree of diversification and sophistication has also been accomplished in this sector. The industrial sector now contributes nearly 43% of India's GDP. The growth has been particularly striking in segments like petroleum products, chemicals, metal products, electronics, electrical machinery, transport equipment and power generation. There have also been some fundamental structural changes for the better. The output of basic and capital goods industries now has a share of 55 per cent in the index of industrial production whereas it had only a share of 20% in 1950. Traditional industries of India have also undergone rapid modernisation during these years. Though it still has a long way to go in this respect, a good beginning has already been made and it augurs well for the future.

A Satellite Survey of Indian Industry

We will make an industry by industry analysis so that we can have a proper understanding of the prevailing industrial base and industrial environment in the country.

- Steel industry
- Engineering industry
- Automobile industry
- Cement industry
- Textile industry
- Chemical industry
- Electronics industry
- Computers
- Small-scale industry and khadi and village industry

✽ Steel Industry

The iron and steel industry of India has registered commendable growth over the years. India has put in substantial investment in the past to build up of this core industry. Today India is the 5th largest producer of iron ore in the world and the 10th largest producer of finished steel. The government of India deleted the steel industry from the list of industries reserved for the public sector and opened it up to private entrepreneurs. With a view to encourage a large volume of fresh investment in the steel sector, the government also included it in the list of high priority industries for foreign investment.

During the first half of 2007, steel consumption grew by 13 per cent. For the period of April-September 2007-08, the total consumption (excluding double counting) of steel was 21.998 MT as compared to the 19.819 MT in the same period last year (as per data from the joint parliamentary committee).

A Credit Suisse Group study states that India's steel consumption will continue to grow by 16 per cent annually till 2012, fuelled by demand for construction projects worth US$ 1 trillion.

With this surge in demand level, steel producers have been reporting encouraging results. For example, the top six companies, which account for 70 per cent of the total production capacity, have recorded a year-on-year growth rate of 11.4 per cent, 12.7 per cent and 9.7 per cent in net sales, operating profit and net profit, respectively, during the second quarter of 2007-08. Tata Steel, the world 6th largest steelmaker, aims to double its returns on investment by 2012. Essar Steel is aiming to enhance its steel capacity from 4.6 million tons to 9 MT in Gujarat.

Government targets to increase the production capacity from 56 million tons annually to 124 MT in the first phase which will come to an end by 2011 - 12. Currently with a production of 56 million tons India accounts for over 7% of the total steel produced globally, while it accounts to about 5% of global steel consumption. The steel sector in India grew by 5.3% in May 2009. Globally India is the only country to post a positive overall growth in the production of crude steel at 1.01% for the period of January - March in 2009.

* Engineering Industry

India has a large and expanding engineering industry; it has grown not only in terms of investment and output but also in terms of structure, composition of products, technological sophistication and self-reliance. There are four major distinct segments in the engineering industry.

1. Machine building segments/heavy engineering segment.
2. Transport equipment and tractors.
3. Heavy equipment.
4. Machine tools.

The engineering industry plays a vital role of the country's total industrial profile. Each of these segments has registered good growth. For example, in machine tools, India has already become one of the top 20 producers in the world. There are 150 units engaged in the manufacture of machine tools at present. And similar development has taken place in the other segments of the engineering industry. The engineering industry of today has emerged as a vital part of the countries total industrial profile. It is providing infrastructure required for the continued industrial expansions in the country. It not only fulfils most of the domestic needs but also makes a very sizeable contribution in the field of exports. The sophistication and structural changes the industry has undergone will be evident from the fact that the share of capital goods turn-key projects in the exports is now in the range of 40-50%.

The engineering industry in India manufactures a wide range of products, with heavy engineering goods accounting for bulk of the production. Most of the leading players are engaged in the production of heavy engineering goods and mainly produces high-value products using high-end technology. Requirement of high level of capital investment poses as a major entry barrier. Consequently, the small and unorganised firms have a small market presence. The light engineering goods segment, on the other hand, uses medium to low-end technology. Entry barrier is low on account of the comparatively lower requirement of capital and technology. This segment is characterised by the dominance of small and unorganised players which manufacture low-value added products. However, there are few medium and large scale firms which manufacture high-value added products. This segment is also characterised by small capacities and high level of competition among the players.

With a scintillating 2.3 million units produced in 2008 the Indian automobile industry bagged the position of being the ninth largest in the world. Following economic liberalisation, Indian domestic automobile companies like Tata Motors, Maruti Suzuki and Mahindra and Mahindra expanded their production and export operations in and across the country and since then the industry has only shown signs of growth. The automobile industry comprises heavy vehicles (trucks, buses, tempos, and tractors), passenger cars, and two-wheelers.

❉ Automobile Industry

The Indian automobile industry seems to come a long way since the first car that was manufactured in Mumbai in 1898. The automobile sector today is one of the key sectors of the country contributing majorly to the economy of India. It directly and indirectly provides employment to over 10 million people in the country. The Indian automobile industry has a well established name globally being the second largest two-wheeler market in the world, fourth largest commercial vehicle market in the world, and eleventh largest passenger car market in the world and expected to become the third largest automobile market in the world only behind USA and China.

Key automobile manufacturers in India

- Maruti Udyog
- General Motors
- Ford India Limited
- Eicher Motors
- Bajaj Auto
- Daewoo Motors india
- Hero Motors
- Hindustan Motors
- Hyundai Motors India Limited
- Royal Enfield Motors
- Telco
- TVS Motors
- DC Designs
- Swaraj Mazda Limited

(a) Passengers cars

Though quite small by world's standards, the passenger car industry of India is on a path of growth and technological change. Currently Maruti Udyog Ltd., produces around 150,000 units per year, including its new export model and holds a dominant share of the market. The new entrant Telco accounts for a small part of the market with 7,000 units. Worlds giants like General Motors, Mercedes, Peugeot, Toyota, Honda, Fiat are working out tie-ups with local passengers car manufacturers.

(b) Light commercial vehicles (LCV)

In the early eighties, following the liberalisation of the automobile industry, the Light Commercial Vehicles (LCV) segment had attracted a spate of new investments and technical collaboration, especially from Japanese LCV majors such as Toyota, Nissan and Mazda.

(c) Two-wheelers

Two-wheelers account for almost 80% of the total automobile output, and within the two-wheeler segment, scooters undergone a veritable metamorphosis in its competitive character. The extent of competition in this business can be easily understood from the fact that nearly 200 units, 100 large sized units and 100 mini cement units are fighting for a share of the cement market.

❊ Cement Industry

Cement is a key infrastructure industry. It was decontrolled from price and distribution on 1st March, 1989 and delicensed on 25th July, 1991. However, the performance of the industry and prices of cement are monitored regularly. The constraints faced by the industry are reviewed in the Infrastructure Coordination Committee meetings held in the Cabinet Secretariat under the Chairmanship of Secretary (Coordination). Its performance is also reviewed by the Cabinet Committee on Infrastructure.

- **Capacity and production**

  The cement industry comprises 125 large cement plants with an installed capacity of 148.28 million tons and more than 300 mini cement plants with an estimated capacity of 11.10 million tons per annum. The Cement Corporation of India, which is a central public sector undertaking, has 10 units. There are 10 large cement plants owned by various state governments. The total installed capacity in the country as a whole is 159.38 million tons. Actual cement production in 2002-03 was 116.35 million tons as against a production of 106.90 million tons in 2001-02, registering a growth rate of 8.84%.

  Keeping in view the trend of growth of the industry in previous years, a production target of 126 million tons has been fixed for the year 2003-04. During the period April-June 2003, a production (provisional) was 31.30 million tons. The industry has achieved a growth rate of 4.86 per cent during this period.

- **Exports**

  Apart from meeting the entire domestic demand, the industry is also exporting cement and clinker. The export of cement during 2001-02 and 2003-04 was 5.14 million tons and 6.92 million tons respectively. Export during April-May, 2003 was 1.35 million tons. Major exporters were Gujarat Ambuja Cements Ltd. and L&T Ltd.

- **Recommendations on cement industry**

  For the development of the cement industry 'Working Group on Cement Industry' was constituted by the Planning Commission for the formulation of 10th Five Year Plan. The Working Group has projected a growth rate of 10% for the cement industry during the plan period and has projected creation of additional capacity of 40-62 million tons mainly through expansion of existing plants. The Working Group has identified following thrust areas for improving demand for cement;

(i) Further push to housing development programmes;

(ii) Promotion of concrete highways and roads; and

(iii) Use of ready-mix concrete in large infrastructure projects.

Further, in order to improve global competitiveness of the Indian cement industry, the Department of Industrial Policy and Promotion commissioned a study on the global competitiveness of the Indian industry through an organization of international repute, viz. KPMG Consultancy Pvt. Ltd. The report submitted by the organization has made several recommendations for making the Indian cement industry more competitive in the international market. The recommendations are under consideration.

Technological change

The cement industry has made tremendous strides in technological upgradation and assimilation of the latest technology. At present 93 per cent of the total capacity in the industry is based on modern and environment-friendly dry process technology and only seven per cent of the capacity is based on old wet and semi-dry process technology. There is tremendous scope for waste heat recovery in cement plants and thereby reduction in emission level. One project for co-generation of power utilizing waste heat in an Indian cement plant is being implemented with Japanese assistance under Green Aid Plan. The induction of advanced technology has helped the industry immensely to conserve energy and fuel and to save materials substantially. India is also producing different varieties of cement like Ordinary Portland Cement (OPC), Portland Pozzolana Cement (PPC), Portland Blast Furnace Slag Cement (PBFS), Oil Well Cement, Rapid Hardening Portland Cement, Sulphate Resisting Portland Cement, White Cement etc. Production of these varieties of cement conform to the BIS specifications. It is worth mentioning that some cement plants have set up dedicated jetties for promoting bulk transportation and export.

❋ Textile Industry

India has a very large textile industry, one of the largest in the world. It is the single largest organised industry of India. It employs over 12 lakh workers. The total sales income of 61 major companies in this industry aggregates to ₹10,000 crore. The industry presents an interesting picture of the coexistence of four sectors- khadi, handlooms, power looms and organised mills. And a cotton textile is the most significant segment in all these sectors.

Indian textile industry largely depends upon the textile manufacturing and export. It also plays a major role in the economy of the country. India earns about 27% of its total foreign exchange through textile exports. Further, the textile industry of India also contributes nearly 14% of the total industrial production of the country. It also contributes around 3% to the GDP of the country. Indian textile industry is also the largest in the country in terms of employment generation. It not only generates jobs in its own industry, but also opens up scopes for the other ancillary sectors. Indian textile industry currently generates employment to more than 35 million people. It is also estimated that, the industry was to generate 12 million new jobs by the year 2010.

Indian textile industry is one of the leading textile industries in the world. Though was predominantly unorganised industry even a few years back, but the scenario started changing after the economic liberalisation of Indian economy in 1991. The opening up of economy gave the much-needed thrust to the Indian textile industry, which has now successfully become one of the largest in the world.

Indian textile industry can be divided into several segments, some of which can be listed as below:

- Cotton Textiles
- Silk Textiles
- Woollen Textiles
- Readymade Garments
- Hand-crafted Textiles
- Jute and Coir

❋ Chemical Industry

The chemical industry is one of the three largest groups of industries in India, along with iron & steel and textiles. The chemical industry also exports goods to the tune of ₹5000 crore per annum. Inorganic chemicals/heavy chemicals, organic chemicals, petrochemicals, fertilisers, drugs and pharmaceuticals form the important components of India's chemical industry. The current annual turnover of the industry is over ₹40,000 crore, excluding petroleum products. In inorganic chemicals, India has a very strong manufacturing base, annual production of caustic soda and soda ash are in the range of 1.2 and 1.5 million tons respectively; production of sulphuric acid is upwards 3 million tons. In organic chemicals too, India has a strong manufacturing base, especially in products like acetic acid, formaldehyde, methanol, and phenol and phthalic anhydride.

Globalisation poses several changes to the industry that has predominantly developed in a protected environment. With World Trade Origination (WTO) assuming an increasing role in international economics, there is an inevitable move towards an interlinked global economy. However, there have been cases where certain segments of the industry such as pharmaceuticals and biotechnology have performed exceedingly well even at a global level.

The industry needs to address a number of imperatives to achieve the aspirations. These imperatives apply to each segment albeit in different ways to bridge the USD 40 billion gap between the base case and the aspirational scenario.

❋ Petrochemicals

India has a large petrochemicals industry. It has steadily grown and today, both the sectors of this industry i.e., raw material manufacture and conversion are fairly well established. Between 1980-81 and 1990-91, consumption of plastics in India went up steadily, increasing at an average rate of 11 per cent per annum.

The petrochemical industry in India has been one of the fastest growing industries in the country. Since the beginning, the Indian petrochemical industry has shown an enviable growth rate. This industry also contributes largely to the economy of the country and the growth and development of manufacturing industry as well. It provides the foundation for manufacturing industries like construction, packaging, pharmaceuticals, agriculture, textiles etc.

The Indian petrochemical industry is a highly concentrated one and is oligopolistic in nature. Even till a few years back, only four major companies viz. Reliance Industries Ltd (RIL), Indian Petrochemicals Corporation Ltd. (IPCL), Gas Authority of India Ltd. (GAIL) and Haldia Petrochemicals Ltd. (HPL) used to dominate the industry to a large extent. The recent amalgamation of IPCL with RIL has made the industry more concentrated further, as they jointly account for over 70% of country's total petrochemical capacity. However, the scene is a bit different for the downstream petrochemical sector, which is highly fragmented in nature with over 40 companies existing in the market.

India has a large petrochemicals industry. The current consumption of major commodity plastics like polyethylene (PE) of all types, polypropylene (PP), polyvinylchloride (PVC) and polystyrene is over one million tons and the current manufacturing capacity of these major plastics also stands at the same level. The country's present requirements of the high-volume low-priced commodity plastics such as LDPE and HDPE are totally met from indigenous sources; the medium-volume medium-priced engineering polymers are also manufactured indigenously to a limited extent.

❋ Synthetic Fibres and Fibres Intermediates

In the synthetic fibre and fibre intermediates segment, the country made the first strides in 1962, when two plants were commissioned for making nylon filament yarn. The early eighties witnessed the commissioning of many plants of larger capacities and different types in the filament sector.

❋ Fertiliser Industry

The fertiliser industry presents one of the most energy intensive sectors within the Indian economy and is therefore of particular interest in the context of both local and global environmental discussions. Increases in productivity through the adoption of more efficient and cleaner technologies in the manufacturing sector will be most effective in merging economic, environmental, and social development objectives. A historical examination of productivity growth in India's industries embedded into a broader analysis of structural composition and policy changes will help identify potential future development strategies that lead towards a more sustainable development path. Issues of productivity growth and patterns of substitution in the fertiliser sector as well as in other energy intensive industries in India have been discussed from various perspectives.

Historical estimates vary from indicating an improvement to a decline in the sector's productivity. The variation depends mainly on the time period considered, the source of data, the type of indices and econometric specifications used for reporting productivity growth. Regarding patterns of substitution most analyses focus on inter fuel substitution possibilities in the context of rising energy demand. Not much research has been conducted on patterns of substitution among the primary and secondary input factors: capital, labour, energy and materials. However, analysing the use and substitution possibilities of these factors as well as identifying the main drivers of productivity growth among these and other factors is of special importance for understanding technological and overall development of an industry.

❋ Drugs and Pharmaceutical Industry

India's drugs and pharmaceuticals industry presents a picture of fast development. Today, India manufactures most of its requirements of bulk drugs and formulations, in fact, more than 30,000 different pharmaceuticals formulations worth over ₹5,000 crore are manufactured and sold in India.

❋ Electronics Industry

Electronics Today contains a regular Pull- out- **Smart Cards** Today, which brings out the latest news and developments in Smart Cards, RFID, biometrics, e-Security and Mobile communications technologies and industries. In addition to the regular 400,000 readers of Electronics Today, **Smart Cards** Today is read by about 100,000 additional readers in the Government, banking, retail industry, transport, academic and R&D institutions and other user segments of these technologies.

In recent years the electronics industry is growing at a brisk pace. It is currently worth US$32 billion and according to industry estimates it had the potential to reach US$150 billion by 2010. The largest segment is the consumer electronics segment. While is largest export segment is of components.

The electronics industry in India constitutes just 0.7 per cent of the global electronics industry. Hence it is miniscule by international comparison. However the demand in the Indian market is growing rapidly and investments are flowing in to augment manufacturing capacity

The output of the electronic hardware industry in India is worth US$11.6 billion at present. India is also an exporter of a vast range of electronic components and products for the following segments

- Display technologies
- Entertainment electronics
- Optical storage devices
- Passive components
- Electromechanical components
- Telecom equipment
- Transmission & signaling equipment
- Semiconductor designing
- Electronic manufacturing services (EMS)

This growth has attracted global players to India and leaders like Solectron, Flextronics, Jabil, Nokia, Elcoteq and many more have made large investments to access the Indian market. In consumer electronics Korean companies such as LG and Samsung have made commitments by establishing large manufacturing facilities and now enjoy a significant share in the growing market for products such as televisions, CD/DVD players, audio equipment and other entertainment products.

❖ Computer Industry

The high growth in PC sales is attributed to increased consumption by industry verticals such as telecom, banking and financial services, manufacturing, education, retail and BPO/IT-enabled services as well as major e-Governance initiatives of the central and state governments. Significant consumption in the small and medium enterprises and increased PC purchase in smaller towns and cities was witnessed during the year. It is expected that increased Government focus on pan-India deployment of broadband at one of the lowest costs in the world will soon lead to accelerated PC consumption in the home market.

The growing domestic IT (information technology) market has now given impetus to manufacturing in India. The year witnessed not only capacity expansion by the existing players, but also newer investments in hardware manufacturing. India is also high on the agenda of electronics manufacturing services companies.

❊ Small-scale Industry and Khadi and Village Industry

An analysis of the entire Indian industrial scene would not be complete without a reference to India's small-scale industry and khadi and village industry. These sectors constitute nearly 50% of India's industrial production. They also contribute substantially to the export earnings of the country. The small-scale sector has ventured into totally new and sophisticated fields including production of TV sets, cardiac pacemakers, ECG (electrocardiograph) machines and hearing aids. Small-scale units also supply parts and components to large-scale industries.

❊ The Consumer Goods Scene

Indian market size has enormous potential to become a major global force to reckon with the credit for having a huge market size in India is largely attributed to the fact that the India is the second most populated country in the world. Owing to the liberal government policies, the Indian market size has increased of late as it has witnessed the entry of new players to the Indian market scene. It is very difficult to gauge the full extent of Indian market size due to the extremely heterogeneous nature of the various elements within the country. The Indian market size can be broadly classified into four components:

- Labour Market
- Money Market
- Commodity Market
- Capital Market

The **labour market** in India is among one of the cheapest in the world. Besides, there are a large number of English knowing technically qualified workforce in the country. This increases the Indian market size vastly and also makes India one of the favourite destinations for overseas companies to set up branches. The labour market consists of workforce in the entire three sectors primary, secondary and tertiary sector.

The **money market** in India deals with all the aspects related to the lending and borrowing of funds. Since the Indian market size is huge; performance in the country's money market depends on a variety of factors. The money market is closely connected to the foreign exchange market.

The **commodity market** comprises exchange of goods that is estimated in terms of the domestic currency. The wholesale market and the retail market are important components of the commodity market.

Capital market deals with all the assets of the country. Here both the government and public companies can raise short term and long term funds, depending on their requirements. The bond market and the share market come under the capital market.

Demand for consumer goods (figures in '000)

	1995-96	2001-02	2005-06	2009-10 (Estimated)
Cars	276	788	1560	3466
Motorcycles	760	2599	4663	8369
CTV Regular	1785	4580	6295	9957
Refrigerators	1850	3006	4335	6774
White Goods	3437	6024	8727	13149

An increase in the demand for consumer goods means that the production requirement naturally increases. The rapid rise in the income patters of the population in India has ensured that the demand for consumer goods increased at an even faster pace. Today, the numbers of people who own consumer goods are far larger than they were a decade ago. Indian market size has witnessed tremendous change over the last few years due to this. Besides the quantum jump, the consumer goods scene has also witnessed a great enlargement of the range of products on sale. A number of new products in durables as well as non-durables categories which were hitherto nonexistent in the Indian market have now become a part of the regular fare. In addition, many of the older products acquired new strengths and new marketing dimensions. Television sets, audio systems, VCRs, quartz watches, computers, two-wheelers, refrigerators, cooking ranges, vacuum cleaners and other home appliances, processed foods and soft drinks have been some of the most rapidly growing product groups of this period. Today, the consumer goods market of India includes practically all the products and services that are used by the consumption communities of the affluent world.

We shall pick up a few specific segments and illustrate the developments in the consumer goods scene.

1. Entertainment electronics
2. Refrigerators
3. Washing machines
4. Pressure cookers
5. Other durables
6. Processed foods & convenience foods
7. Modern services
8. Credit cards
9. Courier service
10. Car rental service

11. Value-added telecom services
12. Fax service
13. E-mail
14. Videoconferencing

❊ Entertainment Electronics

Entertainment electronics is perhaps the most striking example of high growth in consumer durables in recent years. The first big spurt materialised between mid-seventies and mid-eighties; during this period sale of entertainment electronics has registered a tenfold increase from ₹103 crore to ₹1,045 crore. The trend still continues.

❊ Refrigerators

By the beginning of the nineties, refrigerators constituted a ₹1,200 crore business in India. The production of refrigerators in the country increased from 2.8 lakh units in 1980 to 14 lakh units in 1990 recording a compound annual growth rate of 16%. More significant developments have been taken place in the business in recent times, new players like Videocon and BPL entered the market, existing players introduced new models, they also went for expansion and some of them became increasingly aggressive, thus Indian refrigerator market was becoming the battleground of international white goods majors.

❊ Washing Machines

Washing machines became an essential fixture in Indian middle-class homes in the nineties just as mixers and refrigerators were during the previous decade. Today, there are nearly more than 25 brands of washing machines in the market. Videocon entered with a semi-automatic washing machine in 1986, made with collaboration of Matsushita of Japan.

❊ Pressure Cookers

Pressure cookers, which constituted a part of the well-established kitchen appliance market, also witnessed good growth in the early nineties. It became a ₹150 crore market, with hundreds of brands, and sales in the region of 4.5 million pieces per year.

❊ Other Durables

Besides refrigerators, washing machines, pressure cookers and dishwashers, the durables boom of the nineties also embraced products like microwave ovens, geysers, air coolers, and air conditioners, vacuum cleaners. Milton Plastics manufacturer of household plastic brought in a wide variety of new products, in 1982, when they entered the market their initial products were a mere water bucket, a jug and ice-pail, by the early nineties they had a range of 250 products.

❋ Processed Foods and Convenience Foods

A wide range of processed foods is now produced and marketed in India. It consists of two main categories–traditional products and products that are quite new as far as the Indian market is concerned. Processed fruits and vegetables, processed seafoods, biscuits and bakery products, malted milk beverages, coco-based products, etc.

❋ Soft Drinks and Fruit Drinks

Soft drinks and fruit drinks have also become big business in India in recent years. The soft drinks business underwent major changes with entry of Pepsi and re-entry of Coke; Coke's takeover of the Parle brands, in particular, changed the competitive profile of the business. The other major manufacturers of soft drinks include Parle, Pure Drinks. Parle has been the market leader till now with some of the most popular brands like Thums Up and Limca. It also has the largest number of franchisee. The government has created a separate ministry for food processing and entrusted it with the task of developing food processing into a modern industry. Government identified this sector as a thrust area for exports under its new trade policy.

❋ Modern Services

The environment in respect of modern and sophisticated services too, has changed for the better in recent years. Modern services include facilities such as credit cards, courier service, car rental service and new business communication services like value-added telecom services, fax services, e-mail, videoconferencing, etc.

❋ Credit Cards

It was only in the eighties that credit cards, the symbol of consumption communities entered the Indian market. Diners Club of India was the first to introduce credit cards in India by acquiring the franchise for India from Diners Club Inc. of the USA, which incidentally is the agency that introduced the credit card concept in the world. Diners Club of India started with 2000 charter members.

The early nineties thus saw not only a quantitative expansion, but also a new dynamism in the credit cards business; the entry of the multinational banks into the business contributed greatly to this dynamism. Today, the number of credit cardholders in India exceeds one million. And the experts in the business predict that soon India would be the second largest credit card market in the world next only to the USA.

❋ Courier Service

Private courier service, also known as the express industry, has grown rapidly in the past few years and has become a ₹400 crore per annum industry. It is currently growing at 30 to 35 per cent per annum. Simultaneously, the structure of the business too has undergone a rapid change; there has been a quick proliferation of the number of operators. There are about 4,500 medium and small-scale players and a dozen major players. DHL, Skypak, Blue Dart, Elbee Services, and Overnite Express are some of the major players.

The liberalisation and the new emphasis on exports have given a push to this industry. The proliferation of financial services has also offered new opportunities for this industry. Emergence of air taxis has helped the industry enlarge its means of transportation. The earlier monopoly of state-run airlines caused many hurdles. Today's competition in the skies has proved another blessing for the courier business.

❊ Car Rental Service

Car rental service too is now becoming active in India. The Indian law now allows companies to offer self-driven cars to their clients, thereby opening up rent-a-car-business in the country. Companies like Hertz, Europcar and Budget who have already established themselves in this business the world over, are now in India, introducing a variety of service packages for the benefit of the corporate and leisure travellers in the country. To start with, the international companies are operating through joint ventures. The Transport Corporation of India's Hertz franchisee; Sapna Travel Agency is the master licensee for Budget; and Travel House is the sole licensee for Europcar. The three main players are carving out niches in the car rental market. Sixty per cent of the business is coming from the corporate sector–domestic as well as foreign travellers bring in the balance. Hertz is concentrating on the self-driven segment. Hertz is already operating the service in 11 cities. It has also a database of 6,000 frequent users of its services; Hertz sends them a quarterly newsletter, update. Europcar, with a fleet of 200 cars and operations in Delhi, Bangalore and Jaipur, is focusing on the corporate of corporate clients. The Surlux group–which is expected to enter this market shortly–plans to concentrate on the luxury travel segment, especially the foreign tourist segment, by investing in a fleet of Mercedes-Benz and opening offices in Mumbai, Delhi, Agra and Jaipur. All these companies have on offer self-driven services, chauffeur-driven options and renting options on long-term lease.

❊ Value-Added Telecom Services

The new telecom policy and the opening up of the telecom services to the private sector, Indian as well as foreign, has changed the telecom scene radically. Telecom switching factories have been set up by multinational companies like Alcatel of France and Erricson of Sweden.

❊ Fax Service

In recent years, fax service has grown in India very rapidly. Estimates show that it is doubling every year and the number of connections is poised to touch the 1,00,000 mark, almost as large as today's PC population. Ever since the Government threw open the import doors, as a part of the liberalisation measures, India has been flooded with dozens of Fax models.

❊ E-mail

India is fast catching up with E-mail as well. As a communication tool, E-mail bypasses the postal, telex and facsimile systems, saves a great deal of time and money and provides for faster, almost instant information flow. E-mail lets people to work together despite physical boundaries and changes the very style in which an organisation works.

In the communication sphere, ITI Equatorial Satcom Limited has started offering VSATs (Very Small Aperture Terminal) or micro earth stations, a satellite communication tool that takes computerisation to total communication.

❊ Videoconferencing

Videoconferencing is the other new tool of business communication now spreading in India. It enables people in different locations to come face to face and confer live with the help of video images and audio impulses transmitted to different centres. With this facility, executives of Indian companies can now have instant national and global conferences without having to travel.

❊ Social Scenario

On the social scene, the emergence of a large middle class is perhaps the most significant of all developments, from the marketing point of view. Recent studies have placed India's middle class at 150 to 200 million. This middle-class explosion has been the result of several socio-economic developments. There was the evaluation of a new group that received a steady and reasonable income. The trade class also expanded considerably. While the landed gentry became a vanishing tribe, a large well-to-do agricultural group emerged.

❊ The Rural Marketing Scenario

The growth in the markets is perhaps the most significant feature of the marketing environment of India in recent times. Today, rural market of the country accounts for a large share of the expenditure on manufactured and branded consumer goods. The marketing environment governing the rural markets has been undergoing vast changes in the last two decades. For example, tape recorder or two-in ones were practically unheard of in the Indian rural market twenty years ago. Today, they are seen everywhere in rural areas and remote areas. While rural market of India poses a great attraction, tapping the market is beset with a variety of problems. Marketing men find it a new market, involving a new customer and a new marketing situation. Evidently there are two sides of rural marketing, the market provides immense opportunities, it also displays intimidating challenges, it does not lend itself to be tapped through an automatic transfer of the tools and techniques of marketing which proved a success in the urban marketing context.

❋ The Legal Environment

The legal framework prevailing in respect of its economy, trade and commerce has a direct impact on the marketing environment of the country. India is no exception to this reality. The following are the noteworthy legal enactments with a bearing on the marketing environment.

(a) The Prevention of Food Adulteration Act, 1954
(b) The Agricultural Produces Act, 1937
(c) The Drugs Act, 1940
(d) The Companies Act, 1956
(e) The Essential Commodities Act, 1955
(f) The Display of Prices Order Act, 1963
(g) The Packaged Commodities Order, 1975
(h) The Consumer Protection Act, 1986.

The legal environment is generally in favour of the consumer vis-á-vis the manufacturer and the middleman.

❋ The Advertising and Media Scene

Marketing experts often aver that the nature, substance and volume of advertising in a country is a pointer to the marketing environment of the country and the extent of competition prevailing in the country. It therefore makes sense to briefly analyse the advertising scenario in India. Qualitatively too, the advertising business of India has grown considerably. There was a time when Indian ads were mere imitations of the British and American ads. But now, the situation has vastly changed. The ad-men of India have succeeded in giving distinctiveness to Indian advertising. New approaches and new styles to suit the Indian audience have emerged, making advertising in the country a well-developed field of activity.

❋ On the Whole a Robust Marketing Environment

The analysis in the preceding pages would reveal that the marketing environment of India has been steadily acquiring greater dynamism and robustness. The breakthrough in the agricultural sector has been quite significant. The country has also acquired a solid industrial base. And the infrastructure required for further advancement of the industry is right now being developed. All the developments have made a profound impact on the size and structure of India's markets. On the social side, the country has witnessed the evolution of a large middle class. The opening up of the economy in the nineties, as a sequel to the new economic policies and liberalisation measures has given a new impetus to this process.

KEYWORDS

Marketing concept: It gives emphasis to consumer orientation and satisfaction as well as profitability for the organisation.

Need: A human need is a state in which a person feels deprived of something.

Selling: This consists of exchange of a product by the salesman or shopkeeper with the customer for money and, in case of the modern concept of selling, it must result in satisfaction of the company and profitability for the organisation.

Want: A need has to be converted into a want for our product or service through adequate marketing strategy, such as promotion.

Marketing planning: Marketing planning involves objectives and plans with a 2-5 year time horizon and is thus further from day-to-day activity of implementation.

Relationship marketing: Development and maintenance of long-term, cost-effective exchange relationships with individual customers, suppliers, employees and other partners for mutual benefit.

Customer orientation: Business philosophy incorporating the marketing concept that emphasises first determining unmet customer needs and then designing a product/service for satisfying them.

Market: The set of all actual and potential buyers of a product or service.

Demands: Human wants that are backed by buying power.

Buyer: The person who makes an actual purchase.

Exchange: The act of obtaining a desired object from someone by offering something in return.

Product: Anything that can be offered to a market for attention, acquisition, use or consumption that might satisfy a want or need. It includes physical objects, services, persons, places, organisations and ideas.

Potential market: The set of consumers who profess some level of interest in a particular product or service.

SUMMARY

"Marketing is a societal process by which individuals and groups obtain what they need and want through creating, offering, and freely exchange products and services of value with others."

The core functions of marketing are conducted by various organisations based on six alternative concepts or orientations.

1. *The Production Concept*
2. *The Product Concept*
3. *The Selling Concept*
4. *The Marketing Concept*
5. *The Customer Concept*
6. *The Societal Marketing Concept*

The concept of marketing and its tools and techniques are equally applicable in the design, implementation and control of social programmes. To highlight most social causes to be effectively promoted, whether it is family planning or environment pollution, one needs as vigorous a marketing approach as new product or service.

Marketing Environment

1. *Competition*
2. *Customers*
3. *Govt. policies*
4. *Suppliers*
5. *Trade*

1. *Product*
2. *Import tariffs*
3. *Trends*
4. *Technology*
5. *Politics*

Another important concept of marketing is 4 Ps as product, place, price, and promotion. Companies have to choose the optimum marketing mix as per the requirements of the market and the consumers.

Customer needs

1. *Stated needs*
2. *Real needs*
3. *Unstated needs*

4. *Delight needs*

5. *Secret needs*

Marketing management has experienced a number of shifts in recent years as companies seek marketing excellence.

Marketing Mix

1. *It is the tools that an organisation employs to pursue for its marketing objectives in the target market.*
2. *Product, price, place, promotion.*
3. *4 Cs–customer solution, cost, convenience, communication.*

The set of tasks necessary for successful marketing management includes developing marketing strategies and plans, connecting with customers, building strong brands, shaping the market offerings delivering strong brands, shaping the market offerings, delivering and communicating value, capturing marketing insights and performance, and creating successful long-term growth.

ASSIGNMENT

Assignment-1

Case Study 1: Marketing Beyond the Veil

Many marketers think that marketing to Saudi Arabian women is a very difficult task. Women in Saudi remain behind the purdah and it is difficult to talk to them. Saudi Arabia is one of the largest markets in West Asia and is a homogenous society. There exists a wrong notion among some marketers that Saudi women are passive consumers. Many Saudi women are often highly educated. About 3,80,000 women work in Saudi Arabia and the number of female students in the colleges is set to rise about 1,75,000 in the next two years.

Most women work in the traditional fields of health and education. Some are even employed in retailing, designing, publishing and manufacturing. They are exploring ways to sell products to Saudi women since Saudi Arabia is considered a young market. Shopping malls are an utter flop as women find these out-of town malls inconvenient. MNCs have realised that Saudi women are brand conscious and make the buying decision for household items.

MNCs have been searching intensively for women who can act as intermediaries between the company and the clients and those who have links with colleges, women groups, etc. Marketers should now stop underestimating the sophistication of Saudi women as consumers. It is time they recognised that they are the emerging economic force.

A women emerging out of a car fully covered by the purdah, may hold a degree in finance or law or medicine, and so on, and she may be a potential consumer given her educational background and culture.

Source: Master of the Online Supermall,
(Excerpt from Business Today, May 2004)

Questions: List out the differences between consumer behaviour of women in a closed culture (as described by this case) in Saudi Arabia and in a open culture (say, in Western Eupore). Highlight the cultural implications for a woman consumer and also for a marketer in the given context. Think of creative applications of 'reference groups' to market to the Saudi Arabian women, say for a personal care product.

Case Study 2

Amazon.com could well go down in history as a love child born of the heady fling that the stockmarket had with dotcoms in the late 1990s. But the company, founded by Jeff Bezos in July 1995 when the Internet was still an untested business medium, is a survivor-par-excellence. It floundered a bit in the swirl of the dotcom bust, but unlike thousands that were swept away, Amazon.com reinvented itself and emerged stronger.

The 40-year old Bezos, a computer science graduate from Princeton University, is the pioneer of Internet Retailing. His compelling vision introduced a new paradigm for retail, the click-and-buy model; buy goods from a website instead of a physical store, from wherever there is an Internet connection: home, office or cyber-cafe. A model that gave convenience to buyers, and mind-boggling market reach to sellers.

Named after the mighty Amazon river and its numerous tributaries that surge through dense rainforests, Amazon.com was started with an initial investment of a few thousand dollars. In less than three weeks after the website went live, Bezos and his wife Mackenzie were pulling in sales of over $20,000 a week. And soon after going public in 1997, the company had a market capitalisation higher than that of its brick-and-mortar rivals. In 1999, Bezos was chosen as Time Magazine's 'Person of the Year'. But things changed soon after and the dotcom bust saw Amazon.com lose almost 90 per cent of its market cap in 2000.

Bezos didn't give up on his vision. He set about transforming Amazon.com from a website selling books into something much bigger: the world's largest online retailing platform. A series of tie-ups with companies like Toys R Us and Target helped give the website the feel of an online supermall where a customer could buy almost anything. Marketing initiatives followed–from free shipping to highly discounted prices to very customised offerings (based on customer profile) to wide distribution through sites which can divert traffic to Amazon.com for a small commission. But the biggest move was Bezos' decision to make the site 'more global'.

The moves have paid off. The company announced its first full-year profit in 2003. It has been making money now for three straight quarters and revenues have exceeded a billion dollars for the last six quarters. If proof was needed that there is money to be made in online retailing, this is it. And Bezos has proved that the right idea, coupled with perseverance, pays in the end.

Questions

1. How does Amazon.com bring utility or create value for its customers?
2. Explain the marketing framework of *www.amazon.com*.
3. What do you learn about marketing from the Amazon story?

Assignment-2

Think of a recent purchase you made. How did the company provide you with the following utilities?

From _____
_____

Time _____
_____

Place _____
_____

Ownership _____
_____

Assignment-3

The following list consists of some MARKETING MYTHS. Tick the myths you thought about marketing before reading this section? Add some new myths you might have discovered.

1. Marketing and selling are synonymous.
2. The job of marketing is to develop good advertisements.
3. Marketing is pushing the product to the customers.
4. Marketing is transaction-oriented than relationship-oriented.

5. Marketing is a short-term business strategy.
6. Marketing is an independent function of a business.
7. Marketing is part of selling.

Assignment-4

Make a statement to describe each of the stages in the evolution of marketing. You may consider the given examples before coming up with your own statements.

1. Production era
   a. 'Cut costs. Profits will take care of themselves.'.
2. Product era
   a. 'A good product will sell itself.'
3. Sales era
   a. 'Selling is laying the bait for the customer.'
4. Marketing era
   a. 'The customer is king!'
5. Relationship marketing era
   a. 'Relationship with customers determine our firm's future.'

Assignment-5

Match the following

(1) Product marketing	(a) AIDS awareness campaign
(2) Service marketing	(b) Selling iron ore to a steel manufacturer
(3) Consumer marketing	(c) Selling ice creams to adults
(4) Industrial marketing	(d) Disney setting up a park in Hong Kong
(5) International marketing	(e) Setting up an ayurvedic massage centre
(6) Non-profit marketing	(f) Selling electric bulbs

REVIEW QUESTIONS

1. How would you define marketing? Discuss the evolution of marketing?

2. Explain scope of marketing? Illustrate core concepts of marketing?

3. Explain approaches to the study of marketing?

4. Do you think any company in India that has adopted marketing concept? Give suitable example to justify your opinion.

5. Are there companies still operating as production oriented and sales oriented, in your view?

6. Discuss in detail the important principles on which implementation of marketing concept rests.

7. What are the environmental forces? Briefly discuss?

8. Define Green Marketing and its implementation in the present scenario.

9. Discuss the impact on consumption patterns in the Indian society due to cultural changes as a result of latter day marketing activities?

10. In what way are Indian cultural values changing? How are marketers responding to these changes?

11. How environmental influences marketing activities of some foreign companies in India?

12. Discuss micro and macro environment of marketing.

13. Take any one of the following sectors or any other sector of your choice and collect the relevant current information that has been published during the last three months, which indicates the type of marketing effort that is being made to develop and promote these sectors:

    (a) Export promotion
    (b) Family planning
    (c) Tourism
    (d) Quality control movement.

MARKETING RESEARCH AND BUYER BEHAVIOUR

STRUCTURE

- Introduction
- The Context of Marketing Decisions
- Definition
- Purpose of Marketing Research
- Scope of Marketing Research
- Characteristics of Good Marketing Research
- Marketing Research Design Procedure
- Precautions to be Taken in Designing a Good Questionnaire
- Types of Marketing Research
- Applications of Marketing Research
- Marketing Research in Indian Perspective
- The Measurement Concept
- Marketing Decision Support System
- Quantitative Tools Used in MDSS
- Marketing Information System
- Buyer Behaviour
- Importance of Consumer Behaviour
- Models of Buyer/Consumer Behaviour
- Determinants of Buyer/Consumer Behaviour
- The Consumer Decision Process
- Marketing Implications of Consumer Behaviour

2.1   INTRODUCTION

In many areas of management, such as production, finance, and personnel the information required for decision-making is primarily generated within the firm and is easy to collect and analyse. Moreover, in these areas formalised procedures have greatly improved decisions; statistical quality control in manufacturing, PERT (Programme Evaluation Review Technique) in project scheduling, queuing theory in managing large machinery maintenance programmes, etc.

Market research comprises actual and potential buyers available at a place where exchange of goods and products takes place. Market research involves defining the problem and application of systematic and thorough efforts to solve them, related to who, what, where, when, why and how of actual and potential buyers.

2.2   THE CONTEXT OF MARKETING DECISIONS

In the area of marketing, much of the information required for decision-making exists outside the firms, e.g., information on why people buy only certain products and not other products, information about the competitors next move; information about new government rules and regulations which can affect your working, etc.

"Gentlemen, we have a dilemma. Pollution scientists say
it will destroy the ozone—however, Market Research
predict it will sell like hot cakes."

The marketing manager faces a challenging task in attempting to improve his decision-making. The variables involved in the marketing decisions being external to the firm make collection of information cumbersome and expensive. Since the variables are often qualitative and dynamic in nature, their measurement is difficult and the results not always accurate. Thus, the pressure on the marketing manager is very strong to correctly choose the most critical decision variables and seek relevant information about them. And the manager also needs to monitor what is happening in the marketplace and in the general environment of the firm. The only way the manager can monitor all these is through regular market research.

2.3 DEFINITION

Marketing Research (MR) is the systematic and objective identification, collection, analysis, dissemination and one of information for the purpose of improving decision-making related to the identification and solution of problems in marketing.

The American Marketing Association defines Marketing Research (AMA, 1961) "The systematic gathering, recording and analysing of data problems related to the marketing of goods and service".

According to Crisp Marketing Research "The systematic, objectives and exhaustive search for and study of the facts relevant to any problem in the field of marketing".

It would be useful to add the word 'continuous' to these two definitions to make them even more meaningful. A study conducted today may lose much of its relevance by the next year and may need updating, modifications or even an entirely new effort. The rate of change in information would depend on the specific product and customer segment with which you are dealing.

If your firm is marketing readymade cloths for teenagers, you are dealing with a market where a rapid change is its distinguishing characteristic. You would need continuous and extensive market research to find out what design, fabrics, colours, and price will appeal this market segment, this winter, the coming summer and the following winter, and so on. You also need to monitor the fashion scene in Europe and America and see what new trends can be successfully adapted for the Indian market. No matter whether you are in a product line which is generally affected by customer taste, habits, values, attitudes, or dealing in a product which is not that susceptible to environmental influences, you need marketing research to improve and be at least one step ahead of your competitor.

In Procter & Gamble there are two separate in-house research groups, one in charge of overall company advertising research and the other in charge of marketing testing. The staff of each group consists of marketing research managers, supporting specialists and in-house field representatives to conduct and supervise interviewing. Each year Procter & Gamble calls or visits one million people in connection with about 1,000 research projects.

2.4   PURPOSE OF MARKETING RESEARCH

The general purpose of Marketing Research (MR) is to facilitate the decision-making process. A manager has before him a number of alternative solutions to choose from in response to every marketing problem and situation. In the absence of marketing information, he may make the choice on the basis of his hunch. By doing so, the manager is taking a big risk because he has no concrete evidence of this alternative in comparison with others or to assess its problem's outcome. But with the help of information provided by marketing research the manager can reduce the number of alternative choices to one, two or three and the possible outcome of each choice is also known. Thus, the decision-making process becomes a little easier.

The second purpose of marketing research is that it helps to reduce the risk associated with the process of decision-making. The risk arises because of two types of uncertainties; uncertainty about the expected outcome of the decision will always remain no matter how much information you may have collected to base your decision on hard facts. Unforeseen factors have the uncanny ability of upsetting even the most stable apple cart. In the mid-1950s, Ford company in USA had a 25% market share of the automobile market. The company wanted to introduce a new car model which would appeal to young executives and professionals. The decisions was based on research which revealed that this market segment accounted for 25% market share and was expected to grow to about 40%. Ford spent colossal amounts researching and designing the new model which was named Edsel. When introduced in the market the car was utter flop. This happened because of three unforeseen events.

First, the youthful car market segment did not grow as rapidly as the market research had indicated.

Secondly, the recession also set in at about this time and people began looking for economical means of transportation.

Thirdly, there was a sudden change in customer tastes, with people turning away from flashy exteriors, and the flamboyant Edsel was totally out of time with new taste for austerity and functional simplicity.

The above example highlights the fact despite best research effort the outcome can still be unpredictable. As Reynolds, a former Ford executive, commenting on the Edsel fiasco, commented, "it is hard to see how anyone could, given the kind of car market that existed in 1955 and 1956 have anticipated such trends." The techniques of market research are based on scientific methods of collecting, analysing and interpreting data, its findings and projections, at the least provide a definite trend of scenarios for future decision-making.

The third purpose of market research is that it helps firms in discovering opportunities which can profitability be exploited. These opportunities may exist in the form of untapped customer needs or wants not catered to by the existing firms.

2.5   SCOPE OF MARKETING RESEARCH

Marketing Research (MR) is concerned with all the aspects of marketing, relating to product design and development, product-mix, pricing, packaging, branding, and sales, distribution, competition, target customer segments and their buying behaviour, advertising and its impact.

Specifically, the scope of MR includes customers, products, distribution, advertising competitive information and macro-level phenomenon.

(i) Marketing is concerned with identifying and fulfilling customer needs and wants. Thus, MR should precede marketing. The unfulfilled wants should first be identified and translated into technically and economically feasible product ideas which then should be marketed to the customers. Mere identification of customer wants is not enough. Marketing requires continuous effort to improve the existing product, increase sales and beat the competition. For this, it is important to know who the customers are for your products (whether housewives, teenagers, children), what their socio-economic profile is (in terms of income, education, cultural, religious and professional background) and where they are concentrated in terms of location. Besides this information, it is also important for you to know the process by which a prospective customer arrives at a decision to buy your product. If you know the sequential steps in the purchase process positive impact on them, and thus ensure an actual purchase. The study of consumers and their purchase behaviour is so important that there is a separate, special body of knowledge known as consumer behaviour.

(ii) The second area which is of direct concern for MR is the product and product design. MR is helpful in determining the final design of the product and its physical attributes of colour, size, shape, packaging, and brand name. It is useful in arriving at the right combination of product mix, the number of variations of the basic product, accessories and attachments. It can also help decide the quantities to be produced according to the projected demand estimates. MR can also be used to gauge customer reactions to different prices.

(iii) Marketing research helps in discovering what types of distribution channels and retail outlets are most profitable for your product. On the basis of comparative information for different channels and different types of outlets, you can choose the combination most suitable for your product. Distributor, stockist, wholesaler, retailer may represent most kind of distribution channel in contrast to another in which you may use only the distributor and retailer. Consider the below given example:

A firm is marketing refrigerators through distributors and retailers in the eastern zone. The understanding between the firm and distributors is that the latter will provide the after-sales service. Analysing the sales figures, the firm finds that the sales level in eastern zone is much lower than in the other zones. Marketing research reveals that one of the reasons for this low sales performance is the poor after-sales service provided by the distributor. In a high value, durable product such as refrigerator the quality of after-sales service is an important factor influencing the customers' purchase decision regarding the specific brand to buy. The firm decides to do away with the distributor and instead opens its own branch office. The new distribution channel comprising branch office and retailers is operationally more expensive, but the company can now control the quality of after-sales service as well as the other marketing inputs. The result is improved sales and the incremental cost associated with the new distribution network is justified.

(iv) Most companies provide advertising support for their products. In some cases the amount spent on advertising may be small, while in others it may run into crores of rupees. Irrespective of the actual amount spent on advertising, each firm would like to maximise the return on every rupee that it spends. Marketing research can help the firm to do this. Research can provide information on the most cost-effective media to help determine the advertising budget, measure the effectiveness of specific advertisements; advertising campaigns and the entire advertising strategy. Research also provides information on the size and type of audiences for different advertising media channels. This information can be used to refine the advertising strategy to make it more relevant and sharply focused. Advertising research is also useful in determining customer perceptions about the image of specific branches and companies. The various research tools applied in marketing area is impacted for further studies such as:

(a) Demand forecasting
(b) Consumer behaviour
(c) Measuring advertising effectiveness
(d) Media selection for advertising
(e) Test marketing
(f) Product positioning
(g) Product potential.

(v) Marketing research is being increasingly used at the macro level. Government spends colossal amounts on various socio-economic development schemes and projects. If the objectives of these projects are not in tune with the prevailing consumer tastes, attitudes and values, the entire amount may prove to be a total waste. Just as a business organisation needs MR to monitor the efficacy of its strategy in achieving the objectives, so does the government, and its departments.

vi) Organisation research is an interdisciplinary field. Since the men who do the research in organisations, come from a variety of backgrounds. They tend to bring with them different tools, different concepts and different methodological concepts. The organisation research enables the managers to get exposed to many theories and research findings have relevance to organisations.

The role of the manager and the research scientists are often viewed as very different; many of the day-to-day problems are similar to those faced by researches. For example, a manager is confronted with the problem of high absenteeism in one department. Once the problem is identified and the need to take corrective actions is being recognised, the manager must collect reliable information about the problem. The manager should have adequate knowledge of various research methods through which he/she can solve the problems.

(vii) Industrial research laboratory is presumably a pragmatic organisation. This kind of research is benefit for the future prosperity of a particular company. The specific objectives of industrial research are:

(a) To improve the quality of products
(b) To minimise the cost
(c) To run with standardisation
(d) To make innovative methods to capture new markets
(e) To make complete relations with the customer group.

(viii) Production research organisation is never static (constant). It keeps on changing in an innovative manner. But the changes always bring difficulties, if not troubles. Thus, research acts as a backbone for smooth production process in a continuous method. Production research activities normally fall in three categories:

(a) Investigation of a new production method
(b) Investigation of methods of standards and control
(c) Troubleshooting (problem solving)

Marketing researchers have steadily expanded their activities and techniques which is mentioned in the list where 36 marketing activities and the percentage of companies carrying on each activity are given. These activities have been benefited from increasingly sophisticated techniques.

Type of Research	Area	Per cent Doing
(a) Business/Economic and corporate research	1. Industry	83
	2. Acquisition	53
	3. Market-share analysis	79
	4. Internal employee studies	54
(b) Pricing	5. Cost analysis	60
	6. Profit analysis	59
	7. Price elasticity	45
	8. Demand analysis	
	a) Market potential	74
	b) Sales potential	69
	c) Sales potential	67
	9. Competitive pricing analysis	63
(c) Product	10. Concept dev. & testing	68
	11. Brand testing	38
	12. Test marketing	45
	13. Product testing	47
	14. Packaging design studies	31
	15. Competitive studies	58
(d) Distribution	16. Plan/warehouse location	23
	17. Channel performance	29
	18. Channel coverage studies	26
	19. Export and international	19
(e) Promotion	20. Motivation research	37
	21. Media research	57
	22. Copy research	50
	23. Advertising effectiveness	65
	24. Competitive advertising	47
	25. Public image studies	60
	26. Sales force compensation	30
	27. Sales force quota studies	26
	28. Sales force territory	31
	29. Studies of premiums	36
(f) Buying behaviour	30. Brand preference	54
	31. Brand attributes	53
	32. Product satisfaction	68
	33. Purchase behaviour	61
	34. Purchase intentions	60
	35. Brand awareness	59
	36. Segmentation studies	60

Source: Thomas C. Kinnear and Ann R Root, Eds, 1988, Survey of marketing research operations, functions, budget, compensation (Chicago American Marketing Association, 1989) p. 43.

2.6 CHARACTERISTICS OF GOOD MARKETING RESEARCH

1. **Scientific Method:** Effective marketing research uses the principles of the scientific method, careful observation, formulation of hypothesis, prediction, and testing.

> **Ex:** A mail order house was suffering from a high rate (30%) of returned merchandise. The management asked the marketing research manager to investigate the causes. The marketing researcher examined the characteristics of returned orders, such as the geographical locations of the customers, the sizes of the returned orders, and the merchandise categories. One hypothesis was that the longer the customer waited for order merchandise, the greater the profitability of its return. Statistical analysis conformed this hypothesis. The researcher estimated how much the return rate would drop for a specific speed of service. The company did this, and the prediction proved correct.

2. **Research Creativity:** At its best, marketing research develops innovative ways to solve a problem.

3. **Multiple Methods:** Competent marketing researchers shy away from over reliance on any one method, preferring to adapt the method to the problem rather than the other way around. They also recognise the desirability of gathering information from multiple sources to give greater confidence.

4. **Interdependence of Models and Data:** Competent marketing researchers recognise that the facts derive meaning from models of the problem. These models guide the type of information sought and therefore should be made as explicit as possible.

5. **Value and Cost of Information:** Competent marketing researchers show concern for estimating the value of information. It helps the marketing research determine which research projects to conduct, which research designs to use, and whether to gather more information after the initial results are out. Research costs are typically easy to quantify while the value is harder to anticipate.

6. **Ethical Marketing:** Most marketing research benefits both the sponsoring company and its consumers. Through marketing research, companies learn more about consumers needs and are able to supply more satisfying products and services. However, the misuse of marketing research can also harm consumers.

7. **Healthy Skepticism:** Competent marketing researchers will show a healthy skepticism toward given assumptions made by the managers about how the market works.

2.7   MARKETING RESEARCH DESIGN PROCEDURE

Marketing research is undertaken to improve the understanding about a marketing situation or problem and consequently improve the quality of decision-making related to it. The usefulness of the marketing research output will depend upon the way the research has been designed and implemented at each stage of the process. Each of these steps or stages in turn may contain a series of activities. When all these activities are completed in a satisfactory manner, a thesis is produced. The various steps in research design process are shown in the Fig. 2.1.

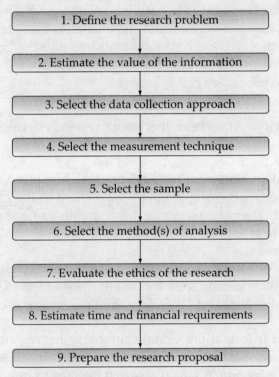

1. Define the research problem

2. Estimate the value of the information

3. Select the data collection approach

4. Select the measurement technique

5. Select the sample

6. Select the method(s) of analysis

7. Evaluate the ethics of the research

8. Estimate time and financial requirements

9. Prepare the research proposal

Fig. 2.1 Steps in the research design process.

Step 1: Define the Research Problem

Problem definition is the most critical part of the research process. Research problem definition involves specifying the information needed by the management. Unless the problem is properly defined, the information produced by the research process is unlikely to have any value.

Research problem definition involves four interrelated steps.

1. Management problem/opportunity clarification
2. Situation analysis
3. Model development and
4. Specification of information requirement.

1. Management's Problem/Opportunity Clarification

The basic goal of problem clarification is to ensure that the decision-maker's initial description of the management decision is accurate and reflects the appropriate area of concern for research. If the wrong problem is translated into a research problem, the probability of providing the management with useful information is low.

2. Situation Analysis

The situation analysis focuses on the variables that have produced the stated management problem or opportunity. The factors that have led to the problem/opportunity manifestations and the factors that have led to the management's concern should be isolated. The situation analysis is seldom limited to an armchair exercise in logic, although this may be a valuable part of it. It also involves giving careful attention to company records; appropriate secondary sources such as census data, industry sales figures, economic indicators, and so on, and interviews with knowledgeable individuals both internal and external to the firm. The persons interviewed will include the manager(s) involved and may include salespersons, other researchers, trade association officials, professionals, and consumers.

3. Model Development

A situation model is a description of the outcomes that are desired, the relevant variable and the relationships of the variables to the outcomes. The researcher is therefore interested in having the manager answer the following questions.

1. What objective(s) are desired in solving the problem or taking advantage of the opportunity?
2. What variables determine whether the objective(s) will be met?
3. How do they relate to the objective(s)?

At least two sources of information may be helpful in this phase of research design. First, secondary data sources beyond those concerned directly with the situation analysis should be reviewed. These sources range from trade journal articles and special reports concerning the variable in a specific situation to more abstract theoretical treatment of the variable.

The second approach for getting information to help the researcher to develop a problem situation model involves using selected case analyses. Assume that a firm is concerned with the sales performance of its various branch offices. The case approach would involve an in-depth comparison of a "successful" branch and an "unsuccessful" branch. Those variables that differed the most between the two branches would then be considered relevant for further study.

At the end of the model development stage, the researchers will have developed a list of variables relevant to the management problem and some known or tentative sets of relationships between the variables.

4. Specification of Information Requirements

Research cannot provide solutions. Solutions require executive judgement. Research provides information relevant to the decisions faced by the executive. The output of the problem-definition process is a clear statement of the information required to assist the decision-maker. A common temptation is to try to collect data on all possible variables. Unfortunately, this is generally impractical and always costly. The best approach for ensuring that any data collected is indeed relevant is to ask questions concerning the ultimate use for the data. The emphasis is on what it will do, or at least, is likely to do, given certain findings.

- **Categories of research**

  A number of researchers have found it useful to consider three general categories of research based on the type of information required. These three categories are exploratory, descriptive, and causal.

- **Exploratory research**

  It is concerned with discovering the general nature of the problem and the variables that relate to it. Exploratory research is characterized by a high degree of flexibility, and it tends to rely on the secondary data, convenience or judgement samples, small-scale surveys or simple experiments, case analyses, and subjective evaluation of the results.

- **Descriptive research**

  It is focused on the accurate description of the variables in the problem model. Consumer profile studies, market-potential studies, product usage studies, attitude surveys, sales analyses, media research, and price surveys are examples of descriptive research. Any source of information can be used in a descriptive study, although most studies of this nature rely heavily on the secondary data sources and survey research.

- **Causal research**

  It attempts to specify the nature of the functional relationship between two or more variables in the problem model. For example, studies in the effectiveness of advertising generally attempt to discover the extent to which advertising causes sales or attitude change. We can use three types of evidence to make inferences about causation:

  1. Concomitant variation
  2. Sequence of occurrence
  3. Absence of other potential causal factors.

  1. Concomitant variation, or invariant association, is a common basis for ascribing the cause.

  2. Sequence of occurrence can also provide evidence of causation. For one event to cause another, it must always precede it. An event that occurs after another event cannot be said to cause the first event.

  3. A final type of evidence that we can use to infer causality is the *absence of other potential causal factors*. That is, if we could logically or through our research design eliminate all possible causative factors except the one we are interested with was the causative factor. Unfortunately, it is never possible to control completely or to eliminate all possible causes for any particular event. We always have the possibility that some factor of which we are not aware has influenced the results. However, if all reasonable alternatives are eliminated except one, we can have a degree of confidence in the remaining variable.

Step 2: Estimate the Value of the Information

The principle involved in deciding whether to do more research is that the research should be conducted only when it is expected that the value of the information to be obtained will be greater than the cost of obtaining it.

Two approaches can be taken to arrive at an assessment of whether the expected value of the information in a proposed research project is greater than its estimated cost: the intuitive and the expected value approaches to the problem.

The Intuitive Approach for Making the Research - Decided Without Research Decisions:

The intuitive approach relies entirely on the private judgement of the person making the assessment. Because it is a private process, it is not possible to specify exactly what kinds of considerations the person(s) involved took into account. We can, however, specify what minimum considerations ought to be weighed in making the decision.

1. The alternative actions that could be taken.
2. The possible states of the market and their payoffs (possible outcomes resulting from uncontrollable factors affecting the market).
3. The degree of uncertainty concerning which state of the market is the actual state.
4. The ability to forecast the actual state of the market given the research findings.
5. The risk preferences of the decision-maker(s).

The Expected Value Approach for Making the Research-Decide Without Research Decision

The expected value approach uses the same five items of information just described for the intuitive approach, but it uses them within an explicit quantitative mode. This model involves the application of Bayesian statistics, a branch of statistics that allows personal (judgemental) probabilities to be used.

Step 3: Select the Data Collection Approach

There are three basic data collection approaches in marketing research:

1. Secondary data
2. Survey data and
3. Experimental data

Secondary data were collected for some purpose other than helping to solve the current problem, whereas primary data are collected expressly to help solve the problem at hand. Survey and experimental data are therefore secondary data if they were collected earlier for another study; they are primary data if they were collected for the present one.

The selection of the data-collection method(s) is one of the key aspects of the research design. Although creativity and judgement play a major role in this stage of the design process, the decision is constrained by the type of information required, its value, and the characteristics of the respondents.

Step 4: Select the Measurement Technique

There are four basic measurement techniques used in marketing research:

1. Questionnaires
2. Attitude scales
3. Observation and
4. Depth interviews and projective techniques

Step 5: Select the Sample

Most marketing studies involve a sample or subgroup of the total populations relevant to the problem, rather than a census of the entire group. The population is generally specified as a part of the problem-definition process. The sampling process interacts with the other stages of the research design.

Step 6: Select the Method(s) of Analysis

Data are useful only after analysis. Data analysis involves converting a series of recorded observations into descriptive statements and/or inferences about relationships. The types of analyses that can be conducted depend on the nature of the sampling process, the measurement instrument, and the data collection method.

It is imperative that the researcher selects the analytic techniques prior to collecting the data. Once the analytic techniques are selected, the researchers should generate fictional responses (dummy data) to the measurement instrument. These dummy data are then analysed by the analytic techniques selected to ensure that the results of this analysis will provide the information required by the problem at hand. Failure to carry out this step in advance can result in a completed research project that fails to provide some or all of the information required by the problem. Further, it sometimes reveals that unneeded data are about to be collected.

Step 7: Evaluate the Ethics of the Research

It is essential that marketing researcher restricts his research activities to practices that are ethically sound. Ethically sound research considers the interests of the general public, the respondents, the client, and the research profession as well as those of the researcher.

Step 8: Estimate Time and Financial Requirements

Once the research design(s) has been devised and checked for ethical soundness, the researcher must estimate the resource requirements. These requirements can be broken down into two broad categories: time and financial. Time refers to the time needed to complete the project. The financial requirement is the monetary representation of personnel time, computer time, and materials requirements. The time and finance requirements are not independent. The programme evaluation review technique (PERT) coupled with the critical path method (CPM) offers a useful aid for estimating the resources needed for a project and clarifying the planning and control process.

Step 9: Prepare the Research Proposal

The research design process provides the researcher with a blueprint, or guide, for conducting and controlling the research project. This blueprint is written in the form of a research proposal. A written research proposal should precede any research project. The word precede here may be somewhat misleading obviously, a substantial amount of research effort is involved in the research planning process that must precede the research proposal. The research proposal helps ensure that the decision-maker and the researcher are still in agreement on the basic management problem, the information required, and the research approach.

2.8   PRECAUTIONS TO BE TAKEN IN DESIGNING A GOOD QUESTIONNAIRE

A questionnaire is simply a formalised set of questions for eliciting information. As such, its function is measurement and it represents the most common form of measurement in marketing research. Although the questionnaire generally is associated with survey research, it is also frequently the measurement instrument in experimental designs as well. When a questionnaire is administered by means of the telephone or by a personal interviewer, it is termed an interview schedule, or simply schedule.

Questionnaire construction involves seven major decision areas:

1. Preliminary considerations
2. Decisions about question content
3. Decisions about question wording
4. Decisions about the response format
5. Decisions about the question sequence
6. Physical characteristics of the questionnaire
7. Decisions about the pretest.

2.8.1   Preliminary Decision

Prior to constructing the actual questionnaire, the researcher must decide exactly what information is to be collected from which respondent by what techniques.

Required Information

Data gained from questionnaires are of limited value if they are on the wrong topic (surrogate information error) or if they are incomplete. The collection of data that are not required increases the cost of the project. The researcher must begin with a precise statement of what information is required to deal with the management problem at hand.

Which Respondent

It is also essential to have a clear idea of exactly who the respondents are to be. In general, the more diversified the potential respondents, the more difficult it is to construct a sound questionnaire that is appropriate for the entire group.

Interview Technique

Finally, one needs to decide on the method or technique of administering the question-naire prior to designing it. It may be necessary to alter the method of administration if attempts at designing an effective questionnaire for the initial method of administration are unsuccessful.

In addition, the researcher must be aware of the general approach that is to be taken with the respondent. This involves such issues as identification of the sponsor, what the respondents are told concerning the purpose of the research, and whether the respondents are to be treated anonymously.

2.8.2   Decisions About Question Content

Decisions concerning question content centre on the general nature of the question and the information it is designed to produce, rather than on the form or specific working of the question. Five major issues, or problem areas, are involved with question content. For each question, the researcher must ascertain (1) the need for the data, (2) the ability of the question to produce the data, (3) the ability of the respondent to answer accurately, (4) the willingness of the respondent to answer accurately, and (5) the potential for external events to bias the answer.

1. **The Need for the Data Asked for by the Question**

   The preliminary decisions will result in a list of informational items required to solve the problem. The next task is to generate one or more questions for each information item.

2. **Ability of the Question to Produce the Data**

   The "double-barrelled" question is one in which two or more questions are asked as one. Questions that require the respondent to aggregate several sources of information in order to answer should generally be subdivided into several specific questions.

3. Ability of the Respondent to Answer Accurately

Inability to answer a question arises from three major sources: (1) having never been exposed to the answer, (2) having been exposed to the answer but forgetting, and (3) being unable to verbalise the answer. The first two categories are concerned primarily with factual information, whereas the third is concerned more with attitudes and motives.

- **Uninformed Respondents**

  Respondents are frequently asked questions on topics about which they are uninformed. "Uninformed" in this sense means that they have never known the answer to the question. Uninformed respondents become a source of measurement error because of reluctance by people to admit a lack of knowledge on a topic. This becomes particularly acute when the content or wording of the question implies that the individual should know the answer.

- **Forgetful Respondents**

  Three aspects of forgetting are of concern to the researcher: (1) omission, which occurs when an individual is unable to recall an event that actually took place; (2) telescoping, which occurs when an individual remembers an event as occurring more recently than it actually occurred; and (3) creation, which occurs when an individual "remembers" an event that did not occur.

- **Unaided Recall**

  Questions that rely on unaided recall result in an understatement of some specific events, such as brands in a choice set, shows watched, or small items purchases. In addition, more popular and known brands tend to be overstated in response to questions asking for this kind of information.

- **Aided Recall**

  Aided recall provides respondents with descriptions of all or some aspects of the original events. The difference between an aided recall and unaided recall questions is similar to the difference between a multiple-choice and an essay examination question.

- **Inarticulate Respondents**

  We buy things from habit, for vanity, and other reasons of which we are not consciously aware. However, when we are asked why we buy a given product or brand we may respond with conventional reasons rather than the actual reasons.

4. Willingness of the Respondent to Answer Accurately

A refusal to answer a question may take on three forms. First, the respondent may refuse to answer the specific question or questions that offend and still complete the remainder of the questionnaire. This is called item non-response.

Another effect of an improper question (from the respondent's viewpoint) is refusal to complete the remainder of the questionnaire. In mail surveys, this generally results in failure to return the questionnaire. In telephonic interviews, it may result in a broken connection.

The third way of "refusing" to answer a question is through distortion providing an incorrect answer deliberately. Thus, the respondent may avoid a particular question by providing acceptable but inaccurate information. This type of refusal is the most difficult to deal with because it is hard to detect.

Why would a respondent refuse to answer one or more questions accurately? There are at least three possible reasons. The information request may be perceived by the respondents as (1) personal in nature, (2) embarrassing, or (3) reflecting on prestige.

- **Requests for Personal Information**

  Most people will provide answers to questions that they think are legitimate. By legitimate, we mean that the questions are reasonable in light of the situation and the role of the person asking the question. However, many respondents who have willingly answered a lengthy series of questions on purchasing and shopping patterns will refuse when suddenly asked without an explanation for their income, age, occupation, or other data.

- **Requests for Embarrassing Information**

  Answers to questions that ask potentially embarrassing information are subject to distortion especially when personal or telephone interviews are used. Questions on the consumption of alcoholic beverages, use of personal hygiene products, readership of certain magazines, and sexual or aggressive feelings aroused by particular advertisements are examples of topics on which questions are subject to refusals or distortions by the respondents.

  Intuitively, it would seem that anonymity would enhance the likelihood that respondents would answer, and answer accurately sensitive questions. However, studies indicate that assurances of anonymity have little effect. Two additional approaches to seeking potentially embarrassing information are the use of counter biasing statements and randomised response techniques.

- **Counter Biasing Statements**

  Counter biasing statements involve beginning a question with a statement that will make the potentially embarrassing responses seem common. Counter biasing effects can also be obtained by carefully structuring the response options to multiple-choice questions.

- **Randomised Response Techniques**

  Another approach to overcoming non-response and measurement errors caused by embarrassing questions is the randomised response technique. It presents the respondent with two questions, one sensitive or potentially embarrassing, the other harmless or even meaningless. The respondent then flips a coin, looks at the last number on his or her social security card to see if it is odd or even, or in some other random manner selects, which question to answer. The chosen question is then answered with a "yes" or "no" without telling the researcher which question is being answered.

  (a) A sensitive question to which the researchers desire a "yes" or "no" answer.

  (b) A neutral question which has known proportions of "yes" and "no" responses.

  (c) A random means of assigning one of the questions to each respondent such that the question assigned a particular respondent is known only to that respondent, but the percentage of respondents assigned each question is known.

Requests for "Prestige" or "Normative" Information

Prestige-oriented questions, such as those dealing with education obtained, income earned, or amount of time spent in reading newspapers, typically, produce answers with an upward bias. For example, readership of low-prestige magazines is often understated when self-report techniques are utilised. The reported consumption of both "negative" products, such as alcoholic beverages, and "positive" products, such as milk, is also subject to distortion.

Similarly, questions with a normative or socially accepted answer to end to have a consistent bias toward social norms. For example, the percentage of survey respondents who claim to have voted in the last election always exceeds the percentage of the population that actually voted.

2.8.3   Decisions About Question Phrasing

Question phrasing is the translation of the desired question content into words and phrases that can be understood easily and clearly by the respondents. In general, questions should be as simple and straightforward as possible.

The primary concern with question phrasing is to ensure that the respondents and the researcher assign exactly the same meaning to the question. There are five general issues involved in question phrasing. (1) Are the words, singularly and in total, understandable to the respondents? (2) Are the words biased or "loaded" in any respect? (3) Are all the alternatives involved in the question clearly stated? (4) Are any assumptions implied by the question clearly stated? and (5) What frame of reference is the respondent asked to assume?

The Meaning of Words

Most of us would agree that questions designed for 8-year olds should have a simpler vocabulary than questions designed for adult respondents. The researcher must take the vocabulary skills of the intended respondent group into account when designing a question. Such terms as innovations, psychographics, and advertising medium should be used only when dealing with specialised respondent groups.

The meanings of some terms are vague to most respondents. Alternative terms may be equally confusing. After substantial protesting a government health survey included a diagram indicating the location of the abdomen as attempts at verbal descriptions proved fruitless.

Biased Words and Leading Questions

Biased or loaded, words and phrases are emotionally coloured and suggest an automatic feeling of approval or disapproval. Leading questions suggest what the answer should be or indicate the researcher's own point to view.

Biased phrases are difficult to deal with because phrases that are neutral to one group may be emotionally charged to another. Phrases such as luxury items and leisure time are neutral to many people, yet carry negative overtones to others. This fact illustrates the need to pretest with respondents who are as similar as possible to those people who will be included in the final survey.

Implied Alternatives

Making an implied alternative explicit frequently, but not always, increases the percentage of people choosing the alternative. For example, the following question:

If there is a serious fuel shortage this winter, do you think there should be a law requiring people to lower the heat in their homes?

Produced 38.3 per cent in favour of the law. Adding the phrase, "or do you oppose such a law"? Reduced the percentage in favour of the law to 29.4 adding the phrase, "or do you think this should be left to individual families to decide?" Produced 25.9 per cent in favour of the law. Clearly, both the presence and nature of stated alternatives can influence the response.

Frame of Reference

The working of the question will often determine which frame of reference or viewpoint the respondent will assume. Consider the following versions of a question to be answered by recent claimants of an automobile insurance company.

Does Allstate provide satisfactory or unsatisfactory settlement of claim?

Do you believe that Allstate provide satisfactory or unsatisfactory settlement of claims?

Were you satisfied or unsatisfied with Allstate's settlement of your recent claim?

Each of these versions provides the respondent with a somewhat different frame of reference. The first version calls for an objective answer that may include the respondent's perceptions of other people's standards for claims settlement and how adequately Allstate meets these expectations. The third question involves only the individuals' own standards and perceptions of the firm's reaction to his or her last claim. The second question probably elicits responses somewhere between the first and the third. Which question is best depends upon the purpose of the research.

2.8.4   Decisions About the Response Format

The first question is an example of an open or open-ended question. The respondent is free to choose any response deemed appropriate, within the limits implied by the question. The second question is an example of a multiple choice response format. Here the respondent must select from among three or more pre-specified responses. The final question represents a dichotomous question. Multiple-choice and dichotomous questions are often referred to as closed questions.

The decision as to which form of question to use must be based on the objective for the particular question. Each has its particular uses, advantages and disadvantages. Most questionnaires contain all three types of questions.

Open-Ended Question

Open-ended questions leave the respondent free to offer any replies that seem appropriate in light of the question.

The degree of openness will vary from question to question. The question "What do you think about cigarettes"? allows almost total freedom to the respondent who may discuss cigarettes in general, particular brands, advertising slogans, health issues, ethics, and a host of other issues. The question "What brand of cigarettes do you generally smoke?"

offers much less freedom. In this case, the respondent is constrained (we hope) to merely naming the brand generally smoked.

Advantages of Open-Ended Questions

Open-ended questions do not influence the respondent with a pre-stated set of response categories. Thus, opinions can be expressed that are quite divergent from what the researcher expected or what others had expressed. Related to this is the fact that open-ended questions particularly suitable for exploratory and problem-identification research.

Open-ended questions can provide the researcher with a basis for judging the actual values and views of the respondents that are often different to capital with more structured techniques. This "feel" for the quality of the information can be conveyed in the final report by the inclusion of quotes from representative responses. Finally, respondents generally like to have at least a few opportunities to express themselves openly.

Disadvantages of Open-Ended Questions

Open-ended questions should be limited on self-administered questionnaires because most respondents will seldom write elaborate answers. Furthermore, these questions are subject to two important sources of error. First, they may measure respondent articulateness. Some respondents will answer clearly and in depth on almost any topic, whereas others, who may have equal knowledge, may be more reluctant to express themselves.

A second source of error is interviewer effects. Interviewers will vary in this ability to record the respondents answers, in their intensity of probing, and in their objectivity.

As an alternative to central coding, each interviewer can code or categorise the respondent's answer without showing the respondent the list of response alternatives. This technique is generally called preceding. The interviewer has, in effect, a multiple-choice question that is presented to the respondent as an open-ended question. The interviewer must select the appropriate response category based on the respondent's verbal reply.

Multiple-Choice Questions

The essential feature of a multiple-choice question is that it presents, either in the questions proper or immediately following the question, the list of possible answers from which the respondent must choose.

Advantage of Multiple-Choice Questions

Multiple-choice questions generally offer a number of advantages over open-ended questions. They are generally easier for both the interviewer and the respondent. Indeed, they tend to reduce the interviewer bias and bias caused by varying levels of respondent articulateness. In addition, tabulation and analysis are much simpler. Multiple-choice questions have an advantage over dichotomous questions whenever the answer naturally involves more than two choices or when some measure of gradation or degree is desired.

Disadvantages of Multiple-Choice Questions

The development of a sound set of multiple-choice questions (or dichotomous questions) requires considerable effort. In addition, showing the respondents the list of potential answers can cause several types of distortion in the resulting data.

If all possible the alternatives are not listed, no information can be gained on the omitted alternatives. Even if an "other (specify)" category is included, there is a strong tendency for respondents to choice from among those alternatives listed. This may occur simply because one of the alternatives sounds familiar or logical, and "not thought about before" may be selected over the alternatives that would have been thought of independently. This particular feature may be good or bad, depending on the precise purpose of the question.

Issue with Multiple-Choice Questions

Number of Alternatives: A crucial issue in multiple-choice questions is how many alternatives to list. The standard answer to this question is that "each alternative should appear only once and all possible alternatives should be included." However, it is frequently impractical to include all possible alternatives. A list of all possible brands of cigarettes, for example, would have to include not only American brands but also all foreign brands that are available in local tobacco shops. A researcher is seldom interested in those brands or alternatives that only a few people will select. Therefore, the general approach is to list the more prevalent choices and an "Other" category, which is often accompanied by a "Please specify" and a short space to write in the answer. If the original list somehow excluded a major alternative, the "Other" category may uncover it.

Balanced or Unbalanced Alternatives: Another important issue concerns the number of alternatives on each side of issue. For example, consider the following two lists of alternatives for the same question:

Is Scars' advertising truthful or misleading?

- Extremely misleading
- Very misleading
- Somewhat misleading
- Neither misleading nor truthful
- Truthful

Versus

Is Scars' advertising truthful or misleading?

- Extremely truthful
- Very truthful
- Somewhat truthful

- Neither truthful nor misleading
- Misleading

The results obtained from the two sets of response categories will differ significantly. Although the preceding example is an extreme one, it is not difficult to find cases where a high degree of imbalance exists. Unless there is a specific reason (such an evidence that all respondents will respond on one side of the issue) to do otherwise, a balanced set of alternatives should be presented.

Position Bias: Which of the two alternative response sets to the following question will produce the highest per cent reporting that they eat out "much more often" than the last year? Or will both sets produce similar results? The two versions of the questionnaire were administered by mail to over 750 respondents each.

Compared to a year my household eats at a restaurant:

- Much more often
- Somewhat more often
- About an often
- Somewhat less often
- Much less often

- Much less often
- Somewhat less often
- About as often
- Somewhat more often
- Much more often

Version A produced twice as many "much more often" responses than version B (10 per cent versus 5 per cent). Similar results were obtained for questions on television viewing and the use of home repair professional versus doing-it-yourself.

It has been found that if three or four relatively long or complex alternatives are read to the respondents, there will be a bias in favour of the last alternative. However, if the alternatives are presented visually and all at the same time, the bias shifts to the alternative appearing at the top of the list.

A list of numbers such as the amount of money spent, and estimates of acts, such as the number of outlets in a given chain store, is subject to a middle-position bias. That is, respondents tend to select those values that are near the middle of the range presented.

A split-ballot technique—using multiple versions of the questionnaire with responses subject to position bias will minimise but not eliminate these effects.

Dichotomous Questions

Dichotomous questions which represent an extreme form of the multiple-choice questions, allow only two responses, such as "agree-disagree," "male-female. . . female," and "did-did not." Often the two categories are supplemented by a neutral category such as "don't know", "no opinion", "both," or "neither."

The advantages of the dichotomous question are similar to those of the multiple-choice questions. It is particularly well suited for determining certain points of fact, such as "Did you purchase a new model car in the past year?" and other clear-cut issues on which the respondents are likely to hold well-crystallised views. However, the researcher needs to be sure that the respondents think about the issue in dichotomous terms before using such questions.

2.8.5   Decisions about the Question Sequence

Question sequence, the specific order in which the respondents receive the questions, is a potential source of error. A number of general guidelines will reduce the probability of generating measurement error caused by the sequence of the questions.

The first question should be simple, objective, and interesting. If the respondents cannot answer the first question easily, or if they find them interesting, they may refuse to complete the remainder of the questionnaire. Similarly, if the questions arose suspicions in anyway, such as causing the impression that the interview really may be a sales call, respondents may distort the answers to later questions. Therefore, it is essential that the first few questions relax and assure the respondent.

2.8.6   Physical Characteristics of the Questionnaire

The physical characteristics of the questionnaire should be designed to make it easy to use. The first and most important objective is to minimise the possibility of recording mistakes. The questionnaire must be designed so that the interviewer or respondent can easily move from one question to the next. This is particularly important when skip, or branching instructions are involved. These instructions require the respondent to answer different questions based on the answer to the current questions.

Branching instructions have been found to confuse respondents in mail surveys and should be avoided if possible.

2.8.7   Decisions about the Pretest

A pretest requires five types of decisions.

- First, what items should be pretested?
- Second, how should the pretest be conducted?
- Third, who should conduct the pretest?
- Fourth, which respondents should be involved in the pretest?
- Fifth, how many respondents should be used?

2.8.8   Errors in Research Design

1. *Measurement Error:* Measurement error is caused by a difference between the information desired by the researcher and the information provided by the measurement process. In other words, not only it is possible to seek the wrong type of information but it is also possible to gather information that is different from what is being sought. This is one of the most common and serious errors. For example, respondents may exaggerate their income in order to impress an interviewer. Measurement error is particularly difficult to control because it can arise from many different sources.

2. *Experimental Error:* Experiments are designed to measure the impact of one or more independent variables on a dependent variable. Experimental error occurs when the effect of the experimental situation itself is measured rather than the effect of the independent variable.

   For example, a retail chain may increase the price of selected items in four outlets and leave the price of the same items constant in four similar outlets, in an attempt to discover the best pricing strategy. However, unique weather patterns, traffic conditions activities may affect the sales at one set of stores and not the others.

3. *Population Specification Error:* Population specification error is caused by selecting an inappropriate universe or population from which to collect data. This is potentially a serious problem in both industrial and consumer research. A firm wishing to learn the criteria that are considered most important in the purchase of certain machine tools might conduct a survey among purchasing agents.

4. *Frame Error:* The sampling frame is the list of population members from which the sample units are selected. An idea frame identifies each member of the population once and only once. Frame error is caused by using an inaccurate or incomplete sampling frame.

5. *Sampling Error:* Sampling error is caused by the generation of a non-representative sample by means of a probability sampling method, for example, a random sample of one hundred university students could produce a sample? Composed of all females (or all seniors or all business majors) such sample would not be representative of the overall student body. Yet it could be using probability sampling techniques. Sampling error is the focus point of concern in classical statistics.

6. *Selection Error:* Selection error occurs when a non-representative sample is obtained by non-probability sampling methods.

   For example, one of the authors talked with an interviewer who was afraid of dogs. In surveys that allowed any freedom choice, this interviewer avoided homes with dogs present. Obviously, such a practice may introduce error into the survey results. Selection error is a major problem in non-probability samples.

7. *Non-response Error:* Non-response error is caused by (i) The failure to contact all members of a sample and (ii) The failure of some contacted members of the sample to respond to all of specific parts of the measurement instruments. Individuals who are difficult to contact or who are relatively easy to contact or who readily cooperate. If these differences include the variable of interest, non-response error has occurred.

For example people are more likely to respond to a survey on a topic that interests them.

If a firm were to conduct a mail survey to estimate the incidence of the athlete's foot among adults, non-response error would be of major concern. Why? Those most likely to be interested in athlete's foot and thus most likely to respond to the survey are current or recent sufferers of the problem. If the firm were to use the percentage of those responding who report having athlete's foot as an estimate of the total population having athlete's foot, the company would probably greatly overestimate the extent of the problem.

2.9   TYPES OF MARKETING RESEARCH

The research always starts with a problem or question and its purpose is to find answers for the related problem in a scientific method and systematic and intensive towards a more complete knowledge of the subject studied. In this aspect, there are various types of research methods which are broadly classified as:

1. *Pure Research:* Pure research is undertaken to satisfy the researcher's thirst for knowledge and it is mainly goaded by the researcher's curiosity, it may be undertaken for designing tools to tackle practical problems. It concerns with singular situation and not suitable to a wide area. The pure research is also applied for the problems

arising in the areas such as sociology, psychology and economics. Thus, pure research enables us to make tools and applied research uses such tools to study a particular problem.

2. *Applied Research:* Applied research is undertaken with the aim of uncovering data to solve an existing problem. The driving force of this research is finding solution to a problem. Applied research aims at application of science to a singular situation. This kind of research is again classified into two categories, (a) problem solving research (b) problem oriented research.

   (a) *Problem Solving Research:* Problem solving research, as the name itself indicates, is concerned with a particular issue or a problem and is usually proprietary in character. The latter characteristic indicates that such a research is undertaken within a firm or by an outside consultant on its behalf.

   (b) *Problem Oriented Research:* In this type of research with a class of issues or problems in which several firms may be interested. This kind of research is usually concerned with conceptual aspects and oriented with applied problems.

3. *Exploratory Research:* When the purpose of research is to gain familiarity with a phenomenon or acquire new insights into it in order to formulate a more precise problem or develop hypothesis, the exploratory studies come in handy. If the theory happens to be too general or too specific, a hypothesis cannot be formulated. Therefore, a need for an exploratory research is felt to gain experience that will be helpful in formulating relevant hypothesis for more definite investigation. Again this research which is supported with some measures such as: (a) survey of literature (b) experience survey (c) case study.

   (a) *Survey of Literature:* A review of the literature helps to identify the hypothesis which may serve as a guide for further investigation.

   (b) *Experience Survey:* A small portion of the existing knowledge and experience is put into written form. Everyday-experience provides opportunity to obtain information required to formulate hypothesis.

   (c) *Case Study:* The focus may be on individual or group or communities. This method of study may lay stress on the examination of the existing records. It may be unstructured interviewing or participant observation or some other approach.

4. *Descriptive Research:* A descriptive study may be simple or complex. It determines who, what, where and how of a topic. It is concerned with describing the characteristics estimating the proportion of the people in a specified population who hold certain views or attitudes and discovering or testing whether certain variables are

associated. It should be remembered by the researcher while gathering information in this category research he/she must be careful about bias and extravagance that may creep at every stage of the study, designing the methods of data collection, selecting sampling, and analysing that data and reporting the findings.

5. *Other Types of Research:* The remaining types of research are variations of one or more of the aforementioned methods. They vary in terms of the purpose of research or the research may either be in the nature of one-time or longitudinal research. While the research is restricted to a single time-period in the former case, it is conducted over several time-periods in the latter case. Depending upon the environment in which the research is to be conducted, it may also be laboratory research or field-setting research, or simulation research, besides being diagnostic or clinical in nature. Under such research, in-depth approaches or case-study methods may be employed to analyse the basic causal relations. These studies usually conduct a detailed in-depth analysis of the causes of things or events of interest and use very small samples and a sharp data collecting method. The research may also be explanatory in nature. Formalised research studies consist of substantial structure and specific hypotheses to be verified. As regards historical research, sources include philosophy of persons and groups of the past or any remote point of time. Research is also categorised as decision-oriented and conclusion-oriented. In the case of decision-oriented research, it is always carried out for the need of a decision-maker and hence, the researcher has no freedom to conduct the research as per his/her own desires. Whereas, under conclusion-oriented research, the researcher is free to choose the problem, redesign the enquiry as it progresses and even change conceptualisation as he/she wishes to. Further, operations research is a kind of decision-oriented research, because it is a scientific method which provides the executive departments a quantitative basis for decision-making with respect to the activities under their purview.

2.10   APPLICATIONS OF MARKETING RESEARCH

The broad areas of application for marketing research are sales and market analysis, product research, advertising, business economics and corporate research, and corporate responsibility.

(i) **Sales and Market Analysis**

  (a) *Determination of market potential:* The market potential is the total amount of a product or product group which could be sold to a market in a specified time period and under the given conditions. Market potential is applicable in case of a new product, a modified version of an existing product, or an existing product to be introduced in a new geographical market.

(b) *Determination of market share:* In case of an existing product, a company may be interested to know the percentage share of the market which their brand commands.

(c) *Sales forecasting:* Sales forecasting is an attempt to predict the sales level at a given point in the future on the basis of the existing information. Sales forecasting is applicable to both existing products as well as new products. The sales may be calculated either in units or in value. Basically, there are two types of forecasts– short-term and long-term. The short-term forecast takes into account seasonal growth pattern of the industry to which the product belongs and the business cycle operating in the industry.

(d) *Design of market segmentation studies:* A market is a group of potential customers which has something in common. The common factors may be a geographical area, sex (after shave lotion is used only by men), age (toys for children under 5, between 5-7, etc.), physical characteristics (weak eyesight, overweight), income, lifestyle.

Children comprise the market for toys. But in this broad category, the market can be viewed to be made up of many smaller markets or segments: one market for pre-schoolchildren, another for school-going children, one market comprised of educational toys, one for mechanical toys, one for electrical toys, one for indoor games, etc. The choice before the marketing manager is whether to cater to the broad market of toys or to only one or two of the specific market segments. MR can help answer questions such as "To what extent should the market segmentation strategy be pursued?" and "What should be the basis for segmentation?"

(e) *Test Market:* This is a controlled experiment to predict sales or profit conse-quences of the various marketing strategies. It refers to trying out something in a particular market before extending it on a larger scale. You may have noticed advertisements for soaps, or snack foods which sometimes carry the message 'available only in Hyderabad' or 'available only in Kolkata.' The firm selling these products is probably test marketing the product. The results of the market test provide the research data for taking a decision whether to extend the marketing to other areas or drop the idea totally. Test marketing also yields information which helps to modify the product and marketing strategy to give it a better chance for success.

(f) *Distribution channel studies:* Market research can be used to determine the most effective and profitable distribution channels for different types of products.

(g) *Determination of market characteristics:* Research surveys can be conducted to collect information about the market characteristics which would help a new entrance plan in entry or help an existing company focus its strategy more sharply for increasing market share. Information can be collected on the number of brands competing in the market, state-of-technology prevailing in the market, geographical concentration and dispersal of customers, nature of outlets selling the products, number of such retail outlets, etc.

(h) *Determination of competitive information:* Research can provide information on the marketing strategies used by various competing brands and the 'unique selling proposition' of each.

(ii) Product Research

This can be used for:

(a) Evaluation of new product ideas

(b) Testing for new product acceptance

(c) Evaluating the need for change in product formulation

(d) Testing package design in terms of aesthetic appeal, protection for the product, and ability to withstand transportation and stocking ordeals.

(e) Testing for product positioning. Should a new brand of tea be positioned on the basis of its fragrance and taste, or colour and strength, or price.

(iii) Business Economics and Corporate Research

(a) Studies of business trends to determine industries with growth potential and those facing a stagnant future.

(b) Pricing studies to estimate the demand level at different prices. Such studies reveal the extent to which customers are sensitive to price changes and provide valuable clues to the market or in assessing the impact of price increase or decrease on the sales.

(c) Diversification studies: These provide information on the profitable new opportunities of business growth which a firm can consider for diversification. The diversification may be into totally new and unknown areas or into allied areas.

(d) Product-mix studies: If a firm considering diversifying into allied product areas, it may like to find out the product mix combinations which would optimise its existing resources and provide synergy for growth. A company in the business of cooking oil would like to do research into one or more of the following products for arriving at a synergistic product-mix: butter, vanaspati, ghee, spices, dehydrated foods, frozen foods, instant food mixes, custard powder, branded wheat flour and rice.

(e) Plant and warehouse location studies: Research is also needed to determine the best possible location for setting up a new plant. Before arriving at a decision, a firm would need to research into factors such as availability of raw material and labour, proximity to marketplace, telecommunication and transport infrastructure, financial, taxation and other incentives applicable to each location. In case of warehouse location, you would research into movement patterns of goods to different cities, high sale potential areas versus low potential areas, number of checks for quality needed en route the destination of final customer, benefit of conducting these checks against the cost of acquiring and maintaining a warehouse and convenient rail/road connections.

(iv) Advertising Research

(a) Audience measurement for advertisements appearing in different media such as newspapers, magazines, journals, radio, TV, outdoor hoardings, kiosks, bus side panels, etc. The objective of this type of research is to estimate the audience size of each media channel (e.g., press) and within that the specific media vehicle (*India Today, Readers Digest, The Indian Express,* etc.). Given the audience size, you would be interested in knowing its age, sex, socio-economic and cultural profile to focus your advertising strategy.

(b) Determining the most cost-effective media plan: Each media channel has its unique advantages and disadvantages, and each media vehicle has its own cost structure. Research can be used to find out the best media vehicle by matching the product characteristics with the audience profiles of different media vehicles and the respective cost of advertising in these.

(c) Copy testing: One approach for researching into the effectiveness of the copy is to test the following elements:

- Basic themes, ideas, appeals
- Headlines, baseline, pictures, jingle, story sequence
- Pre-testing whole advertisements in rough or finished form
- Pre-testing the effect of repetition to simulate a campaign (all the above can be tested under simulated conditions)
- After the advertisements have been released, post-testing them individually in their normal media
- The other approach for conducting research is to assess the copy or the entire advertisement/campaign for the following:
  - Assessing for its attention value, interest value and arousal
  - Test for communication clarity
  - Test for their effect on consumer attitudes
  - Test for their effect on purchase behaviour.

(d) Determining advertising effectiveness: After the advertisements have been released, it is important to monitor their impact in terms of achieving the intended objective(s). To what extent has the advertising achieved its objective of creating brand awareness, creating corporate image, educating the customers about the product usage, and so on. The effectiveness is always determined in relation to the cost incurred.

(v) **Consumer Behaviour Research**

(a) To determine who the customers of the product (men, women, children, working women, housewives, retired people) are and profile them in terms of their socio-economic background, age, religion and occupation.

(b) To find out where the customers are located.

(c) To determine their motivations to purchase your brand of product.

(d) To determine their buying behaviour pattern in terms of identifying sources of information and influence, and sequence of purchase decision.

(e) To find out the post-purchase satisfaction level of customers.

2.11   MARKETING RESEARCH IN INDIA

In India, marketing research (MR) has gained a great deal of recognition and status in recent years. The trend started in the latter half of eighties, and the post-liberalisation period witnessed a new accent on market research. Not only has MR become more visible as an industry, but there has also been a shift from tactical and strategic research. The growth of competition and the sea change in the environment, have turned Indian industry and business towards market research. While many consumer product firms, especially the larger ones, were already using the market research tool, with the intensification of competition in practically every sector and every product category, more and more firms have started looking up to market research for help. Two distinct developments have taken place in this regard, several firms have strengthened their in-house marketing research capability, several others have turned to the professional market research agencies resulting in a substantial growth of independent MR agencies in the country.

There are different marketing research agencies in India. They are:

- Operations Research Group
- National Council of Applied Economic Research
- Indian Market Research Bureau
- Marketing and Research Group
- Marketing Design and Enquiry Service

- Marketing and Business Associates
- Pathfinders India

Marketing research is used equally by companies in both the private and the public sectors. The only difference is that private sector companies tend to use MR more for decisions on diversification, new product, market segmentation, product positioning, and measuring customer satisfaction than do public sector organisations.

The manner in which marketing research is conducted is revealed in the table below.

Marketing Research Channel used by Indian Organisations

Type of Channel	Per cent
Company sales staff	69%
Market research agencies	52%
In-house market researchers	44%
Advertising agencies	35%
Consultants	34%
Syndicate research services	22%

Companies use more than one kind of channel and so the percentage adds up to more than 100

(*Source:* Business India)

2.11.1 Problems of Conducting Marketing Research in India

The biggest problem confronting anyone who sets out to conduct research in India is the meagre secondary data. The census which contains a wealth of data takes many years to be compiled and released for public usage. Data contained in journals and handbooks is usually two to three years old. Thus, whatever data is available is usually obsolete and this greatly reduces its utility.

In collecting primary data, the problems are those of widely scattered sampling units, location of some sampling units in remote and inaccessible areas, and poor communication facilities which compounds the problem of inaccessibility. If the sampling units are the industrial units in the unorganised sector, there is no guide for locating these units. The other kind of problem encountered in collecting primary data is the uncooperative attitude of respondents arising out of sheer lack of knowledge about the nature of MR and its utility. Respondents often view interviewers with suspicion and may refuse to give any information.

Most of the market research organisations are located in the cities and have an urban-bias to the extent that they have neither a penetration/base in the rural areas and nor can they communicate properly with the rural people. Most market research is conducted in the cities for products used by city dwellers.

The state-of-the-art in marketing research has not reached the sophisticated levels as in America or Europe. The marketing research techniques used in India are still relatively unsophisticated and simplistic.

2.12   THE CONCEPT OF MEASUREMENT

Measurement may be defined as the assignment of numbers to characteristics of objects, persons, states, or events, according to rules. What is measured is not the object, person, do not measure the object itself but only its characteristic of being present. We never measure people, only their age, height, weight, or some other characteristics.

The term number in the definition of measurement does not always correspond to the usual meaning given this term by the non-researcher. It does not necessarily mean number that can be added, subtracted, divided, or multiplied. Instead, it means that numbers are used as symbols to represent certain characteristics of the object. The nature of the meaning of the numbers/symbols depends on the nature of the characteristics they are to represent and how they are to represent them.

Measurement and Concepts

A concept is simply an invented name for a property of an object, person, state, or event. The terms construct and concept are sometimes used interchangeably. We use concepts such as sales, market share, attitude, and brand loyalty to signify abstractions based on observations of numerous particular happenings. Thus, the concept car refers to the generalisation of the characteristics that all cars have in common. The concept car is closely related to a physical reality.

Many concepts in marketing research do not have such easily observed physical referents. It is impossible to point to a physical example of an attitude, product image, or social class. Two approaches are necessary to define a concept adequately:

1. Conceptual definition
2. Operational definition

1. Conceptual Definition

A conceptual definition (sometimes called a constitutive definition) defines a concept in terms of other concepts. It states the central idea or essence of the concept. A good conceptual definition clearly delineates the major characteristics of the concept and allows one to distinguish the concept from similar but different concepts. Consider "brand loyalty" as a concept. Under your definition, is one loyal to a brand if one consistently buys it because it is the only brand of the product that is available at the stores at which one shops? Is this individual brand loyal in the same sense as others who consistently select the same brand from among the many brands carried where they shop? An adequate conceptual definition of brand loyalty should distinguish it from similar concepts such as "repeat purchasing behaviour."

2. Operational Definition

An operational definition describes the activities the researcher must complete in order to assign a value to the concept under consideration. Concepts are abstractions, as such, they are not observable. Thus, a conceptual definition should precede and guide the development of the operational definition.

Consider this conceptual definition of brand loyalty: "the preferential attitudinal and behavioural response towards one or more brands in a product category expressed over a period of time by a consumer (or buyer)." Brand loyalty defined in this way can be measured in a number of different ways. However, it is sufficiently precise to rule out many commonly used operational definitions of sequence in which brand loyalty is defined as X consecutive purchases (usually three or four) of one brand of often used. This operational definition is not adequate because it ignores the attitudinal component specified in the conceptual definition.

Scales of Measurement

It is useful to distinguish four different types of numbers of scales of measurement: nominal, ordinal, interval, and ratio which is represented in Table 2.1. The rules for assigning numbers constitute the essential criteria for defining each scale.

Nominal Measurements

Nominal scales comprise numbers used to categorise objects or events. Perhaps the most common example is when we assign a female the number 1 and a male the number 0. Numbers used in this manner differ significantly from those used in more conventional ways. We could just as easily have assigned the 0 to the females and the 1 to the males or we could have used the symbols A and B or the terms male and female. In fact, in the final research report, terms are generally substituted from numbers to describe nominal categories.

A nominally scaled number serves only as a label for a class or category. The objects in each class are viewed as equivalent with respect to the characteristic represented by the nominal number.

An example of the use of nominal measurement is the case of a manager of restaurant located in a shopping centre who wants to determine whether noon customers select the establishment primarily because of its location or primarily because of its menu. The manager randomly selects and questions 100 customers and finds that 70 state that they eat there because of the location and 30 because of the menu. This represents a simple analysis using nominal data. The manager has formed a two-category scale, counted the number of cases in each category, and identified the modal category.

A mean or a median cannot be calculated for nominal data. A mode can be used, however. In the example given, location was the modal reason for choosing the restaurant among the males and the menu was the model reason among females. The percentages of items falling within each category also can be determined. A chi-square statistical test can be conducted to determine if differences between the numbers falling in the various categories is likely to be the result of chance or randomness.

Ordinal Measurements

Ordinal scales represent numbers, letters, or other symbols used to rank items. Items can be classified not only as to whether they share some characteristic with another item but also whether they have more or less of this characteristic than some other object. However, ordinarily scaled numbers do not provide information on how much more or less of the characteristic various items possess.

A significant amount of marketing research relies on ordinal measures. The most common usage of ordinal scales is in obtaining preference measurements. For example, a consumer or a sample of experts may be asked to rank preferences for several brands, flavours, or package designs.

A mode or a median may be used, but not a mean. Then model quality rating is "2" as it is for the median. A mean should not be calculated because the differences between ordinal scaled values are not necessarily the same. The branch of statistics that deals with ordinal (and nominal) measurements is called non-parametric statistics.

Interval Measurements

Interval scales represent numbers used to rank items such that numerically equal distances on the scale represent equal distances in the property being measured. However, the location of the zero point is not fixed. Both the zero point and the unit of measurements are arbitrary. The most familiar examples of interval scales are the temperature scales, both centigrade and Fahrenheit. The same natural phenomenon, the freezing point of water, is assigned a different value on each scale, 0 on centigrade and 32 on Fahrenheit. The 0 position, therefore, is arbitrary. The difference in the volume of mercury is the same between 20 and 30 degrees. A value on either scale can be converted to the other by using the formula F = 32 + 9/5C.

The most frequent form of interval measurement in marketing is index numbers. Are index numbers calculated by setting one number, such as sales, for a particular year equal to 100. This is known as the base period or base value. Other numbers for subsequent years are then expressed as percentages of the base value. The Department of Labour provides a consumer price index with 1967 as the base year (1985 = 320), whereas the Federal Reserve System uses 1977 as the base year for its industrial production index. Since any year or value, including a completely arbitrary value, can serve as the base value, index numbers have an arbitrary zero point and equal intervals between scale values.

Another common type of marketing research data generally treated as interval scale data is attitude measures. A Likert scale, for example, requires the respondents to state their degree of agreement or disagreement with a statement by selecting a response from a list such as the following one:

1. Agree very strongly
2. Agree fairly strongly
3. Agree
4. Undecided
5. Disagree
6. Disagree fairly strongly
7. Disagree very strongly

It is doubtful that the interval between each of these items is exactly equal. However, most researchers treat the data from such scales as if they were equal intervals in nature since the results of most standard statistical techniques are not affected greatly by small deviations from the interval requirement. Where this is a concern, there are ways to transform most ordinal data used by marketers into workable interval data.

Virtually the entire range of statistical analyses can be applied to interval scales. Such descriptive measures as the mean, median, mode, range, and standard deviation are applicable. Bivariate correlation analyses, t-test, analysis of variance tests, and most multivariate techniques applied for purpose of drawing inferences can be used on internally scaled data.

Ratio Measurements

Ratio scales consist of numbers that rank items such that numerically equal distances on the scale represent equal distances in the property being measured and have a meaningful zero. In general, simple counting of any set of objects produces a ratio scale of the characteristic being measured exists. Thus, such common measurements as sales, costs, market potential, market share, and number of purchasers are all made using ratio scales.

Table 2.1 Scales of Measurement

	Basic Empirical		Typical Statistics	
Scale	Operations	Typical Usage	Descriptive	Inferential
Nominal	Determination of equality	Classification: Male-female, purchaser, non-purchaser, social class	Percentages, mode	Chi-square, binomial test
Ordinal	Determination of greater or less	Ranking: Preference data, market position, attitude, measures, many psychological measures	Median	Mann-Whitney U, Friedman two-way ANOVA rank-order correlation
Interval	Determination of equality of intervals	Index numbers, attitude measures, level of knowledge about brands	Mean, range, standard deviation	Product moment correlation t-test, factor analysis, ANOVA
Ratio	Determination of equality of ratios	Sales, units number of customers, cost	Produced	Coefficient of variation

2.13   MARKETING DECISION SUPPORT SYSTEM

A growing number of organisations have added a fourth information service a marketing decision support system (MDSS) to help their marketing managers make better decisions. Little defines an MDSS as:

"*A coordinated collection of data, systems, tools and techniques with supporting software and hardware by which an organisation gathers and interprets relevant information from business and environment and turns it into a basis for marketing action*".

This is shown in Fig. 2.2.

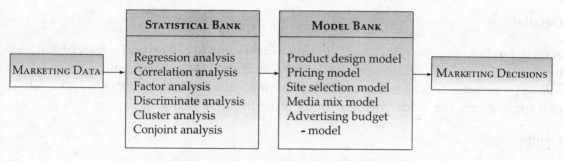

Fig. 2.2 Marketing decision support system.

Suppose a marketing manager needs to analyse a problem and take action. The manager puts questions to the appropriate model in the MDSS. The model draws up data, which are analysed statistically. The manager can then use a program to determine the optimum course of action. The manager takes this action and the action along with other forces, affect the environment and result in new data.

Marketing managers in a growing number of companies now have available computer marketing workstations. These workstations are to marketing managers what the cockpit controls are to airline pilots arming managers with the means of flying the business in the right direction.

New software programs regularly appear to help marketing managers analyse, plan, and control their operations. *Marketing News*, April 27, 1992, lists over 92 different marketing and sales software programs. They provide support for designing marketing research studies, segmenting markets, setting prices and advertising budgets, analysing media, planning sales force activity, and so on. Here are examples of decision models that have been used by marketing managers.

Brand Aid

A flexible marketing mix model focused on consumer-packaged goods whose elements are manufacturers, competitors, retailers, consumers, and the general environment. The model contains sub-models for advertising, pricing and competition. The model is calibrated with a creative blending of judgement, historical analysis, tracking, field experimentation, and adaptive control.

Call Plan

A model to help salespeople determine the number of calls to make per period to each prospect and current client. The model takes into account travel time as well as selling time. The model was tested at United Airlines with an experimental group that managed to increase its sales over a matched control group by 8 percentage points.

Detailer

A model to help salespeople determine which customers to call on and which products to represent on each call. This model was largely developed for pharmaceutical detail people calling on physicians where they could represent no more than three products on a call. In two applications, the model yielded strong profit improvements.

Geoline

A model for designing sales and service territories that satisfies three principles—the territories equalise sales workloads, each territory consists of adjacent areas and the territories are compact. Several successful applications were reported.

Mediac

A model to help an advertiser buy media for a media for a year. The media-planning model includes market segment delineation, sales potential estimation, diminishing marginal returns, forgetting, timing issues, and competitor media schedules.

Some newer models now claim to duplicate the way expert marketers normally make their decisions.

Promoter

Evaluates sales promotions by determining baselines sales (what sales would have been without promotion) and measuring the increase over baseline associated with the promotion.

Adcad

Recommends type of ad (humorous, slice of life, and so on) to use given the marketing goals and characteristics of the product, target market, and competitive situations.

Coverstory

Examines a mass of syndicated sales data and writes an English language memo reporting the highlights.

2.14 QUANTITATIVE TOOLS USED IN MARKETING DECISION SUPPORT SYSTEMS

Statistical Tools

1. *Multiple Regressions:* A statistical technique for estimating "best fitting" equation showing how the value of dependent variables varies with changing values in a number of independent variables.

2. *Discriminate Analysis:* A statistical technique for classifying object or persons into two or more categories. Example: A large retail chain store can determine the variables that discriminate between successful and unsuccessful store location.

3. *Factor Analysis:* A statistical technique used to determine the few underlying dimensions of a larger set of intercorrelated variables.

4. *Cluster Analysis:* A statistical technique for separating objects into a specified number of mutually exclusive groups such that the groups are relatively homogenous. Example, a marketing researcher might want to classify a miscellaneous set of cities into four groups of similar cities.

5. *Conjoint Analysis:* A statistical technique whereby the ranked preferences of respondents for different offers are decomposed to determine the persons inferred utility function for each attribute and the relative importance of each attribute. Example, an airline can determine the total utility delivered by different combinations of passenger services.

6. *Multidimensional Scaling:* A variety of techniques for representing objects as points in a multidimensional space of attributes where their distance from each other is a measure of dissimilarity.

Models

1. *Markov process model:* This model shows the probability of moving from current state to any new state. Example, a branded packaged good manufacturer can determine the period-to-period switching and staying rates for his brand and, if the probabilities are stable, the brand is ultimate brand share.

2. *Queuing model:* This model shows the waiting times and queue lengths that can be expected in any system, giving the arrival and service times and the number of service channels and service speed. e.g., a supermarket can use the model to predict queue lengths at different times of the day given the number of service channels and service speed.

3. *Sales response model:* This is a set of models which estimate functional relations between one or more marketing variables–such as sales force size, advertising expenditure, sales-promotion expenditure, etc. and the resulting demand level.

4. *New product pretest model:* This model involves estimating functional relations between buyer states of awareness, trail, and repurchase based on consumer preferences and actions in a pre-test situation of the marketing offer and campaign. Among the well-known models are ASSESSOR, COMP, NEWS and SPRINTER.

Optimization Routines

1. *Differential Calculus:* This technique allows finding the maximum or minimum value along a well-behaved function.

2. *Mathematical Programming:* This technique allows finding the values that would optimise some objective functions that are subject to a set of constraints.

3. *Statistical Decision Theory:* This technique allows determining the course of action that produces the maximum expected value.

4. *Heuristics:* This involves using a set of rules of thumb that shorten the time or work required to find a reasonably good solution in a complex system.

2.15   MARKETING INFORMATION SYSTEM

Marketing information system is an internal arrangement designed to support management decision-making and action. Marketing information system provides the management with:

(a) Current or conditional future states of the market environment

(b) The market responses to company and/or competitor actions.

According to Professor Brien and Professor Stafford, a marketing information system is *"a structured interchanging complex of persons, machines and procedures designed to generate an orderly flow of pertinent information collected from both intra and extra firm sources for use as the basis for decision-making in specified responsibility areas of marketing management."*

In the words of Professor Alder Lee, marketing information system is *"an interaction, continuing, future-oriented structure of people, equipment and procedure designed to generate and process an information flow which can aid business executives in the management of their marketing programmes."*

Thus, marketing information system is an interacting, ongoing and future-oriented structure of persons machines and procedures designed to generate an orderly flow of evaluated data from internal and external sources for the use of managerial decision-making in the dynamic area of marketing. It collects, sorts out, classifies, analyses and evaluates the data and stores for future decision-making.

The concept of a marketing information system (MIS) is illustrated in Fig. 2.3. As shown marketing research is but one subsystem—the others are concerned with the following.

(i) **Internal Reports**

The internal accounting system that reports such items as sales and order.

(ii) **Marketing Intelligence**

Provides information about relevant developments in the marketing environment.

(iii) **Analytical Marketing**

Consists of advanced techniques for analysing data and problems, includes a statistical bank and a model bank.

The activities performed by an MIS and its subsystems include information discovery, collection, interpretation (which may involve validation and filtering), analysis, and intracompany disseminating (storage, transmission, and/or dumping).

More specifically, the MIS can be tied directly to the decision process. A good MIS will contribute in some way to every part of this process, although not necessarily equally.

The MIS should have the capability to

1. Store and retrieve data easily.
2. Generate reports and analyses, both standard and ad hoc as required.
3. Provide modelling and "what-if" (i.e., spreadsheet-type) analysis.
4. Create high quality visual aids (e.g., graphics)
5. Integrate all of the functions listed above.

A highly developed marketing information system has four major components or divisions, namely:

- Internal marketing information
- Marketing intelligence

- Marketing research
- Management science.

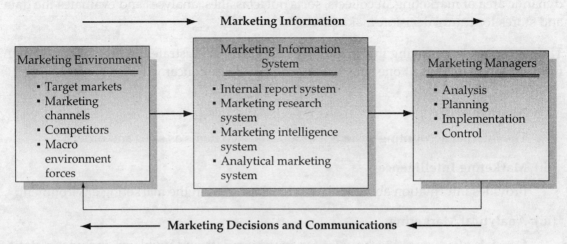

Fig. 2.3 The marketing information system.

A brief explanation of each component is a must to have clear grasp of the marketing information system in any organization. Fig. 2.3 helps us in understanding the same.

1. Internal Marketing Information System

Internal marketing information system is also called internal accounting system. The internal accounting system involves using marketing data available from within the company as a means of indicating the cost effectiveness of the firm. The internal forces and their relationship to good information management influencing the decision-making of marketers are that marketing has become more complex with wideness gamut, it needs faster and sounder decision, it warrants efficient use of resources—particularly time, treasure and talent when they are getting short and use of inexpensive data made possible by information explosion caused by computer technology. The details on internal sales, costs inventories, cash-flows, account receivables and payables, time availability, and so on are provided by internal accounting system.

2. Marketing Intelligence System

Marketing intelligence involves the collection of qualitative and often subjective data about changing conditions in the marketing macro environment. There are external forces that influence the functioning of a given organisation. Marketing intelligence acts as mirror of marketing environmental reflecting clearly how things are going on in the marketplace. It is essentially an organised feedback process in the overall marketing information system of any organisation.

3. Marketing Research System

There has been some confusion regarding the usage of these two phrases "marketing research" and "marketing information system." A close look at these two makes it amply clear that marketing research can only be a part of marketing information system as the latter has wider connotations and coverage. Marketing research offers special in-depth information to the marketing executive on request face and combat typical marketing problems.

The MR efforts are project-oriented involving the studies of behaviour, product or brand preferences, product usage, advertising awareness, sales promotions dealer behaviour, physical distribution, competition and the like hire, the management poses the specific problems or problems which are researched to arrive at the most agreeable solution.

4. The Management Science System

In a nutshell, marketing information system with these four subsystems is a link between the marketing environment and the marketing executives who make decisions. It received the marketing data from the environment evaluates into useful information to the needy and busy executives enabling them to make sounder and quicker decisions.

In a nutshell, marketing information system with there four subsystems is a link between the marketing data from the environment evaluates into useful information to the needy and busy executives enabling them to make sounder and quicker decision.

2.15.1   Questionnaire—A Market Survey on Mineral Water

Questionnaire for Retail Outlets

1. For how many years have you been stocking mineral water?

    ☐ Less than 1 year
    ☐ 1-3 years
    ☐ 3-7 years
    ☐ More than 7 years

2. Which brand of mineral water do you stock?

  ☐ Mohan Meakin
  ☐ Bisleri
  ☐ Any other (please specify) _____

3. If you stock only one brand, why do you stock only this brand?

  ☐ Customers usually ask for this brand.
  ☐ It comes in plastic bottles.
  ☐ It is natural spring water.
  ☐ It is cheaper.
  ☐ We get a large dealer discount.
  ☐ We have a contract with the manufacturer.
  ☐ Better relations with the company salesman.
  ☐ We have had negative experience with the other manufacturers.

  _____

  Please specify who

  _____

  (Any other, please specify)

4a. Do you use any display material for the mineral water?

  ☐ Posters
  ☐ Stickers
  ☐ Neon lighting
  ☐ Hangers

  _____

  Please specify who

  _____

4b. Who pays for the display material?

  _____

5. If no display material is being used, how do you let the customers know that you stock mineral water?

  _____

6. Are you satisfied with the present display set?

    ☐ Not satisfied
    ☐ Satisfied

7. What improvements do you suggest?

_____

8. Are you satisfied with the existing level of advertising done by the manufacturers?

    ☐ Yes
    ☐ No

9. When customers ask for mineral water, do they ask for a specific brand?

    ☐ Yes
    ☐ No

    Which brand _____

9a. Do you give credit to your customers?

    ☐ Yes
    ☐ No

9b. Do you give credit to your customers for other purchases?

    ☐ Yes
    ☐ No

10. Do you provide home delivery to your customers?

    ☐ Yes
    ☐ No

11a. What percentage of your customers?

    ☐ Carry the bottle away? _____
    ☐ Drink the mineral water in the shop? _____

11b. What percentage of your customers are?

    ☐ Foreigners? _____
    ☐ Indians? _____

12. In case of the foreigners, can you tell us the ranking of the following categories of customers?

     □ Resident foreigners _____
     □ Student (resident) _____
     □ Tourists _____

13. How many bottles do your customers purchase from you at a time?

     □ One
     □ Two
     □ Three
     □ Four
     □ 5-7
     □ 8-10
     □ Over 10

14. Do you charge for the bottle in case the customers wish to carry it away?

     □ Yes
     □ No

     How much _____

15. What is the percentage of breakages (of bottles) during delivery?

16. What is the frequency of ordering and the number of bottles ordered per lot?

     □ Daily _____
         □ 1 case
         □ 2 cases
         □ 3-5 cases
     □ Weakly _____
     □ Fortnightly _____
         □ 6-10 cases
         □ Over 10 cases
     □ Monthly _____

17. Could you tell us?

     The price you pay per case? _____

     The price you sell per bottle? _____

     In case of bulk sales per case? _____

18. What credit + discount do you get from the manufacturer?

Give to the customer? _____

For bulk purchases/timely payments? _____

19. What is the nature of delivery?

It is delivered to us _____

We pick it up from the manufacturer _____

Both (varying situation-wise) _____

20. Is the demand for mineral water seasonal?

☐ Yes
☐ No

When + Why _____

21. Name of outlet: _____

22. Address: _____

23. Profile of outlet:

(a) Softdrink vendor
(b) Pan shop
(c) General provision shop
(d) Chemist
(e) Departmental store
(f) Super bazar
(g) Any other

Questionnaire for Potential Indian Customers

1. Do you use water from the tap for drinking purposes?

☐ Yes
☐ No

If yes, what do you think of the hygiene of tap water _____

If no, then why not _____

2. Could you tell us what treatment do you subject tap water to (at home) before you consider it fit for drinking?

☐ Only filter
☐ Filter + boil
☐ Only boil
☐ Filter + boil + chemical
☐ Only chemical treatment
☐ Chemical
☐ Chemical + boil

3a. Home treated water, in your household, is used by:

☐ All members of the household
☐ Only the aged members
☐ Only the children
☐ Only the unwell

Any other (please specify) _____

3b. Home treated water, in your household, is used when:

☐ Travelling
☐ Unwell
☐ Throwing a party
☐ On a festive occasion
☐ All the time
☐ In the rainy season

Any other (please specify) _____

3c. You treat your water at home because:

_____

4. Outside your home, your drinking water habits can best be described as:

☐ Usually drink only at the homes of friends
☐ Carry drinking water along
☐ Drink water only at decent restaurants
☐ Drink water from vendors, dhaba, etc.
☐ Drink only beverages

Any other (please specify) _____

5. What do members of your household do when on an outstation trip?

☐ Carry drinking water from home

☐ Drink from local sources (untreated)
☐ Treat local water before drinking it
☐ Drink only beverages
Any other (please specify) _____

6. What do you feel about the treatment you give to the tap water?

☐ Renders the tap water less than 100% bacteria-free, but fit enough for drinking
☐ Cleans the water only partially ·
☐ Leaves room for risk of infection
☐ Consumers excessive fuel/electricity
☐ Too cumbersome an effort
☐ A time-consuming effort
☐ Worth the trouble

☑ the most relevant blank.

7. If an easily available, safe and hygienic substitute for treated tap water be made available would you use it?

☐ Yes.
☐ No.

8. How much would you be willing to pay for a 1 litre bottle (2 milk bottles = 5 soft drink bottles = 1 litre)

_____

9. You would like to use this substitute in your household:

☐ For children
☐ For the unwell members
☐ For the aged
☐ For special occasions (festivals, parties, picnics)
☐ For foreign guests
☐ When travelling
☐ For daily use for all household members
Any other (please specify) _____

10. Where would you prefer to purchase such a substitute from?

☐ Local grocery shop
☐ Local restaurant/soft drink shop

☐ Departmental store
☐ Chemist
☐ Super bazaar

Any other (please specify) _____

11. What bottle size of this substitute would be most convenient for you?

☐ ½ litre
☐ 1 litre
☐ 1½ litre
☐ 2 litre

Any other (please specify) _____

12. Have you heard of mineral water?

☐ Yes
☐ No.

If yes, could you indicate the source of your information?
☐ Shopping displays
☐ On a trip abroad
☐ From foreign guests
☐ From a hotel menu card
☐ From reading matter

Any other (please specify) _____

13. Have you ever consumed mineral water before?

☐ Yes
☐ No.

If yes, could you indicate how often?
☐ Once
☐ Twice
☐ A few times
☐ Occasionally
☐ Regularly

14. If you have consumed it more than a few times could you mention the occasions of consuming mineral water?

_____

15. Why did you consume it on these occasions?

   _____

16. You think mineral water is:

   - ☐ A medical drink
   - ☐ Natural spring water
   - ☐ Purified water
   - ☐ A tonic
   - ☐ A nutritive water
   - ☐ Water with minerals mixed in
   - ☐ An ingredient for cooking purposes

   Mark ☒ the two most relevant blank.

17. Could you tell us the reason for your not having consumed mineral water on a regular basis to date?

   Mark ☒ the most relevant blanks.

   - ☐ It is too expensive.
   - ☐ It is too much of a bother
   - ☐ You have never felt the need to do so
   - ☐ You don't need mineral water

18. Your occupation _____

19a. Educational qualification:

   Yourself _____

   Your spouse _____

19b. How often did you and your spouse travel abroad

   Yourself _____

   Your spouse _____

19c. Are you/your spouse a member of any club in India?

   Could you name it/them _____

19d. Your monthly income is

   - ☐ ₹5,000
   - ☐ ₹8,000

    ☐ ₹12,000
    ☐ ₹16,000
    ☐ Over ₹16,000

19e. Name _____

Address + Tel _____

Status in family _____

Age 20-30, 30-40, 40-50, 50-60, over 60

For Regular Consumers Only

20. Your monthly consumption of mineral water bottles is:

    ☐ 1
    ☐ 2
    ☐ 3
    ☐ 4
    ☐ 5-10
    ☐ Above 10

21. You purchase mineral water from?

_____

22. Your brand preference is for?

    ☐ Bisleri
    ☐ Aqua Mineral
    ☐ Any other brand
    Why _____

23. Your preference is for?

    ☐ Glass bottle
    ☐ Plastic bottle
    Why _____

2.16   WHAT IS BUYER BEHAVIOUR?

Consumer behaviour is the process through which the ultimate buyer makes purchase decisions. Here is a sample of popular definitions for consumer behaviour:

'... the study of the buying units and the exchange processes involved in acquiring, consuming, and disposing of goods, services, experiences, and ideas' **(Mowen)**.

'... the decision process and physical activity individuals engage in when evaluating, acquiring, using or disposing of goods and services' **(Loudon and Della Bitta)**.

'... reflects the totality of consumers' decisions with respect to the acquisition, usage and disposition of goods, services, time and ideas by (human) decision-making units (over time)' **(Jacob Jacoby)**.

The definition by **Jacoby** can be further illustrated. The totality of consumers' decisions include whether to buy or not, what to buy, why to buy, how to buy, when to buy, where to buy and also how much/how often/how long. The idea of consumption not only includes purchasing and using, but also disposing. The marketer's offering can mean many things—be it product, service, time, ideas, people, and so on. The term decision-making unit obviously refers to the people involved. In a typical purchase, many people may be involved and they play different roles such as information gatherer, influencer, decider, purchaser and user. In a consumer buying context, it may mean a family or group influence whereas in the industrial buying context, it means a cross-functional team with each member of the team performing a particular role in the buying decision. The word 'time' could mean different units of time like hours, days, weeks, months and years.

2.17   IMPORTANCE OF CONSUMER/BUYER BEHAVIOUR

Consumer/buyer behaviour is helpful in understanding the purchase behaviour and preference of different consumers. As consumers, we differ in terms of our sex, age, education, occupation, income, family, set-up religion, nationality and social status. Because of these different background factors, we have different needs and we only buy those products and services which we think will satisfy our needs. In marketing terminology, specific types of consumers buying different products represent different market segments.

To successfully market to different market segments, the marketing manager needs appropriate marketing strategies which can be designed only when he understands the factors which account for these differences in consumer behaviour and tastes.

In today's world of rapidly changing technology, consumers' tastes are also characteristics by fast changes. To survive in the market, a firm has to be constantly innovating and understand the latest consumer trends and tastes. Consumer behaviour provides invaluable clues and guidelines to marketers on new technological frontiers which they should explore. For example, let us consider the advent of colour television in India. When we switched over from black and white transmission to colour transmission in the early eighties, the consumers exhibited a desire to purchase colour TV for closer to life picture viewing.

Consumer behaviour is a process, and purchase forms one part of this process. There are various endogenous psychological and exogenous environmental factors which influence this process. All these factors and the type of influence which they exert on an individual's consumption behaviour can be understood and analysed. Moreover, some of these factors can be further influenced by specific elements of the marketing strategy, so that the consumer behaviour process results in a definite purchase decisions. To the extent that the marketer can understand and manipulate the influencing factors, he can predict the behaviours of consumers. Though predictions can never be absolutely accurate, it certainly reduces the risk associated with different marketing strategies. Thus, the importance of consumer behaviour lies in the fact that the behaviour can be understood and influenced to ensure a positive purchase decision. The marketing manager's interest lies exactly here, i.e., to ensure that his marketing strategy results in purchase of the product.

2.17.1   Types of Consumers

All consumers can be classified into two types—personal and organisational. When you buy a shirt for your own use—you are buying in your capacity as a personal consumer. However, when you are buying a typewriter for use in office you are making the purchase in your capacity as an organisational consumer. Whenever you buy goods and services for your own or family use, you are a representative of a personal consumer. All individuals thus fall in the category of personal consumer. All business firms, government agencies and bodies, non-business organisations such as hospitals, temples, and trusts are organisational consumers of goods and services purchased for running the organisation.

2.17.2   Buyer versus User

Often the person who purchases the product is not the person who actually consumes or uses the product. A father buys toys and clothes for consumption for her young children. The father is the buyer but the actual consumers are children. A car is purchased by the husband or the wife but it is used by all the family members. Thus, in the family context, you may either have the situation where the buyer is distinct from the consumer or the buyer is only one of the many consumers. The question that arises is who should be the subject of study in consumer behaviour? Should we study the buyer or the consumer? To overcome this problem, in many instances it is the household or family and not the individual who is considered the subject of the study.

However, a person involved in marketing, should have a very sharply defined focus for marketing strategy, especially promotional strategy. You must identify the best prospect for your products—weather it is the buyer or the user. But even when the consumer is distinct from the buyer, the consumer's likes and dislikes, taste, etc influences the buyers' decisions to purchase a specific product or brand. Thus, many companies play it safe and focus their promotion at both the user and the buyer. Consider the promotional message of Maggi Noodles and Rasna Soft Drink concentrate, the taste and fun aspects of both these products are meant to appeal to the children who are the major consumers, while the convenience and economy are meant to appeal to the mothers who are the buyers.

2.18   MODELS OF CONSUMER/BUYER BEHAVIOUR

Consumer behaviour is a dynamic, multidisciplinary process. The study of consumer behaviour builds upon an understanding of human behaviour in general. In an effort to understand why and how consumers make buying decisions, marketers borrow extensively from the sciences of psychology and sociology. The work of psychologist Kurt Lewin provides a useful classification scheme for influences on buying behaviour. Lewin's proposition is: $B = f(P, E)$ which means that behaviour (B) is a function (f) of the interactions of personal influences (P) and pressures exerted by outside environmental forces (E). This statement is rewritten to apply to consumer behaviour as $B = f(I, P)$ (i.e.) consumer behaviour (B) is a function (f) of the interactions of interpersonal influences (I).

Such as culture, role models, friends and family—and personal factors (P) such as attitudes, learning and perception. Therefore, inputs from others and an individual's psychological make up both affect a consumer's purchasing behaviour. This model is further explained in the following sections of this lesson. There are many other models of consumer behaviour.

The most generic model of the consumer behaviour suggests a stimulus-response pattern of understanding the consumer's behaviour (Fig. 2.4). The stimulus can be marketing stimuli (which can be manipulated by the marketer) and other external stimuli (like the economy, culture, technology, and so on). The response includes the decision to buy, product choice, dealer choice and choices regarding time, quantity, etc. The consumer is at the centre of this model. The stimulus is applied to this consumer who in turn comes up with a response. The consumer has his/her own characteristics and a multi-staged decision-making process. There are also several influencing factors acting upon the consumer. The influencing factors may include personal and interpersonal influences.

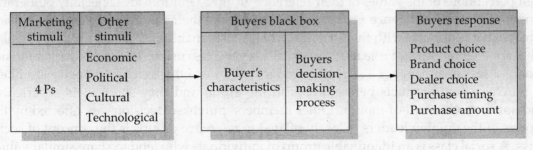

Marketing stimuli	Other stimuli	Buyers black box		Buyers response
4 Ps	Economic Political Cultural Technological	Buyer's characteristics	Buyers decision-making process	Product choice Brand choice Dealer choice Purchase timing Purchase amount

Fig. 2.4 Models of consumer behaviour.

2.19   DETERMINANTS OF CONSUMER BEHAVIOUR

Consumers don't make purchase decisions in a vacuum; rather, they respond to a number of external, interpersonal influences and internal, personal factors. Consumers often decide to buy goods and services based on what they believe others expect of them. They may want to project positive images to peers or satisfy the unspoken desires of family members. Marketers recognise three broad categories of interpersonal influences on consumer behaviour: cultural influences, group influences and family influences.

Cultural influences

Culture can be defined as the values, beliefs, preferences and tastes handed down from one generation to the next. Culture is the broadest environmental determinant of consumer behaviour. Therefore, marketers need to understand its role in customer decision-making. They must also monitor trends to spot changes in cultural values. Marketing strategies and business practices that work in one country may be offensive or ineffective elsewhere because of cultural variations. Hence, cultural differences are particularly important and complex to understand for international marketers. Cultures are not homogeneous entities with universal values. Each culture includes numerous subcultures–groups with their own distinct modes of behaviour.

Group (social) influences

Every consumer belongs to a number of social groups. Group membership influences an individual's purchase decisions and behaviour in both overt and subtle ways. The influences may be informational and/or normative. Every group establishes certain norms of behaviour. Group members are expected to comply with these norms. Difference in group status and roles can also affect buying behaviour. The surprising impact of groups and group norms on individual behaviour has been called the Asch phenomenon because it was first documented by psychologist S.E. Asch. Discussions of the Asch phenomenon raise the subject of reference groups–groups whose value structures and standards influence a person's behaviour. Consumers usually try to coordinate their purchase behaviour with their perceptions of the values of their reference groups. Children are especially vulnerable to the influence of reference groups. They often base their buying decisions on outside forces–what is popular with their friends, what is fashionable and trendy, what is popular, what are their heroes and role models (usually, celebrities) using. In nearly every reference group, a few members act as opinion leaders. They are the trendsetters who are likely to purchase new products before others in the group and they share their experiences and opinions via word of mouth. Other members' purchase decisions are affected by the reports of the opinion leaders. Closely related to reference groups is the concept of social class. A social class is an identifiable group of individuals who tend to share similar values and behaviour patterns different from those of other classes. These values and behaviour patterns affect the purchase decisions.

Family influences

The family group is perhaps the most important determinant of consumer behaviour because of the close, continuing interactions among family members. Like other groups, each family typically has norms of expected behaviour and different roles and status relationships for its members. The traditional family structure consists of a husband and wife. Although these and other members can play a variety of roles in household decision-making.

Marketers have created four categories to describe the role of each spouse: (1) Autonomic, in which the partners independently make equal number of decisions (e.g. personal-care items) (2) Husband-dominant, in which the husband makes most of the decisions (e.g. insurance) (3) Wife-dominant, in which the wife makes most of the decisions (e.g. children's clothing) and (4) Syncratic in which both partners jointly make most decisions (e.g. vacation). Consumer behaviour is affected by many internal, personal factors, as well as interpersonal ones. Each individual brings unique needs, motives, perceptions, attitudes, learning and self-concepts to buying decisions.

Courtesy: Happydent Advertisement

Needs and motives

Individual purchase behaviour is driven by the motivation to fill a need. A need is an imbalance between the consumer's actual and desired states. Someone who recognises or feels a significant or urgent need then seeks to correct the imbalance. Marketers attempt to arouse this sense of urgency by making a need 'felt' and then influence consumers' motivation to satisfy their needs by purchasing specific products. Motives are inner states that direct a person toward the goal of satisfying a felt need. The individual takes action to reduce the state of tension and return to a condition of equilibrium.

Perceptions

Perception is the meaning that a person attributes to incoming stimuli gathered through the five senses–sight, hearing, touch, taste and smell. Certainly a buyer's behaviour is influenced by his or her perceptions of a good or service.

Attitudes

Perception of incoming stimuli is greatly affected by attitudes. In fact, the decision to purchase a product is strongly based on currently held attitudes about the product brand, store or salesperson. Attitudes are a person's enduring favourable or unfavourable evaluations, emotional feelings or actions tendencies toward some object. Because favourable attitudes likely affect brand preferences, marketers are interested in determining consumer attitudes toward their products.

Learning

In a marketing context, learning refers to immediate or expected changes in consumer behaviour as a result of experience (that of self or others). Consumer learning is the process by which individuals acquire the purchase and consumption knowledge and experience that they apply to future related behaviour. Marketers are interested in understanding how consumers learn so that they can influence consumers' learning and subsequently, their buying behaviour.

Self-concept

The consumer's self-concept–a person's multifaceted picture of himself or herself–plays an important role in consumer behaviour. The concept of self emerges from an interaction of many of the influences–both personal and interpersonal–that affect the buying behaviour.

Consumers complete a step-by-step process to make purchasing decisions. The length of time and the amount of effort they devote to a particular purchasing decision depends on the importance of the desired good or service to the consumer. Purchases with high levels of potential social or economic consequences are said to be high-involvement purchase decisions. Routine purchases that pose little risk to the consumer are low-involvement decisions. Consumers generally invest more time and effort to purchase decisions for high-involvement products than to those for low involvement products. For example, a car buyer will probably compare prices, spend time visiting dealer showrooms, read auto reviews and ask for advice from friends before making the final decision. Few buyers invest that much effort in choosing between two brands of candies. They will still go through the steps of the consumer decision process but on a more compressed scale. Purchase decisions can be thought-based (cognitive) or feeling-based (emotive). While it is true that both cognition and emotion will be present in every purchase decision, either one of them will dominate the decision. As a result, we can construct a grid as follows to analyse different consumer purchase decisions which are shown in the Fig. 2.5.

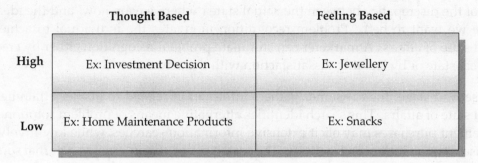

	Thought Based	Feeling Based
High	Ex: Investment Decision	Ex: Jewellery
Low	Ex: Home Maintenance Products	Ex: Snacks

Fig. 2.5 Classification of consumer purchase decisions.

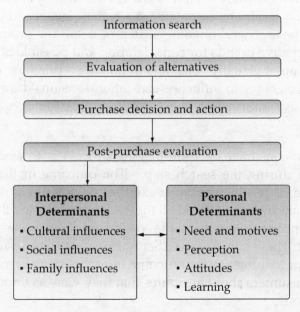

Fig. 2.6 Consumer decision process.

Figure 2.6 represents the five steps in the consumer decision process. First, the consumer recognises a problem or an unmet need. Then he/she searches for goods or services that will fill that need and evaluates the alternatives before making a purchase decision (and the actual purchase). After completing the purchase, the consumer evaluates whether he/she has made the right choice. Much of marketing involves steering the consumers through the decision process in the direction of a specific item. Consumers apply the decision process in solving problems and taking advantage of opportunities. Such decisions permit them to correct differences between their actual and desired states. Feedback from each decision serves as additional learning experience to help guide subsequent decisions.

During the first stage in the consumer decision-making process, the consumer becomes aware of the discrepancy between the actual state ('where we are now' and the ideal state ('where we want to be'). Problem recognition motivates the individual to achieve the desired state of affairs. A marketer can stimulate problem recognition either by creating a new ideal state or by creating dissatisfaction with the actual state.

In the second stage, the consumer gathers information related to his/her attainment of a desired state of affairs. This search identifies alternative means of problem solution. High-involvement purchases may elicit extensive information searches, while low-involvement purchases require little search activity. The search may cover internal or external sources of information. During internal search, stored information, feelings and experiences relevant to the problem-solving situation are recalled from the consumer's memory. An external search gathers information from outside sources, which may include family members, associates, store displays, sales representatives, advertisements and product reviews. The external search may be a general ongoing search or a specific pre-purchase search. The search identifies alternative brands for consideration and possible purchase. The number of brands that a consumer actually considers in making a purchase decision is known as the evoked set. Marketers try to influence consumer decisions during the search process by providing persuasive information about their goods or services in a format useful to consumers.

The third step in the consumer decision-making process is to evaluate the evoked set of options identified during the search step. The outcome of the evaluation stage is the choice of a brand or product in the evoked set or possibly a decision to renew the search for additional alternatives, should all those identified during the initial search prove unsatisfactory. To complete this analysis, the consumers develop a set of evaluative criteria to guide the selection. These criteria can either be objective facts or subjective impressions. Marketers can attempt to influence the outcome from this stage in many ways. First, they can try to educate consumers about attributes that they view as important in evaluating a particular class of goods.

They can also identify which evaluative criteria are important to an individual and attempt to show why a specific brand fulfils those criteria. They can try to induce a customer to expand his/her evoked set to include the product they are marketing.

The search and alternative evaluation stages of the decision process result in the eventual purchase decision and the act of making the purchase. At this stage, the consumer has evaluated each alternative in the evoked set based on his/her personal set of evaluative criteria and narrowed the alternatives down to one. Marketers can smooth the purchase decision and action by helping consumers through financing, delivery, installation, and so on.

The purchase act produces one of the two results. The buyer feels either satisfaction at the removal of the discrepancy between the actual and the ideal states or dissatisfaction with the purchase. Consumers are generally satisfied if purchases meet their expectations. Sometimes, however, consumers experience some post-purchase anxieties, called cognitive dissonance. It is a perception that one has not made the right decision. The consumer attempts to reduce this dissonance by searching for additional information that confirms his/her choice. The marketer can help by providing reassuring information to the buyer and also by positive marketing communications.

2.20   THE CONSUMER DECISION PROCESS

An integrated model of the consumer decision process is shown below.

Consumers complete a step-by-step process to make purchasing decisions. The length of time and the amount of effort they devote to a particular purchasing decision depends on the importance of the desired goods or services to the consumer. Purchases with high levels of potential social or economic consequences are said to be high-involvement purchase decisions. Routine purchases that pose little risk to the consumer are low-involvement decisions. Consumer generally invest more time and effort to purchase decisions for high-involvement products than to those for low-involvement products.

For example, a car buyer will probably compare prices, spend time visiting dealer show-rooms, read auto reviews and ask for advice from friends before making the final decision. Few buyers invest that much effort in choosing between two brands of candies. They will still go through the steps of the consumer decision process but on a more compressed scale. Purchase decisions can be thought-based (cognitive) or feeling-based (emotive). While it is true that both cognition and emotion will be present in every purchase decision, either one of them will dominate the decision. As a result, we can construct a grid as follows to analyse different consumer purchase decisions as shown in Fig. 2.7.

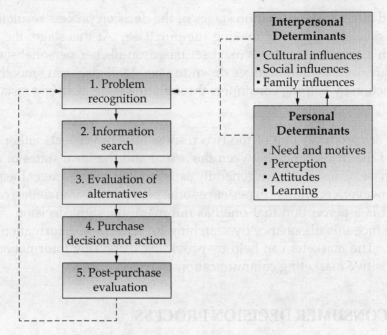

Fig. 2.7 Consumer decision process.

	Thought Based	**Feeling Based**
High effort	Ex: Investment Decision	Ex: Jewellery
Low effort	Ex: Home Maintenance Products	Ex: Snacks

Fig. 2.8 Classification of consumer purchase decisions.

An integrated model of the consumer decision process shown in Fig. 2.7 consists five steps. First, the consumer recognises a problem or an unmet need. Then he/she searches for goods or services that will fill that need and evaluates the alternatives before making a purchase decision (and the actual purchase). After completing the purchase, the consumer evaluates whether he/she has made the right choice. Much of marketing involves steering the consumers through the decision process in the direction of a specific item. Consumers apply the decision process in solving problems and taking advantage of opportunities.

Such decisions permit them to correct differences between their actual and desired states. Feedback from each decision serves as additional learning experience to help guide subsequent decisions. During the first stage in the consumer decision-making process, the consumer becomes aware of the discrepancy between the actual state ('where we are now' and the ideal state ('where we want to be'). Problem recognition motivates the individual to achieve the desired state of affairs. A marketer can stimulate problem recognition either by creating a new ideal state or by creating dissatisfaction with the actual state. In the second stage, the consumer gathers information related to his/her attainment of a desired state of affairs. This search identifies alternative means of problem solution. High-involvement purchases may elicit extensive information searches, while low-involvement purchases require little search activity. The search may cover internal or external sources of information. During internal search, stored information, feelings and experiences relevant to the problem-solving situation are recalled from the consumer's memory. An external search gathers information from outside sources, which may include family members, associates, store displays, sales representatives, advertisements and product reviews. The external search may be a general ongoing search or a specific pre-purchase search. The search identifies alternative brands for consideration and possible purchase. The number of brands that a consumer actually considers in making a purchase decision is known as the evoked set. Marketers try to influence consumer decisions during the search process by providing persuasive information about their goods or services in a format useful to consumers.

The third step in the consumer decision-making process is to evaluate the evoked set of options identified during the search step. The outcome of the evaluation stage is the choice of a brand or product in the evoked set or possibly a decision to renew the search for additional alternatives, should all those identified during the initial search prove unsatisfactory. To complete this analysis, the consumers develop a set of evaluative criteria to guide the selection. These criteria can either be objective facts or subjective impressions. Marketers can attempt to influence the outcome from this stage in many ways. First, they can try to educate consumers about attributes that they view as important in evaluating a particular class of goods. They can also identify which evaluative criteria are important to an individual and attempt to show why a specific brand fulfils those criteria. They can try to induce a customer to expand his/her evoked set to include the product they are marketing.

The search and alternative evaluation stages of the decision process result in the eventual purchase decision and the act of making the purchase. At this stage, the consumer has evaluated each alternative in the evoked set based on his/her personal set of evaluative criteria and narrowed the alternatives down to one. Marketers can smooth the purchase decision and action by helping consumers through financing, delivery, installation, and so on.

The purchase act produces one of the two results. The buyer feels either satisfaction at the removal of the discrepancy between the actual and the ideal states or dissatisfaction with the purchase. Consumers are generally satisfied if purchases meet their expectations.

Sometimes, however, consumers experience some post-purchase anxieties, called cognitive dissonance. It is a perception that one has not made the right decision. The consumer attempts to reduce this dissonance by searching for additional information that confirms his/her choice. The marketer can help by providing reassuring information to the buyer and also by positive marketing communications.

2.21   MARKETING IMPLICATIONS OF CONSUMER BEHAVIOUR

Marketers study consumer behaviour because it has serious marketing implications–be it in marketing strategy (as defined by market segmentation, targeting and positioning) formulation or in designing the marketing mix (defined by the 4 Ps of marketing, viz., product, price, place and promotion). The following is a list of questions related to marketing strategy and marketing mix. The answers obviously arise from insights and findings from the study of consumer behaviour. Consider this.

- **Developing a Customer-Oriented Strategy**

  Market segmentation
  How is the market segmented?
  How profitable is each segment?
  What are the characteristics of consumers in each segment?
  Are customers satisfied with existing offerings?
  Selecting the target market

- **Positioning**

  How are competitive offerings positioned?
  How should our offerings be positioned?
  Should our offerings be repositioned?

- **Developing Products or Services**

  What ideas do consumers have for new products?
  What attributes can be added to or changed in an existing offering?
  What should our offering be called?
  What should our package and logo look like?
  What about guarantees?

- **Making Promotion (Marketing Communications) Decisions**

  What are our advertising objectives?
  What should our advertising look like?
  Where advertising should be placed?
  When should we advertise?

Has our advertising been effective
What about sales promotion objectives and tactics?
When should sales promotions happen?
Have our sales promotions been effective?
How many salespeople are needed to serve customers?
How can salespeople best serve customers?

- **Making Pricing Decisions**

What price should be charged?
How sensitive are consumers to price and prices changes?
When should certain price tactics be used?

- **Making Distribution Decisions**

Where are target consumers likely to shop?
How should stores be designed?

Here are some specific real-life examples to emphasise the marketing implications that arise from the study of consumer behaviour.

Product positioning and competition: Remember the classic ad campaign for CoffeeBite. It talks about the positioning identities–What am I and Who am I. The Axe Deo campaigns strongly bring out the positioning identity of 'For whom am I?' Also the positioning of different supermarkets like FoodWorld, Nilgris, ApnaBazar and Subiksha answer the question 'For whom am I?'. While designing the competitive marketing strategy, one question that bothers marketers is 'Who am I competing with?' For instance, is Xerox competing with other photocopier makers or computer printer makers or printers? With a positioning as 'the Document Company' it protects itself from marketing myopia and positions itself to take on competition even from the substitute products. If Style-Spa, the high-end home furniture retailer considers itself as a home expressions company, it invites competition from antique furniture shops. Similarly, Archies, a social expressions company selling cards and gifts, in reality competes with florists! These insights emerge from an understanding of the consumer needs and motives which is central to consumer behaviour.

Marketers are concerned about how consumers perceive their products. For example, brands like Strepsil (with all its colours and flavours), Crocin (with interesting mass media campaigns) can possibly confuse the consumers–are they pharmaceutical products? Self-help relievers? Are they speciality or commonplace products? Consumer perception determines the evoked set for the problem. No brand wants to be categorised with wrong competition in the evoked set! Itchguard represents a classic case of the creation of a new product category. The consumer need was always there until this brand arrived and addressed this need exquisitely and exclusively. In many markets, orange juice enjoys different perceptions–as a breakfast drink, as a refresher drink, as a health drink and as a health recovery drink. Same product but different consumer perceptions! This understanding is vital for a brand like Tropicana which sells orange juice in different markets. Also the use of celebrity endorsements (as reference groups, opinion leaders) is attributed to its role in consumer behaviour. The use of cricketers like Sachin Tendulkar and Bollywood stars like Aishwarya Rai in advertisements attempts to shape and influence consumer behaviour in favour of the brands they endorse. Another classic example is the 'Got milk?' campaign featuring several celebrities in support of milk as a healthy drink and endorsing its consumption. Check out for more about this campaign at www.whymilk.com. In Eastern cultures, group values are stressed over the individuals. So the appeal to normative beliefs takes on greater significance while designing marketing communications in the Eastern cultures.

A study of consumer learning reveals how consumers generalise related marketing stimuli. Based on this, there are several marketing applications–product-line extension (Pepsi Lemon), product-form extension (Pepsi can), product-category extension (Aquafina), Family branding (Nestle's Maggi, HP Pavillion), Licensing (Tommy, CK, Disney–in several product categories to several merchandisers), usage situation generalisation (an all-hair shampoo).

The study of consumer behaviour is an exciting field of marketing. Marketing begins and ends with consumers. As a result, the study of consumer behaviour permeates all of marketing.

KEYWORDS

Consumerism: A social force within the business environment designed to aid and protect buyers by exerting legal, moral and economic pressures on businesses.

Buyer behaviour: Process by which consumers and business buyers make purchase decisions.

Consumer behaviour: Buyer behaviour of ultimate consumers.

Reference group: Group with which an individual identifies strongly enough that it dictates a standard of behaviour.

Opinion leader: Trendsetters likely to purchase new products before others and then share the resulting experiences and opinions via word of mouth.

Evoked set: Number of brands that a consumer considers buying before making a purchasing decision.

Cognitive dissonance: Post-purchase anxiety that results from an imbalance among an individual's knowledge, beliefs and attitude.

Primary data: Data which is collected originally for the current investigation.

Secondary data: Data which has already been collected by an agency or individual and available in published or unpublished form.

Sample: A small group drawn from the population or universe and which has all the characteristics of the population and is a true representative of it.

Survey: A method of collecting primary data. In the survey method data is gathered from the sample with the help of a questionnaire. The data may be gathered personally, over the telephone or by mail.

Questionnaire: An organised and written format which contains all the relevant questions for gathering data from the sample.

Respondents: An individual in his personal capacity or representing an institution who fulfils all the requirements of a sampling unit and is used for collecting data. He is known as respondent because he responds to the questionnaire.

Perception: Process of selection, organisation and interpretation of stimuli into cohesive, coherent picture.

Attitudes: Enduring and learned tendencies to act in a particular consistent way with regard to a given object or idea.

Learning: Process of applying results of past experiences to evaluate a new situation or modify future behaviour.

Demographics: The technique of measuring lifestyle using psychographic character such as attitudes, opinions, and interest.

Lifestyle: An individual's pattern of living in the world as expressed by the manner in which he spends money and time on various activities and interests, and the opinions that he holds.

Social class: Division in a society comprising people sharing same social, values, beliefs, attitudes, and exhibiting a distinct preference for certain products and brands.

Sub-culture: Culture within a culture distinct group of people grouped on the basis of nationality, religion, geographic region or race and having their own distinct motives, values and behaviour patterns.

Diffusion of innovation: Process by which the acceptance of an innovation is spread by communication to members of a society and the adoption of the innovation in terms of actual purchase of the product.

SUMMARY

Marketing Research (MR) as a tool for decision-making is gaining wide acceptance. Marketing decision involves variables which are often external to the firm, dynamic in nature, uncontrollable by the firm and interact with each other in a complex manner. Because of their dynamic and uncontrollable nature, the uncertainty associated with them is very high, which in turn leads to the situation that in most marketing decisions the associated risk factors is also very high.

The marketing manager is always on the lookout for ways and means to reduce this risk. One way that the risk can be reduced is through the use of MR which by providing information reduces uncertainty and converts the unknown risk factor into a known calculated risk.

MR can be used for gathering information about the market structure, competitors' activities, consumer behaviour, testing the efficacy of various elements of the marketing strategy and making forecasts. MR can be used for pre-testing a strategy before actually implementing it, monitor it during implementation, and after implementation monitor the results to assess its impact. Apart from its usefulness in the areas of marketing, MR is also used for monitoring socio-economic projects.

Every MR project involves five steps. These are: problem definition, research design, field work, data analysis and report presentation and analysis.

The manager must make the decision regarding the utility of MR on the basis of the cost involved in conducting the research and the benefits expected to accrue from it.

Measurement may be defined as the assignment of numbers to characteristics of objects, persons, states, or events, according to rules. What is measured is not the object, person, state, or events, according to rules.

Marketing information system is an internal arrangement designed to support management decision-making and action. Marketing information system provides the management with:

(a) Current or conditional future states of the market environment and

(b) The market responses to company and/or competitor actions.

A questionnaire is simply a formalised set of questions for eliciting information. As such, its function is measurement and it represents the most common form of measurement in marketing research.

Questionnaire construction involves seven major decision areas: (1) Preliminary considerations, (2) Question content, (3) Question wording, (4) Response format, (5) Question sequence, (6) Physical characteristics of the questionnaire, and (7) Pretest.

Consumer behaviour is the study of why, how, what, when, where, and how often do consumers buy and consume different products and services.

The study of consumer behaviour also provides an insight into how consumers arrive at the purchase decision and the variable which influences their decision. Once the influencing variables have been identified, the marketer can manipulate them so as to induce in his consumers a positive purchase decision.

Man is a many faceted, complex psychological being. His consumer behaviour is influenced by his motives, perception, attitudes and learning. Each of these psychological factors provides a unique mental framework for each consumer within which he makes his purchase decisions. For the marketer it is essential to associate his product with the motives and perceptions of his consumers. Also he must ensure that the product concept fits in with the consumer's existing attitudes and beliefs.

Consumers differ from one another in terms of age, sex, education, income, family life cycle, personality, and lifestyle, and other personal characteristics which influence their buying behaviour. Among the various groups such as family, friends, social organisations, professional associations, the strongest influence is exerted by the family.

Culture is the most pervasive influence on our lives and influences all aspects of our behaviour, consumers operate within the cultural framework of their society and purchase only those operate within the cultural framework of their society and purchase only those products which fit in with their cultural norms.

ASSIGNMENT

Assignment 1

Does your organisation use marketing research to improve the quality of decisions? Give a specific instance, describing the marketing situation/problems, in which research may have narrowed down the choice of alternative solutions reduced the risk associated with a decision or helped in identifying a new marketing opportunity. (Compare two organisations and bring out the facts.)

_____

_____

_____

_____

_____

Assignment 2

Construct a brief questionnaire for gathering information about the marketing strategies of the brands competing with each other. Your sampling units would be the distributors/wholesalers/retailers dealing with those brands.

Assignment 3

Suppose you are assigned the job of conducting a survey to determine the levels of post-purchase or post-consumption satisfaction of the customer of your product. Who would you choose in your sampling unit? What socio-economic variables would you consider in detailing the profile of your customers?

_____

_____

_____

_____

_____

Assignment 4

(a) Identify which of the members within your own family are likely to be buyers and users for the following products:

Product	Buyer	User
Shaving Cream	_____	_____
Stereo System	_____	_____
Toilet Soap	_____	_____
Nail Polish	_____	_____
Vegetables	_____	_____
Moped	_____	_____
Bike	_____	_____

(b) In the above analysis, which of your family member plays the buyer's role most of the times? Can you identify the reason?

Assignment 5

1. Draft each of the following appears on a paper questionnaire that respondents find out and return to a research firm. Rephrase or reformat each question so that the respondent is more likely to provide the research firm with information it needs.

   (a) Which brand do you like the most?

   (b) Can you tell how many children you have? Whether they are girls or boys, and how old they are?

   (c) How much say do you have regarding the charities that your church contributes to?

   (d) Are auto manufacturers making satisfactory progress in controlling auto emissions?

2. Levi Strauss's marketing team has determined that the men buy Levi's jeans fall into five categories:

   (a) Utilitarian jeans customer: The level Loyalist who wears jeans for work and play

   (b) Trendy casual: High fashion customers who come to late at night

   (c) Price shopper: Buys on the basis of price at departmental stores and discount stores

   (d) Mainstream traditionalist: Over 45 years old and shops in departmental store accompanied by his wife

   (e) Classical independent: Independent buyer, shops alone in speciality stores, and wants cloths that make him "look right" (the target in this case)

   The marketing team wants to develop a product for the "classic independent" segment. Should the Levi name be used on the new product? Can this product be marketed successfully through Levi's current channels of distribution? What kinds of formal market research should the company conduct to help it make a sound decision on whether to purchase this segment and how?

3. Suggest creative ways to help companies research the following issues:

   (a) A liquor company needs to estimate liquor consumption in a legally dry town.

   (b) A magazine distribution house wants to know that many people read a specific magazine in doctors' offices.

   (c) A men's hair tonic producer wants to know at least four alternative ways to research how men use its products.

Assignment 6

To get preliminary idea about the study and application of consumer behaviour, complete the following table in terms of your own purchase behaviour.

1. What are your reasons for purchasing the following products and services?

    (a) Toothpaste _____
    (b) Tea (packaged tea) _____
    (c) Electrical bulb _____
    (d) Haircutting service _____
    (e) Pressure cooker _____

2. Which brand do you normally purchase?

    (a) Toothpaste _____
    (b) Tea (packaged tea) _____
    (c) Electrical bulb _____
    (d) Haircutting service _____
    (e) Pressure cooker _____

3. How often/how much do you buy at a time?

    (a) Toothpaste _____
    (b) Tea (packaged tea) _____
    (c) Electrical bulb _____
    (d) Haircutting service _____
    (e) Pressure cooker _____

4. From where do you usually purchase?

    (a) Toothpaste _____
    (b) Tea (packaged tea) _____
    (c) Electrical bulb _____
    (d) Haircutting service _____
    (e) Pressure cooker _____

5. Conduct a similar exercise for one of your close friends and compare his/her purchase behaviour with your own. Are there any differences? Identify the reasons for these differences.

    _____

    _____

    _____

CASE STUDY

Case Study-1

That CSR (Corporate Social Responsibility) Thing!

It shouldn't surprise anyone that Indian companies have just discovered the marketing pay-off of their corporate social responsibility (CSR) initiatives. They could get by with focusing on real or perceived product attributes, and with profit-mindedness being considered a coarse sentiment, any CSR programme they launched was far removed from their core businesses, brands, even consumers.

There has been a spate of corporate CSR initiatives over the past few years. Companies have been quick to respond to crises (such as the Gujarat earthquake or the Tsunami that hit the southern parts of the country) or shown inherent goodness in plugging gaps in the government's efforts to provide healthcare and education to all–in a country as vast as India, there will always be gaps–but there has been little effort to link such work to things such as marketing, even corporate strategies. Most CSR activities are, at best, charity, not very different from discrete acts of philanthropy and, at worst, a mere humane façade of a for-profit-only capitalist system.

This is why recent advertising campaigns by the country's two largest fast moving consumer goods (FMCG) companies, Hindustan Lever Limited (HLL) and ITC are significant. The first, a campaign for Surf Excel Quick Wash with the tagline *Do bucket paani ab rozana hai bachain* (I will save two buckets of water a day), has struck a chord in a country where the shortage of water is an endemic phenomenon. "We decided it would be of immense benefit to a household if a technology could be developed that would reduce the water consumed in the washing of clothes and the amount of effort required while rinsing while delivering superlative cleanliness", says an HLL spokesperson. Surf's sales, say sources in the market, have gone up by as much as 15% since the advertisement, starring actress-turned-social-activist and former Member of Parliament, Shabana Azmi, went national (the company had tested the strategy in waterstarved Tamil Nadu last year with another actress-turned-social-activist Revathy Menon).

Then, there is ITC's *working for you, working for India* campaign, one strand of which focuses on the company's e-choupal initiative, an effort that seeks to enhance rural incomes, then, sell a variety of products and services to rural customers (apart from sourcing agricultural produce from them). The tagline itself smacks of old-style image led CSR activity, but given what the e-choupal does, it is actually an attempt to build and position the company's brand around the idea of doing something for the country.

In some ways, ITC's e-choupal is a far stronger example of a CSR-brand linkage than the Surf Excel campaign. It is a programme that is obviously advantageous to the company, yet it is accomplished by enough socially relevant goodies to make it look the way a government programme targeted at rural development ideally should. HLL, coincidentally, has an initiative that fits the bill, its Project Shakthi that uses Women's self-help groups in rural areas to further its reach. "The problem with old-style CSR was that the benefactors were not in control of what they would get", says Vivek Vaidya, a brand consultant. With brand or corporate strategy driven CSR, they are.

Source: Business Today, May 8, 2005

Questions

1. Explain the success of *Do bucket paani ab rozana hai bachain* (I will save two buckets of water a day) campaign for Surf Excel.
2. What consumer behaviour insights can you draw from this case?
3. Identify the personal and interpersonal factors that affect consumer behaviour for the product/service described in the case.

Case Study-2

XYZ Corporation deals with a product 'Body Spray'. Their manufacturing set-up is in Delhi. At present, they want to enter the Chennai market. The product is to be branded and to be positioned in the market. Suppose you are the market researcher and this assignment is given to you for a market study.

Questions

(i) How will you plan the market research?
(ii) How will you brand the product?
(iii) How will you segment and target the product?

Case Study-3

Assume that in your city a leading corporate is planning to open up its retail outlet chain stores. They wanted to know the consumer's factors like their perception and culture, value system, lifestyles. If you have given a chance to do a market research, how will you plan your market research for this corporate retail outlet?

REVIEW QUESTIONS

1. Define marketing research and its basic importance. Illustrate with an example.

2. Explain the process of marketing research and its impacts on organisational objectives.

3. Discuss the types of marketing research and its applications.

4. Construct a brief questionnaire for gathering information about the marketing strategies of the brands competing with each other. Your sampling units would be the distributors/wholesalers/retailers dealing with those brands. And explain the features of good questionnaire and precautions to be taken while preparing a questionnaire.

5. Discuss concepts of measurement and scaling in marketing research.

6. Explain about DSS and how it helps market managers.

7. Define marketing information system and its components.

8. If you are a sales manager for Samsung in India, what methods will you use for forecasting your sales for the next 3 years? Justify your answer.

9. Explain buyer behaviour and its importance.

10. Discuss the model of consumer behaviour with various determinants.

11. Explain the consumer decision process.

12. Define various implications for buyer behaviour.

MARKET SEGMENTATION AND MARKETING MIX

STRUCTURE

- Introduction
- The Concept of Market and Segmentation
- The Logic of Segmentation
- Market Segmentation and Patterns
- Segmentation Analysis
- Bases for Segmentation
- Targeting Approaches
- Selection of Segments
- Positioning the Product and Repositioning
- Marketing Mix
- Product Management Decisions
- The Concept of Optimum Marketing Mix and Specific Situations

3.1 INTRODUCTION

All corporate marketing activities have to be necessarily carried out in such a way that they lead to generation of surplus funds. Even in case of non-profit and non-manufacturing set-ups it becomes to achieve marketing goals in the most economical way. This is so primarily because of budgetary constraints in such organisations. One of the ways to obtain economies in marketing is to concentrate and focus the marketing effort in respect of a well-defined homogenous cluster of potential customers. This approach known as market segmentation helps in optimising the marketing mix. In this unit, we will discuss about market segmentation and the basic concepts of marketing mix.

3.2   THE CONCEPT OF MARKET AND SEGMENTATION

Unless you know the exact market to which your organisation wants to cater, your focusing will be wrong and your planning will be faulty and you will fail to develop an appropriate marketing strategy or effort to meet the needs of your target market. To identify the target market, let us first define the term 'market'.

- ☞ It can be used in respect of the network of institutions like wholesalers and brokers dealing in a product.
- ☞ It can also be used to refer to the nature of demand for the product, as when we speak of the maker for soap.
- ☞ The two meanings are related but are physically distinct. Related because without the wholesalers and other institutions, it will be difficult to serve the customer's (demand).

On the basis of the meaning of market given above, we can reiterate that buyers evaluate criteria about what constitutes the right choice for performing the function. As a consequence different offerings will attract different buyers.

To illustrate, all brands of colour television sets will appeal to some degree to those in the market for a colour TV but some brands will appeal to some groups more than others. But, if there were only one brand of colour TV set, there will be choice for the buyers. But as the market develops, manufacturers seek to cater more closely to some groups than others and the buyer's choice widens as a result.

At the most detailed level every buyer is a market in himself for every buyer's 'want' is probably distinct in some way. But on the basis of similarities and differences, such unique wants can be grouped into subclasses. What means is that wants within a subclass are more related to each other than wants between subclasses.

Based on the above view you can now define market segments and the process of market segmentation.

Market segments refer to the subclasses of the market reflecting subclasses of wants and the process of conceptually distinguishing segments is known as market segmentation.

Why to segment the market?

Market segmentation confers several benefits on the marketing man. In the first place, it helps him distinguish one customer group from another within a given market and thereby enables him to decide which segment of the market should form his target market. It also enables the effectiveness crystallisation of the specific needs of the buyer in the target market and facilitates an in-depth study of the characteristics of the buyers when the buyers are approached after careful segmentation, responses that are predictable would be forthcoming from them. This would help the marketing man develop his marketing programme on a predictable and reliable base. When the need and characteristics of the customer group have been brought into a clearer focus, "marketing offers" that are most suited to the particular customer group can be easily developed, the specialisation that is required in the product mix, the distribution mix, the promotion mix and the pricing policy to suit the particular customer group can be easily achieved, and marketing appeals that fall exactly in line with the requirements of the customer groups can be easily developed.

The resources of any given firms are usually limited. As such, no firm can normally afford to attack the entire market without any delimitation whatsoever. It would be better if the efforts are concentrated on the most productive and profitable segments of the market. By focusing sharply on each of the different customer groups within a market, market segmentation would make the marketing effort more efficient and economical.

3.3   THE LOGIC OF SEGMENTATION

The concept of market segmentation has helped marketing decision-making since the evolution of marketing. The goal of market segmentation is to partition the total market for a product or service into smaller groups of customer segments based on their characteristics, their potential as customers for the specific product or service in question and their differential reactions to marketing programmes. Because segmentation seeks to isolate significant differences among groups of individuals in the market, it can aid marketing decision-making in at least four ways:

1. Segmentation helps the marketer by identifying groups of customers to whom he could more effectively 'target' marketing efforts for the product or service.
2. Segmentation helps the marketer avoid 'trial-and-error' methods of strategy formulation by providing an understanding of these customers upon which he can tailor the strategy.
3. In helping the marketer to address and satisfy customer needs more effectively, segmentation aids in the implementation of the marketing concepts.
4. Ongoing customer analysis and market segmentation provides important data on which long-range planning (for market growth or product development) can be based.

Although it is a very useful technique, segmentation is not appropriate in every marketing situation. If, for instance, a marketer has evidence that all customers within a market have similar needs to be fulfilled by the product or service in question (i.e., an undifferentiated market), one 'mass' marketing strategy would probably be appropriate for the entire market. However, in today's market environment, it is unlikely that one would find either an entirely homogeneous market.

Criteria for Segmentation

If segmentation has to be useful in marketing decision-making, then it must possess the following characteristics:

1. Segments must be internally homogeneous—consumers within the segment will be more similar to each other in characteristics and behaviour than they are to consumers in other segments.
2. Segments must be identifiable—individuals can be 'placed' within or outside each segment based on a measurable and meaningful factor.
3. Segments must be accessible—can be reached by advertising media as well as distribution channels. Only then, the segments can be acted upon.
4. Segments must have an effective demand—the segment consists of a large group of consumers and they have the necessary disposable income and ability to purchase the goods or services.

3.4   MARKET SEGMENTATION

Markets consist of buyers, and buyers differ in one or more respects. They may differ in their wants, purchasing power, geographical locations, buying attitudes, and buying practices any of these variables can be used to segment a market which is represented in Fig. 3.1.

The General Approach to Segmenting a Market

The below Fig. 3.1(a) shows a market of six buyers. Each buyer is potentially a separate market because of unique needs and wants. A seller might design a separate product and marketing programme for each buyer.

For example, Boeing manufactures aeroplanes for a limited number of airline customers and customises its product for each. This ultimate degree of market segments, called customised marketing, is illustrated in Fig. 3.1(b).

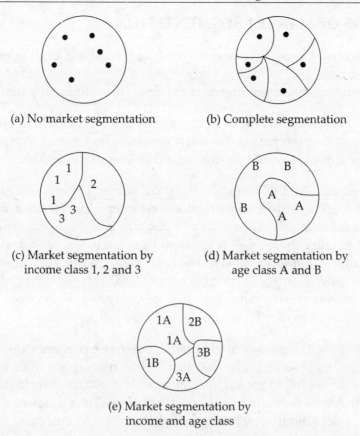

(a) No market segmentation

(b) Complete segmentation

(c) Market segmentation by income class 1, 2 and 3

(d) Market segmentation by age class A and B

(e) Market segmentation by income and age class

Fig. 3.1 Segmentation of a market.

Most sellers will not find it profitable to "customise" their product for each buyer. Instead the seller identifies classes of buyers who differ in their broad product requirements and/or marketing responses. For example, the seller might discover that income groups differ in their wants. In Fig. 3.1(c), a number (1, 2, or 3) is used to identify each buyer's income class. Lines are drawn around buyers in the same income class. Segmentation by income results in three segments, the most numerous segment being income class 1.

On the other hand, the seller might discover pronounced difference between the needs of younger and older buyers. In Fig. 3.1(d), a letter (A or B) is used to indicate each buyer's age. Segmentation by age class results in two segments, each with three buyers.

Now both income and age might influence the buyer's behaviour toward the product. In this case, the market can be divided into five segments: 1A, 1B, 2B, 3A, and 3B. Fig. 3.1(e) shows that segment 1A contains two buyers, and the other segments each contain one buyer.

3.5   PATTERNS OF MARKET SEGMENTATION

Earlier, we segmented a market by income and age, resulting in different demographic segment. Suppose, instead, we ask buyers how much they want of two product attributes. The aim is to identify different preference segments. Three different patterns can emerge.

Homogeneous Preferences: Figure 3.2 (a) represents a market where all the consumers have roughly the same preference. The market shows no natural segments. We would predict that existing brands would be similar and cluster in the centre.

Diffused Preferences: At the other extreme, consumer preferences may be scattered throughout the space (Fig. 3.2(b)), showing that consumers vary greatly in their preferences. The first brand to enter the market is likely to position in the centre to appeal to the most people. A brand to enter the market is likely to position in the consumer dissatisfaction. A second competitor could locate next to the first brand and fight for market share. Or it could locate in a corner to attract a customer group that was not satisfied with the centre brand. If several brands are in the market, they are likely to position throughout the space and show real difference to match consumer-preference differences.

Clustered Preferences: The market might reveal preference clusters, called natural market segments as shown in Fig. 3.2(c). The first firm in this market has three options. It might position in the centre hoping to appeal to all groups. It might position in the largest market segment. It might develop several brands, each positioned in a different segment. Clearly, if the first firm developed only one brand, competitors would enter and introduce brands in the other segments.

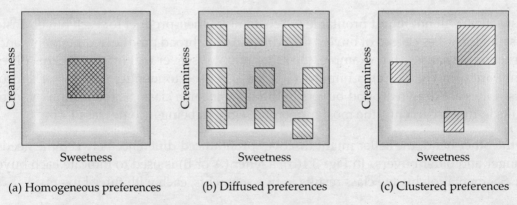

(a) Homogeneous preferences   (b) Diffused preferences   (c) Clustered preferences

Fig. 3.2 Basic market preference patterns.

3.6 SEGMENTATION ANALYSIS

Here is a list of a few general steps, referred to as segmentation analysis, that will be most often followed after the decision to employ market segmentation has been made.

Examples of questions to be answered during each step are also given.

Step-1: *Define the purpose and scope of the segmentation*

- What are our marketing objectives?
- Are we looking for new segments or determining how to better satisfy existing ones?
- Will we use existing data or invest time and money in new research?
- What level of detail will be needed in the segmentation analysis?

Step-2: *Analyse total market data*

- What is the character of the total market? (e.g. size)
- Are there basic differences between users and non-users of the product class?
- Are there any factors which clearly distinguish users from non-users or users of different brands?
- What is our competitive position in the market now?

Step-3: *Develop segment profiles*

- What factor seems to differentiate groups of consumers most clearly?
- Are the profiles of each segment internally consistent?

Step-4: *Evaluate segmentation*

- What are the major similarities and differences among segments?
- Should the number of segments described be reduced or increased?
- How sensitive is this segmentation of the market to growth?

Step-5: *Select target segment(s)*

- Which segment(s) represent our best market opportunity?
- What further details do we know about the target segment's characteristics and market behaviour?
- If complete data on market behaviour for the target segment are not available, can we make reasonable assumptions?
- Are we alone in competing for this target segment?

Step-6: *Designing the marketing strategy for the target segment*

- What type of product do these consumers want?
- What kinds of price, promotion or distribution tactics will suit their needs most?
- Would other segments react positively to a similar strategy? (If so, the segments should probably be merged.)

Step-7: *Reappraisal of segmentation*

- Do we have the resources to carry out this strategy?
- If we wish to broaden or change our target definition in the future, how flexible is the strategy?
- If we wish to change some element of the strategy in the future, how would that change probably influence the target segment?
- Does the target segment/strategic plan meet our objective? Does it fit our corporate strengths?

3.7   BASES FOR SEGMENTATION

After gathering complete information about what they want and also in the market, you have to tackle another important criteria for grouping the buyers into segments.

For this, we might take the following approach:

- ☞ Listening to what those in the market say for example, about their performance.
- ☞ Studying what those in the market are for example, their demographic characteristics.
- ☞ Studying what those in the market do for example, their lifestyle.

The different bases for segmentation put different emphases on what people in the market SAY, ARE, or DO.

Benefit Segmentation

In benefit segmentation you segment the market on the basis of what people say or the benefits they seek from the product. Yenkelovich applied benefit segmentation to the purchase of watches. He found that buyers bought for lowest price (23%), durability and general product quality (46%), and symbols of some important occasion (31%).

One of the most successful benefit segmentation was reported by Russell Haley who coined the phrase benefit segmentation. According to him, the oral hygiene (toothpaste) market can be divided into four distinct benefits segment depending on which of the following is sought.

- Flavour and product appearance
- Brightness of teeth
- Decay prevention
- Low price.

Once we have categories those in the market on the basis of the benefits they seek, they can be identified by what and what they do. For example, in the Russell Haley study, the brightness of teeth seekers were young people in their teens with a personality disposed towards high sociability and an active style. Similarly, decay prevention seekers had large families, were heavy toothpaste users, and were conservative. Each segment also favoured certain brands.

Thus, benefit segmentation requires:

- Determining the major benefits that people look for in the product class, like intrinsic preference, for example, taste, level of performance, snob appeal, price, reputation, etc.
- The kinds of people who look for each benefit
- The major brands that deliver each benefit.

Demographic basis

Instead of focusing on the differences in benefits sought, you might divide people in the market on the basis of demographic variables such as age, sex, family, size, income, occupation, education, social class, family life cycle, location, religion, race and nationality. Demographical variables are the most popular bases for distinguished customer groups. You should use such variables to infer the likely variations in what is sought

Age and Life Cycle Stage: Consumer wants and capacities change with age. Alabe products, a toy manufacturer, realised this and designed different toys for babies as they move through various stages from three months to one year. This segmentation strategy means that parents and gifts buyers can more easily find the appropriate toy by considering the baby's age. Another example General Foods applied age-segmentation strategy to dog food. Many dog owners know that their dog food: Cycle 1 for puppies, Cycle 2 for adult dogs, Cycle 3 for overweight dogs, Cycle 4 for old aged dogs.

Gender: Gender segmentation has long been applied in clothing, hairdressing, cosmetics, and magazines. Occasionally other marketers will notice an opportunity for gender segmentation.

Income: Income segmentation is another longstanding practice in such product and service categories as automobiles, boats, clothing, cosmetics, and travel. However, income does not always predict the best customers for a given product.

Psychographic basis

You can also segment the market on the basis of the lifestyle or mode of living. This helps you to understand what those who are in the market do. Some of the products where lifestyle approach has been used for segmenting the market are cars, women's clothing, cigarettes, cosmetics, alcoholic beverages and furniture.

Social class: Social class has a strong influence on the person's preference in cars, clothing, home furnishing, leisure activities, reading habits, retailers, and so on. Many companies design products and services for specific social class.

Lifestyle: The people's product interest are influenced by their lifestyles. In fact, the goods they consume express their lifestyles. Marketers are increasingly segmenting their markets by consumer lifestyle.

Examples: Manufacturer of women's apparel are following Du Pont's advice and designing different clothes for the "plain women", the "fashionable women", and the "manly women". Cigarette companies develop brands for the "defiant smoker", the "casual smoker", and the "careful smoker".

Companies making cosmetics, alcoholic beverages, and furniture are seeing opportunities in lifestyle segmentation. At the same time, lifestyle segmentation does not always work, Nestle introduced a special brand of decaffeinated coffee for "late nighters", and it failed.

Personality: Marketers have used personality variables to segment markets. They endow their products with brand personalities that correspond to consumer personalities. Currently, Nike is using the personality of certain athletes, such as basketball star Michel Jordan, as a brand identifier to attract Michel Jordan fans to Nike shoes.

Self-image is one aspect of personality that may relate to buyer behaviour. Some marketers use this approach to endow their product with brand image that corresponds to self-image of the consumer. In fact, assumption that buyers seek a match between self-image and brand image is implicit when advertising appeals to certain types of personality.

Behavioural basis

In behavioural segmentation, buyers are divided into groups on the basis of their knowledge, attitudes, use, or response to a product. Many marketers believe that behavioural variables are the best starting point for connecting market segments.

Occasion: Buyers can distinguish according to occasion when they develop a need, purchase a product, or use a product. For example, air travel is triggered by occasion related to business, vacation, or family. Occasion segmentation can help firms expand product usage. For example, orange juice is most usually consumed at breakfast. An orange juice company can try to promote drinking orange juice on other occasions, lunch, dinner, and midday.

User Status: Markets can be segmented into groups of non-users, ex-users, potential users, first-time users, and regular users of a product. Thus, blood banks must not rely on only regular users of a product. Thus, blood banks must not rely on only regular donors to supply blood. They must recruit new first-time donors and contact ex-donors, and each will require different marketing strategy. The company's position in the market will also influence its focus. Market share leaders will focus on attracting potential users, whereas smaller firms will focus on attracting current users away from the market leader.

Other basis

Loyalty Status: A market can be segmented by consumer loyalty patterns. Consumers can be loyal to brands (Coca-cola), stores (Sears), and other entities. Suppose there are five brands: A, B, C, D and E. Buyers can be divided into four groups according to their brand loyalty status.

Hard-Core Loyals: Consumers who buy one brand all the time. Thus, a buying pattern of A, A, A, A, A, A might represent a consumer with undivided loyalty to brand A.

Split Loyals: Consumers who are loyal to two or three brands. The buying pattern A, A, B, A, B represents a consumer with a divided loyalty between A and B. This group is rapidly increasing. More people now buy from a small set of acceptable brands that are equivalent in their minds.

Shifting Loyals: Consumers who shift from favouring one brand to another. The buying pattern A, A, A, B, B, B would suggest a consumer who is shifting brand loyalty from A to B.

Switchers: Consumers who show no loyalty to any brand. The buying pattern A, C, E, B, D, and B would suggest a non-loyal consumer who is either deal prone (buys the brand on sale) or variety prone (wants something different each time).

Buyer-Readiness Stage: A market consists of people indifferent stages of readiness to buy a product. Some are unaware of the product; some are aware; some are informed; some are interested; some desire the product; and some intend to buy. The relative numbers make a big difference in designing the marketing programme. Suppose a health agency wants women to take an annual pap test to detect possible cervical cancer. At the beginning, most women are unaware of the pap test. The marketing effort should go in to high-awareness-building advertising using a simple message. Later, the advertising should dramatise the benefits of the pap test and the risks of not taking it, in order to move more women into desiring the test. A special offer might be made of a free health examination to move women into actually signing up. In general, the marketing programme should be adapted to the different stages of buyer readiness.

Attitude: Five attitude groups can be found in a market: enthusiastic, positive, indifferent, negative, and hostile. Door-to-door workers in a political campaign use the voter's attitude to determine how much time to spend with the voter. They thank enthusiastic voters and remind them to vote; they reinforce those who are positively disposed; they try to win the votes of indifferent voters; they spend no time trying to change the attitudes of negative and hostile voters. To the extent that attitudes are correlated with demographic descriptors, the political party can more efficiently locate the best prospects.

Segmenting the Industrial Markets

Industrial marketing needs to consider two important sets of characteristics of the business buyers: (1) the characteristics of the buyer as a consuming organisation and (2) the behavioural characteristics of the buyer. The first set includes such factors as the type of the organisation, the size, the product requirements, the end use of the product, the organisation capabilities, and so on. The second set includes factors like the buying decision-making process and considers the fact that it is in fact people and the organisation, who take the decision. These characteristics have led to a two-stage approach to industrial market segmentation starting with macro segmentation and then going into a micro segmentation. Between the macro and micro bases of industrial market segmentation, there lie some useful bases of segmentation, as suggested by Shapiro and Bonoma in the nested approach to segmenting the industrial markets. These intermediate bases of segmentation, viz., demographics, operating variables, purchasing approaches, situational factors and personal characteristics, are explained in Table 3.1. The table lists major questions that business marketers should ask in determining which customers they want to serve. By targeting these segments instead of the whole market, companies have a much better chance to deliver value to customers and to receive maximum rewards for close attention to their needs.

Table 3.1 Major Segmentation Variables for Industrial Markets

Segmentation variables	Examples of variables measured	Comments
Demographics	Industry • Company size • Location	Which industries that buy this product should we focus us? What size companies should we focus on? What geographical areas should we focus on?
Operating variables	Technology • User/non-user status • Customer capabilities	What customer technologies should we focus on? Should we focus on heavy, medium or light users or non-users? Should we focus on customers needing many or few services?
Purchasing approaches	Organisation • Power structure • Nature of existing relationship • General purchase policies • Purchasing criteria	Should we focus on companies with centralised or decentralised purchasing? Should we focus on engineering or finance or marketing-dominated companies? Should we focus on companies with which we already have strong relationships or just go after the most desirable companies? Should we go after companies that prefer leasing? Service contracts? Systems purchases? Sealed bidding? Should we focus on companies that are seeking Quality? Service? Price?
Situational factors	Urgency • Specific application • Size of order	Should we focus on companies that need quick delivery or service? Should we focus on certain applications of our product rather than all applications? Should we focus on small or large orders?
Personal characteristics	Buyer-seller similarity • Attitudes toward risk • Loyalty	Should we focus on companies whose people and value are similar to ours? Should we focus on risk-taking or risk avoiding customers? Should we focus on companies that show high loyalty to their suppliers?

3.8 TARGETING APPROACHES

Target market selection is the next logical step following segmentation. Once the market-segment opportunities have been identified, the organisation got to decide how many and which ones to target. Lot of marketing effort is dedicated to developing strategies that will best match the firm's product offerings to the needs of particular target segments. The firm should look for a match between the value requirements of each segment and its distinctive capabilities. Marketers have identified four basic approaches to do this which are also represented in Fig. 3.3.

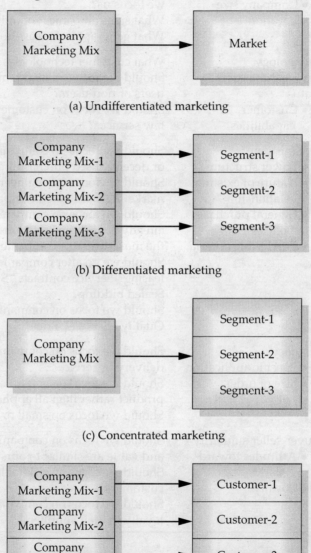

(a) Undifferentiated marketing

(b) Differentiated marketing

(c) Concentrated marketing

(d) Micro marketing

Fig. 3.3 Market targeting approaches.

1. Undifferentiated Marketing

A firm may produce only one product or product line and offer it to all customers with a single marketing mix. Such a firm is said to practice undifferentiated marketing, also called mass marketing. It used to be much more common in the past than it is today. A common example is the case of Model T built by Henry Ford and sold for one price to everyone who wanted to buy. He agreed to paint his cars any colour that consumers wanted, 'as long as it is black'. While undifferentiated marketing is efficient from a production viewpoint (offering the benefits of economies of scale), it also brings in inherent dangers. A firm that attempts to satisfy everyone in the market with one standard product may suffer if competitors offer specialised units to smaller segments of the total market and better satisfy individual segments.

2. Differentiated Marketing

Firms that promote numerous products with different marketing mixes designed to satisfy smaller segments are said to practice differentiated marketing. It is still aimed at satisfying a large part of the total market. Instead of marketing one product with a single marketing programme, the firm markets a number of products designed to appeal to individual parts of the total market. By providing increased satisfaction for each of many target markets, a company can produce more sales by following a differentiated marketing approach. In general, it also raises production, inventory and promotional costs. Despite higher marketing costs, a company may be forced to practice differentiated marketing in order to remain competitive.

3. Concentrated Marketing

Rather than trying to market its products separately to several segments, a firm may opt for a concentrated marketing approach. With concentrated marketing (also known as niche marketing), a firm focuses its efforts on satisfying only one market segment. It may be a small segment, but a profitable segment. This approach can appeal to a small firm that lacks the financial resources and to a company that offers highly specialised goods and services. Along with its benefits, concentrated marketing has its dangers. Since this approach ties a firm's growth to a particular segment, changes in the size of that segment or in customer buying patterns may result in severe financial problems. Sales may also drop if new competitors appeal successfully to the same segment. Niche marketing leaves the fortunes of a firm to depend on one small target segment.

4. Micro Marketing

This approach is still more narrowly focused than concentrated marketing. Micro marketing involves targeting potential customers at a very basic level, such as by the postal code, specific occupation or lifestyle. Ultimately, micro marketing may even target individuals themselves. It is referred to as marketing to segments of one. The Internet allows marketers to boost the effectiveness of micro marketing. With the ability to customise (individualisation attempts by the firm) and to personalise (individualisation attempts by the customer), the Internet offers the benefit of mass customisation–by reaching the mass market with individualised offers for the customers.

3.9   SELECTION OF SEGMENTS

Before we conclude our discussion of market segmentation, we should also discuss how a company should select its segments. Both general factors which one uses to evaluate any economic opportunity and the factors specific to the situation should be considered in evaluating segment opinions against these criteria.

General Factors

The following are some core general factors and these you must consider:

✠ **Company thrust:** The company that is segmenting its market needs to identify the requirements for success in the concerned target market. Next, it must determine what particular business system consisting of marketing, production, finance, personnel, etc. will be needed to meet the requirements for success in that segment. As far as possible the firm's trust should be such that it gives the company a critical advantage in the segment.

✠ **Size and growth potential:** Not only the present size but also the future potential of the concerned target market must be considered. The current market demand by itself may prove misleading. The measurement might also create its own problems.

✠ **Investment needed:** Investment needed for tapping a particular target market is another factor to consider and you must take care to see both entry costs and costs associated with building market share have been included.

✠ **Profitability:** The question of profitability is associated with investment decisions. To calculate it we have to estimate both future sales and costs in the concerned segment. What must also be considered is value-added to the product that is to be marketed in that target segment, for a low value-added product makes profitability more hazardous.

✠ **Risk:** There are the usual risks associated with the extent to which a particular target market would respond. But these are not only ones. Other risks like the new product taking away part of the market share from the existing products of the company in that target market need also be considered.

Specific Factors

- **Segment durability:** Remember, segments based on fads and fashions are of a short duration, that is, their life cycles are ephemeral and your plans to tap such segment must take this into account. Besides, you can't think of making substantial investment in such ventures from the long-term point of view.

- **Mobility:** Mobility means the movement in and out of a segment of members of a target group, if the mobility rate of target group members is high in respect of a certainty product, say hair oils, the company in order to keep its sales stable would have to attract new users to its product.

- **Visibility:** Visibility refers to the extent to which the want of a target market or segment is distinctive. If what is sought by the members of that segment is perceived as very different from what is sought in other segments, the segments 'loyalty' will be greater but those in other segments may regard that offering as very different and something which is not meant for them. Highly different segments, however, are likely to be more stable than other segments of a market.

- **Accessibility:** Those in the segment or the target market should be directly reachable through established communication and distribution channels. If that particular segment cannot be reached, the exercise in market segmentation will be futile.

For evaluating segment options on the basis of these factors, remember that you will have to weigh these factors in the context of your specific situation.

Requirements for effective segmentation

There are many ways to segment a market. Not all segmentations, however, are effective. For example, buyers of table salt could be divided into blond and brunet customers. But hair colour is not relevant to the purchase of salt. Furthermore, if all salt buyers buy the same amount of salt every month, believe all salt is the same, and want to pay the same price, this market would be minimally segmentable from a marketing point of view. To be maximally useful, market segments must exhibit five characteristics:

Measurable: The size, purchasing power, and profile of the segments can be measured. Certain segmentation variables are difficult to measure. An illustration would be the size of the segment of teenage smokers who smoke primarily to rebel against their parents.

Substantial: The segments are large and profitable enough to serve. A segment should be the largest possible homogeneous group worth going after with a tailored marketing programme. It would not pay, for example, for an automobile manufacturer to develop cars for persons who are shorter than four feet.

Accessible: The segments can be effectively reached and served. Suppose a perfume company finds that heavy users of its brand are single women who are out late at night and frequent bars. Unless these women live or shop at certain places and are exposed to certain media, they will be difficult to reach.

Differentiable: The segments are conceptually distinguishable and respond differently to different marketing mix elements and programmes. If married and unmarried women respond similarly to a sale of fur coats, they do not constitute separate segments.

Actionable: Effective programmes can be formulated for attracting and serving the segments. A small airline, for example, identified seven market segments, but its staff was too small to develop separate marketing programmes for each segment.

3.10   POSITIONING THE PRODUCT

When a company introduces a new product, a decision critical to its long-term success is how prospective buyers view it in relation to those products offered by its competitors. Product positioning refers to the place an offering occupies in consumers' minds on important attributes relative to competitive products. Product positioning involves changing the place an offering occupies in a consumer's mind relative to competitive products.

Positioning

Having chosen an approach for reaching the firm's target segment, marketers must then decide how best to position the product in the market. The concept of positioning seeks to place a product in a certain 'position' in the minds of the prospective buyers. Positioning is the act of designing the company's offer so that it occupies a distinct and valued place in the target customers' minds. In a world that is getting more and more homogenised, differentiation and positioning hold the key to marketing success! The positioning gurus, Al Ries and Jack Trout define positioning as: Positioning is your product as the customer thinks of it. Positioning is not what you do to your product, but what you do to the mind of your customer. Every product must have a positioning statement. A general form of such a statement is given below:

Product X is positioned as offering (benefit) to (target market) with the competitive advantage of (competitive advantage) based on (basis for competitive advantage).

Source: skydeckcartoons.com

For example, the positioning statement of toothpaste X may read as follows:

Toothpaste X is positioned as offering to kids' toothpaste made especially for those kids who don't like to brush with the competitive advantage of a mild fruit taste and lower foaming.

One way to think about positioning is to imagine a triangle, with the baseline anchored by the organisation and competitor concerns and the apex, the customers. The marketer's job is to find a positioning of the product or service that is both possible and compatible with organisation constraints which uniquely place the product/service among competitive offerings so as to be most suitable to one or a number of segments of customers.

Positioning can be done along different possibilities. Attribute positioning is when the positioning is based on some attribute of the product. Benefit positioning is when a derived benefit is highlighted as the unique selling propositioning. Competitor positioning is when a comparison is drawn with the competitor and a differentiation from the competitor is emphasised. Product category positioning is when a product is positioned to belong to a particular category and not another category which probably is crowded. Quality/price positioning is when the product is positioned as the best value for money.

For example, a pizza may be positioned on its taste or its natural contents or as an easy meal or with a thicker topping or as the lowest priced offering the best value for money. Each one of them offers a distinct positioning possibility for a pizza. In the positioning decision, caution must be taken to avoid certain positioning errors: Under-positioning is done when a unique, but not so important attribute is highlighted. As a result, the customer does not see any value in such a position. Over positioning is done when the product performance does not justify the tall claims of positioning. Confused positioning is when the customer fails to categorise the product correctly and the product ends up being perceived differently from what was intended.

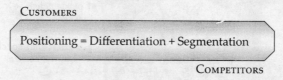

Doubtful positioning is when the customer finds it difficult to believe the positioning claims. Positioning map is a valuable tool to help marketers' position products by graphically illustrating consumers' perceptions of competing products within an industry. For instance, a positioning map might present two different characteristics, price and quality, and show how consumers view a product and its major competitors based on these traits. Marketers can create a competitive positioning map from information solicited from consumers or from their accumulated knowledge about a market. Sometimes, changes in the competitive environment or cultural environment force marketers to reposition a product–changing the position it holds in the minds of prospective buyers relative to the positions of competing products. Nestle's Milkmaid brand has undergone a few repositionings in the last few decades. The original positioning as 'sweetened condensed milk as a milk substitute' became obsolete when India attained self-sufficiency in milk production and milk products. So Milkmaid was repositioned as a 'ready ingredient' in preparing home-made sweets. Recipes started appearing on the labels. It succeeded for a certain period of time. Soon the Indian households were no longer making home-made sweets, but rather consuming ready-made, packaged sweets. If it was an economic environment factor that necessitated a repositioning earlier, it was now the changing demographic of the Indian homes. Milkmaid was then repositioned as a 'central ingredient' in making the desserts at home. The recipes naturally changed. Repositioning helps a firm to tide over the environmental changes and the changes in consumers' preferences. It extends the life of a brand.

Product positioning

Making profit is of paramount importance to any business, a goal that can be achieved in two ways: by selling more or creating a product that would attract more buyers. The later could only be possible when the product is better than the existing ones.

Today's companies and their managements are judged on the basis of their image in comparison to their competitors. It is here that the concept of product positioning shows its importance. Product concept is a concept which is used to motivate customers to select a given product. The greater the strength and number of competitors, the greater the need for positioning to distinguish between a given product and the competitive brands.

Product positioning can be divided into three categories:

1. Category positioning
2. Selling positioning
3. Commercial positioning.

Category positioning is very broad. It refers to the product category in which the brand has to compete, while selling positioning refers to the specific ideas used to market the product. It highlights the distinct attributes of the product like design, package and price. For instance, Lipton has recently distinguished its brand through its unique packaging in the form of its zipped pack and flip flop pack offering the consumer an experience of convenience. It also refers to selling ideas which are placed in the buyer's perception.

These are ideas to which the customer can relate with ease because of their association with a lifestyle or some other frame of reference with which the customers identify themselves. It is evident from the above that our task is to study and understand the needs of the consumers, the element of competition and other environmental factors and thereafter measure the opportunities whereby to decide about the gap in the market. The first important task in the process of gap selection and filling it successfully is to identify the most important dimension used by the consumers to perceive the product. Grouping would make the task of narrowing down of the dimensions easier. The next task is to design the product. No consumer product will sell to the public for a longer period until and unless it does not fulfil a consumer need reasonably well.

The product has to be projected in such a way that the consumer perceives it in the same manner as the seller wants him to perceive. If a product which has superior features, but the consumer fails to perceive it to be so, the opportunity will be lost. Psychological elements are more important in consumer products. We should, therefore, make sure that the Core Benefit Proposition (CBP) is properly communicated to the consumer through advertising and promotion. Identification of product dimensions holds the key to success. Once the dimensions have been identified, the next task of the seller is to determine customer preferences, our own and competitor's strong and weak points by conducting strengths, weaknesses, opportunities, threats (SWOT) analysis and the possible pay-offs of filling certain gaps.

Take the case of restaurants that start spending lot of money on making their food better to beat their competitors, but later on discover that the cause of success of their competitors rested in the environment and not the quality of food. This shows the importance of picking up the right gap techniques to determine customer preference.

The 'expectancy value model' and 'preference regression method' are the two easier and less expensive popular ways to determine customer preferences.

Expectancy value (linear) model: This is not only simple but less expensive model of customer preferences. This model can be used in early design process to get an initial indication of attribute importance. The expectancy value model discovers what the customer believes to be important.

When Burger King started off initially, their approach was to offer hamburgers made specifically to the customer's taste. Their tagline for this was, "Have it your way". This was an excellent tactic to use against other fast food restaurants that gave the customer little or no choice. Keeping this distinctive attribute in mind they opened all their stores within a couple of blocks of existing McDonald's locations.

Preference regression method: The weightage given by the consumer in expectancy value method to different attributes may not always be correct. To avoid being misled, Preference Regression Method may be useful. This statistical technique produces reasonably accurate "average" importance of the perceptual map. Simple regression is sufficiently robust; it is less expensive and easy compared to monotonic techniques. It is used to derive the core benefit proposition.

3.11   REPOSITIONING

Product positioning is not limited to new products alone. It is relevant for occasional face lifting of the existing products. This is evidenced by so called "new and improved products" of almost all kinds such as toilet soaps, shampoos, cosmetics, toothpastes, etc. Repositioning does not mean total change. It sometimes entails strengthening and clarifying an existing identity. Products are like plants. If neglected and not repositioned they will die. A famous garment firm was having a tough time with the sales of its men's shirts. Instead of involving into a futile competition with its competitor, its newly appointed chairman shifted the weight from men's shirts to women's blouses and sports wear. The result was an amazing increase in its profits.

It is not only the product itself which is involved in positioning or repositioning. Several factors combined together make up for the success including change of name and technique of advertising.

Repositioning does not always hold the key to success. In case a product has got into a very bad shape due to prolonged neglect, repositioning effort may turn out to be an exercise in futility. In such cases it would always be better to drop the product.

Two Approaches to Product Positioning

There are two main approaches to positioning a new product in the market.

1. *Head and Head positioning* involves competing directly with competitors on similar products attributes in the same target market.

2. *Differentiation positioning* involves seeking a less competitive, smaller market niche in which to locate a brand. McDonald's initially tried to appeal to the health-conscious segment and introduced its low fat McLean Deluxe hamburger to avoid direct competition with Wendy's and Burger King. Companies also follow a differ nation positioning strategy among brands within their own product line try to minimise cannibalisation of brands sales or shares.

Positioning Milk Drinks for Children

Assume you work for a dairy or soft drink company trying to develop milk drink for school-children that have more nutritional value than soft drinks but more appeal than regular value soft drinks. Here's what companies did:

✠ Finding a position for milk drinks: Marketing managers looked at this kind of perceptual map and picked a position about at point C in the previous page. This is a relatively big gap between regular milk and flavoured drinks and shows the increased nutritional value of the milk drinks.

✠ Developing the product and flavours: In mid-2004, Coca-cola and Cadbury Schweppes PLC both developed "dairy drinks" positioned at point C, with just over half being regular milk and the rest being water, sugar, and flavourings. Although calories and sugar are concerns, these drinks have nutritional value missing in soft drinks. Sample flavours? Cadbury Raging Cow started with five flavours, including Chocolate Insanity, Pina Cholada Chaos, and Jamoach Frenzy.

Positioning Identities

Positioning is creating an identity for your product. This identity is a cumulative of the following four positioning identities.

1. Who am I? It refers to the corporate credentials like the origin, family tree and the 'stable' from which it comes from. For instance, think of the mental associations when a buyer buys a Japanese car and it is a Honda!

2. What am I? It refers to the functional capabilities. The perceived brand differentiation is formed using the brand's capabilities and benefits. For instance, the Japanese cars are known for their fuel efficiency, reasonable price and utility value.

3. For whom am I? It refers to the target segment for the brand. It identifies that market segment for which his brand seems to be just right and has competitive advantage. For instance, the Japanese car makers have traditionally focused on the quality conscious value-seeking and rather serious car buyers.

4. Why me? It highlights the differential advantage of the brand when compared to the competing brands. It gives reasons as to why the customer should select this brand in preference to any other brand. For instance, Japanese car makers have tried to score a competitive advantage on the lines of quality and technology.

Differentiation across the Consumption Chain

A research finding suggests that there are one million branded products in the world today. As a result, the market is increasingly competitive and confusingly crowded. For the customers, it means more choices than they know how to handle and less time than they need to decide. For the marketers, it is hyper-competition and continuous struggle to win the attention and interest of choice-rich, price-prone customers. The tyranny of choice for the buyers is represented by the following facts:

- An average hypermarket stocks 40,000 brand items (SKUs - Stock Keeping Units).
- An average family gets 80% of its needs met from only 150 SKUs.
- That means there's a good chance that the other 39,850 items in the store will be ignored.

The implication is that those that don't stand out will get lost in the pack! The average customer makes decisions in more than 100 product/service categories in a given month. He/she is exposed to more than 1600 commercials a day. Of this, 80 are consciously noticed and about 12 provoke some reaction. The challenge for marketers is: how to get noticed (i.e., *differentiation*) and be preferred (i.e., *positioning*)? Most profitable strategies are built on differentiation (i.e.) offering customers something they value that competitors don't have. A close look at consumer behaviour reveals that people buy on the differences. An ability to create compelling differences remains at the heart of a firm's competitive advantage. The battle has always been (and still is) about differentiation–create winning differences in customers' minds. People pay attention to differences (though at different levels) and tend to ignore undifferentiated products. Here is an example of how Nike (the top-dog sports shoe brand) creates winning differences at cognitive, normative and wired-in levels in the buyer.

1. Cognitive (conscious decisions) Level

'I buy Nike because it's made of engineered materials which enable higher athletic performance'

2. Normative (semiconscious feelings) level

'I buy Nike because it's "in" with my crowd'

3. Wired-in (subconscious determinants) level

'Nike appeals to my desire to be cool, fashionable, strong, aggressive. . .'

Organisations use several differentiation dimensions. The most popular are product differentiation, service differentiation, personnel differentiation, channel differentiation and image differentiation.

3.12 MARKETING MIX

After marketers select a target market, they direct their activities towards profitably satisfying that segment. Although they must manipulate many variables to reach this goal, marketing decision-making can be divided into four areas: product, price, place (distribution) and promotion (marketing communication). The total package forms the marketing mix–the blending of the four elements to fit the needs and preferences of a specific target market. These are the four variables that a marketer can use in different

Table 3.2 Marketing mix.

Elements of the marketing mix	Sub-elements
Product	Product design Product positioning Product name and branding Packaging and labelling Breadth and depth of product line Level and type of customer service Product warranty New product development process Product life cycle strategies
Price	Manufacturer, wholesaler and retailer selling prices Terms and conditions Bidding tactics Discount policies New product pricing (skim vs. penetrating pricing)
Place (distribution channels)	Direct vs. Indirect channels Channel length Channel breadth (exclusive, selective or intensive) Franchising policies Policies to ensure channel coordination and control
Promotion (marketing communications)	Advertising Sales force policies Direct marketing (mail, catalogue) Public relations Price promotions–for the consumers and the channel Trade shows and special events

combinations to create value for customers. Several of the sub-elements in each of the four Ps that constitute the marketing mix are listed in Table 3.2.

Marketing Programmes

A marketing programme is made up of the various elements of the marketing mix and the relationships among them. The concept of the marketing mix emphasises the fit of the various pieces and the quality and size of their interactions. There are three degrees of interaction—consistency, integration and leverage. Consistency is the lack of a poor fit between two or more elements of the marketing mix. For example, to sell a high quality product through a low quality retailer would seem inconsistent. While consistency is the lack of a poor fit, integration is the presence of a positive, harmonious interaction among the elements of the mix. For example, heavy advertising can sometimes be harmonious with a high price, because the added margin from the high price pays for the advertising and high advertising creates the brand differentiation that justifies the high price. Leverage is the situation in which each individual element of the mix is used to the best advantage in support of the total mix.

Once the elements of the marketing mix have met the internal tests of consistency, integration and leverage, the next step is to check that the proposed programme fits the needs of the target customers, the core competencies of the company and the likely responses of key competitors.

The concept of programme/customer fit encompasses development of a marketing programme that fits the needs of the target-market segments. For that, the market must first be carefully and explicitly delineated. If the target has not been defined, it cannot be reached! The programme must not only fit the market, but also fit the company. A marketing programme must match the core competencies of the company that is implementing it. For example, an organisation with extensive mass advertising experience and expertise is more likely to be able to carry out a programme that leans heavily on advertising than an organisation less strong in that particular area. An effective marketing programme must not only fit the company's own core competencies, it must also take account of competitors' programmes. Competitive/programme fit can be defined as the characteristic of a marketing programme that while building on a company's strengths and shielding its weaknesses, protects it from competitors by capitalising on their weaknesses, in the process creating a unique market personality and position.

Like most concepts, the marketing mix is an abstraction and real marketing programmes do not always fit perfectly the product, price, place and promotion paradigm. In fact, several parts of the mix fall at the interface of two elements. For example, brand, which is often viewed as an aspect of product, is clearly also a part of marketing communications and can serve to help coordinate product policy and communication.

3.13 PRODUCT MANAGEMENT DECISIONS

Product decisions start with an understanding of what a product is, viz., the product offering is not the thing itself, but rather the total package of benefits obtained by the customer. This is called the total product concept. For example, a watch from *www.rediff.com* is not just a watch but one shipped within 24 hours of order and unconditionally guaranteed. This broad conception of a 'product' is key to seeing possible points of differentiation from competitors. Fig. 3.4 illustrates the total product concept.

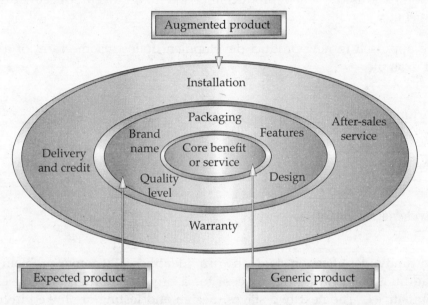

Fig. 3.4 Total product concept.

The 'generic' product is no longer sought (leave alone bought!) by the customers. It merely represents customer need fulfilment. The expected product represents the customers' minimal purchase conditions. When such customer expectations are met, it leads to customer satisfaction. The augmented product represents the customers' wish list. It leads to customer delight. Beyond the augmented product, lies the potential product which represents all that this product can become in the future. It represents the customers' dream.

Taxonomy of product line planning decisions can be developed by considering some product planning decisions firms face. Product line breadth: How many different lines will the company offer? A guiding principle in answering breadth questions is the company's position on desired consistency or similarity between the lines it offers. Product line length: How many items will be there in a line providing coverage of different price points?

Product line depth: how many types of a given product?

Individual item decisions: Decisions on individual items need to be considered within the context of the firm's full product line due to item interrelationships. At the individual item level, decisions to be made are whether to undertake efforts to delete an item from the line (pruning), reposition an existing product within the line (balancing), improve the performance of an existing product to strengthen its positioning (modernisation), introduce a new product within an existing line (filling) and introduce a product to establish a new line (extension). The assortment of product lines and individual product offerings is called as the product mix.

A proactive approach to new product development follows some form of a sequential process, for example,

- Opportunity identification
- Design
- Testing
- Product introduction
- Life cycle management.

In the opportunity identification stage, the firm identifies a customer problem that it can solve. In addition it identifies the concept for a product through idea generation and screening initiatives. The next two stages, design and testing are linked in an iterative process. The firm must first embody the product idea in a concept statement which is tested via presentation to potential customers. After the firm has settled on the product and a supporting plan, it reaches product introduction. Decisions at this stage involve the geographic markets to which the product will be introduced and whether markets will be approached at the same time or sequentially over time. After introduction, a process of Product Life Cycle Management begins. The life cycle stages are introduction, growth, maturity and decline. The marketing objectives vary across these stages–so do the sales, profits and costs. The marketing mix also changes from stage to stage.

The first P of marketing, namely, the product also looks at how firms build and maintain identity and competitive advantage for their products through branding. Functions like packaging and labelling also perform specific functions within the ambit of product management.

Place (Channel Management)

The marketing channel is the set of mechanisms or network via which a firm 'goes to market' or is 'in touch' with its customers for a variety of tasks ranging from demand generation to physical delivery of the goods. The customer's requirements for effective support determine the functions which the members of the channel must collectively provide.

Eight generic channel functions can be identified, viz.,

1. Product information
2. Product customisation
3. Product quality assurance
4. Lot size (e.g. the ability to buy in small quantities)
5. Product assortment (refers to breadth, length and width of product lines)
6. Availability
7. After-sales service
8. Logistics.

Marketers develop channels and formulate distribution plans to ensure that consumers find their products available in the proper quantities at the right time and places. Distribution decisions involve transportation, warehousing, inventory control, order processing and selection of marketing channels. Marketing channels are made up of institutions such as wholesalers and retailers–all those involved in a product's movement from producer to final consumer. The two major decisions in channels are: (1) Channel design–which involves both a length and breadth issue, and (2) Channel management–what policies and procedures will be used to have the necessary functions performed by various parties. An important point with respect to channel design is that while there are options about whether a particular institution (e.g., a distributor) is included in the channel or not, the setting implicates specific tasks which need to be accomplished by someone in the channel. One can eliminate a layer in the chain but not the tasks that the layer performed.

Promotion (Marketing Communications)

The next element of the marketing mix is deciding the appropriate set of ways in which to communicate with customers to foster their awareness of the product, knowledge about its features, interest in purchasing, likelihood of trying the product and/or repeat purchasing it. Effective marketing requires an integrated communications plan combining both personal selling efforts and non-personal ones such as advertising, sales promotion, direct marketing and public relations. Put together, they are referred to as the promotion mix.

A useful mnemonic for the tasks in planning communications strategy is the 6 Ms model:

1. *Market–To whom is the communication to be addressed?*
2. *Mission–What is the objective of the communication?*
3. *Message–What are the specific points to be communicated?*
4. *Media–Which vehicles will be used to convey the message?*
5. *Money–How much will be spent in the effort?*
6. *Measurement–How will impact be assessed after the campaign?*

The marketing communications or promotions mix is potentially extensive–including non-personal elements as well as personal selling. The popular non-personal vehicles are advertising, sales promotion and public relations. Advertising in media is particularly effective in

- Creating awareness of a new product
- Describing features of the product
- Suggesting usage situations
- Distinguishing the product from competitors
- Directing buyers to the point-of-purchase
- Creating or enhancing a brand image

Advertising is limited in its ability to actually close the sale and make a transaction happen. Sales promotions may be an effective device to complement the favourable attitude development for which advertising is appropriate. One trend in advertising is the movement to more precisely targeted media vehicles. Direct marketing to households or email marketing to individuals are just instances of this trend. Sales promotion includes things such as samples, coupons and contests. These are usually most effective when used as a short-term inducement to generate action. The three major types of sales promotion are:

1. Consumer promotions–Used by a manufacturer and addressed to the end consumer
2. Trade promotions–Used by the manufacturer and addressed to the trade partners
3. Retail promotions–Used by the trade partners and addressed to the end consumer

Public relations refers to non-paid communication efforts, such as press releases. These efforts do entail a cost to the firm, but generally are distinguished from advertising by virtue of the fact that the firm does not pay for space in the media vehicle itself. Personal selling as the communication vehicle presents the advantage of permitting an interaction to take place between the firm and a potential customer rather than just the broadcast of information. The importance of personal selling in the promotions mix typically increases with the complexity of the product and the need for education of potential customers. The proper allocation of the budget across the various media vehicles varies greatly depending upon the market situation. A fundamental decision is whether to focus on a 'push' or 'pull' strategy. In a push strategy, focus is on inducing intermediaries, such as a retailer, to sell the product at retail. Advertising's job may be to make the consumer aware of the product, but the closing of the deal is left to the intermediary. Alternatively, a pull strategy means the end consumer develops such an insistence on the product that he or she 'pulls' it through the channel of distribution, and the retailer's role is merely to make the product conveniently available.

Pricing Basis, Objectives and Approaches

One of the most difficult areas of marketing decision-making, pricing, deals with the methods of setting profitable and justifiable prices. It is closely regulated and subject to considerable public scrutiny. In comparison to the other 3 Ps–product, place and promotion–of marketing mix, the price element is the only revenue element whereas the others are cost elements. Also, this is the element which can be easily copied. To a large extent, the combinations of the 3 Ps determine the target customer's perception of the value of the firm's product in a given competitive context. Conceptually, this perceived value represents the maximum price which the customer is willing to pay. This should be the primary guide to pricing the product. Once the firm has created value for customers, it is entitled to capture some of that value for itself to find future value-creation efforts. This is the role of effective pricing.

Pricing Basis and Objective

In most situations, cost should act as a floor on pricing. In some circumstances, a firm intentionally sells at a loss for a time to establish a position in the market, but it is often difficult to increase prices later due to the customer's use of the introductory price as a reference point. With perceived value in mind, the first question is what is the marketing objective and how does the pricing objective derive from that? For example, the price that would maximise short-term profit is typically higher than the one which would maximise market penetration subject even to making some profit on each item. It can be described as a choice between a 'skim' and 'penetration' pricing strategy. In a skim strategy, the focus is on those consumers with high value. Starting with a high price and targeting a segment that is willing to pay this price, skimming happens. Later on, prices are reduced to reach the segments below. In penetration pricing, the firm sets a lower price to generate lots of sales quickly. It is designed to preempt competition and gain a significant number of customers early on. The appeal of a penetration strategy increases to the extent that (1) customers are sensitive to price, (2) economies of scale are important, (3) adequate production capacity is available, and (4) there is a threat of competition. Since customers typically place different values on the product, the firm should consider whether it is worth trying to capitalise on these value variations by charging different customers different prices. In some cases, legal constraints and logistical practicalities can make this infeasible. However, many firms owe their economic well-being to their ability to customise prices. In many cases, for example, prices are varied depending on when the buyer is booking, for how long, for what days of week, and so on.

These characteristics are used as indicators of the value the customer places on the product. Price customisation can be achieved by:

- developing a product line–e.g., developing 'economy' versions of the product
- controlling the availability of lower prices–e.g., select availability in certain stores
- varying prices based on observable buyer characteristics–e.g., new vs. existing customers
- varying prices based on observable characteristics of the transaction–e.g., purchase volume.

Another pricing approach is the product life cycle pricing in which different prices are charged at different stages of the product's life cycle. Since the marketing objective and the cost structure various across the stages, the pricing approach also varies. While product marketing mix consists of the 4 Ps, services marketing brings in additional 3 Ps into an extended marketing mix. The additional 3 Ps–People, Process and Physical evidence–are necessitated by the characteristics of the services. While products are tangible, services are intangible. While products can be manufactured and inventoried, production and consumption take place at the same time and hence are inseparable. While products can be standardized, services cannot be–thanks to the human interaction in service delivery. The perceived quality of service depends on who provides it, when and where it is provided and also to whom it is provided. Because of this, the heterogeneity in services throws a quality challenge. Finally, the services are perishable–so managing the demand and supply is crucial. Because of these characteristics of services, viz., intangibility, inseparability, heterogeneity and perishability, there is a need for industrialising and standardising the services (process), tangibilise the intangibles (through physical evidence) and managing the service personnel (people) who are part of the service. The sub-elements of these additional 3 Ps are shown in the Table 3.3.

3.14   THE CONCEPT OF OPTIMUM MARKETING MIX

The concept of optimum marketing mix relates to the issue of dividing the marketing budget optimally over the elements of the marketing mix:

Table 3.3 3 Ps coordination

Additional 3 Ps in Services Marketing	Sub-Elements
Process	Flow of activities Service script (number of steps) Customer involvement
Physical evidence	Facility design Service ambience Equipment Signage Employee dress Point-of-sale displays Other tangibles (e.g., business cards)
People	Employees • Recruiting • Training • Motivation • Rewards • Teamwork Customers • Education • Training

But in doing so you should remember that the components of the mix are partially substitutable for each other.

The challenge, however, that a marketer faces is to find the optimal marketing mix. Assume that a marketer has identified sales promotion and advertising as two major components of the marketing mix on which marketing budget is to be allocated. In principle, the marketing budget can be divided in a number of ways on these two elements. Associated with every possible marketing mix would be a resulting sales level.

In theory, for a given marketing budget, the money should be divided among the various marketing tools in a way that gives the same marginal profit on the marginal profit on the marginal rupee spent on each tool. This would result in an optimum allocation of a given marketing budget over different elements of the marketing. Such an allocation would provide to be a sales maximising marketing mix.

In devising optimum marketing mix, it is important to know how various marketing mix variables interact in their impact on sales/profit. Here are some examples of the assumption made by marketing managers.

- ✠ Higher advertising expenditure results in reducing buyers' price sensitivity. The resulting interference is that a firm wishing to charge a higher price should more on advertising.
- ✠ Advertising expenditure's have a greater sales impact on how price products than high price products.
- ✠ Higher advertising expenditure reduce the total cost of selling. The logic is that the advertising expenditure pre-sell the customer and sales representative can spend their time advertising objectives and closing the sale.
- ✠ Higher prices lead buyers to attribute higher product quality.
- ✠ Tighter credit terms require much greater selling and advertising effort to move the same volume of goods.

The question arises is: Can we accept these relationships without any future inquiry? The answer is 'no' because while these relationship may hold true for many products, managers of other products should be cautious. That, is a clear direction for such interactions could not be predicted a priori. That is, other factor like the nature of the advertising appeal, the structure of the market, etc., would also have to be taken into consideration.

Another important point that needs to be highlighted in predicting the results of such interaction is that marketing mix variables not only interact with each other but also with non-marketing variables in the firm.

For example, a manager cannot set the product's price and quality at any level he wishes. He has to understand that both price and product qualities are affected by non-marketing variables. The non-marketing variables that will affect price, for example, will be productivity which in turn will be affected by investment decisions and personnel policies. Similarly, product quality will be affected both by production reliability and technology which in turn would be affected by both personnel policies and research and development (R&D) investment.

The conclusion that emerges is that the marketers must not take price and product for granted. Rather they should influence those non-marketing variables that will enable the firm to reduce costs and products higher quality products.

3.15   MARKETING MIX - SOME SPECIFIC SITUATIONS

In this context, we will discuss some specific situations with regard to the development of strategies in relation to some of the elements of the marketing mix. These situations relate to marketing mix decisions with respect to new product development, stages in the life cycle of a product, and the relative role of advertising and pricing in the marketing mix.

New Product Development and Marketing Mix

The product is one component of the marketing mix and is usually the core part, so the product is developed first; there are occasions when the product is designed to fit in some other component of the mix. To illustrate, the product may be developed to fit a price range, an image slot or a channel. But you must not forget that the various elements of a marketing mix are conceptually interconnected to meet somewhat and so there must be a procedural interconnection in designing the various components.

The drawing up of a tentative marketing mix is part of any new product development programme. First let us take the element of promotion. It is a key consideration when the want is likely to be latent or passive for the majority of the members of the target market, in general terms, the motivation to buy is based preferably on some core advantage and the benefits that might be stressed in the advertising copy or sales appeal.

Next, we take price as a strategic element in new product development. Price can be important not just in terms of cost to the consumer but as contributing to the image of the product. Pricing needs to be considered in relation to both the buying inducement and the rest of the offering or mix. Although the introductory price is of introduction interest in terms of new product development, the management needs to plan an overall pricing strategy that might be adopted as the market grows.

Finally, the distribution strategy is new product development. Remember, if distribution, i.e., availability in the target market cannot be assured, all else fails. The role which distribution channels are expected to play must be investigated at the early stages.

You must, however, forget the all important fact emphasised earlier that all the elements of the marketing mix, i.e, promotion, pricing, and distribution strategies need to be brought together and coordinated in the overall marketing mix.

Product Life Cycle and Marketing Mix

Here we will relate the strategic aspects of the elements of the marketing mix to different stages of the product life cycle.

But before that we will explain very briefly the Product Life Cycle concept itself. The objective here is not to explain the concept in all its aspects but to help you to understand how the components of the marketing mix change during different phases of the life cycle curve, we will deal with PLC (Product life cycle) in more detail in the coming chapter.

The belief that sales of a product follow a life cycle has been around from the beginning of the twentieth century. According to this belief, a product through a specific sequence of stages corresponding to the life phases of infancy, growth, maturity and decline. The force in the case of products is on the shape of the sales curve. The assumption is that sales are low during the introductory stage, rapidly rising during the growth stage, reach the peak during the maturity stage and declining during the final stage.

Product life cycle curve is S-shaped of introduction, growth, maturity and decline.

Different products will take different spans of time to pass through the cycle of introduction, growth, maturity and decline. Many classes of products like light bulbs and aspirin, seem to remain indefinitely at the maturity stage in economic growth, a product can also be at the introductory stage in one country, and in maturity stage in another.

The question that arises is whether one should view the PLC concept, as a universal fact or law or as ideal type. The answer is an ideal type. For if it is viewed as a universal fact, every product would achieve to be shown to be following or to have followed the S-shaped curve, which is not there. Even one exception would disapprove the universality of the concept. Therefore, it would probably be best to view it is an ideal type, which means that it is to be viewed as a standard against which to compare or predict real cases. For an ideal type is an abstraction that may or may not correspond too closely with the real world.

After explaining the concept, we revert to the strategic aspects of the elements of the marketing mix during different stages of the product life cycle. This we are doing by listing some of the suggestions relating to different elements of the marketing mix for coping with the different life stages. Table 3.4 shows some strategic relating to the elements of the marketing mix.

The question that arises is what approach should be followed to guide marketing mix as defined in the above stages. One possible answer is that a marketer should seek and identify the stage in the life cycle from the conditions in the market. Probably, it would be helpful for this purpose to try and foresee the next stage and work back to establish the current stage.

Role of Advertising in the Marketing Mix

Generally speaking, there are only a few firms which directly compete with each other in the same target market. Economists call such a situation an oligopolistic situation. In this type of structure or situations, many firms prefer to increase their share by increasing demand through advertising rather than by reducing prices. The question that arises is why firms prefer such a strategy. The reason is that building up an image through advertising can be more difficult to match than a price cut. The assumption behind this preferred approach, of course, is that the firm cost advantage over competition as to make price cutting an attractive pre-empting strategy.

Table 3.4 Typical suggested strategic relating to marketing mix variables in the PLC stages.

Stages in Life Cycle	Product	Pricing	Promotion	Distribution
Introduction	Iron out product deficiencies	Highest	Create awareness of product's potential, stimulate primary demand	Selective distribution
Growth	Focus on the product quality, variations of product introduced	High	Selective advertising of brand, heavy advertising to create image	Extended coverage
Maturity	Product adjustment for further brand differentiation	Moderate	Build and maintain image. Sales promotion facilities	Seek close dealer relationship
Decline	Simplify product line. Seek new product uses, introduce changes to revitalise product.	Low	Primary demand may again be cultivated	Selective cultivated

Role of Price in the Marketing Mix

Price can be the major element in the marketing mix. Generally, however, pricing decisions have to be carefully coordinated with decisions on product, promotion and distribution. The framework for such coordination is the target market strategy, since the chosen target market gives overall direction in determining the marketing mix.

To illustrate: The luxury segment of consumer markets suggests a quality, branded product, extra touches, high class outlets, appeals and media that capture the luxury image and a high price to match.

But you must remember that where there are just a few rival brands, competitors are more likely to react to a lowering of price that to an increase in advertising expenditure. Decreases in price are highly visible and are most often associated with the consent of cut-throat competition.

KEYWORDS

Segmentation: *Dividing a consumer population into several homogeneous groups based on characteristics like geography, demography, psychography and lifestyle.*

Target market: *A homogeneous group of people in a heterogeneous marketplace toward whom a firm markets its goods and services with a strategy designed to satisfy their specific needs and preferences.*

Needs and wants: *The word 'need' is often used interchangeably with 'want' but 'need' suggests a want that is an absolute requirement. Thus, one may want 'idli and dosa' but needs food. Few wants are needs in this sense.*

Factor analysis: *Is a statistical procedure for trying to discover a few basic factors that may underline and explain the intercorrelations among a large number of variables.*

Positioning: *Consumers' perceptions of a product's attributes, uses, quality and advantages and disadvantages in relation to those of competing brands.*

Repositioning: *Marketing strategy to change the position of a product in consumers' minds relative to the positions of competing products.*

Undifferentiated marketing: *Marketing strategy to produce only one product and market it to all customers using a single marketing mix.*

Differentiated marketing: *Marketing strategy to produce numerous products and promote them with different marketing mixes designed to satisfy smaller segments.*

Niche market: *A firm targets its efforts on profitably satisfying only one market segment. It may be a small but a profitable segment.*

Marketing mix: *Blending the four elements of marketing decision-making—product, price, distribution and promotion—to satisfy chosen consumer segments.*

Product strategy: *Element of marketing decision-making involved in developing the right good or service for the firm's customers, including package design, branding, trademarks, warranties, product life cycles and new product development.*

Product mix: *A company's assortment of product lines and individual offerings.*

Product life cycle: *The four basic stages through which a successful product progresses—introduction, growth, maturity and decline.*

Pricing strategy: *Element of marketing decision-making dealing with methods of setting profitable and justifiable prices.*

Distribution strategy: *Element of marketing decision-making concerned with activities and marketing intermediaries that get the right goods or services to the firm's customers.*

Promotional strategy: *Element of marketing decision-making that involves appropriate blending of promotional mix elements, namely, personal selling, advertising, sales promotions, direct marketing and public relations—to communicate with and seek to persuade potential customers.*

R&D (Research and Development): *R&D expenditures are all costs associated with the search for a discovery of new knowledge that may be useful in developing new products, services, processes or techniques, or that might significantly improve existing products or processes. However, the following costs are excluded. These are costs of routine product improvement or seasonal changes of style, market research and testing, quality control and legal costs to protect patents.*

SUMMARY

All the sellers can adopt three approaches to a market. Mass marketing is the decision to mass produce and mass distribute one product and attempt to attract all kinds of buyers. Product variety marketing aims to offer a variety of products to broaden the customer base.

Target marketing is the core decision to distinguish various groups that make design of a market and to construct corresponding products and marketing mixes for each target market. The major steps in market segmentation are STP: **Market Segmentation, Market Targeting, Market Positioning.** *Segmentation impacts are always based on: Measurable, Substantial, Accessible, Differentiable, and Actionable.*

The important aspect which should focus from the seller is that he has to target the best market segmentation: he has to evaluate the profit potential segment towards each, which is a function of segmentation size and growth, segment structural attractiveness, and organisation objectives and resources. Then the seller has to make decision for service.

It is further emphasised that we could seldom be sure that we had segmented the market in the best possible way. For segmentation of a market is not an arbitrary process, but neither is there a unique set of segments to be discovered. It was emphasised that the ultimate aim of segmentation was to relate consumers in the segment and their response to different offerings.

By way of choosing target segmentation, marketers need to consider segment interrelationships and potential segment invasion plans.

Positioning is the main designing of the company's offer and image so the target market understands and appreciates what the company stands in relation to its competitors. The company positioning must be rooted in an understanding of how the target market defines values and makes choice among vendors.

The objective of a marketer is to combine the various elements of the marketing mix, viz., product, promotion and distribution in such a way that he will achieve the necessary volume of sales at a cost that will permit him to make the desired profit.

The elements of a marketing plan are current marketing situation analysis problem and opportunities analysis, objectives, marketing, strategy and programme, marketing budgets and sales volume, cost/profit estimate. The other decisions areas of marketing strategy relate to target markets, market positioning and market expenditure levels.

Decisions are made with respect to marketing mix. For instance, new products are developed and modifications are made in the existing products. Packages are redesigned from time to time. Price and channel policies are established. Decisions are made with respect to the allocation of marketing budget over different elements of the promotional mix, viz., advertising, personal selling and sales promotion. Remember these are largely decisions made by the individual firm for its own situations. They do not necessarily have general applicability, although we do know, for example, that industrial goods manufacturers tend to spend proportionately less for advertising than do consumer goods manufacturers. But these relationships should not be accepted without further inquiry as marketing mix variables interact not only with each other but also with non-marketing variables in the firm.

ASSIGNMENT

Assignment 1

Consider the toothpaste market. Nearly everyone uses it. Yet, the toothpaste manufacturers have found that consumers have different ideas about what they would like the product to do. Prepare a list of what consumers want their toothpastes to do to them.

1.

2.

3.

4.

5.

6.

7.

8.

Assignment 2

Refer to the Assignment 1: From what you have noted down as the 'wants' of toothpaste consumers, match each of those wants with the segmentation variables listed below.

1. Consumer background characteristics

    1.1 Geography -

    1.2 Demographic -

    1.3 Psychographic -

    1.4 General lifestyle -

2. Consumers' market history

    2.1 Product usage -

    2.2 Product benefit -

    2.3 Decision-process -

Assignment 3

Match the following real-life marketing examples with the above-mentioned targeting approaches.

1. Titan now selling fashion eyewear and watches apart from regular watches
2. A promotional email from www.amazon.com based on your previous purchases
3. Air Deccan with its no-frills, single-class airline model
4. The battery-operated, eco-friendly electric car, Reva.

Case Study 1: HLL goes adult with its ice creams
(Excerpt from *Business Today*, May 8, 2005)

The summer looks hot. That isn't the weatherman talking, but the ice cream marketer, who seems to have abandoned an age-old positioning of the product (as a fun, family treat) in favour of a new one: as an adult indulgence. Leading the new strategy is HLL, which has reworked the marketing communication of its Kwality brand to something more risqué. Its TV and billboard ads show adults "pleasuring it up" quite suggestively. What's up?

According to an HLL spokesperson, the repositioning is "a bid to reflect the sensorial awakening in society". "Evidence of which", the spokesperson continues, "is to be found in the spending one sees at malls and multiplexes". At any rate, says the spokesperson, given that half of the country's population is between 18 and 34, its new communication better reflects its image as a youthful and indulgent brand.

Rivals haven't yet followed suit. On the contrary, ones like the Anand-based milk marketing cooperative Amul, whose officials were not available for comment, are sticking to their family-centric campaigns, Will HLL's new positioning put its ₹89 crore (2004 revenue) ice cream business on the boil? Hard to say. For, this is one category where availability plays a bigger role than just branding.

Question

1. What are the market segmentation, targeting and positioning insights that you draw from this case?
2. Why is HLL repositioning its Kwality brand of ice creams?

Assignment 4

Draw a positioning map to describe the toothpaste market. Choose any two characteristics to show how the different brands can be viewed based on these traits.

Assignment 5

Match the following brands with their chosen differentiation dimensions.

1. Apple's iMac (with an innovative product design)
2. Honda's bikes (In the US market, they did an image makeover for bike riders to differentiate from the image created by Harley-Davidson bike riders)
3. Singapore Airlines (highlighting the 'Singapore Airlines girl' in its campaign)
4. Dell computers (Dell becoming synonymous with Direct (channels) selling)
5. Cemex cement (using GPS to deliver ready-mix concrete just-in-time)

Assignment 6

Think of how the petrol banks have evolved over the years—starting from selling a commodity to marketing a branded product in landscaped locations! Is there a way to differentiate selling petrol?

Assignment 7

Illustrate the product hierarchy or 'total product concept' with an example.

Core benefit -
Basic product -
Expected product -

Augmented product -

Potential product -

Assignment 8

Sort the following promotion mix elements in the order of importance for consumer marketing (B2C) and industrial marketing (B2B)

1. Advertising
2. Personal selling
3. Public relations
4. Sales promotions
5. Direct marketing

Assignment 9

Positioning map for the toothpaste market can be drawn based on characteristics like ingredients (herbal vs. chemical), benefits (emotional vs. functional utilities), age (kids vs. adults), usage (normal vs. treatment), price (low vs. high), attribute (taste vs. contents), and so on. Different brands of toothpastes can then be plotted on the map depending on their positioning in the marketplace.

REVIEW QUESTIONS

1. Which companies in India in your opinion follow the product differentiation strategy and which the market segmentation strategy? (For this purpose examine the ads by Indian companies.)

2. Take any consumer product and describe the step-by-step procedure that you will follow in segmenting the market for that product. Some of the products could be

   (a) Premium toilet soap
   (b) Personal computer
   (c) Colour TV
   (d) Soft drinks

3. Select some products say two or three and examine their ads to find how the companies producing these products segment their markets.

4. Define target segment steps involved in it.

5. Define various patterns of market segmentation.

6. Explain product positioning and repositioning of a product.

7. Write out the most precise, yet descriptive definition on marketing mix.

8. Define product management decisions and its importance in marketing mix.

9. Explain the concept of optimum marketing mix and evaluate some specific situations of marketing mix.

10. Why marketing mix is an important determinant of a firm's success? What problems a marketer faces in determining a suitable marketing mix? Illustrate with examples.

11. Marketing Mix Exercise

   Richman Ltd., marketing its own blend of coffee, finds that coffee is not as popular in northern parts as it is in the southern parts of the country. The company now wants that coffee consumptions should increase in the northern parts as well.

   You are required to design complete marketing mix based on the following limited information.

   (a) There are fewer coffee drinkers than tea drinkers in the northern parts of India.
   (b) North Indians are traditionally tea drinkers and not coffee drinkers.
   (c) Coffee drinkers are usually in the upper middle to upper income brackets.
   (d) Coffee drinkers are usually college educated.

   In the above information, describe each of the following

   Target consumer

   _____

   _____

   _____

   Product activities

   _____

   _____

   _____

Promotional activities

_____

_____

_____

Advertising

_____

_____

_____

Personal selling

_____

_____

_____

Sales promotion

_____

_____

_____

Place or distribution activities

_____

_____

_____

Physical distribution

_____

_____

_____

Channel of distribution

_____

_____

_____

Assume that you have to make a presentation of the recommended strategies relating to different elements of the marketing mix to the marketing manager of your company. What aspects of the marketing mix are most likely to be successful? Which ones are most likely to be least successful? Why?

4 CHAPTER

PRODUCT MANAGEMENT

STRUCTURE

4.1 INTRODUCTION

It is a fact that product/service is a 'mixer of ingredients' wherein the manufacturer/service provider who blends various marketing activities in a manner that strengthen the business interests of the firm. Product related decisions form one of the 4Ps of marketing. These decisions include introduction of new products, improvements of existing products, planned elimination of absolute products and packaging and branding. This lesson narrates the important concepts like marketing mix, products, brand, trademark, packing and labelling with suitable examples from Indian marketing environment.

What is a product?

In order to be effective at selling or marketing, it is necessary to have a proper perspective of the meaning of a product, or how it should be viewed from a marketing perspective. You may like to think a little deeply on what is meant by the word 'product'. Let us understand this with a help of an example:

While conducting seminars for experienced salesmen who had been in the field for 10 to 15 years, salesmen were asked a question.

"What are you selling?"

Different answers were received from different groups. One group answered, "Soaps" when asked, "What? What did you say?" the salesman would immediately answer back "Soaps, Soaps and Soaps". They even tried to help seminar leader by putting forward their right hand with the first finger and the thumb holding something rectangular, thereby assisting him to visualise soap.

In case of another consumer products organisation, the salesmen's answer was, "Bulbs", when seminar leader frowned and asked them, "What did you say?" the answer came back, "Bulbs, Bulbs and Bulbs, Sir".

The third group answered "Drills". When asked again, in the same way, they replied "Drills, drills, drills... Brr... Brrr... brrrr... " Thus, they tried to explain, as if the instructor was deaf and could understand the meaning of drills even by making those funny noises.

Before we analyse the answers, let us give you another question. You may like to fill in the blank or complete the given sentence.

"A good salesman does not sell goods. He sells _____".

If your answer to this question was something like the word 'satisfaction' or 'benefits', then you are on the right track.

Remember that the customer is not interested in your foods. He is interested in himself and what "benefits" he will get, and not in your organisation. Thus, a product is the bundle of benefits or satisfaction offered to a customer. This is the meaning which must be accepted in a marketing sense, so that you become consumer oriented. Now you can modify your answers about what they were selling in connection with soaps, builds and drills as given below.

A motor car in terms of marketing is something more than merely assembled pieces of metal, rubber, etc. It certainly provides 'transportation' and that is one of the important benefits provided by a car. However, this is not the only reason why motor cars are bought. Why some people move about in expensive foreign cars? The expensive cars obviously provide a sort of 'image' or a 'status symbol' for the owner.

So it can be said that a product is a combination of several characteristics, physical and psychological. How people personally feel about, or perceive the product is just as important as the actual physical characteristics.

4.2   CONCEPT OF A PRODUCT

The term 'product' is widely used to refer a market offering of any kind. In its broadest sense, this may be anything from the physical to the abstract—an idea or a moral issue. Generally, however, most products are made up of a combination of physical elements and services. This is true in services marketing, where the service offering can include tangible features, such as food in a restaurant, or be a 'pure' service, intangible in nature.

A service product refers to an activity or activities that a marketer offers to perform, which results in satisfaction of a need or want of predetermined target customers. It is the offering of a firm in the form of activities that satisfies needs such as hairstyling done by a barber.

Consumers will buy only what suits them. As customers, we buy different kinds of products and services to satisfy our various needs. We buy toothpaste, butter, shaving cream, pen, scooter, and ticket for the U.S.A. and many other such items in our daily life. As we understand, our decision to buy an item is based not only on its tangible attributes but also on psychological attributes such as services, brand, package, warranty, image, etc. discussions about the marketing of goods apply to services as well. Services have special characteristics that make them different than products.

According to Alderson, W., *"Product is a bundle of utilities consisting of various product features and accompanying services".*

According to Schwarte, D.J., *"A product is something a firm markets that will satisfy a personal want or fill a business or commercial need".*

At the time of product planning, the marketer has to think about five types of benefits which are represented in Fig. 4.1.

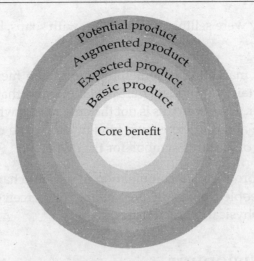

Fig. 4.1 Product levels and benefits.

From Generic to Potential Product: Most of you would be aware that a product has a personality of several components like the physical products, the brand name, the package the label, etc. All of us know that most of the products are undergoing a constant change and the marketing man has been constantly engaged in enriching his product offer. In his attempt to score over competition, he has been bringing about refinement on his basic product offer, but managing the product was becoming more and more difficult. Hence the product travelled various levels:

- The core product
- The generic product
- The branded product
- The differentiated product
- The customised product
- The augmented product
- The potential product

The core product: What does the product mean to the customer? For example, a car offer generic benefits of convenience in travelling.

The generic product: Is the unbranded and undifferentiated commodity like rice, bread flour or cloth.

The branded product: The branded product gets an identity through a 'name'. Moder Bread, Harvest are branded products. We would study in detail about brand name in th brand section.

The differentiated product: The differentiated product enjoys a distinction from other similar products/brands in the market. The differential claimed may be 'real', with a real distinction on ingredient, quality, utility, or service, or it may be 'psychological' brought about through subtle sales appeals.

The customised product: Customer specific requirements are taken into account while developing the product. Commonly practised in the industrial product marketing, where the manufacturer and the user are in direct contact and the product gets customised to the requirements of the customer.

The augmented product

The augmented product is the result of voluntary improvements brought about by the manufacturer in order to enhance the value of the product, which are neither suggested by the customer nor expected by them. The marketer on his own augments the product, by adding an extra facility or an extra feature to the product.

The potential product

The potential product is tomorrow's product carrying with it all the improvements and finesse possible under the given technological, economic and competitive condition. There are no limits to the 'potential product'. Only the technological and economic resources of the firm set the limit.

Product differentiation

It is the act of designing a set of meaningful differences to distinguish the companies offering from competitor's offerings? The number of differentiation opportunities varies with the type of industry. The Boston consulting group has distinguished four types of industries based on the number of available competitive advantages and their size.

1. **Volume industry:** One in which companies can gain only a few, but rather large, competitive advantages.

2. **Stalemated industry:** One in which there are a few potential competitive advantages and each is small.

3. **Fragmented industry:** One in which companies face many opportunities for differentiation, but each opportunity for competitive advantage is small.

4. **Specialised industry:** One in which companies face many differentiation opportunities, and each differentiation can have a high payoff.

Theodore Levitt in one of his books "Marketing Success, through differentiation of anything" explains that in a marketplace, there is no such thing as commodity. All goods and services are differentiable. In a marketplace differentiation is everywhere. All the companies try to distinguish their offers from that of their competitor. This is true of even those who produce and deal in primary metals, grains, chemicals, plastics and money. Starting from technology to plant location to post-sale service firms to the personnel/procedures employed for various functions like sales, production, etc., and companies can differ their offers in many ways. Companies usually choose those functions, which give them greatest relative advantage.

There are different strategy stances that firms can adopts.

It is natural for different firms to take different strategy stances as the requirement; situational design of each is different from the other. One firm might find it appropriate to have direct confrontation with the market leader; another may find it appropriate to keep aloof for some time from the competition; and the third might may find it relevant to chalk out a strategy of sheer survival. No strategy stance is universally valid. Broadly strategy stances can be classified under three heads:

1. Offensive/confrontation strategy
2. Defensive
3. Niche strategy.

1. Offensive Strategy

Is the strategy of aggression usually employed by the firm that is not presently the leader, but aspires to leadership position in the industry. It acts as a challenger and the leader is mostly its target. It tries to expand its market share and utilises all the elements of the marketing mix in attacking the leader.

2. Defensive Strategy

Is usually employed by the leader who has the compulsion to defend his position against the confrontation of powerful existing competitors or strong new entrants trying to remove the leader from the topmost position. The leader has to maintain constant vigilance and defend its position against the attack of the challengers.

3. Niche Strategy

Is usually employed by firms, which neither confront nor defend it. It cultivates a small market segment for itself with unique products/services; supported by a unique marketing mix. Small firms with distinctive capabilities adopt this stance. A market niche to be worthwhile must have characteristics such as reasonable size, profit potential and growth potential.

4.3   TYPES OF PRODUCT

Generally, products are classified into two types, namely,

- Consumer Products
- Industrial Products.

Consumer Products

Consumer goods are those, which are used by ultimate consumers or households and in such form that they can be used without further commercial processing. Consumer goods can be divided into

- Convenience goods
- Shopping goods
- Durable or durable goods, and
- Non-durables or non-durable goods.

Convenience Goods: These are goods which consumers generally purchase and frequently without making an effort or as a habit. The purchase is almost spontaneous and the person has already a predetermined mind. These convenience goods are bought impulsively or spontaneously. These goods includes soaps, newspapers, toiletries, toothpastes, etc., often convenience goods are bought impulsively or spontaneously. For example, when a person goes for shopping around and sees a product, which attracts his eyes he buys it on impulse. Such goods are not purchased on regular basis.

Shopping Goods: These are the goods which are purchased after going around shops and comparing the emphasis on quality, price, fashion, style, etc., are of great importance. A common example: Purchasing of sarees by ladies. Generally, ladies go looking around shop before they make their final selection. Hence, the expression 'shopping goods'.

Durable Goods: These are the goods, which are 'Durable' or which last for some time. Examples of such goods would be electric irons, refrigerators, television sets, etc. The question of after-sales service and repairs is also of importance as 'selling points' or 'benefits' which the customer would like to have.

Non-durable Goods: These goods, which get depleted on consumption. For example, a bottle of soft drink is consumed at one occasion within a matter of minutes. Soap obviously takes a little longer. These are the products that have to be advertised heavily, with a view to inducing people to try them out, and thus, build up brand preference and brand loyalty.

Services are especially mentioned here because it is generally thought that marketing is related to products alone. It should be remembered that marketing ideas and practices are equally applicable to services with slight adaptations in certain decisional areas. For example: hospital offers a service, police, post offices, etc. Apart from government or public sector undertakings, there are non-profit organisations such as museums and charities. The business and commercial sectors which includes airlines, banks, hotels, and insurance companies, and the professionals such as charter accountants, management consulting firms, medical practitioners, etc. need marketing.

Industrial Products

These are the products, which are sold primarily for use in manufacturing other goods or for rendering some service. These include items like machinery, components, and raw materials which from the bulk of industrial goods.

Machinery is also sold generally through the sales force, particularly if it is of the heavy type. It is obvious that the latter cannot be stocked in retail outlets. The type of product determines the type of marketing mix, which has to be adopted. Industrial goods also include supplies and services. Supplies are similar to convenience goods. They are purchased with very little effort and repurchased once the consumer is satisfied. They also marketed through retail outlets. Industrial services include maintenance and repairs. For example, persons having typewriters naturally wants them to be looked after on a regular basis generally by the same (regular) maintenance person who is normally an outsider. Similarly, after purchasing a computer, service is necessary. These services are often provided by small producers or by the manufacturer of the original equipment itself.

(a) **Material and Parts:** These are goods that enter the manufacturer's product completely. They fall into two classes—raw material and manufactured material part.

(b) **Capital Items:** These are long lasting goods that facilitate developing or managing the finished products. They include two groups: installation and equipment.

(c) **Supplies and Business Services:** These are short-listing goods and services that facilitate developing or managing the finished products.

Let us briefly analyse the difference in marketing strategies which might be required for the two types of products, namely, consumer and industrial products. This understanding is important for product line decisions. Industrial products are generally subject to greater standardisation, as against certain consumer products which require frequent changes in fashion and style. Advertising normally is an important promotional tool for consumer products, but may not be so in the case of industrial products. Personal selling and after-sales services is generally more important for industrial products. Industrial products generally involve high value purchase and this involves competitive bidding based on price competition selling is done on the basis of quality or tangible attributes. As against this, consumer products are very often sold for psychological satisfactions. For example, in case of soap offers you a complexion like that of a film star.

Consumer products require elaborate channels of distribution, but industrial products are sold through outlets and often directly by the organisational itself. These are some of the silent features of marketing of consumer products as against industrial products. A more detailed treatment will follow in subsequent units no promotion and physical distribution.

Product Classification

Marketers have traditionally-classified products on the basis of varying products characteristics. The thought is that each product type has an appropriate marketing mix strategy. With this background, we are ready to examine company decisions regarding the product systems and mixes, product lines, and individual products.

Product Systems and Mixes

A product system is a group of diverse but related items that function in a compatible manner. For example, Palm-One handheld and smart-phone product lines come with attachable products including headsets, cameras, computer keyboards, Liquid Crystal Display (LCD) projectors, e-Books, e-Journals, MP3 players, and voice recorders. A product mix is also called product assortment is the set of all products and items a particular seller offer for sale. A product mix consists of various product lines. The consumer product portfolio of Nirma Limited consists of fabric-care products, personal care products, food products, and variants. A company's product mix has a certain width, length, depth, and consistency. These formations are illustrated in Table 4.1 for the consumer-product division of HUL (Hindustan Unilever Limited).

1. *The width of a product mix refers to how many different product lines the company carries. Table 4.1 represents product-mix width of eleven lines, (in fact, HUL has other businesses as well).*

2. *The length of a product mix refers to the total number of items in the mix. In Table 4.1 it is 25. We can also talk about the average length of a line. This is obtained by dividing the total length (here 25) by the number of lines (here 11), or an average product length of less than 3.*

3. *The depth of a product mix refers the number of variants offered of each product in the line. Since Lux comes in four scents (exotic flower petals and jojoba oil, almond oil and milk cream, fruit extracts and honey in milk cream, and sandal saffron in milk cream) and in two sizes, it has a depth of eight. The average depth of HUL's product mix can be calculated by averaging the number of variants within the brand groups.*

4. *The consistency of the product mix refers to how closely related the various product lines are in the end use, production requirements, distribution channels, or some other ways. HUL's product lines are consistent insofar as they are consumer goods that go through the same distribution channels. The lines are, however, less consistent of one considers that they perform different functions for the buyer.*

These four product mix dimensions permit the company to expand its business in four ways. It can add new product lines, thus widening its products mix. It can lengthen each product line. It can add more product variants to each product and deepen its product mix. Finally, a company can pursue more product-line consistency. To make these product and brands decisions, it is useful to conduct product line analysis.

Table 4.1 Product Mix Width and Product Line for Hindustan Unilever Limited.

	Product Mix Width										
	Home and Personal Care							**Food**			
	Personal Wash	Laundry	Skin Care	Hair Care	Oral Care	Deodorants	Colour Cosmetics	Tea	Coffee	Foods	Ice Cream
Product Line Length	Lux	Surf Excel	Fair & Lovely	Sunsilk Naturals	Pepsodent	Axe	Lakme	Brook Bond	Bru	Kissan	Kwality Walls
	Lifebuoy	Rin	Pond's	Clinic	Close-Up	Rexona		Lipton		Knorr Annapurna	
	Liril	Wheel									
	Hamam										
	Breeze										
	Dove										
	Pears										
	Rexona										

4.4 PRODUCT LINE DECISIONS

Let us now understand terms like product item, product line, product mix frequently used in managing products.

A Product or Product Item

The 'product item' refers to a specific product or brand like Hamam or Moti soap. There are companies with only one product and there are others having several products for various reasons, may be higher market share or higher profits or both or any other reasons.

Product Line

✠ A series of related products
✠ A group of products that are physically similar in performance, use or feature and intended for a similar market

- ✠ "A set of products that are closely related."
- ✠ Shoes Nike, Adidas, Reebok, file, new balance, British knight, books, converse, vans, sic, puma notebooks, Toshiba, NEC, TI, Compaq, IBM, DELL, Apple, HP, Hitachi, Mitsubishi, Mutsuhito.

Cannibalisation

- ☞ Situation involving one product taking sales from another offering in a product line.
- ☞ Cannibalisation occurs when sales of a new product cut into (reduce) the sales of a firm's existing products.

It is part of the product strategy to determine whether an organisation will have a single product or more of closely related products. Examples of these would include the Usha line of fans or the Lakme line of cosmetics. In case of product line, very often a product manager or a product line manager is appointed to look after a particular product line. Generally, he tries to enlarge his product line because he wants a higher market share, or growth in volume of sales resulting in more profit. The latter aspect must always be remembered, and the product line manager should be willing to eliminate any product which is found to be unprofitable, or nor required to complete the line of products offered.

Product line decisions have to be taken about how long or short the line should be. The basic considerations being the capacity of the organisation in terms of availability of production facilities, finance, etc. and the profitability of the items in the product line.

Another concept, which is very important and should be known to you, is cannibalisation

When the sales of the firms' new products are due mainly because of decreasing sales of its existing and established product, then we say that cannibalisation has occurred. In brief we can say by this you are actually eating away your own market. A good example of it would be Hyundai Santro, they have introduced Santro Xing as a new product in the market in other way they have cannibalised their own market, like a person who wanted to buy Santro old model will buy Xing as it is latest so they are not capturing new customer but converting their own customers. Only if they are able to make a person buy their product where he was planning to buy some product of Maruti then it is not cannibalisation.

If you want to avoid cannibalisation, the new product should not be identified too closely with the established products. Instead it should be targeted with new appeals to different market segments. Cannibalisation is desirable when margins on new products are higher than those on established products. In highly competitive industries, it is often desirable to induce target customers to trade up to the firm's newer products. This strategy is adopted by Videocon International, which entered the market with a low priced colour TV with basic features and then introduced more sophisticated models up the price scale in order to ensure that customers in all segments would buy only Videocon products.

Product Line Sales and Profits

The product line management needs to know the percentage of total sales and profits contributed by each item in the line. Which is also shown below (Chart 4.1)

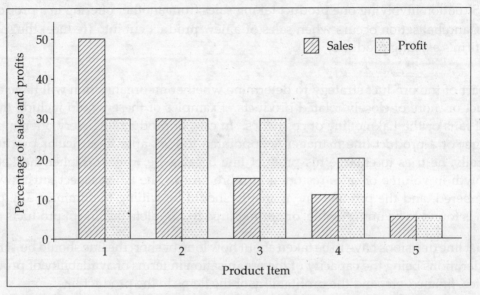

Chart 4.1 Product item contributions to a product line's total sales and profits.

Chart 4.1 shows that a sales and profit report for a five-item product line. The first item accounts for 50 per cent of total sales and 30 per cent of total profits. The first two items account for 80 per cent of total sales and 60 per cent of total profits. If these two items were suddenly hurt by the competitor, the line's sales and profitability could collapse. These must be carefully monitored and protected. At the end, the last item delivers only 5 per cent of the product line's sales profits. The product-line manager may consider dropping this item unless it has strong growth potential.

Every company's product portfolio contains with different margins, supermarkets make almost no margin on bread and milk, reasonable margins on canned and frozen foods; even better margins on flowers, ethnic food lines, and freshly baked goods. A local telephone company makes different margins on its core telephone service, call waiting, caller ID, and voice mail. A company can classify its products into four types that yield different gross margins, depending on sales volume and promotion. For example consider (personal computer) PC;

- **Core Product**: Basic computers that produce high sales volume and are heavily promoted but with margins because they are viewed as undifferentiated commodities.

- **Staples**: Items with lower sales volume and no promotion, such as faster CPU's or bigger memories, these yield a somewhat higher margin.

- **Specialities**: Items with lower sales volume but which might be highly promoted, such as digital movie making or might generate income for services, such as personal delivery, installation, or on-site training.

- **Convenience items**: Peripheral items that sell in high volume but receive less promotion, such as computer monitors, printers, upscale video or sound cards, and software. Consumers tend to buy them where they buy the original equipment because it is more convenient than making further shopping trips. These items can carry higher margins.

The core point is that companies should recognise that these items differ in their potential for being higher or advertised more as ways to increase their sales margins, or both.

Expanding and Reducing the Product Line

As you are aware that there are many models of TV available in the market. There is a large variety of radio sets from Sony. Underlines bras are available in a number of styles. Syrups and crushes are available in many flavours, e.g., Rasna concentrates and Mala's crushes. There are technical products with higher and lesser sophistication. We find many product categories where consumers prefer to have a great variety for their satisfaction. Marketers are adopting strategies of adding new versions with new specifications, while retaining the old versions for the less sophisticated consumers.

Sometimes this addition of new products to the existing line is done to include complementary products, e.g., a toothpaste marketer may add toothbrushes to the product line. Camel may introduce paintbrushes, which go well with its watercolours. Sometimes, there are occasions to delete a product/products from the line. A product, which shows decline in terms of sales, may be abandoned. Non-contributing products may be eliminated. While doing so, it should be seen that other products in the product line are not affected.

Product line length

Now you should ask a question what is the optimum size of a product line? A line is too long if after eliminating a product results into increased profits. A line is too short when any addition to it results into increased profits.

One thing should be clear to you that the company's overall objectives do affect the length of its product line. For instance, a company may have the objective of expanding its market share. It will then have a longer product line. Contribution of individual products to profits may be ignored. However, a company whose objective is to have larger profits will have a shorter product line consisting of those items, which contribute to profits substantially Product lines have a tendency to lengthen over a period of time. Many a time, a firm may, have extra capacity, which is used for developing new items. Sales people and trade put pressure on the management to keep on adding items to a product line so as to satisfy their customers. Lengthening of the line shoots up costs. At some point, this must come to halt. Loss making items are then eliminated. The contribution of items to profits is studied. Thus, in the life of an organisation, there is a cycle of longer product line followed by a pruned product line. This cycle is repeated again and again.

Line stretching

Most of the companies have range of products in its existing product lines, like Videocon has a range of TVs in its product line, right from budget TVs to premium TVs. Line stretching occurs when this range is lengthened. This stretching could be upward, downward or both ways.

Upward stretching

Here a company operates in the lower end of the market. By upward stretch, it proposes to enter the higher end. Perhaps, it is motivated by higher margin of profits, higher growth rate or a position of a full-range marketer. This decision has its own risks. A well-established high-end marketer might assault the stretcher by stretching downwards. Besides, it is a question of credibility of a lower-end marketer, whether he will be able to produce high-quality products. There is one more risk. The existing infrastructure of a low-end marketer may not be competent to deal with the high-end market.

Downward stretch

Let us start with an example: like all of you know Parker. Parker started with pens only at high price but if we look at Parker today we can see products available in the range of 50 rupees which no one could have thought of in older times. Many companies start with high-end products, but later stretch downwards by adding low-priced products. The down-end products are advertised heavily so as to pull customers to the whole line on the basis of price. Videocon advertises its budget line 14" inches TV at ₹8,000. Once the customer is pulled, he may decide to buy a higher priced model–he trades up. This strategy needs careful handling. The budget brand being promoted should not dilute the overall brand image. Besides, the budget brand must be available. Consumers should not get a feeling that they were hooked to bait, for switching later. Downward stretch is practised in the following situations: A competitor stretches upward and challenges the marketer. He counter-attacks him stretching downwards

- Most companies start at the upper end, and then roll downwards.
- The high-end market has a slow growth rate.
- By filling the gap at the low-end, new competition is avoided.

Downward stretch has its own risks. The down-end item might cannibalise the high-end items. Besides, our downward stretch might provoke a competitor to move upward. Down-end product may not be managed properly as the company may not have that capacity. It may dilute the brand image of the company's products. It however, needs careful consideration–a product line should not have a gap at the lower-end. It exposes the company to competition, e.g., American car companies faced the competition from small-sized, Japanese cars at the lower-end of the market.

Two-way stretch

Beside upward and downward stretch you can even stretch in two ways like several companies serve the middle-end market. They can stretch their product line in both the directions. A hotel company operating hotels in the comfort category where each room has a tariff 2000-3000 a day might decide to have elite upper-end hotels with tariffs of ₹5000-7000 a lower-end budget hotels with tariffs of ₹600-1500 a day. Ashoka group of ITC has thus elite 5-star hotels, at the upper-end comfort hotels at the middle-end and budget hotels like Ashoka Yatri Niwas at lower end.

Product Lines and Brands

Most service organisations offer a line product rather than just a single product. Some of these products are distinctly different from one another. Again in response to changing market opportunities, companies may revise the mix of products that they offer. Following example illustrates this concept. British Airways (BA), which explicitly reorganises eight different air travel products–or brand–under the British Airways umbrella. (The company also has equity shares in several other airlines). There are four intercontinental service brands–concorde (supersonic deluxe service), first class (deluxe subsonic service), club world (business class) and world (business class), and world traveller (economy class); two intra–European brands–club world (business class) and euro-traveller (economy class): and within the United Kingdom, the super shuttle brand, offering a graduated economy seat and high-frequency service. In additional, six commuter airlines, flying in British airways colours, operate service in partnership with BA under the British Airways express brand. As described by Douglas, each British Airways brand has a key brand proposition and a set of clearly stated product specifications for pre-flight, in-flight and on-arrival service element. To provide additional focus on product, pricing and marketing communications, responsibility for managing and developing each brand is assigned to a brand management team. Through internal training and external communication, staff and passengers alike are kept informed of the characteristic of each brand.

4.5   CREATING CUSTOMER LOYALTY

Who is the Customer?

This is simple. Anyone can be a customer. It is not just the old lady who goes to the baker to buy the muffins. It is not just the busy traveller who checks into the hotel. It is not just the net savvy teenager who orders a CD from Amazon.com. It is not just the passenger who travels on the bus. The employee is a customer of the manager. The college going student is a customer of the university. Your friend is your customer in many ways. Anyone can be a customer. It is not just a one-way relationship in this case. It can be a two-way relationship also. Take the simple case of an employee and a manager. The employee may be like a customer to the manager but the manager can also be a customer to the employee. Both need to understand each other's needs and build loyalty towards each other for a successful combination. In true business sense, it is important to treat everyone as a customer. The basic essence of a customer relationship is that both parties must benefit. Customers make or break a business. A business that is not focussed towards the customer can never succeed. Small time businesses do not grow until their focus is purely on the customers. Never forget–**your customer is your king**.

What is Customer Loyalty?

Customer loyalty is winning the confidence of the customer in favour of an organisation such that the relationship becomes a win-win situation for both the organisation as well as the customer. Customer loyalty is not a process that finishes with the customer joining the loyalty programme but actually a process that starts with the customer joining the same. Customer loyalty is something more of what an enterprise must get from the customer. As opposed to what the name suggests, is not just something that the customer has to build towards the enterprise. It is not just the customer who is being loyal to the company in the progress but also the company that has to maintain its loyalty to the customer.

Loyalty Programme

The first and foremost thing–the customer feels important at the establishment. Importance gives rise to feeling happy too! This works wonders. For instance, a happy customer at a departmental store is as good as a hungry customer in a food store! The customer will always buy more! However, to the customer, one of the first things that will strike, is the saving in money. This is the reason that more often than not–establishments tend to advertise their customer loyalty programmes as money saving schemes. "Enroll today and save as you buy" is one of the most common themes of customer loyalty programmes. These are the smaller customer loyalty programmes but not to be discounted. Nothing attracts a customer more than a saving. Benefits and awards that customer loyalty programmes carry with them attract some customers. A free cruise or an airline class upgrade is all awards that customers would look forward to entertainment.

One route to achieving customer loyalty is to become friends with your customers. When entertaining customers, choose events that reflect your company's image and set you apart from your competitors.

For your most important customers, entertain on a one-to-one basis.

1. An occasional lunch or an after-work drink can be fitted into most people's schedules.
2. Activities like golf provide a relaxed, non-work environment to get to know people in.
3. Find out what your customer's interests are, and indulge them.

If you need to entertain large number of customers, consider having an annual event. This need not be expensive. For example:

1. A specialised travel company might put on a video or slide show each year, plus an exhibition of customers' photos.
2. An injection moulding company might combine a presentation on state-of-the-art plastics technology (by a suitably high-profile speaker) with some kind of entertainment afterwards.

Customers Rarely Report Bad Experiences

This is not the universal truth but a fact. Customers who have not had a good experience with some employees of the store or maybe some products will not report the bad behaviour to the management of the store. The more likely reaction would be that the customer would stop visiting the store. That is not the only problem–the customer will also start discouraging near and dear ones from using the services of the stores! Nothing can be worse if there is a competition available nearby! This however is a behaviour governed by the geographies. For instance, in the Americas–it is likely that customers exchange or return defective products. In Asia–this is not so prominent. It is a difficult task–exchanging even defective merchandise. The tough part is where the merchandise is not involved. Take hotels as an instance. What would you do if the hotel staff of a hotel were rude to you or if the towels in your bathroom were not replaced by the end of day? You probably will not leave a note citing this instance. If you had an option, you will stay at some other hotel in the future. Losing a customer is definitely easier than getting one. The toughest challenge is retaining one.

Geographies of Customer Loyalty Programmes

Are all loyalty programmes the same? Will the same system work for USA and India? These are some basic questions that crop. With very few minor differences (which arise more due to difference in business practices) the objective of loyalty programmes stays pretty much the same across the globe. The owner of the customer loyalty programmes must create a situation for the customer where the customer keeps feeling special. It is essential to have a system that caters to the world anyway. Travelling abroad on a holiday is in. If you could use my local restaurant loyalty programme points to buy a meal at London Heathrow Airport, you definitely would be pleased! There is the concept of tie-ups between customer loyalty programmes. A customer is happier if not forced to spend all the money earned on one airline to be able to use the facilities on the same airlines only. That is the reason for so many tie-ups in customer loyalty programmes in the airline industry. Relevant industries also need to have the right tie-ups. The benefits of air miles can be used at hotels. This makes sense because people travelling by air would in all probability need places to stay while away from home. A tie-up between a grocery store programme and a hotel programme is unlikely to yield results.

Customer Loyalty in hard times

Customer loyalty will be hard to get in times of a recession. At least harder than it was when the consumer had enough to spend. All loyalty programmes that expect the customer to pay a membership (to join the loyalty system) for the additional small benefits better start planning again. Small reasons will be enough for customers to turn away from putting money into a business. Customers will not put loyalty first but the price will be a major driving force. Also the bigger problem will be the fact that customer loyalty programmes normally drive at long-term benefits and as of now–the consumer confidence being so low–the customer will be influenced by immediate benefits. As such customer loyalty programmes will need to adapt to quicker and possibly immediate awards to the customer. Lower prices as part of the loyalty programme will definitely boost membership to the loyalty programmes but this must be a carefully advertised campaign. Discounts in the store must be treated separate from the benefits of lower price to loyal customers. Loyal customers must be given a feeling that they are being treated specially, even in these times of recession. That is the key to keeping the customers with the business even in these times. Customers need to be better informed now of the benefits that they are getting because of being with the loyalty programme.

Unusual Business Practices a Must

Times have changed. Innovative and unusual business practices are the new business growth strategies. Wal-Mart is a live example. Customers want a change–so do "loyal" customers. They do not want the same stereotype behaviour from the business establishments. What they are looking for now is a change–a definite, positive change! New ideas are more likely to catch attention of consumers rather than conventional ones. Though consumers may not receive new ideas with the fear of having to spend money, they definitely would like to try new ideas where they feel that the returns are high. This must not be confused with the promotional offers that companies might try in hard times. Offers within a loyalty system are different from that category. For instance, a loyalty programme offer could evolve during hard times where the customer gets a higher return faster than it would have come in normal circumstances. Consider the following example: A coffee chain offers a free cup of coffee for every 10 cups of coffee purchased. This specialised coffee chain could now start targeting to give free coffees for every 6 cups purchased! This sounds as a far more reachable figure and clients would easily get into trying this scheme! This is not the end. After working out the economics–the company needs to identify other items that they can offer to the customer as options. Customers always want to see the business flexible to their needs. Nothing evokes more praise than a business that is ready to adjust as per customer needs. For instance, a customer might want a free bagel with every 6 coffees purchased. The company needs to identify these options and work their plans accordingly. With the advent of the web, more innovations came through. *www.MyPoints.com* as a website did wonders by having a loyalty programme for various sites managed by it as an entity. This innovation became popular with the customers feeling the advantage of mixing loyalty points over different programmes. Consider the case of websites. Most customers would wait for a few days more if the shipping were free. This could be a potential idea for loyalty programmes. This might lead to increased customer spending.

Conclusion

The customer is the king and the king needs to be served happily not forcefully!

4.6 DIVERSIFICATION

The meaning of the word diversification is very simple. As soon as a manufacturer offers more than one product, it is described as product diversification. Generally, diversification is categorised into two types:

1. Related diversification
2. Unrelated diversification.

Where the new products introduced in the product mix are similar to the existing product, diversification is described as 'related'. When a company accepts new product which are very different from the existing products, the diversification is said to be unrelated.

Related diversification

Related diversification is the commonest form of diversification, inexpensive and easier. However, in our earlier discussion Hindustan Lever, we can also include other brands of soaps or cleaning materials such as Vim, Surf, or Rin, manufactured by this company as part of related diversification strategy. So far, the relatedness of the products is quite clear. However, this relatedness is sometimes stretched to include other similar items. For example, in case of Hindustan Lever, toiletries would also be included under related diversification. For example, Hindustan Lever produces signal and Close-up toothpaste.

Some of the probable reasons for companies undertaking related diversification are:

1. to make a more effective use of the existing selling and distribution facilities
2. to use its under-utilised production capacity
3. to meet varied customer needs
4. to take advantage of its existing reputation in a particular type of products, and
5. to increase the sale of existing products.

Do you know why Gillette company launched their razor? Surprisingly the answer was not to make more profits through this extra product namely the razor, but to increase the sale of their blades.

Unrelated Diversification

When the new products offered or introductions are quite different from the existing ones, the company is said to have adopted the strategy of unrelated diversification. For example, if a consumer products' manufacturer diversifies into the manufacturer of raw materials such as chemicals or industrial products, such diversification would be described as un-related diversification. This naturally involves heavier costs and management challenges. This is the reason why related diversification is more popular.

Hindustan Lever was basically a consumer products company. It was forced into unrelated diversification because of its desire to grow in the face of Foreign Exchange Regulations Act and Industrial Licensing Policy. Today, this company is a leading manufacturer of sodium tripoly phosphate (STPP), glycerine, nickel catalyst and fine chemicals. It is also producing a plant growth nutrient, a product of its own research innovation branded 'Paras' it is supposed to increase cereals and vegetable yields considerably. Thus, this company has now diversified into unrelated products. Take another well-known company which has a varied product mix–Godrej, it not only makes cosmetics, but also steel furniture, animal feeds and its popular locks. It can be seen that this company has also adopted unrelated diversification as its product mix strategy.

Integrated Diversification or Integration

Backward integration is a term applied where a company diversifies and manufactures products which it previously purchased, that is, industrial products. For example, a company may start manufacturing what it uses as raw materials for its final products. Previously these raw materials was purchased from outside. Now the company has decided to be independent of outsiders and so indulges in backward integration.

The term **forward integration** applies when a company decides to go forward into starting its own distribution system from mere manufacturing. In this way, it gains independence with regard to retail outlets. Bata brand of shoes are largely retailed through company controlled outlets.

At times the expression "**horizontal integration**" is also used. This is where the company starts buying up and getting control over its competitors.

However, it must be remembered that any type of integration or diversification involves several questions, the most important of which concern cost, the possibility of profits, the extent of competition and the ability to meet it and the risk involved. In the final analysis, the product mix strategy or the diversification strategy of an organisation must fit into the organisation's long-term objectives in terms of profits growth and sales stability.

4.7   BRAND AND BRAND DECISIONS

A brand is a name, term, sign, symbol, or design, or a combination of them, intended to identify the goods or services of one seller or group of sellers or group of sellers and differentiate them from those of competitors.   - *American Marketing Association*

Thus, brand identifies the seller or a maker. Under trademark law, the seller granted exclusive rights to the use of the brand name in perpetuity. This differs from other assets such as patents and copyrights which may have expiry dates.

Many consumers' products, their basic features, need attractive packing and a 'brand name'. A brand is a symbol or a mark that helps customers in instant recall, differentiating it thereby from the competing products of a similar nature.

What is the brand?

Too often even marketing professionals don't have an answer and too many have their 'own' answers which make life very confusing. We've trawled though our resources to find some of the best definitions: the dictionary of business and management defines a brand *as a name, sign or symbol used to identify items or services of the seller(s) and to differentiate them from goods of competitors.*

Definitions

According to the American Marketing Association, "A brand name is a part consisting of a word, letter, groups of words or letters to identify the goods or services of a seller or a group of sellers and to differentiate them from those of the competitors."

David Ogilvy defined a brand is not necessarily positive! Building from this idea of a 'mental box' a more poetic definition might be: these are all great definitions, but we believe the best is this: "A brand is a collection of perceptions in the mind of the consumer. A brand is the most valuable real-state in the world, a corner of the consumer's mind". Why is the best? Well, first of all it is easy to remember, which is always useful! But it is also best because it works to remind us of some key point.

This definition makes it absolutely clear that a brand is very different from a product or service. A brand is intangible and exists in the mind of the consumer. This identification helps us understand the idea of brand loyalty and the 'loyalty ladder'. Different people have different perceptions of a product or service, which places them at different point of loyalty ladder. A brand mark is a symbol or a design used for the purpose of identification. For example: Air India's MAHARAJA. The legal version of a brand mark is the 'trademark' e.g., Ashok Masale and Good Health Atta. A brand is given legal protection from being used by others because it is capable of exclusive approbation. A brand distinguishes a product or service from similar offerings on the basis of names are: LUX, LIRIL, REXONA, EVITA, PROTEX, HAMAM and in case of toilet soaps; SURF, ARIEL and NIRMA in case of detergents and NIVEA, OIL OF OLEY, CHARMIS and VASELINE in case of vanishing creams.

The best brands convey a warranty quality, but a brand is even a more complex symbol. A brand can convey up to six levels of meaning.

- ❖ **Attributes:** A brand first brings to mind certain attributes. Thus, Mercedes suggests expensive, well-built, well-engineered, durable, high prestige, high resale value, fast, and so on.
- ❖ **Benefits:** A brand is more than a set of attributes. Customers are not buying attributes they are buying benefits. Attributes need to be translated into functional

and emotional benefits. The attribute durable could translate into the functional benefits.

❖ **Values:** The brand also says something about the producer's values. Thus, Mercedes stands for high performance, safety, prestige, and so on. The brand marketer must figure out the specific groups of car buyers who would be seeking these values.

❖ **Culture:** The brand may additionally represent a certain culture. The Mercedes represents German culture organised efficient high quality.

❖ **Personality:** The brand can also project a certain personality. If the brand were a person, an animal, or an object come to mind?

❖ **User:** The brand suggests the kind of consumer who buys or uses the product. We would be surprised to see a 20-year-old secretary driving a Mercedes. We would expect instead to see a 50-year-old top executive behind him.

All this suggests that a brand is a complex symbol. If a company treats a brand only as a name, it misses the point of branding. The challenge in branding is to develop set of meanings for the brand. When the audience can visualise all six dimensions of a brand, we call it a deep brand; otherwise it is a shallow brand. A Mercedes is a deep brand because we understand its meaning along all six dimensions. An Audi is a brand with less depth, since we may not grasp as easily its specific benefits, personality, and user profile.

Branding Decisions

Having an appropriate brand has emerged as the most important activity in the area of marketing of products especially consumers' products. Several decisions need to be taken, though not simultaneously, with regard to brand selection and its use. These are:

1. Should the product be branded at all?
2. Who should sponsor the brand?
3. What quality should be built into the brand?
4. Should each product be individually or family branded? Should other products be given the same brand name?
5. Should two or more brands be developed in the same product category?
6. Should the established brand be given a new meaning (repositioning)?

Let us consider each of these issues:

1. Whether to brand a product or not is a decision which can be taken only after considering the nature of the product, the type of outlets envisaged for the product, the perceived advantages for branding and the estimated costs of developing the brand. Historically, it is found that brand development is closely correlated with the

increase in the disposable income, the sophistication of the distributing system and the increasing size of the national market. The same trend is visible in India now. Even few years back, nobody could have thought of selling branded rice or refined flour, but several firms in the recent past have become successful even in such product categories. The basic reason is that a class of consumers is willing to pay more for uniform and better quality product represented by the brand. Irrespective of location and from which retailer they buy, customers are always buying the same product attributes when they buy a branded product. Many other such commodities, such spices are also now being branded.

2. The question of sponsorship of a brand refers basically to the decisions as to whether it should be a manufacturer's brand also known as a national brand or a private brand, also known as a middleman's brand. This is a major decision in most developed countries where large-chain departmental stores dominate the retail distribution system. Only super bazaars have started marketing few products which are specially packed and sold under their names. However, if outlets of Super Bazaars, Mother Dairy and National Consumer Cooperative Federation increases in sufficient numbers, it is possible that private brands will also become a reality in future. Some retailer's brand names in the product categories of sarees and car accessories have already been established.

3. A very crucial decision is with regard to the quality and other attributes to be built into the product. The matrix of such attributes will decide the product positioning. A marketer has the option to position his product at any segment of the market, top, bottom or the intermediate. Taking an example, Surf is positioned as a premium quality and high priced product.

4. The marketer also has to decide at the outset whether he would like to adopt a family brand under which all the products of the company would be sold or he would like to brand each product separately. Companies like GE or Philips follow the family name strategy, while GM follows the individual brand strategy. In India, L&T and Kissan are examples of the former, while HLL follows the latter.

These are advantages in either approach:

(a) Family Brand

(i) One of the basic advantages of using the family brand is that it reduces the costs of product launching and ongoing promotional expenditure substantially. The firm has to promise only one brand which, if successful, would be able to sell the entire product line. Lining up the distribution channel members also becomes comparatively easier. A family brand name has been found to be very cost-effective in tyre marketing.

(ii) If one product does exceptionally well, it is perfectly possible that there would be positive fallouts for other products being marketed under the same brand.

(iii) It is however necessary to be cautious following this strategy. It will be a very ill advised strategy if the products being offered are of highly uneven quality. It may not be a good strategy if the marketers are quite dissimilar in terms of consumer profile.

(iv) A greater weakness of this strategy is that it does not recognise that each product can be given a specific identify by a suitable brand which can go a long way to make it successful.

(b) Individual Brand

(i) The weakness, as pointed out above, becomes the principal strength of this strategy. Recent consumer researchers have irrefutably established that a name can have varied associations and conjure diverse images. These psychological factors can immensely influence the buying decisions. Individual brand strategy is in a position to take care of this aspect of marketing.

(ii) The second advantage of this strategy is that if there is a product failure, its damaging effect will be limited to that particular product and will not extend to the entire product line.

(iii) The basic disadvantage lies in the economics of developing an individual brand. It is obviously a costlier strategy than the other.

Courtesy: Maggi

(iv) The other disadvantage is that the brand does not directly derive any benefits from the reputation of a firm.

To take care of these problems, some firms follow a slightly modified strategy. This involves using individual brands but also giving prominence to the company name or logo in all promotional campaigns as well as in product packaging. For example, TOMCO follows individual brand strategy but displays prominently the words. A TATA PRODUCT in many cases a brand extension strategy is adopted. This is really an effort on the part of the manufacturer to secure additional mileage from a particularly successful product for launching either similar or even dissimilar product under the same brand. A recent successful example is the decision to introduce MAGGI range of sauces to capitalise on the image of Maggi brand of noodles.

(v) A firm may decide several brands of the same product which to some extent are competing inter se. The basic reason is that, at least in the consumer products, various benefits and appeals and even marginal differences between brands can win a large following group of customers.

Brand Repositioning

Over the life cycle of a product, several market parameters might undergo a change such as introduction of competing products, shifts in consumer preferences, identification of new needs, etc. All and each of such changes call of a relook as to whether the original positioning of the product is still optimal or not. Stagnating or declining sales also point to a need for reassessment of the original product positioning. For example, Thums Up has been repositioned several times in the recent past, from the young to the professional to the kids and back to the young.

Branding advantages and disadvantages

Branding as an aspect of product marketing can be analysed from two different standpoints. That of buyers and sellers.

(a) **Buyers:** The buyers can drive several advantages
   (i) A brand generally denotes uniform quality.
   (ii) It makes shopping easier.
   (iii) Competition among brands can, over a period of time, lead to quality improvements.
   (iv) Purchasing a socially visible brand can give psychological satisfaction to the buyer.

(b) **Sellers:** A marketer can also derive certain advantages such as

   (i) It helps in product identification.

  (ii) In a highly competitive market, it can carve out a niche for itself through product differentiation.

 (iii) If brand loyalty can be developed through successful promotion, the firm will be able to exert quasi-monopolistic power.

But to obtain the advantages, it is necessary for the manufacturers to invest resources in promoting brand name.

Selecting a brand name

Finding an appropriate name for a new product is a tricky job, basically for two reasons. First, the name should be one which satisfies several marketing criteria some of which are discussed below. Secondly, the name should not be one which is already being used by another firm. The necessitates extensive investigation.

Marketing Criteria: There is no simple solution to the name selection problem. However, though extensive research and accumulated past experience, market researcher have developed certain principles which should be followed:

1. A brand name should reflect directly or indirectly some aspect of the product, viz, benefit, function, etc. For example, the name 'BURNOL' immediately connotes that the product has to do something with burns.

2. A brand should be distinctive, especially if the product requires such distinction. Example: a name like 'CHANCELLOR' for a cigarette conjures up ideas of status, power and opulent lifestyle.

3. A brand name should be easy to pronounce and remember. Examples are VIMAL, HAMAM, etc.

4. It should be such that it can be legally protected, if necessary.

A firm invests substantial amount of money on a brand. It should, therefore, ensure that nobody else takes advantage of the brand illegally. Though there is no foolproof system for trademark position, the steps, as outlined below, can be of substantive help:

1. Use the generic name of the product in association with the trademark. An example is PEARL, PET were PET is the acronym for generic technical product, i.e. Polyethylene Terephthalate while PEARL is the brand associated.

2. Design the brand name as a trademark by actual notice. If the mark is registered, the proper form of notice is the letter R ® enclosed in a circle.

3. Display the mark with some form of special graphic treatment. A trademark is not a noun; therefore, it can be capitalised. If it can be printed in some distinctive logotype, so much the better.

4. Do not use the trademark in the wrong grammatical form. It should not be used as a noun, verb, in the plural, or in the possessive.

5. The trademark should not be altered by additions or abbreviations.

6. Use the trademark for a line of products.

4.8   PACKAGING

Earlier, packaging was considered a major expense in marketing. For some toiletries, packaging costs actually exceeded the costs of contents. Today, it is however, fully recognised that packaging helps in branding and promoting brand loyalty. It also enables the buyers to handle and carry their products with case. Moreover, packaging may cut marketing costs thus adding to profit.

Qualities of Good Packaging

✦ Attractive appearance
✦ Convenient for storage and display
✦ Shield against damage or spoiling
✦ Product description shown on the package.

Function of Packaging Especially for Consumer Goods

1. Protection and presentation are the basic functions of a packaging.
2. Modern marketing methods demand that package be convenient to handle transport requirements.
3. A package must be made to consistent and rigid quality standards. The consumer demands uniformity each time he purchases a product.
4. Transport economics.
5. Every package must be recognisable
6. Every package must have eye appeal.

Packing should satisfy the following conditions:

(a) It should be capable of withstanding the hazards of handling and transport. The cargo may be handled manually and mechanically. The handling methods may differ between places. When manually handled, it may be tilted, draped, thrown, pulled, pushed, rolled, etc. Further it may also be subject to compression due to stacking.

The packing should, therefore, be capable of withstanding such hazards of handling and transportation.

(b) It should be easy to handle. To facilitate easy handling, bulk packs may be provided with handling facilities like hooks, handles, grippers, etc. In case of products which shall not be turned upside down, the position should be clearly indicated like marking 'this side up'. In case of fragile articles, which shall not be subject to rough handling, the size, shape and weight of the pack should be amendable for smooth handling. Further, it should also be indicated on the pack.

(c) It should be amendable to quick examination of contents. It may be remembered that the customs authorities of the exporting and importing countries may want to examine the contents.

(d) It should be easy to identify.

(e) It should be adequately marked.

(f) Unless it is necessary, the contents shall not be disclosed.

(g) It should be easy to dispose of.

(h) Packing must conform to the buyer's specifications, if any and the regulations in the exporting and importing countries, guidelines and regulations by the shipping company, etc. Care should be taken to observe the established has prescribed packing standards for certain goods. The British standard packing code, published by the British Standards Institution and Exporters Encyclopedia, USA, give detailed packing instruction. Shipping companies also given certain packing instructions especially for highly dangerous products. According to the products he intends to export, the exporter has to choose the right type of packing to send the goods in good condition to the destination. A right package always guarantees the right quality of the product at the time of delivery.

Role of Packaging

1. It helps increase sales
2. It adds to the use of a product
3. It helps promote a product
4. It contributes to the safety of a product
5. It helps in storage
6. It helps in product differentiation.

Packaging Decisions

Packaging Design

It is not easy to design a package for various items. For example, all shaving creams come in tubes, but different brands of shaving cream have different packaging. Because of the high cost of packaging some companies have resorted to refill packs.

Colour

Colour is an important factor for determining customer acceptance or rejection of a product. The use of right colours in packaging may help marketers reap huge advantage. Packaging color should be attractive so that it may help promote sales.

Packaging the Product Line

A company must decide whether to develop a family resemblance in the packaging of its several products. Families packaging involves the use of identical packages for all products or the use of packages with some common feature.

Packaging and Sales Promotion

Product package often plays an important role in implementing sales promotion campaigns. Promotion is defined as a short-term special measure to boost sales of a specific product. There are several accepted promotional packaging techniques. Some of these are:

(a) Money off Pack: A 'flash' in distinctive colour is superimposed on the package, announcing the special price discount being offered. This is the most widely used form.

(b) Coupon Pack: A coupon, either as a part of the package or placed separately in the package, of a certain value can be redeemed after the purchase of the product.

(c) Pack in Premium: A premium, i.e., the gift packed within the original product package, viz., a handkerchief in a cosmetic product package.

(d) Premium Package: A specially made package having either a reuse or prestige value, instant coffee packed in glass tumblers having closures is an example of the first type.

(e) Self-liquidator: The buyer has to send a number of packages or parts thereof as evidence of buying the product to the company. In return, he may purchase additional quantity of the same product at reduced prices or be rewarded with a different product. Several companies in India, in the processed foods and beverages industry, occasionally use this technique.

(f) Other applications of packaging as a marketing tool: There are several other innovative ways of packaging that can be used for achieving higher sales. In the area which can guarantee a higher shelf life would be one up on its competition. A new Indian company, Tasty Bite Eatables which is in the area of frozen and pre-cooked foods, identifies the 18th months shelf life of its products as the major strength. The increased shelf life is to a large extent due to better packaging.

Introduction of a new package can also be used as a promotional technique. Till the very recent past, edible oils were packed in tin cans in India which looked messy and dirty. Packaging can also be used ingeniously to avoid direct price comparison with the competing products. This is done by a deliberate choice of odd size, while the competing brands follow a standard size. A recent example in India is the case of Maggi Ketchup which was introduced in the market in 400 grams bottle, while the industry-wise standard size is 500 grams bottle.

Legal Dimensions of Packaging

While managing the packaging function, constant attention needs to be given to the various regulations that the government has laid down in this respect. Government regulations are many and encompass areas such as the use of a specific packaging material for certain products. Among these is the regulations relating to the information and manufacturer is obliged to provide in the package itself on the product. This is commonly known as labelling requirement and covers a host of commodities. Principles among these are food products, cosmetics, pharmaceuticals, etc. Label is regarded as part of marketing because packaging decision-making involves the consideration of the labelling requirements. In international trade, many countries insist that labelling should be done in the absence of such a statutory requirement. Statutory obligations are important aspects of labelling. Many countries have laid down labelling requirements in respect of a number for commodities. According to the regulations labelling of food items should disclose information about a number of aspects like date of manufacturing, expiry date or optimum storage period for good which do not have an indefinite storage period, composition, storage conditions, necessary method of use, if necessary, etc.

A good label is one which helps a potential buyer to make his decision by providing relevant and correct information. Apart from the information which must be statutorily given, the label should therefore provide

(a) Picture of the product, accurate as to size, colour and appearance
(b) Description of raw products used along with methods of processing
(c) Directions for use, including cautions against misuse
(d) Brand name.

Statutory requirements

(a) Net weight, when packed
(b) Date of manufacture
(c) Date of expiry
(d) Maximum retail price including or excluding local taxes
(e) Directions for storage.

4.9   PRODUCT LIFE CYCLE (PLC)

We can now focus on the product life cycle. The product life cycle portrays distinct stages in the sales history of a product. Corresponding to these stages are distinct opportunities and problems with respect to marketing strategy and profit potential. By identifying the stage that a product is in, or may be headed toward, companies can formulate better marketing plans.

To say that a product has a life cycle is to assert things:

- ❖ Products have a limited life.
- ❖ Product sales pass through distinct stages, each posing different challenges to the seller.
- ❖ Profits rise and fall at different stages of the product life cycle.
- ❖ Products require different marketing, financial manufacturing, purchasing, and personnel strategies in each stage of their life cycle.

Most discussions of product life cycle (PLC) portray the sales history of a typical product as following an S-shaped curve which has been represented in Fig. 4.2. This curve is typically divided into four stages, known as introduction, growth, maturity, and decline.

- **Introduction:** A period of slow sales growth as the product is introduced in the market. Profits are non-existent in this stage because of the heavy expenses of product introduction.
- **Growth:** A period of rapid market acceptance and substantial profit improvement.
- **Maturity:** A period of a slowdown in sales growth because the product has achieved acceptance by most potential buyers. Profits stabilise or decline because of increased marketing outlays to defend the product against competition.
- **Decline:** The period when sales show a downward drift and profits erode.

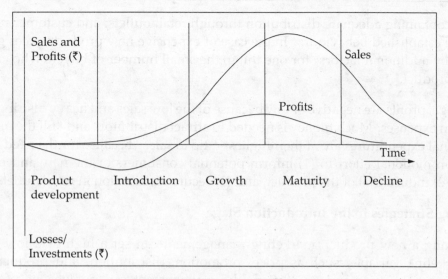

Fig. 4.2 Product life cycle.

Designating where each stage begins and ends is somewhat arbitrary. Usually, the stages are marked where the rates of sales growth or decline become pronounced. Polli and Cook proposed an operational measure based on a normal distribution of percentage changes in real sales from to year.

Those planning to use the PLC concept must investigate the extent to which the PLC concept describes product histories in their industry. They should check the normal sequence of stages and the average duration of each stage. Cox found that a typical ethical drug spanned an introductory period of one month, a growth stage of six months, a maturity stage of 15 months, and a very long decline stage–the last because of manufacturers' reluctance to drop drugs from their catalogues. These stage lengths must be reviewed periodically. Intensifying competition is leading to shorter PLC s over time, which means that products must earn their profits in a shorter period.

Rationale and Appropriate Market Strategies

Introduction Stage

The introduction stage starts when a new product is launched. It takes time to roll out the product in several markets and to fill the dealer pipelines, so sales growth is apt to be slow. Such well-known products as instant coffee, frozen orange juice, and powdered coffee creamers lingered for many years before they entered a stage of rapid growth. Buzzell identified several causes for the slow growth of many processed food products: delays in the expansion of production capacity; technical problems ("working out the bugs");

delays in obtaining adequate distribution through retail outlets; and customer reluctance to change established behaviours. In the case of expensive new products, sales growth is retarded by additional factors: for one thing, the small number of buyers who can afford the new product.

In this stage, profits are negative or low because of the low sales and heavy distribution and promotion expenses. Much money is needed to attract distributors and "fill the pipelines." Promotional expenditures are at their highest ratio to sales "because for the need of a high level of promotional effort to (1) inform potential consumers of the new and unknown product, (2) induce trial of the product, and (3) secure distribution in retail outlets.

Marketing Strategies in the Introduction Stage

In launching a new product, marketing management can set a high or a low level for each marketing variable, such as price, promotion, distribution, and product quality. Considering only price and promotion, the management can pursue one of the four strategies shown in Fig. 4.3.

High   Promotion   Low

	High Promotion	Low
High Price	Rapid skimming strategy	Slow skimming strategy
Low	Rapid penetration strategy	Slow penetration strategy

Fig. 4.3 Four introductory marketing strategies.

A Rapid-Skimming Strategy consists of launching the new product at a high price and a high promotion level. The firm charges a high price in order to recover as much gross profit per unit as possible. It spends heavily on promotion to convince the market of the product merit even at the high price. The high promotion acts to accelerate the rate of market penetration. This strategy is made under the following assumptions; a large part of the potential market is unaware of the product; those who become aware are eager to have the product and can pay the asking price; and the firm faces potential competition and wants to build up brand preference.

A Slow Skimming Strategy consists of launching the new product at a high price and low promotion. The high price helps recover as much gross profit per unit as combination is expected to skim a lot of profit from the market. This strategy makes sense when the market is limited in size; most of the market is aware of the product, buyers are willing to pay a high price and potential competition is not imminent.

A Rapid-Penetration Strategy consists of launching the product at a low price and spending heavily on promotion. This strategy promises to bring about the fastest market penetration and the largest market share. This strategy makes sense when the market is large, the market is unaware of the product, most of the buyers are price sensitive, there is strong potential competition, and the company unit manufacturing costs fall with the scale of production and accumulated manufacturing experience.

A Slow-Penetration Strategy consists of launching the new product at a low price and low level of promotion. The low price will encourage rapid product acceptance; and the company keeps its promotion costs down in order to realise more net profit. The company believes that the market demand is highly price elastic but minimally promotion elastic. This strategy makes sense when the market is large; the market is highly aware of the product; the market is price sensitive; and there is some potential competition.

A company, especially the market pioneer, must choose a launch strategy that is consistent with its intended product positioning.

Growth Stage

The growth stage is marked by a rapid climb in sales. The early adopters like the product, and middle-majority consumers start buying the product. New competitors enter the market, attracted by the opportunities for large-scale production and profit. They introduce new product features and expand the number of distribution outlets.

Prices remain where they are or fall slightly insofar as the demand is increasing quite rapidly. Companies maintain their promotional expenditures the same or at a slightly increased level to meet competition and to continue to educate the market. Sales rise much faster, causing a decline in the promotion-sales ratio.

Profits increase during this stage as promotion costs are spread over a larger volume, and unit manufacturing costs fall faster than price declines owing to the "experience-curve" effect.

The rate of growth eventually changes from an accelerating rate to a decelerating rate. Firms have to watch for the onset of the decelerating rate in order to prepare new strategies.

Marketing Strategies in the Growth Stage

During this stage, the firm uses several strategies to sustain rapid market growth as long as possible.

- ☞ The firm improves quality and adds new product features and improved styling.
- ☞ The firm adds new models and flanker products.

☞ It enters new market segments.

☞ It increases its distribution coverage and enters new distribution channels.

☞ It shifts from product-awareness advertising to product-preference advertising.

☞ It lowers prices to attract the next layer of price-sensitive buyers.

The firm that proposes these market expansion strategies will strengthen its competitive position. But this improvement comes at an additional cost. The firm in the growth stage faces a tradeoff between high market share and high current profit. By spending money on product improvement, promotion, and distribution, it can capture a dominant position. It foregoes maximum current profit in the hope of making even greater profits in the next stage.

Maturity Stage

At some point, a product's rate of sales growth will slow down, and the product will enter a stage of relative maturity. This stage normally lasts longer than the previous stages, and it poses formidable challenges to marketing management. *Most products are in the maturity stage of the life cycle, and therefore most of marketing management deals with the mature product.*

The maturity stage can be divided into three phases. In the first phase, growth maturity, the sales growth rate starts to decline. There are no new distribution channels to fill, although some laggard buyers still enter the market. In the second phase, stable maturity, sales flatten on a per capita basis because of market saturation. Most potential consumers have tried the product, and future sales are governed by population growth and replacement demand. In the third phase, decaying maturity, the absolute level of sales now starts to decline, and customers start switching to other products and substitutes.

Marketing Strategies in the Mature Stage

In the mature stage, some companies abandon their weaker products. They prefer to concentrate their resources on their more profitable products and on new products. Yet they might be ignoring the high potential that many old products still have. Many industries widely thought to be mature–autos, motorcycles, television, watches, and cameras–were proved otherwise by the Japanese, who found ways to offer new values to customers. Marketers should systematically consider strategies of market, product, and marketing mix-modification.

Market Modification: The company might try to expand the market for its mature brand by working with the two factors that make up sales volume:

$$\text{Volume} = \text{number of brand users} \times \text{usage rate per user}$$

The company can try to expand the number of brand users in three ways:

✠ **Convert Nonusers:** The company can try to attract nonusers to the product. For example, the key to the growth of airfreight service is the constant search for new users to whom air carriers can demonstrate the benefits of using airfreight over ground transportation.

✠ **Enter New Market Segments:** The company can try to enter new market segments— geographic, demographic, and so on that use the product but not the brand. For example, Johnson & Johnson successfully promoted its baby shampoo to adult users.

✠ **Win Competitors' Customers:** The company can attract competitors' customers to try or adopt the brand. For example, Pepsi-Cola is constantly tempting Coca-Cola users to switch to Pepsi-Cola, throwing out one challenge after another.

Volume can also be increased by convincing current brand users to increase their annual usage of the brand. Here are three strategies:

✠ **More Frequent Use:** The company can try to get customers to use the product more frequently. For example, orange juice marketers try to get people to drink orange juice on occasions other than breakfast time.

✠ **More Usage per Occasion:** The company can try to interest users in using more of the product on each occasion. Thus, a shampoo manufacturer might indicate that the shampoo is more effective with two rinsings than one.

✠ **New and More Varied Uses:** The company can try to discover new product uses and convince people to use the product in more varied ways. Food manufacturers, for example, list several recipes on their packages to broaden the consumer's use of the product.

Product Modification: Managers also try to stimulate sales by modifying the product's characteristics. This can take several forms.

A strategy of quality improvement aims at increasing the functional performance of the product–its durability reliability, speed, and taste. A manufacturer can often overtake its competition by launching the new and improved machine tool, automobile, television set, or detergent. Grocery manufacturers call this a "pulls" launch and promote a new additive or advertise something as "stronger," "bigger," or "better". This strategy is effective to the extent that the quality is improved, buyers accept the claim of improved quality, and a sufficient number of buyers will pay for higher quality.

Marketing-Mix Modification: Product managers might also try to stimulate sales by modifying one or more marketing-mix elements. They should ask the following questions about the non-product elements of the marketing-mix in searching for ways to stimulate a mature product's sales:

- **Price:** Would a price cut attract new triers and users? If so, should the list price be lowered, or should prices be lowered through price specials, volume or early purchase discounts, freight absorption, or easier credit terms? Or would it be better to raise the price to signal higher quality?

- **Distribution:** Can the company obtain more product support and display in the existing outlets? Can more outlets be penetrated? Can the company introduce the product into new types of distribution channels?

- **Advertising:** Should advertising expenditures be increased? Should the advertising message or copy be changed? Should the media-vehicle mix be changed? Should the timing, frequency, or size of ads be changed?

- **Personal Selling:** Should the number or quality of salespeople be increased? Should the basis for sales force specialisation be changed? Should sales territories be revised? Should sales force incentives be revised? Can sales-call planning be improved?

- **Services:** Can the company speed up delivery? Can it extend more technical assistance to customers? Can it extend more credit?

Decline Stage

The sales of most product forms and brands eventually decline. The sales decline might be slow, as in the case of oatmeal; or rapid, as in the case of the Edsel automobile. Sales may plunge to zero, or they may petrify at a low level.

Sales decline for a number of reasons, including technological advances, consumer shifts in tastes, and increased domestic and foreign competition. All lead to overcapacity, increased price-cutting, and profit erosion.

As sales and profits decline, some firms withdraw from the market. Those remaining may reduce the number of product offerings. They may withdraw from smaller market segments and weaker trade channels. They may cut the promotion budget and reduce their prices further.

Unfortunately, most companies have not developed a well thought-out policy for handling their aging products. Sentiment plays a role:

But putting products to death—or letting them die—is a drab business, and often engenders much of the sadness of a final parting with old and tried friends. The portable, six-sided Pretzel was the first product. The company ever made. Our line will no longer be our line without it.

Logic also plays a role. Management believes that product sales will improve when the economy improves, or when the marketing strategy is revised, or when the product is improved. Or the weak product may be retained because of its alleged contribution to the sales of the company's other products. Or its revenue may cover out-of-pocket costs, and the company has no better use for the money.

Unless strong reasons for retention exist, carrying a weak product is very costly to the firm. The cost is not just the amount of uncovered overhead and profit. Financial accounting cannot adequately convey all the hidden costs: The weak product might consume a disproportionate amount of management's time; it often requires frequent price and inventory adjustment; it generally involves short production runs in spite of expensive setup times; it requires both advertising and sales force attention that might be better used to make the "healthy" products more profitable; its very unfitness can cause customer misgivings and cast a shadow on the company's image. The biggest cost might well lie in the future. Failing to eliminate weak products delays the aggressive search for replacement products.

Marketing Strategies during the Decline Stage

A company faces a number of tasks and decisions to handle its aging products.

Identifying the Weak Products

The first task is to establish a system for identifying weak products. The company appoints a product-review committee with representatives from marketing, R&D, manufacturing, and finance.

Determining Marketing Strategies

Some firms will abandon declining markets earlier than others. Much depends on the level of the exit barriers. The lower the exit barriers, the easier it is for firms to leave the industry, and the more tempting it is for the remaining firms to remain and attract the customers of the withdrawing firms. The remaining firms will enjoy increased sales and profits. For example, Procter & Gamble stayed in the declining liquid-soap business and improved its profits as the others withdrew.

In a study of company strategies in declining industries, Harrigan distinguished five decline strategies available to the firm:

- ❖ Increasing the firm's investment (to dominate or strengthen its competitive position)
- ❖ Maintaining the firm's investment level until the uncertainty about the industry is resolved.
- ❖ Decreasing the firm's investment level selectively, by sloughing off unprofitable cus-

tomer groups, while simultaneously strengthening the firm's investment in lucrative niches.

❖ Harvesting (or milking) the firm's investment to recover cash quickly.
❖ Divesting the business quickly by disposing of its assets as advantageously as possible.

The appropriate decline strategy depends on the industry's relative attractiveness and the company's competitive strength in that industry. For example, a company in an unattractive industry but possessing competitive strength should consider shrinking selectively. However, if the company is in an attractive industry and has competitive strength, it should consider strengthening its investment. Procter & Gamble on a number of occasions has taken disappointing brands that were in strong markets and restaged them.

P & G launched a "not oily" hand cream called Wondra that was packaged in an inverted bottle so the cream would flow out from the bottom. Although initial sales were high, repeat purchases were disappointing. Consumers complained that the bottom got sticky and that "not oily" suggested it wouldn't work well. P & G carried two restaging; First, it reintroduced Wondra in an upright bottle, and later reformulated the ingredients so they would work better. Sales then picked up.

P & G prefers restaging to abandoning brand names. P & G spokespersons like to claim that there is no such thing as a product life cycle, and they point to Ivory, Camay, and many other "dowager" brands that are still thriving.

If the company were choosing between harvesting and divesting, its strategies would be quite different. Harvesting calls for gradually reducing a product or business's costs while trying to maintain its sales. The first costs to cut are R & D costs and equipment investment.

The Drop Decision When a company decides to drop a product, it faces further decisions. If the product has strong distribution and residual goodwill, the company can probably sell it to a smaller firm.

Jeffrey Martin, Inc. bought several "worn-out" brands from Purex Corporation, including Cuticura, Bantron, and Doan's Pills and turned them around. Two Minnesota businessmen bought the Ipana toothpaste name and formula from Bristol-Myers; with no promotion, they sold $250,000 in the first seven months of operation.

If the company can't find any buyers, it must decide whether to liquidate the brand quickly or slowly. It must also decide on how much parts inventory and service to maintain for past customers.

4.10 PRODUCT PLANNING

Meaning of Product Planning

According to Kart H. Tietjen, "Product planning is an act of making out and supervising the search, screening, development and commercialisation of new products; the modification of existing lines, and the discontinuance of marginal or impossible items".

In the words of Prof. Dale Littler, "Product planning involves devising procedures to evaluate the performance of products and planning where necessary, of existing products, aimed at extending their lives: the deletion of those products which have reached the terminal stage of their lives; and the development and marketing of new products."

From the above definitions, it is clear that product planning is a process of deciding by a firm as to what type of products it should develop and sell in the market so that the product serves as an instrument to achieve the marketing objectives. It also involves close monitoring of the product behaviour and deciding whether it should be continued in the product line abandoned or modified so as to choose the changing consumer needs. In other words, product planning is a process of constantly reviewing and revising portfolio of a firm with the objective of securing a balanced sales growth, cash flow and risk. In short, product planning is the process of determining in advance that line of products which can secure maximum net returns from the market targeted.

Objectives of Product Planning

Product planning has certain objectives. Its main objectives are:

1. To design products on the basis of research input provided by marketing research to satisfy the needs and preferences of consumers.
2. To evaluate the performance of the existing products to find out their weaknesses and to modify or to eliminate them, if they are unprofitable.
3. To maintain well-designed product lines.
4. To utilise the firm's resources in sound and profitable product lines.
5. To strengthen the firm's marketing capacity and competing position.

Considerations to be borne in mind in the Product Planning Process

For the success of product planning, certain considerations have to be borne in mind in the product planning process. Those considerations are:

(i) Evaluation of product performance
(ii) Exploring possibilities of modifications of the existing products to meet the changing needs and preferences of consumers.

(iii) Devising strategies for diversification of product mix.

(iv) Devising strategies in product positioning.

(v) Development of new products.

4.11   PRODUCT DEVELOPMENT

Product development refers to the technical activities of product research, engineering and design. It requires the collective participation of production, marketing, engineering and research departments.

Decisions Involved in Product Planning and Development Process

The process of product planning and development involves taking decisions in number of areas. These decisions cover the following:

(a) What products the firm should manufacture in its plant, and what products it should buy in the market?

(b) In what quantity each of the products should be produced?

(c) Whether the firm should expand or simplify its products?

(d) How should each of the products of the firm be made more useful than before?

(e) How should the cost of the products be reduced so as to fix competitive prices for them?

(f) What sales policy the firm should follow to promote the sales of its products?

4.12   NEW PRODUCT DEVELOPMENT AND ITS STRATEGY

With advances in technology and intense competition, the creation of new products has become a way of life in India. However, being a developing country, India is yet to face a situation of too many products chasing a handful of customers. Moreover, the sheer size of the Indian market and the continuing economic development has opened up new vistas for launching new products. This lesson discusses new products development process in detail and also analyses the new product launches in India in the new millennium.

(a) New Products Launches

An analysis of new products development in the recent past shows that these products have been either offshoots of technological development in the west or improvement over the existing products in the areas of their, style, substance or packing. In the recent past, new product launches in India have shown that these launches can be broadly classified into three categories.

(b) Marketing Innovations

Companies have been improving on the existing products and have launched these as new products in the market. For instance, Maggi noodles, soft drink in tetra pack, Shrikh and Pan Parag, etc. are basically slightly alternated version of existing or old products. Here, consumers did not require changing their consumption habits drastically to accommodate these new products. These are examples of improvement in the products whose success was derived more from marketing innovation such as packing, branding and easy availability, rather than any significant change in the substance of the product itself.

(c) Product Improvement

The launch of 100 cc two-wheelers, radical types, pocket size cameras are basically slight innovations on the technology/design of the existing products, although the products category as such already existed in its primitive form. Such new products are generally targeted for a new class of buyers. The success of such ventures depends upon the ability of the marketers to convince the consumer about the improvement in the performance over traditional brand(s) as well as over similar new extract. For example, in the 100 cc two-wheelers vehicle market, TVS Suzuki was the entrant and it had captured a sizable market. Subsequently, Hero Honda became the market leader in this category of motorcycles by virtue of better performance and marketing techniques.

(d) Technological Innovations

The Indian market has experienced a rapid induction of products like personal computers, photocopiers and colour television. Generally, these products require some kind of assembling of improved kits. Although adaptation of such products calls for substantial change in the consumption pattern, yet these products have succeeded in view of their significant utility to the user. Such ventures require an initial awareness building and persuasion to install the product. Initial resistance to change may delay any adoption of new technologies. However, a look at the track record of such new product shows that early entrants have reaped the benefits of leadership. Subsequent entrants have faced difficulty in established themselves.

Sources of New Product Ideas

Customers: Customers are sometimes able to discuss their requirements and offer ideas that will meet those problems.

Competitors: Systematic comparison or benchmarking with the competition may offer good source of new product ideas.

Distributors: Suggestions from distributors and their problems in handling present products often thrown up new ideas.

Creative techniques: Brainstorming, focused interviews and technological forecasting enable one to find out the latent capabilities of innovations.

External world: The external world, especially the use of their technology, offers a good source of ideas for implementation in the home market.

Research and development: Create new product ideas through R&D. From initial generation of ideas to full commercialisation and well into the mature age of a product, the developers should strive to control what is in their power and to monitor what is beyond their control. No single facet of new product development can assure success. Few facets are so detrimental that they cannot be at least alleviated. Because of the probabilistic nature of new product development, planning and assessments must consider long-term repercussions.

Organisational Structure and Staffing

Given a clear strategy, it is necessary to build the organisational capability to meet the challenge. At times this is simply appointing a committee. Other times it is creating an entirely new team and physically separating it from the ongoing organisation. Selecting the right persons for such a team is difficult.

Concept Creation and Development

Once the enabling conditions of strategy and organisation are identified, actual ideation can begin. First, the team must focus on one area of interest or activity, specifically, a product category, a group of team may study floppy discs and try to improve them. Another team may try to find better ways to solve the problems of teachers. Or they may work to develop improved gold balls or golf balls or golf clubs. They may focus on their design capability and find new applications. Or they may focus on combinations of two or more of these areas.

Concept Development

Concept development involves asking question such as the following:

- ☞ **Need:** Do customers find a strong perceived need for the benefit offered?

- ☞ **Trust:** Do they believe that the new product has the benefits claimed?

- ☞ **Communicability:** Do customers easily understand the key benefits being offered?

- ☞ **Usage:** Does it offer easy adoption?

- ☞ **Perceived Value:** Do customers see it as offering value at the price being considered?

After the working area is defined, concept generation begins, often at a hectic pace. Ideas flow fast and in most cases rejection is equally fast. The team looks for the few fast and in most cases rejection is equally fast. The team looks for the few concepts that warrant concepts development–the evolving of an original ideation attempt into a specific statement of need, form and technology that can be evaluated.

Concept Evaluation

Often considered the heart of the new products process, the evaluation state is long, involved, and difficult. Evaluation actually begins when the strategist evaluates the organisation's abilities. And it continues long after a product is marketed since a product often needs revision to remain competitive. Concept testing and other pre-screening marketing research prepare the team for the actual screening evaluation. This evaluation is a full, detailed analysis of the proposal. If the concept passes screening, technical development begins. The technical work produces prototypes, which can then be evaluated and if all goes well, the finished product can be prepared for use testing. Next, the team joins the new product to its marketing plan for a test of them combined called market testing. All of the above data combine to permit a full financial analysis near the end of development.

Commercialisation

The management's decision that the new item is worth marketing either in a test market situation or in a full-scale launch is called the point of commercialisation. Pilot processes are then converted to full-scale manufacturing. Final design specifications are written. Marketing strategy is finalised, including actual brand, packaging, service commitment, etc. The team gradually moves the company from tentative exploration of a concept into production and marketing of a new product.

Review and Evaluation

After the launch the entire project must be reviewed to see how successful the team was, those problems they faced and what they can learn to facilitate the next project.

Analysis of New Product Launches in India

Empirical data suggests that in highly competitive markets such as in the US, the success rate of new launches, depending on the strictness of definition of success, varies from a low of two per cent to a high of 10 per cent. Markets in India are not as competitive as in the West and therefore, the success rate of new launches is likely to be healthier. A study by Abraham Koshy, revealed the following facts.

On an overall basis, out of all the new launches, 53 per cent were successes and the remaining 47 per cent were failures. This implies that, caterius paribus, even at an optimistic level, new launches are likely to have a probability of success of around 50 per cent. In reality, this proportion may even at an optimistic level, new launches in the country today, given the level competitiveness in the market and professionalism of companies, is likely to be less than 30 per cent! This is worse than even the odds when a coin tosses; no company can invest huge resources for new launches if the probability of success is so unfavourable. The message from this insight is clear when the chances of survival are so low; the only way to beat the odds is through a systematic and professional approach to managing new launches. Otherwise it is 50-50.

The mortality rates of new brands indeed tend to be high; only about 36 per cent of new products launched in the market with new brand names survived, the remaining 64 per cent were failures. This is indeed more unfavourable than the overall situation presented in the preceding paragraph. It means that if you do not have a strong brand to leverage and therefore, there is a need to build brand awareness and create brand preferences afresh, then you should be even more thorough in your new launch efforts. Life extensions and brand extensions were significantly more successful than the launch of new brands. Thus, 71 per cent of new launches that were line extensions and 63 per cent of brand extensions were successful in the marketplace. From one perspective, this suggests that your chances of success in a new launch are far greater if you leverage. From a different perspective, it also means that a levering strategy will not automatically guarantee you success; the results show that nearly a third of line extensions as well as brand extensions were failure. These in other words imply that even if you have strong brands, you need to be systematic in configuring your offer in tune with market needs. Inappropriate leveraging of brand names, leveraging weak brands and improper alignment of marketing mix elements are certified formulae for failures.

How can one Influence Success of New Launches?

A perplexing question that a practitioner is often confronted with is the reason for product failures. Marketing literature suggests several reasons for product failures. These reasons are broadly classified under product (or offer) related factors, market by the research team (or consumer) related factors, market by the research team related factors and competition related factors. The latter two reasons, namely, market related and competition related factors provide the context of a firm's marketing operations and hence these are the factors on which the firms can exert little control. All that a firm can do is to understand these given conditions and then align the total market offer based on these realities. And this is given where many firms slip rather badly. Findings of the study conducted by IIM, Kolkata provided interesting insights into the ways in which firms manage their new product activities.

Failure in Utilising/Adopting Marketing Research Technique

The fundamental condition to succeed in any market is a deep understanding of consumers and an excellent appreciation of competitors and their activities. This can come about only if your company has strong systems and methods, not only to collect and analyse market data, but also to disseminate the information thus obtained to relevant decision-makers within the organisation. Studies revealed that nearly 67 per cent of the executives noted that market research agencies are seldom utilised by their companies to collect market data in a formal and structured manner; only the remaining 33 per cent of companies either frequently or almost always used marketing research agencies. Granting that it may be somewhat costly to use market research agencies on a regular basis, the extent of utilisation of internal mechanisms to collect market data also does not seem to be very high. Nearly half the companies do not have strong formal mechanisms to collect systematic data on a regular basis from their own sales people and about a third of the companies rarely collect data from their retailers. If this is the general trend, then it is not very surprising that the success of new brand launches is low. The message, therefore, is that you need to review your internal systems and processes for gathering and utilising market data relating to your consumers and competitors to what your decisions become sharper and data based. Success otherwise will be elusive.

Failure in Identifying Market Opportunities for New Brand Launches

One of the weakest links in many organisations is the absence of any systematic approach for identifying market opportunities, either for introducing new brands and products, or for re-launching and/or repositioning of the existing products. A glimpse at the mindset of companies, obtained from the survey of executives suggests that in most companies, the major source of new products ideas is the top management. These efforts are supplemented with analysis of foreign technology/products or competitors' products. Seldom do companies obtain idea for new product launches from consumers. This is not surprising since the extent of utilisation of market research for new products development. The picture then becomes clearer for new product opportunities; companies depend either on the secondary technology available in some markets. There is hardly any serious and systematic effort to understand consumer's needs and requirement in the context of competing offers and naturally the market opportunities thus imagined to have existed turn out to be here mirages!

Failure in Integrating Customer's Choice/Ideas in New Product Offering

Consumers do not pay for mere ideas; they only buy tangible offers that satisfy their needs. Companies, therefore, need to translate their brilliant ideas for new brands and products into tangible offers that spell out the specific benefits that the new offer will provide, the needs that they will satisfy and the cost that the consumers will have to bear. This phase of transforming new ideas into tangible and viable market offer is very critical stage and is perhaps the stage where the firms commit major resource. But then can any firm take such major decisions without an assessment of likely consumer acceptance of the proposed new offer? In reality, unfortunately, many firms do not seem to be marking sufficient efforts in assessing consumers' reaction abut the new proposal and thus estimating the risks involved before investing huge resource to develop new offers. Further findings of the study suggest that 44 per cent of the firms do not carry out a formal concept testing and another 30 percent do it only occasionally.

Data further suggests that 53 per cent of the companies never or seldom make a assessment of the financial viability of the proposed new products/brand before proceeding further with introduction plans. These indications suggest that many firms let pass occasion's access consumer preference carefully and fine-tune their proposal to reflect the value propositions of consumers. They slide over issues like leverage strengths of brands and appropriateness of equity of the brand for the proposed new product. Many a times firms even underplay the question as to whether or not the whole scheme makes the commercial sense. Given such limited insight into the likely future potential of the new venture, companies end up courting disaster. In fact, many sad endings could have been averted if only companies showed little more diligence in assessing consumer reactions to the new proposal and estimating commercial viability before making major resource commitments.

Failure in Product Testing

If the core product that you are offering to consumers does not provide the functional benefits that it is intended to provide, then no amount of advertisement or publicity can salvage the situation. Therefore, it is extremely important to ensure that the basic product meets consumer requirement.

Research data revealed that nearly 56 per cent of companies do test their products either frequently or almost always. Out of the remaining, 44 per cent either never or rarely test their products. In all probability, the proportion of your offer, you do not have much to worry. However, even a good product will not survive if it needs to be made either before the investment in manufacturing and/or later. Many new brand failures in India today are more failures of concept rather than failures of basic product.

This observation suggests that you not only need to test the product to ensure that the functional performance under the laboratory as well as field conditions is satisfactory, but also it does address the felt needs of consumers better than competitors. This is also an activity, which will provide valid inputs to assess the likely market acceptance of the proposed new brand by way of volume prediction. This input certainly helps in assessing commercial viability of the proposal. Research findings suggest that most of the firms carry out some financial analysis at this stage.

New Product Development Strategy

Many products fail and in order to keep expanding company sales, we must have new products. Some products of Hindustan Lever have failed, but still they remain leading manufacturers because they have continuously added to their lines and added product lines to their product mix. Their **'HIMA'** peas introduced in the 60s flopped, because, in the words of the Chairman of Hindustan Lever, 'India is not yet ready for convenience food, neatly done up in packages.' The product 'concept' requires testing before one goes into product designing and it is very necessary to have an adequate strategy for developing new products and introducing them. Several stages must be defined. Figure 4.4 gives the stages in new product development. These will now be discussed in detail.

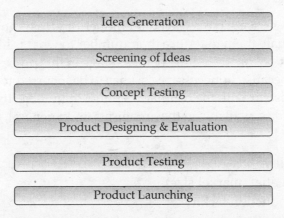

Fig. 4.4 Stages in new product developments.

Generation of New Product Ideas

The first step obviously is to get ideas with regard to possible new products. Can you think of the sources from which you can get such product ideas? Your answer should have been: customers, company salesman, competitors, company executives, and employees within the organisation including technical people.

As marketing is aimed at satisfaction of consumer needs, an alert marketer can get some ideas from the customers for possible new products by keeping his eyes and ear open and more particularly the mind to perceive even needs which are so far unexpressed. For example, in case of refrigerators, someone conceived the idea of having a 'two-door' refrigerators, someone conceived the idea of the ballpoint, which obviated the need for constantly filling fountain pens. Thus, new ideas can come from customer needs or problems requiring solution.

Company salesmen are in excellent position help. This is because they are in constant touch with the market, that is, both consumers and competitors. Watching competitors and what they introduce can also be useful for new ideas. Finally, company executives and even the lower staff can be brought in for discussions. The interesting method here is what is known as brainstorming. This is basically done to have a flow of ideas—good and bad. A number of people, say executives of the organisation, are called together and asked a question for new ideas or ideas for new products. They are asked to mention it without evaluation. None is criticised. The answers are recorded on a tape recorder so that the flow is not interrupted. Thereafter, the answers generated are evaluated as will be explained in the next stage.

Evaluation or Screening of the Ideas

So far, from the first stage, we have received a number of ideas—good and bad. We have now to screen and evaluate them to reduce their number to what is likely to be useful. This is known as the 'evaluation' or 'screening' of ideas stage in this process. Poor ideas must be dropped immediately because unnecessary cost has to be incurred to process them further. The ideas must be consistent with the company's philosophy, objectives and strategies and be in terms of the resources available in the organisation. In general, the ideas are screened in terms of

1. Possible profitability
2. Good market potential (market size)
3. Availability of production facility
4. Availability of raw materials for such a product, if selected
5. Availability of finance
6. Availability of managerial ability
7. Uniqueness of product.

Product Concept Development and Evaluation

Particularly when the product idea is rather revolutionary, the concept itself must be tested. For example, people talk about 'battery driven car's to save on petrol. This is a concept which has to be tested in the environment in which the product is sought to be introduced. As already indicated. Hindustan Lever failed with their Hima peas and fast foods. This was a failure of concept testing. The mention of the failure of Hindustan Lever is not to run down the performance of this excellent company but to emphasise that good companies introduce a number of products some of which may fail.

The introduction by Parle's of the **'Big Bite'** (the hamburger) did fail in some of the regions in Indian market. Was this due to wrong concept? The answer is probably in the negative.

The failure was because the customer got 'soggy' hamburgers at the retail end. Thus, there was lack of 'quality control' at the level of the retail outlets which did not supply freshly cooked hamburgers. So you can see that even if the concept is accepted, a failure can take place in other areas resulting in the ultimate failure of the product itself. This did not deter the company from going further. Parles introduced **Frooti** and **Appy** which are fruit based soft beverages. These are offered in tetra packs. Thus, there is an innovation. The question of whether tetra packs, as packaging material, will succeed in India or not is a question of concept testing of the package.

Product Designing and Evaluation

If the product idea or the concept passes the test, we then proceed to the engineering or the production or the R&D stage. So far what we had was only a description or an idea. Now this has to be converted into a product. Prototypes are developed and tested. The test can be done under laboratory or field conditions. At this stage of product development, the technical problems, if any, must be solved. This is because the product must not suffer from complaints regarding quality in use. Even a small defect might shorten the life cycle of the product as well as spoil the company's image.

Product Testing Stage

Apart from mechanical performance, customer acceptance is essential. In fact, the following can be stated as **requirements for the new product**, after it is designed:

1. Satisfactory performance

2. Customer acceptance

3. Economical production

4. Adequate distribution

5. Adequate servicing arrangements where required

6. Effective packaging and branding.

A market test should, therefore, be conducted before launching the new product. This will help us find out whether the product can be launched successfully on a commercial scale or not.

Launching the New Product

The test marketing may show up something as depicted in Fig. 4.5.

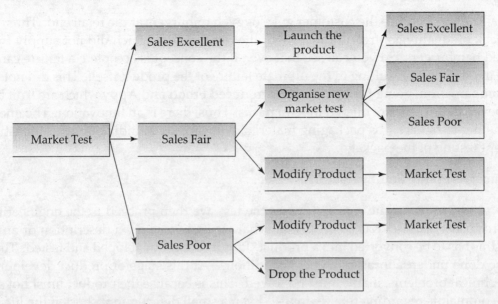

Fig. 4.5 Market test decision tree alternative decisions.

It may show that the sales are 'excellent', in which case, our decision is easy and we can proceed to launch the product. As against this, if it shows that the sales are 'poor', there are generally two alternatives available from a particular viewpoint. We can drop the product or modify it and test it again. If the sales are 'fair', we may modify the product or conduct a new market test. The latter is done when we feel that perhaps there is something wrong with the market test just completed.

An alternative, generally available, is to modify the product in terms of the feedback which has been received from the market test, and then test again before the final decision is taken to launch the product commercially or to drop it. One must, however, remember that constant testing involves further costs. A decision must, therefore, be arrived at as early as practicable.

Hence, we can say that the introduction of a new product is not an easy decision. It has to be weighed very carefully in terms of possible markets, the costs involved and the potential profits.

The question of timing, sometimes, is also relevant. Should the company be the first one to offer a new 'novel' product on the market? In case of small companies, if they do so, they are at a distinct advantage. However, large companies can afford to wait. For example, Philips entered the stereo hi-fi system market relatively later. However, they were able to introduce an attractively priced product, and quickly gained product acceptance because of their long-standing reputation in the market.

The Future of New Products Management

In the new millennium, we are seeing more segmentation there will be even more competition for almost everyone than there is today; and life cycles of products will continue to get shorter or stay short. Similarly, most of the forces acting to increase the costs of innovation will remain high or will increase. In most instances productivity will increase as all producers focus so intently on it as the path to lower costs and higher quality product. On the positive side, three forces acting to at least partially forces acting to at least partially offset the negative forces described above. All three of these positive forces will get stronger, not weaker.

The first, technology, is the strongest of all and that there is little left to invent; we know that this is simply not so. Computerisation, automated manufacturing, molecular biology, fibre optics and surface ceramics are just a few of many fields that offer what almost certainly will be more technological opportunities in the next 25 years than in the past 50. Molecular biology has the potential for outstripping anything else done so far in this century. Moreover, there is an amazing move to invest large sums of money in older technologies, especially in the so-called mature industries. And as a final plus international opportunity continues to grow and contribute new markets, new skills and new concepts of management.

The second positive force is the general willingness of consumers to accept new items otherwise there is absolutely no basis for forecasting. And third, management's general capability has been growing almost exponentially, particularly by taking advantage of the many MBAs entering the workforce and the wide array of continuing education opportunities for managers today. The combined results of these negative and positive forces are mixed, of course, but the negatives had no perceived effect on the development and marketing of home video systems or on the development of new drugs in recent years.

KEYWORDS

Benefits: Physical or psychological offered to a customer.

Brand Name: A word, letter or a group of words or letters representing a product or service of the company.

Branding: Use of a name, term symbol and/or design to identify a product.

Consumer Goods: These are goods which are purchased by the ultimate consumer or user and require no further commercial processing.

Diversification: *This implies that a company has moved from one product item to marketing more than one product.*

Decline Stage: *It is the stage in the product life cycle where the sales and profits shoot down.*

Family brand: *A brand name which is used for several products belonging to the same company.*

Fads: *These are novelty products that come quickly to the public eye and are lost fast. Here the product life cycle is very brief.*

Growth Stage: *It is the stage in the product life cycle when the sales and profits increase happily for the organisation.*

Introduction Stage: *It is the stage where the product is just introduced and is at the beginning of the product life cycle. This is evidenced by slow growth and very small profits.*

Market Testing: *It is the stage where the product is actually tested in the market that is introduced in a consumer setting with a view to ascertain the reactions of consumers and dealers before a final decision to market or launch the product is made.*

Maturity Stage: *It is the stage in the life cycle where the sales stop going up and down because competitors have entered the market and it becomes difficult for a continuous increase in the sales.*

Product or Goods: *A composite of the characteristics and features—physical and psychologist which are offered for purchase by a customer, weather it is a consumer or an industrial purchaser*

Product Item: *Refers to a specific product or a brand.*

Product Line: *It relates to a group of products which are closely related as satisfying a class of need.*

Product Addition: *Adding closely related products or another brand of the same product to the existing product line is called product addition.*

Product Deletion: *Deleting or dropping a group of closely related products or one or more of the brands of the same products from the existing product line.*

Product Mix: *A composite of products which are offered for sale by an organisation and may consist of different types of products related and unrelated.*

Trademark: *Only those words, symbols or marks that are legally registered by company which has the exclusive right to their use.*

SUMMARY

Every product or service must offer certain benefit or benefits in the prospects or likely customer either to satisfy some need or solve problems. Different types of products require different marketing strategies. Personnel selling are an important input in marketing of industrial products, whereas promotion and distribution are of critical importance in case of consumer products. You must have noticed that the area of product planning, product line decision-making and arriving at proper product strategy is an extremely exciting and interesting field. It is challenging and, if not done properly, can result in losses in the organisation.

The product life cycle concept is an extremely important one which, at times, is neglected by even well-known companies. While one may like to add new products to the company's product mix, it should be remembered that it is an expensive process. However, it must be done and one must go through the proper steps.

After the product is properly designed and it is felt that it is appropriate for the markets, it must be actually tested in the market before the final decision is made to launch the new product. After the new product is launched it must be watched throughout its life cycle.

Brand management is one of the most important areas of marketing especially with reference to consumer products. The name gives the product its unique personality, and is so well associated with the product that the brand name sometimes even takes the place of the generic product name Surf and Dalda are two classic examples where the brand names connote the generic product category, i.e., detergent and Vanaspati respectively.

Packaging is another crucial aspect of marketing which plays an important role in determining the success of a product. Marketing decisions such as those related to pricing, distribution are not so obviously critical from the customers viewpoint simply because he is not so aware of them, but the implications of packaging decisions are obvious since the customer confronts is face-to-face.

The other legal requirement is regarding labelling wherein you are required to provide complete and accurate information about the product contents, its usage, possible side effects, and date of manufacture and expiry.

ASSIGNMENT

Assignment-1

What is a motor car manufacturer selling? Put a check mark (✓) against the correct answer. If you feel the answer is something different, put a check mark in the 'any other' portion and then write what you mean

1. Assembled pieces of metal, rubber, paint and other materials   ( )
2. A mass of molecules   ( )

3. A symbol of economic and social status   ( )
4. Transportation   ( )
5. Any other, please specify   ( )

Assignment-2

(a) Write down the types of products which come to your mind or the ones which you are selling:

_____

_____

_____

(b) Identify the customers in each case

_____

_____

_____

(c) How do they differ from one another

_____

_____

_____

Assignment-3

Identify product items in case of the following product lines of various organisations or brands

Brand/Organisation	Product Line	Product Item
Dunlop	Tyres	_____
Godrej	Soaps	_____
Brooke Bond	Package Tea	_____
Oscar	Colour TVs	_____
Telco	Light Commercial Vehicles	_____

Assignment-4

(i) Prepare a list of five family brands. Carefully analyse their products sold under each of these brands.

_____

_____

_____

(ii) Prepare a list of five companies which use different brands for their respective products. Identify their products.

_____

_____

_____

(iii) Based on (i) and (ii), find out what kinds of products have family and individual brands.

_____

_____

_____

(iv) Do you think branding decision in each case is rational one? If yes, why? If not why?

_____

_____

Assignment-5

Identify a leading brand in respect of the products mentioned below. What image is usually associated with these brands by their users?

Product	Leading Brand	Associated Brand
1. Tyre	_____	_____
2. Pen	_____	_____
3. Toothpaste	_____	_____
4. Bread	_____	_____
5. Bicycle	_____	_____
6. Scooter	_____	_____
7. Personal Computer	_____	_____
8. PVC Resin	_____	_____
9. Intercom Instrument	_____	_____

Assignment-6

Identify at what stages of their respective product life cycle are the following products in Indian market context

Product	Stage
1) Colour television	_____
2) Mobile phones	_____
3) Luxury products	_____
4) Air conditioners	_____

CASE STUDY

In the processed meat industry, Sara Lee Meats (SLM) is a star. It owns and operates meat-processing plants in 40 different nations. SLM's business strategy includes product innovation, acquisitions and mergers, and market leadership in a number of different categories. Its growth strategies support an annual 6 per cent growth in sales. Important U.S. brands in the Sara Lee product line are Kahn's, Jimmy Dean, Hillshire Farms, Bryan, State Fair, Best's Kosher, and Tastefuls! According to SLM executive George Chivari, "We work very hard at Sara Lee on brand equity. We have to make sure our new ideas are not only profitable and achieve big volume for our [retail] customers, but also that they are consistent with the quality of the brand and there is a good fit." Tastefuls! is a product that SLM feels is a particularly good fit with the company's other products. The lunch combination features two small sandwiches, chips, and dessert and was developed and marketed by a subsidiary of SLM, Jimmy Dean foods. Up until the development and marketing of Tastefuls!, Jimmy Dean has just made produce sausage.

Questions

1. Given what you have read about Sara Lee Meats, you would think its executives want you to classify the SLM products as
2. One method SLM can use to maintain its brand equity would be to:

REVIEW QUESTIONS

1. Explain the following
   "people do not buy product they buy benefits"

2. Explain the meaning of product mix state the reasons why companies generally diversify their range of products.

3. Explain briefly the product life cycle concept, in marketing management and state why you feel it is useful to understand this concept.

4. Explain how marketing mix has to be changed during the different stages of PLC.

5. Selection and development of a new product are very important steps in the marketing strategy. Explain briefly stages through which you would test the ideas coming up for new products until the final stage of launching the new product.

6. What is product planning? Discuss the decisions involved in Product planning and Development process.

7. Define customer loyalty.

8. Identify the basic favours that prompt a company to brand its products. Select any well advertised brand of your choice and define the personality of that brand.

9. Do you consider branding to be identical importance in marketing (a) industrial products, (b) consumer products, and (c) agricultural products? Give supportive arguments.

10. What are the basic strategies to open a firm? Discuss their relative strengths and weaknesses?

11. One marketing expert strongly urged every manufacture to adopt a nonsense word as the brand what can be the reason for this recommendation?

PRICING STRATEGIES

STRUCTURE

- Introduction
- Determinants of Pricing
- Factors Influencing Pricing
- Pricing Objectives
- Pricing Policies and Constraints
- Consumer Psychology and Pricing
- Pricing over the Life Cycle of a Product
- New Product Pricing Strategies
- Price Sensitivity

5.1 INTRODUCTION

Price is an important element of the marketing mix. It can be used as a strategic marketing variable to meet the competition. It is also a direct source of revenue for the firm. It must not only cover the costs but leave some margin to generate profit for the firm. However, price should not be so high as to frighten the customers. Price is also an element that highly influences the customers and significantly affects their decisions to buy a product. In general, price directly determines the quantity to be sold. That is why electric fans are sold at lower prices and hotels reduce their tariffs during off-season period to attract customers.

In the competitive marketplace, pricing is a game. The struggle for market share focuses critically on price. Pricing strategies of competing firms, therefore, are highly interdependent. The price one competitor sets is a function not only of what the market will pay but also of what other firms charge. Prices set by individual firms respond to those of competitors; they also are intended often to influence competitors' pricing behaviour. All of marketing comes to focus in the pricing decision.

A way to think about making a pricing decision is that price should be set somewhere between what the product costs to make and sell and its value to the customer. If price exceeds the perceived value of the product to potential purchasers, it has no market. If the price is below what the product costs to produce, the business cannot survive for long. Where a price should be set between cost and customer value is a strategic decision. Many factors can influence this decision, viz., competitors' product/price strategies, governmentally imposed constraints and the seller's and the buyer's sense of what is fair. Finally, the most important determinant of price is the marketer's objectives—what is the firm trying to do.

Ancient philosophers recognised the importance of price in an economic system. Some early written accounts refer to attempts to determine fair and just prices. Price continues to serve as a means of regulating economic activity. All the four factors of production, viz., natural resources, capital, human resources and entrepreneurship, depend on the prices that those factors receive. An individual firm's prices and the resulting purchases by its customers determine how much revenue the firm receives. Prices, therefore, influence a firm's profits as well as its employment of the factors of production. Traditionally, price is the major determinant of buyer choice. This is still the case in the poorer economies and with commodity-type products. Although non-price factors have become more important in recent decades, price still remains one of the most important elements determining market share and profitability. Pricing has come to occupy centre-stage in many marketing rivalries. Many reasons can be attributed to this.

Some of them are outlined below:

✠ In some cases, product differentiation is getting blunted, thanks to the homogenisation of technology. This is more relevant in the context of global business where the million dollar question is whether the firms should offer a standardised offering or a differentiated offering.

- There is intense inter-firm rivalry in some industries. It may be attributed to the removal of entry/exit barriers. Also the cost of fighting these marketing wars must be recovered and often, it is transferred to the customer.

- In certain industries, the products and the markets are mature. The only way to differentiate may be through an augmented service or price cuts. Here again, pricing decisions are crucial to the survival of the firm.

- Customers' value perception correlates with the quoted price. To a customer, price always represents product's value. The price-quality perception must be taken into account during the product decision and the price decision.

- Inflation in the economy may also contribute to the significance of pricing decision in a marketing programme. It lowers customer's purchasing power and increases input costs. As a result, the marketer has to make the price decision after careful evaluation.

All the profit organisations and many non-profit organisations set prices on their products or services. Price goes by many titles.

Price is all round us. You pay rent for your apartment, tuition fee for your education, and a fee to your physician or dentist. The airline, railway, taxi, and bus companies charge you interest for the money you borrow. The price for driving your car on Florida's sunshine parkway is a toll, and the company that insures your car charges you a premium. Clubs or societies to which you belong may make a special assessment to pay unusual expenses. Your regular lawyer may ask for a retainer to cover her services. The price of an executive is a salary. Finally, all the economists would disagree that income taxes are the price we pay for the privilege of making money.

Meaning of Price

Price is the exchange value of a product. In fact, price revolves around two elements i.e., utility and value. Utility is the generic property of the product to satisfy a need or want of the consumer. Value is the quantitative worth the consumer attaches to the product, for which he is willing to part with a certain amount of money. Price remains vague until all the details about it are spelt out.

5.2 DETERMINANTS OF PRICING

Pricing decisions are usually determined by costs, demand and competition. We shall discuss each of these factors separately. We take demand first.

Demand: The popular 'Law of Demand' states that "higher the price, lower the demand, and vice versa, other things remaining the same". In a season, due to plentiful supplies of certain, agricultural products, the prices are low and because of low prices, the demand for them increases subsequently. You can test the validity of this law yourself in your daily life. There is an inverse relationship between price and quantity demanded. If price rises, the demand falls and if the price falls, the demand goes up. Of course, the law of demand assumes that there should be no change in the other factors influencing demand except price. If any one or more of the other factors, for instance, income, the price of the substitutes, tastes and preferences of the consumers, advertising expenditures, etc. vary, the demand may rise in spite of a rise in price, or alternatively, the demand may fall in spite of a fall in price. However, there are important exceptions to the law of demand.

There are some goods which are purchased mainly for their 'snob appeal' when prices of such goods rise, their snob appeal increases and they are purchased in larger quantities. On the other hand, as the price of such goods falls, their snob appeal reduces and, therefore, their demand falls. Diamonds provide a good example.

It is necessary for the marketer to know what should be the reaction of the consumers to the change he wishes to make in the price. Let us take some examples: Smokers are usually so addicted to smoking that they will not give up smoking even if the price of cigarettes increases. So also demand for salt or for that matter of wheat is not likely to go down even if the prices increase. Another example of inelastic demand is the demand for technical journals, which are sold mainly to libraries. On the other hand, a reduction in the price of television will bring in more than proportionate increase in demand. Some of the factors determining the price elasticity of demand are the nature of commodity, whether it is a necessity or luxury, extent of use, range of substitutes, urgency of demand and frequency of purchase of the product.

It may also be noted that the price elasticity of demand for a certain commodity and the price elasticity of demand for a certain brand of that commodity may be radically different. For example, while the demand for cigarettes as such, may be highly inelastic, the price elasticity of demand for 'Charms' may be highly elastic. The reasons for this are weak brand loyalty and the availability of substitutes.

Competition

The degree of control over prices which the sellers may exercise varies widely with the competitive situation in which they operate. Sellers operating under conditions of pure competition do not have any control over the prices they receive. A monopolistic, on the other hand, may fix prices according to his discretion. The marketer, therefore, needs to know the degree of pricing discretion enjoyed by him. Let us take these cases individually.

Perfect competition is said to exist when (1) there are a large number of buyers and sellers (ii) each purchasing and selling such a small quantity that their withdrawal from the market will not affect the total demand and supply and demand are at an equilibrium. It is shown in Fig. 5.1.

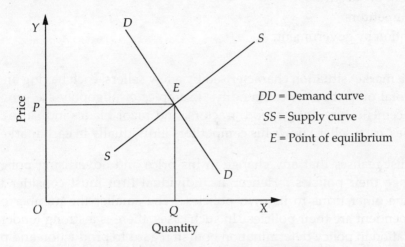

Fig. 5.1 Pricing under perfect competition.

In pure competition, all that the individual seller can do is to accept the price preventing in the market, i.e., he is in the position of a **price taker**. If he wants to charge a higher price, buyers will purchase from other sellers. And he need not charge less since he can sell his small supply at the going market price.

Under **monopoly**, a single producer has complete control of the entire supply of a certain product. Railways and telephones are examples of monopoly. The main features of monopoly are (i) there is only one seller of a particular good or service and (ii) rivalry from the producers of substitutes is so remote that it is almost insignificant, as a result, the monopolistic is in a position to set the price himself. Thus, he is in the position of a **price setter**.

However, even in the case of monopoly, there are limits to the extent to which he can increase his prices. Much depends on the elasticity of demand for the product. This, in turn, depends on the extent of availability of substitutes for the product. And in most cases, there is rather an infinite series of closely competing substitutes. Even railways and telephone organisations must take into account potential competition by alternative services, railways may be substituted by motor transport and telephone calls by telegrams. The closer the substitute and greater the elasticity of the demand for a monopolistic product, the less he can raise the price without frightening away his customers. High price of oil has led to development of alternative sources of energy.

Monopolies are constantly tending the break down due to the following reasons.

1. Shifts in consumer demand
2. Continuous process of innovations and technological developments leading to development of substitutes
3. New competitors
4. Intervention by government.

Oligopoly is a market situation characterised by a few sellers, each having an appreciable share in the total output of the commodity. Examples of oligopoly are provided by the automobiles, cement, tyre, infant food, tractors, and razor blades industries. In each of these industries, each seller knows his competitors individually in each market.

Each oligopolist realises that any change in his price and advertising policy may lead rivals to change their policies. Hence, an individual firm must consider the possible reactions of the other firms to its own policies. The smaller the number of firms, the more interdependent are their policies. In such cases, there is a strong tendency towards close collaboration in policy determination both in regard to production and prices. Thus, oligopolists follow the philosophy of 'live and let live'. Two examples of this may be mentioned here. In response to tenders invited by the Director General of Civil Suppliers and Disposals, the three principal manufacturers of storage batteries, viz., Chloride India, Standard Batteries and AMCO Batteries, quoted almost identical prices.

The **price leader** has lower costs and adequate financial resources, a substantial share of the market and a reputation for sound pricing decisions. Price leaders with the strongest position in the market may offer increase in their prices with the hope that competitors will follow suit. Price followers may delay their prices in the hope of snatching a part of the market share away from the leader.

Monopolistic competition is a market situation, in which there are many sellers of a particular product, but the product of each seller is in some way differentiated in the minds of consumers from the product of the other seller. None of the sellers is in a position to control a major part of the total supply of the commodity but every seller so differentiates his portion of the supply from the portions sold by others, that buyers hesitate to shift their purchase from his product to that of another in response to price differences. At times, one manufacturer may differentiate his own products.

For example, a blade manufacturer in India manufactures more than 25 brands of blades. This differentiation of product by each manufacturer by giving it a brand name gives him some amount of monopoly. If he is able to create a goodwill for his product and he may be able to charge higher prices thereof to some extent, still, his product will have to compete with similar products of other manufacturers which puts a limit on his pricing discretion. If he charges too high a price, consumers may shift their loyalty to other competing suppliers. You can find it out yourself by going to the market, as a large number of consumer goods like toothpaste, soaps, radios, etc. are subject to a large degree of product differentiation as a means of attracting customers.

As long as a consumer has an impression that a particular product brand is different and superior to others, he will be willing to pay that brand of the same commodity. The differences real or illusory may be built up his mind by (a) recommendations by friends (b) advertising and (c) his own experiences and observations.

Product differentiation is more typical of the present-day economic system, than either pure competition or monopoly. And, in most cases, an individual firm has to face monopolistic competition. It tries to maintain its position and promote its sales by either (i) changing its price and indulging in price competition, or (ii) intensifying the differentiation of its product, and/or (iii) increasing its advertisement and sales promotion efforts.

5.3   FACTORS INFLUENCING PRICING

There are two categories of factors—internal factors and external factors. Influence the pricing decisions of any enterprise, in each of these categories, some may be economic factors and some psychological factors, again, some factors may be quantitative and yet others qualitative.

Internal Factors

The firm has certain objectives—long term as well as immediate in pricing, for example, it has certain costs of manufacturing and marketing, and it seeks to recover these costs through price. The firm may have basic philosophy on pricing. The pricing decisions of the firm have to be consistent with the overall objectives of the firm. The firm tries to seek a particular public image through its price policies. The following are the important internal factors that must be considered in pricing a firm's product/service.

❖ **Marketing objectives:** Before setting price, the firm must decide on its strategy for the product. This reiterates the idea that the corporate strategy must precede the marketing strategy and then marketing strategy must precede the pricing strategy. If the firm has selected its target market and positioning carefully, then its marketing-mix strategy (i.e., the 4 Ps) will be fairly straightforward. For example, if the Coimbatore-based Paramount Airways decides to target the corporate/business travellers with its single-class aeroplanes, this suggests charging a high price. Whereas, a no-frills, low cost carrier would charge a low price, as dictated by its targeting and positioning.

Thus, pricing strategy is largely determined by past decisions on marketing strategy. At the same time, the firm may seek additional objectives. The clearer a firm is about its marketing objectives, the easier it is to set price. Some of the common objectives include survival, current profit maximisation, market-share leadership and product-quality leadership.

❖ **Other objectives:** Sometimes a firm might set prices so low as to prevent competition from entering the market as they might lead the competition to regard the market as less attractive. Non-profit organisations may adopt a number of other pricing objectives such as full cost recovery, partial cost recovery or set a social price geared to the distributed income situations of different clients.

❖ **Marketing-mix strategy:** Price is only one of the marketing-mix elements that a firm uses to achieve its marketing objectives. Therefore, logically pricing decisions must be coordinated with product design, distribution and promotion decisions to form a consistent and effective marketing programme. Decisions made for other marketing-mix elements may affect pricing decisions. For instance, the decision to position the product on quality plank will imply that the seller must charge a higher price to cover higher costs and/or to match the price-quality perception in the mind of the customers. It is common for marketers to design a price position wherein a target cost is set, then met and the target price is set. However, some marketers de-emphasise price and use other marketing-mix elements to create non-price positions. The marketer must consider the total marketing mix when setting prices. If the product is positioned on non-price factors, then decisions about quality, promotion and distribution will strongly affect the price. If price is a crucial positioning factor, then it will strongly affect decisions made about the other marketing-mix elements. In most cases, the company will consider all of the marketing-mix decisions together when developing the marketing programme.

❖ **Costs:** Though this topic was dealt with earlier in this chapter, some finer aspects related to costs are described here. Costs set the floor for the price that the firm can charge for its product. A firm's costs may be an important element in its pricing strategy. The firm wants to charge a price that both covers all its costs for producing, distributing and selling the product and delivers a fair rate of return for its effort and risk. The types of costs were explained earlier. To price wisely, managers need to know how costs vary with different levels of production. The concept of economies of scale comes into play here. Also, costs vary as a function of production experience. There is a drop in the average cost with accumulated production experience and this is attributed to the experience curve or the learning curve. Consider the semiconductor industry as an example. It has a strong experience curve effect. As a given chip is produced, manufacturing speeds go up, defect rates drop and costs plummet. These effects are seen dramatically in the PC market, here computing power increases and costs drop every year.

✤ **Organisation for pricing:** The management must decide who within the organisation should set prices. Firms handle pricing in a variety of ways. In small firms, prices are often set by top management rather than by the marketing or sales departments. In large firms, pricing typically is handled by product line managers. In industrial markets, salespeople may be allowed to negotiate with customers within certain price ranges. Even so, top management sets the pricing objectives and policies, and it often approves the prices proposed by lower-level management or salespeople. In industries where pricing is a key factor, companies will often have a pricing department to set the best prices or help others in setting them. Others who have an influence on pricing decisions include sales managers' production managers, finance managers and accountants.

External Factors

In addition to the internal factors mentioned above, any business firm has to encounter a set of external factors while formulating its pricing strategy. In the first place, the nature of the economy and the nature of competition have to be reckoned with. The purchasing power of consumers has to be reckoned with. The bargaining power of major customers groups and supplier groups another important consideration. Sometimes, the Government exercises price controls on certain products. The following are the important external factors that must be considered in pricing a firm's product/service.

☞ **Nature of the market and demand:** While costs set the lower limit of prices, the market and demand set the upper limit. Buyers balance the price of a product or service against the benefits of owning it. Therefore, before setting prices, the marketer must understand the relationship between price and demand for his product. Price-demand relationship varies for different types of markets and how buyer perceptions of price affect the pricing decision. Economists recognise four types of markets, viz., pure competition, monopolistic competition, oligopolistic competition and pure monopoly. Each presents a different pricing challenge and pricing freedom.

1. Under pure competition, the market consists of many buyers and sellers trading in a uniform commodity. A seller cannot charge more than the going price because buyers can obtain as much as they need at the going price. Nor would sellers charge less than the market price because they can sell all they want at this price.

2. Under monopolistic competition, the market consists of many buyers and sellers who trade over a range of prices rather than a single market price. A range of

prices occurs because sellers can differentiate their product/service offering to buyers. Buyers see differences in sellers' offerings and will pay different prices for them.

3. Under oligopolistic competition, the market consists of a few sellers who are highly sensitive to each other's pricing and marketing strategies. The product may be uniform (as a commodity) or non-uniform. Each seller is alert to competitors' strategies and moves. An oligopolist is never sure that it will gain anything permanent through a price cut or a price hike.

4. In a pure monopoly, the market consists of one seller. The seller may be a government monopoly (the Indian Postal service), a private regulated monopoly (a power company) or a private non-regulated monopoly (e.g., Sify, when it introduced Virtual Private Networks for corporate users). Pricing is handled differently in each case. A government monopoly can set the price below cost to make the product/service affordable or set price to recover costs or set a high price to slow down consumption (an instance of e-marketing). In a regulated monopoly, the government permits the firm to set rates that will yield a fair return. Non-regulated monopolies are free to price at what the market will bear. However, they will be careful not to attract competition nor invite government regulation.

5. The price-demand relationship must also be studied before taking the price decision. Each price the firm might charge will lead to a different level of demand. The relation between the price charged and the resulting demand level is described as the demand curve. In the normal case, demand and price and inversely related. For 'prestige' goods, raising the price may result in more sales. In measuring the price-demand relationship, the marketer must not allow other factors affecting demand to vary. They also need to know price elasticity, that is, how responsive demand will be to a change in price. If demand hardly changes with a small change in price, the demand is said to be inelastic. If demand changes greatly, it is said to be elastic. Price elasticity of demand is determined by many situations. For example, buyers are less price sensitive when the product they are buying is unique or when it is high in quality, prestige or exclusiveness. They are also less price sensitive when substitute products are hard to find or when they cannot easily compare the quality of substitute products. Buyers are less price sensitive when the total expenditure for a product is low relative to their income or when the cost is shared by another party.

☞ **Competition**—Another external factor affecting the company's pricing decisions is competitors' costs and prices and possible competitor's reactions to the company's own pricing moves. For so-called commodities (i.e., virtually undifferentiated products), all competitors generally charge identical prices. If one goes above the market price, sales will drop off sharply; if one goes below, all others are likely to follow or risk significant reductions in market share. How much any individual firm is constrained by competitors' prices, therefore, depends largely on how differentiated its product is. A product that is set apart from other market offerings by its functional design, appearance, brand image and the supplier's reputation for service and availability in ways that have value to customers can command a price premium. There are circumstances, however, in which firms will price over competitive levels even though the price differences are not really justified by superior product quality and service. A company may consciously elect, for example, not to meet competitive prices in a strategy of 'milking' the business, that is, yielding market share and gradually withdrawing from the market. It may continue to sell profitably for some time to its loyal customers, in the mean time gradually cutting back on selling and promotional expenses until it eventually phases out of the market. Some companies may choose not to price competitively because doing so would mean selling below cost. These so-called marginal firms eventually go out of business. Some large companies may not elect to meet the low price of a smaller competitor because to do so might mean giving up unit profits on a large sales base. It may be less costly in the short run to hold prices and give up some small percentage of market share. In the long run, the smaller competitor encroaches increasingly on the market positions of its major competitors until it becomes, itself, a major factor. Under shortage conditions, some firms may price opportunistically above the prevailing market levels, knowing that demand far exceeds available supply and that some buyers will pay the high price. Finally, some firms may unknowingly be under-priced by competitors on some of their products. These products may be part of a broad line and the reporting system may not allow for monitoring the sales-profit performance of each item on the list. Thus, the company may be losing sales and market position because of price and never realise, until too late, that the business has gone to more aggressive competitors. Generally, pricing strategies must inevitably be shaped with regard for present and future competition. In this respect, there is significant pricing interdependency among firms in an industry with each being heavily influenced by others' strategies and tactics. Some firms follow price trends; others, the larger ones, seek to lead them. Accordingly, in contemplating price changes, the marketing manager will often seek to anticipate competitive responses.

☞ **Other environmental factors**—When fixing prices, the firm also must consider other factors in its external environment. Economic conditions can have a strong impact on the firm's pricing strategies. Economic factors such as inflation, boom or recession, and interest rates affect pricing decisions because they affect both the costs of producing a product and consumer perceptions of the product's price and the value. The firm also must consider what impact its prices will have on other parties in its environment. How will resellers react to various prices? The firm should set prices that give resellers a fair margin, encourage their support, and help them to sell the product effectively. The government is another important external influence on pricing decisions. In regulated industries such as utilities, transport, and so on, the government has the authority to approve or reject price changes. Finally, social concerns may have to be taken into account. In setting prices, a firm's short-term sales, market share and profit goals may have to be tempered by broader societal considerations.

5.4 PRICING OBJECTIVES

Just as price is a component of the total marketing mix, pricing objectives also represent components of the organisation's overall objectives. The objectives of the firm and its marketing organisation guide the development of pricing objectives, which in turn lead to development and implementation of more specific pricing policies and procedures. For example, a firm might set a major overall objective of becoming the dominant producer in its domestic market. It might then develop a marketing objective of achieving maximum sales penetration in each region, followed by a related pricing objective to set prices at levels that maximise sales. These objectives might lead to adoption of a low-price policy implemented by offering substantial price discounts to channel members. While pricing objectives vary from firm to firm, they can be classified into four major groups:

1. Profitability objectives
2. Volume objectives
3. Meeting competition objectives
4. Prestige objectives

Profitability objectives include profit maximisation and target-return goals. Volume objectives pursue either sales maximisation or market share goals.

Profitability objectives: Classical economic theory bases its conclusions on certain assumptions. It presumes that firms will behave rationally. Theorists expect that rational behaviour will result in an effort to maximise gains and minimise losses. Profits are a function of revenue and expenses.

$$\boxed{Profits = Revenue - Expenses}$$

Revenue is determined by the product's selling price and the number of units sold:

$$\boxed{Total\ revenue = Price * Quantity\ sold}$$

A profit maximising price, therefore, rises to the point at which further increases will cause disproportionate decreases in the number of units sold. A 10% price increase that results in only an 8% cut in volume will add to the firm's revenue. However, a 10% price hike that results in an 11% sales decline will reduce the revenue. Profit maximisation is identified as the point at which the addition to total revenue is just balanced by the increase in total cost. Consequently, marketers set target return objectives–short-run or long-run goals usually stated as percentages of sales or investments. Target return objectives offer several benefits for marketers in addition to resolving pricing questions. For example, they serve as tools for evaluating performance. They also satisfy desires to generate 'fair' profits as judged by the management, stockholders and the public.

Volume objectives: Many marketers argue that pricing behaviour actually seeks to maximise sales within a given profit constraint. They set a minimum acceptable profit level and then seek to maximise sales in the belief that the increased sales are more important than immediate high profits to the long-run competitive picture. Such a firm continues to expand sales as long as its total profits do not drop below the minimum return acceptable to the management. Another volume-related pricing objective–the market share objective– sets a goal to control a portion of the market for a firm's goods or services. The company's specific goal may target maintaining its present share of a particular market or increasing its share. Volume-related goals such as sales maximisation and market share objectives play important roles in most firms' pricing decisions.

Meeting competition objectives: A third set of pricing objectives seeks simply to meet competitor's prices. In many lines of business, firms set their own prices to match those of established industry price leaders. These kinds of objectives de-emphasise more strongly on non-price variables. Pricing is a highly visible component of a firm's marketing mix and an easy and effective tool for obtaining a differential advantage over competitors; still other firms can easily duplicate a price reduction themselves. Because such price changes directly affect overall profitability in an industry, many firms attempt to promote stable prices by meeting competitors' prices and competing for market share by focusing on product strategies, promotional decisions and distribution–the non-price elements of the marketing mix. When price discounts become normal elements of a competitive marketplace, other marketing-mix elements gain importance in purchase decisions. In such instances, overall product value, not just the price, determines product choice. Value pricing emphasises benefits a product provides in comparison to the price and quality levels of competing offers. This strategy typically works best for relatively low-priced goods and services. Value-priced products generally cost less than the premium brands, but marketers point out that value does not necessarily mean cheap. Value is not just price, but is also linked to the performance and meeting expectations and needs of consumers. The challenge for those who compete on value is to convince customers that low-priced brands offer quality comparable to that of a higher-priced product.

Prestige objectives: The final category of pricing objectives, unrelated to either profitability or sales volume, encompasses prestige objectives. Prestige pricing establishes a relatively high price to develop and maintain an image of quality and exclusiveness that appeals to status-conscious consumers. Such objectives reflect marketers' recognition of the role of price in creating an overall image for the firm and its goods and services.

General pricing approaches

The price the firm charges will be somewhere between one that is too low to produce a profit and one that is too high to produce any demand. Product costs set a floor to the rice and consumer perceptions of the product's value set the ceiling. The firm must consider competitors' prices and other external and internal factors to find the best price between these two extremes. Firms set prices by selecting a general pricing approach that includes one or more of these three sets of factors. Let us examine the following approaches:

1. Cost-based approach
2. Buyer-based approach
3. Competition-based approach

1. Cost-based approach

The simplest pricing method is cost-plus or markup pricing—adding a standard markup to the cost of the product. Markups vary greatly among different goods. Some common markups (on price, not cost) in supermarkets are 9% on baby foods, 14% on tobacco products, 27% on dry foods and vegetables and 50% on greeting cards. Markups are generally higher on seasonal items (to cover the risk of not selling) and on speciality items, slower moving items, items with high storage and handling costs and items with inelastic demand. It must be noted that any pricing method that ignores current demand and competition is not likely to lead to the best price. Hence, markup pricing only works if that price actually brings in the expected level of sales.

Advantages

1. It covers all the costs.
2. It is designed to provide the target rate of margin.
3. It is generally a rational and widely accepted method.
4. It is easy to comprehend and a simple method.

Disadvantages

1. The cost calculations are based on a predetermined level of activity. If the actual level of activity varies from this estimated level, the costs may vary, rendering this method unrealistic.
2. If the costs of the firm are higher than its competitors, this method would render the firm passive in relation to price.
3. Another drawback is that sometimes the opportunity to charge a high price is foregone.
4. It ignores the price elasticity of demand.
5. The cost-based pricing would not be helpful for some of the objectives or tasks like market penetration, fighting competition, and so on.
6. It imparts an in-built inflexibility to pricing decisions. Another cost-based pricing approach is breakeven pricing, or a variation called target profit pricing. The firm tries to determine the price at which it will breakeven or make the target profit it is seeking.

2. Buyer-based approach

An increasing number of firms fix their prices on the product's perceived value. Perceived-value pricing uses buyers' perceptions of value, not the seller's cost, as the key to pricing. The company uses the non-price variables in the marketing mix to build up perceived value in buyers' minds. Price is set to match the perceived value. A company using perceived-value pricing must find out what value buyers assign to different competitive offers. Sometimes consumers are asked how much they would pay for each benefit added to the offer. If the seller charges more than the buyers' perceived value, the firm's sales will suffer. Many firms overprice their products, and their products sell poorly. Other firms' under-price. Under-priced products sell very well, but they produce less revenue than they would if prices were raised to the perceived-value level.

3. Competition-based pricing

Many firms follow the dominant competitors, particularly the price leader, in setting the price. The main advantages of this method are:

1. It is a very simple method.
2. It follows the main market trend.
3. It has relevance to the competitive standing of the firm.
4. Holding to the going price will prevent harmful price wars.

The major disadvantages and limitations of following competitors are:

1. If the competitors' price decisions are unrealistic, the follower will also be going wrong on the price.
2. The cost factors of the follower may not be similar to that of the competitors.
3. The pricing objective of the firm could be different from that of the competitors.
4. Sometimes the competitor may initiate price change for wrong reasons.

Competition-based pricing approach may take the form of going-rate pricing or sealed bid pricing. In going-rate pricing, the firm bases its price largely on competitors' prices, with less attention paid to its own cost or to demand. In oligopolistic industries that sell commodities, firms normally charge the same price. It is a popular pricing method. When demand elasticity is hard to measure, firms feel the going price represents the collective wisdom of the industry concerning the price that will yield a fair return. Competition based pricing is also used when firms bid for jobs. Using sealed-bid pricing, a firm bases its price on how it thinks competitors will price rather than on its own costs or on the demand. The firm wants to win a contract and winning the contract requires pricing lower than other firms. Yet, the firm cannot set its price below a certain level. It cannot price below cost without hurting its position. In contrast, the higher the firm sets its price above its costs, the less its chance of getting the contract.

5.5   PRICING POLICIES AND CONSTRAINTS

Firms do their pricing in a variety of ways as discussed earlier. Executives complain that pricing is a big headache and one is wary of committing a go/drop error in the pricing decision. Pricing less than what the customer wants to pay and pricing more than what the customer wants to pay are both costly errors. 'There are two fools in every market: one asks too little, one asks too much', says a Russian proverb. Many companies do not handle pricing well. Some common mistakes are:

1. Price is not revised often enough to capitalise on market changes.
2. Price is set independently of the rest of the marketing mix rather than as an intrinsic element of market-positioning strategy.
3. Price is not varied enough for different product items, market segments, distribution channels and purchase occasions.

The importance of pricing for profitability was demonstrated in a 1992 study by McKinsey & Company. Examining 2,400 companies, McKinsey concluded that a 1% improvement in price created an improvement in operating profit of 11.1%. By contrast, 1% improvements in variable cost, volume and fixed cost product profit improvements of only 7.8%, 3.3%

and 2.3% respectively. Effectively designing and implementing pricing strategies requires a systematic approach to setting, adapting and changing prices.

Procedure for a pricing policy

A firm must set a price for the first time when it develops a new product, when it introduces its regular product into a new distribution channel or geographical area, and when it enters bids on new contract work. The firm has to consider several factors in setting its pricing policy. A useful 6-step procedure to develop the pricing policy is discussed below.

1. **Selecting the pricing objective:** The firm first decides where it wants to position its market offering. The clearer a firm's objectives, the easier it is to set the price. A firm can pursue any of the objectives classified under four major groups, viz., profitability objectives, volume objectives, meeting competition objectives and prestige objectives. This was discussed in earlier section.

2. **Determining demand:** Each price will lead to a different levels of demand and therefore have a different impact on a firm's marketing objectives. The relation between alternative prices and the resulting current demand is captured in a demand curve. In the normal case, demand and price are inversely related: the higher the price, the lower the demand. In the case of prestige goods, the demand curve sometimes slopes upward. However, if the price is too high, the level of demand may fall. The demand curve sums the reactions of many individuals who have different price sensitivities. The first step in estimating demand is to understand what affects price sensitivity. Generally speaking, customers are most price sensitive to products that cost a lot or are bought frequently. They are less price sensitive to low cost items or items they buy infrequently. They are also less price sensitive when price is only a small part of the total cost of obtaining, operating and servicing the product over its lifetime. Firms, of course, prefer customers who are less price sensitive. The following is a list of factors leading to less price sensitivity, as identified by Nagle and Holden.

   ✠ The product is more distinctive.
   ✠ Buyers are less aware of substitutes.
   ✠ Buyers cannot easily compare the quality of substitutes.
   ✠ The expenditure is a smaller part of the buyer's total income.
   ✠ The expenditure is small compared to the total cost of the end product.
   ✠ Part of the cost is borne by another party.
   ✠ The product is used in conjunction with assets previously bought.
   ✠ The product is assumed to have more quality, prestige or exclusiveness.
   ✠ Buyers cannot store the product.

Most firms make some attempt to measure their demand curves using methods like statistical analysis, price experiments and surveys. In measuring the price demand relationship, the marketer must control various factors that will influence demand. The competitor's response will make a difference. Also, if the company changes other marketing-mix factors besides price, the effect of the price change itself will be hard to isolate and measure.

3. **Estimating costs:** The management needs to know how its costs vary with different levels of production. It is important to be aware of the risks presented by pricing based on the experience/learning curve. It assumes that competitors are weak followers. It leads the company into building more plants to meet the demand, while a competitor may be innovating a lower-cost technology. Then the market leader will be stuck with the old technology. Today's firms try to adapt their offers and terms to different buyers. A manufacturer may negotiate different terms with different retail chains. One retailer may want daily delivery (to keep inventory lower) while another may accept twice-a-week delivery in order to get a lower price. The manufacturer's cost will differ with each chain and so will its profits. To estimate the real profitability of dealing with different customers with differing requirements, the manufacturer needs to use activity-based cost (ABC) accounting instead of standard cost accounting. ABC accounting tries to identify the real costs associated with serving each customer. It allocates indirect costs like clerical costs, office expenses, supplies, and so on, to the activities that use them, rather than in some proportion to direct costs. Both variable and overhead costs are tagged back to each customer. Another interesting costing concept is target costing. Costs change with production scale and experience. They can also change as a result of a concentrated effort by designers, engineers and purchasing agents to reduce them through target costing. Market research is used to establish a new product's desired functions and the price at which the product will sell, given its appeal and competitors' prices. Deducting the desired profit margin from this price leaves the target cost that must be achieved. Each cost element–design, engineering, manufacturing, sales–must be examined and different ways to bring down costs must be considered. The objective is to bring the final cost projections into the target cost range. If this is not possible, it may be necessary to stop developing the product because it could not sell for the target price and make the target profit.

4. **Analysing competitors' costs, prices and offers:** Within the range of possible prices determined by market demand and company costs, the firm must take competitors' costs, prices and possible price reactions into account. The firm should first consider the nearest competitor's price. If the firm's offer contains features not offered by the nearest competitor, their worth to the customer should be evaluated and added to the competitor's price. If the competitor's offer contains some features not offered by

the firm, their worth to the customer should be evaluated and subtracted from the firm's price. Now the firm can decide whether it can charge more, the same or less than the competitor. But competition can change their price in reaction to the price set by the firm.

5. **Selecting a pricing approach:** Given the three C's–the customer's demand schedule, the cost function and the competitors' prices—the firm is now ready to select a price. Figure 5.2 summarises the three major considerations in price setting. Costs set a floor to the price. Competitors' price and the price of substitutes provide an orienting point. Customers' assessment of unique features establishes the price ceiling. Firms select a pricing approach that includes one or more of these three considerations. The pricing approaches are cost-based or buyer-based or competition-based.

6. **Selecting the final price:** Pricing methods narrow the range from which the company must select its final price. In selecting that price, the company must consider additional factors, including the impact of other marketing activities, company pricing guidelines, gain-and-risk-sharing pricing and the impact of price on other parties. The final price must take into account the brand's quality and advertising relative to the competition. The price must be consistent with the firm's pricing

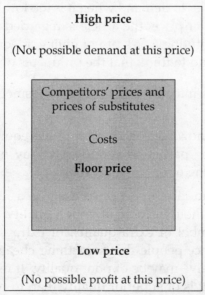

(*Source:* Marketing Management, 12e, Kotler and Keller)

Fig. 5.2 The three C's model for price setting.

guidelines. When a firm establishes pricing penalties, it must be done judiciously so as not to unnecessarily alienate customers. Sometimes, buyers may resist accepting a seller's proposal because of a high perceived level of risk. The seller has the option of offering to absorb part or all of the risk if it does not deliver the full promised value. Management must also consider the reactions of other parties to the contemplated price. For instance, the reaction of marketing intermediaries must be thought about. The reaction of the sales force must be taken note since they will be the ones to sell at that price in the marketplace. All these reactions might hold clues to fine tune the final price.

5.6   CONSUMER PSYCHOLOGY AND PRICING

In a particular situation, the behaviour of one individual may not be the same as that of the other. Some important characteristics of consumer behaviour as revealed by research and experience are detailed below.

1. From the point of view of the consumer, prices are quantitative and precise whereas product quality, product image, customer service, promotion and similar factors are qualitative and ambiguous. It is easier to speculate about what consumers would do if prices rise by 5% than if the quality is improved by 5%.

2. Price constitutes a barrier to demand when it is too low just as much as when it is too high. Above a particular price, the article is regarded as too expensive and, below another price, as constituting a risk of not giving adequate value. If the price is too low, consumers will tend to think that the product is of inferior quality.

3. Price inevitably enters into the consumers' assessment of quality. There are two reasons for this:

   (a) It needs expert knowledge and appropriate equipment to test the quality or durability of some particular products (to say nothing of the time and cost involved in carrying out a proper test).

   (b) Customers tend to look upon price itself as a reasonably reliable of quality. What is costly is thought to be of a high quality. A higher price is ordinarily taken to be a symbol of extra quality, or extra value or extra prestige. It is difficult to convince people that something cheap is of good quality and that something expensive may be of poor quality. It may be easier to prove that an expensive product is of superior quality than to prove that a cheap product is of good quality. This is specially true of durable consumer goods which are very often differentiated, at least psychologically, through branding, packaging and advertising. In such cases, the sale of certain goods could be stimulated more effectively through higher than lower prices for two reasons: (i) the higher price increases the snob appeal of the goods (ii) it also creates confidence in the customer that he is getting a good quality product.

(c) To conclude, in many cases, price is used by the prospective customer as a clue for sizing up the quality of the product. This price quality association is well established.

4. With an increase in income level, the average consumer becomes, quality conscious. An improvement may, therefore, lead to an increase in demand. If this is so, a time may come when a high price results in an increase in demand. This extreme situation may arise if price in increasing affluent societies comes to serve merely as an indicator of quality.

5. Consumers may be persuaded to pay more for heavily advertised goods, a firm's size, its financial success, and even its age are often perceived by consumers as measures of quality. Well-known firms very often assert that by virtue of their reputation they are able to charge 5 to 10 per cent higher than other firms but defiantly not much more.

6. In a comprehensive survey of consumers consciousness, it was revealed that the basic postulate of the demand theory, i.e., the consumers have an appropriate knowledge of market prices, was not fundamentally wrong.

The following types of consumers are most likely to perceive price as an indicator of quality.

(a) Persons trying to achieve status

(b) Occasional consumers who are not knowledgeable in a product area e.g., purchase of a camera

(c) The buyer who is impressed by the importance of quality, but has difficulty in identifying.

An experimental study in India showed that more than 60 per cent of the respondents revised their of ready-made shirts after knowing their prices indicating thereby that prices information does have a significant effect on quality perception.

To conclude, higher prices that increase consumer readiness to buy may sound uneconomic, but may not be unrealistic. The price quality concept has equal relevance to new product pricing which is being learnt in this topic and the producer has considerable flexibility in pricing his products, provided has to create a psychological image of quality.

Pricing of Industrial Goods

For many consumer products, buyers are not usually aware of the prevailing prices. Products falling in the category of luxury goods and items not frequently purchased would constitute such goods. Consumers, of course are usually aware of the regularly purchased items like groceries. On the other hand, buyers of industrial goods tend to be price conscious. They are more keen to check what they get for the price they pay. They also tend to act more rationally than an average buyer of consumer goods. Their knowledge of market is more intensive and exact if not perfect. Very often the buyer of an industrial product knows or at least can make a guess of the costs of the manufacturer.

Product differentiation is easier in industrial goods than in consumer goods by (i) providing better service in connection with delivery, use of installation, and (ii) building a reputation for reliability or quality of workmanship. Moreover, product differentiation results much more from product differences that generate provable claims. Branding, therefore, plays a much less important role in marketing of industrial goods than in the case of consumer goods.

Price leadership is a very common phenomenon in the industrial goods market. The price elasticity of the demand for an industrial product would depend to some extent on how important its price is in the general costs structure of the using firm. If it represents a significant element, a reduction in price may lead to a substantial increase in demand. If it is not, a change in price may not lead to a change in demand. The demand for equipment is a part of the overhead costs which cannot be really identified.

Some characteristics are listed below:

The true price that an industrial customer pays is often different from the list price because of factors like delivery and installation costs, discounts, training costs, trade-in allowance, financing costs, and so on.

- ☞ Pricing is not an independent variable. It is highly intertwined with the product, promotion and distribution strategies. Price for industrial products cannot be set out without considering other products that are compliments or substitutes sold by the firm. Cross elasticities exist, where the price of one item affects sales of other items.

- ☞ Prices can be changed in numerous ways such as changing the quantity of goods and services provided by the seller, changing the premiums and discounts that are offered, changing the time and place of payment, and so on. This implies that pricing is often a more flexible decision than product or distribution decisions.

- ☞ Industrial prices are established, in many cases, by competitive bidding on a project-by-project basis. In a number of cases, prices are resolved through negotiation.

- ☞ Industrial pricing is often characterised by an emphasis on fairness. Industrial buyers, who are experienced and able to estimate the vendors' approximate production costs expect the price increases to be justifiable on the basis of either the cost increases or product improvements.

☞ Industrial prices are affected by a host of economic factors such as inflation, interest rate changes, and exchange rate fluctuations, and so on. This problem is particularly critical for the marketer locked into a long-term contract with no escalation cause.

5.7 PRICING OVER THE LIFE CYCLE OF A PRODUCT

Many products generally have a characteristic known as perishable distinctiveness. This means that a product which is distinct when new, degenerates over the years into a common commodity. The process by which the distinctiveness gradually disappears as the product merges with other competitive products has been rightly termed by Joel Dean as "the cycle of competitive degeneration".

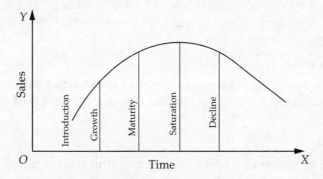

Fig. 5.3 Life cycle of a product.

The cycle begins with the invention of a new product, and is often followed by a rapid expansion in its sales as the product gains market acceptance. Then the competitors enter the field with imitation and rival products and the distinctiveness of the new product starts diminishing. The speed of degeneration differs from product to product. The innovation of a new product and its degeneration into a common product is termed the life cycle of the product. There are five distinct stages in the life cycle of product as shown in Fig. 5.3.

Each phase presents different opportunities and constraints on price.

Introduction phase

During the introduction phase, pricing can be a quandary, especially if you enjoy a temporary monopoly. In that situation, there may be no direct competitor and thus no benchmark for what buyers will tolerate or for their sensitivity to price differences. There may be indirect competitors (substitutes), however, and they can be used as starting points for the pricing decision. The total economic value equation becomes relevant, wherein the price of the best alternative is known but the value of the performance differential of the new product is unknown. Customers themselves may have difficulty in sizing up the value of something that is new and different. They too lack benchmarks of value. In such instances, any of the following strategies may be adopted:

- **Skimming:** Some people will be happy to pay a high price for anything that is new and unique. This strategy, of course, is short term and contains dangers like attracting competition.

- **Penetration pricing:** A low price may have the threefold benefits of (1) getting established as the market share champion, (2) discouraging market entry by competitors, and (3) creating broad-based demand for the product.

- **Cost-plus:** In a monopoly, the producer can administer its own price and cost-plus is one way of determining that price. However, product monopolies are short lived.

Pricing decisions in this introductory phase are not only difficult but also extremely important. Putting too high a price on a newly introduced product may kill it in its infancy, undoing the work of many employees over a long period of development.

Growth phase

The growth phase is characterised by increasing unit sales and accelerating customer interest. If competitors have not yet surfaced (which is an unlikely event), skimming may be appropriate. All the deep-pocketed buyers who simply want to be the first in their neighbourhoods to own the product have already been skimmed in the introduction phase. So now, the price must be reduced gradually, skimming other market segments that are progressively more price sensitive.

A producer that enjoys prime position on the experience curve will also want to progressively reduce prices during this phase. Doing so will maintain its margins even as the strategy expands unit sales and punishes late-into-the-game rivals in the marketplace. Some of these rivals will either take a loss on every sale or simply wind up.

Mature phase

By the time a product enters this phase, growth in unit sales is levelling off and the remaining competitors are trying to find ways to differentiate their products. During this phase, one may see sellers offer different versions of the product, each version trying to colonise a targeted segment. Price is one of the factors used in this strategy (i.e., by developing and pricing good, better and best versions to expand the product line).

Saturation phase

Sales reach and remain on a plateau marked by the level of replacement demand. There is little additional demand to be stimulated.

Decline phase

Competition gets ugly in this phase. Total demand for the product category is now visibly slipping, perhaps because of the appearance of superior substitutes or because of market saturation. Whatever the case, unit sales will continue to decline. Some companies will get out of the business entirely; those that remain will aggressively try to take business away from the rivals. Every player in the market tries to harvest as much as possible from a contracting market. Price tactics include the following:

- ☞ Beat a retreat on price, but work overtime to reduce production costs. Success in the latter will maintain a decent profit margin.

- ☞ Increase the price on the few remaining units in inventory. This is because there may be a small number of customers who still rely on that particular product. This is particularly true of replacement parts. Here the seller hopes that the higher price will compensate for fewer sales. When the inventory is exhausted, the product line is terminated.

Pricing is one of the linchpins of marketing strategy and success. How is the company making its pricing decisions? Are these decisions appropriate for the current phase of the product life cycle? The most reliable method of pricing is to get inside the heads of customers, because how they value the firm's products relative to those of competitors and substitutes matters more than anything else.

5.8   NEW PRODUCT PRICING STRATEGIES

Pricing strategies usually change as the product passes through its life cycle as illustrated in the previous section. The introductory stage is especially challenging. Firms bringing out an innovative patent-protected product can choose between two options, viz., market-skimming pricing and market-penetration pricing.

Market-skimming pricing

Many firms that invent new products initially set high prices to 'skim' revenues layer by layer from the market. At product introduction in the marketplace, the firm may charge the highest price it could give the benefits of its new product over competing products. The firm sets a price that made it just worthwhile for some affordable segments of the market to adopt the new product. After the initial sales slow down, the firm may lower the price to draw in the next price sensitive layer of the customers. In this way, a firm skims the maximum amount of revenue from the various segments of the market. It is important to note that skimming works well only under certain conditions. The quality and image must support its higher price and enough buyers must want the product at that price. Also the cost of producing a small volume cannot be so high that they cancel the advantage of charging more. In the mean time, competitors should not be able to enter the market easily and undercut the price. A skimming strategy offers several benefits to the markets, as listed below:

- It allows a manufacturer to quickly recover its research and development costs.
- It also allows a firm to maximise revenue from a new product before the competitors enter the field.
- A skimming strategy offers a useful tool for segmenting a product's overall market on a price basis.
- It permits marketers to control demand in the introductory stages of a product's life cycle and then adjust productive capacity to match demand.

The chief disadvantage of skimming strategy is: it attracts competition. Potential competitors see innovative firms reaping big financial gains and decide to enter the market. This new supply forces the price even lower than its eventual level under a sequential skimming procedure. However, if patent protection or other proprietary ability allows a firm to exude competitors from its market, it may continue a skimming strategy for a relatively long period.

Market-penetration pricing: Rather than setting a high initial price to skim off small but profitable market segments, some firms set a low initial price in order to penetrate the market quickly and deeply–to attract a large number of buyers quickly and win a large market share. A penetration pricing strategy may also extend over several stages of the product life cycle as the firm seeks to maintain a reputation as a low-price competitor. Since many firms begin penetration pricing with the intention of increasing prices in the future, success depends on generating many consumer trial purchases. Penetration pricing works well under the following conditions:

- A good or service experiences highly elastic demand.
- The market is highly price sensitive and a low price stimulates market growth.
- Production and distribution costs fall with accumulated production experience.
- A low price helps discourage actual and potential competition.

Product-mix pricing: The strategy for setting a product's price often has to be changed when the product is part of a product mix. In this case, the firm looks for a set of prices that maximises the profits on the total product mix. This pricing is difficult because the various products have related demand and costs and face different degrees of competition. The following section outlines the five product-mix pricing situations depicted in Fig. 5.4.

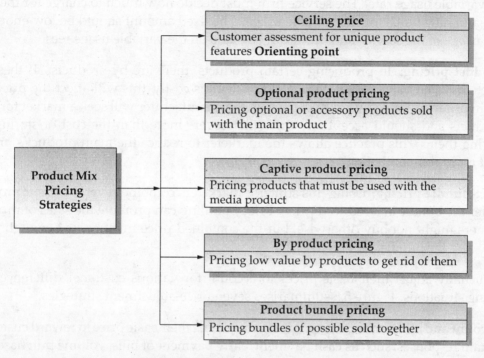

Fig. 5.4 Product-mix pricing strategies.

Product-line pricing: Since most firms market multiple product lines, an effective pricing strategy must consider the relationships among all of these products instead of viewing each in isolation. In product line pricing, management must decide on the price steps to set between the various products. The price steps should take into account cost differences between the products, customer evaluations of their different features and competitors' prices. In many industries, marketers use well-established price points for the products in their line. The customer will probably associate low, average and high quality with the price points. The marketers' task is to establish perceived quality differences that support the price differences.

Optional-product pricing: Many firms use this strategy by offering to sell optional or accessory products along with their main product. These firms have to decide which items to include in the base price and which to offer as options. Often the basic model which is stripped of many comforts and conveniences sought by the customers gets rejected.

Captive-product pricing: Firms that make products that must be used along with the main product use this strategy. Producers of the main products often price them low and set high markups for the supplies. For a competitor who does not sell these supplies, will have to price his product higher in order to make the same overall profit. In case of services, this strategy is called two-part pricing where the price of the service is broken into a fixed fee plus a variable usage rate. The service firm must decide how much to charge for the basic service and how much for the variable usage. The fixed amount should be low enough to induce usage of the service and profit can be made on the variable usage fees.

By-product pricing: In producing certain products, there are by-products. If these by-products have no value and if getting rid of them is costly, this will affect the pricing of the main product. Using by-product pricing, the manufacturer will seek a market for these by-products and should accept any price that covers more than the cost of storing and delivering them. This practice allows the marketer to reduce the main product's price to make it more competitive.

Product-bundle pricing: Using this strategy, marketers combine several of their products and offer the bundle at a reduced price. Price bundling can promote the sales of products consumers might not buy otherwise, but the combined price must be low enough to get them to buy the bundle.

Firms usually adjust their basic prices to account for various customer differences and changing situations. Figure 5.5 summarises seven price-adjustment strategies.

1. Discount and allowance pricing: Most firms adjust their basic price to reward customers for certain responses, such as cash payment, early payment of bills, volume purchases and off-season buying. Some of those adjustments are described below:

❖ **Cash discounts:** A cash discount is a price reduction to buyers who pay their bills promptly. The discount must be granted to all buyers meeting these terms. Such discounts are customary in many industries and help to improve the sellers' cash situation and reduce bad debts and credit collection costs.

❖ **Quantity discounts:** A quantity discount is a price reduction to buyers who buy large volumes. It must be offered to all customers and must not exceed the seller's cost savings associated with selling large quantities. These savings include lower selling, inventory and transportation expenses. Discounts provide an incentive to the customer to buy more from one given seller, rather than from many different sources.

❖ **Functional discounts:** A functional discount (also called trade discount) is offered by the seller to trade channel members who perform certain functions, such as

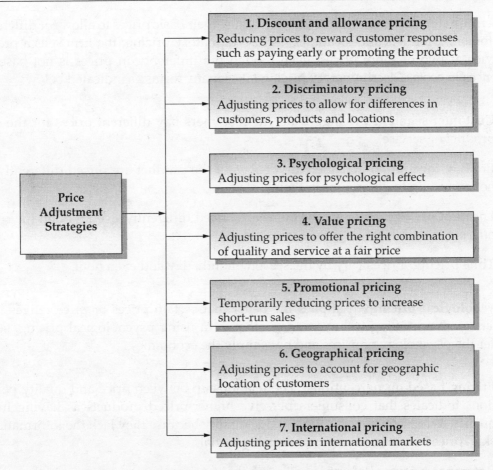

Fig. 5.5 Pricing adjustment strategies.

selling, storing and record keeping. Manufacturers may offer different functional discounts to different trade channels because of the varying services they perform, but manufacturers must offer the same functional discounts within each trade channel.

❖ **Seasonal discounts:** A seasonal discount is a price reduction to buyers who buy out of season. It allows the seller to keep production steady during the entire year.

❖ **Allowances:** They are another type of reductions from the list price. Trade-in allowances are price reductions given for turning in an old item when buying a new one. Promotional allowances are payments or price reductions to reward dealers for participating in advertising and sales-support programmes.

2. Discriminatory pricing: Firms will often adjust their basic prices to allow for differences in customers, products and locations. In discriminatory pricing, the firm sells a product or service at two or more prices, even though the difference in prices is not based on differences in costs. Discriminatory pricing takes many forms as indicated below:

☞ **Customer-segment pricing:** Different customers pay different prices for the same product or service.

☞ **Product-form pricing:** Different versions of the product are priced differently, but not according to differences in their costs.

☞ **Location pricing:** Different locations are priced differently, even though the cost of offering in each location is the same.

☞ **Time pricing:** Prices vary by the season, month, day and even hour.

3. Psychological pricing: It applies the belief that certain prices or price ranges make products more appealing to buyers than others. In using psychological pricing, sellers consider the psychology of prices and not simply the economics.

✠ **Pricing based on perceptions:** The relationship between price and quality perceptions indicates that consumers perceive higher-priced products as having higher quality. When consumers cannot judge quality because they lack the information or skill, price becomes an important quality signal.

✠ **Reference pricing:** Reference prices are those prices that buyers carry in their minds and refer to when looking at a given product. It might be formed by noting current prices, remembering past prices or assessing the buying situation. Sellers can influence or use these consumers' reference prices when setting price.

✠ **Odd pricing:** In odd pricing, marketers set prices at odd numbers just under round numbers. An odd ending conveys the notion of a discount or bargain to the customer.

4. Value pricing: During slow-growth times, many firms adjust their prices to bring them into line with economic conditions and with the resulting fundamental shift in consumer attitudes toward quality and value. Value pricing is offering just the right combination of quality and good service at a fair price. In many cases, value pricing involves redesigning existing brands in order to offer more quality for a given price or the same quality for less.

5. Promotional pricing: In promotional pricing, a lower-than-normal price is used as a temporary ingredient in a firm's selling strategy. Some promotional pricing arrangements form part of recurrent marketing initiatives. Some may be to introduce a promotional model or brand with special pricing to begin competing in a new market. Promotional pricing takes several forms and some of them are described below.

Loss-leader pricing: It happens when retailers drop price on well-known brands to stimulate store traffic in the hope that customers will buy other items also, at normal markups.

Special-event pricing: Sellers use special-event pricing in certain seasons to draw in more customers. The seasonal need of the customers is capitalised on by the sellers using this pricing strategy.

Cash rebates: Manufacturers sometimes offer cash rebates to consumers who buy the product from dealers within a specified time.

Low-interest financing, longer payment times, longer warranties—All these represent the promotional incentives offered by the sellers to the buyers. Since they provide some flexibility and also bring down the perceived risks (in case of longer warranties), buyers are motivated to make the buying decision.

Psychological discounting: The seller may simply offer discounts from normal prices to increase sales and reduce inventories. For the buyer, the motivation to buy below normal prices may be compelling.

6. Geographical pricing: Geographical considerations strongly influence prices when costs must cover shipping heavy, bulky, low-unit-cost materials. Buyers and sellers can distribute transportation expenses in several ways: (1) The buyer pays all transportation charges; (2) The seller pays all transportation charges; or (3) The buyer and the seller share the charges. This choice has particularly important effects for a firm seeking to expand its geographic coverage to distant markets. The seller's pricing can implement several alternatives for handling transportation costs.

- *FOB-origin pricing:* It means that the goods are placed free on board (FOB) a carrier, at which point the title and responsibility pass to the customer, who pays the freight from the factory to the destination. Though it looks fair, the disadvantage is that the firm will be a high-cost firm to distant customers.

- *Uniform delivered pricing:* It is the exact opposite of FOB pricing. The company charges the same price plus freight to all customers, regardless of their location. An advantage is that it is fairly easy to administer and it lets the firm advertise its price nationally.

- *Zone pricing:* It falls between FOB-origin pricing and uniform delivered pricing. The company sets up two or more zones. All customers within a given zone pay a single total price; the more distant the zone, the higher the price.

- *Basing-point pricing:* The seller selects a given city as a 'basing point' and charges all customers the freight cost from that city to the customer location, regardless of the city from which the goods actually are shipped.

- *Freight-absorption pricing:* The seller who is anxious to do business with a certain customer or geographical area might use freight-absorption pricing. This strategy involves absorbing all or part of the actual freight charges in order to get the desired business. It is used for market penetration and to hold on to increasingly competitive markets.

7. International pricing: A wide variety of internal and external conditions can affect a marketer's global pricing strategies. Internal influences include the firm's goals and marketing strategies, the costs of developing, producing and marketing its products, the nature of the products and the firm's competitive strengths. External influences include general conditions in international markets, especially those in the firm's target markets, regulatory limitations, trade restrictions, competitors' actions, economic events, customer characteristics and the global status of the industry. In general, a firm can implement one of three export pricing strategies, as described below.

- *Standard worldwide price*: Exporters often set standard worldwide prices, regardless of their target markets. This strategy can succeed if foreign marketing costs remain low enough that they do not impact overall costs, or if their prices reflect average unit costs. A firm that implements a standard pricing programme must monitor the international marketplace carefully, however, to make sure that domestic competitors do not undercut prices.

- *Dual pricing*: It distinguishes prices for domestic and export sales. Some exporters practise cost-plus pricing to establish dual prices that fully allocate their true domestic and foreign costs to product sales in those markets. Others opt for flexible cost-plus pricing schemes that allow marketers to grant discounts or change prices according to shifts in the competitive environment or fluctuations in the international exchange rate.

- *Market-differentiated pricing*: It makes even more flexible arrangements to set prices according to local marketplace conditions. Effective market-differentiated pricing depends on access to quick and accurate market information.

Product Positioning and Price

By "positioning" we mean the way a product is viewed by the customer in comparison with similar products. All aspects of the marketing mix must be coordinated to place the product in the right position in the market segment aimed at.

Price is just one element of the marketing mix and it must reflect the product position in the market. A toilet soap meant to be a novelty to attract the elite must be sold at higher price. This basic idea behind product differentiation, is to avoid a situation where the product has to compete only on the basis of the price alone.

Non-Price Competition

The basic aim of non-price competition is to alter those characteristics of the product other than price which influence the decision of the buyers. The various forms of non-price competition are

(a) advertising and creating brand loyalty

(b) changes in quality of goods and service of goods and services

(c) prompt deliveries

(d) free gifts and contests

(e) better sales service.

The more complex the product, the greater are the characteristics, which could be modified in response to customer tastes or a result of changes in technology. Among the major factors responsible for the growth of non-price competition are:

(a) the tendency towards price uniformity

(b) desire to hold customers on the basis of attributes other than price, as for example convenience and early deliveries or longer period of guarantee

(c) adoptions of measures necessary even to make price competition effective.

From the point of view of consumers' non-price competition is a boom as they may get better quality goods and services.

5.9   PRICE SENSITIVITY

Price sensitivity however is not just about charging high prices to maximise revenue. It might also make sense to cut prices–sometimes dramatically–to encourage people who may otherwise not be part of the market to use the services or goods being provided. In the *News* article on price sensitivity cited two cases where prices had been reduced to generate additional revenue through encouraging demand. The first was the case of the Little Chef chain of restaurants who have reduced the price of some of their main meals and mugs of coffee by nearly a half. The second was Sunderland Football Club who slashed the prices of its tickets for a Carling Cup game and filled the stadium as a result. The decisions about how to manipulate prices to maximise revenue might seem unfair at times but it is really just a case of businesses using sound logic and the principles of supply and demand to their advantage. We do after all have a choice about whether we buy these goods and services and ultimately it is all about the value we place on these items in relation to what we are being asked to give up to receive them.

The theory behind price sensitivity is based on an understanding of the aims of an organisation and the concepts of **price elasticity of demand** and **consumer surplus**. Most private sector business organisations need to make a profit to survive. This may not translate to a profit maximising approach but nevertheless they will be looking to generate profits from activities.

Revenue and Price

Part of this process will be looking at what happens to revenue. **Revenue** is the amount received from the sale of goods and services and is found by multiplying the price of a product by the quantity sold.

Price has an important function in markets. It acts as a signal to both producers and consumers. For producers it gives them some indication about the returns they can expect from sales in relation to their costs–in other words whether it is worth producing a good or not. For consumers it provides an indication about value. **Value** is a very important concept in economics and business. It is difficult to define because we all have a different interpretation of what value means. In essence, the value we place on a good or service is indicated by the price we are willing to pay to consume that good or service.

If I am willing to pay £60 to watch Chelsea play a football match it implies that I place the enjoyment, excitement and satisfaction that I will gain from watching that match above whatever else that £60 will buy me at that time. In economics, human behaviour is often assumed to be 'rational'. If I get more enjoyment out of activity X than activity Y, then it is rational to assume that I will choose X over Y. This then suggests that if I could also have bought a DVD player for £60 that I would get more satisfaction from 90 minutes of football than using the DVD player.

Opportunity Cost

Opportunity cost is the cost expressed in terms of the next best alternative sacrificed. Opportunity cost is central to the whole study of both economics and business as it is at the heart of the decision-making that characterises the essence of both subject disciplines.

Value helps to explain why the demand curve slopes downwards from left to right. At higher prices, consumers have to sacrifice more utility (the satisfaction gained) from consuming other products. For some in a market, the price they are being asked to pay does not represent value for money—in other words they recognise that the sacrifice of other goods and services they are having to make represents a negative impact on their utility.

Image: Would a dishwasher have price elastic demand or would it be price inelastic?

This is all very theoretical but it is what we do when we make decisions about spending every day. If you go into a shop to buy a chocolate bar, one of the things you will consider is the utility gained from that chocolate bar as opposed to the utility gained from the other chocolate bars on display. If, for example, a Mars bar has gone up in price, you will have to think about whether the amount you are giving up will give you more utility than what you could buy if you spent that same sum of money on other goods.

Businesses therefore have to be concerned about the extent to which consumers are price sensitive. If the price of a Mars bar is increased by £10, it might have a very small effect on the number of people deciding that it is now too expensive and choosing something else instead. However, if a business decided to increase prices for its range of dishwashers by £50, for example, it might have quite a considerable effect on sale.

Consumer Surplus

We have seen earlier how revenue is given by price × the quantity sold. If we look at the demand curve, we can see that at any price, the number of people willing and able to pay that price to acquire those goods or services is given. Thus, the demand curve can give us an indication of the likely total revenue that will be gained at different prices.

In the diagram below, if the price were set at £10, then the quantity demanded would be 100, and total revenue would be £10 × 100 = £1,000. Notice that some people in this market (1 – 99) are prepared to pay more than £10 to acquire this good. They clearly value the product concerned more than £10.

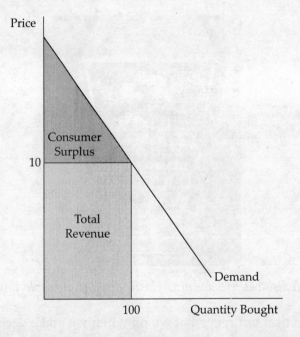

If you think about this in relation to your own purchases it is easy to see what we are talking about here. Think of something you have recently bought. What price was it? Now think about what the maximum amount you were prepared to pay to acquire this product. If this price was higher, then you are getting a degree of surplus value from that product. This is called **'consumer surplus'**.

If you would have been prepared to pay £15 to acquire the product but the price you actually paid was only £10; then you have effectively gained £5 surplus value! Consumer surplus has an interesting application in auctions–eBay is an excellent example. When you use eBay you tend to be bidding for an item in an auction with other bidders. What you are prepared to bid is a reflection of the value you are putting on acquiring that good. You are likely to have an upper level in mind that you are prepared to bid. If, when the auction ends, you get the good for a lot less than you would have bid, then you might be justifiably very pleased. You tell your friends that you got a 'bargain'. What we mean when we talk about bargains is that there is a lot of consumer surplus involved! (Next time you get a bargain, see what the reaction of your friends is by telling them you got a high level of consumer surplus from your purchase!)

For businesses, therefore, they always have to consider how the market will react to pricing levels in terms of the level of demand. They might know that by charging a higher price that they are excluding some people who might want their product. It might be that they do this deliberately as might be the case when trying to pitch the product as being 'exclusive'. But whatever price they charge, they have to think about the level of demand and what revenue it will generate. This will enable them to get some indication as to whether they will be able to make a profit from their activities.

Price Elasticity of Demand

A knowledge of price elasticity of demand is useful in helping make pricing decisions. **Price elasticity of demand** is the responsiveness of demand to changes in price. In simple terms, if the price rises or falls, we know that demand will change but crucially we will want to know how much it changes.

Source: Full house at the Stadium of Light for Sunderland's match against Arsenal in October 2005–all because of price elasticity of demand.

Price elasticity of demand is to do with proportionate changes. If the price is changed by 5% what effect will this have on demand? Will it change by more than 5% or less than 5%? That is really all that elasticity is about! Its importance is that it gives business information about the possible effect on its revenues as a result.

Let's take the example of Sunderland FC's recent experience. Let's assume that the average price of a ticket for a Sunderland home game is around £30. The ground capacity is 47,000. If they sell every seat, then the revenue per home game would be £1,410,000.

Sunderland will know that not every match will sell out–the opposing team may not be very fashionable, the Sunderland team itself might not be as exciting as it could be, and they will need to be mindful of the other options open to potential customers of what they could do with their £30, as well as the income of people in the locality, and so on.

Some games therefore might see relatively low crowds. The cost of staging a match is likely to be pretty much the same however many people turn up and so the marginal cost of filling an extra seat is very low if not zero. For competitions like the Carling Cup, the attendance at grounds across the country is not very high. Let's assume that Sunderland might be expecting a crowd of only 6,000 for such a match. 6,000 fans paying £30 each would yield a revenue of only £180,000. In addition, the atmosphere in the ground would be very poor and would not help the players. Supporters also buy things like programmes, food and drink and thus the revenue generated from associated merchandise sales is likely to be low.

The club decides to offer heavily discounted ticket prices to encourage fans to turn up. The club charged £5 for adults and £1 for children. Let's assume that the average price was £5. The low price encourages people who would not normally go to the match because of the high price of tickets to go to the game. In the event, the game sold out 47,000 fans each paying £5 would yield a revenue of £235,000. Each of those fans might then spend money on programmes, food, drink, and so on and the final revenue for the club would be significantly higher than would have been the case with only 6,000 in the ground.

The below graphs represents how different price elasticities would affect revenue given different price elasticities.

(a) 1) The effect on revenue of reduction in price demand is price inelastic

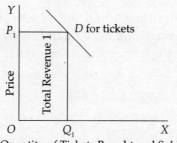

Quantity of Tickets Bought and Sold

(a) 2)

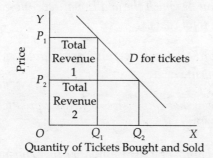

Quantity of Tickets Bought and Sold

(b) 1) The effect on revenue of a rise in price demand is price inelastic

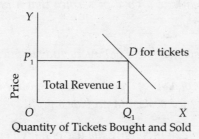

Quantity of Tickets Bought and Sold

(b) 2)

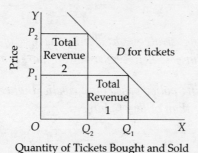

Quantity of Tickets Bought and Sold

In the above example, the demand is price elastic. If the club decided to increase its ticket prices the effect on demand would be to reduce it. But the percentage change in the demand would be greater than the percentage rise in the price and revenue would fall. Again, there would be little point in increasing the price in such circumstances.

Price sensitivity therefore is important to all businesses when considering their pricing strategies. They will need to have some understanding of how their market will react to changes in price and thus what the impact is on their revenue.

KEYWORDS

Price: *The exchange value of a good or service.*

Profit maximisation: *The point at which the additional revenue gained by increasing the price of a product equals the increase in total costs.*

Target return objective: *A short-run or long-run pricing practice intended to achieve a specified return on either sales or investment.*

Value pricing: *A pricing strategy that emphasises benefits a product provides in comparison to the price and quality levels of competing offerings.*

Demand: *A schedule of the amounts of a firm's product that consumers will purchase at different prices during a specified time period.*

Supply: *A schedule of the amounts of a good or service that a firm will offer for sale at different prices during a specified time period.*

Elasticity: *A measure of the responsiveness of buyers and suppliers to changes in price.*

Cost-plus pricing: *The practice of adding a percentage or specified amount (as markup) to the base cost of a product to cover unassigned costs and provide a profit.*

Price skimming: *A pricing strategy involving the use of a high entry price relative to competitive offerings.*

Penetration pricing: *A pricing strategy involving the use of a relatively low entry price as compared with competitive offerings to help secure initial market acceptance.*

Psychological pricing: *A pricing policy based on the belief that certain prices or price ranges make a good or service more appealing than others to buyers.*

Product line pricing: *The practice of setting a limited number of prices for a selection of merchandise.*

Promotional pricing: *A technique that temporarily lowers prices below normal levels in a temporary marketing campaign.*

By-product pricing: *Setting a price for by-products in order to make the main product's price more competitive.*

Captive-product pricing: *Setting a price for products that must be used along with a main product.*

FOB-origin pricing: *A geographic pricing strategy in which goods are placed free on board a carrier; the customer pays the freight from the factory to the destination.*

Going-rate pricing: *Setting price based largely on following competitors' prices rather than on firm's costs or demand.*

Mark-up: *The percentage of the cost or price of a product added to cost in order to arrive at a selling price.*

Product-bundle pricing: *Combining several products and offering the bundle at a reduced price.*

SUMMARY

Pricing is an important element of the marketing mix. Pricing is affected not only by the cost of manufacturing of the product, but also by (i) company objective in relation to market share and sales, (ii) the nature and intensity of competition, (iii) stage of the product life cycle at which the product is currently positioned, (iv) nature of product whether as consumer or industrial product and if the former whether it is a luxury or necessity. Before making any pricing decision it is important to understand all these factors.

The four most commonly used methods are full cost pricing, for a rate of return going rate pricing and customary pricing. While the first two methods are based on the costs incurred, the latter methods are based on the competitor's pricing. Thus, in many cases high price associated with good quality and vice versa.

Before designing the pricing strategy in which the choice is between penetrative and skimming pricing. The marketer must fully understand the connotation of price to a customer. In some a reduction in price may lead to an increase in sales. While in other cases it may not. This is especially true in case of industrial products, where the buyer may be more concerned with quality, reliability, delivery schedules, and after-sales services of the product rather than merely the price. Rather than a reduced price, what may be more relevant is price discounts in the form of quantity or cash discounts.

ASSIGNMENT

Assignment-1

The total annual demand for fans in a country in 1987 was established to be 500,000 units. A company manufacturing table fans had 10% market share. The average price of its fans was ₹500/- per unit. This impact on sales as prices were changed was estimated as follows:

Items	Price	Estimated Sales
A	150/-	46,000
B	520/-	44,000
C	480/-	56,000
D	450/-	100,000

Would you recommend a price change? If yes, what price will you recommend?

Hint: Calculate the sales revenue and gross margin for each of the price levels

_____

_____

_____

_____

Assignment-2

See the following data for a door handle:

Direct labour per unit	₹7.50
Raw materials per unit	₹2.00
Advertising and sales force costs	₹400,000
Other relevant fixed costs	₹100,000
Current going rate (market) price/unit	₹22.00

Questions

1. (a) Find out the contribution/unit
   (b) No. of units to be sold for breaking even (BEP)

2. (a) If profit target is ₹60,000, how many units should be sold?

   (b) If currently 50,000 units are being sold, what is the profit?

3. (a) If owner's investment in the plant is ₹1,000,000 and they desire 20% rate of return before tax after covering all expenses, how many units should be sold?

Case Study: Dynamic pricing–smart pricing?

DHL used to have one-price-fits-all list prices for shipping packages in the United States and around the world, and when potential customers called for rates DHL scared them off by asking for more than FedEx or UPS. With Web pricing tools, DHL tested the market by offering cold callers different prices to see how low prices could go and still make a profit. In the end, DHL wound up changing hundreds of prices. There were plenty of surprises. Most prices did go down, but the company did not have to match the competition. In fact, by lowering prices a bit, DHL's "ad hoc" business not only stabilised but it also grew. For instance, of people who called to get a quote, 17% actually shipper prior to the pricing overhauls. The new prices have increased the ratio to nearly 25%. Constant price revision, however, can be tricky where consumer relationships are concerned. Research shows it tends to work best in situations where there is no bond between the buyer and the seller. One way to make it work is to offer customers a unique bundle of products and services to meet their needs precisely, making it harder for them to make price comparisons. This tactic is being used to sell software, which is vulnerable to price wars because the cost of producing more copies is near zero. Application service providers are 'renting' their software and support by the month instead of selling an unlimited-use licence. The tactic most companies favour, however, is to market perfect pricing as a reward for good behaviour rather than as a penalty. For instance, shipping company APL, Inc., rewards customers who can better predict how much cargo space they ill need with cheaper rates for booking early. Customers are getting savvier about how to avoid buyer's remorse. They are changing their buying behaviour to accommodate the new realities of dynamic pricing–where prices vary frequently by channels, products, customers and time.

Questions

1. Under what conditions will dynamic pricing be smart and successful pricing?
2. Explain the success of DHL's ad-hoc business from a pricing perspective.

Assignment-3

Read the Pricing lesson's learning goals that follow and consider the questions for each goal. Answering these questions will reinforce your understanding of the key concepts in this unit and allow you to check how well you have achieved these learning goals. Where a blank appears before a question, answer with true or false; for multiple choice questions, circle the letter of the correct answer.

Major categories of pricing objectives

1. Pricing objectives include all of the following except

    (a) profit maximisation objectives
    (b) meeting competitors' prices
    (c) market-share objectives
    (d) quality performance objectives
    (e) prestige objectives

2. Profits are

    (a) the most important objective for a firm
    (b) the result of supply and demand
    (c) a function of revenue and expenses
    (d) depend primarily on the quantity of product sold

The concept of price elasticity and its determinants

3. _____ Elasticity measures the responsiveness of manufacturers and distributors to inventory levels.

4. _____ If customers can easily find close substitutes for a good or service, producers tend to encounter elastic demand for it.

Major cost-plus approaches to price setting

5. _____ Cost-plus pricing methods include incremental cost pricing and full cost pricing.

6. _____ Full cost pricing bases decisions on competition and demand for the product.

Major issues related to price determination in international marketing

7. _____ Global pricing strategies almost always depend on demand in the domestic market.

8. _____ A firm's global pricing strategy reflects its global marketing strategy.

Comparing alternative pricing strategies

9. _____ Marketers often practice penetration pricing in industries with few products and little competition.

10. _____ A skimming pricing strategy sets a high market-entry price for a product with little or no initial competition.

Pricing policy decisions that marketers must make

11. _____ Marketers follow pricing policies in making long-term competing pricing decisions.

12. _____ Pricing policy choices includes psychological pricing, price flexibility, product line pricing and promotional pricing.

Relating price to consumer perceptions of quality

13. _____ In general, consumers perceive a high price as a symbol of high quality.

14. _____ Price limits are directly associated with supply and demand.

15. _____ The concept of price limits suggests that unusually low prices may indicate poor quality.

Price negotiations

16. Buyers and sellers negotiate prices most often when.

    (a) Multiple suppliers compete for an order
    (b) Only one available supplier can fill an order
    (c) Contracts over unchanging and routine purchases
    (d) Prices are set once and remain unchanged

Alternative strategies for pricing exports

17. _____ Firms almost always implement the same pricing strategies for domestic and export sales.

18. _____ Market-differentiated pricing allows a firm to price its products according to local marketplace conditions.

REVIEW QUESTIONS

1. What is the most important group of individual factors which influence the price of the product?

2. What type of competitive market structure does your company belong? How much discretion do you have in pricing your products?

3. What would be your pricing strategy if you are faced with an increased excise duty on your product?

4. How do the stage of PLC and product positioning affect the pricing decisions regarding the product of your company?

5. Can you find out some cases where factors other than cost have to be considered for fixing the prices?

6. Define price sensitivity.

7. Can you list some companies who have been able to capture a good market share on the basis of a low price?

8. You are manufacturing washing soap on a small scale. Your capacity is 10,000 cakes per month. Your fixed expenses amount to ₹2000 per year. Variable expenses amount to 40 paise per cake. At what price you would sell your soap, keeping in view the following points.

   (a) You face competition not only from other small but also from large-scale units.
   (b) Other similar soaps sell at 50 to 55 paise per cake.
   (c) You consider your product to be superior to the existing product in the field.
   (d) You cannot afford to have your own distribution organisation?

   What other points would you bear in mind making your decision? Give some reasons for your decision.

DISTRIBUTION AND PUBLIC POLICY

6 CHAPTER

STRUCTURE

6.1 INTRODUCTION

Sales forecasting, though crucial, is one of the grey areas of marketing management. It is crucial because without a proper sales forecast the marketing executive cannot determine the type of marketing programme to use in order to attain the desired sales and marketing objectives. It is a grey area of marketing management in the sense that it is based on a number of assumptions regarding customer and competitor behaviour as well as the market environment, and therefore, its reliability depends upon the extent of culmination of the uncertainty as predicted. Before understanding the various aspects of sales forecasting, let us look at the sales forecasting practices followed by large size companies.

A leading automobile engine manufacturing company determines the sales forecasts of its diesel engines by using two approaches. In the first instance, it uses an econometric model and an estimate of the company's market share to derive the company forecast. Under the second approach the company initiates the process by undertaking a detailed study of the needs of each of its diesel vehicles customers. This study includes an analysis of market factors such as the vehicle manufacturers marketing programme. The resulting forecast is prepared by vehicle manufacturer model, monthwise. These individual manufacturer forecasts are aggregated to produce a company sales forecast which is then compared with the company forecast arrived at under the first approach, and finalised.

6.2 HOW TO PREPARE SALES FORECAST?

The preparation of a sales forecast requires (a) the availability of historical information on the product and industry sales, (b) identification of product sales determinants, (c) predictions regarding the behaviour of market forces for the period under forecast, (d) use of appropriate techniques for forecasting, (e) judgment of executives preparing the sales forecast, and (f) the firm share's objectives. These sales forecasting requirements are given below:

1. An assessment of the total market size.
2. An appreciation of the market trends.
3. Innovations which may have an impact on the market.
4. Market trends in foreign countries where the market pattern is in advance stages of the domestic market.
5. An evaluation of the market share obtained.
6. An evaluation of competitive strengths.
7. The criteria on which purchase decisions are likely to be made.
8. Assessment of elements at work in the market which will influence sales.

9. The influence in the market of competitors.
10. The level of sales needed by the company to obtain optimum use of resources.
11. The image of the company in the market.
12. The market strategy of the company to capitalise on its strength and overcome its weaknesses.
13. An evaluation of the market share which can be obtained.
14. Assessment of factors within the company which will influence sales level.
15. Planned distribution and sales promotion activities by the company.

6.3 APPROACHES TO SALES FORECASTING

There are two general approaches to sales forecasting at the level of the firm–the breakdown approach also called top-down approach, and the market build-up approach.

Breakdown Approach

Under this approach, the head of the marketing function initially develops a general economic and market sales potential for a specific period. The firm's sales potential is then derived from it.

Market Build-up Approach

In this approach, the task of sales forecasting begins by first estimating the sales at the product, product lines, customer groups or geographical area level. The estimates of the different products, product lines, customer groups or geographical areas are then aggregated and received in the light of the firm's objectives, available resources, as well as competition activities before the sales forecast is finalised.

While both the approaches have their own usefulness, the breakdown approach is less time-consuming and costly when it can use aggregate data made available by others. It may, however, lack advantages of greater realism and reliability which result from the use of market build-up approach. Combination of both the approaches though time-consuming seems ideal and worth the effort expended.

6.4 METHODS OF FORECASTING

Let us now consider various methods used for preparing the sales forecast. The methods are commonly grouped into five categories, executive judgement, surveys, time series analysis correlation and regression methods and market share.

1. Executive Judgement

It is an efficient method of sales forecasting. Based on the past performance, insights gained intuition of the executive, this method of sales forecasting works out fairly well particularly when the market is stable. However, this method generally suffers from difficulty in realistic reflecting changes in the market. Sales force composite method and jury of executive opinions are two popular forms of this method of sales forecasting.

2. Surveys

A second way of sales forecasting is by surveying the customers, sales force, experts, etc., and ascertaining their predictions. Customer surveys can provide information relating to type and quantity of products which customers intend purchasing. Sales force surveys can provide estimates of overall territory offtake company's share and the share of the major competitors. Dealer surveys may also form part of the salesforce survey if a firm so desires. Expert surveys provide sales forecast as the expert and industry consultants look at it. A outsider's view to the company internal forecast and helps many a times by adding new dimensions for considerations of management.

3. Time Series Analysis

Using the historical sales data, this method tries to discover a pattern in the firm's sales volume over time. The identification of the pattern helps in sales forecasting.

Time series analysis helps locate the trend, seasonal, cyclic and random factor changes associated with the past sales data. In this way, it improves the predictions from the past sales data. Experience reveals that times series analysis for sales forecasting are quite accurate for short- and medium-term forecasts and more so when demand is stable or follows the past behaviour

Some of the popular techniques of time series analyses are: moving averages, exponential smoothing, time series extrapolation, and Box-Jenkins technique.

4. Correlation and Regression Methods

These methods attempt at examining the relationship between part of sales and one or more variables such as population, per capita income or gross national product, etc. The use of regression analysis is done in order to determine whether any relationship exists between the part sales, and changes in one or more economic, competitive or internal variables to a firm. The accuracy of forecasts made by using correlation and regression methods is generally better than the other methods. Though the correlation method helps in identifying the association between the factors, it does not explain any cause and effect relationship between them.

5. Market Tests

Market tests are basically used for developing one time forecasts particularly relating to new products. A market test provides data about customers' actual purchases and responsiveness to the various elements of the marketing mix. On the basis of the response received to a sample market test and providing for the factor of the market characteristics as well as learning from the market test, product sales forecast is prepared.

6. Combining Forecasts and Using Judgement

Experience brings out that the forecasts resulting from the use of multiple methods in a combined way greatly surpass most individual methods of sales forecasting. Research also supports the combined use of quantitative and qualitative methods of sales forecasting in a given situation rather than using either of the two. Application of judgement to quantitatively arrived forecasts should be done in a structured manner with a view to adding insights and realism to the forecasts so arrived, since a forecast is a prediction and needs the subjective perception too.

Several studies have shown how combining factors by using one or the other methods can improve accuracy of the forecasts. The methods which can be used for combining forecasts are (i) a simple average of two or more forecasts, and (ii) by assigning historical or subjective weights to such forecasts which more closely reflect the changing reality. In short, being aware the firms to prepare for different alternatives forecasts. By monitoring which alternative works better, the firm can learn to achieve its goals more effectively.

6.5 THE EVALUATION OF FORECASTS

Managers face a great deal of difficulty in evaluating their forecasts. The task becomes more difficult when the manager lacks any specific criteria for evaluating the forecasts. Survey of literature suggests the consideration of the following important factors when evaluating forecasts. These factors are: understanding of the state-of-the-art of forecasting techniques, the availability of reliable databases, and knowledge about monitoring environmental changes. The value and outcome process depends on the firm's database and the forecasting manager's experience, the manager's knowledge of the forecasting methods, and models, and his ability to understand the past and present changes.

The Forecasting Audit

In the final analysis forecasting is more of an art than a science, nothing can currently replace experience and good judgements. J. Scott Armstrong of Wharton School, USA suggest a Forecasts Audit Checklist consisting of 16 questions covering the forecasting process, assumption and data, uncertainty and costs. More no's to the questions will indicate negligence on the part of the manager and also lead time to think ideas on how to improve the forecasting process. The suggested checklist appears in Table 6.1.

Table 6.1 Forecasting audit checklist.

Sl. No.	Forecasting Methods	NO	YES
1.	Forecast independent of top management	☐	☐
2.	Forecast used objective methods	☐	☐
3.	Structured techniques used to obtain judgements	☐	☐
4.	Less expensive experts used	☐	☐
5.	More than one method used to obtain forecasts	☐	☐
6.	Users understand the forecasting methods	☐	☐
7.	Forecasts free of judgement	☐	☐
8.	Separate documents prepared for plans	☐	☐
9.	Ample budget for analysis and presentation data	☐	☐
10.	Central data bank exists	☐	☐
11.	Least expensive macroeconomic forecasts and	☐	☐
12.	Upper and lower bounds provided	☐	☐
13.	Quantitative analysis of previous accuracy provided	☐	☐
14.	Forecasting prepared for alternative futures	☐	☐
15.	Arguments listed against each forecasting	☐	☐
16.	Amount spent on forecasting reasonable	☐	☐

It is also seen that the ultimate test of how good a sales forecasts is whether it can improve the firm's marketing strategy.

Computerised Sales Forecasting

The rapid development in computer hardware and software has made it possible for managers to make sophisticated forecasts with the help of computers. The greatest advantage is that managers can introduce subjective inputs into the forecast and immediately test their effects.

Specifically, the last few years have seen sophisticated forecasting models being rewritten using by different databased software programmes for personal computers. Nowadays vast techno has improved in different kinds of software and development in the computers field especially in artificial intelligence system have also enabled the development of expert system models, i.e. the model that the experts use in making a decision. These are of great use when the judgement is an important part of the forecast. In future, we are going to see greater use of computers in sales forecasting in India.

Relating the sales forecast to the sales budget and profit planning

In order to achieve forecasted sales and planned profits, a certain level of sales inputs are must. The required sales inputs when expressed in monetary term result in the preparation of the sales budget. Since the sales inputs have to be deployed in anticipation of the sales results which may or may not be achieved on the expected lines suggest caution to be exercised while expanding the sales budget. Profitable marketing suggests a break-up of the sales budget on product wise territory sales-wise and time period wise in the first instance. The second basic requirement relates to close monitoring of the actual sales against the targets on a continuing basis.

The thumb rule is that not more than 40% of sales budget should be spent in the first six months of the budget year. The underlying logic is that since a sales forecast is based on assumption, sales efforts should be spent in conjunction with the culmination of reality as assumed.

The dynamic nature of the market, therefore, requires that the managers must feel the pulse of the market particularly in relation to the sales budget and profit plan of the firm. For, if forecasting is not practised as a dynamic activity, then there may be little to regulate the continued use of sales budget and erosion of profitability. It is important, therefore, to use simple yet comprehensive sales information formats to monitor the market and conduct sales analysis at a regular periodicity.

6.6   DEFINING DISTRIBUTION CHANNELS

Different people perceive marketing channels in different ways, some see it as a route taken by a product as it moves from the producer to the consumer, and others describe it as a loose coalition of business firms that have come together for purpose of business. Customers may view marketing channels as simply 'a lot of middlemen' standing between the producer and the product. Given all these different perspectives it is not possible to have one single definition for marketing channels. Marketing channels can be defined as the external contractual organisation that management operates to achieve its distribution objectives.

There are four terms in this definition that has to be given a special mention, namely, external, contractual organisation, operates and distribution objectives. The term external means that the marketing channel exists outside the firm. Managing of the marketing channel therefore involves the use of inter-organisational management (managing more than one firm) rather than intra-organisational management (managing one firm). The term contractual organisation refers to those firms which are involved in the negotiatory function as the product moves from the producer to the end user. The function of these firms involves buying, selling and transferring of goods and services. Transportation companies, public warehouses, banks ad agencies do not come under these and are referred to as facilitating agencies. The third term suggests the involvement of management in the channels and this may range from the initial development of the channel structure to the day-to-day management. Finally the distribution objectives explain the distribution goals the organisation has in mind. When the objectives change, variations can be seen in the external contractual organisations and the way in which the management operates. In simpler terms, a channel then consists of producer, consumer and any intermediary. Marketing channel strategy is one of the major strategic areas of marketing. In most cases eliminating middlemen will not reduce prices, because the amount that goes to the intermediaries compensates them for the performance of tasks that must be accomplished regardless of whether or not an intermediary is present. In simple terms, a company can eliminate intermediaries but cannot eliminate the functions they perform.

Need for and Importance of Channels of Distribution

The need for and the importance of the channels of distribution is clear from the role they play and the functions they perform in the marketing of goods. Channels of distribution play a very important part in the marketing of goods. Their importance in the marketing of goods is as follows:

1. Channels of distribution serve as a bridge between the producers and final consumers or industrial users, in the sense that it is through the channels of distribution that the producers deliver their goods to the ultimate consumers or users.

2. The channels of distribution help to move the goods from one place to another, and thereby, add place utility to the goods.

3. They bring the goods to the final consumers or users, whenever they want them, and thereby, add time utility to goods.

4. They helps in the transfer of title to goods, and thereby create position or ownership utility.

5. They make the goods available to the consumers in convenient unit or size, package etc. and thereby, add to the convenience of the consumers.

6. They have vital impact on decision-making in all the areas of marketing. The channel decisions determine the size of the sales force, type of sales force, etc.

6.7 FLOWS IN MARKETING CHANNELS

As discussed a conventional channel of distribution consists of a manufacturer, a wholesaler, a retailer and the ultimate consumer. Not all the channels include all these marketing institutions. At times the product passes directly from the manufacturer to the consumer. There are five most important flows, namely, as represented in Fig. 6.1.

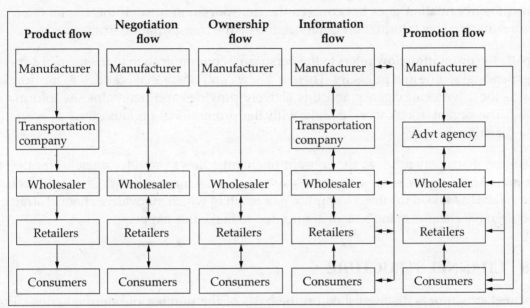

Source: The orgin and concept of flows in marketing channels is generally attributed to Ronald S. Valie, E.T Grether and Reavis Cox

Fig. 6.1 Flows in the marketing channel.

The **product flow** refers to actual physical movement of the product from the manufacturers through all the parties who take physical possession of the product from the point of production to the final consumer.

Negotiation flow represents the interplay of the buying and the selling functions associated with the transfer of title. If you note from the above diagram, you find the transportation firm is not included in the flow because it does not participate in the negotiation function, also you can find the arrows flow in both the directions, indicating the negotiation is mutual at all levels of the channels. The ownership flow shows the movement of the title to the product as it is passed along from the manufacturer to the consumer, here as well we find the transportation function missing since the transportation firm does not take title or is actively involved in the facilitating function. It merely involves in transporting physical products.

In case of the **information flow**, we can see that the transportation function has reappeared and all the arrows are two-directional. All the parties participate in the exchange of information. For example, Coke may obtain information from the transportation company about its shipping schedules and the rates, while the transportation firm may seek information regarding when and in what quantities it plans to ship its products. Sometimes the information bypasses the transportation company directly to the wholesaler or the retailer when the information does not concern the transportation firm. If there is an offer, or a price reduction this information is not needed by the transportation firms.

Finally the **promotion flow** refers to the persuasive communication in the form of advertising, personal selling and publicity. There is a new component that is added to the flow and that is the advertising agency and this actively provides and maintains the information flow. The organisations work closely with the promotional organisations so we find a two-directional arrow.

From the management view, the concept of channel flows provides a useful framework for understanding the scope and complexity of channel management. Changing scenario does make the role of the firms' complex, as a result of which innovative channel strategies and effective channel management are needed to make this happen.

6.8 CHANNEL STRUCTURE

Channel structure is distinguished on the basis of the number of intermediaries. There are different levels in a channel structure. The common levels are zero-level, one-level, two-level, and three-level. Each level presents both opportunities and challenges for the marketer. Figure 6.2 gives a picture of the different levels.

1. **Zero-level** structure is one of the simplest forms of the channel structure. Here organisations like Avon, Eureka Forbes use direct selling mode to take the products from their production houses to the consumers directly. A lot of money has to be spent in order to make this channel structure effective, as there is no third party to take your product to the consumer. Even a bakery can come as a firm, which bakes cakes and sells it directly to the consumers. Marketers who use the mailing services, toll-free numbers are also using this service.

2. **One-level** structure is one in which we have one intermediary acting as a link between the manufacturer and the consumer. Here the retailers procure goods directly from the manufacturer and supply it to the consumers. Retailers like Viveks, Wal-Mart deal directly with the manufacturer. In some cases in order to retain profitable and reputed retailers the manufacturers act as wholesalers. One of the advantages for the intermediaries is the customisation and the discounts they receive.

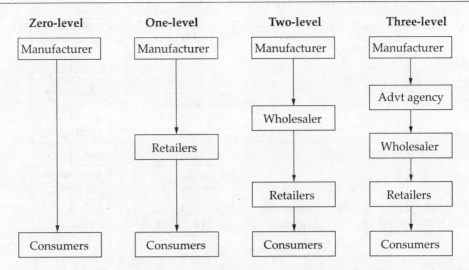

Fig. 6.2 Typical channel structure for consumer goods.

3. **Two-level** channel has two people interceding before the product reaches the consumer. Here there would be a wholesaler and a retailer who takes the efforts for a speedy delivery and this is one of the most commonly used structures for consumer goods. In the case of Metro, most of the small retail and Kirana stores buy all the merchandise from Metro and in turn sell them to the consumer. One of the advantages of the two-level structure is the benefit of using the wholesaler in the distribution of services.

4. **Three-level** channel happens predominantly when the firm plans to go global. When a manufacturer enters another country, it always holds well when he uses the help of agents to operate in that environment. The agents are people who know the legal procedures and who can negotiate with the host country in case of a problem. Most of the airlines that operate in different countries take the help of agents to penetrate the market.

Example of Consumer Markets

When it comes for business-to-business operations, the channels differ from the consumer markets, in this structure, firms predominantly may use their existing sales force to sell the products to the customers, and they may even use industrial distributors to take their products to the industrial customers. Figure 6.3 details the business-to-business model of channel structure.

Mark Andy is one of the big names in the printing machines industry. In India Mark Andy supplies its printing machines to the industrial customers through Heidelberg, an

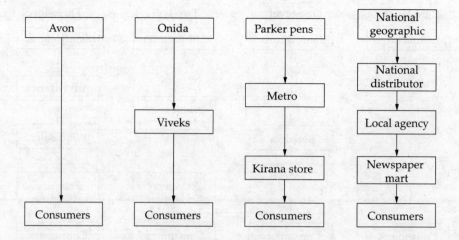

industrial distributor. It also has its own representatives who pitch in when the customer needs information. In case of Industrial Channel, the zero-level, one-level and two-level are the most commonly used methods. When it comes for business-to-business channels agents become the integral point of the whole process, since the characteristic of the business-to-business market is oligopolistic and are huge buyers.

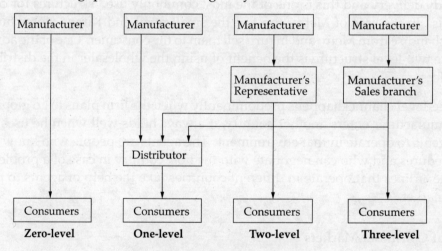

Fig. 6.3 B2B marketing channels.

6.9   FUNCTIONS OF DISTRIBUTION CHANNELS

Some of the major functions performed by the intermediaries are mainly physical distribution, communication and facilitating functions. When we talk about physical functions, they include braking bulk, accumulating bulk, creating assortments, reducing transactions and transporting and storing.

1. Breaking Bulk: One of the important role intermediaries perform is bulk-breaking function. Here these organisations buy in large quantities and break them into smaller quantities and pass them to the retailers, wholesalers or even to the customers. By doing so, the intermediaries reduce the cost of distribution for the manufacturers as well as the consumers. This particular function is also termed 'resolution of economic discrepancies' Fig. 6.4 gives a pictorial description of bulk breaking.

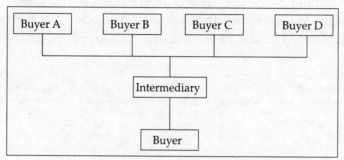

Source: Adapted from William Zikmund & Michael d'Amico

Fig. 6.4 Bulk-breaking function.

2. Accumulating Bulk: At times the intermediaries also do the task of accumulating the bulk. The intermediaries may buy bulk from different small producers, accumulate them and offer to those buyers who prefer large quantities. The intermediaries in accumulating

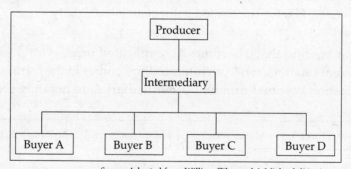

Source: Adapted from William Zikmund & Michael d'Amico

Fig. 6.5 Bulk-accumulating function.

the bulk are mostly found in the agricultural businesses, whereby the intermediary will procure vegetables from local farmers and assemble them and sell it to the wholesalers. Figure 6.5 gives a clear picture on accumulating bulk. Once the marketers accumulate bulk they start to sort the products identifying differences in the quality, grades and classify them into different categories.

3. Creating Assortments: The third important function of the intermediaries is creating assortments. When we take the case of magazines, on an average there are around thousands of magazines being published in a month and it is impossible for a particular newsstand to get it going, here big distributors and agents work in creating assortments and enable a speedy process. This needs a lot of teamwork and timing. Certain magazines become outdated within a certain period of time.

4. Reducing Transactions: One of the biggest reasons that keep the economy moving and the customer smiling is the presence of intermediaries, they reduce the number of transactions necessary to accomplish the exchange of goods. It is represented in Fig. 6.6 that shows the complicated nature of the transaction if an intermediary does not come in place

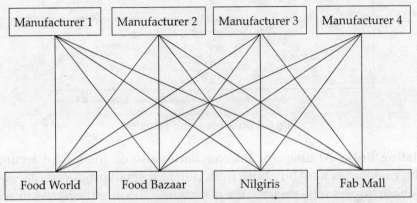

Fig. 6.6 Transaction without an intermediary.

In the above exhibit, we find that it becomes a complicated process for the manufacturers to work on with different retailers, when an intermediary comes in the form of a wholesaler we find the whole situation becomes different. Intermediaries do not only reduce the number

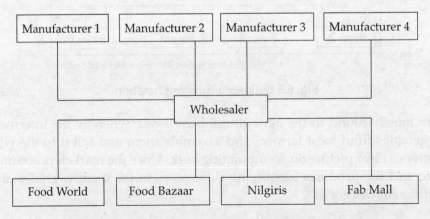

Fig. 6.7 Reduction of transactions by an intermediary.

of transactions but also help in the reduction of the geographical distances that both buyers and sellers have to cover. Channel intermediaries doing the roles of a buying agent for their customer and selling agents for the manufacturers does simplify the process of transaction considerably. From Fig. 6.7, we find the reduction in the number of transactions that happen between the manufacturer and the retailer.

5. Transporting and Storing: Apart from breaking, accumulating, creating assortments and reducing transactions, they also perform two key marketing functions, namely, transporting and storing. The final product has to be moved from the point of production to the point of consumption. This means it involves storing the product along the way till it is delivered. Most of the big retailers hold enough of the product in order to cater to the consumers.

6. Credit Services: Apart from the function of physical distribution the intermediaries also help in offering credit services. Even though there are firms like Metro, which are predominantly cash and carry kind of intermediaries, most of the intermediaries provide credit facility or even paying in parts. Many intermediaries offer about 30 to 45 days to the retailers for paying back.

7. Risk Taking: One of the vital functions of the intermediaries is risk taking. Not every product finds favour in the eyes of the customer, much fallout within few months, as a result of which the intermediaries would be at risk. An uncontrollable factor like floods, earthquakes or even contamination or fire could pose a serious threat. The intermediaries have to bear these risks along with the market risks. These are some of the core functions intermediaries perform enabling goods and services to reach consumers at the right time.

6.10 FACTORS AFFECTING CHANNELS OF DISTRIBUTION

The selection of the proper channel of distribution must be made by a manufacturer or producer through a careful study of the various factors that influence the channel choice. The various factors that influence the selection of the channel of distribution by a manufacturer or producer or the factors affecting channel decisions are:

1. Product Characteristics

Product characteristics refer to the various characteristics of a product such as its class (i.e., whether it is a consumer product or an industrial product and if it is a consumer product, whether it is a convenience product or shopping product or speciality product, and if it is an industrial product, either it is a raw material, or operating supply or fabricating part of a capital equipment), its nature (i.e., whether it is a durable product or a perishable product), its bulk and size, its uses, its price, the rapidity of fashion change, the frequency of its purchase, the sales and after the sales services required by the product, etc. The product characteristics have considerable influence on the selection of the channels of distribution. For instance, perishable goods must be placed in the hands of the consumers as quickly as possible, and so they require direct selling. So also products which have high unit value like speciality goods require either direct selling or selling through selected distributors. On the other hand, convenience goods require the use of a large number of middlemen, especially the retailers.

2. Customer Characteristics

Customer characteristics refer to the number of potential buyers, their geographical dispersion, their frequency and regularity of purchasers, their average purchases, their buying motives, etc. The customer characteristics influence the selection of the channels of distribution considerably. For instance, direct sale or sale through short channels is usually practised when the customers are few in number concentrated in a limited geographical area. And they purchase large units infrequently and regularly. On the other hand, lengthier marketing channels are used when the customers are large in the number and are widely distributed, they purchase small quantities frequently and irregularly.

3. Middlemen Characteristics

Middlemen characteristics refer to the number of middlemen available for distributing the products, their willingness to undertake the work of distribution, their location, their size, and financial strength, their product lines, their sales potentiality, their behaviour, etc. The middlemen characteristics also exert considerable influence on the selection of the channels of distribution.

4. Supply Characteristics

Supply characteristics refer to the number of producers to the suppliers, their concentration or dispersion, the quantum of their supplies, etc. The supply characteristics also influence the selection of the channels of distribution. For instance, if producers or suppliers are few in the number and are geographically concentrated in a limited area, direct selling or selling through short channels of distribution is practised, on the other hand, if producers are large in number and are widely dispersed, then a long channel of distribution is used.

5. Distribution Policies of the Producer or Manufacturer

A concern may adopt the policy or practice of intensive distribution or maximum distribution (i.e., distribution of a product through as many channels as possible) or selective distribution (i.e., the distribution of a product through a selected number of intermediaries) or selected limited agency distribution (i.e., the distribution of a product through a few or limited agencies) or exclusive agency distribution (i.e., distribution of a product through an exclusive or single agency). The distribution policy followed by a concern has a great bearing upon the selection of the channel of distribution.

6. Channels of Rivals

While selecting the channels of distribution, the effectiveness of the channels of distribution adopted by the rivals should be studied. If the channels of distribution adopted by the rivals are found to be effective, it is preferable to adopt the same channels of distribution. This is because these channels are familiar to the purchasers and it is very easy to reach the customers through the familiar channels.

7. Company Characteristics

Company characteristics refer to the various characteristics of the manufacturing company such as its size, financial position, product mix, etc. The company characteristics also play an important role in the selection of the channels of distribution. For instance, a big concern with strong financial position and wide product lines can afford to engage in direct selling. On the other hand, a small and financially weak concern with the narrow product line is forced to use the service of middlemen for the distribution of its products.

8. Economic Conditions and Laws of the Country

Economic conditions influence the selection of the channels of distribution. For instance, when economic conditions are depressed, shorter channels of distribution are preferable. Similarly, the laws of the country also influence the selection of the channels of the distribution, for instance, when there is multi-point tax on sales, naturally, direct selling to consumers or direct selling to retailers or the use of agent middlemen is quite common.

9. Costs of the Marketing Channels

The relative costs of the various channels of distribution also influence the selection of the channels of distribution. Generally, those channels which ensure efficient distribution and secure the desired sales volume at the lowest possible costs are chosen by a manufacturer or producer.

Factors Influencing the Choice of Intermediaries or Middlemen

Just as a number of factors affect the choice of distribution channels. Many factors influence the choice of intermediaries in the channels of distribution. The following factors are:

1. Type and extent of market served by the intermediary.
2. The product line in which the intermediary specialises.

3. The financial position of the intermediary.
4. The market reputation enjoyed by the intermediary.
5. The selling policies of the intermediary compatible with those of the producer.
6. The continued relationship for a long time between the producer and the intermediary.
7. The sales organisation, i.e., the utility and efficiency of the sales force of the intermediary.
8. Other facilities, such as storage facilities, delivery vans, etc. possessed by the intermediary.

6.11   DESIGNING DISTRIBUTION CHANNELS

Channel design refers to those decisions that involve in the development of new marketing channels or modifying the existent ones. The channel design decision can be broken down into six steps, namely:

1. Recognising the need for channel design decision
2. Setting and coordinating distribution objectives
3. Specify the distribution tasks
4. Develop alternative channel structures
5. Evaluate relevant variables
6. Choose the best channel structure.

1. Recognising the Need for a Channel Design Decision

First and foremost task for the organisation is to recognise the need for a channel design. An organisation would go in for a new channel design for the following reasons, namely,

❖ When a new product or product line is developed, mainly when the existing channels are not suitable for the new line.
❖ When the existing product is targeted to a different target market. This is common when an organisation is used to catering the B2B, plans to enter the consumer market.
❖ When there is a change in the marketing mix elements, when an organisation reduces its prices on certain offering the channel worked out will be based on the price points, they may look in for discounters.
❖ When facing major environmental changes namely in economic or technological or in legal spheres.
❖ Finally, when the organisation opens up new geographic marketing areas the list by no means is comprehensive, but gives a picture about some of the most common conditions when channel design decisions are worked out.

2. Setting and Coordinating Distribution Objectives

Once a need for a design is recognised the next task for the channel manager is to work out to develop the channel structure, either from the scratch or by modifying the existing one. It is necessary for the channel manager to carefully evaluate the firm's distribution objectives. In order for the distribution objectives to be effective and well coordinated, the channel manager needs to perform three tasks, namely,

- Become familiar with the objectives and strategies in other marketing mix areas and other relevant objectives and strategies of the firm. In most cases, the person or the group that sets the objectives of the other marketing mix elements will also set the objectives for distribution as well.

- Set the objectives and state them explicitly. A good objective is one, which is clear, and explicit, and has a greater role in achieving the firm's overall objectives. Some examples of a good distribution objectives are as follows, at the start of the new millennium, *Apple Computers set a distribution objective to reach more consumers with what it refers to as the 'Apple experience'. So, Apple reinvigorated and reestablished relationships with large retail chains, which it had neglected in recent years. In the same way, Coca-Cola seeks to broaden its penetration in schools and colleges, as a result of which it has entered into contract with many schools and colleges, whereby these institutions would sell only Coca-Cola products on their campuses.*

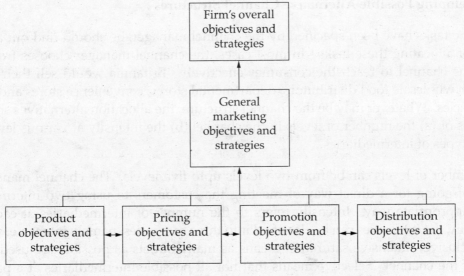

Fig. 6.8 Reduction of transaction by an intermediary.

- Check and see if the distribution objectives are congruent with marketing and other general objectives and strategies of the firm. This involves verifying if the distribution objectives do not conflict with the objectives in the other areas of marketing mix or even to the overall objectives of the company. In order to crosscheck, it is essential to examine the interrelationships and hierarchy of the objectives of the firms. Figure 6.8 gives a clear picture of the same.

3. Specifying the Distribution Tasks

Once the objectives are formulated, a number of functions need to be performed in order for the distribution objectives to be met. The manager, therefore, has to specify the nature of the tasks that need to be carried out in order to meet the objectives. The tasks need to be precisely stated so that it meets the specified distribution objectives. For example a manufacturer of a consumer product, say a high quality cricket bat aimed at serious amateur cricket players would need to specify distribution tasks such as gathering information on target markets shopping patterns, promote product availability to the target, maintain inventory, and timely availability, compile information about the product features, provide hands-on experience using the product, process and fill customers orders, transport the product, arrange for credit provisions, provide warranty, provide repair and service, establish product return to make the offering readily available. Sometimes these functions may appear to be production oriented rather than distribution tasks, but when we talk about meeting customers, they are indeed distribution tasks.

4. Developing Possible Alternative Channel Structures

Once the tasks have been specified by the channel manager, he should find out alternate ways of allocating these tasks. In most cases, the channel manager chooses from more than one channel to reach the consumer effectively. Britannia would sell their biscuits through wholesale food distributors, departmental stores, convenience stores and even in pharmacies. Whatever may be the channel structure, the allocation alternatives should be in terms of (a) the number of levels in the channel (b) the intensity at various levels, and (c) the types of intermediaries.

The number of levels can be from two levels upto five levels. The channel manager can think of going for a direct way of meeting the customers to using two intermediaries as an appropriate way. Intensity refers to the number of intermediaries at each level. Generally, the intensities can be classified into three categories, namely intensive, selective and exclusive. Intensive saturation means as many outlets as possible are used at each level of the channel. Selective means that not all possible intermediaries at a particular level are used. Exclusive refers to a very selective pattern of distribution. A firm like Parle may use intensive distribution channel structure, while Rolex may use high degree of selectivity. The types of intermediaries, third component has to be carefully dealt with. The firms should not overlook new types of intermediaries that have emerged in recent years particularly the auction firms such as Baazee, bid or buy as possible sales outlet for their products.

5. Evaluating the Variables affecting Channel Structure

Once the alternative structures have been outlined, each channel structure has to be evaluated on a number of variables. There are five basic categories, namely

Market variables–Marketing management is based on the philosophy of marketing concept, which stresses on the consumer's needs and wants, the managers have to take the cues from the market. The subcategories that have a greater influence on the market structure are market geography, market size, market density and market behaviour.

Product variables–Some of the most important product variables are bulk and weight, perishability, unit value, degree of standardisation, technical vs. non-technical and newness. Heavy and bulky products have a high handling and shipping costs relative to their value. The manufacturers of such products have to keep in mind to ship in large lots to a fewer possible points. It would always be better if the channel structure remains short. Food products, flowers are considered to be highly perishable. When products are highly perishable, the channel structure should be designed to provide rapid delivery from producers to consumers. One important consideration is lower the unit value of a product, the longer the channels should be as low unit value leaves small margins for distribution costs. Figure 6.9 explains the relationship between the degree of standardisation and channel length. If the product flows directly from manufacturer or producer to the user the degree of customisation is more, but as the product becomes more standardised it passes through many channels. Mostly the B2B machinery has a great degree of customisation as it passes from the manufacturer to the industrial user, while many consumer market are predominantly standardised ones. When it comes for the technical component, the industrial products are mostly distributed through direct channels because of the technical expertise and service while many technical consumer products do use shorter channel structure. When the product is new and is in the introductory stage in order to capitalise on the aggressive promotion, a shorter channel is preferred to gain awareness.

Company variables–The important variables that affect a good channel design are size, financial capacity, managerial expertise and objectives and strategies. Larger the firms in terms of size it enables them to exercise a substantial amount of power in the channel. The size does give flexibility for the firm in picking the channel structures. The same holds true when it comes for the financial capability. Greater capital available with a firm, less dependency is seen on the intermediaries. When a firm is into industrial marketing, it

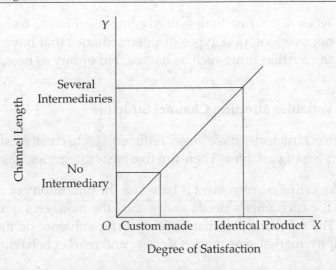

Fig. 6.9 Relationship between degree of standardisation and channel strength.

prefers to have its own sales force, warehousing, order processing capabilities and larger firms with good financial backing are better able to bear the high cost of these facilities. When a firm lacks quality managerial skills, a comprehensive channel structure ranging from wholesalers to brokers are needed to perform the distribution activity, once the firm gains experience it can change or reduce the number of intermediaries. The objectives and strategies a firm has may limit the use of intermediaries. These strategies may emphasise on aggressive promotion and may even alter the distribution tasks. Overall this is one of the prime variables used for evaluating.

Intermediary variables–The important intermediary variables are availability, costs and services offered. The availability is one of the key variables as this influences the channel structure. If we take the case of Dell Computers, due to lack of a proper channel structure it designed a direct mail order channel, which provided a strong technical backup as well. The cost is another variable a channel manager considers. If the cost of using a particular intermediary is too high compared to the services it offers, the manager may consider in minimizing the use of intermediaries. The services performed by the intermediaries is another integral component, a good intermediary is one, which offers efficient services at the lowest cost.

Environmental variables–The uncontrollable or the macro environmental forces may affect the different aspects of channel development and management. Forces like the socio-cultural, economic, technological, legal forces have a significant impact on the channel structure. The other variables are those the organisations can work upon or change to the situation but the environmental forces are those the organisations has to cope up with.

6. Choosing the 'Best' Channel Structure

In deciding the manager should choose an optimal channel structure that would offer desired level of effectiveness at the lowest possible cost. Even though there is not one set method to pick an optimal channel structure, it all depends on the orientation of the firm. If the goal of the firm were profit maximisation, the channel structure would be in line with the goal. Most channel choices are still, however, made on the basis of managerial judgement and the data that is available.

6.11.1 Managing Channel Members and Their Conflicts

After a particular channel is selected, the marketer must manage or administer the channel members or intermediaries. Managing channel members include

(a) Selecting intermediaries
(b) Motivating channel members or middlemen
(c) Controlling or managing channel conflicts
(d) Evaluating performance of channel members

(a) Selecting intermediaries: Selection of intermediaries or middlemen is a continuous process because some of them leave the channel or get terminated by the marketer. Hence, it is not the part of a channel design. It is necessary for the marketer to determine criteria or factors for selection of intermediaries. These criteria differ depending on the type of middlemen and the firm's particular product/market conditions. Some of the common factors considered are financial standing, location, prior experience and type of customers served.

(b) Motivating middlemen: The marketer must continuously motivate his intermediaries to achieve long-term success. Motivating the intermediaries to achieve top performance should start with understanding the middlemen's needs, perceptions and outlook. The quality of support from middlemen will depend on the motivational techniques used and incentives offered.

(c) Controlling channel conflicts: Even though a manufacturer's channel design is well done, there will be some conflict because of the differences in the objectives and perceptions of the channel members. The conflicts or tensions between the channel members can damage channel performance. Marketers should periodically undertake surveys of intermediaries or conduct formal/informal discussions with them to assess the areas or sources of conflicts. Some of the sources of conflict are indicated in Table 6.2.

Table 6.2 Sources of Channel Conflicts

S. No	Sources of Conflict	Examples
1.	Differences in objectives	Manufacturers want long-term profitability but middlemen prefer short-term
2.	Dealings with customers	Middlemen feel cheated when the manufacturer deals with large customers and asks them to serve small customers
3.	Differences in interest	The manufacturer feels that the middlemen are not giving attention to the firm's products. The middlemen are interested in products that are fast moving or have higher margins for them
4.	Differences in perceptions	The manufacturer wants the middleman to carry a higher inventory due to the perception of good market conditions. The middleman does not share this optimism
5.	Competition	Manufacturer's representatives feel that the commission offered by the manufacturer is not adequate. The manufacturer thinks otherwise
6.	Unclear territory boundaries	The territory boundaries between middlemen are not clear, resulting in competition among the firms' intermediaries to secure business from the same customers

The channel conflicts can be controlled or managed in several ways, including:

- Effective communication network
- Joint goal-setting
- Diplomacy
- Mediation
- Arbitration
- Developing a vertical marketing system.

An effective communication network between the manufacturer and the intermediaries can be developed through periodic formal and informal meetings and cooptation of intermediaries in board of directors or advisory committees. In joint-goal setting, the channel members come to an agreement on the superordinate (or fundamental) goals they jointly seek. Such goals can be market share leadership, customer satisfaction or product/service quality in a highly competitive market where survival and success of channel members depend on their performance and cooperation. The channel members may resort to diplomacy, mediation or arbitration, when conflicts are sharp. Diplomacy is used when the conflict is resolved through discussions between the persons from both the parties. In mediation, a neutral third party tries to conciliate the interests of the two parties. In arbitration, both the parties present their arguments to a third party (i.e., the arbitrator) and agree to accept the arbitration decision.

d) Evaluating channel members: It is a good policy for the marketer to evaluate the performance of each channel member periodically. An evaluation is useful to know which intermediaries are achieving favourable results and which are not. The intermediaries not performing well need to be counselled, re-trained, re-motivated or terminated. An evaluation data can also be used while deciding which type of middlemen to be used. The factors or criteria to be used for an evaluation of middlemen's performance can include sales achieved versus sales quota, average inventory levels, customer delivery performance, customer complaints, cooperation in market feedback, support for new products and new customers generated.

6.12   CHANNEL DYNAMICS

Like any other concept, channel systems do change according to the development and the need of the hour. With consumers becoming conscious of where they buy and how they want things to be delivered there has emerged different systems, namely, the vertical, horizontal and multi-channel marketing systems. The conventional or the traditional marketing channel encompasses a producer, one or few wholesalers and one or few retailers. The objective of these different players is to see that they make enough profits, they are highly independent and don't have control over other channel members.

In contrast, the **Vertical Marketing System (VMS)** has the three members acting as one unified team, there is one channel member who owns the other members or allows franchising but ensures a greater role in the execution. Many organisations have started to operate in this format as strong channel members try to dictate terms for the producer as well as when they found the objectives of different channel members differ from that of the producer. There are three variants of vertical marketing system, namely, corporate, administered and contractual vertical marketing system. In case of corporate, the organisation combines the production and the distribution under one roof. Organisations like Asian Paints, Amul are not only involved in the production of the products but they also own a considerable no. of outlets. An administered vertical marketing system coordinates the production and distribution efficiencies but use their size as a dominant influence. HUL commands a greater shelf space or Samsung gets better displays in retail outlets purely because of their size and the reputation they carry with them. The third variant, namely, contractual vertical marketing system coordinates the activities of individual firms at different levels integrating their programmes at contractual levels. Firms like McDonalds, KFC use this type of vertical marketing systems for the integration of their businesses.

The **horizontal marketing systems** is one where two or more unrelated businesses come together pull in resources to exploit the emerging opportunities. Many private players especially banks have got into the act of tie-ups with retail stores or even with fuel outlets in order to gain greater market. ICICI bank has got tied with Big Bazaar, and this has greatly enhanced the reputation of both these firms as well as increasing the customer base respectively.

The **multi-channel marketing systems** as the term simplifies it is one in which a firm uses multiple channels to reach different customer segments. In the present scenario, most organisations have started to use multiple channel method because it helps in the expansion of the market coverage, it costs little when the target segment is small instead of using a bigger channel and mainly helps in customising the offering according to the need of the segments.

When distribution goes overseas they are bound to face a lot of restraints and problems like the host country laws, the laws of the country to which the goods are shipped, the laws of the nations through which the goods pass must be abided by the company. Apart from this, other environmental factors do play an active role when considered from a macro-marketing perspective. In the next chapter, we deal with the role of retailers, wholesalers and logistics in this value chain and how do they facilitate the process of performing the channel function effectively.

6.13   RETAILING

Retailing is one of the largest sectors in the global economy. It employs almost 23 million people in United States alone, generating about \$3 trillion in sales annually. About 50 organisations in the Fortune 500 are from the retail sector. Retail is one among the fastest growing industry. Consider Wal-Mart, the biggest retailer in the world with approximately \$250 billion in sales was started in the early sixties, while Fortune came with its annual ranking of top 500 organisations in 1952, a year when nobody would have dreamt about Wal-Mart. In the early nineties for the first time Wal-Mart became the top organisation according to Fortune Magazine, which it still continues to hold. Retail is the buzzword today and this lesson explores the emerging retail scenario and the strategies available for different retail formats. Figure 6.10 shows that distribution of the product begins from the producer or the manufacturer and ends with the consumer, between them are the retailers who act as a link. The word 'retail' is derived from the French word retailer, meaning 'to cut a piece off' or 'to break bulk.

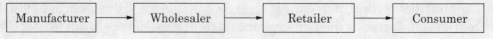

Fig. 6.10 Distribution channel.

Wholesalers buy products from manufacturers and sell them to retailers while retailers take the product from wholesalers to the consumers. While the wholesalers try to satisfy the retailers, the retailers make all the effort in satisfying the needs of the consumers. Retailing has become an intrinsic part of our everyday lives and this has been evident with the nations that have enjoyed the greatest economic and social progress have been those with a strong retail sector. Retailing encompasses selling through mail, the Internet, door-to-door visits apart from brick and motor stores.

Nature and Importance of Retailing

Retailing includes all the activities involved in selling goods or services directly to final consumers for their personal, non-business use. Any organisation that does this selling– whether a manufacturer, wholesaler, or retailer–is doing retailing. It does not matter how the goods or services are sold (by person, mail, telephone or vending machine) or where they are sold (in a store, on the street, or in the consumer's home). On the other hand, a retail store is any business enterprise whose sales volume comes primarily from retailing.

Types of Retailers

Retail organisations exhibit great variety and new forms keep emerging. Several classifications have been proposed. For our purposes, we will discuss store retailers, non-store retailing, and retail organisations.

I. Store Retailers

Consumers today can shop for goods and services in a wide variety of stores. Marketing Environment and Trends describes the most important retail-store types, many of which are found in most countries. Retail-store types, like products, pass through stages of growth and decline that can be described as the retail life cycle.

One reason that new store types emerge to challenge old store types is given by the wheel-of-retailing hypothesis. Conventional store types typically offer many services to their customers and price their merchandise to cover the cost. A large number of shoppers use the conventional stores for deciding what to buy and then drive to the discount stores to make the actual purchase.

New store types emerge to meet widely different consumer preferences for service levels and specific services. Thus, in the past, most consumers purchased shoes in shoe stores, where they were waited on by fitters. Today, most shoes are bought in mass-merchandise outlets where consumers take them off the shelf, and an increasing number of shoes are purchased through the mail. It turns out that retailers in most product categories can position themselves as offering one of four levels of service:

1. **Self-Service Retailing:** Used in many retailing operations, especially for obtaining convenience goods and, to some extent, shopping goods. Self-service is the corner-stone of all discount operations. Many customers are willing to carry out their own locate-compare-select process to save money.

2. **Self-Selection Retailing:** Involves customers in finding their own goods, although they can ask for assistance. Customers complete their transactions by paying a salesperson for the item. Self-selection organisations have higher operating expenses than self-service operations because of the additional staff requirements.

3. **Limited-Service Retailing:** Provides more sales assistance because these stores carry more shopping goods, and customers need more information. The stores also offer services, such as credit and merchandise-return privileges, not normally found in less service-oriented stores and hence they have higher operating costs.

4. **Full-Service Retailing:** Provides sales people who are ready to assist in every phase of the locate-compare-select process. Customers who like to be waited on prefer type of store. The high staffing cost, along with the higher proportion of specially goods and slower moving items (fashions, jewellery, cameras), the more liberal merchandise return policies, various credit plans, free delivery, home servicing of durables, and customer facilities such as lounges and restaurants, results in high-cost retailing.

Types of Retail Stores

1. Speciality Stores: Speciality stores, as the name implies, are ones that carry a narrow products line with a deep assortment within that line. Typically, these jewellery stores like Tribhovandas Bhimji Zaveri in Mumbai and New Delhi, watch stores, garment or apparel stores like in style, Chirag Din in Mumbai, sporting goods stores, book stores, etc. These stores can be further classified on the basis of the degree of narrowness in their product lines. A store like Shoppers Stop that retails readymade garments for the family is called singleline store. Raymond show-shops that retail only men's clothing and accessories is known as limited line store and stores that retail designer cloths for men like Van Henusan, Louis Philip are know as superspeciality stores.

2. Department Stores: A department stores carries several product lines, invariably all those that will be required by a typical household. These lines include food, clothing, appliances, and other household goods. Home furnishings, gifts etc,. In India, these stores are still in introductory phase and they are mainly located in metros like Mumbai, Delhi, and Chennai, and other cities like Bengaluru and Hyderabad. In U.S. market, department stores are believed to be in decline phase of the retail life cycle mainly because of increased rivalry among them. Increased in competition from other types of retail stores like discount stores, and major demographic changes in cities making shopping less of a pleasure.

3. Supermarket: This is a large, low cost, low margin, high volume, self service operations designed to serve the customers need for food, laundry and household maintenance products. Another reason is that the customer is more assured of product quality and freshness when he or she buys his or her requirements from place like Food-land. Moreover the wide range of product mix carried by these stores makes them a favourite retail outlet.

4. Convenience Stores: These are generally food stores much smaller in size than supermarkets. These are conveniently located near residential areas and have long hours of operations, seven days a week, and carry a limited line of high turnover convenience products. In the Indian context, the old and faithful street corner grocery store or cold storage or just the food store are the ones that can be called convenience stores.

5. Discount Stores: As the name implies, discount stores are the ones that sell merchandise at lower price than the conventional merchants or stores by accepting lower margins but pushing for higher sales volume. A true discount store has four characteristics.

- It regularly sells its goods at discounted prices
- It carries national or reputed brands to enhance its image
- It keeps its operational costs to the minimum by emphasising on self-service and no frills interiors.
- Its location tends to be in low rent areas, and it draws customers from even distant locations.

6. Off-price Retailers: When major discount stores traded up, a new wave of off-price retailer stores traded up, a new wave of off-price retailers moved in to fill the low-price, high volume, gap. Ordinarily discounters buy at regular wholesale price and accept lower margins to keep price down. There are three main off-price retailers

- Factory outlets
- Independent
- Warehouse clubs.

Factory outlets are owned and operated by manufacturers and normally carry the manufacturers surplus, discontinued, or irregular goods.

Independent off-price retailers are owned and run by entrepreneurs or are divisions of larger retail corporations.

Wholesale clubs or warehouse clubs sell a limited selection of brand name grocery items, appliances, and clothing and at deep discount to members who pay $25 to $50 annual membership fees.

7. Catalogue Showroom: A catalogue showroom sells a broad selection of high markup, fast moving, brand name goods at a discount prices. These include jewellery, power tools at a discount prices. Catalogue showrooms have been struggling in recent years to hold their share of the retail market.

II Non-store Retailing

Although the overwhelming majority of goods and services are sold through stores, non-store retailing has been growing much faster than store retailing, amounting to more than 12% of all consumer purchases.

1. **Direct Selling:** Direct selling which started centuries ago with street peddlers has burgeoned into a $9 billion industry, with over 600 companies selling door to door, office to office, or at home sales parties. The pioneers include the Fuller Brush Company (Brushes, Brooms, and the like), World Book (encyclopedia), Electrolux (Vacuum Cleaners).

2. **Direct Marketing:** Direct marketing has its roots in mail order marketing but today includes reaching people in other ways than visiting their homes or offices, including telemarketing, television direct response marketing, and electronic shopping.

3. **Automatic Vending:** Automatic vending has applied to a considerable variety of merchandise, including impulse goods with high convenience. In Japan, vending machines have advanced and further dispense jewellery, frozen beef, fresh flowers, whisky, and even names of prospective dating partners. Vending machines offer customers the advantages of 24-hour selling, self-servicing, and unhandled merchandise.

III Retail Organisation

Although many retail stores are independently owned, an increasing number are falling under some form of corporate retailing. The five types of corporate retailing are corporate chains, voluntary chain and retailer cooperatives, consumer cooperatives, franchise organisations, and merchandising conglomerates.

Retailer Marketing Decisions

Retailers today are anxious to find new marketing strategies to attract and hold customers. In the past, they held customers by having special or unique assortments of goods, by offering greater or better services than the competitors, by offering store credit cards to enable their buyers to buy on credit, or simply by being closer and more convenient. All of this has changed. Today, many stores offer similar assortments; national brands such as Calvin Kelvin, Izod, and Levi are now found in most department stores, mass-merchandise outlets, and off-price discount stores. The national brand manufacturers, in their drive for volume, placed their brands well everywhere. The result was that retail stores and assortments looked more and more alike.

For all these reasons, many retailers today are rethinking their marketing strategy. We will now examine the marketing decisions faced by retailers in the areas of target market, product assortment and procurement, services and store atmosphere, price, promotion, and place.

1. Target-Market Decision: A retailer's most important decision concerns the target market. Should the store focus on upscale, midscale, or downscale shoppers? Do the target shoppers want variety, assortment depth, or convenience? Until the target market is defined and profiled, the retailer cannot make consistent decisions on product assortment, store décor, advertising messages and media, price levels, and so on.

Some retailers have defined their target markets quite well. Here are two prime examples whose founders are among the richest men in America:

Leslie H.Wexner borrowed $5,000 in 1963 to create The Limited Inc., which started as a single store targeted to young, fashion-conscious women. All aspects of the store–clothing assortment, fixtures, music, colours, personnel–were orchestrated to match the target consumer. He continued to open more stores, but a decade later his original customers were no longer in the "young" group. To catch the new "young", he started the Limited Express. Over the years, he started or acquired other targeted store chains, including Lane Bryant, Victoria's Secret, Sizes Unlimited, Lerner's, and so on. Today, The Limited operates 4,494 stores in 14 retailing divisions. Sales totalled $6.1 billion in 1991.

The late Sam Walton and his brother opened the first Wal-Mart discount store in Rogers, Arkansas in 1962. It was a big, flat, warehouse-type store aimed at selling everything from apparel to automotive supplies to small appliances at the lowest possible prices to small-town America. More recently, Wal-Mart has been building stores in larger cities. Today, Wal-Mart operates 1,600 stores in 35 states and produces more than $32 billion in annuals sales, making it America's largest retailer Wal-Mart's secret? Target small-town America, listen to the customers, treat the employees as partners, purchase carefully, and keep a tight rein on expenses. Signs reading "Satisfaction Guaranteed" and "We Sell for Less" hang prominently at each store's entrance, and customers are often welcomed by a "people greater" eager to lend a helping hand. Wal-Mart spends considerably less than Sears and K mart in advertising, and yet its sales are growing at the rate of 30% a year. Sam Walton also launched a successful new set of store called Sam's Wholesale Club, which provides members (small businesses, government employees, and so forth) with super discounts on furniture, appliances, supplies, and food products.

2. Product Assortment and Procurement Decisions

The retailer's product assortment must match the shopping expectations of the target market. In fact, it becomes a key element in the competitive battle among similar retailers. The retailer has to decide on product assortment breadth and depth. Thus, in the restaurant business, a restaurant can offer a narrow and shallow assortment (small launch counters), a narrow and deep assortment (delicateness), a broad and shallow assortment (catering), or a broad deep assortment (large restaurant).

3. Services and Store Atmosphere Decisions

Retailer must also decide on the service mix to offer customers. The old mom and pop grocery stores offered home delivery, credit, and conversion, service that today supermarkets have completely eliminated.

4. Price Decisions

The retailer's prices are a key positioning factor and must be decided in relation to the target market, the product and service assortment mix, and competition. All retailers would like to charge high markups and achieve high volumes, but usually the two do not go together. Most retailers fall into the high-markup, lower volume group or the low-markup, higher-volume group. Within each of these groups there are further gradations.

5. Promotion Decision

The retailer must use promotional tools that support and reinforce its image positioning. Fine stores will place tasteful full page ads in magazines such as *Vogue* and *Harper's*. Discount retailers will place loud ads on radio, television, and newspaper touting low prices and specials. Fine stores will carefully train salespeople in how to greet customers, interpret their needs, and handle their doubts and complaints. Discounts will use less well-trained salespeople and use a whole range of sales promotion tools to generate traffic.

6. Place Decision

Retailers are accustomed to satisfying that the three keys to success are "location, location and location". For example, customers primarily choose the nearest bank and gas station. Department store chains, oil companies, and fast food franchisers must exercise great care in selecting locations. The problem breaks downs into selecting regions of the country in which to open outlets, then particular cities and then particular sites.

Retailers can asses a particular stores sales effectiveness by looking at four indicators

1. Number of people passing by on an average day
2. Percentage who enter the store

3. Percentage of those entering who buy
4. Average amount spent per sale

A store that is doing poorly might be in a poorly trafficked, or not enough passersby drop in, or too many dropins browse but not buy, or the buyers do not buy very much. Each problem can be remedied. Dropins are increased by better window displays and sales announcement, and the number buying and the amount purchased are largely a function of merchandise quality, prices, and salesmanship.

Indian Scenario

Retail in India is still at a very early stage. Most retail firms are companies from other industries that are now entering the retail sector on account of its amazing potential. There are only a handful of companies with a retail background. One such company is Nilgiri's from Bangalore that started as a dairy and incorporated other areas in its business with great success. Their achievement has led to the arrival of numerous other players, most with the backing of large groups, but usually not with a retail background. Most new entrants to the India retail scene are real estate groups who see their access to and knowledge of land, location and construction as prime factors for entering the market.

New retail stores have traditionally started operations in cities like Mumbai and Delhi where there has been an existing base of metropolitan consumers with ready cash and global tastes. The new perspective to this trend is that new entrants to the retail scenario should first enter smaller cities rather than focusing entirely on the metros. Spending power in India is not concentrated any more in just the 4 metros (Delhi, Mumbai, Chennai, Kolkata). Smaller but upcoming cities like Chandigarh, Coimbatore, Pune, Ahmedabad, Baroda, Trivandrum, Cochin, Ludhiana, Simla etc will fast be catching up to the metros in their spending capacity.

Cities in south India have taken to the supermarket style of shopping very eagerly and so far the maximum number of organised grocery and department stores are in Chennai, Bangalore and Hyderabad. The north has a long way to go to come up to par. International stores now prefer to gauge the reaction of the public in these cities before investing heavily in a nation-wide expansion. Milou, the Swiss children's wear retailer, recently opened up its first store in Chennai, bypassing Delhi and Mumbai. Besides the urban market, India's rural market has just started to be seen as a viable option and companies who understand what the rural consumer wants will grow to incredible heights. The bulk of India's population still lives in rural areas and to be able to cater specifically to them will mean generating tremendous amounts of business.

Business, specifically retail business must focus on the most important factor in the Indian mindset—value for money. Indian consumers are ready to pay almost any amount of money for a product or service as long as they feel they are getting good Value for Money. This is often misconstrued as being tight fisted or interested in lower priced and/or lower quality products.

In the past decade, international companies entering India (Levi's, Pepe, Tommy Hilfiger, Marks and Spencer, Mango) have generally offered moderately priced to expensive items. They have aimed for the upper-middle and rich classes of Indian society. These are consumers who travel abroad often and can buy these items overseas quite easily. Instead, international companies should be focusing on the lower and lower-middle classes of India. This is where the real potential is, the aspirational class of consumers who want to lead a better lives and believe in education, hard work and absorb knowledge from every possible angle. The phenomenal success of Big Bazaar, Pantaloons version of Wal-Mart, is proof that there is enormous potential in providing products and services to this class of consumers.

Indians are very curious by nature and will try everything at least once before rejecting it. The initial success of KFC in India proved that Indians could make a success of most new ventures entering India but reject a concept once they have tried and tested the offering and found nothing worth going back for. The menu at KFC was rather boring and insipid to the Indian consumer who is used to the innumerable combinations and permutations of street food. For their second run in India, KFC re-thought its menu and has been very successful marketing at specific groups within India, like the Punjabi's who have quite a history of loving the Chicken leg and have made the Chandigarh outlet a huge success!

A company entering India cannot have just one game plan to apply to the entire country as the people, their tastes, the lifestyle, the budgets etc are all too divergent. International entrants must enter each market specifically focusing only on that area to be successful.

The Indian retail sector is estimated to have a market size of about $180 billion; but the organised sector represents only 2% share of this market. Most of the organised retailing in the country has just started recently, and has been concentrated mainly in the metro cities. India is the last large Asian economy to liberalise its retail sector. In Thailand, more than 40% of all consumer goods are sold through the super markets and departmental stores. A similar phenomenon has swept through all other Asian countries. Organised retailing in India has a huge scope because of the vast market and the growing consciousness of the consumer about product quality and services. A study conducted by Fitch, expects the organised retail industry to continue to grow rapidly, especially through increased levels of penetration in larger towns and metros and also as it begins to spread to smaller cities and B class towns. Fuelling this growth is the growth in development of the retail-specific properties and malls. According to the estimates available with Fitch, close to 25mn sq. ft. of retail space is being developed and will be available for occupation over the next 36-48 months. Fitch expects organised retail to capture 15%-20% market share by 2010.

Drivers of Change

- ❖ Changing Demographics–One of the biggest reasons for the growth of retail in India is the changing demographics. The number of middle-income class and the people in the age group 18-35 has been ever increasing and this has changed the consumer's preference. According to a world study, India is considered one of the youngest economies and this is helping in the growth of the sector.

- ❖ Emphasis on Convenience–With the ever-expanding cities and upcoming towns, people are becoming choosier with the things they buy and the places they shop. This has resulted in the emergence of new retail ventures trying to be niche in some area.

- ❖ Explosion of Knowledge and Technology–With the emergence of the Internet, people have become aware of what's happening in the other part of the world and this has led him in comparing the prices, assortment, ambience, etc. To cope up with this knowledge explosion different retail formats have emerged and this has made shopping more of fun and experiences.

- ❖ Added Experimentation–Back in the 1980s, people were highly loyal to the brands they bought and the outlets they shopped, but the present generations of consumers like to experiment. Long back people never felt shopping for vegetables and groceries at retail outlets was a good idea, but things have changed and vegetable retailing has grown by 35 per cent.

6.14   THEORIES OF RETAIL

Like every other industry new retail firms have brought innovative approaches in retailing. Retail development can be looked at from different theoretical perspectives, as no one theory is universally acceptable. The reason for this unacceptability is mainly because of different market conditions, different socio-economic conditions in the market. This section deals with the following theories, namely,

1. Wheel of Retailing
2. Retail Accordion Theory
3. Theory of Natural Selection
4. Retail Life Cycle

1. Wheel of Retailing: This theory talks about the structural changes in retailing. The theory was proposed by Malcomb McNair and it describes how retail institutions change during their life cycle. In the first stage when new retail institutions start business they enter as low status, low price and low margin operations. As the retail firms achieve success they look in for increasing their customer base. They begin to upgrade their stores, add merchandise and new services are introduced. Prices are increased and margins are raised to support the higher costs. New retailers enter the marketplace to fill the vacuum, while this continues to move ahead as a result of the success. A new format emerges when the store reaches the final stage of the life cycle. When the retail store started, it started low but when markets grew their margins and price changed. The theory has been criticised because they do not advocate all the changes that happen in the retail sector and in the present scenario not all firms start low to enter the market which is also represented in Fig. 6.11.

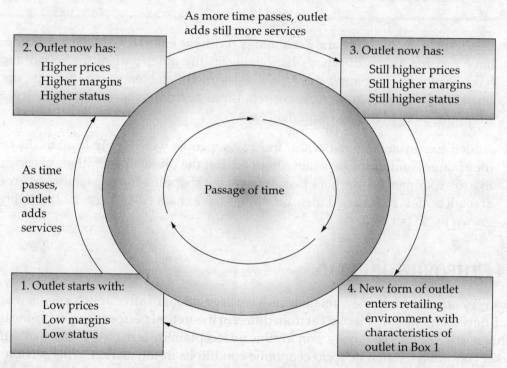

Fig. 6.11 Wheel of retailing.

2. Retail Accordion Theory: This theory describes how general stores move to specialised stores and then again become more of a general store. Hollander borrowed the analogy 'accordion from the orchestra. He suggested that players either have open accordion representing the general stores or closed accordions representing narrow range of products focusing on specialised products. This theory was also known as the general-specific-general theory. The wheel of retailing and the accordion theory are known as the cyclical theories of retail revolution.

3. Theory of Natural Selection: According to this theory, retail stores evolve to meet change in the micro-environment. The retailers that successfully adapt to the technological, economic, demographic and political and legal changes are the ones who are more likely to grow and prosper. This theory is considered a better one to wheel of retailing because it talks about the macro environmental variables as well, but the drawback of this theory is that it fails to address the issues of customer taste, expectations and desires.

4. Retail Life Cycle: Like products, brands retail organisations pass through identifiable stages of innovation, accelerated development, maturity and decline. This is commonly known as the retail life cycle which is represented in Fig. 6.12. Any organisation when in

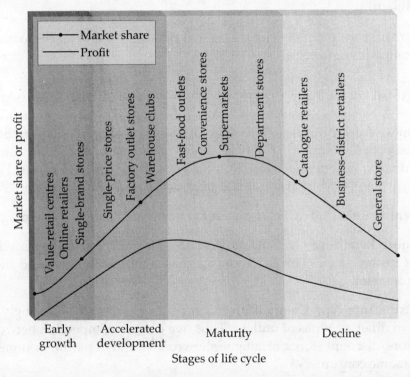

Fig. 6.12 Retail life cycle.

the innovation stage is nascent and has few competitors. They try to create a distinctive advantage to the final customers. Since the concepts are new at this stage, organisations try to grow rapidly and the management tries to experiment. Profits will be moderate and the stage may last for a couple of years. When we talk about our country e-buying or online shopping is in the innovation stage.

In the accelerated growth phase the organisations face rapid increase in sales, competitors begin to emerge and the organisations begin to use leadership and their presence as a tool in stabilising their position. The investment level will be high as there are others who will be creating a lot of competition. This level may go up to eight years. Hypermarkets, Dollar stores are in this stage. In the maturity stage, as competition intensifies newer forms of retailing begin to emerge, the growth rate starts to decline. At this stage firms should start work on strategies and reposition techniques to be in the marketplace. Supermarkets, cooperative stores are in this stage. In the final stage of the retail life cycle, the declining phase where firms begin to lose their competitive advantage. Profitability starts to decline further and the overheads start to rise. Thus, we see that organisations need to adopt different strategies at each level in order to sustain in the marketplace.

Trends in Retailing

We can summarise the main developments that retailers need to take into account as they plan their competitive strategies.

- ✠ **New Retail Forms:** New retail forms constantly emerge to threaten established retail forms. A New York bank will deliver money to its important customer's offices or homes. Adelphi College offers "commuter train classroom education" in which businesspeople commuting between long Island and Manhattan can earn credits toward an M.B.A. degree, American Bakeries stated Hippopotamus Food Stores to allow customers to buy institutional size packages at savings of 10 to 30%.

- ✠ **Shortening Retail Life Cycle:** New retail forms are facing a shortening lifespan.

- ✠ **Non-store Retailing:** Over the past decade, mail order sales increased at twice the rate of instore sales. The electronic age has significantly increased the growth for non-store retailing.

- ✠ **Increasing Intertype Competition:** Competition today is increasingly interpret, or between different types of outlets. Thus, we can see competition between store and non-store, discount stores, catalogue showrooms, and department stores all compete for the same consumers.

- ✠ **Giant Retailers:** Superpower retailers are emerging who through their superior information systems and buying power are able to offer strong price savings to consumers, while causing havoc among their suppliers and rival retailers.

- ✠ **Changing Definition of One Stop Shopping:** Specially stores in malls are becoming increasingly competitive with large department stores in the offering, one stop shopping, customers park once and have a variety of speciality shops available.

- ✠ **Growth of Vertical Marketing System:** Marketing channels are increasingly becoming professionally managed and programmed. As large corporation extend their control over marketing channels, independent small stores are being squeezed out.

✠ **Portfolio Approach:** Retail organisations are increasingly designing and launching new store formats targeted to different lifestyle groups.

✠ **Growing Importance of Retailing Technology:** Retail technologies are becoming critically important as competitive tools. Progressive retailers are using computers to produce better forecasts, control inventory costs, order electronically from suppliers, send electronic mail between stores, and even sell to customers within stores. They are adopting checkout-scanning systems, electronic funds transfer, in store television and improved merchandise handling system.

✠ **Global Expansion of Major Retailers:** Retailers with unique formats and strong brand positioning are increasingly moving into other countries.

Elements of Retail Strategy

The retail strategy is an overall plan and guidelines that guides a retailer. A retail strategy is a clear and well-defined plan that the retail organisations outline to tap the market and create a long-term relationship with the customers. The steps that are involved in strategy formulation are the same in every industry. Figure 6.13 brings out the steps in retail strategy.

Fig. 6.13 Elements of retail strategy.

1. **Situation Analysis** - The first stage in retail strategy is to establish the organisational mission. A mission statement acts as a motivator for the organisation. The mission

statement is one, which inspires the employees in the organisation to stay focus on the goals of the organisation. Evaluating ownership and management options like whether to go it alone or have a partnership or to buy an already existing organisation has to be clearly outlined. Apart from this the merchandise that would be sold should also be evaluated.

2. **Objectives**–These are the long, short and the mid-term goals the retailer hopes to attain the goals may be based on profits that may include ROI, sales which include market share, and the customer and the stakeholders' satisfaction. The objectives need to be well defined keeping in mind the mission of the organisation and should see that the strategies get translated into results.

3. **Identification of customers**–Even though the strategy of a particular retailer may be executable and the mission of the organisation looks inspiring, but if a wrong target market is chosen, it may prove a failure. It is essential for the retailer to understand the needs of the customer. A retailer has three options which he may choose according to his objective, he can try selling different product categories to a broad spectrum of customers which is known as mass marketing or work on one particular segment which is market segment or have two or more segments which is commonly called selective segments.

4. **Overall Strategy**–The overall strategy is broadly classified into controllable and un-controllable factors. The location of the store, merchandise decision, communication, objectives come under controllable factors since the firm has a element of autonomy and deciding about them. In case of uncontrollable factors, the factors that a retailer must try and adapt like the technological changes, legal imperatives, cultural factors, economic situation get categorised. This step is one of the most essential steps in retail strategy because this stage demonstrates the firm's ability to adapt to different changing conditions.

5. **Specific Activities**–This deals with the tactical decisions and the day-to-day operations of the firm. The firm's responsiveness to the environmental factors with the help of the marketing mix elements is the actual functioning of the firm's activities.

6. **Control**–In the final phase of strategy formulation is the review of the firm's performance of a period of time. The firm's strategies and the tactics have to be evaluated to find the effectiveness and if it falls in place with the organisational objectives and then with the firm's mission. In case the firm finds that some of the tactics are time consuming and not much benefit could be figured out the organisation should ensure that such tactics have to be modified or be dropped from the firm's future course of action.

6.15   WHOLESALING

This includes all the activities involved in selling goods and services to those who buy for resale purpose. In the case of wholesaling this excludes manufacturers or producers who are involved directly in the production of the goods. They are the marketing intermediaries that buy from one source and sell it to another. The main function of a wholesaler is facilitating the transportation of the product and at times in the transfer of the titles. The intermediaries performing the wholesaling function is predominantly divided into two types, namely, merchants and agents. The difference between the two forms lies in if they take title to the goods they sell.

Nature and Importance of Wholesaling

Wholesaling includes all activities involved in selling goods or services to those who buy for resale or business use. It excludes manufacturers and farmers because they are engaged primarily in production, and it excludes retailers.

Wholesalers (also called distributors) differ from retailers in a number of ways. First, wholesalers pay less attention to promotion, atmosphere, and location because they are dealing with business customers rather than final consumers. Second, wholesale transactions are usually larger than retail transactions, and wholesalers usually cover a larger trade area than retailers. Third, the government deals with wholesalers and retailers differently in regard to legal regulations and taxes. Thus, retailers and manufacturers have reasons to use wholesalers. Wholesalers are used when they are more efficient in performing one or more of the following functions:

Selling and promotion wholesalers provide a sales force enabling manufacturers to reach many small-business customers at a relatively low cost. The wholesaler has more contacts and is often more trusted by the buyer than is the distant manufacturer.

- **Buying and Assortment Building:** Wholesalers are able to select items and build assortments needed by their customers, thus saving the customers considerable work.

- **Bulk Breaking:** Wholesalers achieve savings for their customers through buying in carload lots and breaking the bulk into smaller units.

- **Warehousing:** Wholesalers hold inventories, thereby reducing the inventory costs and risks to suppliers and customers.

- **Transportation:** Wholesalers provide quicker delivery to buyers because they are closer than the manufacturer.

- **Financing:** Wholesalers finance their customers by granting credit, and they finance their suppliers by ordering early and paying their bills on time.

- **Risk Bearing:** Wholesalers absorb some risk by taking title and bearing the cost of theft, damage, spoilage, and obsolescence.

- **Market Information:** Wholesalers supply information to their suppliers and customers regarding competitors' activities, new products, price development, and so on.

- **Management Services and Counselling:** Wholesalers often help retailers improve their operations by training their sales clerks, helping with stores layouts and displays, and setting up accounting and inventory control systems. They may help their industrial customers by offering training and technical service.

Growth and Types of Wholesaling

Wholesaling has grown in the U.S. at a compound growth rate of 5.8% over the past ten years. A number of factors have contributed to wholesaling growth: the growth of larger factories located some distance from the principal buyers, the growth of production in advance of orders rather than in response to specific orders; an increase in the number of levels of intermediate producers and users; and the increasing need for adapting products to the needs of intermediate and final users in terms of quantities, packages, and forms.

Wholesalers fall into four groups: merchant wholesalers, brokers and agents, manufacturers and retailer's branches and offices, and miscellaneous wholesaler.

Major Wholesalers Types

1. **Merchant Wholesalers:** Merchant wholesalers are independently owned businesses that take title to the merchandise they handle. In different trades they are called jobbers, distributors, or mill supply houses. Merchant wholesalers can be subclassified into full-service wholesalers and limited service wholesalers.

2. **Full-Service Wholesalers:** Full service wholesalers provide such services as carrying stock, maintaining a sales force, offering credit, making deliveries, and providing management assistance.

3. **Wholesale Merchants:** Wholesale merchants sell primarily to retailers and provide a full range of services. General-merchandise wholesalers carry several merchandise lines, while general-line wholesalers carry one or two lines in greater depth.

4. **Industrial Distributors:** Industrial distributors are merchant wholesalers who sell to manufacturers rather than to retailers. They provide several services, such as carrying stock, offering credit, and providing delivery. They may carry broad range of merchandise, a general line, or speciality line.

5. **Limited-Service Wholesalers:** Limited-service wholesalers offer fewer services to their suppliers and customers. There are several types.

6. **Cash-and-Carry Wholesalers:** Cash and carry wholesalers have a limited line of fast-moving goods and sell to small retailers for cash and normally do not deliver.

7. **Truck Wholesalers:** Truck wholesalers perform a selling and delivery function primarily.

8. **Drop Shippers:** Drop shippers operate in bulk industries, such as coal, lumber, and heavy equipment. They do not carry inventory or handle the product. Upon receiving an order, they select a manufacturer, who ships the merchandise directly to the customer on the agreed terms and time of delivery.

9. **Rack Jobbers:** Rack jobbers serve grocery and drug retailers, most in the area of nonfood items. They send delivery trucks to stores, and the delivery person sets up toys, paperbacks, hardware items, health and beauty aids, and so on.

10. **Producer's Cooperatives:** Producers cooperatives are owned by farmer members and assemble farm produce to sell in local markets. Their profits are distributed to members at the end of the year.

11. **Mail-Order Wholesalers:** Mail-order wholesalers send catalogues to retail, industrial, and institutional customers featuring jewellery, cosmetics, speciality foods, and other small items. Their main customers are businesses in small outlying areas. No sales force is maintained to call on customers. The orders are filled and sent by mail, truck or other efficient means of transportation.

Brokers and Agents

Brokers and agents differ from merchant wholesalers. They do not take title to goods, and they perform only a few functions.

1. **Brokers:** The chief function of a broker is to bring buyers and sellers together and assist in negotiation. The party who hired them pays them. They do not carry inventory, get involved in financing, or assume risk. The most familiar examples are food brokers, real-estate brokers, insurance brokers, and security brokers.

2. **Agents:** Agents represent either buyers or sellers on a more permanent basis. There are several types.

3. **Manufacturers Agents:** Manufacturers agents represent two or more manufacturers of complementary lines.

4. **Selling Agents:** Selling agents are given contractual authority to sell a manufacturer's entire output. The manufacturer either is not interested in the selling function or feels unqualified.

5. **Purchasing Agents:** Purchasing agents generally have chases for them, often receiving, inspecting, warehousing, and shipping the merchandise to the buyers.

6. **Commission Merchants:** Commission merchants (or houses) are agents who take physical possession of products and negotiate sales. Normally, they are not employed on a long-term basis. They are used most often in agricultural marketing by farmers who do not want to sell their own output and do not belong to producer's cooperatives.

Manufacturers and Retailers Branches and Offices

The third major type of wholesaling consists of wholesaling operations conducted by sellers or buyers themselves rather than through independent wholesalers. There are two types.

1. Sale Branches and Offices: Manufacturers often set up their own sales branches and offices to improve inventory control, selling, and promotion. Sales branches carry inventory and are found in such industries as lumber and automotive equipment in such industries as lumber and automotive equipment and parts. Sales offices do not carry inventory and are most prominent in dry goods and notions industries.

2. Purchasing Offices: Many retailers set up purchasing offices in major market centres. These purchasing offices perform a role similar to that of brokers or agents but are part of the buyer's organisation.

Miscellaneous Wholesalers

A few specialised types of wholesalers are found in certain sectors of the economy, such as agricultural assemblers, petroleum bulk plants and terminals, and auction companies.

6.16 WHOLESALER MARKETING DECISIONS

Wholesaler-distributors have experienced mounting competitive pressures in recent years.

1. **Target-Market Decision:** Wholesalers need to define their target markets and not try to serve everyone. They can choose a target group of customers according to size criteria (e.g., only large retailers), type of customer (e.g., convenience food stores only), need for service (e.g., customers who need credit), or other criteria.

2. **Product-Assortment-and-Services Decision:** The wholesalers "product" is their assortment. Wholesalers are under a great pressure to carry a full line and maintain sufficient stock for immediate delivery. But this can kill profits. Wholesalers today are reexamining how many lines to carry and are choosing to carry only the more profitable ones. They are grouping their items on an ABC basis, with A standing for the most-profitable items and C for the least profitable. Inventory-carrying levels are varied for the three groups.

3. **Pricing Decision:** Wholesalers usually mark up the cost of goods by a conventional percentage; say 20%, to cover their expenses. Expenses may run 17% of the gross margin, leaving a profit margin of approximately 3%. In grocery whole selling, the average profit margin is often less than 2%. Wholesalers are beginning to experiment with new approaches to pricing.

4. **Promotion Decision:** Wholesalers rely primarily on their sales force to achieve promotional objectives. Even here, most wholesalers see selling as a single salesperson talking to a single customer instead of a team effort to sell, build, and service major accounts. As for non-personal promotion, wholesalers would benefit from adopting some of the image-making techniques used by retailers. They need to develop an overall promotion strategy involving trade advertising, sales promotion, and publicity.

5. **Place Decision:** Wholesalers typically locate in low-rent, low tax areas and put little money into their physical setting and offices. Often the material handling systems and order processing system lag behind the available technologies.

6.17   TRENDS IN WHOLESALING

Manufacturers always have the option by passing wholesalers or of replacing inefficient wholesalers with better ones. Manufacturers' major complaints against wholesalers are as follows. They do not aggressively promote the manufacturers product line, acting more like order takers, they do not carry enough inventory and therefore fail to fill customers orders fast enough, they do not supply the manufacturer with up-to-date market and competitive information. Progressive wholesaler distributors, on the other hand, are those who adapt their services to meet the changing needs of their suppliers and target customers. Nerus and Anderson interviewed leading industrial distributors and identified four ways to strengthen their relationship with manufacturers.

- They sought a clear agreement with their manufacturers about their expected functions in the marketing channel.
- They gained insight into the manufacturer requirement by visiting their plants and attending manufacturer association conventions and trade shows.
- They fulfilled their commitments to the manufacturer by meeting the volume targets, promptly paying their bills, and feedback customer information to their manufacturers.
- They identified and offered value-added services to help their suppliers.

6.18   LOGISTICS MANAGEMENT

Today's retail environment is more complex than ever before, it is no longer just an art, but a science. Over the past century, the business of retailing has transformed itself immensely. Many of the large retailers are now not only operating stores within their own countries but have also shifted their operations across borders. Controlling merchandise as well as store operations especially for chain store retailers within their own borders or even across their borders, has always been a major challenge. Fortunately the advent of cutting edge technologies together with improved distribution system, have been of immense help in simplifying this crucial task of retail operation. It is thus said retailing that if the retailer can get the right merchandise at the right location and at the right time, he has already won half the battle for supremacy over his competition. It is the art of converting this superior technology into real time benefits in retail distribution that finally decides the ultimate winners.

What is logistics management?

The effective and efficient management of logistics is an extremely crucial factor in the success of a retail company. Logistics is the term used to define the entire process of flow of merchandise right from the point where merchandise is sourced to the point of its actual sale to customers. Managing this complex flow across the entire retail distribution network has almost become the deciding factor as to who finally succeeds in the marketplace. In the case of chain store retailers, merchandise flow from the vendors to the distribution centre and then to the stores, while in the case of independent retailers, merchandise flows directly from the vendor to the stores. Unfortunately, most retailers in India have absolutely no idea whatsoever about this fine art of logistics management and in fact only know what merchandise is going into their stores. Until and unless the merchandise is physically counted, they have no clear idea of what is selling and usually rely on their intuition and approximations for all merchandising decisions. As such a retailer is either perpetually stuffed with excess inventory or has a frequent stock out situation and by the time he realises this, it is often too late to implement corrective action such as the purchase of additional merchandise.

The physical flow of merchandise

Logistics, in other words, supplies the physical flow of merchandise across the retail company. In a retail operation it is absolutely essential for the merchandise to flow from the source of supply to the end customer in an efficient manner. While some chain store retailers prefer to maintain elaboration distribution centres, others try to avoid this step and get most of their merchandise delivered directly at their stores. This aspect of a centralised retail operations as well as decentralised operations.

A distribution centre is a warehouse that is responsible for receiving all the merchandise from the multiple vendors, and thereafter for sorting and then sending the same to the respective stores. The size of distribution centre in the global context can range from 100,000 sq ft to even as large as 30 football grounds. These distribution centres are usually constructed at a height of approximately three feet or are at the same level as the base of the trucks.

These distribution centres are usually very well networked not only with the other departments within the same complex but also with their respective stores and their POS terminals and in many instances are absolutely online. The central warehouse thus has an almost up to the minute information of the exact status of each and every SKU at every store and thus able to dispatch the exact quantity required by each store. The operation of the entire system may sound very simple, but it is actually an extremely complex operation and is only simplified with the use of cutting edge information technology.

Distribution centres or warehouses are however, not viable for all types of retailers. As explained earlier if a retailer has only a few outlets, then the substantial expanse of setting up and maintaining a distribution centre may be unwarranted and would, in fact, only complicate matters more for the retailer rather than simplify them. It is true that if the merchandise from the vendors can be consolidated and then delivered to all stores in one area.

Importance of a distribution centre

Distribution decisions have become an increasingly crucial component of a retailer's overall corporate strategy. Retailers have now realised that profit growth cannot be obtained solely through sales growth. As a result, many retailers who have stores in mature, stagnant markets, or in areas where that competition is more intense than in the past, have realised that there is an incredible profit potential in having an efficient distribution system.

Globally, most large retailers such as K-Mart, Safeway and Wal-Mart do both wholesaling as well as retailing. They buy directly from the manufacturers, have the merchandise shipped to their warehouse for storage, and then distribute the merchandise to their stores.

Advantages

1. Retailers with varying demand for specific items at the store level, like CD stores, fashion stores, etc. may essentially need a distribution centre since more accurate sales forecast are possible when demand from the many stores is aggregated at the distribution level.

2. Stores carrying staple merchandise that require frequent replenishment because the entire process right from ordering to receiving. Labelling and shelving, are all very complex and time-consuming tasks which need be attended to in the great detail all day long.

3. Stores that carry a relatively large number of items but usually require less than full case quantities may prefer to receive goods through their distribution centres. Most vendors especially manufacturers do not find it convenient to deliver part cases and hence it would be better for the retailer to receive the sealed cartons at the warehouse and then transfer only the specific quantities required by the respective stores.

4. Retailers with a large number of outlets that are not geographically concentrated within a metropolitan area may also find it difficult to recognise timely delivery from all their vendors. As a result such stores can best be catered to in an efficient manner by maintaining the retailers own central warehouse which could receive all the merchandise from all the vendors and then distribute the same according to the specific requirements of each of his stores.

5. Finally, retail space would be far more expensive than the space allocated for a distribution centre. The latter is thus a much cheaper location for storing merchandise and for preparing it on a regular basis.

Functions of a Distribution Centre

Once the goods are delivered by the vendor to the warehouse, the very first function at the receiving point is to accurately and individually check and count the merchandise to ensure that there are no damaged goods and that the quantities received are accurate. Therefore, the merchandise may or may not be shelved on pallets for reasons indicated earlier. A 'pillar' is a platform on which a number of cartons may be stored together, and it is usually made of wood. However, in this era of the green revolution, pallets made of other plastic material have also become popular.

Therefore, all the products would have to be labelled very carefully as every single piece of every single item must contain the code number allotted to the respective SKU. Every label usually also contains the selling price of the item though many international retailers avoid this exercise and prefer to have the price labels on the shelves only. In fact, in many parts of the world, retailers do not have much labelling to do at all since the items themselves contain a printed label with their respective code numbers. Once the merchandise is received at the central warehouse, the goods must be immediately prepared and processed to be shipped to the respective stores at the earliest. While on some occasions it may be necessary to store the merchandise temporarily at the warehouse for a few days, on other occasions, the merchandise is immediately shipped to the respective stores on the very same day. In fact, it is strongly believed that much success of Wal-Mart, undoubtedly the largest and the most profitable retailer worldwide, is attributed to the high level of efficiency that it has achieved in this regard. Wal-Mart uses a logistic technique popularly known as 'cross-docking' whereby the merchandise received on one side of the warehouse is immediately re-loaded on to the waiting trucks on the other side that are being loaded for taking the goods to their stores. By implementing this method, the company was able to save immensely and it is estimated that the cost of sales of the company was reduced by approximately 2-3 per cent.

6.19 PHYSICAL DISTRIBUTION

Producers of physical products and services must decide on the best way to store and move their goods and services to their market destinations. They typically need to engage the services of physical distribution firms, warehouse and transportation companies, to assist in this task. Producers know that their physical distribution firms warehouse and transportation companies, to assist in this task. Producers know that their physical distribution effectiveness will have a major impact on customer satisfaction and company costs.

Nature of physical distribution

Physical distribution involves planning, implementing, and controlling the physical flow of materials and final goods from point of origin to points of use to meet customer requirements at a profit. The aim of physical distribution to manage supply chains, that is value-added flows from suppliers to ultimate users, as represented in Fig. 6.14.

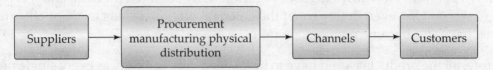

Fig. 6.14 Physical distribution channel.

Thus, the logistic task is to coordinate the activities of suppliers, purchasing agents, marketers, channel members, and customers.

Companies manage their supply chains through information. Major gains in logistic efficiency have resulted from information technology advances, particularly computers, point of sale terminals, uniform product codes, satellite tracking, and electronic data interchange (EDI), and electronic funds transfer (EFT). These developments have made it possible for companies to make or require promises such as "The product will be at dock 25 at 10 a.m., tomorrow", and controlling this promise through information.

6.20   STEPS INVOLVED IN PHYSICAL DISTRIBUTION

The first is sales forecasting on which the company schedules production and inventory levels. The production plans indicate the materials that the purchasing department must order. These materials arrive through inbound transportation, enter the receiving area, and are stored in raw material inventory. Raw materials are converted into finished products. Finished goods inventory is the link between the customer's orders and the company's manufacturing activity builds it up. Finished goods flow off the assembly line and pass through packing, in plant warehouse, shipping-room processing, outbound transportation, field warehousing, and customer delivery and servicing. The entries steps process is shown in Fig. 6.15.

Companies lose customers when they fail to supply goods on time. In the summer of 1976, Kodak launched its national advertising campaign for its new instant camera before it had delivered enough cameras to the stores.

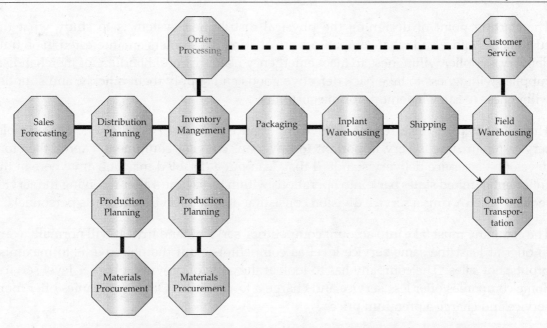

Fig. 6.15 Major activities involved in physical distribution.

Traditional physical distribution thinking starts with goods at the plant and tries to find low-cost solutions to get them to customers. Marketers prefer market logistics thinking that start with the marketplace and works backward to the factory. Here is an example of market logistics thinking.

At one time, German consumers purchased individual bottles of soft drinks. A soft drink manufacturer decided to test a six-pack. Consumers responded positively. Retailers respond positively because the bottles could be loaded faster on the shelves, and more bottles would be purchased per occasion. The manufacturer designed the six-packs to fit on the store's receiving rooms. Factory operations were redesigned to produce the new six packs. The purchasing department let out bids for the new needed materials. Once implemented, the manufacturer's market share rose substantially.

The Physical Distribution Objective

Many companies state their physical distribution objective as getting the right goods to the right places at the right time for the least cost. Unfortunately, this provides little actual guidance. No physical distribution system can simultaneously maximise customer service and minimise distribution cost. Maximum customer service implies large inventories, premium transportation, and multiple warehouses, all of which raise distribution cost. A minimum distribution cost implies cheap transportation, low stocks and few warehouses.

The starting point of designing the physical distribution system is to study what the customers require and what competitors are offering. Customers are interested in on time delivery, supplier willingness to meet emergency needs, careful handling of merchandise, supplier willingness to take back defective goods and supply them quickly, and supplier willingness to carry inventory for the customer.

The company has to research the relative importance of these service outputs. For example, service repair time is very important to buyers of copying equipment. Xerox therefore developed a service delivery standard that "can put a disabled machine anywhere in the continental united states back into operations within three hours after receiving the service request". Xerox runs a service division consisting of 12000 service and parts personnel.

The company must take into account competitors' service standards. It will normally want to offer at least the same service level as competitors. But the objective is to maximise profits, not sales. The company has to look at the costs of providing higher-level service. Some companies offer less service and charge a lower price. Other companies offer more service and charge a premium price.

Decisions in Physical Distributions

1. How should orders be handled (order processing)
2. Where should stocks be located (warehousing)
3. How much stock should be held (inventory)
4. How should goods be shipped (transportation).

1. **Order Processing:** Physical distribution begins with a customer order. A key need in companies today is to shorten the order to remittance cycle, that is the elapsed time between an order placement and payment companies are making great progress in speeding up order handling, thanks to computers. General Electric operates a computer's credit standing and weather and where the items are in stock. The computer issues an order for new stock, and relays the message back to the sales representative that the customers order is on its way, all in less than 15 seconds.

2. **Warehousing:** Every company has to store its finished goods until they are sold. A storage function is necessary because production and consumption cycles rarely match. Many agricultural commodities are produced seasonally, whereas demand is continuous. The storage function overcomes discrepancies in desired quantities and timing. The company must decide on a desirable number of stocking locations. More stocking locations means that goods can be delivered to customers more quickly.

   Companies use storage warehouse and distribution warehouses. Storage warehouses store goods for moderate to long periods of time. Distribution warehouses receive goods from various company plants and suppliers and move them out as soon as possible. For example, Wal-Mart stores, Inc operates four distributions centres. One centre covers 4,00,000 square feet on a 93-acre site. The shipping department loads 50 to 60 trucks daily, delivering merchandise on a twice-weekly basis to its retail outlets. This is less expensive than supplying each retail outlet from each plant directly.

3. **Inventory:** Inventory level represents a major physical distribution decision affecting customer satisfaction. Salespeople would like their companies to carry enough stock to fill all customer orders immediately. However, it is not cost effective for a company to carry this much inventory. Inventory costs increases at an increasing rate as the customer service level approaches 100%. Management would need to know by how much sales and profits would increase as a result of carrying larger inventories and promising faster order fulfilment times.

4. **Transportation:** Marketers need to be concerned with their company's transportation decisions. Transportation choices will affect product, pricing, on time delivery performance, and the condition of the goods when they arrive, all of which will affect customer satisfaction. Transportation decisions must consider the complex tradeoffs between various transportation modes and their implications for other distribution elements, such as warehousing and inventory. As transportation cost changes over time, companies need to reanalyse in the search for optimal physical distribution arrangements.

6.21   PHYSICAL DISTRIBUTION TASKS

There are several tasks that have to be accomplished as a part of physical distribution. These are:

1. **Location of Manufacturing Facilities:** There are two related issues firstly where to locate the manufacturing facility and secondly how many facilities should be set up. The basic decisional parameters would be the availability of the basic raw material and the location of the market. It may be decided to locate the manufacturing facility nearer to the source of supply and ship the finished outputs to the outlaying markets or to erect the production facility near to the geographical market to be served and arrange the shipment of the inputs. Location of the Mathura Refinery was based on the latter concept while the super thermal power plant of the National Thermal Power Corporation (NTPC) is based on the former. The basic consideration involved obviously is the relative cost of transporting inputs and outputs, including the economics of different methods of transportation which may be used to transport raw materials and finished products. For example, transporting gas via pipeline is

more cost effective than distributing fertiliser through the normal modes of surface transport. The decision regarding the number of facilities to be created will be influenced by the geographical distance among various sub-national markets to be served the complementarities of the product line, and the scale economies of production, among other factors.

2. **Location of Warehouse:** One important consideration in this context is the name of the product being sold. If the product is a household consumption item, such as packet tea, soaps or toothpaste, the retail outlets will be the bottom of the distribution channel success or otherwise of the distribution system would depend upon the ability of the company to ensure availability at that level. This obviously would need a comprehensive organisational structure involving a number of central regional warehouse, a larger number of company depots, field sales staff and an elaborate system of physical transportation of delivery vans, either company owned, leased or contracted our to an outside contractor. A manufacturer of capital equipment on the other hand, can have only one centralised warehouse for the main product but has to maintain a number of service centres to stock spare parts.

3. **Mode and Method of Transportation:** There are several key decisional points in the context which for long were considered the heart of distribution management. These are:

    (a) **Which mode of transportation would be optimal:** The choice of quite wide which include inter alia, trucks, other types of delivery, air, waterways, road-ways, or even post parcel, etc. The factors to be considered would include the relative costs of the alternative modes of transportation, speed, reliability and appropriateness, keeping in view the product attributes. The last named factor is so crucial that it can sometimes outweigh all other consideration, such as the refrigerated vans used in diary corporations which forge a close link between the processing plants and the numerous retailing points for a highly perishable commodity.

    (b) **Mode of physical distribution:** A company may decide to own a fleet of delivery vehicles appoint an outside transport company or lease the vehicles from a leasing company. Alternatives are to be evaluated taking into account the cost of capital in case of company owned vehicles and the cost of managing the fleet and the charges to be paid to the leasing firm or to the outside transporter. The decision, however, cannot be taken only on cost consideration. For example, a company using its own fleet which distinctly displays its logo and brand can derive intangible benefits from higher degree of public exposure and recognition.

4. **Inventory Decisions:** Bulk of the total distribution cost, which generally account for five to twenty-five per cent of the product costs, is incurred on the physical

distribution and costs of holding inventories. Since inventory holding costs are always on the rise due to all around increase in prices as well as cost of capital, very careful attention has to be paid on how much inventory should be maintained, of what items and where. Many of the decisions have to be taken keeping in view the broader corporate objective of service reliability, i.e., the capacity of the firm to deliver on time.

5. **Using External Distribution Agency:** Much of what has been discussed above refers to firms always to do so. A firm may decide that because of resource constraints or lack of in-house expertise, it would like to concentrate on production and leave the task of distribution to outside agency. Even the Gujarat Corporation Milk Federation, the famous producer of Amul brand of dairy products, initially handed over its distribution to Voltas Ltd. There are several firms in India such as Voltas, Spencer Blue Star, etc. which have created extensive distribution networks, including servicing facilities and can therefore provide distribution services to individual producers in a cost-effective way. Whether to contract out distribution or not is a major decision would require an in-depth analysis of the relative cost and benefits, both tangible and intangible of the alternative course of action.

Specific Issues Relating to Maintenance of Stocks

The ultimate proof efficiency of distribution system of a firm lies in its ability to service the demands of its customers at all time and at all places. This, however, is only an ideal and hardly ever achieved. The problems in attaining this ideal are many including

- Inaccurate forecasting of demand
- Non-availability of production
- Failure of the production system
- Congestion in the physical distribution system.

Some of these problems are, however, generic in nature and therefore based on past experience. It is possible to visualise the occurrence of such events and their impact, albeit with certain degree of error. Maintenance of stocks geared to keeping the process of distribution undisturbed, even though some of the above factors are present.

Stocks are maintained, irrespective of the place where they are held basically on two accounts (a) production and (b) demand. Production stocks are of two types (i) an inventory of production inputs to tide over the distribution in the supply chain in the short-terms and (ii) to produce at the economically variable scale, irrespective of the short-term fluctuations in the demand for the finalised output. Some stocks are maintained to take care of the possible divergence between current production and current demand. Production stocks are intensively analysed in materials management and production scheduling. Determination of demand stocks, however, is an important segment of distribution strategy.

Size of the demand stocks to be maintained depends primarily on the following factors:

1. Average order size. The larger the average order size, greater would be the stocks requirements.
2. Average lead time required to replenish the stocks. Longer the lead time, greater the stocks to be held.
3. Volatility in demand. Higher the fluctuations in demand, greater would be the stock requirement.
4. The degree of service to be provided, if the company decides that it would like to provide a very high level of service in terms of product availability, it would have to maintain a corresponding high level of stocks.

The degree of product availability to be maintained is to a large extent conditioned by the product characteristics. For example, when a buyer goes to a shop for a particular brand of soap and toothpaste, he may try another shop nearly. It is not available in the firm's shop. But in case it is not available there too, he might buy another brand. On the other hand, he may be perfectly willing to wait for a few weeks to get delivery of a particular brand of a refrigerator or a typewriter. Sometimes, the brand preference can be so strong that buyers are willing to wait almost indefinitely, as was the case some years back for Bajaj Scooter or EC TV, and presently to some extent for Maruti cars.

Logically, the delivery period can be lengthened without or only a little loss to the company when (i) the products are such whose consumption can be postponed or planned with a long lead time, as in the case of custom built equipment (ii) the brand loyalty is very strong and (iii) the market is essentially a seller's market. It is obvious that the parameters of the Indian market are changing very fast in a direction which would make distribution one of the most crucial Ps of marketing. The recent Maggi brand of noodles is also to some extent due to company's flawless distribution system, including giving display containers to the retailers which also serve as points of purchase advertisement.

6.22   MARKETING AND PUBLIC POLICY

A cursory look at the marketing mix of any firm, whether marketing consumer or industrial goods, would reveal that there is hardly any marketing area, which is unaffected by governmental control. The numerous governmental controls which contribute to an overall public policy framework and in the form of various acts and statutes are a major challenge to any marketing manager. Since in the past decades, several of our industrial sectors suffered from shortages, as a cumulative build-up we have acts which are meant to bring highest possible degree of fairness in the marketing exchange process. In this unit, we will look at a selected list of such acts.

Role of Government in Marketing in Developing Economies

Government tries to influence, regulate or intervene in the marketing system of a country primarily with the objective of ensuring a fair treatment to millions of concerns of various products and services. In addition, the government also seeks to manage shortages through a legislative process. In addition, one of the other expected roles of public policy is to improve the efficiency of marketing systems. These are brought about in three ways:

1. Through normal regulative activities including price controls, control of product quality and quantity, controls over market participation, sales taxation, and antitrust regulations.

2. Through provision of marketing infrastructure and market information. Such resources and services as credit, training, storing, transportation and marketing research are provided by the public sector to help private enterprise especially small-scale private traders and producers.

   For example, providing loans to gem and jewellery exporters helps to promote trade and to expand the export of these items. Another example is that of Bureau of Indian Standards which has developed a large number of products standards facilitating product identification, purchasing, selling and servicing.

3. Through direct entrepreneurial participation in the marketing process. The role of the government in such a case is not necessarily intervention but may rather be one of guidance and leadership in guiding the economy including helping the sick units to become healthy once again.

   *For example, super bazaars in cities of India act as competitors in the marketing of various products. The other example is that of the **National Textile Corporation (NTC)** which is engaged in the production, wholesaling and retailing of textiles in direct competition with private enterprise.*

Still other important examples are that of the Food Corporation of India (FCI), the Cotton Corporation of India (CCI), and the Jute Corporation of India (JCI) which procure and sell agricultural commodities such as food grains, cotton and jute.

Naturally, you will like to ask and understand at this stage as to what is the specific purpose of legislation which spells out normal regulative activities. These purposes are:

1. One, to protect companies from each other. It is with this objective that the government passes laws to define and prevent unfair competition.
2. Two, to protect consumers from unfair business practices. It is with this end in view that the government tries to exercise control on quality, packaging, price, promotion, etc.
3. Three, to protect the larger interest of society against unbridled business behaviour. The main focus here is to charge business with the social costs created in their production processes of products.

Articles 39(b) and (c) of the Constitution of India which spells out the reason for government control and the main control laws affecting marketing are listed in the next section. The marketers should know these laws and also keep track of the evolving interpretations by law courts. They should also know the state and local laws that affect their local marketing activity.

Government Control and Marketing Decision-making Process

A number of laws affecting business have become operational over the years. The important ones affecting marketing are listed below:

1. The Indian Contract Act, 1872
2. The Indian Sale of Goods Act, 1930
3. The Industries (Development and Regulation) Act, 1951
4. The Prevention of Food Adulteration Act, 1954
5. The Drugs and Magic Remedies (Objectionable Advertisements) Act, 1954
6. The Essential Commodities Act, 1955
7. The Companies Act, 1956
8. The Trade and Merchandise Marks Act, 1958
9. The Monopolies and Restrictive Trade Practices Act, 1969 (MRTP Act)
10. The Patents Act, 1970
11. The Standards of Weights and Measures Act, 1976
12. The Consumer Protection Act, 1986.

Some of the legislations mentioned above apply to every undertaking, irrespective of the nature of the product sold or the service provided by it like the Contract Act, the Sale of Goods Act, the Companies Act, the Trade and Merchandise Marks Act and the

Standards of Weights and Measure Act. The MRTP Act, however, does not apply to public undertakings, government-managed private undertakings, financial institutions and cooperative societies.

As against this there are certain legislations listed above which seek to regulate certain decisions of undertakings engaged in the specific industries. These include the Industries (Development and Regulation) Act, 1951; the Drugs and Magic Remedies (Objectionable Advertisements) Act, 1954; the Prevention of Food Adulteration Act, 1954; the Essential Commodities Act, 1955, and the Cigarettes (Regulation of Production, Supply and Distribution) Act, 1975.

It would be too much to expect a marketer to know all about the various Acts listed above well as few others like the Bureau of Indian Standards Act, 1986; the Drugs and Cosmetics Act, 1940, and the Drugs (Control) Act, 1950 that affect his decision-making. But, nevertheless, it is essential for him to have a good working knowledge of the major laws protecting competition, consumers and the larger interests of the society. Such an understanding would help him to examine the legal implications of his own decisions.

According to Articles 39(b) and (c) of the Constitution of India, control exists as a means of achieving a socialist pattern of society. These Articles ensure that "the operation of the economic system does not result in the concentration of wealth and means of production to the common detriment" and that the ownership and control of the material resources of the community are so distributed as best to subserve the common good.

The main reasons for government controls can be summarised as follows:

- ✠ Protecting the welfare of individuals and promoting higher standards of public health, general well-being, safety, etc.
- ✠ Maintaining equality of opportunity for all persons irrespective of the sex, nationality, race or religion.
- ✠ Restraining business from engaging in practices harmful to the interests of the public, like making false and misleading statements about a product or service, manipulating prices for personal gains, failing to support warranties, etc.
- ✠ Protecting small firms from the threats of unfair competition by big firms.
- ✠ Preventing unfair practices resulting from mergers or thereform of combinations like price fixing.
- ✠ Conserving national resources especially forests, fuels, water, energy, etc.
- ✠ Preventing pollution of the environment.
- ✠ Preventing concentration of economic power and industrial wealth.
- ✠ Encouraging widely dispersed industrial growth and the growth of small-scale industries.

✠ Protecting the economy from dominance by foreign inventors and helping save the valuable foreign exchange resources.

You should, however, remember that ours is a planned economy and it is not a case of natural growth but of a nurtured growth and the measures of government control and intervention are a reflection of the government's desire to achieve a desired direction or pattern in investment, production and distribution or consumption.

1. Indian Contract Act (1872)

Regulates the economic and commercial relations of citizens. The scope of this Act extends to all such decisions which involve the formation and execution of a contract. The essentials of a valid contract are specified and examined in detail.

A contract is an agreement enforceable at law made between two or more persons by which rights are acquired by one or more to acts or forbearances on the part of the other or others.

The Act also specifies provisions for the creation of an agency and the rights and duties of a principal and an agent.

2. Indian Sale of Goods Act (1930)

Governs the transactions of sale and purchase. A contract of sale of goods is defined as a contract whereby the property in goods is transferred or agreed to be transferred by the seller to the buyer for a price. The Act also lays down rules about passing of property in goods and the rights and duties of the buyer and seller, rules regarding the delivery of goods as well as the rights of the unpaid seller.

3. Industries (Development and Regulation) Act (1951)

It is through this Act that the industrial licensing system operates. In effect it empowers the government to license (or permit) new investment, expansion of licensed units, production of new articles, change of location by the licensed units and also to investigate the affairs of licensed units in certain cases and to take over the management thereof, if conditions so warrant. The objectives behind these powers are, of course, development and regulation of important industries involving fairly large investments which have an all-Indian importance. It is in the actual implementation of these objectives that the relevant aspects of the industrial policy are expected to be fulfilled.

Industrial licensing is a form of direct state intervention in the market to overrule its forces. The underlying assumption here is that the government is the best judge about the priorities from the national point of view and also that it can do the allocation in a better and socially optimal way. It must, however, be understood that there are economic costs involved in the measures of control and the benefits that are expected to accrue at least equal to or more than the costs involved.

4. Prevention of Food Adulteration Act (1954)

Prohibits the production, storage, distribution and sale of adulterated and misbranded food articles and to ensure purity in the articles of food.

5. Drugs and Magic Remedies (Objectionable Advertisements) Act (1954)

Prohibits the publication or issue of advertisements tending to cause the ignorant consumer to resort to self-medication with harmful drugs and appliances.

Advertisements for certain drugs for preventing diseases and disorders like epilepsy, prevention of conception, sexual impotency, etc. are also prohibited. The Act also prohibits advertisements making false claims for the drugs.

6. Essential Commodities Act (1955)

Provides for the control of production, supply and distribution in certain commodities declared as essential under Section 2(a) of the Act, in the public interest. Under Section 3(a) of this Act, the government can fix the price of such a commodity.

7. Companies Act (1956)

It is a piece of legislation which has far reaching effects on business by its regulation of the organisation and functioning of companies. With more than 650 sections, it is one of the longest legal enactments. It is meant to regulate the growing uses of the company system as an instrument of business and finance and possibilities of abuse inherent in that system.

8. Trade and Merchandise Marks Act (1958)

Deals with the trade and merchandise marks registered under this Act.

A mark includes a device, brand, heading, label, ticket, name, signature word and letter of numeral or any combination thereof.

A trademark is a distinctive symbol, title or design that readily identifies the company or its product. The owner of the trademark has the right to its exclusive use and provides legal protection against infringement of his right. A trademark is registered for a maximum period of 7 years and is renewable for a similar number of years, each time the period of 7 years expires.

Further, no such trademark should be used which is likely to be deceptive or confusing, or is scandalous or obscene or which hurts the religious sentiments of the people of India.

9. Monopolies and Restrictive Trade Practices Act (1969) (MRTP Act)

Provides that the operation of the economic system does not result in the concentration of economic power to the common detriment, for the control of monopolies, for the prohibition of monopolistic, restrictive and unfair trade practices and for matters connected therewith or incidental thereto.

It may be of interest for you to know that the first country to pass such legislation was the United States which has a free enterprise system. There such an Act was passed as far back as 1890 and is called the Sherman Antitrust Act. But so far as the United Kingdom is concerned it was only in 1948 that the Monopolies and Restrictive Practices (Inquiry Control) Act was passed. In 1956 and 1964 two more Acts were added, viz., Restrictive Trade Practices Act and the Resale Prices Act respectively. Our Act is modelled on the lines of the above three Acts.

10. Patents Act (1970)

Provisions of this Act are attracted especially where the company intends to produce patented products. A patent is the exclusive right to own, use and dispose of an invention for a specified period. The patent is a grant made by the Central Government to the first inventor or his legal representative.

11. Standards of Weights and Measures Act (1976)

Specifies the quantities in which certain products can be packed. The products are bread, butter, cheese, biscuits, cereals and pulses, cigarettes, cigar, cleaning and sanitary fluids, cleaning powder, condensed milk, tea, coffee, cooking oils, cosmetics, honey, ice cream, jams, sauces, milk powder, soaps, spices, toothpaste, etc.

12. Consumer Protection Act (1986)

Consumer Protection Act is the latest addition to the list of the legislations regulating marketing decisions in India. The Act is in addition to and not in derogation of the provisions of any other law which influence marketing decisions. The Act is intended to provide better protection of the interests of consumers and for that purpose makes provisions for the establishment of Consumer Councils and other authorities for the settlement of the consumer disputes and for matters connected therewith. It does not exclude or exempt from the purview of the regulatory measures the public enterprises, financial institutions, and cooperative societies, which enjoyed a privileged position under the MRTP Act being immune from any action even against those marketing practices of theirs which were considered against consumer or public interest. With the enforcement of the Consumer Protection Act, the consumer can get the redressal of his grievance even against the Public Railways, Delhi Transport Corporation (DTC) and other State Transport Corporations, etc. In particular, this Act provides a new challenge to a large number of public sector undertakings engaged in manufacture or distribution of consumer goods and provisions of consumer services.

The new Act comes with sharper teeth. One of the weaknesses of earlier legislations was the confusion regarding the burden of proof. They never made it sufficiently clear whether the onus of proof rested with the manufacturer, the trader or the consumer. The new Act establishes a landmark in the sense that for the first time the onus has been shifted to the manufacturer and the seller.

The new Act provides the consumer the right

- To be protected against marketing of goods which are hazardous to life and property
- To be informed about the quality, quantity, potency, purity, standard and price of goods
- To protect the consumer against unfair trade practices (the term 'unfair trade practice' has been defined under the MRTP Act, under Section 36-A.
- To be assured, wherever possible, access to an authority of goods at competitive prices.
- To be heard and to be assured that consumers interest will receive due consideration at appropriate forums
- To seek redressal against unfair trade practices or unscrupulous exploitation of consumers
- To get consumer education.

These objects are sought to be promoted and protected by the Consumer Protection Councils to be established at the Central and State levels.

To provide speedy and simple redressal to consumer disputes, a quasi-judicial machinery is sought to be set up at the District, State and Central levels. These quasi-judicial bodies will observe the principles of natural justice and have been empowered to give relief of a specific nature and to award, wherever appropriate, compensation to consumers. Penalties for non-compliance of the orders given by the quasi-judicial bodies have also been provided.

One could say that the scope of this legislation is much wider than any of the existing legislation. But the success will depend on whether the required infrastructure, particularly at the district and State levels, will get created and whether there will be necessary enthusiasm not only to create the machinery but also implement the provisions of the Act.

Environment (Protection) Act (1986)

The Environment (Protection) Act provides for the protection and improvement of environment and for the prevention of hazards to human beings, other living creatures, plants and property.

Environment includes, water, air and land and the interrelationship existing between them and the human beings, living creatures, plants, etc. Any solid, liquid or gaseous substances present which may tend to be injurious to environment is an environmental pollutant and the presence thereof is pollution.

The present enactment covers not only all matters relating to prevention, control and abatement of environment pollution but also powers and functions of the Central Government and its officers in that regard and penalties for committing offences.

Bureau of Indian Standards Act (1986)

The Bureau of Indian Standards Act provides for the establishment of a Bureau for the harmonious development of the activities of standardisation, marking and quality certification of goods and for matters connected therewith or incidental thereto.

It has been provided that the Bureau of Indian Standards will be a body corporate and there will be an Executive Committee to carry on its day-to-day activities. Staff, assets and liabilities of the Indian Standards Institution will perform all functions of the Indian Standards Institution. It has also been stipulated that access will be provided to the Bureau's Standards and Certification Marks to suppliers of like products originating in General Agreement on Trade and Tariff (GATT) code countries.

The Act does not make any change in existing law except to prive a new forum for deciding the cases effectively and without delay.

When the Indian Standards Institution was established in 1947, the industrial development in the country was still in its infancy. Since then there has been substantial progress in various sectors of the Indian economy and hence the need for a new thrust to be given to standardisation and quality control. A national strategy for according appropriate recognition and importance of standards is to be evolved and integrated with the growth and public sector and private sectors including small-scale industries have to intensify efforts to produce higher standard and quality goods to help in inducing faster growth, increasing exports and making available goods to the satisfaction of the consumers.

It was to achieve the above objectives that the Bureau of Indian Standards has been set up as a statutory institution.

Government Agencies

To enforce the laws, the Government has established a number of regulatory agencies, like, the Bureau of Industrial Costs and Prices, the Agricultural Prices Commission and the MRTP Commission.

The Bureau of Industrial Costs and Prices was established by the Government in 1971. Its job is to conduct enquiries about industrial products and recommend prices.

The Agricultural Prices Commission was set up in January 1965 to advise the government on pricing policies for agricultural commodities.

The Government has also framed rules like the Prevention of Food Adulteration Rules, 1955 and the Standards of Weights and Measures (Packaged Commodities) Rules, 1977 to enforce the provision of the related acts. The enforcement of these Acts is the responsibility of the Central and the State Government.

The **MRTP** Commission has been established by the Government under section 5 of the **MRTP Act, 1969**. The Commission may inquire into any restrictive trade practice

(i) upon receiving a complaint of facts which constitute such practice from any trade or consumers association having a membership of not less than twenty-five persons or from twenty-five or more consumers, or

(ii) upon a reference made to it by the Central Government or a State Government, or

(iii) upon an application made to it by the Registrar of Restrictive Trade Agreements (RRTA), or

(iv) upon its own knowledge or information (also known as suo moto inquiries).

As far as monopolistic trade practices are concerned, an inquiry can be made either upon a reference made by the Central Government or upon its own knowledge or information.

A complainant is different from an informant since the latter is not recognised by the Act. In such cases the MRTP Commission has to decide whether any informant in any case is a person interested in the subject matter of the proceedings.

In respect of complaints received from consumer and trade associations directly, the MRTP Commission has to make a preliminary investigation through its Director General of Investigation to satisfy itself that the complaint deserves a full-scale inquiry.

Public interest groups have also grown up during the last one decade or so. These groups try to influence both government as well as business to pay more attention to consumer rights. They even take the matter to a law court to get justice to affected consumers against unfair dealings on the part of business enterprises.

6.23   IMPACT OF GOVERNMENT CONTROL ON PRODUCT, PRICE, PROMOTION, AND DISTRIBUTION DECISIONS

The following are the relevant laws and other provisions which need to be discussed in this context.

1. The Industrial (Development and Regulations) Act, 1951

The provisions of this Act not only influence the product decisions but also the pricing and distribution decisions of companies in India. The concerned provisions relating to pricing and distribution decision have been expressed at appropriate places while the provisions affecting product decisions here.

According to Section 11 of the Act, the manufacturing of a product listed in the first schedule of the Act who carries on production in a factory must register the new industrial undertaking in the prescribed manner within 3 months from the date it becomes such an undertaking.

A factory for this purpose means any premises in which a manufacturing process is being carried on either with the aid of power employing 50 or more workers or without the aid of power employing 100 or more workers.

Therefore, no person or authority, accept the Central Government can establish any new industrial undertaking without a licence from the Central Government if it proposes to manufacture one or more of the products listed in the first schedule and the production is to be carried on in a factory.

Production of a New Article by an Existing Undertaking

In case an existing undertaking proposes to manufacture any new article not already licensed, a fresh permission is required if the new article is one which is listed in the first schedule of the Act or which bears a mark as defined in the Trademarks Act, 1940 or which is a patented article.

Exemption to Small-Scale and Ancillary Units

Small-scale units are exempt from licensing provided that the conditions given below are satisfied.

First the undertaking should not belong to one or other following categories:

1. Undertakings covered by Section 20(a) of the MRTP Act, 1969, i.e., undertakings whose own assets together with the assets of interconnected undertakings if they are ₹100 crore or more.

2. Undertakings belonging to foreign concerns. These include foreign companies, their branches or subsidiaries and companies in which more than 40% of the paid-up equity capital is held directly by foreign companies, their branches or subsidiaries or by foreign national or non-resident Indians.

3. That they are not subsidiaries of or owned by any other undertaking.

Second the product should not belong to:

1. Industries listed in schedule A of the Industrial Policy Resolution, 1956.

2. Specified industries subject to special regulation like coal, textiles manufactured, produced or proceed on powerlooms, milk foods, malted foods, oilseeds crushing, vanaspati, leather, matches, brewing alcoholic drinks.

Preference to Small-Scale Sector

The Government also pursues the policy of proactive reservation for exclusive development under small-scale sector. The Government and its organisations show preference in making their purchases from small-scale industries. In order to ensure regular supply of raw materials to small-scale units, the government has liberalised the import policy and streamlined the distribution of critical raw materials. Small scale industries units including ancillaries located in backward areas qualifying for investment subsidy are eligible to procure machinery on hire purchase basis from the National Small Industries Corporations Ltd., at liberalised terms and conditions.

Industrial units set up by backward areas or by graduates or diploma holders in professional subjects or by ex-serviceman and persons belonging to schedule castes and schedule tribes can avail of special concessions for import of raw materials.

2. The MRTP Act 1969

The MRTP Act is largely concerned with the size including growth and expansion even though the size of Indian companies is far below that of competitors overseas. The Act also regulates the monopolistic and restrictive trade practices followed by companies. You should, however, remember that the Act does not apply to government public undertakings any undertaking owned by a cooperative society and public financial institutions. The major influence of this Act from the point of view of a marketer is felt in the area of product, pricing and distribution channels. In this subunit, we shall principally concentrate on those provisions which affect product decision.

Regulation of Restrictive Trade Practices

The Act also prohibits restrictive trade practices of companies which are covered by it if these are found to be prejudicial to the public interest on an inquiry by the MRTP Commission or otherwise.

Section 2(O) of the Act defines a restrictive trade practice to mean a trade practice which has, or may have, the effect of preventing, distorting or restricting competition in any manner and in particular.

3. The Essential Commodities Act (1956)

The Essential Commodities Act affect production pricing and distribution decisions of a company. Its objective is to control, in the interest of the general public, the production, supply, and distribution of trade and commerce in certain commodities declared essential under the Act. Section 2 of the Act defines essential commodities and lists a large number of products that are included under it.

4. The Prevention of Food Adulteration Act (1954)

The Prevention of Food Adulteration Act also affects decisions of companies manufacturing food products in respect of more than one element of the marketing mix, viz., production, promotion and distribution.

The objective of the Act is to protect the health of the public by prohibiting adulteration of food articles. The Act prohibits storage, distribution and sale of adulterated and misbranded food articles and ensure purity in the articles of food.

5. The Patents Act (1970)

The Patent Act is another piece of legislation which affects company's product decisions. The first thing to understand in this connection is what is patent?

A patent is an exclusive right to own, use and dispose of an invention for a specified period. This is right which is granted by the Central Government to the firms or to his legal representative. An invention as used in the above definition means any new and useful are, process, methods, or manner of manufacture, machine, apparatus or other article and substance produced by the manufacturer.

6. The Trade and Merchandise Marks Act (1956)

The Trade and Merchandise Marks Act not only influences the company's product decisions but also its advertising decisions, so far as they relate to the use of trade and merchandise marks registered under this Act.

A 'mark' includes a device, brand, heading, label, ticket, name, signature, world and letter of numeral or any combination thereof. A trademark is a distinctive symbol, title or design that readily identifies the company or its product. The registration of trademark under this Act endows on its owner the right to its exclusive use and provides legal protection against infringement of his right.

Initially a trademark is registered for a maximum period of 7 years and is renewable for similar number of years, each time the period of 7 years expires.

7. The Standards of Weights and Measures Act (1976)

This is another piece of legislation which affects product decisions of a company. The Act specifies the quantities in which certain products can be packed. The products so covered are bread, butter, cheese, biscuits, cereals and pulses, cigarettes, cigar, cleaning and sanitary fluids, cleaning powder, condensed milk, tea, coffee, cooking oil, cosmetics, honey, ice cream, jams, sauces, ketchup, milk powder, soaps, spices, toothpaste, etc.

Thus, in relation to the product, the government exercise control with the help of a number of Acts which influence not only whether a product can be produced or not but also the quality of production, plans for future expansion, production of new article, the ingredients like colour, flavour, etc. can be used, as well as the packaging, labelling and branding of the products.

6.24 PRICING DECISIONS

The government control in the area of pricing is yet another feature of the interrelationship between government and business in India. The fixation of prices by the government of articles considered essential for the society was introduced in India for the first time during the Second World War. This was essentially a temporary measure to meet a situation of scarcity created by conditions of war. This policy not only was considered a safeguard against profiteering by business and scarcities of many essential manufactured products but the government was influenced by other consideration as well as which in many ways were more important.

The present position is that government regulates the price of the product mainly through three Acts, viz.

- The Industries (Development and Regulation) Act, 1951
- The Essential Commodities Act, 1955 and
- The MRTP Act, 1969.

We shall discuss the relevant provisions of these acts one by one to understand the scope of control under each one of them.

1. The Industries (Development and Regulation) Act (1951)

Section 15 of the Industries Act empower the government to investigate the working of a schedule industrial undertaking when there is a substantial fall in the volume of production, a marked deterioration in the quality of the product, a rise in the price of any article related to that industry without proper justification and to take suitable measures including control of the price or regulating the distribution.

Section 18(g) empowers the government to pass an order for controlling the prices at which schedule products or class thereof may be bought or sold.

2. The Essential Commodities Act (1955)

The Essential Commodities Act, 1955 provides for the control of the production supply and distribution in certain commodities declared as essential under Section 2(a) of the Act, in the public interest. Under Section 3(2)(c) of this Act, the government can fix the price of such a commodity.

Public distribution system: The Government through the public distribution system also aims at controlling and stabilising the prices of certain essential commodities like foodgrains.

Price fixation formula

The formula for price determination is based on accounting principles but in its actual working many complexities arise such as

1. Item of expenditure not to be taken into consideration for determining cost of manufacture
2. Capacity utilisation
3. Return on capital employed

The policy of allowing a return by way of fixed rate on capital employee without considering its other implications has done great harm to the economy in general and the industries concerned in particular. The rate of return once fixed by the government has been enforced on the industries despite the changed money market conditions, for long periods.

3. The MRTP Act (1969)

Collective price fixing agreements, resale price maintenance (RPM) and agreements for price control to eliminate competition or competitors are the three main restrictive trade practices in the area of price fixation which attract the provisions of the MRTP Act.

The collective price fixing agreements or cartels are those agreements wherein sellers agree on certain price level or on the adoption of certain methods for determining prices, cartels may also provide for rebates, commission or discounts to be allowed to the buyers. The aim and result of every price fixing agreement is maximisation of profits by the participating parties.

The MRTP Commission may, however, exempt the goods of the following description from the operation of the provisions relating to minimum resale price maintenance of the commission is satisfied that in default

- The quality of the goods and variety of the goods would be substantially reduced to the detriment of consumer or user of those goods, or
- The prices at which the goods are sold by retail would, in general and, in the long run, increased to the detriment of consumers or users, or
- Any necessary service actually provided in connection with or after the sale of goods by retail would cease to be so provided or would be substantially reduced to the detriment of consumers or users.

6.25   PROMOTIONAL DECISIONS

Promotional mix which includes advertising, sales promotion and personal selling is another element of the marketing mix with respect to which it is essential for the marketing executive to know the implications of his own decisions.

A marketing executive has to particularly careful with the legal implications of objectionable promotion. To be on the safe he must satisfy himself on three counts in respect of persuasive communications, viz.

- ❖ Is the message or communication fraudulent?
- ❖ Does the message or communication misrepresents?
- ❖ Is the message or communication opposed to public policy?

The specific legal constraints which affect decision-making in the area of promotion, the following arrangement will be expressed in the relevant provisions of the various Acts.

- MRTP Act
- Income Tax Act
- Preventation Food Adulteration Rules
- Standards of Weighs and Measures Rules

- Drugs and Magic Remedies Act
- Sales Promotion Employees Act

6.26   DISTRIBUTION DECISIONS

The overall objective of regulation of this element of the marketing mix as with respect to other elements is to promote the healthy marketing environment in the country. More specifically the regulatory framework relating to channel and distribution decisions aims:

- ✠ To prevent restrictions on free flow of goods and services
- ✠ To promote competitive conditions in industry by preventing all restrictive elements like tie-up sales, boycott, exclusive dealing, full line forcing, etc.
- ✠ To prevent trade agreements which often protect less efficient from the efficient ones alone are able to survive, and
- ✠ To protect the consumer.
- ✠ To promote efficiency of the industry manufacturing and distribution units.

KEYWORDS

Administered Prices: The term is often used in the context of regulation of prices by the government. It may assume two forms: one, the price may be set by some government agency like the Bureau of Industrial Costs and Prices (BICP) or the Traiff Commission and in that case the firm has no choice but to abide by it. Two, the price may be set by a firm within the framework or on the basis of a formula given by the government.

Broker: An intermediary whose function is only to establish a link between the manufacturer and customer. He does not himself buy or sell any goods on his own account.

Common Agent: An intermediary who actually buys products from the manufacturer and in turn sells in final customers and in return gets a percentage commission on sales.

Company Sales Forecast: The value and volume of a product that a firm actually expects to sell during a specific period at a given level of company marketing activities.

Channel of Distribution: Those institutions which perform all the activities and functions necessary for moving a product and its title from production to consumption.

Expert Forecasting Survey: Preparation of sales forecasts by experts, such as economist, management consultants, or other professional outside the firm.

Guarantees and Warranties: *The guarantee is the general policy of the manufacturer with regard to defective products. Often used as a promotional device, it usually makes broad promise (such as offering "complete satisfaction") that may or may not be legally binding. The warranty 'however' must specify the exact terms under which the manufacturer will repair or replace its merchandise. Customers often misunderstand the limits of a warranty or fail to read presale posted warranties and may accidentally misuse the products.*

Horizontal Marketing System: *Two or more unrelated businesses come together pull in resources to exploit the emerging opportunities.*

Market Potential: *The maximum sales possible for one company's product as the firm's marketing efforts increase relative to competitors.*

Marketing Channels: *The external contractual organisation that management operates to achieve its distribution objectives.*

Multi-channel Marketing System: *A firm uses multiple channels to reach different customer segments.*

One Level Structure: *One intermediary acting as a link between the manufacturer and the consumer.*

Retailer: *One who sells to the actual customer. The last link in the chain between the manufacture and customer.*

Service: *Service means service of any description which is made available to potential users and includes the provision of facilities in connection with banking, financing, insurance, transport, processing, supply of electrical or other energy, broad or loading or both, entrainment, amusement or the purveying of news or other information Sec(2 (0)) of the Consumer Protection Act.*

Sales Potential: *The maximum sales possible for one company's product as the firm's marketing efforts increases relative to competitors.*

Seasonality Analysis: *A method of predicting sales in which a manager studies daily, weekly or monthly sales figures to evaluate the degree to which seasonal factors, such as climate, festivals and holiday activities, influence the firm's sales.*

Top Down Forecasting: *Analysis of sales for the purpose of forecasting from world, to natural industry to firm level.*

Three Level Structures: *Firms when go global they use the help of agents to take their products to the wholesalers and then to the retailers before reaching the end consumer.*

Two Level Structure: *Two people interceding before the product reaches the consumer.*

Vertical Marketing System: *Members acting as one unified team, there is one channel member who owns the other members or allows franchising but ensures a greater role in the execution.*

Wholesaler: *An intermediary who buys products from the manufacturer and in turn sells them to retailers.*

Zero Level Structure: *The product moves from the manufacturer directly to the consumer without any intermediary.*

SUMMARY

Sales forecasting, though crucial, is one of the grey areas of marketing management. It is crucial because without a proper sales forecast the marketing executive cannot determine the type of marketing programme to use in order to attain the desired sales and marketing objectives. Managers face a great deal of difficulty in evaluating their forecasts. The task becomes more difficult when the manager lacks any specific criteria for evaluating the forecasts. Survey of literature suggests the consideration of the following important factors when evaluating forecasts. Different people perceive marketing channels in different ways, some see it as a route taken by a product as it moves from the producer to the consumer, and others describe it as a loose coalition of business firms that have come together for purpose of business.

At times the product passes directly from the manufacturer to the consumer. There are five most important flows namely

- *Product flow*
- *Negotiation flow*
- *Ownership flow*
- *Information flow*
- *Promotion flow.*

Channel design refers to those decisions that involve the development of new marketing channels or modifying the existent ones. The channel design decision can be broken down into six steps namely:

1. *Recognising the need for channel design decision*
2. *Setting and coordinating distribution objectives*
3. *Specify the distribution tasks*
4. *Develop alternative channel structures*
5. *Evaluate relevant variables*
6. *Choose the best channel structure.*

Like any other concept, channel systems do change according to the development and the need of the hour. With consumers becoming conscious of where they buy and how they want things to be delivered. There have emerged different systems namely the vertical, horizontal and multichannel marketing systems.

Retailing includes all the activities involved in selling goods or services directly to final consumers for their personal, non-business use.

1. *Wheel of Retailing*
2. *Retail Accordion Theory*
3. *Theory of Natural Selection*
4. *Retail Life Cycle*

Wholesaling

This includes all the activities involved in selling goods and services to those who buy for resale purpose. In the case of wholesaling this excludes manufacturers or producers who are involved directly in the production of the goods.

The effective and efficient management of logistics is an extremely crucial factor in the success of a retail company. Logistics is the term used to define the entire process of flow of merchandise right from the point where merchandise is sourced to the point of its actual sale to customers.

Government Control and Marketing Decision-making Process

A number of laws affecting business have become operational over the years. The important ones affecting marketing are listed below:

1. *The Indian Contract Act, 1872*
2. *The Indian Sale of Goods Act, 1930*
3. *The Industries (Development and Regulation) Act, 1951*
4. *The Prevention of Food Adulteration Act, 1954*
5. *The Drugs and Magic Remedies (Objectionable Advertisements) Act, 1954*
6. *The Essential Commodities Act, 1955*
7. *The Companies Act, 1956*
8. *The Trade and Merchandise Marks Act, 1958*
9. *The Monopolies and Restrictive Trade Practices Act, 1969 (MRTP Act)*
10. *The Patents Act, 1970*
11. *The Standards of Weights and Measures Act, 1976*
12. *The Consumer Protection Act, 1986.*

The Government control in the area of pricing is yet another feature of the interrelationship between government and business in India. The fixation of prices by the government of articles considered essential for the society was introduced in India for the first time during the Second World War.

The present position is that government regulates the price of the product mainly through three Acts, viz.

- *The Industries (Development and Regulation) Act, 1951*
- *The Essential Commodities Act, 1955 and*
- *The MRTP Act, 1969.*

The overall objective of regulation of this element of the marketing mix as with respect to other elements is to promote the healthy marketing environment in the country. More specifically the regulatory framework relating to channel and distribution decisions aims:

❖ *To prevent restrictions on free flow of goods and services*

❖ *To promote competitive conditions in industry by preventing all restrictive elements like tie-up sales, boycon, exclusive dealing full line forcing etc.*

❖ *To prevent trade agreements which often protect less efficient from the efficient ones alone are able to survive, and*

❖ *To protect the consumer.*

❖ *To promote efficiency of the industry manufacturing and distribution units.*

ASSIGNMENT

Assignment 1

Suggest some useful techniques for sales forecasting in each of the following

1. City telephones
2. City bus service
3. Readymade textiles
4. A hairdresser
5. Room coolers
6. Cameras
7. Television
8. Electric bulbs

Assignment 2

By interviewing relevant persons, try to find out how the following forecast the sales of their merchandise

(a) Shopkeeper _____

_____

_____

(b) Wholesaler _____

_____

_____

(c) Manufacturing _____

_____

_____

Assignment 3

Visit the wholesaler and retail markets in your town and interview some intermediaries to find out the commission structure for leading brands of the following products.

	Distributor Wholesaler Commission	Retail Commission markup
(a) Table fan	_____	_____
(b) Shaving blades	_____	_____
(c) Common salt	_____	_____
(d) Soft drinks	_____	_____

Can you explain why there are differences in the commission/markup for various products?

Assignment 4

Three purposes of government control have been spelt out earlier. Read carefully the reasons for government control as listed with Article 39 (b) and (c) of the constitution of India and classify these reasons under these three purposes, viz. to protect companies from each other, to protect consumer from unfair business practices, and to protect the larger interest of society against unbridled business behaviour.

_____

_____

_____

_____

_____

Assignment 5

You may recall that up to 1978 we used to have a very popular soft drink marked in India under the brand name of Cola-Cola. Try to gather some facts from published sources and find out as to which laws were used by the then government to force the exit of their soft drink from India.

_____

_____

_____

_____

Assignment 6

What are the different categories of products whose prices are controllable under Industrial Act and Essential Commodities Act?

_____

_____

_____

_____

Assignment 7

Would you use exclusive, selective or intensive distribution for the following products?

- Maruti Automobiles
- MTR food products
- Samsung Electronics

Assignment 8

Visit a nearby Kirana store and a departmental store, try to find out what different activities the retailers provide for the customers and the suppliers. Discuss your findings in a group. Check if you can find more activities that the retailers perform.

Assignment 9

Case Study 1

David Rosenzweig of Lynden Air Freight recently created a lead prospecting method that saved his 60 sales representatives time and helped the company reap $120,000 in profits in 6 months. As part of the method, qualified leads are sent to the sales force and postcards that outline Lynden's capabilities are sent Beth Cocchiarella knew her company needed a better way to qualify prospects when she accidentally made a cold call to the competition.

"I was mortified," says the sales rep for Lynden Air Freight, a Seattle-based business-to-business airfreight service company. "You're shooting in the dark when you're cold calling." While pounding the pavement for new business is vital to the growth of any company, it can also be a waste of time and money when reps do not have access to qualified prospects.

"Reps had really hot leads to go after, and their close ratio increased by seventy percent," says Rosenzweig, author of Spend Less Sell More, 13 Ways to Grow Your Business (Irwin Professional Publishing). Here's how Rosenzweig's system work: Potential prospects are first identified through Dun & Bradstreet's MarketPlace, a CD-ROM product that groups companies by standard industrial classification (SIC) codes, geographic locations, and annual sales revenue. Next, temporary workers call the decision-maker of each company and conduct a survey on the airfreight industry. Information gleaned from the survey allows Lynden to identify those prospects that best fit their model.

"When put to them in sort of a survey question, people were more likely to tell us who they're using, and their criteria for selecting a service provider," Rosenzweig says. Qualified leads are sent to the sales force, and postcards that outline Lynden's capabilities are mailed to each qualified prospect to increase visibility.

Katsy Gracey, a Lynden district manager, says the lead qualifying system has expanded her division's business one new account, for example, brings in as much as $35,000 a month. And her two sales reps, one of whom is Cocchiarella, have more of a focus on where to sell within the division's large territory, which includes the entire Dallas/Fort Worth area. Says Cocchiarella: "I don't do cold calling anymore. And let me tell you, I don't miss it."

Questions

1. What is a cold call and what are its disadvantages?
2. What was the lead prospecting method designed by David Rosenzweig?
3. What are qualified leads?
4. How is this system better than cold calling?
5. Will this strategy be effective in India? If so why? If not, why not?

Case Study 2

Creating an alternative distribution channel

Clerical Medical Investment Group feared its main means of product distribution would be adversely affected when the UK's Financial Services Act was introduced in 1988, placing much tighter restrictions on insurance sales practices and culminating in Disclosure, which took effect January 1, 1995. To counter that threat, Clerical Medical created the Financial Planning Service, a new distribution arm that is supported by laptop computers and a Windows-based point-of-sale system developed by Intuitive Systems. The system has made a positive impact on persistency, speed and accuracy of policy processing and overall customer service and has enhanced the company's efforts to reach a greater number of potential clients.

When Great Britain's Financial Services Act was introduced in 1988, placing much tighter restrictions on insurance sales practices and culminating in Disclosure, which took effect on Jan. 1, 1995 (requiring disclosure of commissions and expenses generated through the sale of most financial products), Bristol-based Clerical Medical Investment Group feared its main means of product distribution could be adversely affected. But the strategy Clerical Medical adopted to counter that threat—creation of a new distribution arm that is supported by laptop computers and a Windows-based point-of-sale system developed by Intuitive Systems (Stevenage Hearts, U.K.)—is boosting sales and doing much more than monitoring legal procedures. Even before it has been completely installed, it appears the point-of-sale system will have a positive impact on persistency, speed and accuracy of policy processing, and overall customer service. It also is enhancing the efforts of Clerical Medical, which offers a full range of products—including pensions, protection, annuities, investment products, and mortgage protection products—to reach a greater number of potential customers. "Legislation was the main driver for the need for an additional distribution channel, because it would have been limiting to depend on just one distribution channel, especially if that channel was shrinking," says Bill Stevenson, programme manager. He oversaw IS development within the multi-million-pound operation, which started doing business last year. The channel that could potentially decline–both by attrition and because of the sales and disclosure legislation–was that of the Independent Financial Advisor. IFAs in Great Britain have their own offices, and consumers come to them for advice and service in buying financial products. The advent of the Financial Services Act and Disclosure, which requires insurance companies to disclose, at the point-of-sale, the commissions the IFA (or any other type of sales professional) will earn in the sale of most financial products, did not originally bode well for this means of distribution.

"The legislation meant that there was a potential for the considerable reduction of our main channel," Stevenson recalls. "We felt that our strength would be enhanced with an additional channel." That became the Financial Planning Service in U.S. terms, a field force that by the end of the year will number about 100, with eventually about 300 professionals covering the U.K. "With the Financial Planning Service, we seek out the customers ourselves, through such avenues as advertisements, affinity groups, referrals, etc.," Stevenson explains. "We're selling a service, with a range of products. The emphasis is on long-term planning, encompassing not only advice on our own products, but also building society products and national savings."

But simply creating an additional delivery channel did not address other parts of the legislation, which specify inappropriate sales practices and require documentation of the financial planner/client interaction to make sure the rules have not been violated. This is where the point-of-sale technology came in. Intuitive's client/server-based sales and marketing systems include the Financial Advisor's Workbench (needs analysis); Channel Management Workbench (lead allocation, performance monitoring); Quotation Builder Workbench; and Telemarketing Workbench. These were adapted by Intuitive for Clerical Medical's Financial Planning Service, and run on IBM notebook computers used by the financial planners. The system facilitates the requirement to do what is called a Fact Find–examination of a potential client's financial and personal circumstances, existing protections, assets and investments, as well as current and future financial needs. According to the legislation, the Fact Find must be followed by Best Advice: "We can't be seen as selling clients a product that doesn't meet their particular needs," Stevenson says. "We have to provide an audit of the Fact Find showing that we actually went through the client's circumstances, to make sure that the product the client is sold is under Best Advice, and something the client actually needs. The Fact Find part of the Intuitive system captures that data and records it," Stevenson says.

Another part of the system is Needs Analysis. "That takes details from the Fact Find, and works out what the current financial position is, what the shortfalls are, and sees what can be done to fill those shortfalls," Stevenson says. "What the system won't do, and what we deliberately didn't want it to do, is recommend a particular product. It identifies the shortfall, and the financial planner, as a result of discussions with the client, will recommend a [particular financial product], under Best Advice." Eventually, the point-of-sale system also will allow for electronic transmission of applications, as well as a more streamlined creation of customer information databases. Stevenson acknowledges that, with the regulatory circumstances that led to the development of the Financial Planning Service, the insurer stands to reap a number of business benefits from both the installation of the point-of-sale system and the implementation of some of the sales practices now required by law. "We have to provide persistency information to the regulators. If there are things like high lapse rates or paid-up policies, we're going to be asked why that is, it may be an indication that some mis-selling is taking place," Stevenson says. "The whole idea of automation is that we should get much better customer service–not only in speed, but in accuracy. The quality of data capture is much higher, as is the information that one can get in terms of the client and his needs, because you have captured that information automatically." Part of that improved service will be the ability to identify when clients may require new services or changes in existing coverage. "We can have updates on a regular basis from the client, and can monitor that and do needs analysis updates," says Stevenson, adding a caveat inspired by the new regulatory restrictions: "But we've got to be careful–we can't sell financial products to people who don't want or need them."

Questions

1. What was the problem faced by Clerical Medical Investment Group?
2. What strategy did they use for solving this problem?
3. How did this strategy help them improve their service?
4. Is this strategy effective in all industries? If so why? If not, in what type of industries this strategy would be useful?

Assignment 10

Tick the Most Appropriate Answer

1. Creative selling, which requires a salesperson to recognise the potential buyers need and then to provide the prospect with the necessary information, is performed by sales position called

    (a) Order taker
    (b) Missionary salesperson
    (c) Technical salesperson.

2. Learning about the potential buyer, the buyers' purchasing process and needs, and anything else that could be helpful in the selling process is the activity of

    (a) The Approach
    (b) The Preapproach
    (c) Qualifying.

3. The most effective short-term sales promotion incentive results from

   (a) Price-off

   (b) Coupons

   (c) Premiums

   (d) Contests.

4. In establishing sales promotion objectives, marketers

   (a) Focus on consumers

   (b) Focus on trade

   (c) Concentrate on activities that will increase consumer demand

   (d) Align objectives with overall organisation objectives.

REVIEW QUESTIONS

1. What is Sales Forecast? Why is it important?

2. Under what conditions executive judgment method is useful for sales forecasting? Discuss its limitations.

3. Given below list of products. What kind of distribution channel (direct or indirect) would you recommend for each of these products and why? (a) personal computer ((b) textile industry (c) branded spices (d) industrial lubricants.

4. A new toy manufacturer company is planning to launch its toys in the market and wishes to appoint retail in all major towns. What should be the criteria for selecting appropriate outlets? Specify the distinct features that the company should look for in the retail outlets.

5. Define logistic and its factors under distribution.

6. Define distribution channel. What are the major distribution channels? What is their relative suitability?

7. What are the factors which influences the choice of channel?

8. Explain the services of retailer. And types of retail units.

9. Define theories in retailing.

10. Define physical distribution and its importance in channel of distribution.

11. Explain the marketing and public policy.

12. Explain need for channels of distribution.

13. Discuss the factors affecting channels of distribution.

14. The Consumer Protection Act, 1986 provides

    (a) An effective machinery for speedy and inexpensive redressal of consumer grievance
    (b) A new hope to marketing manager

    Critically examine the above statements.

15. It is alleged that Government control in the form of industrial licensing MRTP, Act administered prices, etc. has affected the marketing efficiency of companies in India do you agree? Discuss.

16. Explain the existing arrangement for controlling prices in India.

MARKETING COMMUNICATION AND PROMOTIONAL STRATEGIES

STRUCTURE

7.1   INTRODUCTION

The word 'communication' derives from Latin meaning 'common'. Thus, the term communication has to come to mean sharing something of common use.

However, marketing communication poses a special challenge to the marketing strategies for some unique reasons. First, it is the most visible clue next to the product itself, of marketers' intentions and commitment to consumers. Secondly, it receives a relatively closer security from the policy makers and other consumer interest groups. Thirdly, there has been a significant change in viewing marketing communication.

For a very long time, it had been seen as if promotions formed the only communication bridge between a company and its buyers. The limited view of marketing communication is now being replaced with a more correct and wider proposition that the marketing communication travels beyond promotion. In its linkage with the buyers, it encompasses everything including product, packaging and distribution channels, and forms a vital part of overall marketing efforts towards the buyers and also other sections of society.

With growing competition in the marketplace as well as the customers becoming better informed and more choosy, it is important now that marketing communication of the right kind only be made to the right group of target buyers. In order to understand how the promotion function can be managed effectively, let us begin by first taking a look how the communication works.

7.2   THE COMMUNICATION PROCESS

Marketers need to understand how does communication work? A communication model answers (1) who (2) says what (3) in what channel (4) to whom (5) with what effect.

The communication process itself consists of nine elements: sender, receiver, encoding, decoding, message, media, response, feedback, and noise. Two elements represent the major parties in a communication–**sender** and **receiver**. Two represent the major communication tools–**message** and **media**. Four represent major communication functions–**encoding, decoding, response,** and **feedback**. The last element is **noise** in the system. Marketers must know how to get through to the target audience in the face of the audience's tendencies toward selective attention, distortion, and recall. The total elements and the process flow is illustrated in Fig. 7.1.

Senders must know what audiences they want to reach and what responses they want. They encode their messages in a way that takes into account how the target audience usually decodes messages. The sender must transmit the message through an efficient media that reach the target audience. Senders must develop feedback channels so that they can know the receiver's response to the message.

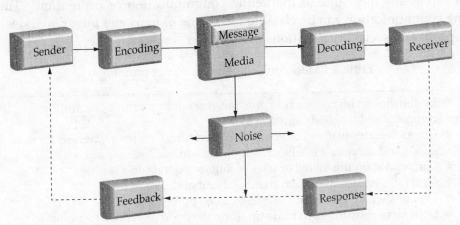

Fig. 7.1 Elements in communication process.

For message to be effective, the sender's encoding process must mesh with the receiver's decoding process. Messages are essentially signs that must be familiar to the receiver. The more the sender's field of experience overlaps with that of the receiver, the more effective the message is likely to be. "The source can be encoded, and the destination can be decoded", only in terms of the experience each has had. This puts a burden on communicators from one social stratum (such as advertising people) who want to communicate effectively with another stratum (such as factory workers).

Fake and **Hartley** have outlined factors that moderate the effect of communication

1. The greater the monopolies of the communication source over the recipient, the greater the change or effect in favour of the source over the recipient.

2. Communication effects are greatest where the message is in line with the existing opinions, beliefs, and dispositions of the receiver.

3. Communication can produce the most effective shifts on unfamiliar, lightly felt, peripheral issues, which do not lie at the centre of the recipient's value system.

4. Communication is more likely to be effective where the source is believed to have expertise, high status, objectivity, or liability, but particularly where the source has power and can be identified with.

5. The social contest, group, or reference group will mediate the communication and influence whether or not it is accepted.

7.3   ROLE OF MARKETING COMMUNICATION

Table 7.1 represents the value of marketing communication or promotion. The role of marketing communication can be classified in dyads of marketer buyer, marketer market and non-profit and social organisations.

Table 7.1 Marketing communication or promotion

- Establishes an image, such as prestige, discount or innovative, for the company and its goods and services
- Communicates features of goods and services o Creates awareness for new goods and services a Keeps existing goods and services popular
- Can reposition the image or uses of faltering goods and services
- Generates enthusiasm from channel members
- Explains where goods and services can be purchased
- Convinces consumers to trade up from one good or service to a more expensive one
- Alerts consumers to sales
- Justifies prices of goods, and services
- Answers consumer questions
- Provides after sale services for consumers
- Places the company and its goods and services in a favourable light relative to competitors

Source: J.R. Evans & B. Berman (1987) "Marketing" 3rd ed. Macmillan Publishing & Co. p. 409.

Communication in Marketer-Buyer Dyad

Marketing communication has a variety of roles to play. To begin with, it brings the marketers and consumers closer to each other in their desire to achieve their respective goals. Thus, a marketing company has such goals as profitability, corporate credibility and market leadership. Similarly, consumers too have such goals as better consumption, staying informed on the new buying alternatives, and a desire for a better quality of life. Examining these goals together, one finds a degree of commonality in the need of satisfaction through mutual efforts. Thus, a product offers the first common vehicle for satisfying these expectations of both marketer and consumers. Consumers buy the product because it is a bundle of need satisfying attributes. Marketers bring out the product because it is the only way they can achieve firm's goals.

The role of marketing communication then is to share the meaning of the firm's total product offering with its consumers in such a way as to help consumers attain their goals and at the same time moves the firm closer to its goals. Figure 7.2 illustrates the linkage.

Fig. 7.2 The role of marketing communication.

Thus, most buyers do not object to the informational content of promotion because it serves to spread the word quickly about innovations. Imagine how much longer would it have taken the buyers to become aware of the functional utility of pressure cookers has it not been communicated by marketers. Similarly, most consumers would also welcome occasional remainders about products they are already familiar with. Thus, even if most buyers of 'Milkmaid' are familiar with its compatibility with creative food preparation, its buyers may still like to receive a reminder and even a new recipe suggestion from it. The persuasive element of communication has, however been a subject of much controversy and some justified criticisms too. Many believe that marketers manipulate consumers though clever marketing communications in making them buy those products and services which they may not need. Usually, emotional appeals in communication are singled out for their cynicism.

Courtesy: ONIDA

Communication in Marketer Market Dyad

Not all marketing communication is directed towards ultimate buyers alone. Many are addressed to other manufacturers and institution, some to the intermediate who engage in resale operations and some to opinion leaders who are in a position to recommend the product. Each of them requires a different message. Thus, while a consumer may be impressed by the look of a particular brand of non-breakable synthetic cookware, dealers may need to know the margins available, its quality and attractions over the competing brands. This example will include the regular publication newsletters to teachers from publishing of houses for book purchase and recommendations.

Communication in Non-Profit/Social Organisation

Finally, communication is vital to non-profit organisations and social institutions too. Thus, the Help Age India of Delhi, and Times of India foundation for Eye Bank would look forward of marketing communication with the same expectation as would probably the P&G. The anti-drug campaign and the family planning and welfare message on TV prime time and Pulse Polio campaigns are handy illustrations of the value of marketing communications in non-profit and social organisations.

7.4   DETERMINING THE COMMUNICATION OBJECTIVES

Marketing communication impacts with these aspects:

1. Marketing communication through product cues
2. Marketing communication through price criteria
3. Marketing communication through place
4. Marketing communication through promotion aspect.

1. Marketing Communication Through Product Cues

The product is a carrier of certain messages, product messages. It concerns with certain explanations through its model of colour, shape, structure and size, and its physical materials, and also its package, brand name, title. A product is no more viewed as a mere living object. It is not even viewed by the consumer as a mere object. Consumers attribute meaning and significance to a product. The product, in turn, projects a personality of its own. All these factors will impact towards product message. There are various elements of a product, function as communicators as such:

- The physical features, like size, shape, design, total product, etc.
- The brand name/title/company goodwill
- The package like colour, label, size and ingredients.

2. Marketing Communication Through Price Criteria

This method is to only evaluate price concept in communication perspective, it shows how price conveys something more than the price with other various aspects into consideration

- Price quality equations
- Price as a core aspect for technological superiority
- Consumers attitude for reasonable price.

3. Marketing Communication Through Place

Always the word of mouth of consumer says for a particular outlet and at a particular location. Because the choice is a more important aspect for reasonable price with a better quality and also the other means is:

1. The store image
2. The level of service
3. A power instrument of store is communication
4. Store choice is linked with store image.

4. Marketing Communication Through Promotion Aspect

As we referred the important three concepts of marketing communication, we are at the stage of promotion it is last but it makes first priority. It is a pointer to its preeminent role in marketing communication. Promotion itself consists of four different components, namely

- Personal selling
- Advertising
- Sales promotion
- Publicity

7.5 THE PROMOTION MIX

In our daily life we are exposed to various tools of promotion aiming at communicating one thing or the other to use. To illustrate, while at home we came across advertisements when reading a newspaper, watching TV, listening to FM or even examining the water, electricity or telephone bills. On our way to the office similar communication faces us on bus panels, roadside hoardings, neon signs, posters and banners etc. And, while at a retail shop these take the shape of traffic builders, product displays, streamers, hangers, bins, etc. all sharing information relating to a specific product of a company.

The above listed are just a few types of the various promotion tools available to a marketer before proceeding further, let us take a look at the definition of the four major methods of promotion. These are: (i) advertising, (ii) personal selling, (iii) sales promotion and (iv) publicity. American Marketing Association defined these components as under.

Advertising: Any paid form of non-personal presentation and promotion of ideas goods, or services by an identified sponsor. It includes the use of such media as magazines, newspapers, outdoor posters, direct mail novelties, radio, TV, catalogues, directories, programmes and circulars.

Personal selling: Oral presentation is a conversation with one or more prospective purchasers for the purpose of making sales.

Sales promotion: Those marketing activities other than personal selling, advertising and publicity that stimulate consumer purchase the dealer effectiveness such as display's shows and exhibitions, demonstration, coupons, contest, and other non-routine selling efforts. These are usually short-term activities.

Publicity: Non-personal stimulation of demand for a product, service or business unit by generating commercially significant news about in published media or obtaining favourable presentation of it on TV or stage. Unlike advertising, this form of promotion is not paid for by the sponsor.

Packaging, Public relations and role of other elements of marketing mix in promotion

Although definitions vary about the number of components that constitutes promotion, marketing practice brings out that almost all marketing activities influence the promotion function. Notably, packaging performs the promotion function in addition to providing protection to the product. By incorporating creativity in its design, a package can add the 'dare to drive' appeal to the product help to communicate its features, uses and benefits more effectively. The promotion aspect of packaging is witnessing a bit of revolution in India nowadays with the introduction of innovative packages in the field of consumer goods. For example, package design of Frooti!

Public relations, likewise perform an important role in promotion insofar as it helps to create a favourable image of the firm and allows the public to experience better satisfaction in dealing with the firm.

High and consistent product quality, provision of superior customer service, price promotions as a way of increasing short-term sales and compatibility between the character of distribution outlets and the product are the other ways which contribute to the promotion function of this firm.

Courtesy: Frooti New Pack

7.6   DETERMINING THE PROMOTION MIX

Marketers rely only on not but promotion method they make use of two or more methods to accomplish promotion and marketing objectives. When a firm makes use of more than one promotion method for one product, the promotion methods used constitute the promotion mix for that product. For example, while TV spots, newspaper and fashion magazine advertisements, and attractive festival displays at the authorised retail shops constitute the promotion mix of Raymond's fabrics; specialised industry magazines constitute the promotion mix of HMT.

Promotion function being linked with the ever changing market environment is a dynamic function. The promotion mix, therefore, acquires the dimensions of dynamism and varies from product to product and over a period of time. Quite similar to the problems faced by a marketer in the determination of the optimal marketing mix are the problems faced in the determination of the promotion mix. The task involved is rather more complex due to cross substitutability of the various promotion methods thereby making the measurement of promotional effectiveness more difficult. Notwithstanding these difficulties, factors as mentioned below act as the major determinants of promotion mix.

1. Type of product
2. Nature of market
3. Stage of product in its life cycle
4. Available budget
5. Company policy

1. Type of the Product: In terms of the promotion task involved, the type of product is the major influence on the promotion mix. For example, a low priced, frequently purchased consumer convenience item, say a toilet soap, a toothpaste or a soft drink need repeat messages influencing and reminding the existing consumers, and persuading the new consumers, be used in a mass manner and at a high frequency. Newspaper and magazines advertisements, TV spots offer incentives to consumers and organisation of contests will, therefore, constitute the 'promotion mix' of such consumer goods. Now let us think of an industrial product, say a special purpose machine tool, which has high unit value, is technical in name, is purchased frequently and requires demonstration and conviction before it gets sold. Personal selling, quite obviously, becomes indispensable for as such a product along with organising product demonstration and exhibitions, holding seminars, etc. These then constitute the promotion mix in the case of an industrial good with newspaper advertising playing only the limited role of keeping the public informed about the company's activities and accomplishments. Publicity, however, to the extent it projects the desired image of the company plays a more important role.

2. Nature of Market: The location characteristics of the customers, intensity of competition in the marketplace and the requirements of wholesalers and retailers influence the promotion mix relating to the product in their own way. For example, if the target audience of a consumer product is both large as well as widely dispersed in different parts of the country, advertising and sales promotions mix comprises publicity, informative advertising, and consumer sales promotions and trade deals. Later, as the product reaches the maturity stage and goals of maintaining brand loyalty and creating brand preference become more important, aggressive brand advertising and dealer promotion become the key components of the promotion mix.

3. Stages in the product life cycle: The promotion mix changes with the movement of the product from one stage to the other in life cycle. For example, when the product is in the introduction and early growth stage, and the tasks involved are that of building and motivating trails of the product, the promotion mix comprises publicity, informative advertising, consumer sales promotions and trade deals. Later, as the product reaches the maturity stage and goals of maintaining brand loyalty and creating brand preferences become more important, aggressive brand advertising and dealer promotion become the key components of the promotion mix.

4. Available Budget: Each method of promotion has certain costs associated with it. The level at which each promotion method is to be used and the selection of the promotion mix is dependent on the promotion budget of the firm. Firms with small promotional budgets have to be content with more localised area activity, using dealer displays, wall writings, personal selling, and other less sophisticated methods. It needs to be emphasised here for the promotion function to be effective, the minimum threshold level must always be exceeded.

5. Company Policy: In the ultimate analysis, an aggregative consideration of the above four determinants clothed in the company's own marketing and promotion policy determine the mix. Important factors here include the conviction of the top management in the role of promotion and its various components, the product market strategy, and the type of corporate image it wants to project. For example, a company even under the seller's market might still believe in keeping a high profile in public and thus may go for extensive publicity and advertising programmes. Yet another company in the same industry may rely more on personal selling and continue to grow by maintaining its promotions at a low key.

7.7   ADVERTISING AND ITS DECISIONS

Modern marketing calls for more than developing a good product, pricing it attractively and making it accessible to the target consumer. Companies must also communicate with the present and potential customers. In this respect, advertising is a potent promotion tool of marketing communication mix, while the rest four are:

1. Sales Promotion
2. Direct Marketing
3. Public Relations and Publicity
4. Personal Selling

Advertising means public announcement. It is a communication of information about a product or service with a view to creating a demand for it. It consists of non-personal forms of communication made through paid media under clear sponsorship.

Its key elements are

- ❖ It is impersonal.
- ❖ Its purpose is to communicate.
- ❖ It is presented by an identified paying sponsor.

Definition of Advertising

The word advertising originates from a Latin word 'advertise', which means to turn to. The dictionary meaning of the term is "to give public notice or to announce publicly".

Advertising may be defined as the process of buying sponsor-identified media space or time in order to promote a product or an idea. The American Marketing Association, Chicago, has defined advertising as "any form of non-personal presentation or promotion of ideas, goods or services, by an identified sponsor."

Various marketing gurus have defined advertising according to their own views:

"Advertising consists of all the activities involved in presenting to a group a non-personal, oral or visual openly-sponsored, identified message regarding a product, service or idea. This message, called an advertisement, is disseminated through one or more media and paid for by the identified sponsor".
-W.Z. Stanton

"To give public notice or to announce publicly".
-Dictionary meaning

"Advertising is mass communication of information intended to persuade buyers so as to maximise profits".
-J.E. Littlefield

To summarise, advertising means any paid form of non-personal presentation and promotion or ideas, goods or services by an identified sponsor.

What Advertisement is?

Advertisement is a mass communicating of information intended to persuade buyers to by products with a view to maximising a company's profits. The elements of advertising are:

(i) It is a mass communication reaching a large group of consumers.

(ii) It makes mass production possible.

(iii) It is non-personal communication, for it is not delivered by an actual person, nor is it addressed to a specific person.

(iv) It is a commercial communication because it is used to help assure the advertiser of a long business life with profitable sales.

(v) Advertising can be economical, for it reaches large groups of people. This keeps the cost per message low.

(vi) The communication is speedy, permitting an advertiser to speak to millions of buyers in a matter of a few hours.

(vii) Advertising is identified communication. The advertiser signs his name to his advertisement for the purpose of publicising his identity.

What is included in advertising?

(i) The information in an advertisement should benefit the buyers. It should give them a more satisfactory expenditure of their money.

(ii) It should suggest better solutions to their problems.

(iii) The content of the advertisement is within the control of the advertiser, not the medium.

(iv) Advertising without persuasion is ineffective. The advertisement that fails to influence anyone, either immediately or in the future is a waste of money.

(v) The function of advertising is to increase the profitable sales volume. That is, advertising expenses should not increase disproportionately.

Advertising includes the following forms of messages:

The messages carried in-

- Newspapers and magazines
- On radio and television broadcasts
- Circular of all kinds, (whether distributed by mail, by person, through tradesmen, or by inserts in packages)
- Dealer help materials
- Window display and counter-display materials and efforts; store signs, motion pictures used for advertising
- Novelties bearing advertising messages and signature of the advertiser
- Label stags and other literature accompanying the merchandise.

What is excluded from advertising?

Advertising is not an exact science. An advertiser's circumstances are never identical with those of another; he cannot predict with accuracy what results his future advertising efforts will produce.

1. Advertising is not a game, because if advertising is done properly, both the buyer and the seller benefit from it.

2. Advertising is not a toy. Advertiser cannot afford to play with advertising. Advertising funds come from sales revenue and must be used to increase sales revenue.

3. Advertisements are not designed to deceive. The desire and hope for repeat sales insures a high degree of honesty in advertising.

Advertising Objectives

Each advertisement is a specific communication that must be effective, not just for one customer, but for many target buyers. This means that specific objectives should be set for each particular advertisement campaign. Advertising is a form of promotion and like a promotion; the objectives of advertising should be specific. This requires that the target consumers should be specifically identified and that the effect which advertising is intended to have upon the consumer should be clearly indicated. The objectives of advertising were traditionally stated in terms of direct sales. Now, it is to view advertising as having communication objectives that seek to inform persuade and remind potential customers of the worth of the product. Advertising seeks to condition the consumer so that he/she may have a favourable reaction to the promotional message. Advertising objectives serve as guidelines for the planning and implementation of the entire advertising programme.

The basic objectives of an advertising programme may be listed as below:

(a) To stimulate sales amongst present, former and future consumers. It involves a decision regarding the media, e.g., TV rather than print.

(b) To communicate with consumers. This involves decision regarding copy.

(c) To retain the loyalty of present and former consumers. Advertising may be used to reassure buyers that they have made the best purchase, thus building loyalty to the brand name or the firm.

(d) To increase support. Advertising impliedly bolsters the morale of the sales force and of distributors, wholesalers, and retailers; it thus contributes to enthusiasts and confidence attitude in the organisational.

(e) To project an image. Advertising is used to promote an overall image of respect and trust for an organisation. This message is aimed not only at consumers, but also at the government, shareholders, and the general public.

Importance

Its primary economic justification is that it adds information utility to goods and services. It tells us what we ought to buy, when we should buy it, and where we can buy it at the best price. We get a basis for choosing among the various brands of the same commodity that are competing for our favour. We are able to buy that brand which suits our pursue and taste best.

Modern advertisement is not a claptrap system it does not make exaggerated statements. On the contrary. It relies on true representation. Advertisement is not waste. It is very profitable investment.

Advertising is one of the most powerful forces in a modern society. By stimulating the public to buy such goods as radios and automobiles. It has helped to develop industries. It has changed peoples 'habits' in food, dress and living. It has accelerated the growth of mass production by creating a mass demand.

Advertising has become increasingly important to business enterprises–both large and small. Outlay on advertising certainly is the voucher. Non-business enterprises have also recognised the importance of advertising. The attempt by army recruitment is based on a substantial advertising campaign, stressing the advantages of a military career. The health department popularises family planning through advertising. Labour organisations have also used advertising to make their viewpoints known to the public at large. Advertising assumes real economic importance too.

Advertising strategies that increase the number of units sold stimulate economies in the production process. The production cost per unit of output is lowered. It in turn leads to lower prices. Lower consumer prices then allow these products to become available to more people. Similarly, the price of newspapers, professional sports, radio and TV programmes, and the like might be prohibitive without advertising. In short, advertising pays for many of the enjoyable entertainment and educational aspects of contemporary life.

Advertising has become an important factor in the campaigns to achieve such societal-oriented objectives such as the discontinuance of smoking, family planning, physical fitness, and the elimination of drug abuse. Though in India, advertising was accepted as a potent and recognised means of promotion only 25 years ago, its growing productive capacity and output necessitates the finding of consumers and advertising plays an important role in this process. Advertising helps to increase mass marketing while helping the consumer to choose from amongst the variety of products offered for his selection. In India, advertising as a profession is in its infancy. Because of this, there is a tremendous scope for development so that it may be productively used for the benefit of producers, traders, consumers, and the country's economy.

1. Product-related Advertising
   (a) Pioneering Advertising
   (b) Competitive Advertising
   (c) Retentive Advertising
2. Public Service Advertising
3. Functional Classification
   (a) Advertising Based on Demand Influence Level
   ❖ Primary Demand (Stimulation)

❖ Selective Demand (Stimulation)

(b) Institutional Advertising

(c) Product Advertising

❖ Informative Product Advertising

❖ Persuasive Product Advertising

❖ Reminder-Oriented Product Advertising

4. Advertising based on Product Life Cycle

(a) Consumer Advertising

(b) Industrial Advertising

5. Trade Advertising

(a) Retail Advertising

(b) Wholesale Advertising

6. Advertising Based on Area of Operation

(a) National Advertising

(b) Local Advertising

(c) Regional Advertising

7. Advertising According to Media Utilised

1. Product-related Advertising

It is concerned with conveying information about and selling a product or service. Product advertising is of three types, viz.,

(a) Pioneering Advertising

(b) Competitive Advertising

(c) Retentive Advertising.

(a) Pioneering Advertising

This type of advertising is used in the introductory stages in the life cycle of a product. It is concerned with developing a "primary" demand. It conveys information about, and selling a product category rather than a specific brand. For example, the initial advertisement for black-and-white television and colour television. Such advertisements appeal to the consumer's emotions and rational motives.

(b) Competitive Advertising

It is useful when the product has reached the market-growth and especially the market-maturity stage. It stimulates "selective" demand. It seeks to sell a specific brand rather than a general product category. It is of two types:

(i) Direct Type: It seeks to stimulate immediate buying action.

(ii) Indirect Type: It attempts to pinpoint the virtues of the product in the expectation that the consumer's action will be affected by it when he is ready to buy.

> *Example: Airline advertising. Air India attempts to bid for the consumer's patronage either immediately, direct action, in which it provides prices, time tables and phone numbers on which the customers may call for reservations; or eventually, indirect action, when it suggests that you mention Air India's name when talking to your travel agent.*

(c) Retentive Advertising

This may be useful when the product has achieved a favourable status in the market–that is, maturity or declining stage. Generally, in such times, the advertiser wants to keep his product's name before the public. A much softer selling approach is used, or only the name may be mentioned in "reminder" type advertising.

2. Public Service Advertising

This is directed at the social welfare of a community or a nation. The effectiveness of product service advertisements may be measured in terms of the goodwill they generate in favour of the sponsoring organisation. Advertisements on not mixing drinking and driving are a good example of public service advertising. In this type of advertising, the objective is to put across a message intended to change attitudes or behaviour and benefit the public at large.

3. Functional Classification

Advertising may be classified according to the functions which it is intended to fulfil.

(a) Advertising may be used to stimulate either the primary demand or the selective demand.
(b) It may promote either the brand or the firm selling that brand.
(c) It may try to cause indirect action or direct action.

(a) Advertising Based on Demand Influence Level

i) Primary Demand Stimulation

Primary demand is the demand for the product or service rather than for a particular brand. It is intended to affect the demand for a type of product, and not the brand of that product. Some advertise to stimulate primary demand. When a product is new, primary demand stimulation is appropriate. At this time, the marketer must inform consumers of the existence of the new item and convince them of the benefits flowing from its use. When primary demand has been stimulated and competitors have entered the market, the advertising strategy may be used to stimulate the selective demand.

ii) Selective Demand Stimulation

This demand is for a particular brand such as Charminar cigarettes, Surf detergent powder, or Vimal fabrics. To establish a differential advantage and to acquire an acceptable sort of market, selective demand advertising is attempted. It is not to stimulate the demand for the product or service. The advertiser attempts to differentiate his brand and to increase the total amount of consumption of that product. Competitive advertising stimulates selective demand. It may be of either the direct or the indirect type.

(b) Institutional Advertising

Institutional advertising may be formative, persuasive or reminder oriented in character. Institutional advertising is used extensively during periods of product shortages in order to keep the name of the company before the public. It aims at building for a firm a positive public image in the eyes of shareholders, employees, suppliers, legislators, or the general public. This sells only the name and prestige of the company. This type of advertising is used frequently by large companies whose products are well known. HMT or DCM, for example, does considerable institutional advertising of its name, emphasising the quality and research behind its products. Institutional advertisements are at consumers or focus them upon other groups, such as voters, government officials, suppliers, financial institutions, etc. If it is effective, the target groups will respond with goodwill towards, and confidence in the sponsor. It is also a useful method or introducing salespersons and new product to consumers. It does not attempt to sell a particular product; it benefits the organisation as a whole. It notifies the consumers that the company is a responsible business entity and is patriotic; that its management takes ecologically responsible action, is an affair-motive action employer, supports the socialistic pattern of society or provides employment opportunities in the community. When Indian Oil advertisements describe the company's general activities, such as public service work, this may be referred to as institutional advertising because it is intended to build an overall favourable attitude towards the company and its family of products. HMT once told the story of the small-scale industries supplying it with component parts, thus indicating how it aided the development of ancillary industries.

(c) Product Advertising

Most advertising is product advertising, designed to promote the sale or reputation of a particular product or service that the organisation sells. Indane's cooking gas is a case in point. The marketer may use such promotion to generate exposure attention, comprehension, attitude change or action for an offering. It deals with the non-personal selling of a particular good or service. It is of three types as follows:-

   (i) Informative Product Advertising
  (ii) Persuasive Product Advertising
 (iii) Reminder-Oriented Product Advertising.

(i) Informative Product Advertising

This form of advertising tends to characterise the promotion of any new type of product to develop an initial demand. It is usually done in the introductory stages of the product life cycle. It was the original approach to advertising.

(ii) Persuasive Product Advertising

Persuasive product advertising is to develop demand for a particular product or brand. It is a type of promotion used in the growth period and, to some extent, in the maturity period of the product life cycle.

(iii) Reminder-Oriented Product Advertising

The goal of this type of advertising is to reinforce previous promotional activity by keeping the brand name in front of the public. It is used in the maturity period as well as throughout the declining phase of the product life cycle.

4. Advertising based on Product Life Cycle

  (a) Consumer Advertising
  (b) Industrial Advertising.

(a) Consumer Advertising

Most of the consumer goods producers engage in consumer product advertising. Marketers of pharmaceuticals, cosmetics, scooters, detergents and soaps, cigarettes and alcoholic beverages are examples. Baring a few, all these products are all package goods that the consumer will often buy during the year. There is a heavy competition among the advertisers to establish an advantage for their particular brand.

(b) Industrial Advertising

Industrial executives have little confidence in advertising. They rely on this form of promotion merely out of fear that their competitors may benefit if they stop their advertising efforts. The task of the industrial advertiser is complicated by the multiple buying influence characteristics like the derived demand, etc. The objectives vary according to the firm and the situation. They are:

- To inform
- To bring in orders
- To induce inquiries
- To get the advertiser's name on the buyer's list of sources
- To provide support for the salesman
- To reduce selling costs
- To help get items in the news column of a publication
- To establish recognition for the firm or its product
- To motivate distributors
- To recognise for the firm or its products
- To motivate distributors, to create or change a company's image
- To create or change a buyer's attitude

The basic appeals tend to increase the rupee profits of the buyer or help in achieving his non-monetary objectives. Trade journals are the media most generally used followed by catalogues, direct mail communication, exhibits, and general management publications. Advertising agencies are much less useful in industrial advertising.

5. Trade Advertising

(a) Retail Advertising
(b) Wholesale Advertising.

(a) Retail Advertising

This may be defined as "covering all advertising by the stores that sell goods directly to the consuming public. It also includes advertising by establishments that sell services to the public, such as beauty shops, petrol pumps and banks." Advertising agencies are rarely used. The store personnel are usually given this responsibility as an added task to be performed, together with their normal functions. The result is that advertising is often relegated to a secondary position in a retail store. One aspect of retail advertising is co-operative advertising. It refers to advertising costs between retailers and manufacturers. From the retailer's point of view, co-operative advertising permits a store to secure additional advertising that would not otherwise have been available.

(b) Wholesale Advertising

Wholesalers are, generally, not advertising minded, either for themselves or for their suppliers. They would benefit from adopting some of the image-making techniques used by retailers–the need for developing an overall promotional strategy. They also need to make a greater use of supplier promotion materials and programmes in a way advantageous to them.

6. Advertising based on Area of Operation

It is classified as follows:

(a) National Advertising
(b) Regional Advertising
(c) Local Advertising.

(a) National advertising

It is practised by many firms in our country. It encourages the consumer to buy their product wherever they are sold. Most national advertisements concentrate on the overall image and desirability of the product. The famous national advertisers are:

- Hindustan Levers
- DCM
- ITC
- TISCO.

(b) Regional advertising

It is geographical alternative for organisations. For example, Amrit Vanaspati based in Rajpura claims to be the leading hydrogenated oil producer in the Punjab. But, until recently, it mainly confined itself to one of the vegetable oil brands distribution to Malihabad district (in U.P. near Lucknow).

(c) Local advertising

It is generally done by retailers rather than manufacturers. These advertisements save the customer time and money by passing along specific information about products, prices, location, and so on. Retailer advertisements usually provide specific goods sales during weekends in various sectors.

7. Advertising According to Media

The most common classification of advertising is by the medium used. For example, TV, radio, magazine, outdoor, business periodical, newspaper and direct mail advertising. This classification is so common in use that it is mentioned here only for the sake of completeness.

7.8   ADVERTISING PLANNING FRAMEWORK

Plans are nothing, planning is everything.

- Dwight D. Eisenhower

The advertising management is mainly concerned with planning and decision-making. The advertising manager will be involved in the development, implementation, and overall management of an advertising plan. The development of an advertising plan essentially requires the generation and specification of alternatives. Decision-making involves choosing from among the alternatives. The alternatives can be of various levels of expenditure, different kinds of objectives or strategy possibilities, and kinds of options with copy creation and media choices. Thus, the essence of planning is to find out the feasible alternatives and reduce them to decisions. An advertising plan reflects the planning and decision-making process and the decisions that have been arrived at in a particular product and market situation.

Planning Framework

Advertising planning and decision-making depends on internal and external factors. Internal factors are situation analysis, the marketing programme, and the advertising plan. The three legs of advertising planning concern are the:

- Objective setting and target market identification
- Message strategy and tactics
- Media strategy and tactics.

The advertising plan should be developed in response to a situation analysis, based on research. Once developed, the advertising plan has to be implemented as an advertising campaign, in the context of social and legal constraints and with the involvement of various facilitating agencies. Let us discuss these factors one after another.

1. Situation Analysis

It involves an analysis of all important factors operating in a particular situation. This means that new research studies will be undertaken on company history and experience.

AT&T, for example, developed a new strategy for its long-distance telephone services-based on five years of research. The research encompassed market segmentation studies, concept testing, and a field experiment. The field experiment increased on testing a new advertising campaign called "Cost of Visit". An existing "Reach Out" campaign although successful, did not appear to get through to a large group of people who had reasons to call but were limiting their calls because of cost. Research based on annual surveys of 3,000 residential telephone users showed that most did not know the cost of a long-distance call or that it was possible to make less expensive calls in off-peak periods. Five copy alternatives were subsequently developed and tested, from which "Cost of Visit" was chosen. This campaign was credited with persuading customers to call during times that were both cheaper for them and more profitable for AT&T and, overall, was more effective that the "Reach Out" campaign. One estimate was that by switching 530 million in advertising from "Reach Out" to "Cost of Visit", an incremental gain in revenue of $22 million would result in the first year and would top $100 million over five years. This example highlights that a complete situation analysis will cover all marketing components and involve finding answers to many questions about the nature and extent of demand, competition, environmental factors, product, costs, distribution, and the skills and financial resources of the from.

2. Consumer and Market Analysis

Situation analysis begins by looking at the aggregate market for the product, service, or cause being advertised, the size of the market, its growth rate, seasonality, geographical distribution. Whereas consumer and market analysis is concerned with the following factors:

Nature of demand

- ❖ How do buyers (consumer and industrial) currently go about buying existing products or services?
- ❖ Can the market be meaningfully segmented or broken into several homogeneous groups with respect to "what they want" and "how they buy"?

Extent of demand

- ❖ What is the size of the market (units and dollars) now, and what will the future hold?
- ❖ What are the current market shares, and what are the selective demand trends?
- ❖ Is it best to analyse the market on an aggregate or on a segmented basis?

Name of competition

- ❖ What is the present and future structure of competition?

❖ What are the current marketing programmes of established competitors?

❖ Why are they successful or unsuccessful?

❖ Is there opportunity for another competitor? Why?

❖ What are the anticipated retaliatory moves of competitors?

❖ Can they neutralise different marketing programmes we might develop?

Environmental climate

❖ What are the relevant social, political, economic, and technological trends?

❖ How do you evaluate these trends? Do they represent opportunities or problem?

Stage of product life cycle

❖ In what stage of the life cycle is the product category?

❖ What market characteristics support your stage-of-life-cycle evaluation?

Cost structure of the industry

❖ What is the amount and composition of the marginal or additional cost of supplying increased output?

Skills of the firm

❖ Do we have the skills and experience to perform the functions necessary to be in the business?

❖ How do our skills compare with those of competitors?

Financial resources of the firm

❖ Do we have the funds to support an effective marketing programme?

❖ Where are the funds coming from, and when will they be available?

3. Competitive Analysis

Advertising planning and decision-making are affected by competition and the competitive situation facing the advertiser. Competition is such a pervasive factor that it will occur as a consideration in all phases of the advertising planning and decision-making process. It should include an analysis of what current share the brand now has, what shares its competitors have, what share of a market is possible, from which competitors the increased share of a market is possible? The planner also has to be aware of the relative strengths and weaknesses of the different competing companies and their objectives in the product category. It is important to look at competition as a precursor to the planning process.

The Advertising Plan

As pointed out earlier, advertising plan and decision-making focus on three crucial areas; objectives and target selection, message strategy and tactics, and media strategy and tactics. Let us elaborate on these points:

1. Objectives and Target Selection

Objectives in advertising can be understood in many ways. An important part of the objective is the development of a precise, disciplined description of the target audience. It is often tempting to direct advertising at a broad audience; but everyone is a potential customer. It is best to consider directing the advertising to more selected groups to develop stimulating copy. It is quite possible to develop several campaigns, each directed at different segments of the market, or to develop one campaign based on multiple objectives.

2. Message Strategy and Tactics

Messages strategy must decide what the advertising is meant to communicate–by way of benefits, feelings, brand personality, or action content. Once the content of the campaign has been decided, decisions must be made on the best–most effective–ways of communicating that content. The decisions, such as the choice of a spokesperson, the use of humour or fear or other tones, and the selection of particular copy, visuals, and layout, are what we call "message tactics".

3. Media Strategy and Tactics

Message strategy is concerned with decisions about how much is to be allocated to create and test advertising copy, media strategy concerns decisions on how many media rupees to spend on an advertising campaign. Media tactics comprise the decisions on which specific media (television, radio, magazines, etc.) or media vehicles (Reader's Digest, etc.) to spend these dollars.

External Factors

The external factors in the planning framework are environmental, social and legal considerations. To a considerable extent, these exist as constraints on the development of an advertising plan and decision-making. In developing a specific advertisement, there are certain legal constraints that must be considered. Deceptive advertising is forbidden by law. What is deceptive is often difficult, because different people can have different perceptions of the same advertisements. Thus, an advertiser who attempts to provide specific, relevant information must be well aware of what constitutes deception in a legal and ethical sense and of other aspects of advertising regulation. Even more difficult consideration for people involved in the advertising effort are broad social and economic issues as stated below.

- Does advertising raise prices or inhibit competition?
- Is the use of sex or fear appeals is appropriate? Women and minority groups are exploited in advertising by casting them in highly stereotyped roles.
- Is it more irritating than entertaining?
- Is it an intrusion into an already excessively polluted environment?
- Advertising directed at children.

Advertiser and the Advertising Agency Interface

From a situation analysis point of view, the advertiser needs to know what kinds of facilitating agencies exist and the nature of the services they provide. From a planning point of view, much local advertising is done without the services of an advertising agency or a research supplier. On the other hand, a national advertiser may have under contract many different agencies and research suppliers, each serving one or more brands in a product line. Many advertising decisions involve choosing facilitating agency alternatives.

1. What advertising agency should be chosen?
2. What media should be used?
3. What copy test supplier will be best for our particular situation?

Concerning the question of agency selection, characteristics such as the quality of personnel, reputation, integrity, mutual understanding, interpersonal compatibility and synergism were very important.

Advertising Industry

The advertising industry consists of three principal groups:

(a) Sponsors
(b) Media
(c) Advertising agencies or advertising departments.

Advertising agencies are of two basic types, viz., independent and house. An independent agency is a business that is free to compete for and select its clients. A house agency is owned by its major client. A house agency is not completely free to serve other clients. The advertising department is an integral part of the organisation it serves. The advertising agency provides for the client a minimum of:

(i) Media information, such as the availability of time and space
(ii) Creative skills, such as "campaign planning" and "appeal planning"
(iii) Research capabilities, such as providing brand preference data.

7.9 ADVERTISEMENT COPY AND AGENCY

The first thing to be done in an advertising campaign is the preparation of an advertisement copy. An advertisement copy is the message that is to be conveyed to the public. It consists of text or the subject matter of the advertisement. The aim of an advertisement copy is to influence the prospective customers to act in the desired way when they read it.

Before an advertisement copy is prepared, the advertiser must consists certain factors. First, the product and its market must be carefully studied. The advertiser must know who will buy his product, how much at will be bought, how often it will be bought, and how it compares with other competing products.

Secondly, the advertiser must decide what kind of appeal he will make for his product. Appeals are of three main types–price appeal, reason appeal, and suggestive appeal. Price appeal is used by businessmen who deal in necessaries of life. For instance, grocers know that they need not persuade us to buy our daily food. Instead, they use advertising to attract us to their particular stores on the score of lower prices, better quality or superior services.

Clothing is often advertised similarly, but quality and style are emphasised. Reason (why) appeal is adopted by businessmen who place new substitutes on the market. To sell a new soap or blade that competes with similar reason for changing to the new brand.

He must present to buyers a definite reason for changing to a new brand. He must persuade consumers that the new product is a better one. He must explain to them in what respects his product is superior to others. Suggestion advertising is used mainly for luxury articles. The suggestions may come from a testimonial or a pictorial representation. The object of an appeal is to arouse one or another of the desires. The desire for the economy for comfort for wealth, or social position, for health and security which prompt men to action.

Thirdly, he has to decide whether to make appeal through the eyes, ears or through both. For example, advertisement in newspaper and magazines appeal through the eyes and radio advertisement through the ears, and TV through both.

Fourthly, he has to decide the choice of the advertising medium through which the product can best be advertised i.e., in the press or on the radio? Tests may often be made on various media in order to discover which gets the best results in selling the given product.

Lastly, he must consider the objectives to be obtained whether to create a new demand or to increase the existing demand or to maintain it.

The effect of an advertisement depends more on the presentation of matter than on the matter itself. Effective presentation goes a long way in attracting the attention of the readers and also in making an effective appeal.

Essential requisites of a good copy of advertisement

1. **Attention or display value:** The purpose of an advertisement is to convey the message to the prospective customers. Therefore, it should be capable of drawing the attention of the reader and including him to go through it. Hence, a copy should have attention value. This value is acquired by means of using coloured or ordinary illustration and big type or by leaving a blank space around the copy. Moving figures, switch light and attractive borders and headlines are some other devices that are adopted for this purposes.

2. **Suggestive value:** The copy on its being seen or heard should be able to make suggestions to the reader. It should suggest to him the advantage of buying and using the article. Presentation of the matter with a suitable picture can be more suggestive than mere description. Pictorial representation can serve two purposes at a time. It can add to the attractive value to it. Suggestions are a very powerful force. When an idea suggested by the advertisement, the impulsiveness of the human mind enforces it. Hence, the desired result follows miraculously.

3. **Convincing value:** There is no use of merely attracting the reader and suggesting something to him. The copy should also be capable to convincing the reader as regards the merits of the article advertised. The reader must be convinced if he is to be influenced to action. Statement accomplished by facts and figures will be more convincing.

4. **Remembrance value:** It is necessary that the advertisement must be remembered by the reader till he buys the product. Therefore, a copy should possess remembrance value; constant repetition of advertisement through slogans will go a long way towards this end.

5. **Sentimental and instinctive value:** The purpose of an advertisement is achieved when it influences the reader to action. For this purpose, the copy should be able to induce him to do, something to acquire the article which is advertised. The best method of doing this is to appeal to the emotions. He is forced to act when his sentiments and instincts are clearly aroused by the advertisements. For instance, a dealer in medicine may appeal to the instinct of the self preservation. Hence, a copy should also possess sentimental and instinctive value.

6. **Simplicity:** Simplicity is yet another request of a good advertisement copy; the matter should be expressed as briefly as possible. Simplicity is necessary for the sake of easy remembrance and economy in the cost of advertisement. But simplicity should not be the cost brevity. Catch words and titles may be used for this purpose, e.g., "Earn While You Spend".

Advertising Agency

An advertising agency acts as a consultant to the client, the advertiser, in formulating the advertising plans and translating them into an advertising campaign.

Another role of the agency is placing the advertisement in the media, since it has a traditional association with the media. The placement aspect has assumed considerable importance wing to media boom and the resultant complexities.

An advertising agency can be defined as an independent organisation of creative business people who develop, prepare and release the advertisements for the sellers seeking to find customers for their goods and services.

In India, there are about 7,000 advertising agencies out of which 700 ad agencies are recognised by the Indian Newspapers Society (INS). INS is a regulatory organisation regulating ad agencies for

- National Income Accounting
- Annual Billing
- Creditworthiness.

The relationship between an advertiser and its advertising agency represents profession-alism to the core. At the same time, capability in terms of culture and style of the two parties and the concerned persons is highly facilitator for a fruitful relationship. Courage and candidness on the part of the agency can contribute much towards getting the client to appreciate the constructive use of a creative approach. It is in the interest of the client to provide the required reassurance to the agency so that communication is inhibited. The selection of an agency by a potential client has a degree of mutuality. A well-considered and wise selection can pave the way for a productive relationship.

Functions of Ad Agencies

An ad agency will be in a position to take an objective view of the advertiser's plan and proposals and thus venture to put forward its opinions and comments. Creative qualified and trained personnel are required for an advertising agency. It may not be worthwhile for an advertiser to have on its permanent staff all the variety of skill required to produce appropriate advertisements.

An agency provides an opportunity as well as flexibility for various combinations of agency personnel from different departments to form a team to work as per the specific requirements of their varied clients. An advertising agency has regular contacts with various support systems required for the production of appropriate ad material. A major advantage of an agency is its regular dealing with the media and the expertise in developing advertisements to suit the requirements of its clients. The ad agency's skills can also be useful in the preparation of campaigns where the risks involved are high such as in the introduction of new products.

Clients' Expectations

+ **Account Service:** Responsive–prompt–accessible–listens–economical.

+ **Creativity Review:** Provide innovative proposals–ideas–visuals.

+ **Production Review:** Quality–timeliness–accuracy–economical.

+ **Media Planning:** Innovative media strategies–capable of coping with the budget changes–provide media trends update.

+ **Buying Media Space:** Explore cost-effective alternatives–ability to negotiate attractive terms.

+ **Market Research:** Relates to existing studies to the specific situation of the client–organise timely and meaningful research.

+ **Retail Advertising and Sales Promotion:** Innovative ideas–POP material, creative events–timeliness–economical.

+ **Financial Control:** Detailed estimates–accuracy in billing–reasonable rates–mutual trust.

7.10 ADVERTISING MEDIA

The advertisement copy is presented through different channels. The channels through which the advertising message is conveyed to the public are called advertising media. Again the media can be either indoor or outdoor. They are of two kinds, viz., primary media and adjuncts. The former are the main media, while the latter are supplementary to the format. Again, the media may be either indoor or outdoor. The important media are:

1. Press
2. Circular and catalogues
3. Prospectus and poster
4. Placards and posters
5. Other media of outdoor publicity

6. Window display
7. Cinema
8. Films
9. Fairs and exhibitions
10. Radio
11. Television
12. Internet.

The selection of media depends on the class of the people for whom the message is meant and the nature of the goods for which the advertisement is made.

1. **Press:** The press consisting of newspaper, periodicals, and magazines is the best media for advertisement. It is considered to be the primary indoor media. Advertisement through the press is the cheapest mode of giving information to the largest number of people. The circulation of daily papers and magazines is wider and the message is conveyed to a large number of readers. Daily newspapers offer facilities for presenting the matter daily in a new light. They are also useful for making timely announcements of new departures. Moreover, they provide scope for variations in advertising techniques. However, they are not suitable for presenting a long copy, as their life is short. "Classified advertisement" in newspapers offers a special attraction.

   Magazines and periodicals, on the other hand, offer greater scope for a long copy as they are read during leisure time. Their life is longer and the advertisements inserted in them are more likely to be noticed more than once by regular subscribers and other readers. They also create a lasting effect. Moreover, magazines and periodicals offer facilities for colour printing, picture advertising and elaborate advertisement. Magazines such as sports journals, medical journals, law journals, etc. offer another facility of directly approaching the particular class of consumers. Thus, advertisement for medicines and medical appliances may be advertised in medical journals, law books in law journals, and so on. The major disadvantage of magazine advertising is that it cannot be planned quickly and cannot be made in time.

2. **Circular letters:** Circular letters are widely employed by modern business concerns as a media of publicity. They are used both as a primary media and as adjuncts. A mailing list is prepared and circular letters are sent to the addresses contained in the list by way of personal letters whenever there is need for conveying any new information. Circular letters command a special advantage. They provide greater scope for conveying detailed information regarding the goods or services offered than is provided by newspapers and periodicals. The effect of circular letters is further increased by enclosing with them order forms and addressed business envelopes ready for use.

When they are used as adjunct material they help to get orders from the parties who have made enquiries in response to an advertisement. Such enquiries should be answered with due care and without any exaggeration in a persuasive style. Persistent efforts should also be made to gain continued patronage by means of a well-directed follow-up system.

3. **Prospectus and Catalogues:** Manufacturers, traders and others make use of prospectus and catalogues as adjuncts to the primary advertisements. These are generally sent in reply to enquire. They are made out in convenient sizes to facilitate both posting and filling. Full scope is provided for display or attractive value. Care is devoted to the getup and contents of these publications. To create a good impression at the outlet itself the covering page is designed attractively and printed in bright colours. Good quality paper is used. The object of these publications is to describe and discuss the merits of the article and to explain its outstanding features. Therefore, pictorial illustrations are included and simple but emphatic language is adopted.

The subject matter is arranged is such a way as to maintain the sustained interest is arranged in such a way to maintain the sustained interest to the reader throughout the literature. Testimonials may also be included to convince the readers about the merits of the goods.

Catalogues furnish particulars about the quality, dimensions, weights, packing and method of selling. The prices may be stated in the catalogues or supplied in a separate price list. Catalogues and advertising literature are generally sent with a view to simplify the work of a travelling salesman. It is also customary to enclose order forms with catalogues when orders are to be received by post. Mail order houses generally employ this form of advertisement.

4. **Placards and posters:** These outdoor media are used as adjuncts to the primary media. They serve as remainders. They help to keep alive the interest of the public in the subject matter already advertised. They lend themselves easily to colour combinations and artistic picture displays. They are very useful for localised advertisement and mass appeal. They have the advantage of rendering rapid results. They are particularly useful for effective display of trade marks and trade names. However, placards and posters are expected to be glanced at casually while the people pass by a street. So the advertisement made through them should be short but impressive. Catch headings in bold types and suggestive pictures prominently displayed will make these advertisements more effective. Another point to be remembered in this connection is that the posters and placards should be fixed up in appropriate places like main roads, theatres and painted walls.

5. **Other media of outdoor publicity:** Distribution of leaflets, display of electric switch lights, advertising, distribution of leaflets is often accompanied by beating of drums or other musical instruments and attracts a large number of passers-by the use of electric switch-lights is costly and should therefore be tried only in prominent localities where a large number of people congregate at night, e.g., near theatres pleasure resorts, restaurants or railway stations. Neon-lights and floodlights can also be used with great benefits. They are the most spectacular of all outdoor advertising. Advertising placards are also displayed in railway compartments and buses. This form of advertising provides an excellent opportunity to impress thousands of cosmopolitan travellers with the merits of the articles advertised. Those who notice this advertisement are most likely to remember the name of the brands advertised and are induced to action. The sandwich board is particularly useful for announcing the latest innovations and seasonal alterations. Metal signs are generally used for advertisements of permanent value. The obvious advantage derived from the use of metal signs is that the subject matter is not spoiled by the effects of weather. They are generally displayed on railway platforms and sidings and on prominent street corners.

6. **Window display:** Window display is another attractive and useful method of advertising. Displaying the articles behind glass windows makes a strong appeal and thus attracts customers. Window dressing is an art in itself. Windows are generally trimmed on artistic lines so as to hold the attention of the observer within the compass of the trimming. Careful attention is required in displaying the articles. Articles of the same class are to be grouped together. Besides appropriate articles are to be displayed during each season, e.g., winter garments in winter. Articles displayed in the windows are often marked with prices. This strongly appeals to the passers-by who ultimately become buyers of such articles. Articles should also be rearranged now and then in order to display as large a variety as possible and also to avoid monotony. This frequent shifting of articles helps to keep alive the interest of a large number of people who pass by the shop daily. During the night colour electric lights may be used. Other attractions like moving figures and music may be made to form part of window display. Modern manufacturers have set up their own "showrooms" to exhibit their products by way of a window display. Retail shops particularly departmental stores organise window display in a more thorough manner.

7. **Cinema and theatrical programmes:** Advertisements are also inserted in theatrical or cinema programmes. Attractive advertisement slides are designed and shown during the interval in a film show. The copy must be very brief as the time allotted for it is very short. The text should contain an appeal presented in a happy and amusing tone. Advertisement of sweets, toilet articles, fancy goods, etc., is appropriately made through this common media.

8. **Films:** In some cases, manufacturers produce a short term film relating to the meritorious use of their articles and distribute it among the various cinema houses for above. It is shown either with other information films or during the interval. The modern cinema talkies appeal both to the eye and to the ears and hence an advertisement brings the greatest possible advantage. However, the form of advertisement is not suitable when specific class is being addressed as the class of people attending cinemas is varying and diverse. The most important point attending cinemas is varying and diverse. The most important point to be remembered in this connection is that the firm must consist of educative and entertainment "No entertainment No result" should be the watch word of film advertisements.

9. **Fairs and Exhibition:** Fairs and exhibitions constitute a common media for periodical advertisements usually organised once in a year by municipalities, corporations and trade associations. They include a variety of entertainments which attract a large number of people. Hence, advertisements in exhibitions appeal to a greater number of people. Retail stores and other business houses as well as public utility concerns set up stalls in exhibitions to display their articles or services. These stalls are designed in an attractive manner so as to draw the attention of the visitors.

10. **Radio:** The wireless is also used as a media of advertisement in this case the advertiser buys time on a broadcasting station broadcasting advertisements. This provides great scope to approach a large number or people. It conveys the message to the customer when he is in a relaxed mood at his residence. However, the success of this advertisement is left to the listeners. The success of this type of advertisement depends on the use of radio by the general public.

The main drawback of radio advertisement is that its message is less permanent than a printed one. Constant repetition is needed to drive home the advertising appeal. Another drawback is that radio advertisement is incapable of supplying visual identification.

11. **Television:** TV is the latest addition to the media of advertising. The potentialities of televisions are greater than those of radios. The user of television advertisement finds that the impact of this advertisement is greater than that of any other medium they have used.

The main limitation of TV advertisement is limited coverage, because relatively a few communities have adequate facilities for telecasting. Various communities have adequate facilities for telecasting. Various forms of film are commonly used for television advertisements. The forms range from a mere slide which is static, to an animated film in which the characters move and speak. The advertisements should be accompanied by entertainment. The usual method by introducing a comic situation or a humorous twist. Care should be taken to avoid monotonous repetition of the same comedy or a tone that is out of harmony with the programme.

12. **Internet:** The Internet has become an efficient means of everything from gaining free exporting information and guidelines to conducting market research and offering customers several time zones away a secure process for ordering and paying for products. "Global abroad" on the Internet does pose special challenges.

Major marketers doing e-commerce range from automakers (GM) to direct-mail companies (L.L Bean and Lands' End) to running- shoe giants (Nike and Reebok) to Amazon.com. Marketers like these are using the Web to reach to new customers outside their home countries, to support the existing customers who live abroad, to source from international suppliers, and to build global brand awareness.

7.11 SALES PROMOTION

Sales promotion consists of a variety of promotional devices designed to stimulate market response. These devices may be grouped under three categories.

(a) Consumer promotional devices
(b) Trade promotional devices
(c) Sales force promotion devices

Factors

The factors influencing sales promotion include proliferation of brands competition, trade pressures arising out of the growth of supermarkets, chain stores and other retailers' adverse economic conditions like recessions.

(a) Consumer Promotions

Sampling: This involves distribution of free samples, sampling is an expensive but a powerful promotion tool, and regular size packages or special sizes are used.

The sample might be delivered from door to door, or be offered in a retail store, at fairs, or featured in an advertising offer. This is suitable for introducing new products, such as soaps, detergents, cigarettes, toothpaste, etc.

Couponing: A coupon is a certificate that entitles the consumer to specify saving on the purchase of a specific product. These coupons are usually issued by the manufacturers either directly to mail or through the retailers.

Premiums or bonus offers: The offer of extra amount of product at no cost to consumers who buy a stated amount of a product or a special pack thereof is called premium offer or bonus offer. There are four types of premium offers:

- A with pack premium
- A free in the mail premium
- A self-liquidating premium
- A reusable premium

Money refund offers: This offer is usually described in media advertising as one in which the manufacturer returns within a stated period, all of the purchaser's money if he is not completely satisfied.

Contest or sweepstakes: This is another popular device used for brand promotion. An opportunity is provided for consumers to participate in a sweepstake, contest or game with chances of winning cash prizes, free air trips or goods.

Trading stamps: Trading stamps have not yet become popular in India. In western countries trading stamps have become very popular. Trading stamps are issued to consumers through retailers in proportion to their purchases.

Price off promotion: This involves an offer to consumers of a certain amount of money of the regular price of a product. Such an offer is prominently printed on the label or package. Special introductory offers of new brands as well as established brands are made this way.

Demonstrations: A new brand is promoted this way. The demonstrations are staged at exhibitions and fairs, temple festivals or even on a door-to-door basis. These are particularly employed for promoting cosmetics, household appliances and new beverages.

(b) Trade promotions

Buying allowances: The buying allowance is offered to the dealer to induce him to buy a new product introduced by the manufacturer. It offers the dealers a percentage on a minimum quantity of product purchased during a stated period of time.

Count and recount allowances: This method of promotion is particularly useful to clear the distribution channels of an old product or package.

Buy-back allowances: This method of promotion is practised to prevent a post-deal sales decline. Under this method the manufacturer offers a certain amount of money for additional purchases based on the quantity of purchases made on the first trade deal.

Free goods: This is also a buying allowance but in the form of goods. An offer is made of a certain quantity of a product to wholesalers and retailers at no additional cost to them on every purchases of stated amount of the same or another product, e.g., 1 free with every 10.

Merchandise allowances: These are short term in character and are given to compensate the dealers for promotion expenses incurred by them. These include advertising allowances, display allowances etc. The allowance is given upon proof of performance.

Co-operative advertising: Here a manufacturer agrees to pay an advertising allowance to retailers for each unit of the product purchased on a contract for specified period. Retailers are to run advertisements against the advertising allowances, due to them and claim payment upon proof of performance.

Dealer listed promotion: Here, the advertisement or other publicity materials, like calendars issued by the manufacturer carry the names and addresses of retailers who stock the product or who are operating in the promotion.

Push money or (PMs): This is an incentive payment in cash or a gift to the retailer or salesman to push the manufacturer's brand at so many rupees per article sold. It proves to be an expensive method of promotion for the manufacturer as the push money or gift is to be given on all sales whether they are really pushed or not.

Sales contest: It is a device used to stimulate and motivate distributors, dealers and their sales staff. Each seller is made to feel that he has some chance of winning and thus participate in promoting the sales. These contests have only short-term effects.

(c) Sales force promotions

Personal selling is by far the most important method of sales promotion. To make it highly effective, sales force promotion is felt necessary. The tools of sales force promotion are bonus, sales force contests, sales meetings and salesmen's conventions are conferences.

Bonus to sales force: A quota is set for a year or for a shorter period. Bonus is offered on sales in excess of the quota. In view of the general tendency on the part of salesmen to start a belated sales drive towards the close of the year when the quota is fixed for the entire year, sales quotas are fixed for each quarter.

Sales force contest: Sales force contests are announced to stimulate company salesmen to redouble their selling efforts over a stated period of time, with prizes going to the top performers. The competitive spirit in men usually responds to this stimulus. However, some salesmen may consider contests as juvenile. They contend it is unfair to extract work from all to reward only a few.

Sales meetings, salesmen's conventions and conferences: These are conducted for the purpose of educating, inspiring and rewarding the salesmen. New products and new selling techniques are also described and discussed.

In view of their importance of 'personal selling' in promotion mix, now let us turn our attention to 'personal selling' and 'salesmanship'.

7.12   PERSONAL SELLING–ITS PROCESS

Personal selling is oral presentation in a conversation with the prospective buyers for making sales. It involves direct personal contact between the seller or his representative and the buyer. It is the oldest method of promotion.

Salesmanship is defined as "the ability to persuade people to want what they already need". It is "the art of satisfying the need of the customer with the goods and services thereby establishing continuous and profitable relations between buyer and seller" salesmanship consists of winning a buyer's confidence for the sellers' house and goods, thereby winning a regular and permanent customer. It is the art of persuading a prospective buyer to become a real buyer promotes the interest of the buyer is salesmanship. The ideal of service to the buyer is the keynote of salesmanship.

The ideal of service to the buyer is the keynote of salesmanship. The salesman who holds this ideal really serves three parties–his customer, his employer and himself. He serves the customer by aiding him in the direction that best satisfies his needs. He serves his employer by building up a clientele of satisfaction consumers for his product. He serves himself by establishing a name for good service.

People buy goods as a means to an end. To make good sales, the salesman must therefore discover the buyers aim and indicate how the article will assist him attaining that aim. This is the fundamental principle of salesmanship.

Importance

Salesmanship is an important auxiliary to modern trade. Production in anticipation of demand is the order of the day. But production cannot go on, unless the products are sold. So, through advertising, a demand is created. Salesmanship is employed to convert that demand is to a sale. Moreover keen competition prevails in the fields of both production and sale. So sale has to be made in the face of resistance by using the appeal of the competing products. Salesmanship helps to overcome this resistance. Scientific salesmanship helps to maintain demand. It helps to establish equilibrium between demand and supply. It makes mass production a success by means of mass distribution.

Salesmanship is complimentary to advertisement. An advertisement which is not followed by effective salesmanship is futile. So both advertising and salesmanship are closely allied to one another. People may like to see the advertised article for themselves. The salesmen should know all about the advertised article and explain its merits and uses to the prospective customers. Hence, the need for a perfect co-ordination between the advertising and sales departments.

Objectives of Personal Selling

Personal selling has been defined as the oral presentation to prospective customers of one's goods and services for the purpose of ultimately making a sale. All selling processes contain the same basic steps, though the detail of each step and time required to complete it, will vary according to the product that is being sold. For example, a door-to-door sales representative may go through all the steps from prospecting to closing of sale in a matter of ten to fifteen minutes; in contrast, the selling process for computer or electronic typewriter may take several visits, even years, for getting an order. The selling process is shown in Fig. 7.3.

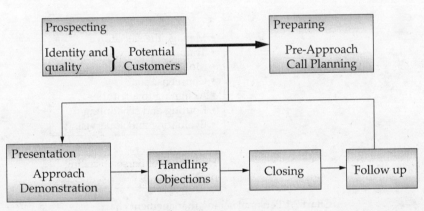

Fig. 7.3 Selling process.

Source: Sales-management concepts, practice and case by Eugene M. Johnson David Kurtz, McGraw -Hill Book Company.

Objectives of personal selling can be briefly stated as sales, profits and growth for the organisation in a continuum in order to ensure its survival. The following objectives are achieved through personal selling, as represented in Chart 7.1.

1. To carry out the complete selling job when some elements of the promotion mix are missing.
2. To serve the existing customers efficiently and effectively.
3. To look for new prospective customers for new/more orders.

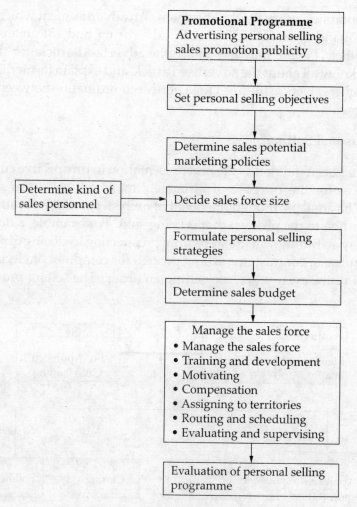

Chart 7.1 Personal selling management chart.

4. To encourage the existing customers for their co-operation in the promotion of the various products of the company.
5. To keep the consumers informed time after time about the various changes in aspects of the marketing strategy and the product line of the company.
6. To provide complete assistance to the customers for selling the product line.
7. To provide proper assistance and advice to the customers regarding certain complicated products and the products for specific uses.
8. To assist and advise regarding the training programmes for the sales personnel of the middlemen/dealers.
9. To help the dealers in their management and related problems.
10. To collect recent information regarding the market and report this to the company (information of company's use)

The quantitative objectives are assigned for a short term and they keep on changing depending upon the market situation from time to time. They are:

1. To retain the existing market share and try for increasing it.
2. To increase the sales volume and hence the profits. It also includes striking of a proper balance between the different elements of the marketing mix of the different products of the company.
3. To make attempts to open new accounts and maintain the existing ones properly, effective and efficiency.
4. To exercise expense management and to keep the expenses within limits.
5. To achieve the targets and try to exceed them.

Selling Process

A salesperson must become accomplished at performing the selling steps. These steps are:

Step 1: Preparation

Before starting the selling job, a salesperson should make a valuable investment of time to know the products he will be selling, to know the customers to whom he will be selling, know the competitors against whom he will be selling and finally know the philosophy policies and range of products of his company. In short, he should be well equipped with the fundamentals of selling.

Step 2: Prospecting

This step of the selling process deals with locating and preparing a list of prospective customers. Prospects can be located through (1) identifying the potential of buying more in existing customers (2) recommendations of existing customers (3) winning back lost customers (4) attracting competitor's customers (5) customers information requests from advertisement (6) newspaper announcement (7) public records (8) directories like telephone, trade associations, etc. (9) other salesmen (10) reference from friends, neighbours and business associates and (11) cost canvassing that is, going from door-to-door

The located prospect should first be qualified broadly in terms of (1) whether they want the product and how intense their want is (2) whether they have the adequate purchasing power, and (3) whether and who possesses the power or authorisation to purchase and spend the required money. The qualifying of prospects is the process of separating the prospects from suspects.

It is worth mentioning here that the ability to prospect is the most essential ability of a successful salesperson. A good salesperson keeps examining, weeding out the already tapped prospects and updating his lists of prospects, and remain in constant search of new prospects.

Step 3: Pre-approach

The qualifying process of separating prospects from suspects further require that the salesperson should possess detailed information relating to the prospects in terms of existing products consumed, their scale of operation, product range, their buying size, frequency, budget and the process, etc. in short, obtain customer orientation. The sources of information for the purpose include company annual reports other salespersons, other suppliers to the prospects, census of manufacturers, professional journals, newspaper and market intelligence. The availability of the above information in as detailed a manner as possible will help the salesperson in ranking the prospect in terms of their priority to the company. Good salesperson use the above information in classifying the prospects in A, B and C categories in terms of the immediacy of the attention to be given to them.

Step 4: Approach

First impression counts. As such, this step needs to be carefully planned. This step has two distinct parts. One, of meeting the customer with a positive set of mind, and the second, is make an impact on him. For the former, referrals of reliable persons known to prospects, calling after fixing an appropriate, use of door openers, help, for the latter the salesperson should equip himself with the key benefit to the emphasised samples or new literature to be handed over, etc.

Step 5: Sales Presentation

Through advance information relating to the prospect every effort should be made to match the product offered to the needs/problems faced by the customer. The sales presentation should generally go according to the AIDA-attention, interest, desire, and action approach. How can this be done? Use of key benefit or a problem solver, or a unique act of the salesperson results in gaining attention. When used alternative this part provides opportunity to get the main point of the initial statements made by the prospect.

The flexibility of the sales presentation can range from the 'canned' or previously prepared presentation, to those allowing the salesperson complex freedom in the presentation. Though both the extremes, and even the hybrid of the two, have their own situational suitability, the important point to note is that salesmanship, being a downman ship function, must arouse active participation of the prospect in the presentation process. This can be done by introducing some action which would keep the prospect captivated. One possible way would be a joint review of the problem faced by the prospect. Another is helping the prospect imagine the projected benefits of owing the product.

Step 6: Handling Objections

It is in the last phase of the sales presentation step that the prospects start expressing doubts or raising objections whether relating to price, need for more time to think, satisfied with the existing product/supplier or product quality claims.

These doubts or objections should be welcome and they should be answered with confidence. There is certainly no doubt that the prospect has to be thoroughly convinced that the product would satisfy his need. The ability of the salesperson relating to the prospects enables him to anticipate the prospect's objectives and reactions.

The golden rules for handling objections are (1) Welcome the objections and show respect to the prospect, and (2) Do not argue with the prospect. Even when the objections raised are half-baked or trivial in nature, the salesperson should handle the situation tactfully. Only in extreme necessity, should a salesperson ask the prospect to adequately explain his problem faced. Even under these circumstances, courtesy should not be lost sight of, and while the discussion is on, the salesperson should start recounting the benefits of the product agreed upon, and lead the prospect to make a favourable decision. It should be remembered that handling objections sharpens the selling skills of the salespersons.

Step 7: Closing Sale

Closing is that aspect of the selling process in which the salesperson asks the prospect to buy the product. There is critical point during each presentation when the salesperson should ask for the order. Pending the location of the critical point, as the objections are being met, the salesperson should help reduce the choice of options, summarises the benefits of buying, and the consequences of not buying, and if the need be, make use of the big idea appeal of buying 'now' at that moment.

Step 8: Post-sale Follow-up

The selling process does not come to an end by writing the order. A few repetitions reassuring the benefits of the product keep the customer sold. Follow-up provides an opportunity to ensure that the product is being rightly used, and if necessary to re-explain the method of using, handling, and storing of the product when not in use. This builds favourable feelings and nurtures strong buyer-seller relationships. Post-sale follow-up not only reinforces the customers' confidence in the salespersons and his company but also tends to keep competition out. This also helps generate repeat business and valuable word-of-mouth publicity. The following up is a good source of freeback too.

Let us conclude this concept by stating that although the eight steps of the selling processes are essential in sprit, these may not always be followed. This could be partly be (1) the selling situation involved (e.g., in the case of insider order taker or retail salesperson, the first three steps of the selling process are generally not applicable as the customer walks the store for buying a product, (2) the experience of the salesperson or (3) the seller's market of the product where customers generally queue up for the product.

Let us also look at the findings of a study by Robertson and Chase on the subject. They pointed

1. The more closely matched the physical, social and personal characteristics of the customer and salesperson, the more likely is the sale.
2. The more believable and trustworthy, the customer perceives salespersons to be, the more likely is the sale.
3. The more presudable a customer is, the more likely is a sale
4. The more a salesperson can make prospective buyers view themselves favourably the more likely a sale is.

Personal Selling and Sales Promotion

No doubt, sales promotion merges on the side into advertising and, on the other hand, into personal selling. But it is different from personal selling in some respects.

The main differences between personal selling and sales promotion are:

1. Personal selling is generally, a recurring event, i.e., it is undertaken continuously year after year. But sales promotion is a non-recurring event, i.e. it is undertakes only during a specified period.
2. Personal selling involves the use of salesmen. But sales promotion may or may not involve the use of salesmen.
3. Personal selling, no doubt, induces the prospectus to buy the product. But sales promotion provides an extra stimulus to the prospectus to buy the product.
4. Personal selling may be adopted by the producers or by the dealers. But sales promotion is always the responsibility of the producers.

However, both personal selling and sales promotion are complementary to each other.

7.13 THEORIES OF SELLING

Old Approach: Generally, the selling theories emphasised 'What to do' and 'How to do' rather than 'Why to do'. The theories are based upon the practical and experimental knowledge accumulated from the years of "living in the market", rather than on a systematic, fundamental body of knowledge.

The second or the *new approach* made use of the findings of the behavioural sciences. Theories according to the new approach:

1. AIDAS theory of selling–Seller oriented
2. 'Right set of the circumstances' Theory of Selling–Seller oriented.
3. 'Buying Formula' Theory of Selling–Buyer oriented
4. 'Behavioural Equation' Theory–Buyers' decision process.

AIDAS Theory of Selling

In this theory AIDAS stands for

- A–Attention
- I–Interest
- D–Desire
- A–Action
- S–Satisfaction

This theory tells about the consumer readiness stage. It is a psychological theory of selling which tells us about the consumer mind–the stages through which the mind passes. These stages are attention, interest, desire, action and satisfaction. This theory tells about the fact that the salesman should make the consumer pass through these five stages so that the purchase should occur.

Phase-I: Securing Attention

1. Get the appointment with the consumer.
2. Salesperson must show mental alertness and be a skilled conversationalist.
3. He should establish a good rapport at once and should be a conversation opener.
4. He should do his homework properly.
5. Good conversation opener causes the prospect to relax and sets stage for the overall presentation.

Phase-II: Gaining Interest

This deals with the evolvement of the strong interest of the consumer in the product, to develop a contagious enthusiasm for the product and to give facts and figures about the product. There should be a strong selling appeal to make their interest in the product. There should be a strong selling appeal to make their interest in the product very effective. Also the attitudes and the feelings toward the product should be clarified. Salesperson must take all these into account in selecting the appeal to be emphasised.

Phase-III: Kindling Desire

Here the interest of the consumer is to be converted into the desire for buying the product. The ways should be found to face and dispose of the sales obstacles, the consumer objections, external interruptions, digressive remarks, etc. The consumer should be satisfied in all respects and all of his doubts should be cleared.

Phase-IV: Inducting Action

The perfect presentation results in the readiness of the consumer to buy the product. All this requires experience of the sales personnel as the buying is not automatic and it should not be closed until the salespersons are positive that the right time has come. Most prospects find it easier to shy away from the hints than from frank requests for an order.

Phase-V: Building Satisfaction

After the purchase generally the customer passes through the state of mental cognitive dissonance in post-purchase anxiety. Now this is the job of the salesperson to relieve him of this tension and convince him that him decision was correct. Building satisfaction means thanking the customer for the order and also to make the customer feel delighted and also to assure him of the promises made by the salesman.

'Right set of circumstances' **Theory of Selling:** This theory is the 'situation response' theory which tells that everything was right for the sale. It also states that the skills of the salespersons have a lot of effect on the sales to take place. Also, if the salesperson presents the proper stimuli or appeals, the desired response will result. This theory tells about two types of factors which constitute the set of circumstances. The factors are internal and external. This theory stresses the external factors at the expenses of the internal factors. This is a seller-oriented theory and stresses the importance of the salespersons in the process of selling of a product.

The major drawbacks of this theory are:

1. It does not take care of the internal factors.
2. It fails to attach appropriate weight to the response side of the situation-response interaction.

'Buying Formula' **Theory of Selling:** This theory is buyer-oriented theory. This is a psychological theory and takes care of the buyer-related problems and revolves round the buyer. This theory explains the cognition process which goes on in the mind of the buyer when he has to take the decision regarding to buy or not to buy. This theory has come through various stages of its development are shown in Fig. 7.4.

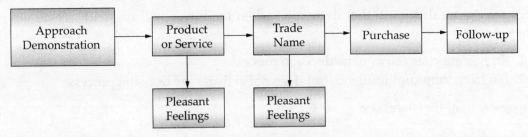

Fig. 7.4 Building satisfaction.

When a buying habit is being established, the buyer must know why the product or service is an adequate solution to the need or problem, and why the trade name is the best one to buy. This theory tells that:

1. The need should be created/emphasised.
2. The relation between the need and the product or service should be emphasised.
3. The brand image should be created.
4. The need, product/service and the trade name/brand image should be associated with each other.
5. The brand loyalty and the customer delight should be emphasised.

'Behavioural Equation' **Theory:** This theory takes care of the buyer's decision-making process and goes in the detail of the process at the micro/internal level. The buyer goes through various stages of learning process. The essential elements of the learning process are:

1. Drive (motivation)
2. Cue
3. Response
4. Reinforcement.

Drives are strong internal stimuli which impel the buyers' response. These drives are of two types. They are:

1. Innate drives–psychological or biogenic drives
2. Learned drives–social drives.

Cues are the weak stimuli that determine when the buyer will respond. There are two types of cues:

1. Triggering cues activate the decision process.
2. No triggering cues influence but does not activate the decision process.

Response is what the buyer does.

Reinforcement strengthens the buyer's tendencies to make a particular response. Hence, this theory takes care of the behavioural aspects of the buyer and how it influences his decisions and his learning process. This also tells about the salesperson's role in all this to make it happen and at the same time it reduces buyer dissonance.

7.14   SALES STRATEGIES

Sales strategies are the policies which are made to provide the guidelines for taking key decisions in personal selling. It includes the following:

1. Size of the sales force required
2. Kind of the sales force required
3. Roles of the salesperson
4. Assigning of the sales territories.

The effectiveness and the efficiency, with which these roles are played by the sales force, determine the extent to which overall personal selling objectives are achieved. The company's competitive posture is shaped by:

1. Product market analysis
2. Salesperson's order securing analysis
3. Choice of the basic selling style:
    (a) Trade selling
    (b) Missionary selling
    (c) Technical selling
    (d) New business selling.

The size of the sales force can be determined by utilizing one or more of the following methods in combination with each other:

1. Work Load Method
2. Sales Potential Method
3. Incremental Method.

Individualising selling strategies to customer

The acid test of the appropriateness of personal selling strategy comes when particulars salespersons interact with particular customers. The management makes its the first key decision on personal selling strategy. When it determines the size of the company's sales force, each salesperson must individualise his own dealing with each customer. The decisions of the above kind are implemented after the required kind and size of the sales force has been recruited, trained and assigned their fields and territories. The strategies should be such so as to benefit the customer and help the firm in achieving its objectives. The strength of the sales force depends upon its communication and convincing power to persuade the customer to buy the product. The approach of the salesperson towards different buyers is a matter of his selling skills. This skill is the function of the preplanning and performance on the call of the salesperson itself. The individual members of the sales force determine the success and failure of the company's overall personal selling strategy and sales management. The efficiency and effectiveness of the sales management in the personal selling field. The salespersons should combine their efforts in such a way so as to achieve their personal objectives through the achievement of the firm's objectives.

Qualifications of a salesman

It is not true that salesmen are born. There may be born salesmen. But they can also be made if a careful selection is made and organised training is provided.

A successful salesman requires certain qualities. First, he should possess an attractive personality. Good looks are a potent force and a long way in attracting customers. Neat dress adds to one's appearance. Personality includes intelligence factor and true sympathy. Secondly, he should be cheerful and possess pleasing manners. A cheerful person can draw others towards him. A Chinese proverb says "A man without smiling face must not open a shop". Similarly, good manners are an asset to a salesman. They always command respect.

Thirdly, a salesman should know all about the goods or services which he offers to sell. Otherwise he would not be able to explain their merits and benefits to the customer. The weakness of many salesmen is the lack of thorough knowledge of the goods. Complete knowledge creates a feeling of confidence and in consequence, a mental attitude which commands success. In the case of plant and machinery, the salesman should be capable of actually demonstrating the working of the concerned plant or machinery. For example, a salesman who deals with typewriters must know typing and he should be well versed with its mechanisms.

Fourthly, he should possess the knack of persuading others. He may include a prospective buyer to action by conveying him about the desirability of the goods which he deals in. But, in the name of persuasion the salesman should not pester to customer to buy an article which he does not like. A salesman will lose customers if he pesters them.

Fifthly, he should be a fluent speaker for he has to explain everything he knows about the goods to the customer. A powerful speaker always impresses the listener. Forceful speech is necessary if the salesman is to "sell" his point of view and convince the customer.

Sixthly, a salesman should be courteous and be prompt in his service. Once he knows the particular thing the customer needs, he should not make the customer to wait unreasonably. He should satisfy his needs without delay. Undue delay in serving may irritate the customer and drive him away from the seller.

Seventhly, a salesman should possess enthusiasm. "Enthusiasm is earnestness and the downright earnest man gets results. Enthusiasm is to a business what patriotism is to an army; it gives zeal and inspiration, his words, the tone of his voice, and all his actions must present the sprit of goodwill, enthusiasm and earnestness.

Above all, he must have the right attitude. That is, he must have the interest of the buyer at heart. The law underlying success is true service. Therefore, he should keep the ideal of service ever in mind.

A good salesman services not only his employer but also his customer. He serves the former by helping him to market his products efficiently. He serves the latter by guiding him in the proper selection of goods.

Sales strategy and technique

Before a salesman proceeds to approach a prospective customer, he must make certain preparations for a same effort. First, he must compile a summary of the special features of his product with proof or evidence of its merits. He must select the specific advantages of his product in order to offer them when he calls on the consumer.

Secondly, he must determine the various motives or instincts to which he must appeal, and classify the various points of advantage in relation to these motives. This study of motives is most important for when an appeal is made for the right motive, there is an irresistible urge to buy the goods.

7.15 DIRECT MARKETING OR DIRECT SELLING

Direct marketing is one of the most important promotional tools. It is now widely used in consumer markets (i.e., sales of goods to final consumers) and business-to-business markets (i.e., sales of goods between business houses).

Meaning of Direct marketing

According to the Direct Marketing Association (DMA), *"Direct marketing is an interactive marketing system that uses one or more advertising media to effect measurable response and/or transaction at any location"*.

This definition places emphasis on a measurable response (i.e., a customer order) as the basic aim of direct marketing. For this reason, sometimes, direct marketing is called direct-order marketing.

Characteristics of Direct Marketing

Direct marketing has certain characteristic features. They are:

1. It is non-public. That is, the message of direct marketing is not addressed to the masses or the general public. It is normally addressed to a specific person.

2. It is customised. That is, the message of direct marketing is customised to appeal to the addressed individual.

3. It is up-to-date that is, under direct marketing, a message can be prepared very quickly for delivery to an individual.

4. It is interactive. That is, in direct marketing, the message can be altered depending upon the person's response.

Benefits of direct marketing

Direct marketing or direct selling offers some benefits. Those benefits are:

1. It is convenient to consumers. Many consumers feel that direct marketing like home shopping is convenient and hassle-free.

2. It saves consumers' time in shopping.

3. It introduces consumers to large selection of merchandise.

4. It helps consumers to do comparative shopping by browsing through mail catalogues and online shopping services.

5. It is also helpful to industrial customers or users. Industrial customers like learning about available products and services without wasting their time in meeting sales people.

6. It is also advantageous to marketers or sellers. Direct marketers can try a mailing list containing the names of any group, and then, personalise and customerise their messages.

7. It helps direct marketers to build a continuous relationship with each customer.

8. It can be timed by direct marketers to reach prospectus at the right moment.

9. It material receives higher readership, because it is sent to more interested persons.

10. It permits the listing of alternative media and messages in search of the most cost-effective approach.

11. It makes direct marketers offer and strategy less visible to competitors.

12. It helps direct marketers to measure response to their campaigns to find out the most profitable ones.

Criticisms against Direct Marketing

Direct marketing is not free from criticisms. The various criticisms against direct marketing are:

(a) Direct marketing is considered by many consumers a nuisance. The increasing number of direct marketing solicitation irritates the customers.

(b) There are instances of unfairness in direct marketing promotional tools.

(c) There are also cases of outright deception and fraud in direct marketing.

(d) There is also the issue of invasion of privacy in direct marketing. That is, the names, addresses, etc. of persons entered in the database of a firm are used by other firms.

Essentials for the Success of Direct Marketing

To ensure the success of direct marketing, direct marketers must do the following:

1. They must plan their campaigns carefully.
2. They must decide on their objectives.
3. They must target their markets and prospectus precisely.
4. They must design the offer's elements wisely.
5. They must test the offers elements carefully.
6. They must establish measures to determine the success of their campaigns.

Besides undertaking the above activities, direct marketers must have customer database, i.e. an organised collection of comprehensive data should be used by the direct marketers to identify the prospectus and to decide which customer should receive a particular offer.

Important tools of direct marketing

There are many tools of direct marketing or selling. Some of the important tools of direct marketing are:

1. Sales call, i.e. sales force calling on the marketer's prospectus, which is the oldest form of direct marketing.
2. Direct mail marketing, involving sending of offer, announcement reminder, etc. to a person at a particular address using the mailing list, fax mail, e-mail and voice mail.
3. Telemarketing.
4. Television direct response marketing and home shopping channel.
5. Kiosk marketing (i.e., marketing through customer-order machines installed in important places.)
6. Online marketing (i.e., marketing through computers and modems).

7.16   PUBLICITY

Publicity is non-personal stimulation of demand for a product, service or business unit by placing commercially significant news about it in a published medium or obtaining favourable presentation of it upon radio, TV or stage that is not paid for by the sponsor.

The crucial aspect of publicity is that it should emanate from a neutral and impartial source such as editorial material and is not paid for by the sponsor. To achieve the aim of credibility it should not raise any doubts regarding interested sponsorship. Publicity and public relations have a lot in common. In fact, publicity is one of the tools of public relations.

Use of publicity

Publicity which is essentially aimed at building positive image, goodwill or favourable visibility has acquired a sound footing to assist a company in its marketing efforts. Specifically, it has a vital role in disseminating information regarding new products warranty terms; product replacement policies and customer service arrangements, new R&D findings, successful bids or contracts won, contributions made to the promotion of sports, culture, and technology, employees welfare policies dealer training and promotion activities; membership of top and senior employees in government and international bodies; community development programmes; promotion of company trade mark and slogans; and issues of public interest and welfare from time to time.

Need for Planning

With significant potential for doing good to the corporate promotion efforts, publicity needs to be systematically planned and suitably handled.

Also a coordinated effort is needed to manage the mishaps and negative occurrences as well as to prevent rumours and damaging stories from circulating about a company. Though surprising, at times, the companies may even make use of advertising space to overcome or reduce the impact of the media bias and to communicate correct picture or offer classification to the public

One of the recent instances of the usage of advertising space to rebut a negative story is the one inserted by Air India about an *India Today* story. The story in *India Today* is said to contain serious allegations against Air India in the matter of leasing freight aircraft and purchasing a Boeing 747 to replace the ill fated Kanishka. The article had suggested, according to Air India's advertisements, "that Air India had manipulated these deals, as a result of which foreign exchange has been lost and the operations 'became costlier' in the long run". The advertisement released by Air India defined any irregularity and berated India today. The result of the advertisement has been both 'dramatic and immediate'. Chief PR manager of Air India opined that the larger outcome of the Air India decisions to go public through advertising space was that pressman would now be a great more circumspect before rushing into print. Air India's action would, therefore, have a statutory effect on the entire press fraternity.

Measuring effectiveness of publicity

Ratings received on corporate image studies carried out by independent bodies awareness of the company's effort, and change in attitudes of the public towards the company are the major methods through which the effectiveness of the publicity can be measured. Both periodic surveys as well as before and after event surveys can be conducted to gauge the level of exposure, awareness and the type of opinions and attitudes held by public. Publicity when used in an integrated way with other elements of the promotion mix adds punch and provides considerable mileage to a firm's promotion efforts.

7.17   PUBLIC RELATIONS

Today, public relations have become one of the elements or components of promotion mix. Every firm tries to create good public relations so as to give good public publicity about itself and its products. To improve public relations, every firm sets up to separate department called public relations department.

Meaning of Public Relations

Public relations refer to an effort to create a favourable attitude towards a firm among employees, shareholders, suppliers, customers, the government and the society at large. In other words, public relations to the firm's communication and relationship with various sections of the public such as employees, shareholders, suppliers, customers, Government and the other sections of the society. In short, public relation means the total process of maintaining good relations with the public and improving the image of the firm in the eyes of the public.

Objective of Public Relations

Public relations programme has a broad objective as compared to other promotional tools like advertising, salesmanship and sales promotion. Its main objective is to improve the image and prestige of the firm.

Importance of Public Relations in Marketing

Today, public relations also play an important role in marketing. Public relations programme has become an integral part of promotional strategy, though its main object is to improve the image of the firm.

The importance of public relations is clear from the following facts.

1. Like advertising, salesmanship, sales promotion and publicity, public relations also help to influence the consumers to buy the product of the firm.
2. The cost of public relations is small as compared to the cost of advertising, salesmanship and sales promotion.
3. Public relations provide an efficient indirect communication channel for promoting the sales of the firm's products.
4. Public relations create a good image of the firm among the public and create a favourable atmosphere for the firm for conducting business.
5. Public relations complement advertising by creating product and service creditability.

However, the success of public relation programmes depends upon competent management, effective co-ordination with the marketing department and sustained efforts.

7.18 THE INTEGRATED MARKETING COMMUNICATION

Integrated marketing communication (IMC) is the practice of unifying all marketing communication tools and corporate and brand messages to communicate in a consistent way to and with stakeholder audiences (that is, those who have a stake or interest in the corporation). An IMC campaign plan is even more complex than a traditional advertising plan because it considers more message sources, more communication tools, and more audiences. IMC programmes are designed to coordinate all the various communication messages and sources. We can group these messages as planned (or controlled) messages by the company and unplanned (or uncontrolled) messages. In addition, unconsidered messages–those delivered by other aspects of the marketing mix (price, product, and distribution) and other contact points (such as the appearance of the parking lot outside the store)–communicate important information to stakeholders that can negate the advertising.

The Tools of IMC

The tools used in an IMC campaign include traditional marketing communication tools such as advertising and sales promotion. However, the IMC approach recognises that other areas of the marketing mix too. The price of the product signals a level of quality. The cleanliness of the store and helpfulness of the customer service department send powerful messages. The product's reliability also communicates. IMC planners should consider all message sources and marketing communications that reach stakeholder audiences.

Stakeholder Audience

In addition to managing the total communication programme, IMC campaigns also address a wide variety of stakeholders, all of whom have a different stake or interest in a company and its brand messages. The different stakeholder audiences are as follows:

Corporate Level

- Employees
- Investors
- Financial community
- Government regulators.

Marketing Level

- Consumers
- Target markets
- Retailers
- Distributors
- Competition
- Suppliers
- Vendors.

Marketing Communication Level

- Consumers
- Target audiences
- Trade audiences
- Local community
- Media
- Interest groups
- Activist groups
- General public.

Why is IMC concerned with all these audiences? The support (or lack of it) that each stakeholder group gives to the company can affect that company's brands positively or negatively. Maintaining consistent communications from all message sources to stakeholders is particularly difficult. It works only if a company or brand has a focused business philosophy or mission, clearly understood core values, and a strong corporate culture. Even though different areas of the company may be sending messages, the person on the receiving end is an individual who has to make sense of all the messages, impressions and experiences. As IMC experts Don Schultz, Starley Tannenbaum, and Robert Lauterborn explain, IMC realigns marketing communication "to look at it the way the consumer sees it as a flow of information from indistinguishable sources". If the messages don't reflect some central core values and deliver a consistent image, they may contradict and create confusion.

Coordination

Coordinating all these messages is an organisational problem best solved through cross-functional management which means using teams of people who are from different parts of the company, outside agencies, or both. These teams manage the planning process and monitor the way the plan is implemented. Cross-functional management may even mean getting different agencies together who are producing the marketing communication.

The Structure of a Campaign Plan

A campaign, whether advertising or IMC, is a complex set of interlocking, coordinated activities. A campaign results from a comprehensive plan for a series of different but related marketing communication efforts that appear in different media and marketing communication areas across a specified time period. The campaign is designed strategically to meet a set of objectives and to solve some critical problem. It is short-term plans that usually run for a year or less. Many advertisements are single-shot ads. In other words, they are free-standing ad unrelated to ads that preceded or followed them. Companies that create one ad at a time and constantly change the core message are not involved in a campaign process. However, a great deal of national advertising is developed as part of a campaign with an umbrella theme that extends across time, different stakeholder audiences, and different advertising vehicles or marketing communication opportunities. A campaign may focus on one specific product attribute or one audience, or it may cover a variety of attributes and reach all the audiences. A campaign plan summarises the marketplace situation, the underlying campaign strategy, the main creative strategies and tactics, media, and the other marketing communication.

The following table gives a bird's eye view of various elements involved in IMC campaign.

1. Situation Analysis
   - Product and company research
   - Consumer and stakeholder research
   - Market analysis
   - Competitive situation
   - Industry analysis
   - Marketplace analysis
2. SWOT Analysis
   - Internal factors: strengths and weaknesses
   - External factors: opportunities and threats
   - Problem identification
3. Campaign strategy
   - Objectives
   - Targeting
   - Positioning
   - Scheduling strategy
4. Communication strategy
   - Message development research
   - The creative theme
   - Creative tactics and executions
5. Media plan
6. Other marketing communication activities
7. The appropriation and budget.

Situation Analysis

The first step in campaign plans is a situation analysis that summarises all the relevant information available about the product, the company, the competitive environment, the industry, and the consumers. Sometimes called a business review, this information is obtained using primary and secondary research techniques. The six most important research areas are:

1. Product and company research
2. Consumer and stakeholder research
3. Market analysis
4. Competitive analysis
5. Industry analysis and
6. Marketplace analysis.

SWOT (Strengths, Weaknesses, Opportunity and Threats) Analysis

Situation analysis evaluates the significance of the research. During the situation analysis planners compile all the information they can about the brand and its competitive situation, marketplace factors such as the health of the category, and the behaviour of consumers toward this brand and some recast this information in terms of internal factors (strengths and weaknesses) and external factors (opportunities and threats). Once the information is gathered and sorted into SWOT categories, the analysis begins. In this stage, the key areas on which the campaign strategy has to be built are identified. Problem identification focuses on a set of serious communication problems that this campaign must address. These problems differ from year to year and situation to situation. For example, in one year's marketing plan, a brand may be launching a line extension, which means the advertising will address the problem of launching a new product under a familiar brand name. The next year the marketing plan may focus on increasing distribution, so the advertising probably address opening up new territories where the brand is unknown. Each type of problem calls for a different advertising and marketing communication strategy. Different audiences are reached with different messages; different marketing communication tools may be used and different communication objectives are set.

Campaign Strategy

After the situation analysis and the SWOT analysis, most advertising campaign plans focus on the key strategic decisions that will guide the campaign. The strategy section of a campaign plan identifies the objectives that will solve the key problems identified at the end of the SWOT analysis. It will also specify the target stakeholder audiences and how the strategy will handle competitive advantage and the product's position. Other strategic decisions revolve around the scheduling and timing of the different phases of the campaign act.

Objectives

As objectives provide the goal, they can then be used at the end of the process to measure the campaign's results. These objectives are established based on an understanding the hierarchy of effects and the various ways advertising can affect its audience.

Targeting

Potential target markets are pinpointed and segmented into groups identified by certain demographic or psychographic characteristics, such as environmentalists, bikeriders, or mall teens. These target audiences (that is, groups of people to whom a marketing communication message is directed) shift with each campaign, its situation, key problems, and objectives. For example, if you are launching a line extension, you will probably targets the current users of the brand. However, if you are opening up new territory there aren't current users, so you will have to target competitors' users. For both audiences, however, the objective may remain the same, which is to convince the target audiences to try a new product.

Positioning

Although objectives and targeting differ from campaign to campaign, the product's positioning remains the same. Does the position mean the same thing to familiar brand users considering a new line extension? What would it mean to entirely new users in a new market territory who are unfamiliar with the brand? They may not respond to the position in the same way, which means that the way the position is presented in the message strategy may need to be adjusted to the target audience's needs, interests, and level of knowledge.

Scheduling

Timing and scheduling are an important part of the media plan and are also tied into the overall campaign strategy. Many campaigns have phases, such as the launch, the continuing campaign, and the close. In some cases, particularly with campaigns that continue for a number of years, such as the classic "Milk Mustache" campaign, the campaign may be launched with one strategy that evolves into another strategy as the campaign matures.

Media Plan

The media plan and the creative plan are equally important and are developed simultaneously. The overall appropriation, or available money for the campaign, determines the media. Initial decisions about which media to use usually reflect the availability of a budget big enough to use television, which is the most costly of all media. The media mix is created by selecting the best combination of media vehicle traditional media, and marketing communication tools to reach the targeted stakeholder audiences. If a product has awareness problem, widespread mass media will probably use to increase the general level of awareness. If the problem is one of trial, sales promotion may be the most important tool. However, if the product only appeals to a small target such as martial arts clothes for aikido devotees, direct mail (assuming, of course, that can find a list or build one) and the Internet may be more effective ways to reach that target. In fact, although there may be a lead tool, such as advertising, often a mix of supporting media is used to reach different stakeholder groups. Media planners allocate media dollars to accomplish reach and frequency objectives. In a high-reach campaign, money is spent to get the message to as many people as possible. In a high-frequency campaign, the money is spent on fewer media reaching fewer people, but repetition of the message is increased. The media plan includes media objectives (reach and frequency), media strategies (targeting, continuity, timing), media selection (the specific vehicles), geographic strategies, schedules, and the media budget. Usually, a pie chart is used to show how the budget is allocated to the various media activities.

Other Marketing Communication Activities

The decision about which tools to use is based on an analysis of the strengths and weaknesses of the various marketing communication tools. The tools are then matched to the problem identified in the situation analysis. In other words, which area can best reach a mass audience (advertising), involve an audience (events), or build credibility and believability (public relations)? This is a process called zero-based planning. Subsections of the plan are devoted to these other important marketing communication areas. A competitive sales campaign targeted business owners and managers during competitors' sales canvassing periods.

The Appropriation and Budget

The amount of money available from the client, or advertiser, governs all strategic decisions. Some sense of the amount of money that has been appropriated for the campaign is used at the beginning of the planning to determine the general scope and scale of the campaign effort. Then, after the plan has been developed, a budget is developed that costs out the various recommendations. If this budget is much higher than the appropriation, either costs have to be shaved or the appropriation has to increase. The budget size for advertising and marketing communication programmes has a tremendous range. If you are working on a campaign for a major marketer, you may have plenty of money or the most expensive form of television advertising. Most campaigns are somewhere in between and their planners rarely have as much money as they feel they need to do the job right. Once the appropriation is set, the money can be allocated among the various advertising and marketing communication activities.

Evaluating the Campaign Plan

The final step in campaign plan is to prepare a proposal stating how the campaign will be evaluated. The key part of an evaluation plan is to measure a company or brand's effectiveness against its stated objectives. If not done formally through a research project, some sort of evaluation is always done informally to determine whether the effort was successful. This information is concerned with questions of effectiveness: Is the campaign working? What were the results? It is also concerned with questions of taste and judgement. Is the campaign fair and accurate? Is it building the brand or corporate reputation?

KEYWORDS

AIDA: *Attention, Interest, Desire, and Action. The stages consumers go through before the actual purchase takes place.*

Advertising Campaign: *Advertising effort relating to a specific product or service extending over a specified time period.*

Advertising Target: *The group of people towards which advertisements are aimed.*

Bounce Back Offer: *An additional offer made with an earlier self-liquidating premium offer on a usually related product.*

Canned Presentation: *A structured sales presentation made of an inflexible mature*

Cold Canvassing: *Door-to-door conviction and sale of products.*

Corporate Advertising: *Advertising aimed at promoting the image of a firm as a whole instead of any of its specific product or service.*

Dealer Leader: *A premium given to a dealer in return for an order of a specified value.*

Decoding: *Giving meaning to a communication by the receiver.*

Encoding: *Representing the idea to be communicated through symbols, figures, words, etc.*

Feedback: *The receiver response to the message received.*

Hierarchy of effect: *A consumer response model to promotion, awareness, knowledge, liking, preference, conviction, purchase.*

Hostess Gift: *A gift given to a housewife who provides for a product demonstration to be conducted in her home.*

Layout: *The arrangement in which various design elements of an advertisement such as headline, illustration, body copy, and signature appear so that the desired impact is achieved.*

Media Plan: *The plan that specifies the media mix and the date time, and sequence in which advertisements are scheduled for release.*

Point of Purchase: *Promotional material displayed in the retail store to encourage sales.*

Price Deal: *Short-run price decrease.*

Prospecting: *The step during which probable customers are found for the product of a product which qualifies a customer to receive a premium or refund.*

Prospecting: *Sales promotion activities directed at the wholesaler and retailer levels.*

Pull: *Promotional methods directing the end consumer to demand specified products or services. One popular form is advertising.*

Push: *Promotional strategy directing the dealers and the sales force to achieve marketing communications and sales objective.*

Promotion: *The marketing communication aimed at informing and persuading consumers to respond positively.*

Promotion Mix: *The specific combination of promotion methods used for a particular product or service.*

Receiver: *The individual group or organisation that decodes a coded message.*

Reinforcement: *Efforts to keep the existing customers sold and advising them to get the maximum satisfaction from the product.*

Trade Deals: *A type of sales promotion that stimulates the trade and to carry the marketers products and markets the product aggressively.*

Traffic Builder: *Low cost premiums offered free as an inducement to visit a store. Also includes the organisation of product demonstration or unique display of products.*

Unaided Recall: *Post testing of advertisements by asking audience to identify what they have seen or heard but without giving any clues to aid their memory.*

Window display: *A display placed in the window of a retail store facing outside to attract the attention of the passers.*

SUMMARY

Communication deals with sharing of information. This is a key function of marketing. The marketing techniques used to communicate with existing and potential customers are called promotion. The four major promotion methods available to a market are: Advertising, personal selling, sales promotion and publicity. packaging, public relations and other elements of the marketing mix supplement the promotion efforts of the marketer in their own way.

The promotion budget is set by using one or more of the following methods: per cent of sales, fixed sum per unit, affordable funds, competitive party and objective and task method. Among these methods, the approach used in objective and task method is most logical. Marketing communication being persuasive in nature and aiming behaviour in the consumer should skilfully manage.

Advertising is an impersonal mass selling and communication method. It makes use of various types of media to reach the target public in short term. Being persuasive in nature, advertising broadly aims at gaining exposure, creating awareness, changing attitudes of target customers in favour of sponsor's products and services, and also at effecting sales and improving corporate image. Besides, it can also act as a good offensive/defensive tool in managing competition.

Advertising decision is complex and capable of getting influenced by various forces. The decisions arrived at should, therefore, be evaluated in a regular manner so that remedial measures and corrective action could be taken before it is also too late. Pre-testing of advertising campaigns before release and post-testing in terms of recall and recognition studies as well as their impact on sales or the number of inquiry coupons received back are some of the ways through which advertising agency proves by and large advantageous to the company.

Personal selling is a direct person-to-person selling and promotion method. The specific role goals of personal selling vary from firm to firm depending upon the nature of goods marketed, distribution system used, and the sales strategy adopted by a firm. The changing market environment calls upon the sales force to transform it in order to perform a more creative role.

Based on the degree of creativity required, McCurry classifies the sales promotion into seven types—merchandise deliverer, inside order taker, outside order take, missionary salesperson, sales engineer, tangible product seller intangible product seller.

Sales promotion, of late, has emerged as one of the most popular methods of promotion in the case of consumer goods. Stated simply promotion deals with offering something extra as an incentive to motivate in early purchase. Sales promotions can be offered at the level of the consumer, trade and sales force. Sales promotion aids in achieving both the paths pull element of a promotion strategy, sales promotion schemes used to attain consumer pull include free samples, price offs, premium give away, coupons and contests. Promotion is a marketing function of each firm. And, rare will be a firm which makes use of only promotional method. The commonality is the ultimate goal of all promotional methods apart, their limited suitability in influencing only a specific part of the consumer adoption process calls for the need to use the promotional mix as an integrative manner.

The finalised sales forecast will be greater utility if it is related to the sales budget and profit plan of the firm. Close monitoring of actual sales against the sales forecast and a thorough probe in case of substantial deviation can forewarn the unrecognised expanding of the sales budget.

Distribution is the all important link between a manufacturer and his customer. The concern is for designing strategy to facilitate the smooth physical flow of products from the manufacturer to the place from where the customers can buy them.

To ensure, smooth and shortest possible route for the physical movement of goods, the manufacturer has to decide the location of manufacturing facilities, warehouse, and the type of transportation to be used. Proper inventory management is also important so that there are always goods when there is demand for them.

ASSIGNMENT

Assignment 1

Identify three instances of television commercials which seek to informm remind and persuade its buyers.

1. _____
2. _____
3. _____

Assignment 2

For a consumer durable product that you purchased recently, identify all the communications that you received which were related to the purchase.

_____

_____

_____

_____

Assignment 3

What promotion mix would you suggest for each of the following products? Answer you have budget, in each case give reasons for your answers.

(a) Chewing gum
(b) Colour television
(c) Sports footwear
(d) Automatic lathe
(e) Light commercial vehicle.

_____

_____

_____

_____

Assignment 4

1. The Economic Times in one of its recent issues came out with an half page write up commending Air India for making profits despite recessionary conditions in the world market. From Air India's point of view, this was a case of

   (a) Sales promotion
   (b) Publicity
   (c) Advertising

2. Getting immediate feedback and having knowledge of customer's needs are advantage of which promotion mix ingredients?

   (a) Advertising
   (b) Publicity
   (c) Sales promotion
   (d) Personal selling

3. The communication process of choosing symbols that convey thoughts is called

    (a) Decoding

    (b) Encoding

    (c) Messaging

4. Advertising effectiveness during an advertising campaign is usually measured by

    (a) Post-test

    (b) Inquires

    (c) Pre-test

    (d) Sales comparison

5. The mailing rate is cost consumption indicator for

    (a) Magazines

    (b) Radio

    (c) Outdoor

    (d) Newspapers

Assignment 5

What general procedure should be followed when qualifying prospects? How can the key prospects for photocopying machines be identified and qualified?

_____

_____

_____

_____

_____

Assignment 6

The sales promotion budget manager of an established lower priced washing powder in planning the sales promotion programme for the next year. Suggest a suitable programme for his consideration.

_____

_____

_____

Assignment 7

Which advertising media you suggest for advertising the following products? Why?

(a) CTV   (b) Surgical instruments   (c) Automobiles

Assignment 8

Write a short note favouring radio as the advertising medium compared to TV.

Assignment 9

From the recent magazines, select one advertisement each of an industrial product and a consumer product. For both the advertisements (a) describe the target market for each advertisement, and (b) offer your observation on their effectiveness.

Assignment 10

Identify some publicity about a product or a firm that is positive. Explain how the firm might have generated this publicity. What are some of the limitations of publicity?

_____

_____

_____

CASE STUDY

Case Study 1

Volkswagen

Volkswagen, the fifth-largest automaker in the world, was founded in 1937. The first prototype was actually built in 1935 by Ferdinand Porsche, founder of the car company bearing his name, who had been commissioned by Hitler to build a "People's Car." Volkswagen began selling its Beetles in North America in 1949, a year in which only two of the vehicles sold in the United States for $995 each. By 1955, the company had sold one million vehicles worldwide. Today, Volkswagen manufactures a number of other car brands, including Audi, Lamborghini, Bugatti, Bentley, Rolls-Royce, Skoda, and Seat.

Growth Years

With the help of creative and effective marketing, Volkswagen became a household name in America during the 1960s. The company's marketing programme in the United States during this decade was designed to make the brand's underdog status an advantage. This was accomplished with self-depreciating advertising that made light of the Beetle's shortcomings. Some memorable slogans for the Bug include "Think Small," "It's Ugly but It Gets There," and "Nobody's Perfect." These self-effacing slogans ran counter to the advertising tradition of U.S. automakers, which usually involved lofty descriptions of a car's style, power, grace, and superior design. The classic Beetle rapidly became a cult favourite, then a popular favourite, and eventually was to become the number-one selling car in history with over 22 million units sold. Volkswagen was not afraid to use the occasional hard sell. One particularly persuasive print ad paired a Volkswagen with a snowplow and a heavy blanket of snow on the ground and asked, "What do you think the snowplow driver drives to work?" Volkswagen also developed a stylish automobile called the Karmann Ghia, which was humorously advertised as the car "for people who can't stand the sight of a Volkswagen."

Decline and Recovery

After sales of VW cars in America peaked at 569,000 units in 1970, cut-throat competition among compacts, especially from Japanese manufacturers, hurt Volkswagen's sales. The company also made an unfortunate marketing move that compounded its problems. It "Americanised" its image, by advertising the opening of an VW assembly line in Pennsylvania–the first U.S. assembly line set up by a foreign auto maker–at a time when imports were popular. The 1980s were not much better for the company, as sales continued to decline. By 1990, Volkswagen was looking for ways to revitalise its business in the United States. Sales had slipped to a mere 1.3 per cent of the American market from a high of 7 per cent in 1970. The company developed an advertising campaign that centred on the word Fahrvergnugen, German for "driving pleasure." This strategy was considered a risk at the time because many assumed Americans would not adopt a German word as a slogan. The hard-to-pronounce word nevertheless became an instant pop-culture buzzword, but U.S. sales continued to drop to under 50,000 units. The company clarified its brand message under the umbrella of the "Drivers Wanted" slogan in 1995, and U.S. sales rose 18 per cent to 135,907 cars in 1996.

Classic Influences Tempt Consumers

In 1998, Volkswagen released a modernised version of its iconic Beetle to a car-buying public nostalgic for the vintage style. Ads for the New Beetle echoed the irreverent humour of the ads from the 1960s, with one ad reading "If you sold your soul in the '80s, here's your chance to buy it back." Another ad emphasised the difference between the modern engine and notoriously underpowered traditional Beetle with the slogan "Less Flower, More Power." American buyers leapt at the chance to buy the classically influenced–but clearly modern– cars, often at well above sticker price. Waiting lists for the new cars, which sold more than 55,000 units in 1998, were common. The company also experimented with the Internet as a marketing and sales medium, holding a special Web–only launch of 2,000 New Beetles in two previously unavailable colours, Reflex Yellow and Vapour Blue. Volkswagen sold out its inventory immediately. By drawing consumers into Volkswagen showrooms, the New Beetle helped the company achieve 50 per cent growth in sales volume between 1998 and 1999. In 2001, the company unveiled its latest retro offering–the Microbus–as a concept car. The car, not expected to be available to the American public until 2003, will likely set off another wave of nostalgia and help the company achieve further sales growth. Other new models slated for introduction include a sport utility vehicle and a luxury V-8 Passat sedan designed to compete with BMW and Mercedes. Volkswagen's history of brilliant marketing will likely lead to success for these new models.

Source: Marketing Management, Philip Kotler

Questions

1. What are some of the ways in which Volkswagen epitomises the meaning and value of the marketing concepts in the text?
2. Suggest creative extensions of VW's marketing tactics and strategies in applications of advertising, promotion, public relations and other promotional techniques.

Case Study 2

Sales Force Compensation

Some people might say executives at outer circle products are out to lunch. Three years ago, Outer Circle, a small, privately held company with 11 salespeople, eliminated sales incentive pay because it clashed with the company's all for-one culture. Salespeople, management reasoned, should be paid like everyone else in the company, with strict base salaries. The manufacturer of lunch boxes and coolers doesn't regard its salespeople as the most important employees in the company. It rejects sales quotas and contests. And, in the corridors of the company's Chicago headquarters, commission may as well be a four-letter word. Despite what most salespeople would consider their cue to leave, Outer Circle reps contend they welcomed the change in the compensation plan. "I was happy," says Sid Mickle, a rep who was recently promoted to national field sales manager. "In our culture, you can't have a department on a different plateau." Mickle's nearly 20 years of sales experience leads him to believe that quotas motivate salespeople to manipulate numbers and make decisions that will benefit their wallets, not their customers. "[Without commissions] there's no benefit to playing with quotas and over shipping," Mickle says.

So instead of receiving incentive pay for hitting a target, reps earn a base salary that Stacy Shane. Director of Human Resources, calls "very generous". In addition, all employees receive a portion of the company's profits. Each fiscal year employees complete a personal-performance plan that includes such objectives as implementing a new training programme, fixing a quality problem, or furthering a relationship with a key customer. Management then uses this plan as a basis for increasing or decreasing people's piece of the pie.

Outer Circle employees can use their earnings from the profit sharing plan to invest back into the company. With the help of an accountant, Outer created a stock programme that allows employees to grow their investment as the company profits. "It's a way for us to tie people into a privately held company and make them feel like an owner in the company rather than taking that check and buying new clothes," Shane says.

But can a sales force really thrive without commissions? No way, says Russ Riendeau, a sales recruiter with Thomas Lyle & Company in Palatine, Illinois. In fact, at least 60 per cent of his clients have changed their compensation plan in the past two years to include more performance-based incentives. The opposite approach, he says, produces a complacent sales force. What's more, "if you don't give them that carrot to chase, [reps] become viable candidates to be plucked away from the organisation," he says. "Based on thirteen years of recruiting, I believe it's growth suicide to remove incentive plans from salespeople." Yet Outer Circle is growing at a respectable pace. Between 1995 and 1997, revenues doubled, and in the past five years, only one rep has left. What's the company's secret? It hires people who fit into its extraordinary culture. Says Shane, the HR director: "The person who sees [the compensation plan] as a negative is not the right candidate for this company."

Pros and Cons of fixed compensation plan

PROS

- Energises salespeople to pursue new business aggressively.
- Separates and rewards top performers.
- Prevents reps from defecting to competitors.

CONS

- Pressures salespeople to manipulate numbers.
- Motivates them to place undue pressure on customers.
- Places reps on a pedestal and may engender resentment among other company divisions.

Questions:

1. What was the sales force compensation plan followed by Outer Circle Products?
2. What are the arguments of Mickle in support of such a plan?
3. What is the view of Russ Riendeau?
4. What kind of compensation plan will be effective for different types of products in Indian companies?

Case Study 3

The Match Fixing Scandal

In April 2000, one of the biggest scandals to hit the world of cricket was unearthed by the New Delhi police. While investigating a local corruption case, officials recorded phone conversations between Hanse Cronje, the captain of the South African cricket team and

Sanjeev Chawla, a London based businessman. The conversation in the tapes seemed to implicate both men in illegal betting on a match played in February 2000 in India. After initial denials, Cronje confessed that he had accepted $15000 to fix the match. The news shocked cricket lovers and the media alike and Cronje's face was smeared with black paint on posters across the country.

Siyaram Silk Mills, one of India's leading textile companies, was particularly affected by this controversy, since Cronje was one of the main endorsers for their J. Hampstead brand of clothing. The campaign, featuring Cronje had been running successfully in all the media for about a month. Siyaram and their advertising agency watched in dismay as their celebrity endorser turned into a hated figure overnight. The scandal also provoked a heated debate in advertising circles regarding the dangers of using celebrity endorsements. Siyaram was forced to withdraw its campaign from all the media and other Indian companies began to rethink the rules of using celebrity endorsements as an integral part of their advertising strategy.

Company Overview

Siyaram was a part of the Siyaram Poddar Group of companies, which had a turnover of $209 billion in 2000–2001. Established in 1954, the Group was into the textile (yarns, fabrics and garments), paper/paperboards and tyre (rubber tyres and tubes) businesses. Siyaram's businesses comprised fabrics and readymade garments. Its popular brands included Oxemberg shirts, trousers and jeans and J. Hampstead wool fabric.

Siyaram was incorporated in June 1978 as a private limited company and was converted into a public limited company in 1980. Siyaram manufactured and marketed textiles, cotton, woollen synthetics and synthetic blends–the main product being polyester blended worsted fabrics. In July 1993, Siyaram came out with a ₹153 million rights issue to part finance a ₹165 million expansion cum modernisation project.

Siyaram had a strong presence in the lower and medium segment of the domestic suitings market. The company had three manufacturing plants situated at Thane and Raigad in Maharashtra and Silvassa in the Union Territory of Dadra and Nagar Haveli, producing over 27.5 million metres of fabric annually. It had a 4% market share in the ₹50 billion suitings and shirtings market. The other players included Vimal, Mayur, Raymond, Digjam, Gwalior and Reid & Taylor. Siyaram retailed its products through 25 exclusive showrooms, besides its distributor network of about 400 wholesale dealers and 50,000 retailers across the country. The company also exported its products to Europe, South America, South Africa, the Far East and the Gulf countries.

Advertising Strategy

Siyaram was one of the few FMCG companies in India that was known for its lavish advertisements. The "Coming Home to Siyaram" campaign was reported to be one of India's most expensive campaigns The company believed that good commercials helped it to effectively position its suitings on a global platform. Percept advertising agency had conceptualised the "Coming Home to Siyaram" campaign. Over the years, the campaign established the brand's association with true love for the motherland, by showing successful men maintaining lasting, strong ties with their families. The campaign was largely responsible for Siyaram's high brand recall and positive consumer feedback.

As part of its brand building efforts, the company also sponsored major sporting events, such as the Triangular Cricket Series–Siyaram's Cup, 1997 and Siyaram's Celebrity Soccer, 1998. It also held Siyaram fabric shows, aimed at increasing awareness among its target audience about the company's range of products. In 2001-2002, the advertising budget was increased to ₹300 million from ₹200 million for the previous year.

The J. Hampstead Story

J. Hampstead was a very popular suiting brand in Europe, renowned for its premium 100% wool suitings woven from rich natural fibres like merino wool, cashmere and woolsilk. In 1995, Siyaram tied up with J. Hampstead for marketing its suitings in India. The company imported the fabric from Italy. It was priced in the range of ₹1500–₹1600 per metre. In September 1997, Siyaram decided to begin manufacturing the brand at its plants with technical assistance from J. Hampstead. Siyaram set aside around ₹50 million for the marketing, sales and promotion of J. Hampstead. The first phase of this promotion was in the form of commercials featuring Indian tennis superstars Leander Paes and Mahesh Bhupathi. These commercials aimed at positioning the brand in the premium segment with the positioning line "The finest fabric in the world."

In September 1999, the company held a tennis carnival to promote J. Hampstead, where several Hindi film stars were invited to play tennis with the brand ambassadors. Soon after, Siyaram faced problems with the tennis duo when they decided to break their partnership, reportedly due to personal problems. In spite of this, the advertisements were continued on the ground that "the sport is bigger than the players."

In February 2000, Siyaram signed the South African cricket team for promoting the brand. The multimedia promotion was spread over television, satellite channels, print, outdoor and point of purchase advertising. The idea was to associate themselves with the number one cricket team, so that it would enable the brand to be globally focused and convey the message that the brand was of international quality.

The company signed up the entire team and not just one individual, since the South African team had a clean image. Hansie Cronje had several years of experience and a high success rate as captain. The ads featured the entire team wearing the J. Hampstead premium suitings.

The Cronje scandal came to light within a month of the campaign being released. Siyaram had to withdraw the campaign a few days later, but denied that the Hampstead brand image had been affected, on the ground that "the brand is bigger than the individual." The advertising agency also felt that the damage done was not great, since the campaign involved the entire team and not just a single player.

Siyaram's strategy of using multiple brand endorsements seemed to have softened the impact of the scandal on the brand. Though company officials denied that they had given up the celebrity endorsement route for J. Hampstead, the dangers of using this strategy began to be seriously examined by Indian companies and advertising agencies.

Questions

1. In your opinion, what are the benefits and disadvantages of using celebrity endorsements in advertising, based on the facts of the case?
2. A wrong choice of celebrity can ruin the image of a brand. What criteria should be taken into consideration when selecting a celebrity?
3. Should Siyaram continue the celebrity endorsement approach in the aftermath of the Cronje controversy? If not, what alternative approach would you recommend for their advertising campaigns for J. Hampstead?

Case Study 4

Dalda–Persuading the Consumer through Emotional Appeals

Consumers had a strong prejudice towards Dalda, a hydrogenated vegetable oil. They complained that Dalda gave a tickle in the throat and led to stomach upsets. Dalda was blamed as the cause of all known and unknown physical ailments. The marketing director of Hindustan Lever, the company that manufactured the oil was of the opinion that the advertising should project Dalda as a superior product of international standards, in order to remove negative associations with the product. A new ad campaign was prepared, highlighting the fact that Dalda was rich in Vitamin A and in Vitamin D, besides being rid of cooking fat and that Dalda would make one strong and healthy.

In spite of the advertising efforts, research revealed that the old prejudices against Dalda still remained. Even those housewives who were using Dalda were ashamed of it and tried to conceal the fact that they were using it. It was then decided to do motivational research to find out the subconscious reasons for consumers' negative attitudes towards Dalda. The finding that emerged was that people had transferred aggression from being deprived of ghee because of its high price. Dalda had become a substitute for ghee and was being blamed for the so called "aches and pains."

The creative team from Lintas, Lever's advertising agency then changed the ad campaign, incorporating an emotional appeal in place of the earlier rational appeal, based on purely informative advertising. The ad no longer highlighted the vitamin and fat content. Instead, the new campaign was built around the theme "Tested on the touchstone of mother's love." What the ad tried to convey was that Dalda was accepted by mothers in the interests of the family. The campaign had immediate results–Dalda soon became an acceptable product, since consumers were left with the feeling that a mother's choice is always the best one and cannot be rejected.

Questions

1. Based on the above case, for which kind of products do you think emotional appeals would be more effective than rational appeals in advertising? What are some of the other factors that would determine the choice of emotional or rational appeals?

Case Study 5

Soaps and Detergents Ads

Most detergent brands highlight stain removal as their unique selling proposition (USP). However, their ads do not really stand out above the clutter. Nirma came out with an advertising execution for its washing powder that tried to be different.

The television commercial features a family at a dining table whose members get provoked by the critical remarks of another member. They start becoming aggressive and throwing food at each other, soiling their clothes. Luckily, they are carrying packets of Nirma which comes to their rescue and helps to remove the stains. The commercial ends with the jingle " Rekha, Geeta, Jay aur Sushma Sabki Pasand Nirma!" The commercial is one in a series of commercials based on the theme of aggression, featuring the same family members. Each time, Nirma comes to their rescue.

Both Sangeetha Bijlani and Shilpa Shetty have remained models for Nirma. Nirma highlights the old property of stain removal, but attempts to execute it in a different manner. It tries to distinguish itself through its four characters–Rekha, Geeta, Jay aur Sushma, who are so different, yet so like-minded.

Questions

1. In your opinion, how effective is the Nirma ad campaign in terms of generating attention, comprehension and retention?

2. What is Nirma's advertising strategy behind the advertising execution described in the above case?

REVIEW QUESTIONS

1. "Money spent on advertisement is not wasteful." Critically examine this statement.

2. What are the objectives of advertising? Discuss the major ones.

3. What are the uses of advertising to various parties? Discuss.

4. How are the advertising functions organised in an organisation?

5. Differentiate between the advertising and salesmanship.

6. What is advertising? Discuss its objectives and point out the problems of advertising in India.

7. How is attention value secured in an advertisement copy?

8. Define sales promotion. What are its objectives? Describe the various steps to be taken for promoting the sales of a big concern.

9. Define sales process.

10. What are the various steps to be followed in planning the sales promotion?

11. Mention briefly the source from which you can get sales personnel as new recruits.

12. Explain the need for non-financial motivation for salesmen and mention some of the methods through which this can be achieved.

13. Distinguish between personal selling and sales promotion.

14. Explain the features of direct marketing.

15. What is public relation? Discuss the role of public relations in marketing.

16. Mention briefly the factors that have to be considered in order to objectively determine the sales territories' for allocation to salesmen?

MARKETING OF SERVICES

STRUCTURE

8.1   INTRODUCTION

Economists have divided all industrial and economic activities into three main groups: primary, secondary and tertiary. Primary activities include agriculture, fishing and forestry. Secondary activities cover manufacturing and construction, and tertiary activity refers to the services and distribution. In the pre-industrialised era, primary activities were the mainstay of the economy. The Industrial Revolution marked the beginning of increasing importance of secondary activities and the gradually decreasing status of agriculture and allied activities. The period following World War-II saw USA become the world's first service economy with more than fifty per cent of the working population employed in producing services.

Today, 80 million, Americans are employed in the service sector and as much as seventy per cent of the US economy is service oriented. This led a New York Congressman to remark that America is becoming a nation of people who are "serving each other hamburgers or taking in each other's laundry". However, the US service industry is a very technical and sophisticated one comprising computer and software development, business consultancy, telecommunications, banking and insurance sectors.

This system of economic development is not universally applicable to all countries. In many African and Asian countries, the agriculture sector is still the dominant one. In countries like, India, we can observe the growing importance of the manufacturing and service sectors while agricultural still continues to retain its stronghold on the economy. The manufacturing and service sectors are growing not only in volume but also in sophistication and complexity. The wide array of services found in the metropolitan cities of Mumbai, Bengaluru, Delhi, Kolkata, Chennai compare favourably with those found anywhere in the universe.

8.2   MARKETING OF SERVICES AND CHARACTERISTICS

Service is the action of doing something for someone or something. It is largely intangible (i.e., not material). A product is tangible (i.e., material) since you can touch it and own it. A service tends to be an experience that is consumed at the point where it is purchased, and cannot be owned since it quickly perishes. A person could go to a caf one day and have excellent service, and then return the next day and have a poor experience.

Services Marketing

Services marketing is marketing based on relationship and value. It may be used to market a service or a product. Marketing a service-base business is different from marketing a product base business.

There are several major differences, including:

1. The buyer purchases are intangible.
2. The service may be based on the reputation of a single person.
3. It's more difficult to compare the quality of similar services.
4. The buyer cannot return the service.
5. Service marketing mix adds 3 more Ps, i.e., people, physical environment, process service and follow-through are keys to a successful venture.

When one markets a service business, one must keep in mind that reputation, value, delivery of "managing the evidence" refers to the act of informing customers that the service encounter has been performed successfully. It is best done in subtle ways like providing examples or descriptions of good and poor service that can be used as a basis of comparison. The underlying rationale is that a customer might not appreciate the full worth of the service if they do not have a good benchmark for comparisons.

However, it is worth remembering that many of the concepts, as well as many of the specific techniques, will work equally well whether they are directed at products or services. In particular, developing a marketing strategy is much the same for products and services, in that it involves selecting target markets and formulating a marketing mix. Thus, Theodore Levitt suggested that "instead of talking of 'goods' and of 'services', it is better to talk of 'tangibles' and 'intangibles'". Levitt also went on to suggest that marketing a physical product is often more concerned with intangible aspects (frequently the 'product service' elements of the total package) than with its physical properties. Charles Revson made a famous comment regarding the business of Revlon Inc.: 'In the factory we make cosmetics. In the store we sell hope.' Arguably, service industry marketing merely approaches the problems from the opposite end of the same spectrum.

Characteristics of Services

Intangibility

They cannot be seen, handled, smelled, etc. There is no need for storage because services are difficult to conceptualise, marketing them requires creative visualisation to effectively evoke a concrete image in the customer's mind. From the customer's point of view, this attribute makes it difficult to evaluate or compare services prior to experiencing the service.

Prior to purchase, much service promotion must rely on performance attributes which can only be measured after a purchase experience (tangible goods have search qualities). Also professional services have credence qualities. Need to use promotional tools to help customers perceive a service as highly tangibility.

1. Develop tangible representation of the service, i.e., credit card serves as the physical product with own image and benefits. Make advertising easier. Airlines use an aircraft. Traveller's umbrella.
2. Develop a brand image–seek out U Haul as opposed to a truck service
3. Word of mouth very important due to intangibility.
4. Offer discounts and free samples/service to customers who encourage friends to come
5. Offer tangible benefits in sales promotions, must be consistent with customers needs/want
6. Establish a clear product position, i.e., 24-hour outside service for repair of industrial equipment.

Intangibility also presents pricing problems. How should an auto mechanic charge for his/her services?

Visibility of the service may be a problem. Although a problem may have been fixed, you don't understand why? Need to explain the time needed for repair, and functions that were performed if you want the repair to be more tangible.

Psychological role of price is magnified since customers must rely on price as the sole indicator of service quality when other quality indicators are absent.

Perishability

Unsold service time is "lost", that is, it cannot be regained. It is a lost economic opportunity. For example, a doctor that is booked for only two hours a day cannot later work those hours–she has lost her economic opportunity. Other service examples are airplane seats (once the plane departs, those empty seats cannot be sold), and theatre seats (sales end at a certain point).

1. Inventory

Services cannot be stockpiled. Need to avoid excess unsatisfied demand and excess capacity leading to unproductive use of resources. To resolve inventory issues:

- market services to segments with different demand patterns
- market new services having counter cyclical demand patterns from the existing services
- market new services to compliment the existing services
- market service extras at non-peak times
- market new services not affected by the existing capacity constraints
- train personnel to do multiple tasks
- hire part time (PT) employees during peak hours
- educate consumers to use service at non-peak hours

- offer incentive, i.e., reduce price at non-peak times, this will not work in all instances, i.e., travel at non-peak hours.

2. Lack of transportability

Services tend to be consumed at the point of "production" (although this doesn't apply to outsourced business services).

3. Lack of homogeneity

Services are typically modified for each client or each new situation (customised). Mass production of services is very difficult. This can be seen as a problem of inconsistent quality. Both inputs and outputs to the processes involved providing services are highly variable, as are the relationships between these processes, making it difficult to maintain consistent quality.

4. Labour intensity

Services usually involve considerable human activity, rather than precisely determined process. Human resource management is important. The human factor is often the key success factor in service industries. It is difficult to achieve economies of scale or gain dominant market share without it.

5. Demand fluctuations

It is difficult to forecast demand (which is also true of many goods). Demand can vary by season, time of day, business cycle, etc.

6. Buyer involvement

Most service provisions require a high degree of interaction between the client and the service provider.

7. Inconsistency

Lawn care service cannot mow a lawn precisely the same way each time, but need to make the service as efficient and consistent as possible. Remedy: Use technology to help make the service provider more consistent...or replace workers with technology.

Inseparability

Leads to direct (short) channels of distribution. In some cases, it is possible to use intermediaries, travel agents, ATMs, etc. Close provider-customer relationship–employee interpersonal skills the very important. "Relationship managers", quality of relationships determines the probability of continued interchange with those parties in the future. Customers may become loyal to a particular employee as opposed to the company, prevalent in the advertising industry. Therefore, must make sure that multiple employees are capable of performing the same tasks.

The Extent of Services in the Economy

US is the world's first service economy. More than 75% of the workforce in the private sector is employed in the service industry. It accounts for more than $3 billion in output and contribute 60% of GNP. 60% of services are consumed by the final consumer. The increase in the service sector is a result of LT growth in the US economy deriving demand for additional services

- Travel
- Financial services
- Entertainment
- Personal care

Dual income families need for convenience. Increase in health awareness.

Service delivery

The delivery of a service typically involves five factors:

1. The service providers (e.g., the people)
2. Equipment used to provide the service (e.g., vehicles, cash registers)
3. The physical facilities (e.g., buildings, parking, waiting rooms)
4. The client
5. Other customers at the service delivery location

The **service encounter** is defined as all activities involved in the service delivery process. Some service managers use the term "moment of truth" to indicate that defining point in a specific service encounter where interactions are most intense.

Many business theorists view service provision as a performance or act (sometimes humorously referred to as dramalurgy, perhaps in reference to dramaturgy). The location of the service delivery is referred to as the stage and the objects that facilitate the service process are called props. A script is a sequence of behaviours followed by all those involved, including the client(s). Some service dramas are tightly scripted, and others are more general. Role congruence occurs when each actor follows a script that harmonizes with the roles played by the other actors.

In some service industries, especially health care, dispute resolution, and social services, a popular concept is the idea of the caseload, which refers to the total number of patients, clients, litigants, or claimants that a given employee is presently responsible for. On a daily basis, in all those fields, employees must balance the needs of any individual case against the needs of all other current cases as well as their own personal needs.

The Service-Goods Continuum

The dichotomy between physical goods and intangible services should not be given too much credence. These are not discrete categories. Most business theorists see a continuum with pure service on one terminal point and pure commodity good on the other terminal point. Most products fall between these two extremes. For example, a restaurant provides a physical good (the food), but also provides services in the form of ambience, the setting and clearing of the table, etc. And although some utilities actually deliver physical goods–like water utilities which actually deliver water–utilities are usually treated as services.

Fig. 8.1 Service Goods Continuum.

In a narrower sense, service refers to quality of customer service: the measured appropriateness of assistance and support provided to a customer. This particular usage occurs frequently in retailing the overall continuum process is represented in Fig. 8.1.

8.3   LIST OF ECONOMIC SERVICES

The following is an incomplete list of service industries, grouped into rough sectors. Parenthetical notations indicate how specific occupations and organisations can be regarded as service industries to the extent they provide an intangible service, as opposed to a tangible good.

1. Business functions (that apply to all organisations in general)

   - consulting
   - customer service
   - human resources administrators (providing services like ensuring that employees are paid accurately)

2. Child care

3. Cleaning, repair and maintenance services

   - janitors (who provide cleaning services)
   - gardeners
   - mechanics

4. Construction

   - carpentry
   - electricians (offering the service of making wiring work properly)
   - plumbing

5. Death care

   - coroners (who provide the service of identifying corpses and determining time and cause of death)
   - funeral homes (who prepare corpses for public display, cremation or burial)

6. Dispute resolution and prevention services

   - arbitration
   - courts of law (who perform the service of dispute resolution backed by the power of the state)
   - diplomacy
   - incarceration (provides the service of keeping criminals out of society)
   - law enforcement (provides the service of identifying and apprehending criminals)

- lawyers (who perform the services of advocacy and decision-making in many dispute resolution and prevention processes)
- mediation
- military (performs the service of protecting states in disputes with other states)
- negotiation (not really a service unless someone is negotiating on behalf of another)

7. Education (institutions offering the services of teaching and access to information)

- library
- museum
- school

8. Entertainment (when provided live or within a highly specialised facility)

- gambling
- movie theatres (providing the service of showing a movie on a big screen)
- performing arts productions
- sexual services (where legal)
- sports
- television

9. Fabric care

- dry-cleaning
- laundromat (offering the service of automated fabric cleaning)

10. Financial services

   (a) accounting
   (b) banks and building societies (offering lending services and safekeeping of money and valuables)
   (c) real estate
   (d) stock brokerages
   (e) tax return preparation

11. Food service industry

12. Hairdressing

13. Health care (all health-care professions provide services)

14. Information services

- data processing
- database services
- language interpretation
- language translation

15. Risk management

   - insurance
   - security

16. Social services

   - social work

17. Transport

   - service car rental

18. Utilities

   - electric power
   - natural gas
   - telecommunications
   - waste management
   - water industry

The Services Marketing Mix

Cowell states that what is significant about services are the relative dominance of intangible attributes in the make-up of the "service product". Services are a special kind of product. They may require special understanding and special marketing efforts.

The provision of the continuing education contains the element of the tangible and intangible. It usually provides a learning materials (physical good) and also number of the service activities (teaching processes, contact with customers, organisation of the courses, etc.). The distinction between physical and service offering can, therefore, be best understood as a matter of degree rather than in absolute term. The continuing education is service-based since the value of this product is dependent on the design and delivery of the Continuing Education (CE) courses rather than the cost of the physical product (teaching materials, CDs, etc.).

The **services marketing mix** is an extension of the 4 Ps framework. The essential elements of *product, promotion, price* and *place* remain but three additional variables—***people, physical*** *evidence* and *process*—are included to 7 Ps mix. The need for the extension is due to the high degree of direct contact between the CE providers and the customers, the highly visible nature of the service process, and the simultaneity of the production and consumption. While it is possible to discuss people, physical evidence and process within the original-Ps framework (for example, people can be considered part of the product offering) the extension allows a more thorough analysis of the marketing ingredients necessary for successful services marketing.

People—Because of the simultaneity of production and consumption in services the CE staff occupies the key position in influencing customer's perceptions of product quality. In fact, the service quality is inseparable from the quality of service provider. An important marketing task is to set standards to improve quality of services provided by employees and monitor their performance. Without training and control employees tend to be variable in their performance leading to variable service quality. Training is crucial so that employees understand the appropriate forms of behaviour and trainees adopt the best practices of the andragogy.

Physical evidence—This is the environment in which the service is delivered and any tangible goods that facilitate the performance and communication of the service. Customers look for clues to the likely quality of a service also by inspecting the tangible evidence. For example, prospective customers may look to the design of learning materials, the appearance of facilities, staff, etc.

Process—This means procedures, mechanism and flow of activities by which a service is acquired. Process decisions radically affect how a service is delivered to customers. The service in CE includes several processes, e.g., first contact with customers, administrative procedure regarding course delivery, preparation, delivery and evaluation of the courses. The following guidelines can be useful for successful CE management:

- Ensure that marketing happens at all levels from the marketing department to where the service is provided.
- Consider introducing flexibility in providing the service; when feasible, customise the service to the needs of customers.
- Recruit high quality staff, treat them well and communicate clearly to them: their attitudes and behaviour are the key to service quality and differentiations.
- Attempt to market to existing customers to increase their use of the service, or to take up new service products.
- Step up a quick response facility to customer problems and complaints.
- Employ new technology to provide better services at lower costs.
- Use branding to clearly differentiate service offering from the competition in the minds of target customers.

The Differential Advantage and Branding

Only few products are unique. Often the challenge lies in finding a way to differentiate your products from a rival's near-identical offerings. The basic question says: "How can I get an advantage over the competitor?"

When your products are better than those of your competitors, and when customers recognise this superiority, you have a real advantage. Few organisations are in this position. Most find that there is a little or nothing to distinguish their own products from competitors. To gain competitive advantage, uncover not just differences but also attributes that customers value. Make sure the differences are meaningful to customers, so that your product is preferable to the others available. Often it is the little things that count. Customers may choose your product over a competitor's identical product because they prefer your lecturers or because you give them coffee while delivering the courses. Pay attention to details that could make a difference. A genuine customer-centric approach will differentiate you from competitors. Show your commitment to customers and ensure that staffs are emphatic. Review company systems and processes to make them more customers focused. Strong, well-known products provide companies with a real competitive advantage. Use the power of branding to imbue your products with personality and meaning, ensuring they achieve a prominent position in the marketplace.

The right name helps to sell products and services. It bestows individuality and personality, enabling customers to identify with your offerings and to get to know them. It makes products and services tangible and real. Choose name that enhances your company's image and that are appropriate for the products and its positioning in the marketplace. Establish trust in your brand and customers will remain loyal.

Branding means developing unique attributes so that your products are instantly recognisable, memorable, and evoke positive association. Some brands have a solid and reliable personality, others are youthful and fun. Choose your company and product name, corporate colours, logo, design and promotional activity to help convey a personality and build a brand. Customers should be able to look at one of your products and assimilate all that you stand for in a second by recalling the brand values. But remember: *A strong brand is not a substitute for quality but an enhancement to it.*

The service attributes are friendliness, creativity, courtesy, helpfulness and knowledge ability. The creation of a corporate identity is a vital element of branding. Present an integrated, strong, instantly recognisable, individual image that is regarded in a positive way by your customers, and seize every opportunity to strengthen your corporate identity. It is important to maintain corporate identity consistently by issuing written guidelines for staff.

Marketing Strategy

A strategy gives business a defined route to follow and a clear destination. Build a marketing strategy and you will ensure that marketing is a long-term way of working, not a one-off activity.

A marketing strategy provides organisation with shared vision of the future. All too often, an organisation will perform a marketing task, such as direct mail shot, then sit back and see what happens. A strategic approach will ensure that you maximise returns on your marketing spending and boost the profits of your organisation.

Strategic marketing manager

- has a clear picture of the future
- anticipates changes in the market
- works towards clear long-term goals.

Non-strategic marketing manager

- lives day-to-day without planning
- reacts to changes in the market
- has only short-term objectives.

During the creation of the marketing strategy, the marketing manager should proceed as follows:

1. Create the team
2. Review current situation
3. Set objectives
4. Plan action
5. Implement strategy
6. Review strategy

Create your team

The first steps during preparation of the marketing strategy are the hardest part. It is important to bring together a strong team to help to prepare the marketing plan. The strategic elements must be understood by every member of team in order to assure the marketing success.

It is important to involve the people whose function touches on marketing, and those whose job involves considerable customer contact. Before embarking on your marketing strategy, establish common ground by agreeing definitions and purpose. Build the team unity; perhaps by organising an away day at a pleasant venue to discuss shared marketing issues and concerns. Show that you recognise the contribution each team member can offer.

Review Current Situation–Perform A SWOT Analysis

SWOT (Strengths, Weaknesses, Opportunities and Threats) Analysis of these four factors provides information on how to shape your marketing strategy. Devise objectives aimed at strengthening weak areas, exploiting strengths, seizing opportunities, and anticipating threats.

Setting objectives

Draw up your objectives carefully, because your entire marketing strategy will be structured around them, and ensure that they are measurable so that you can evaluate their success. Short-term objectives can be staging posts on the way towards fulfilling long-term goals. Analyse your situation and then ask: "What if we do nothing?" Will products become out of date? Will your competitors grow more powerful? Spend time asking "what if?" to help you realise the effects of not keeping up with customer needs and competitor activities. It can serve to spur action. If you have devised a set of objectives around which to build your marketing strategy, seek agreement for them across the organisation. Marketing is a discipline that cuts through many departmental boundaries. Marketing activity will have a knock-on effect in various parts of the operation so, for it to be effective, you will need the support of colleagues. Ensure they understand the need for these objectives and the impact they may have on their work.

Plan action: Investigate constraints, such as time and money, and then create a timetable of activity to give you a working marketing plan. The activities on your marketing timetable should be manageable and workable. The costs of not undertaking certain marketing activities, both in missed opportunities and the effect on your reputation, should be taken into consideration. Look at your marketing ideas and work out the costs of each. Remember that marketing involves meeting customer needs at a profit. To be justified, marketing activity should have a positive impact on the balance sheet. Examine not only the costs but also the benefit. An advertising company may cost a lot of money, but if it reaps profit amounting to several times its costs, it is cheaper.

Implementing strategy

Some organisations invest considerable effort in developing a strategy but enthusiasm and energy wane when it comes to implementation. Ensure that your marketing strategy is put into the action, not let to gather dust on a shelf. Assign each task or activity due for implementation within the next 12 months to a named person.

Review strategy

The world is not static. Things within your organisation or within your market are likely to change over the time. If they do, you might need to redefine your objectives. Review your objectives for every six-months or annually to check that you are till on track. Answering the following questions will help you evaluate the success of your marketing strategy:

1. Have profits increased since the strategy was implemented?
2. Have we seen an increase in our customer base?
3. Have we attracted a greater number of orders, or larger individual orders?
4. Has the number of product/service enquiries risen?
5. Has awareness of our organisation and its products or services increased?

Marketing in Non-profit Organisations

Non-profit organisations attempt to achieve some other objectives than profit. This does not mean that they are uninterested in income as they have to generate cash to survive. However, their primary goal is non-economic, e.g. to provide education.

Marketing is of growing importance to many non-profit organisations because of the need to generate funds in an increasingly competitive arena. Even organisations who rely on government-sponsored grants need to show how their work is of benefit to society: they must meet the needs of their customers. Many non-profit organisations rely on membership fees or donations, which means that communication to individuals and organisation is required, and they must be persuaded to join or make a donation. This requires marketing skills, which are being increasingly applied.

Characteristics of non-profit marketing

❖ *Education versus meeting current needs:* Some non-profit organisations see their role as not only meeting current needs of their customers but also educating them new ideas and issues, cultural development and social awareness. It can be done in harmony with providing CE as an additional value of CE course.

❖ *Multiple publics:* Most non-profit organisations serve several groups or publics. The two broad groups are donors, who may be individuals, trusts, companies and governmental bodies, and clients, who include audiences and beneficiaries. The need is to satisfy both donors and clients, complicating marketing task. For example, a community association providing also the CE courses may be partly funded by the local authority and partly by other donors (individuals or companies) and partly by clients. To succeed all the groups must be satisfied.

❖ *Measurement of success and conflicting objectives for profit-oriented organisations is measured ultimately on profitability:* For non-profit organisations measuring success is not so easy. In universities, for example, is success measured in research terms, number of students taught, the range of qualifications or the quality of teaching? The answer is that it is a combination of these factors, which can lead to conflict: more students and larger courses may reduce the time needed for research. Decision-making is therefore complex in non-profit oriented organisation.

❖ *Public scrutiny:* While all organisations are subject to public scrutiny, public sector nonprofit organisations are never far from public's attention. The reason is that they are funded from taxes. This gives them extra newsworthiness as all taxpayers are interested in how their money is being spent. They have to be particularly careful that they do not become involved in controversy, which can result in bad publicity.

8.4   DELIVERING QUALITY SERVICES

Service quality is very important for customers as well as service providers. To achieve competitive advantage, the service organisations are focusing more on the quality. The concept of quality has drawn massive attention in academic and business circles.

There are many definitions of quality. The word quality means different things to different people. To address such issues as the measurement of service quality, the identification of causes for shortfall in service quality and the design and implementation of corrective actions, it is essential for the service providers to have a common understanding of the concept of quality.

David Garvin identifies **five** perspectives on quality:

1. The transcendent view of quality is synonymous with innate excellence; a mark of uncompromising standards and high achievements. This viewpoint is often applied to the performing and visual arts. It argues that people learn to recognise quality only through the experience gained from repeated exposure. From a practical standpoint, however, suggesting that managers or customers will know quality when they see it is not very helpful.

2. The product-based approach sees quality as a precise and measurable variable. Differences in quality reflects differences in the amount of an ingredient or attribute possessed by the product. Because this view is totally objective, it fails to account for difference in the tastes, needs, and preferences of individual customers.

3. The premise that quality lies in the eyes of the beholder is the basis for user based definitions. These definitions equate quality with maximum satisfaction. This demand-oriented, subjective perspective recognises that the wants and needs of each customer is different.

4. The manufacturing oriented approach is basically supply based and is concerned with engineering and manufacturing practices. The manufacturing based approach focuses on conformance to internally developed specifications, which are often driven by productivity and cost containment objectives.

5. Quality is defined in terms of value and price by value-based definitions. Quality comes to be defined as 'affordable excellence' by considering the trade off between performance and price.

These views of David Garvin help us to explain the conflicts that arise between managers in different functional areas. In many senses quality is subjective. For many people quality implies excellence or luxury. Quality can also be measured in terms of fitness for purpose. In seeking quality service, customer needs and expectations may vary. Service quality is not easy to measure in precise manner.

The nature and characteristics of services can have an impact on quality issues.

- It is very difficult to measure and assess the service quality because of the intangibility of many services.
- Inseparability of the service from the service provider highlights the role and influence of the people in the service transaction, and on quality levels.
- A service is never exactly repeated and will always be variable to certain extent because of the heterogeneous characteristic of service.
- The perishable nature of services can lead to customer dissatisfaction if demand cannot be met.

The most appropriate approach in defining and measuring service is the user-based approach. The idea that quality is subjective and will be strongly linked to the individual's needs and expectations recognizes that customers have different criteria for judging service quality.

Valarie and her associates developed a survey research instrument called "**SERVQUAL**" to measure customer satisfaction with different aspects of service quality. This instrument is based on the assumption that the customers can measure a firm's service quality by comparing their perceptions of its service with their own expectations. "SERVQUAL" can be applied across a broad spectrum of service industries as a generic measurement tool. Reflecting the five important dimensions of service quality such as **tangibles, reliability,**

responsiveness, assurance and empathy, the scale contains 21 perception items in its basic form and a series of expectation items. On a wide range of specific service characteristics, the respondents complete a series of scales that measure their expectations of companies in a particular industry. Respondents are subsequently asked to record their perceptions, using those same characteristics of a specific company whose services they have used. When perceived performance ratings are lower than expectations, this is a sign of poor quality. The reverse indicates good quality.

The Tangibles Dimension

In forming the evaluations, the consumers often rely on the tangible evidence that surrounds the service because of the absence of a physical product. The tangibles dimension of 'SERVQUAL' compares consumer expectations with the firm's performance regarding the firm's ability to manage its tangibles. A firm's tangibles consist of a variety of objects such as carpeting, desks, lighting, wall colours, brochures, daily correspondence and the appearance of the firm's employees. The tangibles component in 'SERVQUAL' is two-dimensional—one focusing on equipment and facilities, the other focusing on HR & communications materials.

The tangibles component of 'SERVQUAL' is obtained via four expectations questions, i.e. E1 to E4 and four perception questions, i.e. P1 to P4. The perception questions apply to the specific firm under investigation whereas the expectations questions apply to excellent firms within a particular industry. Comparing the perception scores with the expectation scores provides a numerical variable that indicates the tangibles gap. The smaller the number, the smaller the gap, and the closer consumers' perceptions are to their expectations. The items that pertain to the tangibles dimension are given below.

Tangibles Expectations

E1-Excellent firms will have modern-looking equipment.
E2-The physical facilities at excellent firms will be visually appealing.
E3-Employees of excellent firms will be neat in appearance.
E4-In an excellent firm, the materials associated with the service will be visually appealing.

Tangibles Perceptions

P1-Firm ABC has modern-looking equipment.
P2-Firm ABC's physical facilities are visually appealing.
P3-Firm ABC's personnel are neat in appearance.
P4-Materials associated with the service are visually appealing at firm ABC.

The Reliability Dimension

The reliability dimension reflects the consistency and dependability of a firm's performance. Consumers perceive the reliability dimension to be the most important of the five 'SERVQUAL' dimensions. Failure to provide reliable service generally translates into an unsuccessful firm. 'SERVQUAL' measures the reliability gap as shown below:

Reliability Expectations

E5-When excellent firms promise to do something by a certain time, they will do so.
E6-When customers have a problem, excellent firms will show a sincere interest in solving it.
E7-Excellent firms will perform the service right the first time.
E8-Excellent firms will provide their services at the time they promise to do so.
E9-Excellent firms will insist on error-free records.

Reliability Perceptions

P5-When firm ABC promises to do something by a certain time, it does so.
P6-Firm ABC shows a sincere interest in solving your problem whenever you have a problem.
P7-Firm ABC performs the service right the first time.
P8-Firm ABC provides its services at the time it promises to do so.
P9-Firm ABC insists on error-free records.

The Responsiveness Dimension

A service firm's commitment to provide its services in a timely manner is reflected in responsiveness. The concern of the responsiveness dimension of 'SERVQUAL' is the willingness and/or readiness of personnel to provide a service. Sometimes the customers may face a situation in which the employees are busy in their own talk with their other colleagues while ignoring the needs of the customers. This is an example of unresponsiveness. The preparedness of the firm to provide the service is reflected in responsiveness. The 'SERVQUAL' expectation and perception items that address the responsiveness gap are given below:

Responsiveness Expectations

E10-Employees of excellent firms will inform the customers exactly when services will be performed.
E11-Employees of excellent firms will give genuine service to customers.
E12-Employees of excellent firms will always be willing to help customers.

E13-Employees of excellent firms will never be too busy to respond to customer requests.

Responsiveness Perceptions

P10-Employees of ABC firm will inform their customers when the service will be performed.
P11-Employees of ABC firm will give prompt and genuine service to customers.
P12-Employees of ABC firm are always willing to help customers.
P13-Employees of ABC firm are never too busy to respond to customer requests.

The Assurance Dimension

The competence of the firm, the courtesy it extends to its customers and the security of its operatives are addressed by the assurance dimension of 'SERVQUAL'. Competence in this context is the firm's knowledge and skill in performing its service courtesy refers to how the firm's employees deal with the customers and with their possessions. Courtesy includes such aspects as politeness, friendliness, and consideration for the customer's property. Security is also an important component of the assurance dimension. Security reflects a customer's feelings that he is free from risk, danger and doubt. The 'SERVQUAL' items used to address the assurance gap are given below.

Assurance Expectations

E14-The behaviour of personnel of excellent firms will instill confidence in customers.
E15-Customers of excellent firms will feel safe in their transactions.
E16-Personnel of excellent firms will be consistently courteous to customers.
E17-Personnel of excellent firms will have the knowledge to answer customer questions.

Assurance Perceptions

P14-The behaviour of personnel of ABC firm instills confidence in customers.
P15-Customers feel safe in their transactions with firm ABC.
P16-Personnel of firm ABC are consistently courteous to their customers.
P17-Personnel of firm ABC have the knowledge to answer the customer questions.

The Empathy Dimension

The ability to experience another's feelings as one's own is called as empathy. Empathetic firms have not lost touch with what it is like to be a customer of their own firm. Empathetic firms understand the needs of their customers and make the services accessible to their customers. Firms that do not provide their customers individualised attention and that offer operating hours convenient to the firm and not to its customers fail to demonstrate empathetic behaviour. The empathy dimension of 'SERVQUAL' addresses the empathy gap in the following manner.

Empathy Expectations

E18-Excellent firms will give individual attention to its customers.
E19-Excellent firms will have operating hours convenient to all their customers.
E20-Excellent firms will have personnel who give customers personal attention.
E21-Excellent firms will have the customers' best interest at heart.
E22-The specific needs of the customers will be understood by the employees of excellent firms.

Empathy Perceptions

P18-Firm ABC gives individual attention to customers.
P19-Firm ABC has operating hours convenient to all its customers.
P20-Employees of firm ABC give personal attention to all its customers.
P21-Firm ABC has customers' best interest at heart.
P22-Employees of firm ABC understand their customer's specific needs.

Limitations of 'SERVQUAL'

'SERVQUAL' though an excellent instrument for measuring service quality is not free from several limitations. The service providers must be well versed with the limitations of the instrument and also the gap theory methodology on which it is based. The major limitations of the 'SERVQUAL' instrument are discussed below:

1. The 'SERVQUAL' measures the expectations of the customers in an ideal firm in a particular service industry. This may or may not be relevant to the capabilities of a particular service firm or the group of service firms available to a customer.

2. Another frequent criticism of the 'SERVQUAL' instrument is its generic nature. Since it is not industry particular, it does not assess variables which may be industry specific.

3. Length of the 'SERVQUAL' questionnaire is another major issue of criticism. A combination of perception and expectation items of 'SERVQUAL' results in a 44 item survey instrument. The argument is that the 44 items are highly repetitive and unnecessarily increase the length of the questionnaire. Further argument is that the expectations section of the instrument is of no real value and that the perceptions section along should be used the measure the service quality.

4. Another limitation of 'SERVQUAL' instrument related with the gap methodology used for assessing the level of service quality. Evaluating consumer expectations after a service has been provided will bias the responses of consumers. If the customers had a positive experience, they will tend to report lower scores for their expectations, so

there is a measurable gap between what they expected and the service they received. If a customer had a negative experience, the opposite occurs. Customers tend to report higher scores for their expectations, so there would be a negative gap between expectations and perceived level of service.

5. Another frequent criticism of the 'SERVQUAL' instrument is that the five proposed dimensions of service quality—reliability, responsiveness, assurance, empathy and tangibles—do not hold up under statistical scrutiny. Consequently, opponents of 'SERVQUAL' question the validity of the specific dimensions in the measurement instrument.

6. The sixth major criticism of 'SERVQUAL' relates to the instrument's ability to predict consumer purchase intentions. Research has indicated that the perception section alone of the 'SERVQUAL' scale is a better predictor of purchase intentions than the combined expectations-minus-perception instrument. The 'SERVQUAL' instrument is criticised on the point that the satisfaction has a more significant effect on purchase intentions than does service quality.

Concluding Remarks about 'SERVQUAL' Instrument

1. **The relevance of employees of customer relations department:** The 'SERVQUAL' instrument highlights many important points that service providers should consider while examining service quality. The attitudes and performance of customer relations executives determine heavily the perceptions of customers about the services. The interaction between are employees and the customers directly determine the responsiveness, empathy and assurance dimensions. The tangible dimension depends partly on the appearance and dress of the employees of the service provider.

2. **Process is equally important as outcome:** The customers judge the service based on the final outcome and also the process through which the service passes through. The nature and frequency of the service is also important in addition to its delivery. Finally, the customer satisfaction depends on the production and consumption of the services.

3. **Difficulty in predicting consumer perceptions:** There are several factors outside the control of the organisation that may not be readily apparent, but the ratings of service quality dimensions will be influenced to a large extent by such factors.

Despite its limitations 'SERVQUAL' continue to be a frequently used instrument to measure service quality and is presently being modified to take into consideration the service quality issues in e-business. When used in conjunction with other forms of measurement, 'SERVQUAL' provides a valuable diagnostic tool for measuring the firm's service quality performance.

8.5   MARKETING OF DIFFERENT SERVICES

Classification of Services

The following flow charts 1 and 2 visualise various classes of services along with the organisations that provide them.

Flow Chart 1:

Consumer Services

Unlike consumer services, industrial services are offered to the business organisations, although there may be some variable common in both.

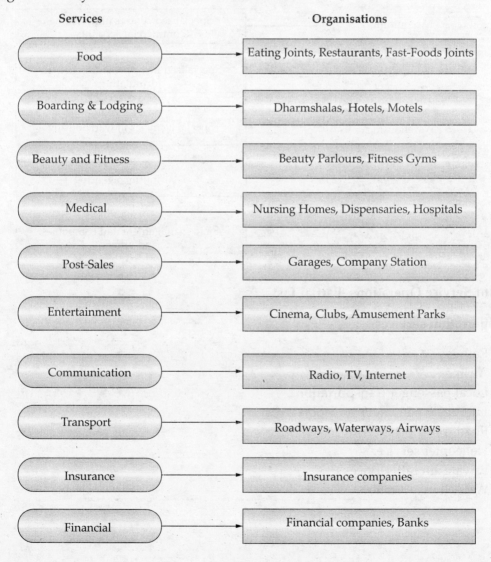

Services	Organisations
Food	Eating Joints, Restaurants, Fast-Foods Joints
Boarding & Lodging	Dharmshalas, Hotels, Motels
Beauty and Fitness	Beauty Parlours, Fitness Gyms
Medical	Nursing Homes, Dispensaries, Hospitals
Post-Sales	Garages, Company Station
Entertainment	Cinema, Clubs, Amusement Parks
Communication	Radio, TV, Internet
Transport	Roadways, Waterways, Airways
Insurance	Insurance companies
Financial	Financial companies, Banks

Flow Chart 2:

There is a tremendous market for services in the large-scale, medium-scale and small-scale sector as well. A partial list of services is given below.

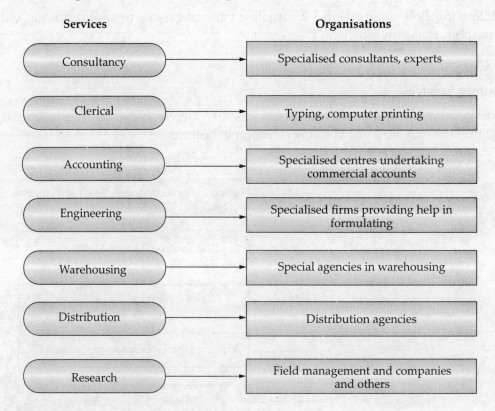

Services	Organisations
Consultancy	Specialised consultants, experts
Clerical	Typing, computer printing
Accounting	Specialised centres undertaking commercial accounts
Engineering	Specialised firms providing help in formulating
Warehousing	Special agencies in warehousing
Distribution	Distribution agencies
Research	Field management and companies and others

Type of Service Operations–Partial List

Transportation services

- Railway
- Airlines
- Local passenger transportation
- Inter-state passenger transportation
- Road transportation
- Helicopter service
- Private aircraft services
- Water transportation

Public utilities services

- Water supply services
- Electric supply
- Gas supply

Communication services

- Telephone
- Postal and courier
- Radio and TV broadcasting
- Telecommunication
- Teleconferencing
- Satellite

Trading services

- Wholesaling and retailing

Financial and insurance services

- Banking
- Leasing
- Security and brokerage
- Investment banking
- Retail banking
- Insurance
- Credit reporting

Real estate services

- Renting
- Investment consultants
- Property consultants
- Building and real estate management

Marketing related services

- Marketing consultancy

- Advertising
- Telemarketing
- Sales promotion
- New product development
- New product testing
- Market research

Government provided services

- Infrastructure
- Defence
- Police
- Transport
- Broadcasting
- Education
- Medical and others

Engineering services

- Equipment inspection
- Designing
- Construction design
- Architectural
- Facility planning
- Technical research
- ERP

Entertainment services

- Motion pictures
- Video parlours
- Game parlours
- Theme parks
- Party
- Event management
- Discos
- Bowl parks
- Clubs

Business and professional services

- Records management
- Management consultancy
- Legal
- Accounting
- Meeting facilities
- Office management

Hospitality services

- Hotels and restaurants
- Catering
- Home delivery

Others services

- Janitorial
- Security
- Public relations
- Landscaping/Lawn care
- Printing
- Data processing
- Speech writing
- Professional speaking
- Educational
- Training
- Travel related
- Courier
- Health and hospital
- Equipment rental
- Interior designing
- Laundry and cleaning
- Computer programming
- Personal grooming
- Fax
- Old age homes
- Warehousing
- Window dressing

- Repair and maintenance
- Home-help

1. Financial Services

Bank Marketing

The banking industry is undergoing a revolution caused by deregulation. The causes for bank marketing can be seen as:

✠ Rising customer needs and expectations due to improvements in general standard of living.

✠ Entry of foreign and private sector banks in India.

✠ Economic liberalisation of Indian economy.

✠ Phenomenal growth of competition due to economic liberalisation.

✠ Rise in the Indian middle class with considerable resources.

✠ Government intervention in protecting the interest of consumers.

Thus, the significance of bank marketing in Indian banking system is undeniable if they have to survive in the competitive environment. Bank marketing is not just advertising and promotion campaign but a managerial process by which services are matched with markets. This indicates evolving a suitable marketing strategy, which suits the needs of the customer. The major step in this direction is to blend the marketing variables—product, price, place, promotion, people, process and physical evidence, to satisfy the requirements of the customer.

ICICI Bank

The way ICICI Bank has promoted itself to become a leader in consumer perception has few parallels in the Indian service industry, especially when you consider the fact that it was earlier a state development bank in the unglamorous business of project financing, and significantly owned by the government. At least in the public perception, it was a typical government bank, until it literally changed its colours to an attractive orange-red. Along with a spanking new logo, and aggressive marketing which included print, television, and personal selling through mailers and telemarketing, the ICICI Bank almost blanketed the landscape and the consumer's mind space in the years 2000-02, to emerge as a leading player in the retail banking industry.

From an NBFC to a Bank: Kotak Mahindra's Strategic Shift

Kotak Mahindra, which started as an NBFC (non-banking financial services company) and has now become a bank. A major paradigm shift is taking place in the way corporate finance is structured. Traditionally, banks in India approached corporate and said "here is our bag of money". I don't think that is sustainable any longer. You have to go to the supply chain and look for gaps.

If you take the automobile sector, for instance, we are end-to-end providers. We have done car financing at one end of the retail chain. Now we are going to the other end, financing the ancillary units and suppliers. We do about ₹2,000 crore of car financing a year. At any point of time, we have about ₹300 crore of dealer finance. We do about ₹1,000 crore of commercial vehicle financing. We are targeting another ₹500 crore at the auto ancillary unit level. The total churn or the transaction volumes in the auto sector would be in excess of ₹5,000 crore a year. We are number three in auto financing, behind ICICI and HDFC Bank. As a vertical, it is a large part of our balance sheet.

If you are in end-to-end financing, we can compensate the reductions, if any, in fee income. But the auto sector is growing at 30 per cent. We are trying to replicate the auto financing model in other sectors–in FMCG, pharmaceuticals, tractors, etc. Don't look at the profits of Kotak Primus in the normal way. That is because there is a very large royalty that Kotak Primus pays the bank, under our agreement with Ford. If you look at Kotak Primus's operating profits (before the royalty payments), it is quite good. Spreads have been under pressure. But even today, I can get a customer for car finance at 15 per cent and 7 per cent. it depends on the risk profile that you want to take on. This is true to some extent. As you go deeper, you get higher returns, but you also run higher risks. We cover the top 60 to 70 cities now. Primarily, we'll stay there. But as a bank, we do have the obligation to go to rural areas and we will do that. We see the conversion as conferring a longer term advantage. We did not have access to call money earlier. No doubt there is a branch cost, but that is met not only by deposits but also by investment products. We see this as a stronger model.

If you have ₹100, you'll put ₹80 in various products. But leave around ₹20 in the SB account. We need to capture that and make it grow bigger. There is a fundamental change happening, globally.

The trick to get stable money for us is to be in the middle of the flow. As we do have more of investment products, and keep on the churn, some part of the flow will keep on getting left behind and the residue will gradually grow. Other banks, which are focused on the stock, may not be able to hold on to it.

Insurance Marketing

The term insurance marketing refers to the marketing of insurance services with the motto of customer-orientation and profit-generation. A fair blending of profit-generation and customer-satisfaction makes the ways for development and expansion. The insurance marketing focuses on the formulation of an ideal mix for the insurance business so that the insurance organisations survive and thrive in the right perspective. The quality of services can be improved by formulating a fair mix of the core and peripheral services. The persuasion process can be speeded up with the support of creative promotional measures. The premium and bonus decisions can be made motivational, the gap between the services-promised and services-offered can be bridged over, the quality and value based personnel can make possible performance-orientation and these developments can make the insurance organisations stronger enough to face the challenges and threats in the markets. It is meant managerial proficiency, which makes an assault on unethical and unfair practices by regulating profiteering. The organisations thus are found successful in increasing the market share, maximising the profitability and keeping on the process of development. In the Indian perspective where rural-orientation needs a prime attention, the insurance marketing may prove to be a device for combating regional imbalance by maintaining the sectoral balance. As an investment institution, the rural development oriented projects make ways for the transformation of rural society. The selection of risks (product planning), policy writing (customer service) rating or actuarial (pricing) and agency management (distribution)—all marketing activities make up an integrated marketing strategy. We can't neglect that during the yester decades, there have been considerable developments in the perception of customer servicing firms like banking and insurance companies. Particularly in the developing countries like ours, the organisational objectives advocate spreading of insurance services much more widely and in particular to the rural areas and especially to the economically backward classes with a view to reaching all insurable persons. This naturally necessitates an integral marketing strategy. In other words, market orientation in place of sales orientation is need of the hour. Hence, the marketing concept in the insurance business focuses on the formulation of marketing mix or a control over the whole group of marketing activities that make up an integrated marketing strategy.

Insurance Marketing in India

The insurance sector plays a vital role in the economic development of our nation. It acts as a mobiliser of savings, financial intermediary, and promoter of investment activities, stabiliser of financial markets and a risk manager. India is still an under-insured country in the world. It is at the 18th position among life insurance markets and 28th in non-life insurance markets in the world. This indicates that there is a huge potential, yet to be explored. The business of life insurance in India in its existing form started in India in the year 1818 with the establishment of the Oriental Life Insurance Company in Kolkata. To survive in the industry, they analyse the emerging requirements of the policy holders/insured and they are in the forefront in providing essential services and introducing novel products. Thereby they become niche specialists, who provide the right service to the right person in right time.

ING Vysya Mutual Fund

The ING Vysya mutual fund is still a relatively small player in the country's ₹1 lakh crore-plus asset management industry. It has, however, gone through significant modifications in the recent times, ones that are expected to support its expansion programmes. The mutual fund (MF), which currently manages a few basic schemes, has proposed to introduce a couple of others in the near future. One, the ING group has increased its equity stake in Vysya Bank to 43.99 per cent from the 20 per cent it held earlier. The bank has been renamed as ING Vysya Bank subsequently. The group now operates as ING Vysya in India through over 500 branches spread across the country. Two, there has been an infusion of fresh capital in ING Investment Management (1) Pvt. Ltd, which is the asset management company. This has been done to strengthen its presence. The fresh infusion came with ING Vysya Bank acquiring a stake of about 26 per cent in the AMC. This reflects the nature of ING's long-term commitment to the Indian market. At the moment it is present in eight cities with more than ₹1,100 crore of assets under the management. It is believed that the inherent strengths can be leveraged to formulate more schemes with a view to create better value. The liquid and short-term products are already among the top-rated names in their respective categories. The future looks bright for the asset management industry and only those players with strong corporate backing would be the likely survivors. The bigger ones absorb small and individual fund houses could do well. This would make competition even more aggressive. It is proposed to come out with a monthly income plan (MIP) and an index linked product. These would be in line with the attempt to cater to the ever increasing needs of investors. The MIP, which would be launched immediately, is aimed at high net worth individuals, retired people and pensioners, among others. To be armed with certain additional services, which would set it apart from other simple MIPs, it would enable them to secure a steady, regular stream of income.

2. Health Services

Health Industry

Until recently the health care industry was at the crossroads, still unsure which way to go. Today, it is in for exciting times. Low costs, combined with excellent facilities, have provided the perfect formula for India to become a major player in the $2.8 trillion worldwide health care industry. Today, the cost of health care in India is only one-tenth the cost in the US in cases of major surgeries. With costs of providing health care low, and with global standards available, the world cannot compete with us. The cost of a heart surgery at Apollo is $2,500 as compared to $30,000 in the US. Bone marrow transplants cost $50,000 in India as against $400,000 in US. India's attraction as a low cost, high-quality centre for health care may be new but the signs are visible. In 1998-99, Apollo Hospitals conducted heart surgeries on 91 patients from Tanzania. In Chennai, Apollo treats around 30 Sri Lankans a day. Daily 40 patients are from Muscat registered in Apollo hospitals in Delhi, Chennai and Hyderabad for treatment. "Health care not only brings in direct purchase of health care, but it also encourages a lot of expenditure, on travel, lodging and boarding which, translated, means foreign exchange". And India has enough embassies and tourism development corporations to spread the message.

Outdoor sport:

- Golf
- Water sports–jet-ski, windsurfing, boating
- Tennis
- Adventure sports–'paint ball' battle games, hot air ballooning, skydiving

Indoor sport:

- Snooker
- Gymnasia and health clubs
- Ice and roller-skating
- Ten-pin bowling

Hospital Services

Marketing has grown in importance for hospitals, looking to strengthen their position in a increasingly competitive health care marketplace. A world-class hospital is a multidisciplinary superspeciality medical centre of international standards. Most hospitals today are well equipped with the most advanced diagnostic and treatment facilities. They try for total health care preventive and curative. Most hospitals in India have grown to a truly world class stature over the years. Some hospitals have even obtained ISO 9002 certification.

Ex., Mallya hospital, Bangalore. ISO 9002 quality assurance is a structured and user-friendly set of systems, which allows the staff at all levels of the hospital to follow simple procedures, which make the most complex tasks easy and efficient. It frees the senior management of everyday stress in observing and monitoring tasks, which have to be completed on daily basis.

Virtual Hospital Strategy

Hospital will soon go hi-tech, not so much in terms of sophisticated medical equipment, but in that a patient's kith and kin can virtually visit him/her from any part of the world and the patient too can communicate with them and relieve their undue anxiety. Bangalore has emerged as a pioneer in the design of an interactive website used in making virtual visits to hospitals, thus introducing a human element hitherto unthought of. This breakthrough in the usage of information technology for patients was achieved by the Bangalore-based Think Ahead Incorporated, designing the website for a hospital here. The primary advantage of this technology is the mitigation of undue anxiety of relatives particularly sons and daughters, children of patients who are settled abroad–who cannot at the bed side of patients undergoing treatment for a heart ailment or a major surgery. The 'Virtual Family Visit' allows relatives to see real-time images of patients through audio-video files which can be downloaded on their computer by entering the hospital website through the Internet. These files of the patient are shot by the hospital using a Webcam (web camera) to show the convalescing patient and his message for his family members. The files are then unloaded in the hospital website. The family members can also communicate with the patient by way of sending on-line get well cards to patients. Besides, they can also get reports of the patient's condition from the doctor-in-charge, if the relative so desires.

Wockhardt Hospital, where the virtual family visit is in use, the relatives are physically able to see their near and dear ones recuperating from the treatment which avoid emotional trauma. This facility in hospital is particularly useful, when a relative is unable to rush to the hospital to be physically present due to various reasons. Besides, the patient himself is on the road to faster recovery when he communicates with his loved ones. The use of web technology for virtual hospital visit here is said to be the first of its kind in the world. The claim may be true considering that family bonds in the country are very strong and even extends to close relatives. It may also be one of the reasons, why such a facility had not been thought of in other parts of the world. Besides, scaled-down joint families are still prevalent, where this technology would come in handy.

3. Hospitality Services Including Travel, Hotels and Tourism

Transport Marketing

The environment in which the corporations are functioning is unique and it is entirely different from that of commercial and industrial enterprises. Some of the important elements of marketing environment for transport services are presented below followed by brief analysis of each of the elements. One of the important and unique features of demand for transport service is that it is a derived demand. Because, the demand for transport service arises due to the demand for other goods and services arise. For instance, if Mr. X wants to purchase a television set he has to travel from his place to the place where the television set, is available. Thus, the demand for goods and services creates demand for transport service, as one has to travel from one place to another to attend to some work or to affect some purchases. Hence, the demand for transport services is derived out of the demand for others.

Before anatomising other dimensions of marketing management, the conceptual exposition of transport marketing is presented. The term transport marketing is identification of the most profitable markets now and in future, assessing the present and future needs of the users, setting business development goals and making plans to meet them and further managing the services and promoting them to achieve the plans—all in the context of the changing business environmental conditions to cater to the changing socioeconomic needs. The aforesaid facts make it clear that the term transport marketing is application of marketing principles by the transport organisations in which the marketing professionals make sincere efforts to market the services in such a way that generation of profit, satisfaction to users and protection of social interests are made easier.

Airlines, Cruise and Ferry Lines, Passenger Railways, Coach and Bus Travel, Car Hire: The range of airline services has increased considerably, not only in terms of frequency of flights and number of destinations, but also in terms of different services, and differing levels of service to meet different passenger needs. This shows the important role marketing plays as competition and demand intensifies.

Passenger rail services have also changed, and their role in tourism is wide as with, for example, Eurorail tickets allowing extensive international travel at a basic (service) standard for students and budget tourists, to the luxury of the Venice-Simplon Orient Express where the train voyage is the holiday. Cruise lines are operating different services tailored to consumers' budgets, and other shipping lines involved in the tourist industry, especially the car ferry operators, are broadening and upgrading their range of services and facilities to meet consumer expectations, and to remain competitive. Coach and bus companies have acted in a similar fashion and these, together with car rental companies, are also included in this sector.

Tour Operators

Package Tours, Speciality Tours

Tour operators are the firms which specialise in providing the whole holiday package, incorporating travel and accommodation needs for the consumer. They range from highly specialised operations such as Abercrombie and Kent who take small groups on safari or expedition-type holidays, to large operators offering services at all different levels to cater for budget, family, or singles holidays to 'near' or 'faraway' destinations. Thomas Cook is one of the best known of such operators; they also offer travel agency and financial services to their consumers. An independent local coach firm may also be a tour operator, and indeed, many transportation companies also offer holiday packages.

Tourism Destination Operators

Theme Parks, Heritage Centres

This is a new category in many senses, as it is an area of the tourism industry which has seen massive growth in the development of theme parks and other types of artificial tourist destinations in recent years. However, Disneyland and Disneyworld in America were the forerunners of this development in tourism marketing, and they have been well established for decades. It is due to the recent growth, and the continuing trends, which make it an area which should be considered separately as a tourism industry. The new Euro Disney theme park in France is an example of a tourism destination operation. On a smaller scale, heritage parks which are being developed from Britain's industrial wasteland such as Wigan Pier, which attracted over half a million tourists in 1991 and similar attractions, now represent a significant amount of tourism activity. All the above sectors of the tourism industry, while quite distinct in themselves, have many aspects in common. There are certain features of tourism marketing which differ from other industries. The impact of environmental forces, for example, can provide different pressure opportunities for tourism than for other service sector industries.

Airline Marketing

The air transport is the modern and efficient component of the transportation system. The expansion of air transport through the world has been post-Second World War phenomenon. India did not lag behind in developing air transport. Its progress after the commencement of the First Five-Year Plan has been accelerated keeping in view the growing economic activities in the country.

In the field of international passenger originating or terminating in a particular destination, air transport plays a very important role as far as passenger traffic is concerned. In international passenger traffic, air transport is fast developing and capturing the traffic handled by sea transport. Air transport, which handled almost an equal number of passengers as sea transport, now accounts for nearly four times the traffic by sea. Airlines play an important part in the tourism world. The measures taken to increase capacity and speed means that their part will continue to increase in future. For some years the airline companies have sought to increase their traffic by using modern aircraft and by a pricing policy taking into account the purpose of travel and elasticity of demand. The policy is determined by increased capacity coming from new aircraft, on one hand and the stiff competition chartered air transport companies on the other hand. Services are by their nature intangible. They cannot be inspected or sampled in their purchase; therefore, an element of risk is involved on the part of the purchaser. The travelling cannot be seen but can only be felt. This makes marketing much more difficult for service products have many drawbacks, the fact that a travel agent does not have to pour products before selling them to clients, reduces the agent's commitment to the sale and hire particular brands. Tourism marketers must overcome the drawbacks posed by the intangibles and there are a number of ways in which this has been achieved in practice. During and before oil prices sent air fares rocketing, seats were made available to the public at very low fares to enable prospective purchases to 'sample' the experience of flying. More recently, British Airways experimented with low price flights to help prospective passengers overcome their fear of flying.

Secondly, services are heterogeneous and airline services are not exception to this. The official, checking the baggage is unlikely to treat passengers with the same consideration all the time; similarly it is difficult to obtain consistent service from the airhostess on all the flights. While good quality control procedures can help avoid variations in performance, they cannot overcome the human problems inherent in the performance of airline services. The airline product is a highly perishable one. An airline seat not sold today is lost forever. This factor is of great importance for marketing, particularly while pricing. The 'stand-by' fares offered by airlines reflect their need to off-load products before their sale potential is lost. Substantial reductions are also offered during off-season or periods of low demand. Further, airline services are highly personalised, the production being the outcome of the seller. In an airline service whatever be the quality of the food in the flight, however comfortable the seating facility is, however, attractive the doctor, services is much an integral part of the product that it would be unlikely that we should be prepared to purchase it from a poor representative. The airline stewards who cater to our needs en route is an essential element of the product, we are purchasing and their social skills in dealing with us are very important. Hence, there are several important considerations to take into account while marketing airlines. It is a fascinating product to create and sell.

There are three important domestic airlines in India (1) Indian Airlines–the biggest one but in the public sector, (2) Jet Airways and (3) Sahara Airlines, both in the private sector. The Mumbai–Delhi Sector is the one which provides the maximum volume of business and is being handled by all the three. Sahara Airlines started the fare war in July 1999 by reducing the airway fare to ₹3,555 and added a bonus of gift of ₹500 for every passenger flying Sahara on this route. Jet Airways followed suit and reduced the fare to ₹4,111. Indian Airlines did not remain behind and reduced the fare to ₹3,800. Not only the fares were slashed, many value-added benefits were provided to the passengers. Jet Airways was hit the hardest and approached the Indian Airlines but the latter did not seem to be in a mood to respond.

A survey by the Marketing and Development Research Analysis (MDRA) concluded, "65.4 per cent of the airline passengers choose their airline on the basis of price". *The Economic Times* feels that fare war may spread to other sectors as well. But by making flying affordable for a much larger number of Indians it may lead to an increase in the growth of civil aviation in India.

Jet Airways–A Services Marketing Case Study: This case examines the success and problems of Jet Airways in the domestic airline industry from a service perspective. Various aspects of services marketing in the airline industry and some innovations brought about by Jet are also highlighted for analysis. With revenues of ₹3000 crore and 6.4 million passengers in 2002-03, and in the tenth year of its operations, Jet Airways has managed to be India's most popular domestic airline. The customer-oriented approach and on-time performance and schedules ensured that Jet continued to be the first choice of air travellers. However, the year 2003 was not a favourable one for the company. The cash profits were slender, the market share had stagnated, and falling seat utilisation rates had started posing problems. With stiff competition from Sahara in the same services cape and the newly created Air Deccan, will Jet Airways survive the turbulence and remain the leader in the domestic aviation service business? Can its legendary excellence on ground and in-flight service, largely responsible for its 'super brand' status, and a source of competitive advantage for the company, enable it to maintain its leadership position in the aviation industry? Jet launched its first customer loyalty programme in 1994, which until 1999 had fetched 30,000 customers. With a view to increasing the loyal customer base, Jet redrafted and relaunched the loyalty programme in December 1999, christening it as "Jet Privilege" (JP). JP customers were not required to pay a membership fee unlike the other loyalty programmes in the market. JP did not require passengers to produce boarding cards or other proof of travel. A passenger started earning free JP miles (points) the moment he or she took the first flight and later the concept of retro-credit was also introduced. JP was a 3 tier frequent flyer programme (blue, silver, gold), with different levels of privileges depending on the number of miles and flights the customer accumulated. Typical benefits included access to special louges, tele-check-in, guaranteed reservations, extra baggage allowance, hotel discounts, and others. JP also involved a joint cooperation with British Airways and KLM/North-west. The miles earned on domestic Indian routes could be redeemed on international flights. In 2001, Jet Airways introduced an in-flight shopping programme-Jet Mall offering travellers the advantage of ordering products from a catalogue. The intention was to provide additional services to customers. It was introduced keeping in mind the busy schedules of the business travellers and flexibility for them to shop on-board without wasting any time. The specially designed catalogue featured quality products - both branded and unbranded at attractive prices. The customer had to complete the order form, along with their credit or charge card number and hand over the same to the cabin crew or alternately post the order form later. The products were to be home delivered to them within two to four weeks. Jet excelled at managing customer expectations. In 2002, customers of Jet Airways received a communication from the airline that requested their cooperation in observing the revised check-in timing and helping the airline in working towards on time flight departures. The communication explained that the need heightened security checks was leading to delays and in an effort to prevent this; the airline had revised is check-in-timings. While sending out this communication, the airline placed in perspective the main reason behind flight delays (most airline passengers simply assume that the airline is at fault) and solicited its passengers' cooperation in ensuring that flights leave on time. The other benefit in such an exercise is that the airline's frontline personnel were more effectively supported when faced with passenger ire at flight delays as well as late check-ins. Jet adopted three ways to keep an eye on its performance in areas that were important to customer service (called key result areas or KRAs in JET jargon). The first was feedback from its customer service department whose staff strength. The second was part-time consultants flying undercover and the third was the customer service questionnaire placed on all Jet flights and answered by about 700 of the 17,000 passengers who took Jet's 255 flights daily. The KRAs where it constantly tried to improve its performance were as follows: (a) Check-in: The process normally took 40 seconds, but if an error at the counter pushed the time taken to much more than 2 minutes, it exceeded the threshold of customer tolerance, as per international standards. In November 1998, 91 per cent of Jet passengers felt that the airline was able to check them in less than two minutes. (b) Customer complaints: When customers at some airports complained of long check-in waiting period, Jet used the allotted space to create more counters and reduced waiting time to within international standards. The customer feedback also prompted them to introduce 'through check-in', a service offered by all international airlines. (c) In-flight meals: Customer feedback on the eye appeal, taste and quality was regularly sought. Finding that more than 50 per cent travellers preferred Indian cuisine, appropriate modification were undertaken. (d) Boarding experience: wherever possible, effects were made to use aerobridges to reduce boarding time to within 8 minutes. (e) Cabin crew service: This included friendliness, efficiency and clarity of announcements made. (f) Baggage arrival: The aim was to release baggage before the first business class passenger was ready to claim it and ensure priority baggage was given due priority in practice. (g) Overall efficiency of service: This was measured in terms of efficiency (combination of speed and accuracy), friendliness and willingness to help. On-time performance reports were checked everyday. All the 30 airports sent their feedback to Jet's Mumbai head office by the first week of every month. This was collated by the 15th to draw up a customer service performance map for the entire Jet network, after which specific points were studied. And when something would go wrong, the responsibility would lie with the station head. A written receipt was to be given to the complainant and a reply to be given within 48 hours. It was rectified through counselling, if the error was human, or by identifying and closing loopholes if it was a system's error. The underlying objective of these elaborate measures was to improve customer service.

Konkan Railway Corporation's roll-on, roll-off (ro-ro) Service: The Konkan Railway Corporation's roll-on, roll-off (ro-ro) service is a success, not only for the corporation but also among the truckers for whom it is intended. Introduced in January 1999, the corporation transports loaded trucks on wagons—called flats in railway parlance—between different destinations. Last financial year (2002-2003), the corporation earned ₹7.50 crore from the ro-ro service, according to Mr D G Diwate, Director (Way & Works), Konkan Railway Corporation.

The service, he says, helps in an indirect saving in fuel cost, and reduces vehicle operating costs in terms of wear and tear of tyres and vehicle maintenance. The service is available between Kolad, about 145 km south of Mumbai in Maharashtra's Raigad district, and Verna, in Goa. The ro-ro service saves a 430-km stretch of travel to Goa from Verna on the national highway. The truck drivers need not drive on the that section. The time taken to transport the wagons on rail is less than 12 hours while the transit time by road is much more. By using the ro-ro service, the transporters use the same fleet of trucks for more number of trips. The service also ensures on-time, intact cargo delivery, free of any risk factor and free from multiple handling of consignments, says Mr Diwate. According to him, the ro-ro service was launched when the corporation did not have enough freight traffic. One service is being operated daily in both directions and each train carries up to 28 trucks. "The response has been overwhelming and now truck operators need to book in advance to use the facility," Mr. Diwate said. The trucks mostly carry building materials, including marble, cement and iron rods. The truck operators get to optimise the fleet utilisation and achieve faster turnaround, he adds. For a two-axle truck (up to 25 tonnes gross weight), the transportation cost from Kolad to Verna is ₹5,100 and for a three-axle vehicle, it is ₹7,650. For every additional tonne, the cost is ₹200. In the return direction, the cost is ₹4,800 and ₹7,200. The corporation plans to move containers in a similar manner, according to Mr Diwate. There is not much of difference in the freight between the ro-ro service and transportation by road, he says.

Hotels

Accommodation includes hotels, ranging from the biggest international chains recognisable worldwide such as Hilton and Holiday Inn to small independent establishments. In order to gain recognition in an increasingly competitive marketplace, many smaller independent hotels have grouped together, adopting a consortium approach. Under a central brand name, they can offer central reservations services, for example, and present a recognisable identity to consumers, which enable them to compete against the larger, more established chains. Other types of accommodation are also well-established in tourist markets, notably self-catering apartments and 'club'-type complexes. Centre Parcs are today's answer to the Butlins-type holiday camps of the 50s and 60s, while Mark Warner Holidays are also successful in their inclusive 'club' formula.

Kadavu resorts Kadavu Resorts was set up in the year 2001 in the then sleepy fishing village of Azhinhillam on the banks of the river Chaliyar in the northern districts of the state of Kerala. Designed to inculcate architectural designs of the local Maplah and Hindu culture, Kadavu was intended to be a luxury resort-cum-business hotel with the distinct charm of the serene Kerala landscape. The most differentiating factor of Kadavu Resort was its entrance. "The unique view that one gets as one enters the lobby is outstanding. Spread over 10 acres of prime waterfront land, the landscape using plants and trees, enhances the ethnic feel of the entire resort. It is built from a special rust stone indigenous to the Malabar region and the architecture here harmoniously blends the Maplah with the Hindu styles giving the resort an absolutely unique appearance. The hotel has 17 independent cottages and 57 elegantly styled rooms or suites. The rooms are centrally air-conditioned with views that offer a breathtaking blend of the crystal clear backwaters surrounded by coconut plantations. Moreover, the lucid movements of the 'vallams' (local canoes) or fishermen in their 'vanchis' (local canoes) or fishermen in their vanchis (local fishing canoes) on the backwaters provide a panoramic view. Apart from all these, the hotel also provides an Ayurvedic rejuvenation centre offering traditional ayurvedic therapies, amphitheatre with a daily cultural programme, a coffee shop and a multicuisine restaurant serving Malabar delicacies.

It also has one of the largest amoeba shaped swimming pools in south India with a Jacuzzi and a separate children's pool, a children's park and play area and a tennis court. For meeting and banquet functions, the hotel also has facilities like 'Chaliar" - the Conference Hall, 'Thekkini' - the banquet space and pool side lawns which can seat 20 to 1,200 people. Unlike most traditional hotel structures which follow a matchbox design, wherein most service outlets and rooms are within a 30-40 metre radius of the elevator or production area, Kadavu resorts adopted a spread-out layout, wherein here was a series of cottages along with a combination of rooms on the main block. The coffee shop was built away from the main building as were the convention hall and the conference rooms. This design provided its own problems in terms of providing quality service within acceptable time limits. The service staff had to walk several minutes from the main kitchen, up a flight of stairs and negotiate small hillocks to provide room service orders to guests on the cottages. To prevent the inevitable customer complaints that would arise due to the delays that may arise from such a long process, Banerjee made efforts to discourage guests from ordering from their rooms and instead coax them to visit the restaurants and coffee shops. The room service menus were deliberately made limited so that guests who prefer more dining choices would come down to the restaurants. The lavish buffet spreads as well as the complimentary evening tea were provided to tempt the resident guests to visit restaurants. The tea/coffee makers and mini-bars were provided in the rooms so that the most frequent beverage orders could be avoided and the accompanying pressure on the service system could be relieved. The kitchenettes were provided even in the cottages.

Tourism Marketing

A clear perception of tourism marketing requires a brief analysis of marketing. We are well aware of the fact that there have been fundamental changes in the traditional concept of marketing, which has been influenced by the multidimensional changes in the business environment. A transformation in the attitudes, lifestyles, and expectations is the result of a number of developments. Professionalism paves the ways for excellence, which opens doors for quality generation vis-à-vis competition. Almost all the organisations producing goods or generating services have no option but to assign an overriding priority to quality upgradation that requires innovations. This necessitates a change in the concept of marketing which determines its functional boundaries. We find satisfaction of users the focal point around which all the functional areas of marketing cluster. While clarifying the perception of tourism marketing, it is essential that we assign due weightage to the three important considerations, the first generation of profits by the tourist organisations, second world-class services to the tourists which help in satisfying them and the third positive contributions of tourist organisations to the process of social transformation and ecological balance. In view of the above, the following points emerge regarding tourism marketing:

- Tourism marketing is a process of creating a product or providing a service.
- Tourism marketing comprises fact-finding, data gathering, analysing (marketing research), communication to inform and promote (promotion), ensuring and facilitating sales, selection of marketing, planning (distribution), coordination, control and evaluation (marketing, planning and auditing) and developing professionally sound personnel (people).
- Tourism marketing is an integral effort to satisfy tourists and more so, it is a device to transform the potential tourists into the actual tourists.
- Tourism marketing is the safest way to generate demand, expand market and increase the market share.
- Tourism marketing is a managerial process to promote business. Tourism is a very complex industry due to its multiple activities, which satisfies the needs of the tourist (customer).

Tourism embraces transportation, accommodation, food catering, tourist attraction, as well as organisers like tour operators and travel agents. The various sub-sectors of tourism, namely, lodging, transport, are themselves a complete industry. Moreover, a tour consists of different requirements of different people and it is not a homogenous product. The main problem lies in maintaining standards for these components. Considering the plethora of activities in tourism, it requires professionalism in major decisions and its success is governed by excellence. While boosting tourism globally, the growing influence of the Internet is filling up some coffers and drying up some, putting the travel industry intermediaries on notice, much to the delight of the consumer. Margins are shrinking and business drifting away for the middleman, be it a tourist operator or a travel agent. The real paradox, however, is that what is being taken away by the Net is compensated by new business generated through the Net. For most intermediaries in the sector, the loss on the outbound sector is made up by the gain on the inbound traffic. By directly contacting tour operator here, foreign tourists get cheaper accommodation package. Booking a hotel accommodation through a tour operator in their country would cost them 25 per cent more. Having eliminated one intermediary in the chain, Indian tour operators are also benefiting since they pin a markup on direct sales. The bonanza, however, may not last long since hotels are also directly marketing their products on the Net. Even the tourism department is getting into action, touch screen terminals are being set up at airports for tourists to make hotel bookings directly. "Those who have not done advance reservations can use this facility and rates would be transparent". Efforts are on to include all major hotels into the new facility to give tourists a wider choice. While the optimism about e-commerce revolutionising tourism is unmistakable, there are also voices of concern. "Steps should be taken to check frauds and false bookings." Other area of concern is undercutting. Most operators only give details of their package on their websites and the rates are not mentioned since it might encourage rivals to undercut. The drawbacks and apprehensions may be there but the 'notification' of tourism is here to stay.

Kerala Tourism: God's Own Country?

Kerala had always been considered the 'backwaters' of India–in a negative way, tourists thought of it as a nice but far away place, to be visited if you had the time, after covering the more popular destinations like the Taj Mahal, Delhi, Jaipur and Goa. But all that has changed, with a single great campaign, based on a memorable line–God's Own Country. As tourism marketers know, a tourist destination sells imagery first, and then depends on the tourists themselves to recommend the destination to their friends, relatives and peer groups. For a long time, Kerala had advertised its boat races held at Alleppey (now known as Alappuzha) and the elephant ritual at 'Thrissur Pooram', and gained some mileage from these too. However, the advertising really started getting into the limelight after the tagline "God's Own Country" was added to the beautiful images. In addition to the foreign tourists, the campaign successfully drew the attention of domestic tourists, and as a result Kerala has successfully entered the tourist map of the world. New investments in Kerala include tourism-related projects at Bekal in the Malabar (north Kerala) region. Tangible things such as good air and road/rail connections, and availability of different types of hotels and resorts also helped, along with the cosmopolitan food habits of Kerala, which is probably the only state apart from Goa where meat and seafood of all types are easily available, to cater to the palates of foreigners who may be predominantly non-vegetarian. Ayurveda practitioners also abound in Kerala, and the oil massages add to the mystique of the destination. Apart from traditional hill stations like Munnar, Kerala offers a forest experience at Thekkady (Periyar wildlife sanctuary), and in the hills of Wayanad district bordering Tamil Nadu and Karnataka.

4. Professional Services

Protech BPO Protech, a Raipur based BPO firm was established in April 2003. It offers comprehensive IT-enabled services, data processing services, software solutions, consulting and training to its clients across the country. Protech makes it easier for their customers to understand the impact of technology on their businesses and help them to conceptualise business transformation initiatives. Hence, it provides cost-effective, flexible and quality solutions for the contemporary complex marketplace. Protech has created a sustainable, economically feasible business model in the area of services and solutions. Presently, it has a seventy member team with expertise in various domains and technologies and is positioned to double its strength by the end of the year 2003. The management team comprises individuals with experience in business solutions and consulting. The employees at Protech have shown their tremendous learning capacity with a learning curve of more than 60 per cent. The Protech problem lies in getting the contract. It has no history to back its stupendous performance and claim a contract, nor does it have access to direct US and other foreign markets. Just serving as a subcontractor to big companies is not bringing in sufficient revenue for the company. Related to the revenue problem is the high attrition rate as compared to industry. Protech is facing a serious problem of retaining its talented pool due to very low wages paid to them. The location of the company has also been a major hurdle. For instance, at times the contracts required a large number of talented professionals, particularly lawyers and accountants. In a city like Raipur, the availability of such professionals in large numbers turned out to be a daunting task. The company even lost a few contracts due to this hurdle. Being a very new set-up the entire process of the company is yet to be put in place. Companies operating in the industry should compete on the process or system they have in place. Having such a process/system helps them to provide very high level of service. Therefore, increasingly the companies operating in this field are going for CMM certification. The CMM guarantees the kind of process, which a firm has in place. It is used as a marketing tool. Protech can be classified as a CMM 1 level company on a scale of 5.

5. Public Utility Services

The Dabbawalla Business Model

The concept of dabbawalla delivery system started in Mumbai in the mid-1880s. The city's population then was a mere 10 lakhs as against the more than 1.30 crores it is today. There were no buses or suburban railways at that time, and the dabbas were transported on bicycles, hand carts, bullock carts and tangas (horse carriages). The service cost its customers around 2 annas (12 paise). Over the years, this evolved into a complex network of delivery, and in their peak days in 1955, the dabbawallas were delivering close to 2 lakh tiffins per day.

The core factor that has sustained this business model is the desire of the average middle-class Mumbaiker to eat home-made food. The dabba or aluminium box consists of discrete compartments, which hold rice, roti, dal, curd, etc.–the staple diet of most North Indians. Eating out of the dabba comes closer than anything else to the feeling of eating at home. The second important factor is the highly evolved transportation system in Mumbai. Mumbai's suburban electric trains and BEST buses efficiently connect disparate and far-flung regions of Mumbai making the food delivery system a viable model.

The above factors are coupled with the fact that the dabbawallas charge a pittance for their delivery - the charge (in the year 2001) is around ₹200 for an entire month. This is far less than what it would cost for a person to eat in hotels or other eateries. Thus, healthy, home-made food delivered at a highly competitive rate made the dabbawalla business an unbeatable model–at least till the late 1990s. The dabbawalla delivery network runs on the principle of a relay system. The dabbas are passed on from one dabbawalla to another with sometimes the lunch boxes changing hands upto 4 or 5 times before finally reaching the customer. The entire network is divided into clusters of roughly 20 men. The process begins with the first group picking up the aluminium boxes from homes or a central kitchen. Depending upon the distance to be covered, dabbas are collected from these places between 8 and 9 in the morning. Each dabbawalla covers roughly 20 houses. Covering these many houses quickly is not easy in a city like Mumbai. The heat during summer and waterlogged roads during the monsoons, with the peak hour traffic thrown in, make reaching each home the toughest part of the process. At each dabba a receiving point, the dabbawalla has to park his cycle at the gate, go to the client's house, which in Mumbai would invariably be a flat in a multi-storied building, collect the lunch and then come down again. These dabbas are then carted off to railway stations on bicycles where they are loaded on to the specified local train. A second set of workers unload them at the local stations like Andheri or Churchgate.

The third set of carriers waiting at the respective station sort out and assemble the dabbas. The sorting process is done effortlessly–thousands of tiffins are sorted in a matter of minutes–thanks to an efficient, evolved coding system. This sorting process is repeated across many stations for area-wise distribution. Each lunch box/dabba has marked on it a circle of a specific colour and an identity number, for example, "K-BO-10-19/A/15" where K is the identity letter of the dabbawalla, BO stands for the area from where the lunch box is to be collected, (Borivali), the number 10 refers to a more specific locality like Nariman Point area and 19/A/15 refers to the 19th building and the 15th floor in Nariman Point area where the box is to be delivered.

At each station, after the sorting is finished, hundreds of dabbawallas pour out of the railway stations with long wooden crates packed with the sorted-out lunch boxes. These are in turn handed over to the huge number of waiting delivery persons who set off on their bicycles to offices across the city. The lunch boxes reach their respective destinations between 11:45 a.m. and 12:30 p.m. covering the journey from start to finish in a matter of about 4 hours. After lunch hour is over, the entire process is repeated in reverse. The dabbawallas again visit the workplaces in the afternoon to collect the empty tiffins and deliver them to the stations where trainwise sorting is done and the dabbas are loaded on to the respective trains. The local carriers at the suburban station collect them, sort them out and proceed to deliver the empty tiffins back to the residences.

The dabbawallas work 12 hours a day, year round-in the sweltering heat of May and the drenching monsoon of June, July & August. They cycle distances of up to 15 km in the city, and push trolleys stacked with tiffin-carriers through the chaos of Mumbai's traffic jammed streets always delivering on time. As is obvious, the entire system depends on teamwork and meticulous timing. In the words of a dabbawalla, "Once you have the boxes with you, you can't even stop to go to the toilet because if you're late by even five or 10 minutes the chain gets disrupted".

So integral have the dabbawallas become to Mumbai's way of life that the railways have given them a special reserved compartment next to the guard's cabin on certain suburban trains. What makes the entire process amazing is the astonishingly low level of mistakes the dabbawallas make despite the fact that most of these persons are semi-literate and illiterate.

In spite of the complexity and sheer volume of the business, the 5,000 dabbawallas make a mistake only about once in every two months which works out to one error in every 8 million deliveries, or 16 million if the return trip is included. "If we made 10 mistakes a month, no one would use our service," says a dabbawalla. It is accuracy generated by sheer necessity.

The dabbawallas became world famous when a few years ago US business magazine Forbes gave them at 6 Sigma performance rating, or a 99.999999 percentage of correctness which technically means one error in every six million transactions. The dabbawallas, in reality, with one mistake in 16 million deliveries, are even better than the 6 Sigma standards. The dabbawallas now routinely deliver talks to high-flying corporates and b-school students on teamwork and how they "manage operational hurdles and still sustain quality".

Till 2004, the dabbawallas of Mumbai functioned as a loose and unorganised association of people. Each dabbawalla would charge about ₹200 per person per month. After paying the Western Railway for transport, the rest would go to the dabbawalla. The dabbawallas had an association called the Mumbai Tiffinmen's Association where each would make a contribution of ₹10 per month. The ₹50,000/- collected would, after meeting minimal administration expenses, go towards charitable causes like feeding the poor. The purpose of organising themselves into a company was twofold. It gave them increased bargaining power and ensured the existence of a social security/pension-like pooling of funds for the dabbawallas when they retired from work.

A most important reason was the dabbawallas' ambitious plans to branch out into other cities of India. The dabbawallas reasoned that in cities across India there would exist prospective clientele who would still prefer home-made food and they hoped to capitalise on this.

Jewellery Marketing Strategies

Broadly speaking many and varied are the jewellery habits. It varies on different aspects. Some such are based on culture, religion, financial viability, custom, changing trend in fashion, love for novelty, style, flexibility in bargaining, post-purchase service, brand image, product quality, and goodwill of the retailer, along with the clients on the part of the buyer, whose purchasing power is presumptive. Craze for status and false prestige in addition to the necessity imposed by ceremonial rites and rituals, make it mandatory. Of late the fairly knowledge-based society, and globalisation make their sway on the consumers' buying behaviour, well defined.

Adornment jewellery

Jewelleries can conveniently be dually classified as adornment ones and asset oriented, which once again lends itself for further rectification as human and idol wearings for beautification. Religious favour rooted in ancient beliefs too, sometimes urges even the unaffordable buyer, to go in for them adducing the motive on religion.

Human jewellery

Interesting feature with the human jewellery is its further scope for division as male and female usable. Watch, chains, cigarette cases, bracelets, belt buckles, pocket book frames, and rings go under the banner of men's wares while necklace, chins studs, bracelets, anklets, hair decorative items and bangles fall under female jewelleries category.

Children jewellery

A third division as children jewellery also is as much noteworthy as earlier mentioned adult ones. They receive love attribute association, besides bearing testimony for their parents' richness and affection.

Saving jewellery

The absence of a well-defined banking system, fairly well to do people were bent upon the purchase of 22 carat jewelleries for the purpose of savings. We may venture to call it as lack of self-control on their part, who feared money may get squandered impulsively. Another greatly contributing factor for such habits is the liquidity of such assets. They under unavoidable circumstances pledge them for capital immobilisation to meet the exigencies. Agricultural pursuit, as many others, is one of the seasonal needs normally and usually felt by agrarian community. Even here the golden jewelleries, as against the gems embedded ones, enjoy the privilege of being the price fixation instrument. The former ones do fetch comparably great value against the latter ones, while pledged for capital mobilisation. Many a families thrive on the jewellery making pursuit for generations together by virtue of their fineries making nuances and intricacies.

Artistic jewellery

The price of artistic jewellery is not calculated on the basis of metal contents but on the artistic value imbibed or developed by the craftsman.

Aesthetic jewellery

The mechanised production has paved way for the entry of novice in the field. They consolidate their position with their knowledge of the marketing strategies and tactics. The festival occasion aesthetics create artificial scarcity and price hike. Now the software professionals ensure the reasonable income resulting in reasonable disposal. The buyer stands to gain. This leading pursuit needs to develop design and strategies for capturing the reasonable share in the gold market. India has enormous potential to compete in the world market, if she develops to adapt new marketing strategies that can counter the marketing strategies of competitors. The strategies can aim at maximisation of product or promotion strategies. It is time for making paradigm shift in strategies formulation for accruing its due share in the world market. The quality assured variety and its designs, can be the focal point of the strategies formulation. The brand building, brand machine and brand extension will ensure growth in sales. The domestic rivalry will lead to the development of new design and exploration of new market.

6. Communication Services

Pricing a Courier Service

India's postal system has undergone a revolution since the private courier service providers made an entry into what was a one-organisation industry–in other words, totally dominated by the Indian Postal Department. Like all other industries where brand proliferation has taken place, India soon had a spate of new service providers–regional, national and international names made their appearance. In the late 90s, yet another technology leap has found a lot of takers–the Internet. This technology has revolutionised communication, both business and personal, to such an extent that personal letter writing suddenly became extinct among those who had access to the net.

The courier industry, though, continued its existence under increasing competitive pressures, mainly due to increasing demand from the business community for the transportation of business documents. Besides, the industry could also cash in on the existing demand for the transportation of bulk packages within the country and abroad. A drop in prices has led to courier services becoming more affordable. Taking stock of the existing market situation, the postal department has also introduced its own branded high-speed courier service–the Speed Post.

In the environment of 2003, a new company would like to enter the courier services business. The promoter, Mr Darbari Singh, an NRI who has returned to India, believes that the service levels offered by many of the Indian players leave a lot to be desired. Based on an analysis of the current players in the courier (documents and packages) industry, their profitability, market shares, etc. advice Mr. Singh on target market selection, entry pricing and long-term prospects.

CTV (Colour Television)

In India the television industry has made steady growth. A number of new players including foreigners are expected to step in the market. The industry will consolidate within around three or four years. But the country has a huge high untapped demand. It is sad to note that 95 colour TV sets are sold per 1000 persons in India against 400 per thousand in China. The rural market for TV sets accounts for around 40 per cent of the CTV sales. The television industry started in India in 1970 with the production of black and white TV sets, which were all 20 inch sets, 14 inch TV sets were launched in 1984. In 1982 when Asian Games (ASIAD) was held in India, colour TV sets were introduced. Setting up of Doordarshan Kendras in many parts of the country, India's victory in the Prudential World Cup in cricket in 1983, etc., provided a great impetus to CTV demand. The Central Government also encouraged this sector. Various state governments came up with their own TV companies, e.g., Uptron, Keltron and Meltron. In 1989, the old players like Weston, Dyanora and Televista also diversified into CTVs. By 1989, there were about 200 players in the market. In 1991, due to initiation of economic liberalisation programme, the growth of CTV scaled high. There was reduction in excise and import duties. Then the opening up of Indian skies to foreign satellite channels in 1991-92 and the coming of cable TV, gave Philips for the growth of TV industry. Simultaneously private and more aggressive domestic players like Videocon, BPL, etc., consolidated their presence in the CTV market, focusing an product promotion and technology. Then the global brands such as Akai, Aiwa, Sansui, Toshiba, etc., have entered the market by having tie-ups with Indian players. At last the other multinationals like Sony, LG, Samsung, etc., entered into the field and quickly captured the imagination of the market with innovations in product quality and features.

Cable Television

The cable industry originated in the late 1980s with a single video channel and DD channels distributed through coaxial cable in a single building/society called MA TV system, extended to the societies nearby thus migrated to CATV (Community Access Television) Systems.

The increase in the penetration of cable and satellite TV has ben a prominent driver of demand for TV sets and satellite households to toal television households rose from about 11% in 1992 to around 50% in 2002. Now their access has been estimated over 40 million households. The urban penetration is about 60% while rural penetration is about 34.3%. Thus, there is rapid growth in the number of channels, particularly in regional languages, which enabled demand proliferation for cable TV (and indirectly for TVs) in the country.

Digital TV

Digital TV presents crystal-clear picture. It has about ten times more picture details than the conventional TV, the black bars are placed at the top and bottom of the screen one can see the complete picture in HDTV (High Definition Television).

Flat Television

The Indian colour television industry is witnessing a major transition with significant growth in the flat TV market. Due to declining price margins and aggressive thrust by CTV manufacturers to upgrade consumers to the flat TV technology, the flat TV in the consumer electronics industry is increasingly becoming the first choice of CTV buyers in India. This segment recorded an approximate 10 per cent growth during 2003-04 with total sales estimated at 1.45 million sets. 21-inch flat TV is a major volume driver in this segment and is reducing the share of mid-sized conventional TVs. So there is phenomenal growth in demand for sound based 21 inch and large screen flat TVs. Thus, the flat-panel TVs (Plasma and LCD), the latest models have promising performance with ever increasing sale. The main advantages of these TVs are their size and shape. They are sleek and can be fitted on the wall-like a painting picture. Flat TV companies are trying to rationalise prices with growing volumes.

Thus, Indian television market has made steady progress. Many new players, particularly foreign, are expected to enter the market. No doubt television industry will soon consolidate its market. As far as urban areas are concerned, television market is encouraging. Thanks to the mushrooming of cable connections which helps to penetrate TV sets in semi-urban and rural areas.

7. Educational Services

Education is a service that is geared primarily to the consumer market. There is a category of consumers for whom education and the pursuit of knowledge are expressive motives. Educational institutions in developing countries have always faced more demand than they could cope with. Formal education begins at the school age and depending upon the choice, vocation and circumstances of the pursuant, it matures into intermediate and higher levels of learning, ramifying into professional and specialised fields. Apparently, the benefits sought from higher and professional or vocational courses are more tangible or measurable in terms of (a) entry qualifications to a chosen profession, (b) certification to enable practising a profession or (c) relative ease of access to a suitable form of livinghood. Covering the field of marketing of education per se, in its entirety is somewhat impossible. The focus here is, therefore, limited to the coaching centres that provide guidance for Common Aptitude Test (CAT).

The CAT is a qualification test for all the students in India and abroad to enrol themselves in one of the six IIMs (Indian Institute of Management) and a host of other reputed management institutions. The number of institutes providing coaching for the same across the country runs into four figures. This is probably the reason why the industry is as big as 120 crore rupees per annum.

Coaching Institutes for Cat Examination

(A) Institute of Management Studies (IMS)

Located in almost every major town/city in the country, the IMS recently celebrated its 25th anniversary. With personal counselling, huge course material, best faculty attracted to its ranks, and an unmatched reach all over the country, the IMS gives its students, an edge that takes them a notch above the rest. An unmatched leader in its category, IMS claims that every second IIM grad has enrolled with IMS. Recognised as the 44th most trusted brand in service industry*, it is ranked fourth in the education sector after Kendriya Vidyalaya, Indian Institutes of Technology (IITs) and Delhi Public School. Surprisingly, the survey rated the IMS a rank above Indian Institute of Management (IIMs), which happens to be the bread and butter of IMS's business. The IMS was a pioneer in many initiatives in its sector like the 'mock CAT', which is a national level test, intended to give the students a feel of real competition.

Some of the well-known courses in classroom offerings of IMS are:

- IMS CAT Foundation (for students not comfortable in Maths and English)
- CATapult (long-term extensive training starting from basic areas: 12 months)
- CAT Classic (medium-term training focusing on CAT and other exams: 6 months)
- CAT Cruncher (short-term training spanning across 9 weeks)

All courses are provided through the 54 IMS centres located across the country. However, the fee structures vary across the centres.

(B) Career Launcher

Career Launcher is a relative newcomer in the industry compared to IMS. With more than 50 centres located in India and the Middle East, it caters its service to almost 15000 students every year. With divisions like Student Services, Institutional Services and Academic Support Services, it caters to the classroom needs of both Indian and international students for the MBA entrance examinations in India. Its competitiveness lies in the extensive technological investment that has done to supplement its core entrance preparation programme. Its classroom course offerings include.

- Pegasus Extended (Full length; 18 months)
- Pegasus Foundation (40 hrs-8 weeks programme for those who have lost touch in Maths/DI)
- Pegasus Integrated (160 hours full stretch programme)
- Pegasus Gallop (Medium length; 6-12 months)

A comparison of all the four classroom coaching offerings is given in Table 8.1.

Table 8.1 Classroom coaching

Features	Pegasus Integrated	Pegasus	PGL Integrated	Pegasus Gallop
Classroom Training (Fundamental + Speed Building)	Y	Y	N	N
Classroom Training (Exercise Driven)	N	N	Y	Y
Course Material	Y	Y	Y	Y
Seminars	Y	Y	Y	Y
Student Information System	Y	Y	Y	Y
Video Library	Y	Y	Y	Y
Magazine	Y	Y	Y	Y
All India Test Series	Y	Y	Y	Y
PDP	Y	N	Y	N

As mentioned above, the state-of-the-art technology has placed Career Launcher on the top of aspirant's mind.

(C) Career Forum

Career Forum is one of the smaller service providers that is in operation since last twelve years. It is located in only six cities and has 24 centres. What makes it stand apart is the high pressure rate (approximately 520 interview calls from each city) which is probably attributed to the fact that it is located in major cities which provides maximum number of students to the IIMs. Besides, it has a significant presence in Western and South India (only two centres in Delhi and no location in the eastern part of the country). The classroom offerings of Career Forum are:

❖ **FocusCAT:** The generic classroom coaching that has three versions (a) long-term (10-month programme) (b) medium-term (5-6 months programme) (c) Weekend batches (spans across 5-6 months)

❖ **CATscan:** All India 'mock CATs' which gives students an exposure to CAT-like environment.

❖ **CAT Express:** It is for the students who are confident enough to get a call from IIMs and want to start preparation as soon as they have given the CAT.

❖ **CAT Clincher:** This programme is meant for all students who have received an Interview call from IIMs or one of the six premier institutes (XLRI, S P JAIN, FMS, NITIE, NMIMS & JBIMS).

❖ The strong point of Career Forum is the focus that apart from the regular faculty they have part time faculty also that are mostly on a short-term basis and usually plan to appear for the CAT. This ensures that the faculty identifies the needs of the student in a succinct manner. Besides, the permanent faculty is suggested to take the exam themselves to complement the visiting faculty. Apart from that, the Career Forum invite fresh IIM students (who might be currently in their MBA programme) to conduct the interviews. This gives quite a lot of confidence to the aspirants.

(D) TIME Institute

The TIME Institute has its branches spread in select places all over India and extensively in the southern part of the country. Headquartered in Hyderabad, it is not a technology-oriented institute. It has targeted mostly the second rung cities and towns in an aggressive manner. Knowing that there is a significant chunk of places where other big institutes have not reached, it has already spread its branches accordingly and has significantly made its presence known. In places like Calicut, it is so established that even institutes like IMS had to wrap up their business because of the strong brand equity that TIME has enjoyed in such places. However, it is worth noting that TIME has a decent presence in metros as well, but probably it is not doing that well there as far as results are concerned. The nature of courses that are offered are similar with a flat fee structure across branches.

TIME remind us of the South West Airlines who have made their motto as 'No Frills' airline providing the minimal basic necessities. Similarly, TIME has focused quite a lot on classroom, faculty and flat course structure. Probably, this is the reason why they have only the following courses to offer: (a) Regular long-term (b) Regular medium-term (c) Regular short-term. All three come with an option of (a) Weekend batch (b) Weekday batch (c) Morning/evening batch. Not a very technology savvy organisation, it does not have a website of its own. Besides, the e-mail ids they use do not have their own domain name. Their official e-mail ids are all based on www.eth.net, which belongs to "education to home" group. However, it is worth noting that the headquarters have a strong hold on to all the franchisees keeping a tab on each and everyone. Any complaint if heard is dealt with very severely. This is the reason why despite being located in not so high flying cities, the TIME has been able to give good service to all those who were earlier ignored by IMS, Career launcher and Career Forum.

8.6 CUSTOMER RELATIONSHIP MANAGEMENT

Customer Relationship Management (CRM) is gaining importance in corporate circles in recent years. It is emerging as the business theme for the 21st century. Companies have realised the value of long-term relationship with individual customers and other business partners in the light of rapid change in technology and consumer expectations. Enhancing lifetime value of customers and developing a relationship with profitable customers has become the central focus of companies' strategy. The change in business focus was aptly pointed out by Jill Dyche, in his words "The so-called typical customer no longer exists, and companies have been learning this lesson the hard way. Until very recently, business was more concerned about the 'what's' than about the 'who's'. In other words, companies were focused on selling as many products and services as possible, without any regard to who was buying them. Most corporations cling to this product-centric view even today, basing their organisational structures and compensation plans on the products they sell and not on the customers".

What is CRM?

CRM stands for Customer Relationship Management. It is a strategy used to learn more about customers' needs and behaviours in order to develop stronger relationships with them. After all, good customer relationships are at the heart of business success. There are many technological components to CRM, but thinking about CRM in primarily technological terms is a mistake. The more useful way to think about CRM is as a process that will help bring together lots of pieces of information about customers, sales, marketing effectiveness, responsiveness and market trends.

Once a business organisation selects its target market, it has to collect customer data and develop customer preference. The relationship cannot be a one-sided approach. It should involve the other side equally with value sharing proposition. Hence, CRM can be defined as development of lasting strategies alliances with customers on a value sharing basis. This definition implies future orientation and win-win proposition between the seller and the customer. The benefits that the business concerns in order to make CRM effective and future oriented.

Relationship marketing is a philosophy of doing business on strategic orientation that focuses on keeping and improving current interactions with the parties concerned rather than acquiring new parties. The philosophy has an underlying assumption that the customers prefer to have an ongoing relationship with an organisation than to switch continually in search for values. James L Schorr explains the importance of relationship by proposing a theory called **'Bucket Theory of Marketing'**. He views the market as a big bucket. The sales, adverting and promotional programmes pour businesses into the top of the bucket. As long as these programmes are effective, the bucket stays full.

Goals of CRM

The idea of CRM is that it helps businesses use technology and human resources to gain insight into the behaviour of customers and the value of those customers. If it works as hoped, a business can:

- Provide better customer service
- Make call centres more efficient
- Cross sell products more effectively
- Help sales staff close deals faster
- Simplify marketing and sales processes
- Discover new customers
- Increase customer revenues.

It doesn't happen by simply buying software and installing it. For CRM to be truly effective an organisation must first decide what kind of customer information it is looking for and it must decide what it intends to do with that information. For example, many financial institutions keep track of customers' life stages in order to market appropriate banking products like mortgages or IRAs to them at the right time to fit their needs.

Next, the organisation must look into all the different ways information about customers comes into a business, where and how this data is stored and how it is currently used. One company, for instance, may interact with customers in a myriad of different ways including mail campaigns, Websites, brick-and-mortar stores, call centres, mobile sales force staff and marketing and advertising efforts.

Solid CRM systems link up each of these points. This collected data flows between operational systems (like sales and inventory systems) and analytical systems that can help sort through these records for patterns. Company analysts can then comb through the data to obtain a holistic view of each customer and pinpoint areas where better services are needed. For example, if someone has a mortgage, a business loan, an IRA and a large commercial checking account with one bank, it behooves the bank to treat this person well each time it has any contact with him or her.

Need for a CRM project

But one way to assess the need for a CRM project is to count the channels a customer can use to access the company. The more channels you have, the greater need there is for the type of single centralised customer view a CRM system can provide.

How long will it take to get CRM in place?

A bit longer than many software salespeople will lead you to think. Some vendors even claim their CRM "solutions" can be installed and working in less than a week. Packages like those are not very helpful in the long run because they don't provide the cross-divisional and holistic customer view needed. The time it takes to put together a well-conceived CRM project depends on the complexity of the project and its components.

CRM cost

A recent (2001) survey of more than 1,600 business and IT professionals, conducted by the Data Warehousing Institute found that close to 50% had CRM project budgets of less than $500,000. That would appear to indicate that CRM doesn't have to be a budget-buster. However, the same survey showed a handful of respondents with CRM project budgets of over $10 million.

What are some examples of the types of data CRM projects should be collecting?

- Responses to campaigns
- Shipping and fulfilment dates
- Sales and purchase data
- Account information
- Web registration data
- Service and support records
- Demographic data
- Web sales data

Successful CRM implementation

- Break your CRM project down into manageable pieces by setting up pilot programmes and short-term milestones.
- Starting with a pilot project that incorporates all the necessary departments and groups that gets projects rolling quickly but is small enough and flexible enough to allow tinkering along the way.
- Make sure your CRM plans include a scalable architecture framework.
- Don't underestimate how much data you might collect (there will be LOTS) and make sure that if you need to expand systems you'll be able to.
- Be thoughtful about what data is collected and stored. The impulse will be to grab and then store EVERY piece of data you can, but there is often no reason to store data. Storing useless data wastes time and money.
- Recognise the individuality of customers and respond appropriately. A CRM system should, for example, have built-in pricing flexibility.

CRM project to run

The biggest returns come from aligning business, CRM and IT strategies across all departments and not just leaving it for one group to run.

CRM projects to fail

Lack of communication in the customer relationship chain can lead to an incomplete picture of the customer. Poor communication can lead to technology being implemented without proper support or buy-in from users.

For example, if the sales force isn't completely sold on the system's benefits, they may not input the kind of demographic data that is essential to the programme's success. One Fortune 500 company is on its fourth try at a CRM implementation, primarily because its sale force resisted all the previous efforts to share customer data.

10 tips for implementing customer self-service

- ✠ Learn everything about your customers.
- ✠ Conduct focus groups to ensure that they want self-service.
- ✠ Define clear business goals.
- ✠ Evaluate the technology for its technical and financial merits.
- ✠ Does it match your customer base? Will it boost profitability?

⌗ Work as a team. Have customer support, IT and other departments involved every step of the way.

⌗ Offer training to employees.

⌗ Expect this to be an iterative process that requires making changes as you learn more about your customers.

⌗ Develop an effective way to measure results.

⌗ Under-promise and over-deliver.

Customer relationship management is a business strategy to select and manage the most valuable customer relationships. CRM requires a customer-centric business philosophy and culture to support effective marketing, sales, and service processes. CRM applications can enable effective customer relationship management, provided that an enterprise has the right leadership, strategy, and culture."   -The CRM Primer, *www.crmguru.com*.

Traditional Marketing Vs Relationship Marketing

Traditional marketing is transaction oriented and as such it is also called transaction marketing. The changing business scenario has forced many business organisations to shift their focus from transaction orientation to customer relationship orientation. Table 8.2 shows some of the differences that are identified between the two types of marketing.

Table 8.2 Difference between transaction marketing and relationship marketing

Transaction Marketing	Relationship Marketing
Focus on Making Sales	Focus on Making a Customer Loyal
Product Features are Focused	Product Benefits are Focused
Short-Term Focus	Long-Term Focus
Little Emphasis on Customer Service	High Customer Service Emphasis
Customer Commitment is Low	Customer Commitment is High
Moderate Customer Contact	High Customer Contact
Customer Satisfaction	Customer Retention

8.7   CRM IN MARKETING

There are 3 approaches to relationship marketing. They are:

1. Customised relationship
2. Organisation to group relationship
3. Non-personal relationship

1. Customised Relationship: Customised relationships are person-to-person or organisation-to-person relationships. Each relationship will be considered special and a unique strategy will be adopted to build, maintain and enhance the relationship with the party. Situations where the parties have greater influence on the business activities and where the parties have expectations of special recognition and treatment this approach can be considered the best. Since customised relationship involves high cost and operational complexities, organisation cannot have costs and operational complexities, organisations cannot have such a relationship with larger groups. They have to be selective in this respect.

2. Organisation-to-Group Relationship: Organisation-to-group relationships are possible when different groups related to the organisation have more or less homogenous characteristics and common expectations as far as the relationship with the organisation is concerned.

3. Non-Personal Relationship: Management of non-personal relationship is somewhat difficult when compared to the other two approaches. Under this approach, an organisation develops relationships with customers who are far away through non-personal communication media. This approach is particularly suitable when the organisation wants to establish relationship, with a fairly large group, and that too spread widely. This is possible only when the group has low expectations from organisation beyond the transaction and there is low involvement problem solving in either buying or selling processes. Service companies have to separate to manage relationship within the organisation among the employees in various divisions and among various divisions in the organisation and with parties outside the organisation.

a) Relationship within the Organisation: The importance of relationship within the organisation has been accepted all over the world and greater orientation is now being given to convert the formal structured interactions into informal relationships. Team sprit, group cohesiveness, objective orientation, high level of motivation and morale, less labour turnover, total quality management, work performance, and so on are the fruits of effective relationships within the organisation. Supervision and control can be reduced to the lowest point, if relationship is to be built on sound lines. The abundance of intelligence, skill, knowledge and expertise that is available in the human resource of the organisation can be exploited for the betterment of the future of the organisation through relationship. The entire organisation will be transformed to a strategic body. Good relationships within the organisation prove to be a great strength.

b) Relationship with Outside Parties: Relationship with parties outside the organisation is helpful in many ways to service companies. Apart from gaining competitive advantage in transactions, the relationships are helpful in having referred markets, employment markets, good quality and a distinctive image. The relationships act as a barrier against minor failures of the organisation and provide a chance for rectification, without losing the party. The long-term orientation in relationship also helps in the planning process by offering some amount of certainty in future.

8.8 CUSTOMER RETENTION

The trend in marketing towards building relationship with customers continues to grow and marketers have become increasingly interested in retaining customers over the long run. Marketing analysis have identified satisfaction as a key determinant in a customer's decision-making, relating to keeping or dropping a given product or service relationship. According to Oliver, satisfaction is the consumers' fulfilment response. It is a judgement that a product or service feature, or the product or service itself, provided a pleasurable level of under or over fulfilment.

Companies do spend a lot of money through different media to attract new customers to the business. Attracting new customers requires substantial skills and effort. However, these skilful efforts will be of little use if the company suffers from high customer churn. Unless organisation pursues customer retention strategies, the problem cannot be solved. Every company needs to define and measure its retention rate. Each company must also distinguish the reasons for losing customers and identify those causes that can be managed better. It is important to know how much loss the company makes when it loses customers. According to an estimate, the lost profit in the case of an individual customer is equal to the customers' lifetime value.

The likely to customer retention is to offer continuous satisfaction to customers. According to Philip Kotler, a highly satisfied customer

1. Stays loyal longer
2. Buys more as the company introduces new products
3. Pay less attention to competing brands and advertising and less sensitive price
4. Offers product or services ideas to the company
5. Costs less to serve than making new customers because transactions take place in a routine manner.

It is necessary, therefore, to measure customer satisfaction regularly by surveying the customers to know whether they are highly satisfied, satisfied, indifferent, dissatisfied or highly dissatisfied. Customers' complaints made by the customers make a vast difference in consumer perception. In other words of Allbrecht and Zemke, between 54% and 70% of the customers who register a complaint, will do business again with the organisation if their complaint is resolved.

The key customer retention is relationship marketing. The service company should develop over time the means of monitoring and evaluating the quality of relationships. There are two basic approaches that can be pursued to monitor the relationships—Relationship survey and customer database.

Current customers should be surveyed in order to understand their value perception of the services, the quality and satisfaction. Customer database in relation to names, addresses, phone numbers, demographics, lifestyle, usage patterns, activities, interest, opinions, and so on forms the basic foundation for designing customer retention strategies. In addition, trailor calls, complaint monitoring and lost customer surveys also help to develop a relevant database for developing strategies.

Berry and Parasuraman have developed a framework which suggests that retention marketing can occur at three different levels. Each successive level of strategy results in ties that bind the customer a little closer to the firm. The following are the three levels of retention strategies.

1. Level One: Financial Bonds
2. Level Two: Financial and Social Bonds
3. Level Three: Financial, Social and Structural Bonds

Financial Bonds: At this level, customers are offered financial incentives either for greater volume purchases or for continuation of relationship for a long time.

Financial and Social Bonds: At this level, the firm intends to develop long-term relationship with customers through social as well as financial bonds. The customers are identified by name and services are customised to fit individual needs. Marketers are looking for ways to keep in touch with their customers by providing a personal touch and building informal relationship.

Financial, Social and Structural Bonds: Financial, Social and Structural Bonds: The strategy is to develop structural bonds along with financial and social bonds. Structural bonds are created by providing highly customised service to the clients. Specific customer needs are bought into the organisational system to design new ways to improve the offerings to the clients. In service business, sometimes, there is possibility of things going wrong. Under such circumstances, a recovery strategy needs to be designed for retaining customers. Effective recovery is essential to save and even build relationships. Quick problem solving and empowering the frontline to solve problems are very important directions for the service organisations to follow.

8.9 SUCCESSFUL APPROACHES TO CRM

The approaches can be defined in two methods. They are:

1. Customers as friends
2. Customers as guests.

1. Customers as Friends: In several businesses, personal relationship and warmth are critical to success. A small automotive repair business in Mexico has blazed a new trail in service leadership by treating customers as friends. At Servicious Automatrices Echegary (SAE) Proprietor Alfredo Gomez impresses upon his employees, through personal example, that customers must be treated as friends. The following are his guiding principles.

(a) Do not make abnormal and unfair profits out of friends. SAE bases its repair pricing on labour costs a 40% margin. As most of its customers are themselves automotive experts, there is no point in even trying to hoodwink them.

(b) Do not make margin on a friend cause. The discounts offered by suppliers should be passed on to friends.

(c) Try to share your friend's concerns. Learn more about his vehicle, what is causing him trouble and keep him cautioned on what could cause a problem in the future. Take a ride with him in his vehicle to understand his concerns fully.

(d) Drive with him when he comes to collect the car, and ensure that he is fully satisfied with the repair. Do not compromise on this.

(e) Friends should spend time together. So make a party of your job. Allow your friends to participate in what you are doing and how you are doing it. Share with them whatever you do and plan to do. Encourage them to help you fix their cars and maintain them.

(f) Friends will give you a chance for they know that no one is prefect. Even if you make a mistake they may be willing to overlook it. Just let them know that you are doing your best. Track your performance and keep improving so as to help your friends better. Get back to school (to learn new and advance and update technology)

2. Customers as Guests: Bruce Lavel, a former senior Vice President at Disney, coined a term 'Guestology' to focus everyone's attention on the importance of guest behaviour and expectations. Guestology turns traditional management thinking upside down. Instead of focusing on organisational design, managerial hierarchy and production systems to maximise organisational efficiency, it focuses the firm to look systematically at the customer experience from the guest point of view. Guestology involves systematically searching for the key factors that determine quality and value in the eyes of the guest, analysing them, measuring their impact on the customer experience, testing various strategies that might improve the quality of experience and then providing a combination of factors or elements that attracts loyal customers. Only after developing this total guest's orientation, can the rest of the organisation issues be addressed. The goal is to create and sustain an expertise that can respond to the customers' needs and expectations and still make a profit

From their study of customer preferences, Disney's guestologists learned that an important reason for the customers' satisfaction with its theme parks is its cleanliness. Disney therefore stresses on keeping the parks clean, and this has become one of its greatest assets. Keeping a theme park clean is a big job. So the Disney organisation encourages its customers to help out by disposing of their own trash. In studying customer behviour, Disney learned two things about trash disposal. First, if cast members constantly pick up even the smallest bins of trash, park visitors would emulate rather than litter. Cast members' practice and respect cleanliness, and so they are role models for the customers. Second, if trashcans are their own trash into them. Disney locates its trashcans 25 to 27 paces apart. Understanding how customers respond to environmental cues and using that knowledge to help maintain a high standard of cleanliness is guestology in practice.

8.10   CRM SUCCESS FACTORS

While clear intention fuels the power of CRM, there are several other success factors to consider. We will focus on five of the most important here. Organisations that implement CRM with a strong return on investment share these characteristics.

1. Strong internal partnership around the CRM strategy: We said earlier that CRM is a way of doing business that touches all areas of your organisation. This means that you and your management peers need to form strong internal partnerships around CRM. If you and your organisation are early on the road to CRM implementation, now is the time to bring your CRM needs to the table, and to be open to listening to the CRM needs of the other areas. You may find that you have requirements that are, at least potentially, in conflict. Resist the temptation to go to the war for what you need.

If your organisation has gone off the partnership road with CRM, then now is the time to come back together and rebuild partnership with the area that is currently championing CRM. Let them know that you appreciate what they have done. Let them know what data you have to offer and help them understand how you plan to use the data you request from them.

2. Employees at all levels and all areas accurately collect information for the CRM system: Employees are most likely to comply appropriately with your CRM system when they understand what information is to be captured and why it is important, they are also more likely to trust and use CRM data when they know how and why it was collected.

3. CRM tools are customer and employee-friendly: CRM tools should be integrated into your systems as seamlessly as possible, making them a natural part of the customer service interaction. A major manufacturer of speciality pet foods redesigned the pop-up screens for its toll-free consumer phone line. In the original design, the final pop-up screen prompted the representative to ask the caller's name and address. Yet, representatives had found that it was easier and felt more natural to ask, "What's your name?" and "Where are you calling from?" and "What's your pet's name?" at the start of the call.

4. Report out only the data you use, and use a data you report: Just because your CRM tool can run a report doesn't mean it should. Refer back to your CRM strategy, and then run the data you will actually use. And share that data with your team.

5. Don't go high-tech when low-tech can do: At Harley-Davidson outside of Milwaukee, WI during the summer they often leave open the big metal doors to the manufacturing facility to let in any breeze and the cooler evening air. Unfortunately, open doors occasionally let in other things, including skunks. A team met to consider the problem and possible solutions. After discussing the pros and cons of screens, half-doors, or keeping the doors shut, they came upon ideal solution. When a skunk wanders in, just leave it alone and wait till it wanders back out. Skunks may be Harley fans, but they never stay long. Organisations that successfully implement their CRM look for the simplest solution when implementing their CRM strategy.

8.11   ECRM (ELECTRONIC CUSTOMER RELATIONSHIP MANAGEMENT)

With ECRM, manufacturers have the opportunity to take customer interaction to new levels of effectiveness by integrating customer information otherwise hoarded by customer service, marketing, and sales departments and making it available across the organisation to improve the overall customer experience.

Some large companies are gaining significant competitive advantage by using Information Technology (IT) and business to analyse and manage their relationship with each customer. This trend is relevant to many larger companies. While smaller companies tend to rely on people, rather than computers, to track and manage their customer relationships, this trend is still relevant to them because—

Most IT driven changes in large companies sooner or later are adapted by progressive smaller companies, as relevant software packages suited to the needs and budgets of Small and Medium Entrepreneurs (SMEs) are developed. Any SME planning an overall medium term eBusiness/IT strategy thus needs to consider whether aspects of CRM are likely to be relevant to that strategy. The ability of large companies to provide a holistic approach to customers may partly erode one of the competitive advantages enjoyed by SMEs, namely, their ability to provide a much more personalised service than their larger competitors.

CRM is the three-letter acronym for Customer Relationship Management. CRM packages are software tools that allow the user to keep a record of all interactions with a customer. Typical examples of these interactions are:

- Complaints
- Queries
- Requests for quotations
- Instructions, and so on

As the user is recording the interactions, the user can have access to all the customer information that exists on the system. Information such as:

- Account balance and transaction history
- Order status
- Shipping status

And static details such as name, address, phone, e-mail, etc. The level of information available is dependent on the level of functionality of the CRM tool or the degree of integration with the company ERP package. ERP packages process accounts, sales order processing, stock movements, purchases, and so on. The CRM tool also has functionality:

1. To assign actions (arising out of an interaction) to different users
2. Keep a record and status on all actions that have been taken against a particular transaction
3. Classify an interaction as being 'open' until all the desired actions have been completed.

The strength of CRM is that any employee within the company can access the interaction record at any time to review the status and update it. The customer cannot catch the employee, who has access to the CRM tool, unaware. This gives the customer the 'VIP feeling' because the customer feels that every employee in the company is aware of the customer and the customer's issues.

CRM originally evolved from the recording and fixing of complaints to the current level where packages are now available on the Internet. In the latest eCRM generation, the customer may record the complaint and could change the customer's own static details using a web browser.

CRM systems also allow for proactive dealings with potential and existing customer (e.g. quotes) and electronic mail-shots. Records are kept of these interactions in the same way as complaints and other 'reactive' interactions are stored.

The normal operational transactions (such as sales order processing, order picking, dispatch, invoicing, and so on) would not normally be stored on a CRM tool as this functionality is readily available in ERP packages. However, some of the Tier 1 CRM solutions have started to store this type of information also. The most well-known CRM tool is provided by Siebel Systems.

Competitive Advantage through CRM

European manufacturers have been slow in adopting customer relationship management. Without explicit retention goals, programmes for improving customer loyalty go nowhere with sub par business performance as a frequent result. But while many companies have such goals in place, fewer are achieving them. The success of many non-European manufacturers in Europe over the last two decades has a lot to do with their forward thinking practices in managing their customer relationships.

With customers embracing "imported" brands like Nike, Procter & Gamble, and Colgate-Palmolive in consumer products, Dell in personal computers, and General Electric in appliances, many European manufacturers' notions about customer loyalty are being called into question. The impact of competitors that excel at anticipating and serving customer needs is beginning to be felt. Despite many European manufacturers' hesitation in adopting CRM practices and principles to date, they now have a unique opportunity to quickly take a lead position. Having sat on the sidelines and let the first wave of CRM initiatives pass them by; these companies can now use the Internet to rethink their customer interactions from scratch. Rather than getting on the traditional CRM bandwagon, they can leapfrog the competition by leveraging the more advanced capabilities of customer relationship management in the digital world: eCRM. Indeed, eCRM gives companies far greater opportunities to improve marketing and customer satisfaction than traditional CRM approaches. Most traditional CRM initiatives predate the World Wide Web and tend to be in silos such as customer service, sales, or marketing functions. For example, many companies installed CRM software in their customer call centres to create deep databases on customers, repair and other service records, and the company's product and service information. By implementing CRM, these companies made improvements in certain narrow areas of the business. For example, their service reps became more knowledgeable about each customer and better able to handle their issues after the purchase. But the primary benefits of the system were limited to the customer service function often the call centre representatives. Sales people typically did not gain access to the data, which they might have used to help make a sale.

Traditional CRM rarely provided a consistent enterprise-wide picture of the profitability and needs of individual customers. In essence, while helping give a better customer experience, those traditional CRM efforts did little to help companies decide where to invest next or how to improve their product offerings or sales process.

As we discuss later, without this holistic, integrated, 360-degree view of the customer, most of the value of CRM efforts dissipates quickly as competitors have little trouble in catching up. Flexible enterprise-wide eCRM systems can create a "digital loyalty cycle" across marketing, sales, and customer service. This provides customers with the optimal price, quality, quantity, brand, pre-sales and after-sales service experience. This is becoming the benchmark for successful customer relationship management in the digital age.

With eCRM, manufacturers have the opportunity to take customer interaction to new levels of effectiveness by integrating customer information otherwise hoarded by customer service, marketing, and sales departments and making it available across the organisation to improve the overall customer experience. Traditional knowledge and analysis of product and geographic markets are becoming relatively less useful as the understanding of individual customers, their purchase history, requirements, and lifetime value is becoming the ultimate unit of analysis. The battleground is moving from scale and market-share to customer profitability and wallet-share. Without investments in stronger eCRM capabilities, however, a complete, actionable picture of individual customers is often unavailable for most companies. This means that strategic marketing decisions today are often founded upon quicksand. As a result, customer loyalty is becoming more and more a subject to the now infamous mouse click. An eCRM system or Web-based CRM system is fundamentally less cumbersome and less expensive to implement than traditional CRM because eCRM can be extended more easily to users everywhere in the company through the Internet. As common standards for exchanging product, service, and customer data emerge, such as eXtensible Markup Language (XML) standards, partners in the sales and distribution channels can be linked more easily to the system and share in the benefits. The cost savings can be sizeable. For example, GE estimates the cost of taking a phone order at around 5 for simple products and as much as 80 for its higher-tech offerings. In contrast, an order placed online costs an average 20-cent. With GE getting 20 million phone calls a year in its appliance business alone, the savings from Internet-based CRM technology could become immense. But the value of eCRM goes way beyond cutting cost. The technology allows companies to capture customer feedback at more of the "touch points" between a company and its customers across channels and functions e.g. meetings with sales people, customer service inquiries, purchases over the Internet, customer surveys, user groups, and the like and use it to improve relationships and value for individual customers.

European manufacturers have been slower to adopt many key enterprise technologies, such as the installation of an enterprise resource planning (ERP) system, for effectively managing millions of customer interactions. Without an ERP system to track the status of a customer's order from the factory to the customer's door, a manufacturer cannot tell a customer some of the most important things he or she wants to hear these days: Where is my order and when do I get it?

Unresponsiveness to customers' concerns, if not rectified, will threaten the sustainability of many manufacturers. The continuing integration and expansion of the European market and the arrival of the Euro are both opportunities and threats. Certainly, those forces have put European manufacturers on more of an equal footing with their competitors based elsewhere, particularly in the United States. An even bigger factor pushing European industrial companies to get much better at managing customer relationships is the Internet. The global communications network eliminates much of the age-old geographic and information advantage that many manufacturers have had over their customers. Customers of everything from cars and appliances to computers and books can now get information on pricing, product features and other buying criteria from a broad array of sellers without leaving their home or office, and they can often complete the transaction electronically. Unlike many services (such as haircuts and hotel services), most manufacturing products can be transferred across borders and are easily comparable across geographies in terms of price, quality, quantity, delivery, and so forth. As consumers become more familiar with the Net, as bandwidth increases and access cost falls, Internet usage will continue to soar. Even if consumers do not buy online, the information they gain on the Internet can still affect prices. Companies must understand that, not unlike the impact of imports on competition, it takes only a small percentage of total sales to go through Internet channels to seriously affect value propositions, prices, and profits.

From Product and Geography Focus to Customer-Centric Strategies

The combined impact of the Euro and the Internet has highlighted pricing disparities across Europe and will no doubt begin to erode them for manufactured and other internationally tradable goods and services. As manufacturers traditionally have reaped the rewards from differential pricing strategies in each country and region, these developments will undoubtedly cause already slim profit margins to become even slimmer. An interesting example of this is to compare prices online for the same technology items in different countries from multinational IT suppliers such as Dell.

While many regional differences will persist within Europe such as those determined by culture, language, government policies, and payment systems manufacturers will have to move beyond product and geography-centric sales, marketing, and customer service practices and start to put the customer at the centre of attention. If increasingly knowledgeable customers can make price comparisons from country to country, the only way for manufacturers to retain price premiums and increase shareholder value will be to offer greater value through improved customer service and target customers with differentiated offerings. That is, they will have to maximise the way they treat each and every customer or segment. The entire customer interaction, including what goes on after the sale, will become even more important. Customer loyalty and retention are bound to become the ultimate platform for competition.

Customer Loyalty and Profitable Growth

Because it costs significantly more to continually attract new customers than to retain the current ones, and because the value of most customer relationships increases over time, companies that increase revenue without holding onto their best customers wind up roding profitability and, thus, shareholder value. When we look at the business performance of customer-centric manufacturers, we find clear indications of the underpinnings of success. Customer-centric manufacturers are more likely to exceed their goals for return on assets and market share compared to non-customer centric companies. They are also much more likely to exceed key operational goals for inventory reduction, parts shortages, labour costs, and organisational learning.

Designing the Digital Loyalty Cycle

If customer loyalty is the goal, eCRM is the tool. Although companies can use eCRM to pursue benefits in any one part of the business, the greatest benefits come from using it to link every operation in a business that affects the customer experience. Integrating and leveraging efforts across pricing, product quality, marketing, sales, and customer service through the digital loyalty cycle will increasingly become the hallmark of successful companies. By always working from a real-time perspective, for example, frontline staff and strategic partners can continuously improve the way they interact with individual customers and segments. In doing so, they not only can improve the customer experience, they can also improve the way feedback from customers is leveraged across product development, manufacturing, marketing, sales, and service.

When executed correctly, eCRM implementations are designed as a digital loyalty cycle that continuously improves to create lasting competitive advantage. When a manufacturer uses eCRM technology and redefines its business processes in customer acquisition and retention, it strengthens its capabilities in key areas that determine a customer's purchase decision including pricing, product quality, marketing, sales, and customer service to create a virtuous, digital loyalty cycle. The impact of eCRM strategies is beginning to show. In traditional call centres alone, eCRM lets companies shift much of the people-intensive customer service transactions to online transactions that let customers serve themselves if they wish. Considering the enormous cost of running call centres to serve customers in multiple languages and cultures and legal environments across Europe, the

Internet provides a permanent but flexible solution to handle this diverse and costly set of requirements. Content created in one country can be translated through software adapted to other countries in near real-time.

The experience of System Label, the Irish specialist printer of industrial labels equipment, demonstrates how eCRM can increase responsiveness to customer requirements. Since implementing several system developments including a new eCRM package, the company often turns around orders faster than its 5-day target at the outset of the project. With eCRM, customer-centric manufacturers can use customer information to better predict customers' buying patterns, which allows them to better manage pricing and marketing decisions in real time. Behind the scenes of the eCRM systems are conventional, perhaps, but crucial components for success: business processes, technologies, and people. When it comes to business processes, manufacturing companies must understand the customer loyalty cycle and use an integrated approach across the organisation to strengthen loyalty. That is, they must synchronise and differentiate everything that affects an individual customer's loyalty: brand, quality, price, sales, and service experience. It is no small task, but by first focusing on the customers that are most profitable and key to future survival, companies can leverage eCRM where it matters most. In terms of technology, companies must use IT to gather, analyse and disseminate information from customers across the enterprise. Enterprise resource planning (ERP) systems can serve as the foundation. For some, a web-based approach is likely to be both faster and cheaper. Leveraging the Internet technology eases the implementation burden and increases flexibility in designing global and regional manufacturing, distribution, and service networks. The same comparison can be made between traditional CRM and eCRM. That is, a typical installation of a CRM system a few years ago would take, say, around 6-12 months. Today, with eCRM, a similar, enhanced and more flexible system based the on Internet technology is not only less expensive to install but also much quicker, taking just about 3 to 6 months depending on the specific circumstances of the company. People are key to serving customers well. Companies must therefore invest in people through continual learning, such as just-in-time and cross training, to ensure that they have the skills and mindset to achieve customer loyalty goals. In addition, incentives should measure and reward customer satisfaction and loyalty. Base wages and benefits may have to be upgraded, and knowledge systems should be supported. Successful companies understand that employee loyalty is crucial to building customer loyalty.

Overcoming Real and Imagined Barriers to eCRM

Becoming customer-centric does not happen overnight. It requires moving the supply chain from a "push" to a "pull" that is, shifting from producing and distributing products according to internal forecasts to building and delivering to meet actual customer demand in a profitable manner. This shift requires thinking of the "supply chain" as the "demand chain".

The challenges to manufacturers are significant but unavoidable. The good news is that many barriers to change are more perceived than real. Take, for example, the lack of a common payment system in Europe and lack of common rules governing financial institutions. If a company wants to set up accounts with the same bank in each EU country, it may need as many as 900 signatures. Some say this will prevent the Internet from facilitating the free flow of goods and services across country lines. But EU countries have already adopted significant legislative changes designed to facilitate both the single European Market and eBusiness.

The one barrier to eCRM that is very real and very big is complacency. Manufacturers are at risk of losing the game if they cannot change their mindset and take advantage of new tools and technologies to become more customer-oriented. Companies often still believe that if you make a good product, people will buy it. If they continue to focus only on the design and manufacture of products, they will miss important opportunities to learn more about what their customers really want and to provide the profitable after-sale services that customers increasingly need and demand. If, on the other hand, they are willing to view their operations more broadly by adopting eCRM technologies to get closer to customers, they can strengthen their customer interactions, grow, and prosper. In the case of Zomax Ireland, for example, it was customers that drove the company to embrace eCRM and other technologies and this is likely to be the experience of many Irish businesses over the coming years.

The arguments manufacturers typically make for skimping on customer retention practices and capabilities like eCRM are rapidly weakening. The challenge now is to use technology to lead the next revolution by leveraging the online loyalty and creating sustainable business models.

8.12   RECENT TRENDS IN MARKETING

There are many recent trends in marketing. Some of the important recent trends in marketing are:

1. E-business (i.e., Electronic Business)

Introduction

Today, e-business (i.e., electronic business) is gaining importance throughout the world. The whole world is caught up in e-business.

Meaning of E-Business

E-Business means buying and selling of the products or services, effecting payments and exchange of information through electronic means of computers and networks. In other words, it means buying and selling of goods or services online through the Internet.

E-Business Opportunities

E-business opportunities are not just confined to large corporate bodies, and government departments. They are also available to medium and small business houses. Again, e-business opportunities are not just restricted to developed countries. They are also available to developing or underdeveloped countries to enter the prosperous global market.

E-Business Models

There are many models of e-business. The important models of e-business are:

(a) Business to business e-business, B to B or B 2 B.
(b) Business to consumers' e-business, B to C or B 2 C.
(c) Intra-company e-business.
(d) Consumer to business e-business, C to B or C 2 B.
(e) Consumer to consumer e-business, C to C or C 2 C.
(f) Business to government e-business, B to G or B 2 G

Business to business e-business means e-business between one business enterprise and another business enterprise.

Business to business e-business facilitates direct business connections and eliminates the need for intermediaries. Business to business e-business contributes to a very high volume of business transactions.

Business to consumers' e-business means e-business between a business enterprise and consumer.

Business to consumer e-business accounts for a large number of business transactions, through the volume of business per transaction may not be much.

Intra company e-business means e-business within a business enterprise

Intra-company e-business contributes to better communications between the various departments of the enterprise, efficient management, reduction in the cost of management and the staff, etc.

Consumer to business e-business facilitates the communication of consumer's views on price terms acceptable to them.

Consumer to consumer e-business facilitates buying and selling of goods or services between consumers directly.

Business to government e-business means e-business between business enterprises and various levels of government agencies, viz., local, state and Central Government agencies.

Advantages of E-Business

E-business has several advantages. It

   (a) contributes to increased sales opportunities for business firms.

   (b) helps business firms to have access to global market.

   (c) facilitates operations 24 hours a day and 7 days a week.

   (d) contributes to decreased transaction costs.

   (e) contributes to increased speed in the exchange of goods and services or information.

   (f) ensures accuracy of information exchanged between parties.

   (g) contributes to the availability of large variety of products to consumers.

   (h) contributes to customised and personalised transactions or services to customers.

   (i) contributes to quick delivery of goods or services to customers.

Limitations of E-Business

E-business is no doubt, quite advantageous. But it is not free from limitations. It suffers from the following limitations:

1. There are global market issues, such as languages, currencies, political and legal environment, and etc. in e-business.
2. There is the problem of maintaining the security in e-business
3. There is the problem of maintaining reliability in e-business.
4. Shortage of skilled technical staff is another limitation of e-business.

Essentials for the Success of E-Business

There are certain essentials for the success of e-business. They are:

1. **Computer System:** As e-business is conduct of business through the Internet, for the successful implementation of e-business, there should be a computer system. The computer system should be sufficient for handling all business transactions.

2. **Internet connection:** For e-business, there should be Internet connection from any Internet service provider.

3. **Comprehensive website:** The business must possess well-designed website, having detailed information, linked with supporting pictures, graphs and technical data.

4. **Effective telecommunication system:** There should be effective telecommunication lines, capable of handling the traffic on the Internet.

5. **Competent workforce:** E-business needs well-trained competent workforce capable of working with computer network and the Internet with ease. They should be capable of handling all types of business operations.

6. **Security and safety of business transactions:** Though e-business supposed to be safe and secure because of its digital or electronic code system, it is subject to security and safety risks, such as brand hijacking, hacking, i.e. unauthorised entry into a website, which destroys the data and information. Viruses, which can enter the system and clean up the data and information stored up by the computer, etc.

7. **Psyche of the people:** The psyche of the people is one of the factors required for the successful information of e-business. For instance, in India, the psyche of the people is one of the obstacles in the development of e-business. Psychologically, the Indian consumers, at least the older generation, do not like to buy things without touching and feeling them.

8.13   TELEMARKETING

Introduction

Telemarketing has become an important marketing tool in recent years. This is clear from the fact that marketers in U.S.A. have spent billions of dollars on telephone charges to sell their products or services, and an average household or customer in U.S.A. receives about 19 telemarketing calls each year and makes about 16 telephone calls to place orders for goods or services. Telemarketing has popular not only in the U.S.A. and other developed countries but also in developing countries in India.

Telemarketing is a form of direct marketing; here the marketers go direct to the customers, using telecom and information technology facilities.

Meaning of Telemarketing

Telemarketing is the system under which marketers make telephone calls to customers to market their products and services, and the customers make telephone calls to marketers to place orders for goods and services. In other words, it is the system of marketing of goods and services of marketers and the placing of orders for goods and services by customers through telephones.

How does Telemarketing Work?

Telemarketing is usually done through specific contacts established with hundreds of prospective customers selected in a special campaign.

Several telecallers are appointed for telecall operations. The telecallers carry on their telecall operations from the call centre. That means, the call centre is the real operation theatre in telemarketing. The call centre has many telecallers for carrying on the telecall operations, a few supervisors for supervising the operations of telecallers, and a manager in overall charge of the call centre. The telecallers are normally grouped into teams of six or seven, and placed under the charge of a supervisor. The telecallers sit in front of the computer terminals and speak into their headsets as telephone operators do in any telephone exchange. Simultaneously, they access information on the computer terminal, and add fresh data on it as the telecalling progresses. The telecaller opens the call by greeting the prospective customer. Then he politely seeks the prospective customers permission to have a brief conversation. Then he strikes the right cord with the prospective customer and explains the product or service offered. He generates interest in the prospect about the offer, and tries to clinch the order.

The telecallers area usually provided with a script initially with which they practice for their operations. Once they become comfortable, they resort to improvisation as required.

Advantages of Telemarketing

Today telemarketing plays a very important role in marketing of goods and services. Its advantages are:

1. It is used in business marketing (i.e., marketing between business firms) and consumer marketing (i.e., marketing between business firms and consumers).
2. It helps a marketer to reduce the amount of personal selling needed for contacting dealers and customers.
3. It contributes to considerable increase in sales for marketers.
4. It facilitates personalised contact with prospective customers.
5. It gives the marketers better chance to influence the prospectus.
6. It enhances marketing productivity by screening and selecting the prospectus through preparatory conservations, and then, concentrating on the selected prospects.
7. It is less expensive compared to other forms of direct selling.

Essentials for the Success of Telemarketing

1. The marketer has to build up a relevant database of potential customers through a special campaign.

2. The telemarketing campaign should be carefully planned.
3. The telemarketing campaign should first be pre-tested on a small scale.
4. The effectiveness of telemarketing depends on choosing the right telecallers.
5. The telecallers selected should be given good training and incentives to perform their task well.
6. The telecallers should have pleasant voice.
7. The telecallers should have project enthusiasm.
8. The telecallers should initially begin with given script and eventually move towards more improvisation.
9. The opening lines of telephone calls are critical (i.e., very important). There should be brief and start with a good question and catches the listener's interest.
10. The calls should be made at the right time to make calls in late morning and afternoon to reach business prospectus, and evening between 7 and 9 to reach households.
11. The telemarketing supervisor should build up telecallers enthusiasm by offering incentives to good performers.

M-Business (i.e., Mobile Business)

Introduction

M-business (i.e., mobile business) or mobile marketing is an innovation in marketing. M-business has become quite popular in recent years.

Meaning of M-business (i.e., Mobile Business)

M-business (i.e., mobile business) is business through mobile phones or cellular phones. In other words, it is the technology of buying and selling goods through S.M.S. (i.e., short message service) via mobile phones.

Characteristics of M-Business

M-business (i.e., mobile business) has certain characteristic features. Those features are:

1. Mobile business is business through mobile phones.
2. It is carried on by sending or receiving S.M.S.
3. It is an innovative approach in marketing in recent years.
4. It is highly personalized.

Essentials of Text Message Sent through Mobile Phones in Mobile Business:

As stated earlier, mobile business is conducted by sending or receiving short text messages (i.e., S.M.S) through mobile phones. The short text messages sent through mobile phones for conducting mobile business should cover the following aspects:

1. Who is to be addressed (i.e., the persons to whom short text message is to be sent) should be decided first. The marketer should determine whether the text business message should be sent to existing customers or new customers.
2. What is the response expected from the persons addressed should also be determined. That is, what action the marketer wants from the addressee should be determined.
3. What is the message the marketer wants to carry across should also be determined.

8.14   RELATIONSHIP MARKETING

Introduction

Personal selling is transaction-oriented. It aims at helping sales people to close a specific sale with a customer. But in many cases, a business firm is not seeking simply a sale, but wants to target important customers and to win the long-term relationship with them to increase its business. The business firm would like to demonstrate to key customers that it has the capabilities to serve their needs in a superior way, particularly if the two parties (i.e., the business firm and the customers) can form a committed relationship. This has contributed to the emergence of relationship marketing. Today, more business firms are shifting their emphasis from transaction marketing to relationship marketing.

Meaning of Relationship Marketing

Relationship marketing has been defined in different ways by different authorities. It has been defined as "attracting and maintaining and enhancing long-term customer relationship."

It is also defined as "establishing, developing and maintaining successful relational exchanges".

It is also defined as "a business strategy which proactively builds a preference for an organisation with its individual employees, channels of distribution and customers, resulting in increased retention and increased performance".

From the above definitions, it is clear that relationship marketing is a marketing strategy that aims at development and maintaining long-term relationship with important customers, suppliers and distributors in order to retain and enhance the business of the firm. In other words, relationship marketing is the process of attracting, maintaining and enhancing relationships with key people, i.e., with selected customers, suppliers and distributors in order to retain their long-term preference and business. In short, it is the practice building and long-term relationship with key parties, i.e., customers, suppliers and distributors in order to ensure their long-term dealings with the business.

Characteristic features of Relationship Marketing

Relationship marketing has certain characteristic features. These are:

1. It is the practice of building long-term relationship with key parties in order to retain their long-term preference and business.
2. It is the practice of building long-term relationships not only with key customers but also with important suppliers and distributors. It even includes the process of building long-term relationship with key employees.
3. Relationship marketing implies building of long-term relationship only with valued customers. This is because it is not feasible for business enterprise to develop long-term relationship with all its customers.
4. Relationship marketing is based on the philosophy of retaining valued existing customers rather than acquiring new customers, this is because it costs much more to attract new customers than it costs to retain one existing customers.
5. Relationship marketing is ensured by focusing on the provision of good quality products and services to customers at fair prices.
6. The ultimate outcome of relationship marketing is the building of a business asset is called a marketing network. A marketing network consists of the company and its supporting stakeholders, viz., the customers, suppliers, distributors and employees.

Advantages of Relationship Marketing

Relationship marketing has many advantages. These are:

1. Relationship marketing contributes to the building up and retaining of long-term relationships with some valued customers.
2. Relationship marketing helps a business firm to build up a business asset, viz., a marketing network.
3. Relationship marketing has the potential to enhance customer satisfaction.
4. Relationship marketing fetches for the business firm long-term contracts, repeated sales orders over time and more profits
5. Relationship marketing is cheaper than acquisition of more new customers.

Difficulties of relationship marketing

Relationship marketing suffers from certain difficulties. These are:

1. Maintenance of accurate and up-to-date database required for relationship marketing is costly.

2. The management of the business firm may not be willing to lose their powerbase by agreeing to the creation of relationship marketing.
3. The staff of the business firm may not be prepared to take on relationship marketing responsibility.

Essentials of relationship marketing

Relationship marketing (i.e., a long-term commitment to working together) requires certain essentials. Those essentials are:

(a) It requires the development of a set of long-term agreements. According to Rackham, the selling process moves from preliminaries to investigating the prospectus problems and needs, then, demonstrating the supplier's capabilities and finally obtaining a long-term commitment.
(b) Today, customers prefer marketers who can sell and deliver a coordinated set of products and services to many locations, who can quickly solve problems that arise in different locations and who can work with closely with customer teams to improve the products and processed. So for relationship marketing, there should be marketers of the type specified above.
(c) Sales teamwork is the key to winning and maintaining major customer accounts.
(d) Relationship marketing is based on the premise that the important accounts, i.e., customers, need focus and continuous attention. So, sales peoples working with key customers must do more than mere call. They should call or visit customers many times, monitor the key accounts, know their problems, and are ready to serve them in a number of ways.

Steps to be taken for establishing Relationship Marketing Programme in a Business concern

Certain steps are required to be taken for establishing relationship marketing programme in a company. Those steps are:

1. The key customers should be identified. The company should first choose five or ten largest customers and concentrate on them for relationship marketing. Additional customers who show exceptional growth can be added to the list later on.
2. The task of building upon relationship marketing with key customers should be entrusted to marketing managers.
3. The sales persons serving the key customers should be given proper training in relationship marketing.

4. A clear job description should be developed for relationship managers; the job description should describe the relationship manager's reporting relationships, objectives responsibilities and evaluation criteria. The relationship manager is responsible for the client, the focal point for all information about the client and is the mobiliser of company services for the client. Each relationship manager should have only one or a few relationships to manage.

5. An overall manager should appoint to supervise the relationship managers. The overall manager should develop job descriptions, utilisation criteria and resource support to increase relationship managers effectiveness.

6. Each relationship manager must develop long range customer relationship plans. The customer relationship plan should state the objectives, strategies, specific activities and required resources.

Evaluation of Relationship Marketing

If a relationship marketing programme is properly implemented, there will be fruitful results. So there is strong move towards relationship marketing. But it must be noted that relationship marketing is not effective in all situations. Relationship marketing will be quite helpful and effective only with customers who have long time horizon and high switching costs.

8.15 CONCEPT MARKETING

Introduction

Concept marketing is a recent trend in marketing. It helps the marketers or business firms to increase their sales by tapping the hidden needs or wants of consumers.

Meaning of Concept Marketing

Before we discuss the meaning of concept marketing, let us understand the meaning of 'concept'. Concept means an idea or a thought.

Now let us discuss the meaning of 'concept marketing'. Concept marketing is the act of conceiving a new concept or idea regarding a product to meet the hidden needs or wants to customers and converting the new concept or idea into a product for a sale to customers on a commercial scale. In other words, it is the act of conceiving a new product idea to satisfy the hidden needs or wants of consumers, developing and producing a new product on the basis of the new idea conceived and marketing the new product produced on a commercial scale for profit. In short, it is the act of conceiving the new concept or idea, and converting it in to a product for sale.

Steps involved in Concept Marketing

Certain steps involved in concept marketing are:

1. Identifying the hidden needs or wants of consumers.
2. Conceiving of a new product idea to satisfy the hidden needs of consumers.
3. Converting the new product idea into a product, i.e., developing a new product on the basis of the new product idea conceived.
4. Creating awareness among the consumers about the new product developed.
5. Effecting changes in the minds of the consumers and creating a sense of need in the minds of the consumers for the new product.
6. Undertaking the marketing of the new product on a commercial scale to increase sales.

Advantages of Concept Marketing

Concept marketing is of great importance to the marketers as well as the consumers. It offers the following benefits.

1. It helps an entrepreneur to conceive and develop a new product for sale.
2. It helps the marketer to increase his sales as well as his profits.
3. It improves the image of the business firm, if the new product becomes a success commercially.
4. It is helpful to the consumers to satisfy their hidden wants.

Limitations of Concept Marketing

Concept marketing is no doubt, of much significance. But it is not without limitations. It suffers from the following limitations.

1. Identifying the hidden needs or wants of the consumers, required for successful concept marketing, is a challenging and difficult task.

2. Concept marketing will be successful only if the new concept is widely accepted and commercially exploited.

3. In the initial stages, there may be resistance from consumers to the new product concept or idea. There are many types of resistance, such as usage resistance, value resistance, risk resistance and social resistance. Usage resistance signifies that there will be resistance from consumers to the new product, if it (i.e., the new product) is not compatible with the existing habits of the consumers. Value resistance signifies

that the new product does not give to the consumers more value for their money. Risk resistance signifies that the consumers perceive high risk in using the product, if the product is entirely new. Social resistance signifies that there will be social resistance, if the new product does not meet social values.

Essentials for the Success of Concept Marketing

There are certain essentials for the success of concept marketing. Those essentials are:

1. The hidden needs or wants of the consumers must be identified by the business firm.
2. There will be development and production of a new product to satisfy the hidden needs or wants of the consumers.
3. The new product must be widely recognised and accepted by the consumers.
4. The new product should be exploited and marketed on a commercial scale (i.e., on large scale).
5. There must be the creation of awareness in the minds of consumers influencing them to act favourably towards the new product.
6. There should be wide use of communication media by the marketer to ensure that the consumers understand and appreciate the benefits of the new product resulting from the new concept.

8.16   VIRTUAL MARKETING

Introduction

Virtual marketing is one of the methods of direct marketing. It is one of the powerful direct marketing channels to reach customers worldwide at minimum cost.

Meaning of Virtual Marketing

Virtual marketing is the process of conducting marketing activities geographically through electronic means. In other words, it is the process of marketing in which enquiries about the different types of products available, their quality and durability, price, etc. are made, selection of the required products is made after comparing the features of different marketing products available, order is placed for the selected goods payment for the purchases is effected, and the delivery of the goods purchased is ensured at the doorstep of the consumer at a convenient time online. In short, virtual marketing is web marketing, i.e., marketing through website.

Advantages of virtual marketing

Virtual marketing has several advantages. They are:

1. Virtual marketing helps the marketers to have access to worldwide marketing. With web marketing comprised in virtual marketing, a marketer located in any part of the world can have access to the market of the whole world, as opening a website is as good as opening branches everywhere in the world.
2. Virtual market through web market can be adopted even by small business firms. Scale of operations is not a limitation in virtual marketing or web marketing.
3. Through virtual marketing, i.e., through web market, marketers can offer a variety of products and services from a single website.
4. Through web marketing, the marketing process can be completed in a very short time.
5. Virtual marketing helps the marketers to achieve economics in various forms, say in the form of reduced levels of inventory, low set-up costs, minimum workforce, reducing warehousing costs, etc.
6. Virtual marketing reduces the communication and channel costs of marketing.
7. Virtual marketing reduces the span of operating cycle because of minimum number of activities involved in web marketing.
8. Virtual marketing helps the marketers to enhance customer value. That is, the consumers get more value for their money through virtual marketing, i.e., web marketing.
9. Like other direct marketing methods, virtual marketing, i.e., web marketing also helps the marketers to build up relationship marketing.
10. Virtual marketing, i.e., Web marketing, helps the marketers to adjust their activities to changing marketing conditions very quickly.
11. Web marketing comprised in virtual marketing, provides high degree of transparency about the various business transactions.

Essentials for the Success of Virtual Marketing

There are certain essentials for the success of virtual marketing. They are:

1. There should be informative and user-friendly web for the success of virtual marketing, because web is the readily accessible means of bringing the sellers and buyers together.
2. The website's goals and objectives should be clearly determined.
3. The website's target audience should be clearly determined.

KEYWORDS

Assurance: *The ability to perform promised service dependably and accurately.*

Analytical CRM: *Analytical CRM is a consistent suite of analytical applications that help the firm to measure, predict, and optimise customer relationships.*

CRM: *Stands for Customer Relationship Management. It is a strategy used to learn more about customers' needs and behaviours in order to develop stronger relationships with them.*

Customer Information Database : *A customer database is an organised collection of comprehensive information about individual customers or prospects that is current, accessible, and actionable for such marketing purposes as lead generation, lead qualification, sale of a product or service, or maintenance of customer relationships.*

Customer privacy: *Customer privacy measures are those taken by commercial organisations to ensure that confidential customer data is not stolen or abused.*

Hybrid service: *This kind of service consists of equal part of goods and services. Restaurants for example, are patronised both for their food and their service.*

Intangible: *That which cannot be seen, touched, smelt or tasted but can only be perceived.*

Inseparable: *Cannot be separated from the person responsible for providing the service.*

Loss Leader Pricing: *Initial low pricing to attract more customers/repeated usage or consumption at subsequently higher price.*

Perishable: *If not used or consumed will be lost forever. Cannot be stored*

Physical Evidence: *Building, dcor, lightening, logo, letterhead, tables, design of product, physical representative which contributes to the 'looks' and 'atmosphere' of the service organisation.*

Pure service: *This service consists of psychotherapy elements and which are tangible in nature.*

Reliability: *The willingness to help customers and to provide prompt service.*

Service: *Is any act or performance that one party can offer to another that is essentially intangible and does not result in the ownership of anything. Its production may not be tied to a physical product.*

Variability: *Services are highly variable, since they depend on who provides them and when and where they are provided.*

SUMMARY

Service can be distinguished from products on the basis of their characteristics of intangibility, inseparability, heterogeneity, lack of ownership and perishability. These characteristics pose a challenge to the marketing manager who has to find solutions to constraints imposed by these features.

The marketing of services requires an extended marketing mix comprising production, packaging, promotion, and distribution as well as people, physical evidence and process. The marketing has put to great stress on the last three elements of the marketing strategy and combine them with the first to achieve a harmonious blend which fulfils the customer's want-satisfaction.

The basic reasons for the development of the service sector are the growth in intermediate demand from various manufacturing organisations that are in the process of unbundling and direct demand from customers. A marketing approach to the service organisations is a recent trend. Increased competition in this sector and growing public awareness, expectations and changing technological and business propositions made service organisations think of a marketing approach to deliver satisfaction to the consumers.

The marketing mix of services consists of seven Ps in addition to 4 Ps of the traditional marketing mix. Service marketing mix have three additional components; physical evidence, people and process. Service firms should make the elements of marketing mix dynamic as well as adaptable to changes in the marketing environment. A marketing strategy formulated in accordance with the organisational goals needs to be implemented with efficiency.

Customer relationship management is emerging as the central theme of corporate strategy. Service companies need to change from their traditional marketing philosophies that are transaction-oriented to relationship-oriented marketing philosophy. They should work on building, maintaining and enhancing customer relationships. Customer retention strategies need to be developed to gain lifetime value of the customers.

Service customers are also interested in building relationships with service providers due to varied reasons. Therefore, relationships should be planned on win-win propositions between the seller and the buyer.

With eCRM, manufacturers have the opportunity to take customer interaction to new levels of effectiveness by integrating customer information otherwise hoarded by customer service, marketing, and sales departments and making it available across the organisation to improve the overall customer experience.

CRM links in e-Business: E-Commerce and Customer Relationships on the Internet.

ASSIGNMENT

Assignment 1

Team Assignment–Differentiate your product

Answering the following questions, try to identify the differential advantage of your CE centre

1. Why should customers buy from us rather than from our competitors?
2. What makes us different from our competitors?
3. How are we better than our rivals?
4. What strengths do we have that we can effectively capitalise on?

Assignment 2

Team Assignment–Marketing SWOT analysis

Identify your four strengths, weaknesses, opportunities and threats answering the questions below:

1. Do you use your strengths to full advantage? Could you do more to capitalise on them?
2. Are there current or future opportunities you could exploit? Are new markets emerging or are there existing, untapped customer groups?
3. What threats do your competitors pose? What threats exist in wider marketplace?
4. What lets you down? What are you not good at? What do your competitors do better?

Assignment 3

If your firm is engaged in marketing services

(a) Identify the need or want satisfaction provided by the service.
(b) Describe the nature of service which your firm is providing.
(c) Describe how your firm is differentiating its services as compared to that provided by the competing firms.

_____

_____

_____

Assignment 4

What are the services which your firm uses on a regular basis in the area of marketing, finance, and government dealing? Against each service, describe the nature of organisation providing the service (viz. individual firm, government agency, etc)

_____

_____

_____

Assignment 5

Identify and describe the tangible aspects of the service provided by the following:

1. Hospital
2. Petrol station
3. Property station
4. Beauty parlour
5. Dry-cleaner

Are any of these a pure tangible product or pure intangible service?

_____

_____

_____

_____

Assignment 6

Identify the controllable elements in the following service organisations

(a) Airlines
(b) A lawyer's firm
(c) A firm which undertakes contract for maintenance and repairs of air-conditioners and refrigerators

Attempt to evolve procedures and standards for these controllable elements with the objective of improving the overall, performance of the service.

Assignment 7

Describe the components of physical evidence in case of railways and banks. Also describe the role of service personnel in these organisations. How can customers influence other customers in these service organisations?

_____

_____

_____

_____

Assignment 8

Team assignment Marketing of non-profit organisation

Consider that your CE centre is non-profit organisation. How does marketing in non-profit organisation differ from that in profit-oriented organisations?

Discuss the extent to which marketing principles can be applied and try to identify two marketing procedures which fit mostly for non-profit organisations

Assignment 9

Team Assignment–people, physical evidence and process

Identify six most important marketing mix elements (people, psychical evidence and process) for your selected market segments.

CASE STUDY

Case Study-1

Impacts of key trends in Indian telecom industry

Indian telecom industry is going through a phenomenal growth in the past five years. Many trends that shaped the direction of this industry have emerged during this period. This article discusses the key trends in the Indian telecom industry, its driver and the major impact of such trends affecting the operators, vendors and customers.

1. People go wireless: Indian customers are embracing the mobile technology in a big way (average four million subscribers are being added every month over the past six months). They prefer wireless service compared to wireline service, which is evident from the fact that while wireless subscriber base has increased 75 per cent from 2001 to 2006, the wireline subscriber base growth rate has been negligible during the same period. In fact, many customers are returning their wireline phones to their service providers. The main drivers for this trend are quick service delivery for mobile connections, affordable pricing plans in the form of prepaid cards and increased purchasing power among 18 to 40 years age group, prime market for this service. Some of the positive impacts of this trend are as follows: According to a study, 18 per cent mobile users are willing to change their handsets every year to newer models with more features, which is a good news for the handset vendors. The other impact is that while the operators have only limited options to generate additional revenues through value-added services from wireline service, the mobile operators have numerous options to generate non-voice revenues from their customers. Some examples of value-added services are ring tone download, ring back tone, talking SMS, etc. Moreover, there exists great opportunity for content developers to develop applications suitable for mobile users like mobilegaming, location based services, etc. On the negative side, there is increased threat of virus, spread through mobile data connections and Bluetooth technology, in the mobile phones making it unusable sometimes. This is good news for anti-virus solution providers who will gain from this trend. Moreover, according to the study conducted by any international organisation, prolonged mobile usage could lead to more health related issues, which is a bad news for heavy mobile users.

2. Telecom equipment manufacturing: The telecom equipment deployed in the Indian telecom network is primarily manufactured in other countries and exported to India. However, there is growing trend of telecom equipment manufacturing in India. Many equipment and handset vendors have either set up their manufacturing facilities or in process of setting up such facilities in India. The main drivers for this trend are availability of low cost and high quality human resources, favourable government policies encouraging investment in telecom manufacturing, and tender norms of telecom operators requiring the vendors to have local manufacturing facilities. Some of the positive impacts of this trend are as follows: Availability of local telecom hardware manufacturing will enable Indian companies to transform into new product innovators from being mere software solution developers. Moreover, with manufacturing factories and their supply chain in place in India, telecom equipment will become cheaper compared to being imported from other countries. Also, the operators could enjoy the benefits of quick turn around time for their telecom equipment repairs because EXIM procedure takes approximately 60 days to get the telecom equipment repaired abroad. Finally, the new telecom manufacturing facilities could lead to more economic development in those cities.

3. Managed services: Usually, telecom service providers operate their networks taking care of all activities like managing outside plant wiring and all the way up to total network management, on their own. However, there is a growing trend among the new operators, especially mobile operators, to outsource majority of their network operations to third party service providers. Typically, the complex network management work is outsourced to telecom equipment vendors. The main drivers for this trend are as follows: Since the new operators lack experience to manage their network efficiently, they need expert's help to manage their network. This will help them to focus on their core competencies like marketing the telecom services to their customers. Moreover, in the competitive job environment, the employers find it difficult to manage the churning of their high-skilled manpower that is needed to manage the complex network. The major impacts of this trend are as follows: The outsourcing model will work efficiently when the network is simple or consists of network components from the same vendor. However, when the operator has complex network with the network elements from multiple vendors, end-to-end network management will be very difficult without active participation of operator, which means that the operators have to invest in developing in house skills.

The other impact of this trend is although the operator gets predicted operating expenses by outsourcing network operations, sometimes, that may not be the better deal for them compared to doing on their own. This is because when there are limited vendors for the outsourced activity like complex network management, the operators do not have flexibility to get better price from their vendors.

4. More revenues from copper base: Another major trend in the telecom industry is that the wireline operators want to extract more revenues out of their huge installed copper base (approximately 45 million homes are connected by wire) by introducing new services. The operators have deployed ADSL gear to offer broadband connections to the customers. Moreover, many telecom operators have signed deals with major enterprises to interconnect their offices creating VPN through their wireline network. Also, some telecom operators have started offering IPTV service in selected regions through ADSL lines. The major drivers for this trend are eroding revenues from wireline business due to competition from wireless and cable TV operators, technological advances like ADSL2+ and MPEG4-AVC enabling transmission of commercial quality video content at bandwidths supported by ADSL and increased demand of broadband connections with availability of low cost PCs. The major impact of this trend is that telecom operators have to increase their capex investments on their backbone network in the near future because the current backbone bandwidth is not enough for new services like video content distribution for their IPTV service. Moreover, the increased competition between telecom operators, cable TV operators in broadband access, and video content distribution will drive down the cost of various services benefiting Indian customers. The other positive impact is that the enterprises do not have to build and maintain the VPN connecting their office networks through dedicated T1/E1 lines. The trends in telecom industry have positive impacts on the operators, vendors and the end customers so far. However, with more technological changes and aggressive competition from other industries like cable TV, new trends having the potential to change the direction of telecom industry in either way could emerge in the future.

Questions

1. Give a detailed analysis of the above trends and their impact on various stakeholders involved.
2. How far the projected trends would be conducive to the new entrants in the sector?

Case Study-2 -

Sahara's Loss is Passenger's Gain

In the dynamic world of Indian aviation, failure of the $500-million plan to merge Jet Airways with Air Sahara has introduced a series of new twists and turns. While there are several winners and losers, passengers are emerging as immediate beneficiaries. Air Sahara operating independently means one more player competing for market share while Jet's muscle to influence the market is weaker. Consolidation, in any case, is not known to benefit customers and moves in the other direction should produce better options for passengers. Since lean season is setting in with the monsoon, cheaper fares are flooding the market and the failed deal is acting as a catalyst to benefit passengers. The confusion arising out of the failed deal has also enthused a number of players like Kingfisher, Air Deccan, Indian and SpiceJet in marketing their products. Air Sahara has also added to the mood by introducing attractive fares on key trunk routes. In any case, the Sahara Group airline had always played a key role in the price-sensitive market by pushing competitive tariffs and incentives. Air Deccan, Kingfisher and SpiceJet are also gaining market share giving Jet a run for its money. Another key factor is the advantage that new airlines are gaining in terms of 'poaching' of pilots and engineers from Jet as well as Sahara. This would help them ramp up operations faster and enhance competition. Some players like IndiGo–looking at launch of operations this year–also stand to gain since it has become far easier to hire pilots and engineers from the two warring airlines. The situation could change if one of the existing players, say Kingfisher, takes over Sahara to gain instant market share. That would lead to limited competition in the full-service segment which now controls 72% market share. While the low-cost segment would remain unaffected, it will be left to Jet Indian, Kingfisher and Sahara to fight for market share. That will bring in the consolidation factor which may not be great news for customers while the industry stands to gain.

At this juncture, however, all the key players are losing money and the Centre for Asia Pacific Aviation (CAPA) feels that profits are at least a year away. "The industry will lose money till the middle of 2007 and airlines which withstand the turbulence will stand to gain," said Kapil Kaul, chief executive for CAPA in the Indian subcontinent and West Asia. Industry leaders like Vijay Mallya acknowledge that the going would be tough if oil prices remain high and infrastructure is not beefed up in double quick time. While Capt G. R. Gopinath of Air Deccan has been following 'rapid expansion' strategy, other players like SpiceJet have been following a strategy of steady growth to keep losses in check. The consensus among all players, including Jeh Wadia of GoAir, is that deep pocket is the name of the game and no airline can make profits right from inception. Increase in capacity deployment in the coming months would also play a key role in pushing fares down, says Ankur Bhatia of Amadeus India. There will be more pressure on fares, he added. Industry veterans feel rapid growth in the industry was helping most players to carry on despite high input costs and increasing competition. Most of the growth in the sector was due to easy availability of cheaper tickets, they feel. "Bottom line pressure will continue in the short run," concedes Mr Gopinath. He feels that mergers help the industry as long as it does not create monopolies, leading to better utilisation of available resources. Most low-cost players feel that there would not be any direct fallout on their business due to the Jet-Sahara tussle. As Air Sahara gets aggressive to retain market share and build up customer confidence, there will be price pressure on most players.

According to an official of airlines "We are targeting a different customer segment and will continue to do so".

Source: Economic Times 30th June, 2006

Questions

1. Elaborate on the impact of merger failure on the working of the airlines industry as such.
2. Do you really feel that this merger failure would really be in the benefit of the air travellers?

REVIEW QUESTIONS

1. Define services marketing.

2. Explain the emergence of marketing thought for services.

3. List out 10 major service industries.

4. What are the underlying themes of service quality? Suggest illustrations of each theme.

5. Explain how a manager might use the conceptual model of service quality to improve the quality of his or her own firm.

6. What are the criticisms of SERVQUAL? What are its developer's responses to these criticisms?

7. You have been hired by a firm to develop the firm's service quality information system. What are the components of this system?

8. What evidence do you see of organisations implementing quality programmes and continually improving service quality? How do you measure service quality?

9. What are the important aspects of CRM that will help managers in running the organisation more efficiently?

10. What are the different approaches for CRM?

11. Explain CRM practices of a service organisation of your choice.

12. How do you manage customer relations? Explain the role of CRM in marketing.

13. Explain the concept of lifetime value of customers.

14. What do you mean by eCRM? Explain its significance in today's competitive and dynamic business environment.

15. What is e-business? Explain the advantages of e-business.

16. Explain the various models of e-business.

17. What is telemarketing? Explain the advantages of telemarketing.

18. Write a short note on M-business.

19. What is relationship marketing? Explain the advantages and limitations of relationship marketing.

20. What is virtual marketing? State the advantages of virtual marketing.

21. Explain the concept marketing in detail.

MANAGING PERSONAL COMMUNICATION

STRUCTURE

9.1   INTRODUCTION

Sales Force Decision is generally termed the backbone of marketing. Brech defines it as "overall management of sales and it refers to only a socialised application of the process of management as a whole." According to the American Marketing Association the "planning, direction and control of the personal selling activities of a business unit include recruiting, selecting, training, equipping, assigning, rating, supervising, paying and motivating as these tasks apply to the personal sales force." The ultimate objective of Sales Management is to influence the consumers of the target market to get sales orders. A sales force serves as a company's personal link to customers.

According Louis Robert Stevenson that "everyone lives by selling something" U.S. firms spend over $140 billion annually on personal selling more than they spend on any other promotional method. Over 8 million Americans are employed in sales and related occupations. Sales forces are found in non-profit as well as profit organisations. College recruiters are the university's sales force arm for attracting new students. Churches use membership committees to attract new members. The U.S. Agricultural Extension service sends agricultural specialists to sell framers on using new farming methods. Hospitals and museums use fund raisers contact and raise money from donors. Selling is one of the classical professions.

The term sales representatives covers a broad range of positions in our economy. *McMurray* devised the following classifications of sales positions.

- *Deliverer:* Positions where a salesperson is job is predominantly to deliver the product (e.g., milk, bread, fuel, oil)

- *Order Taker:* Positions where the salespersons is predominantly an inside order taker (e.g., the haberdashery salesperson standing behind the counter)

- *Missionary:* Positions where the salesperson is not expected or permitted to take an order but is called on only to build goodwill or to educate the actual or potential user (e.g., the medical "detailer" representing an ethical pharmaceuticals house)

- *Technical:* Positions that demand the creative sale of tangible knowledge (e.g., the engineering salesperson who is primarily a consultant to the 'client' companies)

- *Demand Creator:* Positions that demand the creative sale of tangible products (e.g., vacuum Cleaner, refrigerators siding, and encyclopedia) or of intangibles (e.g., insurance, advertising services, or education)

The positions range from the least to the most creative types of selling. The first jobs call for servicing accounts and taking new orders, while the latter requires seeking prospects and influencing them to buy.

9.2 SALES FORCE OBJECTIVES

Sales force objectives must be based on the character of the company's target markets and the company desired positions in these markets. The company must consider the unique role that personal selling can play in the marketing mix to serve customer needs in a competitively effective way. Personal selling happens to be the most expensive contact and communication tool used by the company.

Companies typically set different objectives for their sales forces. IBM's sales representatives are responsible for selling, installing, and upgrading customer computer equipment.

- *Prospecting:* Sales representatives find and cultivate new customers.

- *Targeting:* Sales representatives decide how to allocate their scarce time among prospects and customers.

- *Communicating:* Sales representative skilfully communicates information about the company's products and services.

- *Selling:* Sales representatives know the art of "salesmanship", approaching, presenting, answering objectives, and closing sales.

- *Servicing:* Sales representatives provide various services to the customers consulting on their problems, rendering technical assistance, arranging, financing, and expediting delivery.

- *Information gathering:* Sales representatives conduct market research and intelligence work and fill in call reports.

Companies typically define specific sales forces objectives. One company wants its sales representatives to spend 80% of their times with current customers and 20% with prospects, and 85% of their time on established products and 15% on new products.

Functions of a Sales Organisation

1. Analysing markets and sales policy.
2. Sales planning and sales forecasting.
3. Deciding prices and terms of sales.

4. Selecting, training and controlling the sales force.
5. Deciding sales programmes and sales promotion.
6. Advising about advertising and publicity.
7. Deciding and allocating territory and setting targets.
8. Preparing and maintaining customers records, etc.
9. Preparing sales reports.

Steps in Designing and Managing a Sales Force

- Setting of Objectives
- Training for Sales Policies
- Designing Sales Force Structure and Size
- Deciding Sales Force Compensation
- Recruiting and Motivating Sales Force
- Guiding and Motivating Sales Force
- Performance Rating of Sales Force.

Organising and Managing a Sales Force

Sales force is regularly assigned particular territories. Various factors are taken into account in deciding on the physical size of a territory, transportation links within territory, purchasing power of consumers and their educational and living standards. Therefore, a sales force is deployed according to the geographical and product or consumer requirements. A company should also devote considerable effort in training and development of its sales force. There are two types of training which can be provided to sales force: (a) in-house training, and (b) on-the-job training. It is also necessary for a company to arrange periodic meetings and discussions with its sales force. Finally, the performance can be evaluated on the basis of targets and actual.

Sales Manager's Duties and Responsibilities

The sales manager is the most important person in a sales organisation. All activities are based on his functions and responsibilities. The following are some of the prime duties of a sales manager.

1. Organising sales research, product research, etc.
2. Getting the best output from the sales force under him.
3. Setting and controlling the targets, territories, sales expenses, distribution expenses etc.

4. Advising the company on various media, sales promotion schemes, etc.
5. Monitoring the company's sales policies.

9.3 OUTLINE FOR COMPILING SALES JOB DESCRIPTIONS

Sales

- ✠ Make regular visits
- ✠ Market the full line
- ✠ Handle questions and objections
- ✠ Check finished goods stock
- ✠ Interpret sales points of the line to the customer
- ✠ Explain company policy on credit, merchandising, stock rotation, etc.
- ✠ Get the order
- ✠ Instal product displays and other POPs (Point of Purchase Display)
- ✠ Report product weaknesses, complaints
- ✠ Handle adjustments, returns, and allowances
- ✠ Handle request for credit
- ✠ Handle special orders for customers
- ✠ Establish priorities, if any

Territory Management

- ✠ Arrange route for best coverage.
- ✠ Balance effort with the customer against his potential volume.
- ✠ Maintain sales and important territory records.

Sales Promotion

- ✠ Develop new prospects and accounts
- ✠ Make calls with customer's salesmen in areas where "stockist" are in force
- ✠ Train the personnel of wholesalers, distributors, stockist, etc. whenever requested by them.

Sales Executives

- ✠ Each night makes a daily work plan for the next day.
- ✠ Organise field activity for minimum travel and maximum calls
- ✠ Prepare and submit special report on trends, competition
- ✠ Prepare and submit daily reports to home office.
- ✠ Collect and submit daily reports to home office.

⊞ Attend sales meetings
⊞ Collect overdue accounts
⊞ Collect credit information.

Goodwill

⊞ Counsel customers on their problems
⊞ Maintain loyalty and respect for the company

Sales Supervision

Sales supervision consists of giving instructions to sales force and seeing that they are carried out. Good supervision involves the development of skills in working with people and influencing them to do what you want them to do, and do it well. It is true that salesmen are made, they are not born because, and they are trained by their superiors. Personality, the ability to get along with people, was considered all-important. There are three areas in which sales trainer can impart the training to the sales force:

1. Product Training

It is most important that a salesman must be thoroughly familiar with his product as well as product ranges. Proper emphasis should be given to teach product information in terms of the benefits which can be obtained by the customer. Salesmen must know the following aspects of the products:

- Technical features
- Technology
- Quality
- Packaging
- Grading
- Branding.

2. Selling Areas

- Product history for sales quota attainment in each territory.
- Sales ratios
- Workload per salesperson
- Bills receivable analysis
- Sales analysis report.

3. Selling Skills

The salesperson should be good in human relations and should have the following qualities:

- Good appearance
- Good communications
- Self-confidence
- Creative
- Proud of his association
- Satisfy the curiosity of customers
- Up-to-date knowledge of products.

9.4   DEVELOPING A SALES ORGANISATION

Developing a sales organisation structure is not an easy task. The key to organisational design are consistency and coherence. The importance is highlighted as "spans of control, degrees of job enlargement, and forms of decentralisation, planning systems and matrix structure should not be picked and chosen at random. Rather, they should be selected according to internally consistent groupings, and these groupings should be consistent with the situation of the organisation–its age and size, the conditions of the industry in which it operates, and its production technology". This means that sales managers must recognise, and then deal with, some basic organisational issues when developing a sales organisation. The five major issues are:

1. Formal and Informal Organisations

Every organisation has a formal organisation and an informal organisation. The formal organisation is the creation of management, whereas the informal organisation is often developed from the social organisation. Also called the grapevine, the informal organisation is basically a communication pattern that emerges to facilitate the operation of the formal organisation. Consider the case of a field salesperson that is responsible for collecting certain competitive information, such as prices and trade discounts. If this information were forwarded through the formal organisation, the data would be outdated and would be useless to the management. The informal communication system, however, allows the information to be transmitted directly to the director of marketing research. Flow Chart 9.2 shows an informal communication pattern that might exist in a marketing organisation.

Flow Chart 9.1 shows a lengthy formal communication channel.

Flow Chart 9.1 Lengthy formal communications channel.

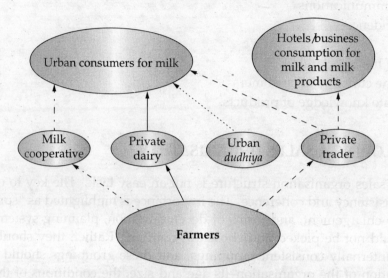

Flow Chart 9.2 Informal organisation.

2. Horizontal and Vertical Organisations

Sales force can have either horizontal or vertical organisational format. The arrangement

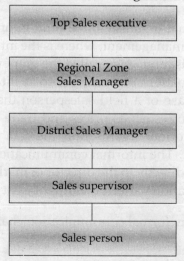

Flow Chart 9.3 Vertical sales organisation.

varies among companies, even within the same industry. The factor that determines whether a vertical or horizontal organisational structure should be employed is the effective span of control. The span of control refers to the number of employees who report to the next higher level in the organisation. Flow Charts 9.3 and 9.4 show the formats of vertical sales organisation and horizontal sales organisation.

Flow Chart 9.4 Horizontal sales organisation.

3. Centralised and Decentralised Organisation

In a decentralised organisation, responsibility and authority are delegated to lower levels of sales management. In a centralised sales organisation, the responsibility and authority for decisions are concentrated at higher levels of management. A related concern is the degree of centralisation in the sales organisation. This issue has to do with the organisational location of the responsibility and authority for specific management tasks. A decentralised organisation structure is ineffective unless commensurate responsibility and authority accompany the assignment of decision to a specific level of sales management.

4. Line and Staff Organisation

Marketing organisations also feature line and staff components. A line function is a primary activity and staff function is a supporting activity. In a marketing organisation, the selling function is the line component, whereas advertising, marketing research, marketing planning, sales training and distributor relations are usually considered staff roles.

Flow Chart 9.5 represents a 'line marketing organisation' and a 'line and staff marketing organisation' is represented in Flow Chart 9.6.

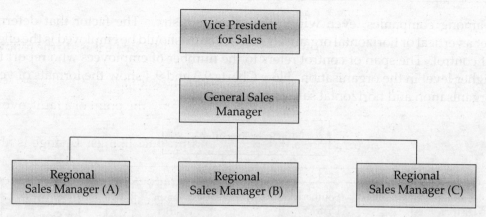

Flow Chart 9.5 A line marketing organisation.

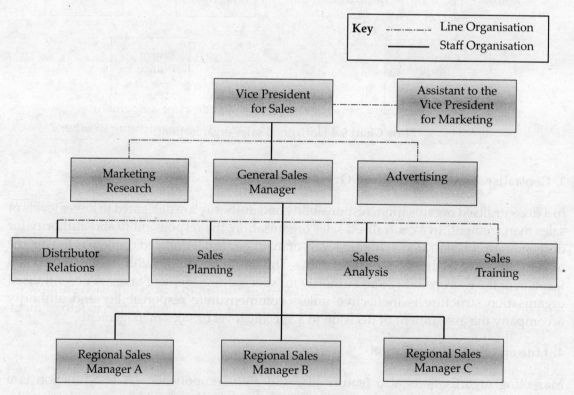

Flow Chart 9.6 Line and staff marketing organisation.

Motivating and Leading the Sales Force

There are several rules which help a sales manager in developing sales force through motivation and leadership.

Rule 1

- Work with sales team and not as members of groups. To achieve this, do the following:
- Know your sales force personally
- Give extra time for discussion and personal problem solving.
- Do proper home work on sales assignments, be clear to the point of a fault, avoiding personal affront.
- Explain your reason for change in territory and product likings. Change is always for the better.
- Learn from your sales force about their hopes, aspirations, abilities and self worth.
- Develop creative personality traits, for example, self-esteem, self-confidence, self-worth to become a self-starter and freedom from fear of failures.
- Assume responsibility for mistakes, that is, be proactive.
- Be internally motivated.

Rule 2

- Set high standards but realistic ones for your sales force.
- Set high personal examples and accept mistakes as errors of judgement.
- Ensure frankness in criticism which is self-rewarding and educating to others.

Rule 3

Ensure that sales force are collaborative among themselves, that is, they work as a team and make full use of each other for collective goal achievement through

- Good means of communication, open and purposive.
- Fostering full cooperation among seniors and juniors.
- Developing individual capabilities, creative attitude and respect for each employee.
- Encourage juniors to settle their own grievances themselves, rather than letting them rush up to you.

Rule 4

Fight for your people and for your ideas:

- You are responsible for people under you; so protect and promote them.
- Support the men in trouble, don't be afraid of telling the faults of superiors against the juniors.
- Help them in progress, get promotions, get noticed and remunerated.

Rule 5

- Retain the principle of accountability as a check on exercise of delegated authority. Promote the right 'men', pay right salaries and perks and put them in positions as deserved by them.
- Pursue the policy of promotion from within as a win-win strategy.
- Accept sales force feelings. Encourage them to open up, to address you as a friend in need.

9.5 SALES STRATEGIES

Sales strategies are the policies which are made to provide the guidelines for taking key decisions in personal selling. It includes the following:

1. Size of the sales force required
2. Kind of the sales force required
3. Roles of the salesperson
4. Assigning of the sales territories.

The effectiveness and the efficiency, with which these roles are played by the sales force, determine the extent to which overall personal selling objectives are achieved. The company's competitive posture is shaped by:

- Product market analysis
- Salesperson's order securing analysis
- Choice of the basic selling style:
  1. Trade selling
  2. Missionary selling
  3. Technical selling
  4. New business selling.

The size of the sales force can be determined by utilizing one or more of the following methods in combination with each other:

1. Workload Method
2. Sales Potential Method
3. Incremental Method.

Individualising selling strategies to customer

The acid test of the appropriateness of personal selling strategy comes when particular salespersons interact with particular customers. The management makes its first key decision on personal selling strategy. When it determines the size of the company's sales force, each salesperson must individualise his own dealing with each customer. The decisions of the above kind are implemented after the required kind and size of the sales force has been recruited, trained and assigned their fields and territories. The strategies should be such so as to benefit the customer and help the firm in achieving its objectives. The strength of the sales force depends upon its communication and convincing power to persuade the customer to buy the product. The approach of the salesperson towards different buyers is a matter of his selling skills. This skill is the function of the pre-planning and performance on the call of the salesperson itself. The individual members of the sales force determine the success and failure of the company's overall personal selling strategy and sales management by the efficiency and effectiveness of the sales management in the personal selling field. The salespersons should combine their efforts in such a way so as to achieve their personal objectives through the achievement of the firm's objectives.

Sales Force Structure

The sales force strategy will have implications for structuring the sales force. If the company sells one product line to one end–using industry with customers in many locations. The company would use a territorial sales force structure.

If the company sells many products to many types of customers, it might need a product or market sales force structure

A good example is expressed of the problem of designing a sales force structure is provided by Wilkinson Sword USA, which had a 7.9% U.S. market share in 1974 but lost most of it in subsequent years. In 1984 Wilkinson decided to rebuild its U.S. market share by setting a goal or recruiting 34 new sales people. Here are the steps it took.

- ❖ **Account identification:** Wilkinson identified 25 leading supermarket chains and hired two national account managers to handled them out of Wilkinson's Atlanta headquarters.

- ❖ **Geographical territories:** The United States was portioned into three divisions east, west, and central. Each division was divided into roughly five areas, and each area was further subdivided into a few territories.

- ❖ **Staffing and training:** Wilkinson looked for people with five or more years of selling experience in top health and beauty aid companies and offered them a competitive package. The first year was spent in staffing and training.

❖ **Trade relations:** Wilkinson hired a vice president of trade relations as well as retail merchandise to handle stocking and stock outs, monitor prices, and so on.

Sales Force Size

Once the company clarifies its sales force strategy and structure, it is ready to consider sales force size. Each sales representative is one of the company's most productive and expensive assets. Increasing their number will increase both sales and costs.

Once the company establishes the number of customers it wants to reach, it can use workload approach to establish sales force size. This method consists of the following steps.

Customers are grouped into sizes classes according to their annual sales volume. The desirable call frequencies are established for each class. The number of accounts in each size class is multiplied by the corresponding call frequency to arrive at the workload for the country, in sales calls per year. The average number of calls a sales representative can make per year is determined.

Suppose the company estimates that there are 1,000 A accounts and 2,000 B accounts required in the nation. And A accounts require 36 calls a year and B accounts counts 12 calls a year. This means the company needs a sales force that can make 1,000 calls a year. The company would need 60 full-time sales representatives.

Sales Force Compensation

To attract sales representatives, the company has to develop an attractive compensation package. Sales representatives would like income regularity, extra reward for an above average performance, and fair payment for experience and longevity. On the other hand, management objectives, such as economy, will conflict with sales representatives "objectives" such as financial security. No wonder that compensation plans exhibit a tremendous variety among industries and even within the same industry.

The company must next determine the components of compensation: a fixed amount, a variable amount, expenses, and fringe benefits. The fixed amount, might be salary or a drawing account, is intended to satisfy the sales representative need for income stability. The variable amount, which might be commission, bonus, or profit sharing, is intended to stimulate and reward greater effort. Fringe benefits such as paid vacations, sickness or accident benefits, pensions, and life insurance are intended to provide security and job satisfaction.

Managing Sales Force

Having established the sales force objectives, strategy, structure, size, and compensation, the company has to move to recruiting, selecting, training, directing, motivating, and evaluating sales representatives. Various policies and procedures guide these decisions.

9.6 RECRUITING AND SELECTING SALES REPRESENTATIVES

Importance of Careful Selection

At the heart of a successful sale force operation is the selection of effective sales representatives.

What makes a good sales representative?

Selecting sales representatives would be simple if one knew what traits to look for. One good starting point is to ask customers what traits they like and prefer in salespeople. Most customers say they want the sales representative to be honest, reliable, knowledgeable, and helpful. The company should look for these traits when selecting candidates.

In defining sales profile, the company must consider the characteristics of the specific sales job. Is type a lot of paper work? Does the job call for much travel? Will the salesperson confront a high proportion of rejections.

Recruitment Procedures: After the management develops its selection method, it must recruit. The personal department seeks applications by various means, including soliciting names from current sales representatives using employment agencies, placing jobs ads, and contacting college students. As for college students, companies have found it hard to sell them on selling. Few students want to go into selling as a career. The reluctant ones gave such reasons as, "Selling is a job and not a profession", it calls for deceit if the person wants to succeed, and "There is insecurity and too much travel," To counter these objections, company recruiters emphasise starting salaries, income opportunities, and the fact that one fourth of the presidents of large U.S. corporations started out in marketing and sales.

Applicant-Rating procedures: Recruitment procedures, if successful, will attract many applicants, and the company will need to select the best ones. The selection procedures can vary from a single informal interview to prolonged testing and interviewing, not only of the applicant but of the applicants spouse.

Training Sales Representatives

Many companies send their new sales representatives into the field almost immediately after hiring them. They are supplied with samples, order books, and a description of their territory. And much of their selling is ineffective. A vice president of a major food company spent one week watching 50 sales presentations to a busy buyer for a major supermarket chain. Here is what he observed:

The majority of salesmen were ill prepared, unable to answer basic questions, uncertain as to what they wanted to accomplish during the call. They did not think of the call as a studied professional presentation.

Today's customers cannot put up with inept salespeople. The customers are more demanding and face many more suppliers. Customers expect salespeople to have deep product knowledge, to add ideas to improve the customer's operations, and to be efficient and reliable. This has required a much higher investment in training.

Training programmes, of course, are costly. They involve large outlays for instructors, materials, and space; paying a person who is not yet selling; and losing opportunities because he or she is not in the field. Yet they are essential. Today's new sales representatives may spend a few weeks to several months in training. The median training period is 28 weeks in industrial products companies, 12 in service companies, and four in consumer products companies. Training time varies with the complexity of the selling task and the type of person recruited into the sales organisation. At IBM, new sales representatives are not on their own for two years! And IBM expects its sales representatives to spend 15% of their time each year in additional training.

The training programmes have several goals:

✠ **Sales Representatives Need to Know and Identify with the Company:** Most companies devote the first part of the training program to describing the company's history and objectives, the organisation and lines of authority, the chief officers, the company's financial structure and facilities, and the chief products and sales volumes.

✠ **Sales Representatives Need to Know the Company's Products:** Sales trainees are shown how the products are produced and how they function in various uses.

✠ **Sales Representatives Need to Know Customer's and Competitor's Characteristics:** Sales representatives learn about the different types of customers and their needs, buying motives, and buying habits. They learn about the company's and competitor's strategies and policies.

✠ **Sales Representative Need to Know How to Make Effective Sales Presentations:** Sales representatives receive training in the principles of selling. In addition, the company outlines the major sales arguments for each product and may provide a sales script.

✠ **Sales Representatives Need to Understand Field Procedures and Responsibilities:** Sales representatives learn how to divide time between active and potential accounts; how to use the expense account, prepare reports, and route effectively.

Directing Sales Representatives

New sales representatives are given more than a territory, a compensation package, and training–they are given supervision.

Developing norms for prospect calls

Companies often specify how much time their sales forces should spend prospecting for new accounts. Spector Freight wants its sales representatives to spend 25% of their time prospecting and to stop calling on a prospect after three unsuccessful calls.

Using Sales Time Efficiently: Sales representatives need to know how to use their time efficiently. One tool is the annual call schedule showing which customers and prospects to call on in which months and which activities to carry out.

Another tool is time and duty analysis: The sales representative spends time in the following ways:

- ☞ **Travel:** In some jobs, travel time amounts to over 50% of total time. Travel time can be cut down by using faster means for transportation–recognising, however, that this will increase costs. Companies encourage air travel for their sales force, to increase their ratio of selling to total time.

- ☞ **Food and Breaks:** Some portion of the sales forces workday is spent in eating and taking breaks.

- ☞ **Waiting:** Waiting consists of time spent in the outer office of the buyer. This is dead time unless the sales representative uses it to plan or to fill out reports.

- ☞ **Selling:** Selling is the time spent with the buyer in person or on the phone. It breaks down into social talk and "selling talk."

- ☞ **Administration:** This consists of the time spent in report writing and billing, attending sales meetings, and talking to other in the company about production delivery, billing, sales performance, and other matters.

Motivating Sales Representatives

Sales representatives will put forth their best effort without any special coaching from the management.

- **The Nature of the Job:** The selling job is one of frequent frustration. Sales representatives usually work alone; their hours are irregular; and they are often away from home. They confront aggressive, competing sales representatives; they have an inferior status relative to the buyer; they often do not have the authority to do what is necessary to win an account; they lose large orders that they have worked hard to obtain.

- **Human Nature:** Most people operate below capacity in the absence of special incentives, such as financial gain or social recognition.

- **Personal Problems:** Sales representatives are occasionally preoccupied with personal problems, such as sickness in the family, marital discord, or debt.

9.7   WORD-OF-MOUTH(WOM) COMMUNICATION

Arndt defines WOM as ". . . oral person-to-person communication between a receiver and a communicator whom the receiver perceives as non-commercial, regarding a brand, product or service." (1967, p. 291) However, it is important to point out that WOM need not necessarily be brand, product or service-focused. It may also be organisation-focused. Neither need WOM be face-to-face, direct, oral or ephemeral. The electronic community, for example, generates virtual WOM which is not face-to-face, not direct, not oral, and not ephemeral.

One of the most widely accepted notions in consumer behaviour is that WOM plays an important role in shaping consumers' attitudes and behaviours. In an early study, Whyte (1954) investigated the diffusion of air-conditioners in a Philadelphia suburb. He concluded, on the basis of anecdotal evidence, that the pattern of ownership could be explained only in the presence of a vast and powerful network consisting of neighbours exchanging product information. In a more formal study, Katz and Lazarsfeld (1955) found that WOM was the most important source of influence in the purchase of household goods and food products. It was twice effective as radio advertising, four times as effective as personal selling, and seven times as effective as newspapers and magazines.

Subsequent investigations of the WOM phenomenon have confirmed the dominance of personal influence in choice decisions. Engel et al. (1969), for example, found that almost 60 per cent of consumers cited WOM as the most influential factor regarding their adoption of an automotive diagnostic centre. Similarly, Arndt (1967) showed that respondents who received positive WOM about a new food product were three times more likely to purchase it as those who received negative WOM. More recent research is provided by Herr et al. (1991). They observed that WOM communication had a much stronger impact on brand evaluations than information from neutral sources such as the 'Consumer Reports' magazine.

The power of WOM communication stems from various factors. First, consumer recommendations are usually perceived as being more credible and trustworthy than commercial sources of information (Day, 1971). It is common to assume that another consumer has no commercially motivated reasons for sharing information (Engel et al., 1993). Also the discussions with either friends or family tend to be friendly and can offer support for trying certain behaviours. Second, the WOM channel is immediately bidirectional and interactive which allows for a 'tailored' flow of information to the information seeker (Gilly et al., 1998). The third strength of consumer WOM comes from its 'vicarious trial' attributes. Potential consumers of a product, for example, can gain some of the product experience by asking somebody who has an actual experience with the product.

WOM is of particular importance to the services sector. The typical characteristics of services such as intangibility, simultaneous production and consumption, perishability, heterogeneity and the need for the consumer participation results in the fact that suppliers are not able to present the product in advance of the purchase (Helm and Schlei, 1998; Zeithaml and Bitner, 1996). Services, therefore, are high in experience and credence properties which the consumer can only ascertain after purchase and use (Zeithaml and Bitner, 1996). As a consequence, consumers of services rely to a large extent on personal communication and the exchange of experiences with other customers since their experiences of serve as a 'vicarious trial'. Empirical support for the importance of WOM when purchasing services is provided by Murray who found that services consumers prefer to seek information from family, friends and peers rather than sponsored promotional sources.

Characteristics of WOM

According to Buttle (1998), WOM can be characterised by valence, focus, timing, solicitation, and intervention.

❖ **Valence:** From a marketing point of view, WOM can be negative as well as positive. In the case of negative WOM, consumers convey information on poor performance, lack of service, high prices or rude salespersonnel. Positive WOM is the mirror image. Assael (1992) notes that dissatisfied consumers complain to approximately three times as many friends and relatives as when they are satisfied. Additionally, Mizerski (1982) indicates that a consumer is more likely to pay attention to negative than to positive information. A study by Heath (1996), however, shows that people do not display a simple preference for bad news. Instead, they pass along information that matches the emotional valence of the conversation topic.

According to File et al. (1994), valence and volume of post-purchase WOM can be influenced by management policy. More specifically, they cite work that provides evidence for the contention that the handling of the complaints process, services recovery programmes and unconditional service guarantees influence the frequency and direction of WOM. Richins (1983), for example, shows that if complaints are encouraged, the retailer has the chance to remedy legitimate complaints and win back a customer who may also make positive reports to others, enhancing goodwill.

❖ Focus. WOM activity is not only limited to consumers. In fact, the extent of WOM activity can be seen as a function of the following: the people with whom the company and its employees come into contact (customers, suppliers, agents, competitors, the general public, and other stakeholders); its communications; and the inherent interest in the company as a result of its actions (Haywood, 1989). Similarly, the S.C.O.P.E. model (suppliers, customers, owners or investors, partners and employees) of relationship marketing indicates that WOM is not only restricted to consumers. WOM, for example, is an important source of information in the recruitment of employees (Buttle, 1998). However, the majority of management writings on WOM is that of the satisfied customer communication with a prospect. The assumption is that positive WOM draws customers on the loyalty ladder as shown below thereby converting a prospect into a customer

Prospect → Customer Client → Supporter → Advocate → Partner

The loyalty ladder [adapted from: Buttle, 1998, p. 101]

- **Timing:** WOM may be uttered at different stages of the decision-making process, i.e. before or after a purchase. WOM that operates as an important source of pre-purchase information is referred to as input WOM. Output WOM, on the other hand, is uttered after the purchase or the consumption experience.

- **Solicitation:** Not all WOM communication is customer-initiated. WOM may be offered with or without solicitation; it may be offered even though it is not sought. If authoritative information is thought, however, the consumer may see the input of an influential or opinion leader.

- **Intervention:** The power of WOM has not gone unnoticed. An increasing number of companies are proactively intervening in an effort to stimulate and manage WOM activity. Some even consider customer WOM as the most effective marketing tool and also the one with the lowest cost (Wilson, 1994). Specifically, marketers seek to influence opinion leaders directly, stimulate WOM communication in advertising and/or portray communications from opinion leaders. Additionally, marketers try to curb, channel and control negative communications.

9.8 CORPORATE SOCIAL RESPONSIBILITY (CSR)

The primary goal of any business is to make money and in today's world, it is not just about making money and profits. More and more large organisations are beginning to understand that there needs to be a good balance of both evil and good. Evil in the sense of making money and good where the organisation considers the interests of both environment and humanity.

Why CSR? Here are Some Benefits of CSR

Source: Pierotonin

1. Enhanced reputation and brand image

Reputation is an important sustainable competitive advantage, because it is very hard to build and cannot be easily mimicked by competitors. An organisation's reputation results from trust by its stakeholders. A strong reputation in ethical environmental and social responsibility can help an organisation build this trust. Several major brands, such as The Body Shop & the Cooperative Group are built on ethical values.

2. Increased profit and customer loyalty

Several academic studies have shown a direct correlation between socially responsible business practices and positive financial performance:

  ✠ A 1997 DePaul University study found that organisations with a defined corporate commitment to ethical principles do better financially (based on annual sales/revenues) than organisations that don't.

✠ An 11-year Harvard University study found that "stakeholder-balanced" organisations showed four times the growth rate and eight times the employment growth when compared to organisations that are shareholder-only focused.

✠ According to the Millennium Poll on CSR, the majority of 25,000 people interviewed in 23 countries want organisations to contribute to society beyond making a profit.

✠ Research has shown that there is a growing desire by consumers not only to buy good and safe products, but they also want to know that what they buy was produced in a socially and environmentally responsible way such as "sweatshop-free" and child-labour-free clothing, smaller environmental impact.

3. Creating new business opportunities

Experience gained through addressing CSR challenges also provides opportunities for organisations to create new business opportunities.

4. Increased ability to attract and retain employees

An organisation's dedication to CSR can be an important aid to recruitment and retention compared with competitors. People want to work for a organisation that is in accordance with their own values and beliefs.

1. 78% of employees would rather work for an ethical and reputable organisation than receive a higher salary. (The Cherenson Group, www.csreurope.org)
2. In interviewing 150 top employees in 24 organisations, the UK consulting firm, Stanton Marris, learnt that employer reputation was a key factor in accepting a job offer.
3. 76% of those polled by the Cone/Roper Corporate Citizenship Study said organisation's "commitment to causes" was an important consideration in deciding where to work.

5. Increased productivity and morale

Committing CSR internally to improve working conditions, lessen environmental impacts can lead to increased productivity and staff morale where the workforce is more reliable, enthusiastic and efficient.

6. Attracting investors and business partners

Organisations addressing ethical, social, and environmental responsibilities have easier access to capital through investors and better conditions for loans on international money markets. It is also easier to do merger/acquisition negotiations, finding business partners and suppliers as well as smoother workforce integration.

A 2001 study showed that 12% of total investment in the USA was of a socially responsible nature. Likewise, there are 313 green, social and ethical funds operating in Europe in June 2003, showing a 12% increase in the last eighteen months.

7. Managing risk

The more an organisation is committed to CSR, the better it is able to manage risk. Large corporations and well-known brands are the first target of litigation for CSR misconduct such as the highly publicised "Nike sweatshops". The consequences could be huge in terms of market share or capital loss. A tarnished reputation might require years to rebuild and cost a large sum of money.

8. Preferential government and regulatory treatment

Governments and regulators are more lenient with organisations that are more committed to CSR. Preferential treatment may be given when applying for permits or permission to do something and less intervention in their business through taxation and regulations.

Some believe that CSR programmes are often undertaken in an effort to distract the public from the ethical questions posed by their core operations. Some that have been accused include British Petroleum (BP) and British American Tobacco (BAT).

9. Increased operational efficiency and reduced operating costs

Operational efficiency can be increased by reducing waste production and operating costs can be reduced by less water usage, increasing energy efficiency and selling recycled materials. At a broader scale, such CSR actions can result in environmental, social and economic benefits.

10. Innovation in market through cooperation with local communities

CSR requires cooperation with the local communities and relationships can be improved. This can help organisations in tailoring products and services as well as more rapid acceptance to local markets. Now, how do you implement a CSR plan/model?

There are few things to think about before you begin a CSR plan. Begin with a big picture; can you do a better job in making our planet, its environment and its inhabitants a better world to live in? If yes, think about how your organisation can impact our world; its people and how you as an organisation can create a better, fair, just and compassionate world.

To achieve success, such ethical, social and environmental values need to be embedded in your business culture: business practices, vision and plan which begin at the highest level.

To begin, you need to do a self-assessment of what priority areas you need to implement based on your unique business strengths. Key stakeholders should be involved in the process where discussions can happen so that everybody can buy into the concept. First, identify any risk that may cause reputation and/or financial risk to your organisation. Second, identify those socially responsible initiatives that are the most cost effective to implement. Once you have developed your CSR priorities, you need to establish a code of principles conduct, clear value statement where the whole organisation needs to commit. You then need to develop policy to formalise and articulate this commitment, and create programmes to implement this policy. To make the programmes meaningful, organisations need to provide training and education, and plan visible, memorable activities. The CSR plan should be implemented across the organisation. It should be localised for different markets and it should have measurement techniques. Open communication with stakeholders (community, employees, customers, shareholders, suppliers and the environment) is also vital as they need to feel that they can respect and trust a company's values. Finally, report the success of the programmes and measure the progress as your CSR investment needs to be justified to shareholders.

Corporate Social Responsibility (CSR) and Ethics in Marketing

Kotler and Levy, in their book, *Corporate Social Responsibility* define corporate social responsibility as "**a commitment to improve community well-being through discretionary business practices and contributions of corporate resources**".

Some of the benefits of being socially responsible include (a) enhanced company and brand image (b) easier to attract and retain employees (c) increased market share (d) lower operating costs and (e) easier to attract investors. A socially responsible firm will care about customers, employees, suppliers, the local community, society, and the environment. CSR can be described as an approach by which a company (a) recognises that its activities have a wide impact on the society and that development in society in turn supports the company to pursue its business successfully and (b) actively manages the economic, social, and environmental and human rights. This approach is derived from the principles of sustainable development and good corporate governance. Marketing managers within different firms will see some social issues as more relevant than others. The relevance of a given social issue is determined by the company's products, promotional efforts, and pricing and distribution policies but also by its philosophy of social responsibility.

  ✠ Focus entirely in profits (and profitable firms typically serve society well).
  ✠ Explicitly incorporate social responsibility into its day-to-day marketing decisions to minimise negative effects on society and enhance positive effects.

✠ Go even further and engage in social projects that are unrelated to the corporate mission and even detrimental to profits (which could be socially undesirable).

✠ The success strategies of a business formed out of abundance and grounded in ethics and cooperation are powerful and long-lasting and they help you feel good about yourself even while bringing in profits (Shel Horowitz).

The management must decide which of these three levels of social responsibility to adopt and which social issues are relevant to its business.

Ethical Conflict faced by the Marketers

Marketers must be aware of ethical standards and acceptable behaviour. This awareness means that marketers must recognise the viewpoints of three key players: the company, the industry, and society. Since these three groups almost always have different needs and wants, ethical conflicts are likely to arise. Ethical conflicts in marketing arise in two contexts: First, when there is difference between the needs of the three aforementioned groups (the company, the industry, and society) a conflict may arise. Second and ethical conflict may arise when one's personal values conflict with the organisation. In either case, a **conflict of interest** is a possible outcome. An example of the first type of conflict is the tobacco industry. Cigarettes have for many decades been a lucrative business. So, cigarette and tobacco marketing have been for companies and good for the tobacco industry. Many thousands of people around the world are employed in the tobacco industry. So, the world economy has been somewhat dependent on cigarettes and tobacco. However, cigarettes are harmful to society. There is documented proof that cigarette smoking is harmful to health. This is an ethical conflict for cigarette marketers. An example of the second type of conflict, when one's personal values conflict with the organisations occurs when a leader in the company seeks personal gain (usually financial profit) from **false advertising**. "Cures" for fatal diseases are one type of product that falls into this category of ethical conflict: In their greed to make a profit, a marketer convinces those who may be dying from an incurable disease to buy a product that may not be a cure, but which a desperately ill person (or members of his or her family) may choose to purchase in an effort to save the dying family member from suffering. Promoting and marketing such products violates rules of marketing ethics.

Ethical dilemmas facing marketing professionals today fall into one of three categories: tobacco and alcohol promoting, consumer privacy, and green marketing. Standards for ethical marketing guide business in efforts to do the right thing. Such standards have four functions: to help identify acceptable practices, foster internal control, avoid confusion, and facilitate a basis for discussion.

Relationship Marketing and Ethics

Nowadays, most ethicists believe that relationship marketing is a reasonable practice leading to positive relationships between buyers and sellers. Relationship marketing requires that rules are not necessarily contractual. Relationship marketing allows buyers and sellers to work together. However, there are disadvantages to this approach–relationship marketing requires time to develop a list of expected conduct or "rules of behaviour." According to a recently published book on this subject, a shift in emphasis in marketing ethics–towards buyer's interests and away from seller's interests–characterises the new country. If this is true, new challenges are presented for marketing ethics and professionals in the field of marketing who want to conduct business in an ethical way.

Social Marketing and Ethics

Social marketing is defined as the use of marketing principles and techniques to influence a target audience to voluntarily accept, reject, modify, or abandon behaviour for the benefit of individuals, groups or society as a whole. Social marketing is usually done by a non-profit organisation, government, or quasi-government agency. The goal is either to steer the public away from products that are harmful to them and/or society (e.g., illegal drugs, tobacco, alcohol, etc.) or to direct them towards behaviours or products that are helpful to them and/or society (e.g., having family meals, praying together, etc.).

Ethical Norms and Values for Marketers

Professional associations and accrediting bodies have identified guidelines for ethics in marketing. According to one of those associations, the American Marketing Association, the following rules guide marketing behaviour. The American Marketing Association commits itself to promoting the highest standard of professional ethical norms and values for its members. Norms are established standards of conduct that are expected and maintained by society and/or professional organisations. Values represent the collective conception of what people find desirable, important and morally proper. Values serve as the criteria for evaluating the actions of others. Marketing practitioners must recognise that they not only serve their enterprises but also act as stewards of society in creating, facilitating and executing the efficient and effective transactions that are part of the greater economy. In this role marketers should embrace the highest ethical norms of practising professionals and the ethical values implied by their responsibility toward stakeholders (e.g., customers, employees, investors, channel members, regulators and the host community).

1. **Responsibility of the marketer:** Marketers must accept responsibility for the consequences of their activities and make every effort to ensure that their decisions, recommendations, and actions function to identify, serve, and satisfy all relevant publics: customers, organisations and society

2. Honesty, integrity and quality are far more important than quick profits. (Shel Horowitz)

3. **Rights and duties in the marketing exchange process:** Participants should be able to expect that products and services are safe and fit for intended uses; that communications about offered products and services are not deceptive; that all parties intend to discharge their obligations, financial and otherwise, in good faith; and that appropriate internal methods exist for equitable adjustment and/or redress of grievances concerning purchases.

4. **Organisational relationships:** Marketers should be aware of how their behaviour influences the behaviour of others in organisational relationships. They should not demand, encourage, or apply coercion to encourage unethical behaviour in their relationships with others.

5. Conduct your business so as to build long-term loyalty. When you get a customer, you want to keep that customer and build a sales relationship that cannot only last years, but also create a stream of referral business. (Shel Horowitz)

6. Marketers must do no harm. This means doing work for which they are appropriately trained or experienced so that they can actively add value to their organisations and customers. It also means adhering to all applicable laws and regulations and embodying high ethical standards in the choices they make.

7. Marketers must foster trust in the marketing system. This means that products are appropriate for their intended and promoted uses. It requires that marketing communications about goods and services are not intentionally deceptive or misleading. It suggests building relationships that provide for the equitable adjustment and/or redressal of customer grievances. It implies striving for good faith and fair dealing so as to contribute toward the efficacy of the exchange process.

8. Marketers must embrace, communicate and practice the fundamental ethical values that will improve consumer confidence in the integrity of the marketing exchange system. These basic values are intentionally aspiration and include honesty, responsibility, fairness, respect, openness and citizenship.

Role of Social Responsibility in Indian Companies

In a global CSR study undertaken in 7 countries (viz., India, South Korea, Thailand, Singapore, Malaysia and Indonesia) by the U.K. based International Centre for CSR in 2003, India has been ranked second in the list. This ideally shows the value that is important to customers in India. Bharat Petroleum and Maruti Udyog have been ranked as the best companies in the country. The next comes in the list are Tata Motors and Hero Honda. Canara Bank, Indal, Gujarat Ambuja and Wipro are involved in community development work of building roads, running schools and hospitals. ACC has been rendering social service for over five decades. They are setting up schools, health centres, agro-based industries and improving the quality of rural life. Bharat Heavy Electricals Ltd (BHEL) is actively involved in the welfare of the surrounding communities that is helping the organisation to earn goodwill of the local people. BHEL is also providing drinking water facilities, construction of roads and culverts, provision of health facilities, educational facilities, and so on. Companies like Oil Natural Gas Corporation (ONGC) are encouraging sports by placing good players on their payrolls. Tata Steels (TISCO), Telecommunication Network for Cooperative Driving (TELCO) and Hindustan Aluminium Corporation (HINDALCO) won the award for excelling in CSR, jointly given by Federation of Indian Chambers of Commerce and Industry (FICCI) and Business world for the 2003. ONGC has also committed resources by adopting a few villages to implement former president Dr. Abdul Kalam's idea of PURA (Provision of Urban Amenities in Rural Areas). National Thermal Power Corporation (NTPC) has established a trust to work for the cause of the physically challenged people. Similarly, in the private sector companies like Infosys, Wipro and Reliance are believed to be most socially responsible corporations.

In 1999, Kofi Annan of the United Nations invited corporate leaders for a **Global Compact** to promote nine principles covering three areas: human rights, labour rights, and sustainable development. Today, India can be legitimately proud to have had the second largest number of companies from any country subscribing to the Global Compact. Several public sector companies have joined together to form the Global Compact Society of India.

9.9   INTERNAL AND EXTERNAL MARKETING

We agree with this view that services are predominantly people-based. In the services generating organisations, we find personnel of the marketing department as well as others very much instrumental in performing the marketing function. This makes it essential that we clearly understand the common purpose and spirit of the tasks to be performed and its backward and forward linkages with the other tasks. Internalising the marketing function is an important task found of critical nature. This makes an advocacy in favour of internal marketing with the motto of employing quality people.

Bringing home the concept of internal customer focuses on marketing internally to the internal market of employees, this makes an advocacy in favour of employing a higher number of skilled personnel in the service generating organisations. The service firms valuing investments in people as much as investments in machines, using technology to support men or people on the front line, making recruitment and training as crucial for sales clerks and housekeepers as for managers and senior executives and linking compensation to performance for employees at every level not just at the top need a new model for managing services.

The task of internal marketing is simplified considerably with the help of internal interactive communication, internal mass communication, market and image research, external mass communication and advertising. The task of raising the customer consciousness is difficult and the following issues are found to have a far reaching effect.

- ☞ Sponsoring employees for training programmes in the areas of marketing. The behavioural management needs an intensive care.
- ☞ Increasing the involvement of staff in activities like deposit mobilisation, customer service campaigns, undertaking market surveys, formulation of branch budget or so.
- ☞ Organising the marketing conference and workshops, activating capsule course relating to the marketing of services.
- ☞ Sharing of the findings of customer surveys, image and other studies.
- ☞ Motivating the staff by offering awards and rewards both on an individual and a group basis.
- ☞ Provision for guiding on the customer service with the help of a house journal, special newsletters and other printed leaflets.
- ☞ Setting up of marketing/customer cells.
- ☞ Maintaining visibility through strengthening public relations activities.

Increasing Business Mindedness

An important task is to increase the business mindedness of employees. The following activities may be helpful in the process:

Sharing of performance results vs. budgets and problems facing the organisations.

- Allocation of specific goals to staff and close monitoring of the day-to-day developments.
- Training for the development of detailed customer call programmes.
- Exposure of staff to the criteria of cost-benefit.
- Development of teamwork among staff.
- Promotion of education programmes.
- Encouraging the use of suggested services.

The personal commitment is an important dimension for increasing the business mindedness and the service generating organisations need to develop employees so that performance-orientation is made possible. We can't negate that employee-orientation would make the ways for performance orientation which focuses on enriching the credentials and making the compensation plans attractive. Responding to the specific characteristics of service markets described above does mean that, unlike many tangible goods situations, it is extremely difficult to separate marketing activities from all the other functions being undertaken within the firm. Furthermore, the nature of the buyer-seller interaction which occurs at the production/consumption interface can have a significant impact on the customer's repeat buying decisions (e.g., if a customer arrives at a hotel to discover that a mistake has been made over a reservation and the room is no longer available, the way in which the receptionist handles this problem will have a significant influence on whether the customer can be placated or is 'lost forever' as a future guest).

Eigler and Langeard (1977) have proposed three main categories of resource's involved in the buyer-seller interaction: contact personnel, who interact directly with the customer. Physical resources that comprise the human and technical resources used by the organisation in undertaking the production, delivery and consumption of the service offering. The customer, who is the person forming a purchase, loyalty decision based on the quality of service received to date. Gronroos (1984) has proposed that management of these three variables is a marketing task which differs from traditional F.M.C.G. marketing because it involves assets not usually part of the mainstream marketing operation, but instead is drawn from across the entire cost-generating production resources within the organisation. Gronroos has proposed that in service firms there exist three marketing tasks. He describes these as 'external marketing' (i.e., the normal formal processes associated with the management of the 4Ps), interactive marketing (i.e., the activities which occur at the buyer-seller interface) and internal marketing. The latter variable is concerned with all of the activities associated with ensuring every employee is (a) customer-conscious and (b) committed to the philosophy that every aspect of their personal role must be oriented towards achieving total customer satisfaction. The suggestion that internal marketing is a holistic process which integrates the multiple functions of the organisation by ensuring employees understand all relevant aspects of organisational operations and are motivated to act in a service-oriented manner, creates the very difficult problem of how one measures the effectiveness of the customer-organisation interaction. Although a number of writers have suggested that the objective of service satisfaction is to minimise the gap between customers' desires and actual experience, developing feasible techniques for the measurement of expectations and perceptions has proved somewhat more problematical.

One of the most important contributions to measuring these variables has been made by Parasuraman, Zeithmal and Berry (1985; 1988; Zeithmal, Parasuraman and Berry, 1990) who from 1983 onwards have implemented a carefully sequenced research project aimed at delivering an effective model for assessing the effectiveness and quality of the service provision process. The first stage of their research was to identify some common variables, which could be used to categorise customer expectations. By the use of focus groups, they identified the following five variables:

9.10   COMPANY HUMAN AND TECHNICAL RESOURCES

Three marketing forms within the service provision process

1. Reliability–The ability to perform the promised service dependably and accurately.
2. Tangibles–The images created by the appearance of physical facilities, equipment, personnel and communication materials.
3. Responsiveness–The willingness to help customers and provide prompt service.
4. Assurance–The process by which the knowledge, ability and courtesy of employees engenders customer trust and confidence in the service provider.
5. Empathy–Created by the caring, individualised attention which employees offer the customer.

Internal marketing involves such basic elements as listening to customers and communicating to others in the customer-supplier chain. This involves everyone at every level and they are to be motivated by appropriate means. Also it involves formation of groups and group interaction to be encouraged by initiating suitable listening and communicating techniques. All these lead towards overall internal effectiveness. Establishment of quality circles throughout the customer supplier chain will facilitate more efficient activities in determining product attributes, package design, launching strategies, promotion measures distribution method and the like.

External Marketing

External marketing is concerned with the process of identifying, segmenting and targeting external customers for the purpose of positioning the product by means of appropriate marketing mix strategy designed. The CORE method (Customer Orientation for Results) involving four steps, namely, understanding customer viewpoint, carrying needed changes, establishing new direction and working together for customer profit, necessitates a blend of both internal and external marketing towards achieving marketing goals.

Until recently, service firms lagged behind manufacturing firms in their use of marketing. Many service businesses are small (auto repair shops, dry cleaners) and often consider marketing unneeded or too costly. Other service businesses (colleges, hospitals) once had so much demand that they did not need marketing until recently. Still others (legal, medical, and accounting practices) believed that it was unprofessional to use marketing.

Still, just like manufacturing businesses, good service firms use marketing to position themselves strongly in chosen target markets. Southwest Airlines positions itself as "Just Plane Smart" for commuter flyers–as a no-frills, short-haul airline charging very low fares. The Ritz-Carlron Hotel positions itself as offering a memorable experience that "enlivens the senses, instills well-being, and fulfils even the unexpressed wishes and needs of our guests." These and other service firms establish their positions through traditional marketing mix activities. However, because services differ from tangible products, they often require additional marketing approaches. In a product business, products are fairly standardized and can sit on shelves waiting for customers. But in a service business, the customer and front-line service employee interact to create the service. Thus, service providers must work to interact effectively with customers to create superior value during service encounters. Effective interaction, in turn, depends on the skills of front-line service employees, and on the service production and support processes backing these employees.

Thus, successful service companies focus their attention on both their employees and customers. They understand the service-profit chain, which links service firm profits with employee and customer satisfaction. This chain consists of five links:

- Healthy service profits and growth–superior service firm performance, which results from ...
- Satisfied and loyal customer–satisfied customers who remain loyal, repeat purchase, and refer other customers, which results from ...
- Greater service value–more effective and efficient customer value creation and service delivery, which results from ...
- Satisfied and productive service employees–more satisfied, loyal, and hardworking employees, which results from ...
- Internal service quality–superior employee selection and training, qualities work environment and strong support for those dealing with customers.

Therefore, reaching service profits and growth goals begins with taking care of those who take care of customers.

The concept of the service-profit chain is well illustrated by a story about how Bill Marriott, Jr., chairman of Marriott hotels, interviews prospective managers:

Bill Marriott reels job candidates that the hotel chain wants to satisfy three groups: customers, employees, and stockholders. Although all of the groups are important, he asks in which order the groups should be satisfied. Most candidates say first satisfy customers. Marriott, however, reasons differently. First, employees must be satisfied. If employees love their jobs and feel a sense of pride in the hotel, they will serve customers well. Satisfied customers will return frequently to the Marriott. Moreover, dealing with happy customers will make employees even more satisfied, resulting in better service and still greater repeat business, all of which will yield a level of profits that will satisfy Marriott stockholders.

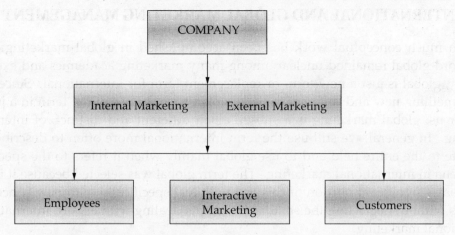

Flow chart 9.7 Three types of marketing in service industries.

All of this suggests that service marketing requires more than just traditional external marketing using the four Ps. Flow Chart 9.7 shows that service marketing also requires both internal marketing and interactive marketing.

Internal marketing means that the service firm must effectively train and motivate its customer-contact employees and all the supporting service people to work as a team to provide customer satisfaction. For the firm to deliver consistently high service quality, everyone must practice a customer orientation. It is not enough to have a marketing department doing traditional marketing while the rest of the company goes its own way. Marketers also must get everyone else in the organisation to practice marketing. In fact, internal marketing must precede external marketing.

Interactive marketing means that perceived service quality depends heavily on the quality of the buyer-seller interaction during the service encounter. In product marketing, product quality often depends little on how the product is obtained. But in service marketing, service quality depends on both the service deliverer and the quality of the delivery, especially in professional services. The customer judges service quality not just on technical quality (say, the success of the surgery) but also on its functional quality (whether the doctor showed concern and inspired confidence). Thus, professionals cannot assume that they will satisfy the customer simply by providing good technical services. They have to master interactive marketing skills or functions as well.

Today, as competition and costs increase, and as productivity and quality decrease, more marketing sophistication is needed. Service companies face three major marketing tasks: They want to increase their competitive differentiation, service quality, and productivity.

9.11 INTERNATIONAL AND GLOBAL MARKETING MANAGEMENT

Although much conceptual work has been accomplished in global marketing, the use of the word global remained unclear among many marketing academics and executives. For many, global is just a new term or replacement term for international. Since, it does mean something new and different to us, we plan to make use of the term in a judicious way. For us, global marketing is a subset, albeit different and distinct, of international marketing. In general, we still use the term international more often to describe factors that relate to the entire field and to use global mainly when it refers to the specific new phenomena in international marketing. The term global was selected because it indicates clearly that a significant portion of this text will deal specifically with new concepts and strategies without neglecting the standard concepts dealing with export, international, or multinational marketing.

Having examined the scope of international and global marketing, we are now able to define it more accurately. Any definition has to be built, however, on basic definitions of marketing and marketing management, with an added explanation of the international dimension. We understand marketing as the performance of business activities directing the flow of products and services from producer to consumer. A successful performance of the marketing function by a firm is contingent upon the adoption of the marketing concept, consisting of (a) a market focus, (b) a customer orientation, (c) an integrated marketing organisation, and (d) customer satisfaction. Marketing management is the execution of a company's marketing operation. Management responsibilities consist of planning, organising, and controlling the marketing program of the firm. To accomplish this job, marketing management is assigned decision-making authority over product strategy, communication strategy, distribution strategy, and pricing strategy. The combination of these four aspects of marketing is referred to as the marketing mix.

For international and global marketing management, the basic goals of marketing and the responsibilities described above remain unchanged. What is different is the execution of these activities in more than one country. Consequently, we define international marketing management as the performance of marketing activities across two or more countries.

Management Orientation

The form and substance of a company's response to global market opportunities depend greatly on management's assumptions or beliefs—both conscious and unconscious—about the nature of the world. The worldview of a company's personnel can be described as ethnocentric, polycentric, regiocentric, and geocentric. Management at a company with a prevailing ethnocentric orientation may consciously make a decision to move in the direction of geocentricism. This orientation is collectively known as the EPRG framework.

Ethnocentric

A person who assumes his or her home country is superior compared to the rest of the world is said to have an ethnocentric orientation. The ethnocentric orientation means the company personnel see only similarities in markets and assume the products and practices that succeed in the home country will, due to their demonstrated superiority, be successful anywhere. At some companies, the ethnocentric orientation means that opportunities outside the home country are ignored. Such companies are sometimes called domestic companies. Ethnocentric companies that do conduct business outside the home country can be described as international companies; they adhere to the notion that the products that succeed in the home country are superior and, therefore, can be sold everywhere without adaptation.

In the ethnocentric, international company, foreign operations are viewed as being secondary or subordinate to domestic ones. An ethnocentric company operates under the assumption that "tried and true" headquarters' knowledge and organisational capabilities can be applied in other parts of the world. Although this can sometimes work to a company's advantage, valuable managerial knowledge and experience in local markets may go unnoticed. For a manufacturing firm, ethnocentrism means foreign markets are viewed as a means of disposing of surplus domestic production. Plans for overseas markets are developed, utilising policies and procedures identical to those employed at home. No systematic marketing research is conducted outside the home country, and no major modifications are made to products. Even if consumer needs or wants in international markets differ from those in the home country, those differences are ignored at headquarters.

Nissan's ethnocentric orientation was quite apparent during its first few years of exporting cars and trucks to the United States. Designed for mild Japanese winters, the vehicles were difficult to start in many parts of the United States during the cold winter months. In northern Japan, many car owners would put blankets over the hoods of their cars. Tokyo's assumption was that Americans would do the same thing. Until the 1980s, Eli Lilly and Company operated as an ethnocentric company in which activity outside the United States was tightly controlled by headquarters and focused on selling products originally developed for the U.S. market.

Fifty years ago, most business enterprises and especially those located in a large country like the United States could operate quite successfully with an ethnocentric orientation. Today, however, ethnocentrism is one of the biggest internal threats a company faces.

Polycentric

The polycentric orientation is the opposite of ethnocentrism. The term polycentric describes management's often unconscious belief or assumption that each country in which a company does business is unique. This assumption lays the groundwork for each subsidiary to develop its own unique business and marketing strategies in order to succeed. The term multinational company is often used to describe such a structure. Until recently, Citicorp's financial services around the world operated on a polycentric basis. James Bailey, a Citicorp executive, offered this description of the company: "We were like a medieval state. There was the king and his court and they were in charge, right? No. It was the land barons who were in charge. The king and his court might declare this or that, but the land barons went and did their thing." Realising that the financial services industry is globalisation, CEO John Reed is attempting to achieve a higher degree of integration between Citicorp's operating units. Like Jack Welch at GE, Reed is moving to instill a geocentric orientation throughout his company.

Regiocentric and Geocentric Orientations

In a company with a regiocentric orientation, management views regions as unique and seeks to develop an integrated regional strategy. For example, a U.S. company that focuses on the countries included in the North American Free Trade Agreement (NAFTA)–the United States, Canada, and Mexico–has a regiocentric orientation. Similarly, a European company that focuses its attention on Europe is regiocentric. A company with a geocentric orientation views the entire world as a potential market and strives to develop integrated world market strategies. A company whose management has a regiocentric or geocentric orientation is sometimes known as a global or transnational company.

The geocentric orientation represents a synthesis of ethnocentrism and polycentrism; it is a "worldview" that sees similarities and differences in markets and countries, and seeks to create a global strategy that is fully responsive to local needs and wants. A regiocentric manager might be said to have a worldview on a regional scale; the world outside the region of interest will be viewed with an ethnocentric or a polycentric orientation, or a combination of the two. Jack Welch's quote at the beginning of this chapter that "globalisation must be taken for granted" implies that at least some company managers must have a geocentric orientation. However, recent research suggests that many companies are seeking to strengthen their regional competitiveness rather than moving directly to develop global responses to changes in the competitive environment.

The ethnocentric company is centralised in its marketing management, the polycentric company is decentralised, and the regiocentric and geocentric companies are integrated on a regional and global scale, respectively. A crucial difference between the orientations is the underlying assumption for each. The ethnocentric orientation is based on a belief in home country superiority. The underlying assumption of the polycentric approach is that there are so many differences in cultural, economic, and marketing conditions in the world that it is impossible and futile to attempt to transfer experience across national boundaries.

9.12   BENEFITS OF INTERNATIONAL MARKETING

The importance of international marketing is neither understood nor appreciated by consumers though they are carrying out international marketing daily. Government officials, especially bureaucrats, seem to always point a negative aspect of international business. Many of their charges on international marketing are imaginary than real. Hence, it is essential that the benefits of international marketing be explicitly discussed. These benefits are

1. Endurance
2. Progress of overseas markets
3. Sales promotion
4. Diversification
5. Inflation and wholesale price index
6. Employment and placement
7. Standard of lifestyle
8. Understanding marketing process.

Endurance

Every country is not as fortunate as America in terms of infrastructure, size, resources and opportunities. Hence, they must trade with other countries to survive. Similarly, every country is not as fortunate as India, which has abundant natural resources and a treasure of biodiversity that it can survive within its resources even if there is a resource crunch. Even then it has to carry out trading with other countries to get oil and armaments for its own survival. Hong Kong cannot survive without food and water from China. The countries of Europe have had similar experience since most European nations are relatively small in size. Without a foreign market, European firms would not have sufficient economies of scale to allow them to be competitive with US firms. Switzerland lacks natural resources, forcing it to depend on trade and adopt the geocentric perspective. Similarly, Japanese firms are dependent on raw material from other countries but they have better technical know-how as a result of which they are the world leaders in electronics and software industry.

Progress of overseas markets

Developing countries, in spite of a poor economy with serious marketing problems, are excellent markets. The US has found that India is the biggest market in the world for consumer and engineering products. According to a report prepared by the US Trade Representative US Congress, Latin America and Asia are experiencing the worst economic recession though they have potential in the world market. The Conference Board's study of some 1500 companies found that US manufacturers, with factories or sales subsidiaries overseas, outperformed their counterparts during 1980s in terms of growth in 19 out of 20 major industrial groups and higher earnings in 17 out of 20 groups. American market cannot ignore the vast potential of the international market. The world market is four times larger than the US market. In the case of Amway Corporation, a privately held US manufacturer of cosmetics, soaps, and vitamins, Japan represents a larger market than the US.

Sales promotion

Foreign markets constitute a large share of total business of many firms that have cultivated markets abroad. Many large US companies have done very well because of their overseas customers. IBM and Compaq sell more computers abroad than at home. The case of Coca-Cola clearly emphasises the importance of overseas markets. Coca-Cola is coming up with milk-based products as majority of Indians and Asians do not relish the taste of aerated drinks which are supposed to have caffeine which is addictive.

Diversification

In the international market, cyclical factors such as recession and seasonal factors such as climate affect the demand for most products. Due to these variables, there are sales fluctuations, which are frequently substantial enough to cause lay off of personnel. One way of diversifying a company's risk is to consider foreign markets as a solution for variable demands. For example, cold weather may depress demand for cold drink consumption. All countries do not enter the winter season at the same time and some of the countries are warm round the year.

Inflation and wholesale price index

The best way to control inflation is to earn foreign exchange through exports. Imports can also be highly beneficial to a country because they constitute reserve capacity of the local economy. Without imports, there is no incentive for domestic firms to moderate their prices. The lack of imported product alternatives forces consumers to pay more, resulting in inflation and excessive profits for local firms. This development usually acts as a prelude to workers to demand higher wages, further exacerbating the problem of inflation. Import quotas imposed on Japanese automobiles in 1980s saved 46,200 US production jobs but at a cost of $160 thousand per job per year. This huge cost was a result of the addition of $400 to the prices of US cars and $1000 to the prices of Japanese imports. This windfall for Detroit resulted in record high profits for US automobiles.

Employment and placements

Tariff barriers and trade restrictions in certain countries had contributed significantly to the Great Depression of 1930 and have the potential to cause widespread unemployment again. Unrestricted trade, on the other hand, improves the world's GNP and enhances employment generally for all nations. With the liberalisation of economic policy, 1991, India has gained tremendously with the inflow of foreign direct investment as a result of which employment in the country has tremendously improved.

Standard of living/style

Trade affords countries and their citizens a higher standard of living than is otherwise possible. Without trade, product shortages force people to pay more for less. Products taken for granted such as coffee and bananas may become unavailable overnight. Life in most of the countries will be more difficult were it not for the many strategic metals that must be imported. Trade also makes it easier for industries to specialise and gain access to raw materials, while at the same time fostering competition and efficiency.

Marketing process

International marketing should be considered a special case of domestic marketing. It has earlier been explained that there is very little difference between domestic and international marketing. Only thing is that the word multinational has been added in the international marketing process. Otherwise, the marketing mix is the same for both. With improvements in information technology, the international markets have become easily accessible and the whole world has become a small global village.

9.13 SCOPE OF GLOBAL MARKETING

The foundation for a successful international marketing programme is a sound understanding of the marketing discipline. Marketing is the process of focusing the resources and objectives of an organisation on environmental needs and opportunities. The first and the most fundamental fact about marketing is that it is a universal discipline. The marketing discipline is equally applicable from China to India, United States to Japan and Australia to Zanzibar. Marketing is a set of concepts, tools, theories, practices and procedures and experience. Although the marketing discipline is universal markets and customers are quite differentiate. This means that marketing practices must vary from country to country. Each person is unique and each country is unique. This reality of differences means that we cannot always directly apply experience from one country to another. If the customers, competitors, channels of distribution and available media are different, it may be necessary to change our marketing plan.

The scope of international marketing is to have a borderless world like the multinational companies–Coca-Cola, Pepsi, McDonald, Gillette, and so on. Their products and body marketing mix elements are both international and local in nature. A central issue in international marketing is how to tailor the international marketing concept to fit a particular product or business.

9.14   OBSTACLES TO INTERNATIONALISATION

Companies attempting to establish and maintain an international presence are likely to encounter obstacles to internationalisation both from within the company and from outside. Such obstacles can be financial in nature: The company might not have the finances to expand beyond national frontiers. Others are psychological: Fear of an unknown international environment or of local business practices may keep the company away from international engagement. These two types of barriers, however, could equally affect the company's local expansion efforts: Companies may not have the finances to expand beyond a small regional market, or they fear going into new markets where consumers may not be familiar with their products and hence may not respond to their marketing strategy.

Some obstacles are encountered only by firms in their process of internationalization-obstacles that they are unlikely to encounter in other expansion efforts. They are the self-reference criterion, government barriers, and international competition.

Self-Reference Criterion

Of crucial importance to international operations is the ability of the firm, and especially of its marketing program, to adapt to the local business environment in order to serve the needs of local consumers and to address the requirements of local government, industry, and channels of distribution. An impediment to adaptation is the self-reference criterion, defined as individuals conscious and unconscious reference to their own national culture, to home-country norms, values, as well as to their knowledge and experience, in the process of making decisions in the host country. "Cultural Influences on International Marketing" illustrates a number of situations in which self-reference can lead to a breakdown in communication between parties from different cultures. For example, an employee of a large multinational company from the United States conducting business in Japan who has been trained by career counsellors in the U.S. that looking one's counterpart in the eyes conveys directness and honesty is likely to be perceived as abrasive and challenging.

Similarly, if the same employee proceeds directly to transacting the business deal in Latin America or Southern Europe (instead of first interacting in a social setting in order to establish rapport), he/she would be perceived as arrogant, interested only in the bottom line, rather than in a long-term working relationship.

A first step to minimising the impact of the self-reference criterion is selecting appropriate personnel for international assignments. Such employees are sensitive to others and have experience working in different environments. Second, it would be important to train expatriates to focus on and be sensitive to the local culture, rather than limit their personal interactions to own country nationals or to expatriates from countries with cultures that are similar to one's own. In fact, an organisation-level general orientation that instills and demonstrates sensitivity to international environments and openly spurns value judgements and national stereotyping should be instilled at the firm level.

Government Barriers

Local governments, especially governments in developing countries, keep a tight control over international market entrants, permitting or denying access to international firms based on criteria that are deemed important for national industry and/or security considerations at a particular point in time. Among formal methods used by national governments to restrict or impede entrance of international firms in the local market are tariffs and barriers such as import quotas, or policies of restricting import licence awards, foreign exchange restrictions, and local content requirements, among others. Member countries of the World Trade Organisation, signatories of the General Agreement on Tariffs and Trade, or members of regional economic integration agreements such as NAFTA and the European Union find it very difficult to use tariffs as a means of restricting international expansion of companies in the countries territories. Increasingly, they are using non-tariff barriers, such as cumbersome procedures for import paperwork processing, delays in granting licences, or preference given to local service providers and product manufacturing for all contracting work.

International Competition

Although competition can be a driver of internationalisation, competitors can also erect barriers to new entrants in a market. They often do so by employing strategies such as blocking channels of distribution, binding retailers into exclusive agreements, slashing prices temporarily to prevent product adoption, or engaging in an advertising blitz that could hurt a company's initial sales in a market and cause it to retrench. With heavy competition from new and lesser brands in Asia, Central and Eastern Europe, and North Africa and the Middle East, Marlboro has created a strong defensive strategy for its cigarettes: It slashed prices by as much as a third, and advertised heavily anywhere it was legal, especially on billboards in the centre of different capital cities and towns in the provinces. As an example, sales of Marlboro in South-Eastern Europe were hurt by various local competitors and, in particular, by a successful international brand, Assos from Greece. Assos was rapidly gaining a leading position in a number of markets in the region when Marlboro went on the offensive, limiting Assos's market share to a point where the company was forced to abandon many of its markets. Marlboro effectively put in question the international expansion of many new European and Asian brands, as well as new brands from the United States (it decimated, for instance, sales of new brands of American cigarettes created specifically for the Russian market).

9.15 PROTECTIONISM

Protection of local markets from foreign companies constitutes an important mandate for national and local governments alike. Many political careers have been built and defended on market protection rhetoric. "We will not sell our country" has been a slogan of countries resisting foreign economic and political dominance in the past. Today, it is a slogan used against multinationals that are rapidly expanding, taking over emerging markets, and bringing with them a consumption culture perceived to go against local culture and traditions. These multinationals also are seen as eliminating small local producers and service providers, bankrupting formerly productive factories, and replacing abundant local labour with more efficient advanced technology, increasing local unemployment and disrupting political stability. All actions by national and local governments are aimed at protecting local markets from foreign competitor.

Some of the arguments for **protectionism** are indeed valid. The infant industry argument is aimed at protecting an emerging national industry from powerful international competitors, which could easily squeeze out a newcomer to the business merely with its brand name resonance and with pricing strategies that a new industry could not possibly sustain in the long-term. The argument stressing the industrialisation of developing countries also is valid for similar reasons. The national defence argument is regarded as justified in international trade forums and is widely accepted as a reasonable argument for protectionism. There is also the argument for environmental protection and/or protection of natural resources and the need for maintaining standards to the benefit of all humankind; this line of arguments is also soundly reasoned. The problem with this defence of protectionism arises when the standards imposed are, in fact, simple protectionist arms that require foreign competition to go through excessive and unwarranted bureaucratic exercise, or when these requirements are imposed on international firms but not on local firms–or not to the same degree.

In general, it is believed that consumers pay the final price for the cost of strategies of protectionism. Arguments for protectionism ignore the economic advantages of free trade and the importance of adopting open market mechanisms for optimal long-term market performance. In fact, history has amply demonstrated that a government's right and authority to pick and choose winners among industries and firms could be corrupted and distorted by local influential firms, power-seeking politicians, and favour-seeking lobby groups. Politicians, particularly in the United States, favour trade barriers and vote for imposing them because such strategies appeal directly to the concerns of their constituencies regarding the possibility of losing their jobs. What these politicians do not consider is the subsequent retaliatory action of other governments which will negatively affect the domestic economy, the higher consumer prices attributed to the tax imposed to subsidise the domestic industry, and higher prices attributed to the reduction in competition in the local market.

Arguments for Protectionism

The following arguments are most often advanced to justify the imposition of tariff and non-tariff trade barriers or protectionism.

Protection of Markets with Excess Productive Capacity

Markets that have excess productive capacity have committed significant resources to the production facilities. In the case of Central and Eastern Europe, for example, the standard for production during the central planning years under communism was represented by mammoth factories employing hundreds of thousands of workers, each charged with minuscule repetitive tasks under an elaborate division-of-labour programme. The goal of such programmes was both to ensure productivity and to assure a place of work to every individual, qualified or not. Such factories had, in addition to the workers, structures with directors and Para directors, all served by several secretaries whose specialisations varied from typing to answering telephones, to making coffee, to taking care of the director's family's personal shopping.

After the fall of communism, the new factory owners (often foreign) quickly realised that they needed only a fraction of the workers for optimal production and proceeded to fire the rest, leading to regional unrest. Currently, remaining factories are protected from foreign buyouts and are managed locally. Often they are state-owned enterprises. National governments protect them from foreign investors. They also protect these enterprises by limiting the entrance of competing products, such as superior steel and higher-performance tractors, by arguing that such restrictions are instituted to protect a market with excess productive capacity.

Employment Protection and Protection of Markets with Excess Labour

Under the scenario presented in section (a), the markets of Central and Eastern Europe– especially those in the countries of the former Soviet Union are now experiencing high levels of excess labour and underemployment, all of which led to flares of social unrest. As a result, local politicians actively lobby against granting import licences for products competing with locally produced goods that are established in the market. Arguments invoking employment protection are used to ensure that competing multinationals do not import products manufactured elsewhere that might drive local manufacturers out of business and create local unemployment. The argument also is used against multinationals that might purchase local plants and fire most of the redundant workers to create acceptable levels of profitability. A related argument, invoking the protection of markets with excess labour, is also used to prevent more efficient multinationals from taking over local businesses and streamlining local operations.

Infant Industry Arguments and Arguments Related to the Industrialisation of Developing Countries

The infant industry arguments and arguments related to the industrialisation of developing countries are considered valid: Developing countries need to protect their markets from competitors with an established industrial base. Foreign competitors would be able to offer higher quality products at lower costs and would undoubtedly undercut local manufacturers attempting to break into the market. Foreign competition would present the greatest challenge to local industries in their infancy.

Natural Resources Conservation and Protection of the Environment

The resource conservation argument is considered to be valid in international trade organisation forums, especially in light of worldwide shortages of raw materials. Similarly, a balance sometimes has to be struck between free trade and legitimate arguments such as those entering on environmental protection, but governments still need to find a way of agreeing when curbs on trade can be an acceptable way to pursue a greater good.

The problem with these two arguments arises when they are used arbitrarily, with a clear bias against international firms, either imposing the standards only on foreign firms or requiring them to meet higher standards than local firms.

Protection of Consumers

Protection of consumers is an often-echoed argument that ultimately favours local, over international, business. Standards that are rigidly applied against foreign businesses, quality controls that necessitate layers of costly bureaucracy, and arbitrary product origin requirements, among others, are invoked as a basis for this argument. Politicians in the European Union have argued that they were protecting consumers by imposing standards on imported beef: Listening to the unified voices of their constituencies and attempting to protect the local beef industry against the high-quality, cheap, corn-fed U.S. beef, the European Union banned its import, invoking the use of growth hormones in the United States. With cattle in many countries of the European Union plagued by mad-cow and/or hoof-and-mouth disease, the primary option available to European consumers is expensive Argentine beef. This is an unequivocal demonstration that consumer-protection gone-too-far is not necessarily in the interest of the consumer.

National Defence Interests

The national defence argument is also perceived as valid, and it is often invoked in international trade forums. Publications that attempt to destabilise the government, armament, and other similar products are often under an import ban. More recently, the national defence argument has been advocated by developing countries and/or by countries that attempt to control and restrict access of their population to Western influence. Such nations may perceive a threat in the unrestricted imports of information-based services through electronic channels; countries such as China, Singapore, and Saudi Arabia impose restrictions on and even ban ownership of satellite dishes, whereas other nations are attempting to control citizen access on the World Wide Web (www).

Tools of Government Protectionism

Tariff and non-tariff barriers

(a) Tariffs

Tariffs are any type of tax imposed on goods entering a particular country. Tariffs are imposed to:

- Discourage imports of particular goods, such as consumer goods, which often are not considered essential in developing countries.
- Penalise countries that are not politically aligned with the importing country, or countries that are imposing tariffs or non-tariff restrictions on goods from the importing country.
- Generate revenues for the importing country.

In general, tariffs that are assessed by the United States are relatively low, less than 10 per cent. Some developing countries set tariffs higher than 100 per cent for products that compete with an infant industry. For example, countries attempting to develop their own automobile industry are likely to impose very high tariffs to all automobiles imported into the country.

(b) Non-tariff Barriers

Non-tariff barriers include all measures, other than traditional tariffs, that are used to distort international trade flows; they raise prices of both imports and import-competing goods and favour domestic over foreign supply sources by causing importers to charge higher prices and to restrict import volumes.

In the past twenty years, in an attempt to keep markets closed without going against the General Agreement on Tariffs and Trade (GATT) and the World Trade Organisation, governments have created new non-tariff barriers, such as orderly market arrangements, voluntary import expansion, and voluntary export restraints, which limit market access for foreign businesses. Many countries have erected these non-tariff barriers, but most are imposed by the United States, members of the European Union, and by other industrialised countries on exporting countries such as Japan, South Korea, and developing countries. Other, more traditional, non-tariff barriers include quotas, currency controls, and standards–such as environmental, quality, performance, and health standards, which are expensive to provide and to evaluate. Boycotts, embargoes, and sanctions are the most severe barriers to trade that are imposed usually to punish a company or a national government.

Import Quotas and Orderly Market Arrangements

Import quotas specify a maximum quantity (unit limit) or a value (usually specified in the national currency) of a product that may be imported during a specified period. Quotas are administered either on a global first-come, first-served basis or on a bilateral basis to restrict shipments from a specific supply source such as the Multifibre Arrangement.

The Multifibre Arrangement was initiated as a temporary measure in 1974 (but lasted 21 years). Its articulated goals were to expand trade, to reduce barriers to trade, and to initiate a progressive liberalisation of world trade in textile products, while ensuring the orderly and equitable development of this trade and avoiding disruptive effects in individual markets and on individual lines of production in both importing and exporting countries. In reality, this was an orderly market arrangement, an intricate process of establishing quotas in the textile and apparel industries, initiated by the United States and Europe, whose textile operations were moving to Asia to take advantage of cheaper labour. The Multifibre Arrangement was nullified under the Uruguay Round of the General Agreement on Tariffs and Trade in 1995 but has since been replaced by very similar non-tariff barriers.

Non-automatic Import Licences

Non-automatic import licences are issued on a discretionary basis and are used to restrict imports of a given product. Licensing requirements can restrict the volume of imports, as do quotas, or they can be used to impose on the exporter or importer specific conditions that will result in fewer imports. It should be mentioned that the World Trade Organisation presently requires member countries to ensure transparency of the import-licence granting process; they are asked to do so by publicising information concerning administration of restrictions, by listing information regarding the licences granted over the most recent period, and, where practicable, by providing additional import statistics of the products concerned.

Automatic Import Licences

Automatic import licenses are granted freely to importing companies. Automatic licences are used by the importing country's government for the purpose of import surveillance: The licences have the potential to discourage import surges, they place additional administrative and financial burdens on the importer, and they may also raise costs by delaying product shipments.

Voluntary Import Expansion (VIE)

Under a voluntary import expansion (VIE), a country agrees to open its markets to imports. Voluntary import expansions increase foreign access to a domestic market, while increasing competition and reducing prices. Voluntary import expansions are not voluntary at all: A country agrees to import products as a result of pressure from another country. An example of voluntary import expansion is Japan's decision to avert U.S.-imposed trade sanctions by importing U.S. semiconductors.

Voluntary Export Restraints (VER)

Voluntary export restraints (VERs) are self-imposed quotas and constitute a barrier to trade often used in the 1980s to protect local industries. The United States, for example, used voluntary export restraints to protect local steel and automobile industries. Voluntary export restraints are agreed upon by the importing country and the exporting country. A country that is subject to voluntary export restraints limits the quantity of products it exports to another, primarily because it attempts, by doing so, to avoid more severe, future mandatory import restrictions. Voluntary export quotas are still used today even though they have been banned by the Uruguay Round of the General Agreement on Tariffs and Trade (and now by the World Trade Organisation) since 1999. The United States is imposing them informally, for example, for Japanese steel imports; this protection mechanism has been used since 1969 in the long history of trade protection of the U.S. steel industry.

Price Controls: Paratariff Measures

Paratariff measures are charges that increase the costs of imports in a manner similar to tariffs. Such measures include allowing an initial number of product units to enter, the country duty-free and charging tariffs to subsequent shipments in excess of this quota; they also include advance import deposits, additional import charges, seasonal tariffs, and customs charges. The United States uses many of these paratariff measures to discourage shipment of certain agricultural products from developing countries.

Local Content Requirements and Foreign Ownership: Percentage Requirements

Governments of many emerging market economies mandate that a certain percentage of the products imported are locally produced. They mandate a local content requirement. Manipulating and/or assembling the product on the territory of the importing country, usually in a foreign trade zone can often meet this requirement. China, for example, has always presented a challenge to importing firms. Multinational firms often join with Chinese partners and agents to either package or manufacture enough of the product to have it qualify based on local content requirements; firms often do tricky calculations on local services and part values to meet such local content edicts.

It should be mentioned that service industries in particular are subjected to regulations that invoke foreign ownership restrictions. Creative strategies that employ an ambiguous legal environment are used to block entry of international service providers or to place them at a disadvantage relative to local competitors.

Currency and Capital Flow Controls

Strategies involving currency and capital flow controls are used in economies that are under tight government control and/or that are experiencing hard-currency shortages. In the case of capital flow, countries use arguments of self-determination to ensure that regions in the country are uniformly developed or that there would not be a capital flight from the country. Such strategies affect international businesses in that they restrict market-dictated activity in the name of protectionism.

Governments use currency flow restrictions primarily to influence the stability of the national currency. Such restrictions, however, directly affect the flow of imports into the country, by giving priority to desirable goods and restricting the import of less desirable goods and services. Among the currency controls used by governments are the following:

- Blocked currency
- Differential exchange rates
- Foreign exchange permits

Blocked Currency

A country using a blocked currency strategy does not allow importers to exchange local currency for the seller's currency. This strategy can be used as a political weapon, to create obstacles for international business attempting to enter the country. More often, however, the strategy is used because the country is experiencing acute balance-of-payments difficulties. Firms fortunately have at their disposal counter trade strategies to address this type of barrier. Under a typical scenario, the exporter sells goods in exchange for local currency and uses the proceeds to purchase local goods for sale abroad; U.S. companies in the past often bought goods from Mexico and from Eastern Europe with local currency to address this barrier.

Differential Exchange Rates

Two types of differential exchange rates can be used. The first, which is government imposed, refers to a strategy the government uses to promote imports of desirable and necessary goods, such as armament and petrol, and to discourage imports of less desirable and necessary goods, such as consumer goods and services, entertainment, and the like. Offering a less favourable exchange rate for international products and services reflects a government strategy that ultimately increases the cost of this second category of products to the final consumer and discourages its purchase.

A second type of differential exchange rate is favourable to the international firm importing products into this market. In this situation, a difference exists between the black market exchange rate and the official government exchange rate, with the black market rate being higher than the government rate. The rate difference is a reflection of economic distortion: A high black market exchange rate can signal a likely depreciation of the local currency, or foreign exchange rationing by the government, or both. A large difference between the government and the free exchange rate can also be interpreted as a tax on exports and a subsidy on imports, stimulating the diversion of resources from the official to the black market sector.

Foreign Exchange Permits

Countries attempting to control foreign exchange often require the use of foreign exchange permits. Such permits are typically provided by the Central Bank. They also give priority to imports of goods that are in the national interest and delay access to foreign exchange for products that are not deemed essential. An exchange permit can also stipulate differential exchange rates. Most countries that experience a shortage of hard currency require foreign exchange permits. China and countries in sub-Saharan Africa currently require such permits. In the past, Latin American and Eastern European countries relied heavily on the use of foreign exchange permits for imports.

9.16   DIRECT MARKETING

The history of direct marketing (and its antecedents, direct mail and mail order) reflects the socioeconomic development of the United States. This is the constant and underlying factor in the direct marketing story. This relationship is as true today as it was in 1872 when Aaron Montgomery Ward produced his first catalogue, ushering in the modern era of mail order as we have known it for more than 100 years. This also explains why long-term success in direct marketing has been inextricably linked to two essential factors: (1) the ability of management to predict the impact of socioeconomic change on the marketplace and on lifestyles, as seen in the recession that hit the U.S. in the early 1990's and (2) the implementation of a sound strategy and marketing programme that offers products and services that satisfy changing needs, wants, and interests of the consumer, as seen in the response by direct marketers to consumers' alarms regarding the environment beginning in 1990.

The Evolution of the Term "Direct Marketing"

As far as can be determined, the first use of the term "direct marketing" occurred on October 1, 1961, in a speech by Lester Wunderman to the Hundred Million Club (now the Direct Marketing Club of New York). The term was used again and elaborated upon by Wunderman in a speech at MIT on November 29, 1967. He said, "I believe the term 'direct marketing' is more appropriate than 'mail order selling' direct marketing where the advertising and buying become a single action."

In May 1968, Pete Hoke changed the name of The Reporter of Direct Mail to Direct Marketing Magazine. From then on, he became the outstanding proponent and missionary for the term "direct marketing," helping to define its meaning and to broaden its scope and significance. The term "direct marketing" has been accepted in advertising, marketing, and business circles, in print and in electronic media, in academia, and, not least, in increasing number of consumers.

The Direct Marketing Association was also acutely aware of the wave of change in the industry. As mentioned earlier, DMA began in 1917 as the Direct Mail Advertising Association, which located the focus of the industry on direct mail. By 1973, the name changed to Direct Mail/Marketing Association, which reflected the broader scope of the membership brought about by the emergence of new media. Although the traditional mail order components of DMA will always be its staple, in 1983, it became the Direct Marketing Association, Inc., reflecting the evolution of multimedia approaches of direct marketing.

Changes in the Marketplace

Throughout the first half of the 20th century, cataloguers experienced tremendous success simply by selling discount merchandise out of one huge catalogue that appealed largely to rural consumers. However, increasing competition and declining sales in the 1970's caused marketers to look more closely at the marketplace, and they found that some dramatic changes were taking place that warranted gross adjustments in the way they did business.

The Increase in Working Women

Probably the most dramatic socioeconomic change occurring during the mid-1960s was the increase in the proportion of women working. It has completely transformed markets, products, families, homes, workplace conditions—essentially, the fundamental lifestyles of the entire U.S. population.

More than 60 per cent of women over the age of 16 now earn paychecks, compared with 43 per cent in 1970. By the year 2000, it is estimated that 82 per cent of all women between the ages of 25 and 34 will be in the labour force. More mothers than ever before are also entering the workforce—50.8 per cent of mothers with children under one year old are working, and that percentage increases as children get older.

This trend has been a real boon to direct marketers. Lack of time is a primary dilemma cited by many women today. They do not have enough time to go shopping or to relax during leisure time. Catalogue marketers began to realise that they should exploit the time-saving offered by catalogue shopping and that they should offer merchandise that appeal to working women. As two-income families became the norm, women began to control more discretionary income and to desire better products. Direct marketers began to see a need for upscaling their products to appeal to this new market.

Direct Marketing and Package Goods

Because of declining effectiveness of traditional media, the struggle for shelf space, and erosion of brand royalty, package goods manufactures, particularly tobacco companies (due in large part to broadcast media advertising restrictions), have long used direct marketing to promote their products. Although the standard promotion vehicle for these companies has traditionally been coupons, more and more packaged goods marketers have discovered direct marketing for its database-building potential.

Kraft General Foods (KGF), a division of Philip Morris Companies, is the largest U.S. manufacturer of packaged goods with more than 30 food brands. The company's success with using the targeted approach of direct marketing has energised sagging sales of several of KGF's brands lines, including Kool-Aid and Maxwell House Coffee. To revamp Kool-Aid's image and to build loyalty among pre-teens, the Wacky Wild Campaign was launched. By collecting points found on every soft drink package, children could order products from the Wacky Warehouse. KGF was then able to capture the child's name, address, and birthday. As a result of this campaign, KGF has experienced a 20-point gain.

Philip Morris, RJR Nabisco, Colgate-Palmolive, Eastman-Kodak, and Sara Lee are few of the many large packaged goods corporations that are using state-of-the-art direct marketing methods successfully to promote their products. As technologies become more advanced, these companies are realising the database-building opportunities offered by direct marketing and participation in the medium will likely increase in the future.

Direct Marketing and the New Technologies

Forecasting the future, particularly where technology is concerned, is a difficult task. While technology has always had an impact on direct marketing, its impact had never been greater. Nor has the rate of technology-driven change ever been so faster than it is today. One does not need a crystal ball to see that the future of the industry, and the survival of many of its current players, will be dictated by the use or neglect of technology. Change is coming in many ways. Direct marketing itself will become fundamentally different as new, powerful entrants—bolstered by the innovative application of technology—change the nature and scope of the industry. Through a variety of marketing devices, including 900-number telephone service promotions and "smart cards," large consumer products companies are gathering customer information and targeting their marketing efforts directly to their customers. In addition, these companies are likely to form partnerships with retailers, their main channel of distribution, to improve the effectiveness of retail promotions. This changing relationship between retailers and their suppliers will likely have considerable impact on direct marketing by bringing new players into the field who are large enough to change some of the rules of the game.

Growth in direct marketing fostered advances in technology that have enabled direct marketers to take advantage of the changing market conditions and manage the direct marketing process. Today, the direct marketer can use technologies to perform functions related to every element of business:

✠ Advances in computer hardware and sophisticated database management systems enable direct marketers to store, access, and manipulate data cost-effectively.

✠ Direct marketers can perform complex analysis on workstations on their desks.

✠ Innovations in communicating information to and receiving a response from consumers include 800 and 900 numbers, electronic kiosks, complex call management, and integrated voice and telecommunications networks.

✠ Marketers can cost-effectively produce marketing materials through in-house desktop publishing and electronic prepress.

✠ Function-rich software is available to improve the marketer's ability to respond to consumer inquiries and complete consumer transaction.

✠ A number of technologies are oriented toward labour-saving and rapid response to support fulfilment, including bar-coding and electronic data interchange.

In the coming years, technology will bring many large and powerful new entrants to direct marketing. The industry will change radically as consumer products companies and retailers gain expertise in direct marketing methods. Both of these new players will bring significant marketing experience and well-developed technology infrastructures to the field. They will change the way that consumers and direct marketers do business.

Database Marketing

Technology improvements in the 1980s resulted in the growth of the most powerful tool today in direct marketing—the database. Keeping track of a consumer's preferences and purchases became increasingly affordable as the cost of accessing and maintaining data fell dramatically this decade. Marketers could now capture an amazing amount of information electronically that could help make them much more efficient.

Today, databases include not only names, addresses and phone numbers of customers, but also credit status, language preference, how often a customer buys, when last bought, how paid, even feelings about the company and its products. Customer information can also be overlaid with geographic, demographic, and lifestyle information. So future offers can be targeted to just the right person. It is also the answer to responding to an American society that has become fragmented into many specialised niches. Thus, database marketing now makes it easy to promote sales, cross-promote, explore new channels of distribution, built lifetime customer loyalty—the possibilities are endless. Database marketing is a prime example of how technology has and will change the scope of direct marketing from mass marketing to an exact science.

Direct Marketing and the Environment

On April 22, 1990, the 20th anniversary celebration of Earth Day renewed public concern about the state of the environment. Prior to the celebration, a paperback called *Fifty Simple Things You Can Do to Save the Earth* was published, and it became an immediate best-seller and was one of the most talked-about publications of the year. The book listed "Stop Junk Mail" as the first action consumers can take to save our planet. This caused a tremendous media and public outcry against direct mail.

Although this attack ignored the environmental benefits of direct marketing and shopping at home, and the fact that more than 50 per cent of the U.S. population purchased merchandise by mail or telephone in 1990, the industry has responded, and many direct marketers are taking proactive stances. Some—such as Sears, Land's End, and Patagonia— have established recycling programmes and some are printing their catalogues, or portions of their catalogues, on recycled paper. Several cataloguers are participating in Global ReLeaf, a tree-planting programme sponsored by the American Forestry Association, and several cataloguers are adding environmentally conscious products to their merchandise offerings. Many new packaging methods have emerged to eliminate the waste of non-recycled plastic "peanuts" to package products.

Seventh Generation, a catalogue that sells "products that promote a healthy environment" has undergone a tremendous expansion as a result of the company's new environmental awareness. The company maintains an active role in the environment, educates its customers on environmental fact and fiction, and bases many business decisions on their anticipated impact on the environment. For example, the company chooses to use paper tape to increase the recyclability of its paper packaging, and it chooses local suppliers to reduce transportation costs, energy consumption, and air pollution. It also participates in AFA's Global Relief programme. The company contributes one per cent of its gross sale to various environmental organisations.

Many new environmental magazines that are devoted solely to Earth issues cropped up in the early 1990s. Two such periodicals, Garbage and Buzzworm, had paid circulations of 86,000 and 75,000, respectively, within a few months of their introductions.

Late in 1989, DMA formed a Task Force on Environmental Issues as a natural outgrow of the concern expressed in the one-on-one communication between direct marketers and their customers. The task force is served by a number of industry leaders and focuses on the role that direct marketing businesses should play with the consumer to make the direct marketing process environmentally sound. By self-regulating, marketers can relieve public concerns about direct marketing's environmental impact and avoid governmental legislation, which could prove harmful to the way they do business. As the 1990s were ushered in, an economic recession hit the country, slowing consumer spending and alarming marketers from coast to coast. Adding to the impact of the recession, direct marketers, especially cataloguers, have had to deal with substantial postal rate increases. In 1988, third-class rates increased, on average, by 20 per cent. However, rates for catalogues rose almost 32 per cent. In 1991, the average third-class increase was 25 per cent, but again, cataloguers rates rose more, in some cases in excess of 40 per cent.

Quite a few cataloguers, including J. Crew, L.L. Bean and Spiegel, reported disappointingly slow sales during the 1990 Christmas season. To remain afloat, direct marketers have had to adapt rapidly to changing market conditions.

In order to keep customers buying, many cataloguers have concentrated on improving communication with their customers, convincing them that their catalogue is the best source for their items. Others are dedicating their efforts to target potential customers as efficiently and cost-effectively as possible. Customer service is emerging as one of the single most important factor in keeping customers loyal.

9.17   RURAL MARKETING

"Rural marketing is real marketing"

India is a land of diversity and about 75% of the Indian population lives in villages. These villages contribute in the economic development of the nation through the production of food grains, vegetables, fruits, etc. Export of these agricultural commodities result in the generation of capital and earnings of foreign exchange.

Indian rural market has a vast size and demand base. Before going into more aspects on rural marketing, let us understand how rural is defined.

The Census figures defines urban India as *"All the places that fall within the administrative limits of a municipality, cantonment board, etc. or have a population of at least 5,000 and have at least 75% male working population in outside the primary sector and have a population density of at least 400 per square kilometre. Rural India, on the other hand, comprises all places that are not urban based"*.

To expand market tapping the countryside, more and more MNCs are foraying into India's rural markets. Among those that have made some headway are HUL, Coca-Cola, LG, Britannia, Colgate & Palmolive and other telecom industries.

Rural Marketing

Rural marketing involves the process of developing, pricing, promoting, distributing rural specific product and a service leading to exchange between rural and urban market which consumer demand and also achieves organisational objectives. This is represented in Fig. 9.1.

Fig. 9.1 Rural marketing process.

It is a two-way marketing process wherein the transaction can be measured in three ways:

- **Urban to Rural:** It involves the selling of products and services by urban marketers in rural areas. These include pesticides, FMCG (Fast Moving Consumer Goods) products, consumer durables, etc.
- **Rural to Urban:** Here, a rural producer (involved in agriculture) sells his produce in urban market. This may not be direct. There generally are middleman, agencies, government cooperatives, etc. who sell fruits, vegetables, grains, pulses and others.
- **Rural to Rural:** These include selling of agriculture tools, cattle, carts and others to another village in its proximity.

Features of Indian Rural Markets

- **Large, Divers and Scattered Market:** Rural market in India is large, and scattered into a number of regions. There may be less number of shops available to market products.

- **Major Income of Rural Consumers is from Agriculture:** Rural prosperity is tied with agriculture prosperity. In the event of a crop failure, the income of the rural masses is directly affected.

- **Standard of Living and Rising Disposable Income of the Rural Customers:** It is known that majority of the rural population are below the poverty line and with low literacy rate, low per capita income, low savings, etc.

- **Traditional Outlook:** Villages develop slowly and have a traditional outlook. Change is a continuous process but most rural people accept change gradually. This is gradually changing due to literacy especially in the youth who have begun to change the outlook in the village.

- **Rising Literacy Levels:** It is documented that approximately 50% of rural Indians are literate. Hence, awareness has to be made in the framers about our globalisation. They are also educating themselves on the new technology around them and aspiring for a better lifestyle.

- **Infrastructure Facilities:** The infrastructure facilities like CC roads, warehouse, communication system, and financial facilities are inadequate in the rural areas.

The Indian government is making continuous efforts to make economic development towards rural areas with innovative technology and also rural market offers a big attraction to the marketers to explore markets that are untapped.

Barriers for Indian Rural Markets

There are several barriers for rural market to come up. Marketers encounter number of barriers with physical, logistic, distribution, and also with deployment of sales force and effective marketing communication when they enter rural markets. The major barriers are discussed below:

1. **Standard of Living:** The number of people below the poverty line is more in rural markets. Thus, the market is also underdeveloped and marketing strategies have to be different from those used in urban marketing.

2. **Low Literacy Levels:** The low literacy levels in rural areas lead to a problem of communication.

3. **Low Per Capita Income:** Agriculture is the main source of income and hence spending capacity depends upon the agriculture produce.

4. **Ineffective Distribution Channels:** The distribution chain is not very well organised and requires a large number of intermediaries, which in turn increase the cost and creates administrative problems.

5. **Lack of Communication System:** Quick communication is the need of the hour of smooth conduct of business, but it continues to be a far cry in rural areas due to lack of communication facilities like telegraph and telecommunication systems.

6. **Seasonal Demand:** Demand may be seasonal due to dependency on agriculture income. Harvest season might see an increase in disposable income and hence more purchasing power.

7. **Dispersed Markets:** Rural population is highly dispersed and requires a lot of marketing efforts in terms of distribution and communication.

The entire points which are focused above challenges to the marketer, he tries to uncover newer ways to market his product as he cannot afford to miss this huge opportunity existing in rural markets. He tries to identify solutions to these marketing problems.

Remedies towards Barriers of Rural Markets

The barriers for rural markets in India, the following suggestions can be adopted by marketers:

1. Regarding the problems of physical distribution, the marketer may have a joint network of stockist clearing-cum-forwarding agents at strategic location for facilities of physical distribution for its products in the rural markets. The main advantage of this scheme is that the cost of physical distribution can be shared by the companies and stockist.

2. The rural market is composed of a number of retail sales outlets along with fair prices shops under the public distribution system. It is suggested that the government should encourage private shopkeepers and cooperative stores to come forward and establish their business in rural areas instead of the weekly market known as weekly bazaar.

3. To solve the problems of sales management, it is suggested that the company takes the care in the recruitment and selection of sales people because the traits they require are different from urban and suburban salespersons. For the rural markets, only those sales people should be preferred for selection who are willing to work in rural areas.

4. Always the company must make media mix like TV, Radio, cinema and POP (Point of Purchase) advertising. Television is gaining popularity in the rural areas but due to poor supply of electricity, radio is performing significantly better. The sales people should always concern rural leaders like Sarpanch, Pradhan and other elderly

persons. They can be approached by the marketers to propagate their messages; these persons can prove to be effective communicators within the rural masses.

5. The markets must come up with innovative ideas through which the villagers also get involved in getting business from their respective villages.

The Indian rural market is quite fascinating and challenging. It provides tremendous opportunities which beckon a marketer to explore.

9.18   RURAL CONSUMER BEHAVIOUR

The rural consumers are classified into the following groups based on their economic status:

- **The Affluent Group:** They are cash rich farmers and a very few in number. They have affordability but not from a demand base large enough for marketing firm to depend on. Wheat farmer in Punjab and rice merchants of Andhra Pradesh fall in this group.

- **The Middle Class:** This is one of the largest segments for manufactured goods and is fast expanding. Farmers cultivating sugar cane in UP and Karnataka fall in this class.

- **The Poor:** This constitutes a huge segment. Purchasing power is less, but strength is more. They receive the grants from government and reap the benefits of many such schemes and may move towards the middle class. The farmers of Bihar and Orissa fall under this category.

Profile of Rural Consumers

According to IMRB (Indian Market Research Bureau) and NCAER (National Council for Applied Economic Research) have made available a few studies based on which rural consumer profile can be arrived at:

1. **Literacy:** Mearly 30% of rural Indian population is illiterate and people are getting added to this list year after year. There are still some villages which are underdeveloped.

2. **Income:** An average rural consumer has a much lower income than his urban counterpart. The disposable income has increased in the recent years to considerable extent. In spite of this, the common traits of rural consumers are low purchasing power, low standard of living, low per capita income and low economic and social positions.

3. **Density:** Rural population is scattered across 7 lakh villages. This implies that rural demand is scattered and urban demand is concentrated.

4. **Influences:** There are many reference groups in a village. These include teachers, doctors, health workers, bank managers, and others.

5. **Occupation:** The main occupation is agriculture. The size and ownership of land determines the basis for differentiation and consumption patterns.

6. **Culture:** Rural consumers are traditional in their needs.

7. **Language:** English is not a language of rural India. Hence, a marketer should aim for communication in the local language.

8. **Media Habits:** TV, radio, video are some traditional media that a rural consumer identifies with.

The above are some of the factors that differentiate the rural consumers from his urban counterpart. A marketer has to decide on all the above parameters while designing a marketing plan.

Changing Profile of Rural Consumer

Rural consumers as studied are dependent on agriculture and were not very literate about the products and services available. This scenario is slowly changing due to increase in literacy and disposable income. Rural markets today are critical for every marketer–be it for a branded shampoo or a television. Earlier marketers thought of van campaigns, cinema commercials and a few wall paintings to entice rural folks under their folds. Many companies are foraying into the rural markets and educating them on newer products and services.

The rural youth today are playing a far more significant role in influencing the purchase decisions. They travel frequently out in the village and are the drivers of purchase decisions regarding radios, televisions, automobiles and other goods.

Penetration levels of consumer durables in the rural sector have risen dramatically in the last decade or so. Even the rural woman is coming out of the closet. She is exercising her choice in selecting categories–the choice of brands may still be with the males of the household.

Influencing the Rural Consumers

The biggest challenge in today's scenario is to develop a scalable model of influencing the rural consumers mind over a large period of time and keep it going. This needs to be achieved in a limited or a reasonable budget. That's where the marketers who really understand rural markets and advertising agencies can make a difference and develop a scalable media communication model.

The mass media has the drawback that the time gap between the point of exposure and the time of purchase is long hence it is difficult to use it in rural communication. The most important element in rural communication is that the marketer has to integrate three things:

1. Exposure of a message
2. Trial or demonstration
3. Final sale.

There is a minimal brand loyalty consumer in rural area. This is mainly due to a bigger problem of brand recognition. There are a lot of look alikes in the rural market. The challenge is to create communication that would help the rural consumer in recognising brands, logos, visuals, colours, etc. so that he or she actually buys the actual brand and not something else.

9.19   MARKETING ORGANISATIONS

Over the years, marketing has evolved from simple sales function to a complex group of activities, not always well integrated themselves or in relation to the firm's non-marketing activities. Some questions were raised between marketing managers at headquarters and salespeople in the field, about the future of brand management, about the need for a corporate vice president of marketing, about marketing relations to manufacturing, R&D, and finance, and so on. We will examine how marketing departments evolved in companies, how they are organised, and how do they interact with other departments.

The Evolution of the Marketing Department

The modern marketing is the product of a long evaluation. At least five stages can be distinguished, and companies are found in each stage.

Stage 1: Simple sales department

All companies start out with five simple functions, someone must raise and manage capital (finance), hire people (persons), produce the product or service (operations), sell it (sales), keep the books (accounting). The selling function is headed by a sales vice-president, who manages a sales force and also does some selling. When the company needs marketing research or advertising, the sales vice-president also handles those functions as is shown in Fig. 9.2.

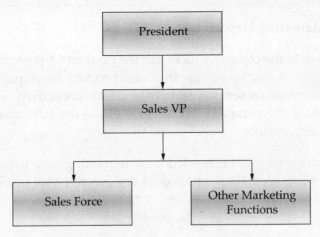

Fig. 9.2 Simple sales department.

Stage 2: Sales Department with Ancillary Marketing Functions

As the company expands to serve new types of customers or new geographical areas, it needs to strengthen certain marketing functions other than sales.

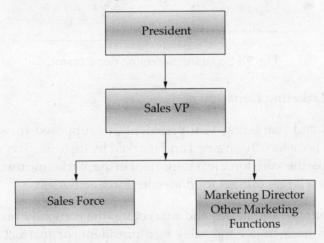

Fig. 9.3 Sales department with ancillary marketing functions.

For example, an East Coast firm that plans to open in the West will first have to conduct marketing research to learn about customer needs and market potential. If it opened business in the West, it will have to advertise its name and products in the area. The sales vice-president will need to hire specialists to handle these other marketing activities. The sales vice-president might decide to hire a marketing director to manage these functions as shown in Fig. 9.3.

Stage 3: Separate Marketing Department

The continued growth of the company increases the productive potential of investments in other marketing functions, marketing research, new product development, advertising and sales promotion, and customer service, relative to sales force activity, which is represented in Fig. 9.4. Eventually the company president will see the advantage of establishing a separate marketing department.

The marketing department will be headed by a marketing vice president, who reports, along with sales vice-president, to the president or executive vice president.

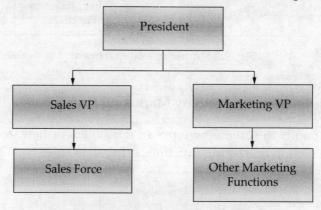

Fig. 9.4 Separate marketing department.

Stage 4: Modern Marketing Department

Although the sales and marketing vice president are supposed to work harmoniously, their relationship is occasionally strained and marked by distrust. The sales vice-president resents efforts to make the sales force less important in the marketing mix, and the marketing vice-presidents seek a larger budget for non-sales force activities.

If there is disharmony between sales and marketing, the company president might place marketing activities back under the sales vice president, or instruct the executive vice president to handle conflicts that arise, or place the marketing vice-president in charge of everything, including sales force.

Stage 5: Modern Marketing Company

A company can have a modern marketing department and yet not operate as a modern marketing company. The latter depends how the other company managers view the marketing function. Marketing is not only a department but also a through going company philosophy. Only then does a company turn into a modern marketing company. Both the stages are shown in Fig. 9.5.

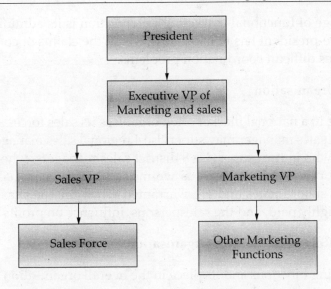

Fig. 9.5 Modern marketing department & company.

9.20 WAYS OF ORGANISING THE MARKETING DEPARTMENT

Modern marketing departments take on numerous forms. All marketing organisations must accommodate four dimensions of marketing activities that are:

1. Functional Organisation

The most common form of marketing organisation consists of functional marketing specialist reporting to a marketing vice-president, who coordinates their activities as shown in Fig. 9.6.

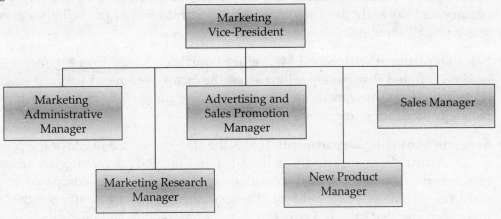

Fig. 9.6 Functional organisation.

632   Marketing Management

The main advantage of functional marketing organisation is its administrative simplicity. The marketing vice-president has to constantly weigh the claims of competing functional specialists and faces difficult coordination problems.

2. Geographical Organisation

A company selling in a national market often organises its sales forces along geographical lines. The national sales manager may supervise 4 regional sales managers, who supervise 6 zone managers, who in turn supervise 8 district sales managers, who supervise 10 sales people. The span of control increases as we move from the national sales manager to give more time to subordinates and are warranted when the sales task is complex. The salespersons are highly paid, and the salespersons, influence on profits is substantial.

3. The Changing Role of Marketing Organisation

Role of the marketing functions and its place in the overall organisation has been changing over time. From a situation where marketing was treated as a selling arm of the factor, it has come a full circle where marketing, 'dictates' what is to be produced. With the passage of time, not only has the organisation of the marketing activity undergone many changes but its growing importance has also influenced the entire concept of viewing a business. More and more firms are now adopting the 'marketing orientation' i.e. the customer and his needs from the nucleus of all the activities of the firm. All the activities and tasks are organised around the customer.

The firms with marketing orientation come into after passing through many distinct phases. These are explained below.

❖ **Simple Sales Department:** The three most basic functions needed for every business are those of production, finance and marketing. Towards the end of the nineteenth century and the early twentieth product was considered of prime importance and was given all attention.

❖ **Sales Department with Some Marketing Function:** As the firm expanded its operations it found that merely selling what the factory produced was not enough to sustain the growth momentum. A firm aspiring for growth and leadership must match its production to customer needs.

❖ **Separate Marketing Department:** This is the stage when the need for the complete range of marketing function is felt and a full-fledged marketing department is established. The sales activity continues to dominate but as compared to other activities, its importance is reduced. The root cause of all such conflicts is the lack of understanding that sales is a part and parcel of marketing and needs the support of other departments to be truly effective.

❖ **Integrated Marketing Department:** This is the stage where the sales and marketing are integrated and organised into a single department. The department is headed by a marketing director with the sales manager reporting to him. The other activities such as marketing research, promotion and advertising, marketing information, customer service and new product development are also organised in this department under the marketing director below matching represents the overall view.

4. Organisation of Corporate Marketing

As the company expands, it becomes necessary to decentralise at least some of the activities and establish separate and branch offices. Necessarily, some of the marketing operations are also handed over to the division and branch offices. What type of support should the corporate marketing office provide to the marketing organisations at the branch office to choose from:

1. **No corporate marketing support:** All marketing activities are handled at the branch or divisional level. The State Trading Corporations have organised themselves on these lines, to offices in various countries operate with lot of independence.

2. **Minimal corporate marketing support:** The major bulk of the marketing function is handled in the individual divisions. Only a few marketing activities are organised at the corporate level, these are:

   (a) scanning for new market new product opportunities and evaluating them.
   (b) providing marketing support on specific request from a division.

3. **Moderate corporate marketing:** Apart from the functions spelt out in the minimal corporate marketing organisation, here the corporate marketing provides centralised

service for advertising, marketing research, sales promotion, and recruitment and training of personnel.

4. **Strong corporate marketing:** All major marketing activities are performed to control by the corporate marketing organisation, and the divisions simply carry out the instructions given to them. This approach is followed by India Tourism Development Corporations for promoting its hotels in various towns.

Commonly Occurring Pitfalls While Structuring the Market Organisation

While structuring the marketing organisation, one has to carefully avoid certain imperfections and anomalies that commonly creep into the structure. These include the following:

❖ Haphazard grouping of the functions resulting in overlapping of responsibilities and duplication of efforts

❖ Vagueness regarding responsibilities assigned to different executive positions, resulting in lack of role clarity

❖ Dual control or absences of unity of command

❖ Unequal or distorted allocation of functions among personnel

❖ Improper delegation either the delegation is inadequate throughout the organisation or there is only delegation of responsibility, but no delegation of authority

❖ Overformalisation: The organisation structure has too much compartmentalisation resulting in tension, and adversely affecting efficiency.

Such pitfalls has avoided while structuring a marketing organisation. They can be avoided only by a correct understating of the role and functions of each department and each executive's position. The final aim of the organisation has to be kept in focus while grouping the functions and deciding the hierarchy.

KEYWORDS

Industrial Salesman: Salesman who deals with the industrial market, i.e. deals with organisations who buy goods and services to produce other products or services which are thereafter sold again to others.

Job Description: This describes the job in detail, indicating what the salesman will have to do including the difficulties that he may have to face in selling the company's product.

Man Specifications: *This provides the qualities which are required of the salesman who can best fill the job as described in the job description.*

Personal Selling: *Oral presentation by a salesman in a conversation with one or more prospective purchasers with a view to effect the sale.*

Pre-approach: *This is the stage just before the salesman actually approaches the customer, in which, he tries to find out as much as he can know about the prospect so that his job at the time of approach would become easy.*

Presentation and Demonstration: *This is the stage where the salesman tries to affect sales by actually showing the product and demonstrating it in use.*

Prospecting: *This is the stage where the salesman collects information of possible customers known as prospects.*

Sales Quota: *A sales goal or quota set for a product line, or representative or even a company division for defining and stimulating sales effort by such individual or unit.*

Sales Territory: *This is the geographical area which is assigned to a particular salesman for his operation with a view to sell or carry out his selling activities in that area.*

Sales Analysis: *Measuring and evaluating actual sales in relation to goals.*

Sales Variance Analysis: *A measure of the relative contribution of different factors to a gap in sales performance.*

Domestic Marketing: *Marketing that is aimed at a single market, the firm's domestic market, is referred to as domestic marketing.*

Export Marketing: *The field of export marketing covers all those marketing activities involved when a firm markets its products outside its main (domestic) base of operations and when products are physically shipped from one market or country to another.*

International Marketing: *When practising international marketing, a company goes beyond exporting and becomes much more directly involved in the local marketing environment within a given country or market.*

Global Marketing: *Over the years, academics and international companies alike have become aware that opportunities for economies of scale and enhanced competitiveness are greater if they can manage to integrate and create marketing strategies on a global scale.*

Direct Marketing: *The use of consumer direct (CD) channels to reach and deliver goods and services to customers without using marketing middleman.*

SUMMARY

Now let us recollect what we have covered. We have realised that we are on a very important aspect of managing the human resource. People are difficult to handle and yet, if you provide the correct environment they will be able to manage and motivate themselves. It is therefore essential to provide a proper system for motivation rather than have a detailed controlling procedure.

You have understood the importance of the selling effort and the functions of the sales manager. Basically, sales manager has to get the targeted sales, i.e., sales as decided by the marketing manager or the top level of the organisation. He has to do this through the sales force at his disposal. He must therefore select very carefully. Once you have recruited somebody, it is not necessary that he would have proper ability. Adequate training must therefore be provided so that he understands more about your company, your products and your policies as well as philosophy.

We have to appreciate how financial incentives can be provided to the salesman. Finally, some extent of controlling the sales personnel is essential.

The term global marketing has only been used for some ten years and began to assume widespread use in 1983 with the seminal article by Ted Levitt. Prior to that, international marketing or multinational marketing was the term used most often to describe international marketing activities. However, global marketing is not just a new term for an old phenomenon;

Marketing that is aimed at a single market, the firm's domestic market, is referred to as domestic marketing. In domestic marketing, the firm faces only one set of competitive, economic, and market issues and, essentially, must deal with only one set of customers, although the company may serve several segments in this one market.

When practising international marketing, a company goes beyond exporting and becomes much more directly involved in the local marketing environment within a given country or market. The international marketer is likely to have its own sales subsidiaries and will participate in and develop entire marketing strategies for foreign markets.

Thus, global marketing is the last stage in the development of the field of international marketing. While global marketers face their own unique challenges that stem from finding marketing strategies that fit many countries, the skills and concepts of the earlier stages are very important and continue to be needed.

Indian rural marketers have a vast size and demand base. Rural marketing involves the process of developing, pricing, promoting, distributing rural specific product and a service leading to exchange between rural and urban markets which satisfies consumer demand and also achieves organisational objectives.

The rural market in India is quite fascinating and challenging in spite of all the difficulties existing. The potential is enormous. Even though, these marketers have weaknesses they also have tremendous opportunities which should be availed by the marketers. The marketers have to come up with innovative ideas through which the villagers also get involved in getting business from their respective villages.

The rural consumers are classified into: the affluent group, the middle class and the poor based on their economic status.

The rural youth today are playing a far more significant role in influencing the purchase decisions. They may not be the end customers but often are the people who influence the purchase of high value products and they decide on which brands to choose.

The biggest challenge today is to develop a scalable model of influencing the rural consumers over a large period of time and keep it going.

An organisation design is a function of the objectives which it has to accomplish—the diversity and complexity of the tasks to be performed and the environment in which the organisation operates. Similarly, a marketing organisation design is a function of the diversity of products, markets and product/market combinations that it is involved with and the marketing objectives. Depending on the combination of these factors, and the relative importance of each of them in achieving the market objectives, you can design an organisation which is suited to your specific requirements.

The four commonly used organisation designs in marketing are based on functions, products, markets and combination of these three factors. Each type of organisation is useful under specific conditions and has its own advantages and disadvantages. While choosing amongst different types of organisation, you must evaluate each on the basis of its effectiveness in accomplishing the specified objectives, its amenability to managerial control and the cost involved.

ASSIGNMENT

Assignment 1

What do you understand by selling and managing?

Selling consists of

_____

_____

_____

Managing consists of

_____

_____

_____

Assignment 2

Examine the salesman recruitment and selection process in a large and a small company. Compare how the selection processes differ from each other. Examine the reason for each difference.

_____

_____

_____

_____

Assignment 3

Examine the various dimensions of salesman training in your organisation. Just in case your organisation does not have selling activities, you may visit some other organisation and study how they train there newly recruited salesman. Are there any differences in the training approaches that you have examined? Can you suggest some modifications?

_____

_____

_____

_____

Assignment 4

Collect the reporting formats used by a salesman working for a marketing organisation. Analyse them and record the various types of information provided by the salesman. Comment on the usefulness of such information.

_____

_____

_____

_____

Assignment 5

If the marketing organisation in your company is differentiated on the basis of function make out a detailed organisation chart, against each position, note the specific tasks/decisions which are performed. Make your own position in the organisation. You may attempt this activity in the context of another organisation, just in case your own organisation does not undertake marketing operations.

_____

_____

_____

_____

_____

Assignment 6

Evaluate of your own firm the role and importance of the marketing organisation vis-à-vis the production and finance organisation. At what stage of evaluation is the marketing organisation in the firm?

In case your firm/organisation is not involved in marketing activities, you may get in touch with some of your friends and interview them to complete this activity.

_____

_____

_____

Assignment 7

Make a detailed analysis of the existing marketing organisation in your firm or any other firm on the basis of the following questions:

1. What are the areas of strength of the marketing organisations?

2. What are the specific weaknesses in the organisation?

3. Can the weakness be overcome, wholly partially? If yes, describe in detail the steps necessary for making up the deficiencies.

If the marketing organisation is functionally organised, evaluate each function individually as an area of strength or weakness. In case of a product management organisation, evaluate each product group separately. Similarly, in case of market centred organisation, each individual market has to be evaluated. For a matrix organisation, besides evaluating each function, product matrix, you would also need to evaluate it from the viewpoint of coordination and overlaying of one basis on another such as function and markets.

Assignment 8
Tick the Most Appropriate Answer

1. Creative selling, which requires a salesperson to recognise the potential buyers need and then to provide the prospect with the necessary information, is performed by sales position called

   (a) Order taker
   (b) Missionary salesperson
   (c) Technical salesperson

2. Learning about the potential buyer, the buyers' purchasing process and needs, and anything else that could be helpful in the selling process is the activity of

   (a) The Approach
   (b) The Preapproach
   (c) Qualifying

3. The most effective short-term sales promotion incentive results from

   (a) Price-off
   (b) Coupons
   (c) Premiums
   (d) Contests

4. In establishing sales promotion objectives, marketers

   (a) Focus on consumers
   (b) Focus on trade
   (c) Concentrate on activities that will increase consumer demand
   (d) Align objectives with overall organisation objectives

REVIEW QUESTIONS

1. "Sales management is primarily a matter of selecting and training men, then evaluating their performance"?

2. Define sales force management and sales strategies.

3. What is sales management? What are the various functions of sales management?

4. Mention briefly the sources from which you can get salespersonnel as new recruits.

5. Mention briefly the factors that have to be considered in order to objectively determine the sales territories for allocation to salesman.

6. Define social responsibility towards marketing.

7. Discuss internal marketing and external marketing with illustrations.

8. How and why does global marketing differ from domestic marketing?

9. Explain the scope of global marketing.

10. Why is the task of the global marketer more complex and difficult than that of the domestic marketer?

11. Distinguish among ethnocentricity, polycentricity and egocentricity.

12. What is rural marketing and how do you define rural markets?

13. "Rural marketing cannot be neglected." Elaborate.

14. Who are the rural consumers? Explain their profiles.

15. Define word of mouth communication.

16. Explain about direct marketing and its characteristics.

REFERENCES

1. Philip Kotler, 2007, Marketing Management, 11/e, Pearson.
2. Rajan Saxena, 2006, Marketing Management, 2/e, TMH.
3. V.S. Ramaswamy & S. Nama Kumari, 2009, Marketing Management, 4/e, Macmillan.
4. Philip Kotler and Kelvin Lane, 2007, Marketing Management, 12/e, Pearson Education.
5. Tapan K. Panda, 2003, "Marketing Management", Macmillan.
6. Adrian Palmer, 2007, "Introduction to Marketing Theory and Practice", Oxford University press.
7. Erdener Kaynak, 1982, Marketing in the Third World, Praeger: New York.
8. Joeal R. Evans & Barry Berman, 2008, Marketing Management, Cengage.
9. Peter Chevton, 2009, Key Marketing Skills, Kogan Page.

APPENDIX

APPENDIX - A
CASE STUDIES

CASE STUDY - 1

PATAGONIA: SOCIAL GOOD AND PROFIT

Patagonia's bright blues, reds, and purples are often spotted on adventurers shooting white water rapids, climbing mountains, whizzing down ski slopes, or occasionally just lying around anywhere in the world. Patagonia is a study in contrasts. It succeeds even though it tries to discourage consumption; it sells millions of items even though its goods are higher-priced, and it focuses on profits even though it's a leader among socially responsible business firms. Where did such a firm come from, and in what sort of economic soil does it grow?

A young Californian, named Yvon Chouinard founded Patagonia in 1957 to sell his handmade mountain climbing equipment. Sales grew slowly until 1972, when Chouinard decided to include clothing-rugby shirts and canvas shorts-in his small outdoor equip-ment catalog. To move these products, he offered a money-back guarantee, which was feasible only because he sold high-quality, high-priced, and durable products. As sales grew, Chouinard began to introduce newer, more innovative fabrics and designs, making products such as foam back rain gear, pile and bunting outerwear, and polypropylene underwear. Patagonia's strategy has been to compete on innovation rather than on cost. The company is known not for low prices, but for developing new materials and designs.

The 1980s provided the perfect growth environment for Patagonia. Consumers wanted quality. They had discovered adventure travel. Style, individualism, and image were "in". Magazine articles celebrated Chouinard's idea of work-spending six to eight months a year hiking, fishing, climbing, and surfing to "test" his new designs and develop new product ideas. As a "fun hog", he was devoted to any non-motorised, outdoor activity. And as "Patagonia's outside man", he was able to gauge the durability, comfort, and usefulness of the outdoor gear he sold.

Concern for the environment sets Patagonia apart from other cataloguers and clothing manufacturers. For example, as early as 1972, Chouinard abandoned production of traditional mountain climbing pitons in favour of chocks that could be inserted into cracks in a rock face, leaving no holes or other damage. Other climbers willingly followed Chouinard's lead by switching to the more environmentally responsible chocks. To emphasise its continuing commitment, Patagonia adopted a mission statement that says all life on earth is facing a critical time and we must all make decisions in the context of this environmental crisis.

How can a firm like Patagonia make decisions with positive environmental effects? Patagonia practices what it preaches by tracing the environmental impact of its products and then identifying changes it can make to reduce this impact. In 1991, Patagonia began a comprehensive Environmental Review Process to examine all the methods and materials used to produce the company's clothing. The study showed there were parts of the clothing process the company had the power to change and other parts it could not change.Take nylon and polyester. Patagonia management realised it couldn't have much impact on the oil extraction and refinement processes used in manufacturing these materials. But it could develop recycling options. With the help of two vendors, Patagonia introduced PCR (post consumer recycled) Synchilla fleece-made from recycled soft drink bottles. The fleece is warm and cozy, and it dries quickly, looks great, and consumes about 25 bottles per jacket.

With cotton, Patagonia realised that it could have a significant impact on production of the raw material. How? By shifting to organic cotton. Today's standard method of producing cotton uses 811 million pounds of pesticides and an additional 4 pounds of chemicals per acre. Some of this spill into rivers, killing fish, and some is inhaled by farmers or anyone else nearby. Pesticide use is growing: it has increased 150 percent since 1962. After reviewing these facts, Patagonia switched to organic cotton in 1996. Although initially there were problems with pilling and shredding of cuffs and ribbing, Patagonia stuck with its decision until it solved the problems.

Although the introduction of PCR Synchilla and organic cotton products has been successful, other moves by Patagonia have not worked as well. In the late 1980s, Patagonia introduced buttons made from resins produced by the tagua nut, which grows in Brazilian rainforests. Unfortunately, these nuts crack open and germinate during periods of intense rain and heat, actions that are desirable in the rain forest but not in your washer and dryer. When the buttons cracked and customers returned garments by the thousands, Patagonia learned a major lesson. Do your homework-follow the materials throughout their life cycles and subject them to rigorous tests. Otherwise, money-back and replacement guarantees will leave you sewing on tens of thousands of replacement buttons.

What has the introduction of PCR Synchilla and organic cotton meant to consumers? Mostly higher prices: both materials cost more. Prices for these products are about 25 percent higher than prices for competing products, and the garments are not visibly different or better. So the next step in the Patagonia strategy is to communicate to consumers why they should buy these more expensive goods, Patagonia pushes this story aggressively.

In the spring of 1991, the Patagonia catalogue began with "Everything we make pollutes"- no shying away from the issues by this company! In a long essay, Patagonia pointed out that all clothing production has a negative impact on the environment. With each additional catalogue, it has announced and explained actions by the company aimed at reducing that environmental impact. In addition to using PCR Synchilla and organic cotton, Patagonia has taken many other steps. To encourage reduced clothing consumption, the company has purged 30 percent of its clothing lines and reduced the number of styles it offers (for example, it sells only two styles of ski pants). It has also eliminated the use of mailing lists, cut back on advertising, reduced the size of its catalogue, and limited the number of catalogues produced each year. The company's clothing is multifunctional-such as jackets that can be used for skiing, hiking, and kayaking, and that have no extra buttons, zippers, or frills. It uses less harsh dyes and no formaldehyde. All these actions affect consumers directly.

Less apparent to consumers is Patagonia's environmental grant program. Each year since 1985, the company has given away 10 percent of its pretax profits-usually in small amounts of from $1000 to $3000-to less-well-known environmental groups. Today, it donates 1 percent of sales or 10 percent of pretax profit, whichever is greater. To date, the company has given away more than $8 million, along with free goods that organisations can sell or auction off to raise funds.

Other environmentally responsible actions include major recycling programs with suppliers and the construction of a 170,000 square foot distribution centre in Reno, Nevada that uses innovative heating and cooling technology. To cope with Reno's hot summers and cold winters, the building is cooled by a nighttime system which admits cool air through roof vents and a radiant-heating system that uses 30 percent less energy than conventional heating. Solar-tracking skylights increase the level of natural light. Occupancy sensors dim lights when people leave an area and increase brightness as daylight fades. The results have been twofold. First, energy consumption and costs are down. Second, improved materials handling and picking equipment in this building has produced nearly 100 percent shipment accuracy and 24 hour turnaround on mail orders. The lower energy costs and fewer returns help Patagonia absorb some of the additional cost of the organic cotton it uses.

Even with all these efforts, Patagonia admits that it still uses some materials that are environmentally destructive, such as polyester buttons and zippers and synthetic dyes.

Why? Because the alternative products cannot meet Patagonia's high quality standards. Although the company has gone further toward environmental sustainability than most other firms, it willingly admits it still has a long way to go.

In thinking about the future, Patagonia's management believes that sustainable business necessitates changes in thinking by two groups. First, shareholders must expand their definition of value to include environmental considerations. Patagonia's cotton products are an example. They had to be more than good looking, long lasting, and well performing-they also had to contribute to the quality of life. Shareholders will have to look at more than the bottom line. They will have to recognise that true value includes a long-term plan for environmental quality and sustainability. Second, the public's perception of value will have to change. Consumers will have to demand that companies pay closer attention to the effects of their operations on the world around us. This requires consumer education and activism.

Consumers are frequently unaware of the contents of their garments-what the buttons, zippers, and pull tabs are made of and what dyes and coatings are used on the fabrics. Without such information, the best intentioned consumers can do little about the environmental impact of the garments they buy. To remedy this, Patagonia engages consumers in a continuing dialogue. Besides information placed on its garment tags, Patagonia uses its Web site (www.patagonia.com) and encourages its managers to give speeches informing consumers.

Patagonia does not take its eye off the profit picture completely. In an Inc. magazine article, author Jim Collins interviewed Yvon Chouinard and found that Chouinard spent as much time talking about the importance and mechanics of profit as about the need for social change. Notes a previous Patagonia CEO, "The one thing I'm clear about is that Chouinard demands 10 percent pretax profit". Collins concludes, "Patagonia might be a social vehicle, but it runs on an economic engine. It's not a question of social good or business profit, but social good and business profit."

Questions for Discussion

1. How does Patagonia exemplify the marketing concept? The societal marketing concept?

2. What consumer needs and wants does Patagonia attempt to satisfy? How does it create customer satisfaction?

3. How does Patagonia establish relationships with consumers?

4. How does Patagonia manage demand?

5. How does Patagonia attempt to meet the challenges of the twenty-first century?

Sources

[1] *Can Slower Growth Save the World?*, Business and Society Review, Spring 1993, pp. 10-20.

[2] Staci Bonner, *Patagonia: A Green Endeavor*, Apparel Industry Magazine, February 1997, pp. 46-8.

[3] Jim Collins, *The Foundation for Doing Good*, INC., December 1997, pp. 41-2.

[4] Fleming Meeks, *The Man is the Message*, Forbes, April 17, 1989, pp. 148-152.

[5] Gary Forger, *New Warehouse Doubles Productivity for Patagonia*, Modern Material Handling, June 1997, pp. 34-6.

[6] Edward O. Welles, *Lost in Patagonia*, INC., August 1992, pp. 44-57.

[7] Jil Zilligen, *Ecological Sustainability*, speech given at the Academy of Management Conference, August, 1996, Cincinnati, Ohio.

[8] Jacquelyn Ottman, *Proven Environmental Commitment helps Create Committed Customers*, Marketing News, February 2, 1998, pp. 5-6.

NIKE: RUNNING OVER THE COMPETITION

Nobody takes the admonition "Just do it" more seriously than Nike, the company for whom the slogan was written. Whether it's entering a new sport, moving into a new geographic market, or developing a new product, Nike approaches its mission with the dedication and single-mindedness of an athlete training for competition. And whatever the task, the goal is always the same: To turn in a peak performance, one that leaves no doubt as to who the best is. That's because at Nike, winning isn't merely a corporate philosophy-it's the company's business.

"This brand is all about building products for athletes, high-performance products, very authentic products, innovative products, bringing new technology to athletes so they can perform better at a higher level in their sport," says Bill Zeitz, global director of advertising development at Nike.

Liz Dolan, the company's marketing director, puts it in even more basic terms. "We have a really incredibly simple mission, which is, 'serve the athlete'. If you're in product development that means you have to make sure that the products really work, that they're really great for whatever sport you are assigned to. If you're in the communications area, it means that you have to communicate with an authenticity about the sports experience, what athletes know to be true of what it feels like to win a basketball game, or run a marathon, or whatever."

This near-obsession with authentic athletic performance comes naturally to the Beaverton, Oregon, company started in the 1960s by Phil Knight, a sports enthusiast and runner who believed the needs of serious athletes were being neglected by Adidas and Puma, the German companies that dominated the athletic shoe industry. With the help of Bill Bowerman, his former track coach at the University of Oregon, Knight set out to develop a shoe that would make a difference in a runner's performance.

The rest, as they say, is history. Nike has become a dominant player in sports apparel. With track, basketball, tennis, and other traditional sports in the "win" column, Nike recently has turned its attention to building its franchise in soccer, cricket, rugby, hockey, and in-line skating, among others. After all, Dolan explains, being a global sports brand requires an intensely local focus.

Being a global brand is extremely important to Nike because its home market, the United States, is nearing saturation. According to John Horan of the newsletter *Sporting Goods Intelligence*, sporting-goods chains have over expanded and profit margins are threatened.

When Nike announced that its second quarter earnings in 1997 would not live up to Wall Street's expectations, its stock dropped 13 percent. With these spurs at home, Nike has to look overseas there it has only 27 percent of sales compared to 43 percent in the U.S. to generate additional revenues.

But going overseas is not a sure win for Nike. "Understanding what sports the people in [a] country play, and then being great at those sports... that's always the challenge. In the U.K., for instance, we are a really good basketball brand, but they don't play that there. And we are a really good tennis brand, but they kept telling us. 'Other than the two weeks during Wimbledon, nobody in the U.K. really cares about tennis.' So in the U.K. soccer is what they play. Rugby is what they play. So we had to really concentrate on being great at two sports that were not really something that came from our American tradition at all. That took years of product development and talking to consumers about, 'What does this sport really mean to you when you play it, and what does it really mean to you when you watch it?' The brand attributes for Nike in the U.K. are the same. We really want to be the authentic sports brand but the sports that are the building blocks for that are very different in the U.K. than they would be in the United States or than they would be in Japan."

Outside the United States soccer is the main sport, and Nike has pursued the soccer player and fan with a vengeance. In the United States, Nike has signed a multiyear contract with major league soccer that calls for it to spend $3.75 million a year to sponsor 5 of the league's 10 teams. In addition, the contract contains a clause that allows Nike to retain sponsorship of half of the League's teams as it expands. Overseas, Nike spent $20 million in a sealed bid process to sponsor the Italian national team. During last year's European championships, it bought up all the billboards around stadiums where matches were held, effectively undermining the event's official sponsor, Umbro. In the spring of 1997, it sponsored a worldwide soccer tour that featured top teams. It has also spent millions on global advertising campaigns and signed leading national soccer stars such as Eric Cantona (captain of the national champion Manchester United soccer team in the U.K.) to highly lucrative contracts.

But nothing matches Nike's sponsorship agreement with the Confederacao Brasil de Futebol, Brazil's soccer federation, which cost the company a breath-taking $200 million. Why Brazil? It won the 1994 World Cup soccer match. The contract is a 10-year deal that includes appearances in Nike-produced exhibition matches and community events. Nike will supply Brazil's national teams with sports kits. In return, the teams will participate in five annual friendly soccer games that Nike is arranging, and to which Nike retains the television rights. Nike will also have access to training clinics in Brazil and to the infrastructure of the game.

Nike has applied the same technical skill and drive to soccer shoes that it applied to the basketball shoes. For example, when Nike couldn't find equipment for testing the best stud configurations and traction in cleated soccer shoes, it decided to build its own. The goal is to create the world's best soccer shoe, but that won't be easy. First, the competition isn't yet ready to roll over and play dead. Adidas retains sponsorship of many top teams and players, including the national teams of Germany, Spain, and France. It also sponsors World Cup 1998, with the rights to sell official soccer balls and sports apparel. Further, Adidas has invaded Nike's home turf, sponsoring three U.S. teams and featuring players from those teams in its U.S. advertising."We don't think that anybody can get near to us on the product side," says Peter Csandai, an Adidas spokesman. Reebok, Nike's main competitor in the U.S., has also signed contracts with at least 30 professional soccer clubs throughout the globe.

And there's competition at home from firms such as Vans, a small California company that aims directly at the teenage market by targeting the California adolescent—an Internet-surfing latchkey kid. As the number of teenagers in the United States grows from 25 million in 1997 to over 31 million in 2010, this move could prove shrewd. These kids are not into team sports; instead they are attracted by individual sports such as skateboarding, snowboarding, surfing, and mountain biking. Within two years of entering the market for snowboard boots in 1995, for example, Vans has become the third largest company in the business. So, it's in a position to make a move on Nike.

Competition is not Nike's only problem; some of its actions haven't left fans cheering either. Signing bad boy Eric Cantona generated a lot of criticism and infuriated the soccer establishment in the U.K. In 1996, Nike flew eight of soccer's hottest players to Tunisia to film an advertisement in which the athletes competed against the devil. Not surprisingly, this ad drew angry letters from many offended fans. Even the Brazil deal has been heavily criticised. As part of that deal, Nike had to pay Umbro an undisclosed amount to cover the remaining two years of its contract with the Brazilian federation. "Nike is going in and almost encouraging teams to break contracts," says James R. Gorman, president of Puma North America. Finally, not all soccer athletes are convinced Nike is better. Many pro players continue to get their equipment from companies such as Umbro, Puma, and especially Adidas, which has been part of the sport for decades, not just the last few years like Nike.

Still, with over $8 billion in sales in 1997, Nike remains the biggest player in the game. Adidas is a distant second with $3 billion. With its free spending, Nike appears to have changed the economics of the game. Nike intends to be the number one supplier of soccer gear by World Cup 2002, but so far its efforts have produced only $200 million in annual sales. It has a long way to go before it scores a match-winning goal in the global soccer market.

Questions for Discussion

1. What is Nike's mission and how does the company accomplish it?

2. Using either the Boston Consulting Group or GE Matrix approach, analyse Nike's business portfolio. How would you characterize its basketball, running, and soccer businesses? What is Nike's growth strategy?

3. What are Nike's markets and how is Nike positioned in these markets? How does it reach these markets?

4. What is Nike's proposed positioning in the global soccer market? Describe the company's global soccer marketing mix?

5. What marketing recommendations would you make to help Nike achieve its quest for global soccer dominance? How serious is the threat of a firm like Vans? Is Nike likely to be successful in global soccer?

Sources

[1] Linda Himelstein, *The Swoosh Heard Round the World*, Business Week, May 12, 1997, pp. 76-80.

[2] *In the Vanguard: Trainers, Sneakers, and Shoes*, The Economist, June 7, 1997, pp. 62.

[3] Geoff Dyer, *Nike Puts Its Hands on Ultimate Trophy*, The Financial Times, December 14, 1996, p. 9.

[4] Patrick Harverson, *Putting Their Shirts on Soccer Deals*, The Financial Times, November 1, 1997, p. 15.

LEVIS: AIMING AT THE ECHO BOOMERS

In 1986, Levi Strauss & Company found that the best way to stay true blue to its customers was to change its colors. Riding high on the results of a recent "back to basis" campaign with its flagship 501 brand, Levi's was enjoying reinvigorated jeans sales. But the good news was followed by bad. Research showed that baby boomers, the core of the company's customer franchise, were buying only one or two pairs of jeans annually, compared to the four to five pairs purchased each year by 15 to 24-year-olds.

Born between 1946 and 1964, the baby boomers had adopted jeans as a symbol of their break with the tastes and traditions of their parents. They had, in the words of Steve Goldstein, vice president of marketing and research for Levi's, helped turn the company into an "international global colossus" in the apparel industry. Now, however, the baby boomers were looking for something different. They still wanted clothing that was comfortable and made from natural fabrics, but fashion had become more important. Many worked in environments with relaxed dress codes, so they sought clothing that combined style and versatility—something appropriate for both professional and leisure activities.

"We set ourselves out to answer the big question," Goldstein says. "How could we keep the baby boomer generation in Levi's brands when they weren't wearing so many pairs of Levi's jeans? And the answer was Dockers, something between the jean that they loved and the dress pants that their parents expected them to wear when they got their first job."

Dockers created a product category—new casuals. Blue denim was out; cotton khaki (in brown, green, black, and navy, but mostly traditional tan) was in. Positioned as more formal than jeans yet more casual than dress slacks, Docker's satisfied an unfulfilled need. They were the right pants for a variety of occasions, an unpretentious alternative to dressy, tailored slacks.

The challenge in marketing dockers was to leverage the Levi's name and heritage while establishing the independence of the new brand, and to do so without detracting from Levi's core jeans focus. According to Goldstein, the company briefly considered not using the Levi's name at all, but realised that this would be "sort of like trying to put a space shuttle up without any launch rockets". So the original theme for Dockers was "Levi's 100 percent cotton Dockers. If you're not wearing Dockers, you're just wearing pants."

Response from retailers and from the target market of 25- to 49-year-olds was everything Levi's hoped for. All the top menswear accounts across the country placed the new product in their stores, and in only five years, Dockers became a $1 billion brand. Brand awareness among men 25 and older was 98 percent, and 70 percent of target consumers had at least one pair of Dockers in their closets.

With the new brand sailing along smoothly, Levi Strauss & Company began to dissociate Dockers from the company brand name. In 1993, the Levi's name and the words "since 1850" were removed from the Dockers logo. Robert Hanson, vice president of marketing and research for Dockers, claims the change was needed to "allow the Levi's brand to be focused on the core teen target because it's the quintessential icon of youth culture".

Still following the baby boomer market, Levi's in 1996 brought out Slates, an extensive line of wool, polyester microfiber, and fine-gauge cotton dress pants. "We thought there was room in a man's closet for a third brand," says Jann Westfall, president of the Slates division. "That's why Slates was created to [fill the gap] between khakis and suits." To Levi Strauss & Company, it seemed a natural evolution—the guy who wore Levi's in the '70s and Dockers in the '80s would be ready for Slates in the '90s. Slates would be the high end of casual, neatly filling the "lunch with client/salary review with boss" role in the Docker man's wardrobe.

Consumer research told Levi's that consumers found shopping for dress pants a chore: slacks departments were dreary; finding the right size was difficult; and getting alterations was frustrating. Consumers wanted cash and carry, off-the-rack dress pants. So Levi's devised a carefully crafted strategy to overcome the typical male distaste for dress pants shopping. Slates were sold in scientifically tested selling areas consisting of mahogany-toned circular store displays that allowed easy access to the various styles and sizes. Levi's also responded with off-the-rack pants that require little altering. Whereas most dress pants come only in even waist sizes, forcing alterations for off-size men, Slates also come in odd sizes. All Slates are hemmed and cuffed and have double pleats in the front. For customers with larger waist sizes, the pleats are more kindly placed.

Levi's backed Slates with $20 million in advertising, beginning with television ads at the opening of the National Football League season. To charm potential customers, Levi's agency designed ads such as one showing a guy springing up from lunch with his partner to tango with his waitress. "The ads are stylish but they are not over [the market's] heads," said Nancy Friedman, vice-president of research and development. "The trick is to rein it back in so it isn't so chi-chi that people can't relate to it." A year later, everyone agreed that Slates was a dynamite brand. Levi's had turned on the Dockers customer to dress slacks just when "corporate casual" started to "dress up". Noted one industry insider, "Slates and other labels have pushed the envelope. This has created a tremendous consumer awareness for slacks in general." Some retailers found that their tailored pants business was up 15 to 20 percent.

However, just like the good news about Levi's "back to basics" move a decade earlier, the good news about Slates has been accompanied by bad news—plummeting market share in the core jeans market. Although Levi Strauss had 30.9 percent of the U.S. blue jeans business in 1990, it had only 18.7 percent seven years later. Worse yet, Levi's sales to teens, the core blue jeans buyers, had dropped from 33 percent in 1993 to 26 percent in 1997. Once the darling of the 15- to 24-year-old buyer, Levi's now faces indifference in this segment and an attitude that Levi's are "your dad's pants". The bottom-line message: Levi's are uncool. Male teenagers increasingly prefer brands like Tommy Hilfiger and Old Navy. Even the young women who have been more inclined buy Levi's are moving toward brands such as Calvin Klein, Gap, and Guess. Levi's is being squeezed by upscale brands like Tommy Hilfiger and Ralph Lauren on one end and private label or store brands on the other.

It's a classic marketing goof: Levi's lost sight of the market that launched it to success. By concentrating on Dockers, and more recently on Slates, executives were distracted from the threat to the core jeans business. "They missed all the kids and those are your future buyers," says Bob Levi, owner of Dave's Army & Navy Store in New York. "It's very important that you attract this age group," says Gordon Hart, vice-president of the Lee brand at VF Corp. "By the time they're 24, they've adopted brands that they will use for the rest of their lives." Moreover, the younger segment sets fashion trends that influence older shoppers. The mistake has been costly: falling sales and market share forced Levi's to lay off 1,000 salaried workers in February 1997, and to shutter 11 plants and lay off one-third of its North American workforce in November of that year.

What is Levi's doing to fix the problem? It's pumping up the Silver Tab brand, an eight-year-old jeans line considered more stylish among young consumers. Silver Tab has a baggier fit and uses non-denim fabrics. The median age of a Silver Tab buyer is 18, compared to 25 for Levi's other products. Levi's plans to expand the line to include more tops, more trendy styles, and new khaki pants. The company also plans to boost Silver Tab promotional spending fivefold for events such as concerts in New York and San Francisco, for up-and-coming bands playing music known as Electronica, and for outfitting characters on hot television shows such as Friends and Beverly Hills 90210.

Levi's is also taking action on the retail front. In 1998, Levi's will introduce jazzier, more colourful packaging aimed at giving its products a more exciting, youthful look. It has dropped plans to open 100 new stores in malls across the country in favour of Nike Town-type stores, which will serve as the company's flagship outlets in large cities.

Holding nothing sacred in its quest to reposition itself in younger segments, Levi's is also searching for a new ad agency to replace Foote, Cone and Belding, which has been the Levi's agency for more than sixty years. And the company is recruiting more outside managers. "[Levi Strauss & Company]" has always been insular, paternalistic, and, quite frankly, a little smug" says Isaac Lagnado, president of Tactical Retail Solutions. All that appears to be changing.

Will the new strategy work? Many industry insiders think that Levi's has the money and market clout to pull it off. But didn't we just read that some of those trendy new styles for Silver Tab include khakis? Doesn't that sound like Dockers? And speaking of Dockers, Levi's may have a problem making that brand relevant to the next generation of young men. Baby boomers who are ageing out of the Dockers' target market have refused to leave the brand behind. Consequently, the Dockers brand that has been positioned for consumers just moving out of their core jeans-wearing years may now be thought of as "my dad's brand" by the next generation of young men moving into this segment. Thus, the "dad's brand" problem that hit Levi's in the blue jeans segment now threatens the Dockers market. Even as Levi's is working to get its core jeans business back on track, it will have to contend with a similar problem with Dockers.

Questions for Discussion

1. What actors and forces in Levi Strauss & Company's microenvironment and macro environment have affected its marketing position?

2. Why was Levi's so successful in designing products for the baby boomers?

3. How and how well has Levi's responded to changes in its marketing environment?

4. Evaluate Levi's strategy for the Silver Tab brand. Is the strategy likely to succeed? Does it meet the concerns of younger buyers? How does Silver Tab compare with the competition?

5. What marketing recommendations would you make to Levi's management?

Sources

[1] Elaine Underwood, *Levi's New Dress Code*, Brandweek, August 19, 1996, p. 22.

[2] *Denim Dish: Dream Jeans for Teens*, Womens' Wear Daily, December 11, 1997, p. 12.

[3] Becky Ebenkamp, *Slates Speaks Directly to Men*, Adweek, September 8, 1997, p. 5.

[4] Stan Gellers, *Tailored Slacks Follow the Mainfloor Leader: Slates Boom Trickles-Up to Better Makers in Casual Fabrics and Golfwear*, Daily News Record, September 24, 1997, p. 3.

[5] Linda Himelstein, *Levi's Is Hiking Up Its Pants*, Business Week, December 1, 1997, pp. 70, 75.

CASE STUDY - 4

MERCEDES BENZ: LOOKING FOR ANSWERS

You probably would agree with Janis Joplin when she sings, "Oh Lord, won't you buy me a Mercedes Benz". Certainly Mercedes hopes so. With a sales goal of over 125,000 cars in the United States by 2000, the luxury car maker has to motivate a lot of customers to buy a Mercedes without waiting for divine intervention. Mercedes' sales peaked in the United States in 1986 at 99,314 cars and slid to 61,899 in 1993. Many factors such as the economy, competition from other luxury cars (introduction of the Lexus and Infiniti), and changes in consumer attitudes have contributed to the loss of sales. To determine why sales were down, Mercedes Benz conducted attitudinal research. It used a series of focus groups and dealer showroom interviews to gather consumer feedback. The good news from the research was that the well-known Mercedes tagline–"Engineered like no other car in the world"–worked for consumers. Customers applauded Mercedes for its quality, engineering, and integrity. The bad news was that they didn't like Mercedes' aloofness, its distance from buyers.

With this research in hand, Mercedes set out to reposition its cars, to convince customers that Mercedes means fun as well as quality. The target market is baby boomers-individuals in their mid to late thirties, forties, and early fifties. This is the single largest age group in the market and people in this age range have achieved the financial success necessary to buy a Mercedes. Reaching baby boomers is not easy, however. "There's a general shift going on in the luxury segment," says Mike Jackson, executive vice president of marketing. "Baby Boomers, by definition, are very young-minded. To keep your relevancy you must connect with them on an emotional level." The key phrase here is "emotional level". The purchase of a Mercedes is not driven by rational motives; it's driven by emotion–strong feelings about the car. People must *want* to buy a Mercedes.

Mercedes upped the emotional level when it launched its E-class car using the concept of fun. Having fun produces strong positive emotions. To inject its promotional campaign with fun, the company used a tongue-in-cheek TV spot that shows a driver passing supermodel Paulina, space aliens, and Ed McMahon with a $10 million check without stopping. The car was so much fun to drive, they didn't need to stop. To appeal to older baby boomers, Mercedes used the song by Janis Joplin, who symbolises the hippie lifestyle associated by baby boomers with their youth. For these consumers, Janis Joplin has always evoked strong emotions.

Other promotions by Mercedes include the introduction of a Website, direct mail to 300,000 current and prospective Mercedes owners, and airplay in theatres for one of its new

TV spots. The company will sponsor an Elton John concert in New York to showcase the E-class among younger consumers and will pay $40 million to sponsor the tennis ATP Tour, in which the Mercedes' logo will be emblazoned on the tennis net itself during telecasts. In December 1995, the company teamed with publisher Hachette Filipacchi to produce *Mercedes Momentum*, a magazine that is distributed to 500,000 dealers and Hachette subscribers. This lifestyle publication carries stories on everything from cigars and wine to ultramarathoners and New England fishermen. Of course, it also provides details on Mercedes models amid the feature articles. "Rather than doing a car book, we decided to focus on lifestyle," says Al Weiss, director of national marketing communications. By featuring Mercedes as part of the lifestyle of baby boomers–actual or desired–the magazine also increases the emotional attachment to Mercedes.

Although all these efforts seem intuitively to be on target, it's the job of Bob Baxter, director of marketing research, to assess how successful each is. Baxter's staff regularly collects information about the economy, the auto industry, and Mercedes in particular. In addition, a staff of trained telephone interviewers can quickly conduct nationwide surveys of customers, dealers, and sales personnel. Other interviewers can conduct in-showroom and focus group interviews. Baxter's staff also conducts written surveys, and his crews of statistical experts analyse the data produced. It is important to gather market research information from a number of sources to help establish its validity. If six separate pieces of research produce the same result, then it must be valid, and if the same research done over and over produces the same result, it must be reliable.

Besides being valid and reliable, marketing research should also be representative. This means that the right sample should be selected. For example, the fun emphasis of advertising for the E-class car is aimed at the under-40 market, whereas the Janis Joplin ads and the Elton John concert are aimed at an older audience. The *Mercedes Momentum* targets both groups. Research must distinguish among the opinions and attitudes of these different segments. Good research requires a thorough understanding of marketing program goals. Research usually aims to answer a specific question. For example, the goal of E-class advertising is to change the way target consumers think about Mercedes. Thus, E-class research seeks to answer questions about changing consumer image perceptions. One way to find out if the advertising worked is to interview viewers of the ads. Although Baxter could have his staff conduct focus groups to gauge the impact of the ads, this technique would not be particularly appropriate. Focus groups are usually exploratory in nature, and evaluation of an ad campaign is primary research which falls in the problem-solving, decision-making arena.

For each marketing research effort, Baxter and his staff have to make sure that they are researching the right question, with the right group of people, using the right technique. Given all the recent Mercedes promotional efforts, they have lots of issues to research. The research can be costly, but to Baxter's way of thinking, the returns are worth every penny.

Questions for Discussion

Develop a marketing research plan for evaluating each of the following:

1. Consumer reaction to the Janis Joplin advertisement.

2. Consumer reaction to the "fun" ad for the E-class auto launch.

3. Success of the Mercedes Website.

4. Audience response to the Elton John concert in New York.

5. Consumer attitudes toward sponsorship of professional tennis.

6. Audience response to Mercedes Momentum.

In each case, list appropriate research questions that Mercedes might attempt to answer. Specify the type of research you would use (exploratory, problem solving, secondary or primary) and describe how the research should be conducted. Finally, indicate the characteristics of who should be researched.

Sources

[1] Steve Gelsi, *Benz Revs Up New Pitch*, Brandweek, March 18, 1997, pp. 20-22.

[2] Joshua Levine, *Give Me One of Those*, Forbes, June 3, 1996, p. 134.

[3] The Mercedes Benz web site at www.mercedes.com.

ROLLERBLADE: ON TOP OF THE MARKET

What's the hottest sports/leisure activity in the United States? Basketball? Soccer? Running? Dancing? None of these: It's *in-line skating*. Since 1995, when in-line skating jumped from third to first place, more Americans have put on their skates and taken to the asphalt than have joined any other participation sport. And as all those Americans hit the asphalt, companies such as Rollerblade have produced a flood of new in-line skate models and types. Knowing that idols such as Madonna and J.F.K., Jr., like to in-line skate enhances the popularity of the sport even more.

The number of new models and skates attests to the wide ranging motivations Americans have for skating. For some, it's just fun–afternoon exercise in the park and a chance to get some fresh air and sunshine. For others, in-line skating is serious exercise ideal for maintaining fitness. Still others race or compete on skates or participate in sports associated with in-line skates, such as hockey.

To keep up with the market, manufacturers of in-line skates carefully study market statistics, looking for changes. For example, an examination of data on the Rollerblade Website (www.rollerblade.com) indicates rapid growth in the total number of in-line skating participants, even if growth is slowing a bit. Between 1994 and 1995, in-line skating participation grew 20 percent (compared to growth rates higher than 30 percent in the preceding five years.) Growth reached 22 percent between 1995 and 1996.

What do changes in the popularity of in-line skating mean for a company like Rollerblade? Rollerblade pioneered in-line skating in the United States when Brennan and Scott Olson decided to sell in-line skates to hockey players during the off-season in the early 1980s. Throughout most of the 1980s, Rollerblade had market shares of around 80 to 100 percent. But as in-line skates sales grew, so did the competition. Firms such as K2 entered the market and the competitive pressures forced all firms to create distinctive differences between their brands. With its early jump on the competition and aggressive marketing, Rollerblade has maintained a market share greater than 40 percent, but doing so requires paying close attention to the market. Recent declines in the growth rate call for examining market data even more closely.

To understand the market, you must first answer the question, "Who skates?" Thirty-five percent of all skaters are children under 12, and 29 percent are teens. But the greatest growth in number of skates in 1996 versus 1995 occurred among adults aged 35 to 54 years (a 61 percent increase). When you couple that with the fact that baby boomers–yes, those same 35- to 54-year-olds–are the largest age group in the United States, it doesn't take a rocket scientist to figure out where the potential market growth is. Nor does it take much science to realise that the kids, teens, and adults skate for different reasons.

Kids and teens may be in the sport for fun, transport, or sports. Adults are more likely to skate for fitness. Ageing baby boomers are attracted to in-line skating because a 30-minute workout on skates burns the same number of calories as a 30-minute run. But it has less impact shock on joints, stronger cardiovascular benefit than stair-stepping machines, and higher activity for muscles of the hips, thighs, and shins than running or cycling. Furthermore, because they find in-line skating to be more fun, participants tend to skate longer than they run or cycle.

Besides understanding customer motivations for skating, Rollerblade needs other information, such as where skaters live, how frequently they skate, their skill levels, and other facts. An examination of statistics on the Rollerblade Website indicates that big states like California, Texas, and New York have the largest *numbers* of skaters; smaller states such as Utah, New Mexico, and North and South Dakota have a greater *percentage* of skaters. Thus, the big states are attractive markets because of their size, but in smaller states, in-line skating is actually more popular and sales may be easier to obtain.

Children are the most frequent skaters–they skate 11 times per month. Teens skate about 10 times a month and adults only seven times. Overall, the average skater skates about 30 days per year. What does information about usage rates mean to Rollerblade? Heavier usage might be associated with more frequent skate purchases to replace worn out equipment or to trade up to skates with different features such, as faster wheels, better brakes, better fit, and greater comfort. For these skaters, Rollerblade has to design new models in colors and styles that appeal to each age group. As a result, there may be more models and styles aimed at kids and teens than at adults. Statistics tend to support this reasoning–more children (83 percent) and teens (84 percent) are classified as advanced skaters than adults (66 percent). More advanced skaters typically will pay more for skates than beginners. A *Money* magazine article indicated that beginners should purchase skates that cost about $100 but more advanced skaters might well pay as much as $339.

In-line skaters are evenly divided between men and women. But men and women often have different motivations for skating and look for different skate styles and colors, prompting Rollerblade to think in terms of men's versus women's skates. In-line skaters also tend to be more upscale, with an average household income of $53,000 versus the U.S. average of $46,000. This could be interpreted to mean that this is an upscale sport–reserved for those with the money–or that companies such as Rollerblade have priced themselves above the mass market. Believing the latter, in 1992 Rollerblade introduced its Blade Runner line of affordable skates, protective gear, and accessories for kids and adults.

These products are sold by mass merchandisers to separate them from the more expensive products found in speciality and sporting goods shops.

In order to maintain leadership in an industry, a firm must sell to the market segment that sets the industry standard. In many industries, that's the high-end, high-price product segment. For in-line skates, it's the segment of aggressive skaters who are the ultimate consumers and who set the standard for performance. For this market, it is extremely important that a brand be distinguished from the skates their parents use. For them, Rollerblade has developed a new line of skates with a logo consisting of a backward R and a B. To understand the needs and wants of these users, and to build a stronger relationship with this segment, Rollerblade invites aggressive skaters such as Chris Edwards to its facilities several times a month to work with its R&D people and to test skates.

Competition also forces changes. K2 came out with an athletic shoe on wheels, which forced Rollerblade to take a close look at this concept. In fact, Rollerblade brought out the Synergy line of soft–shell skates-not a fabric skate but also not the hard model skates of the past. Although Rollerblade officials think most consumers will like the feel of fabric skates in the store, they worry that customers might well be turned off to in-line skating if the fabric skates don't last very long or give poor performance. Skating with your toe poking out the front of the shoe is neither fun nor safe. Moreover, fabric shoes fail to give sufficient ankle support and to transmit energy, with the result that they are slower. The Synergy line is intended to remedy some of the defects of fabric skates while still providing the consumer with a softer shoe.

In a market with a slowing growth rate, firms must look for sales in areas beyond their core products. For Rollerblade, these additional sales come mostly from selling active wear. For example, Jacques Moret, an apparel firm, signed a three-year contract with Rollerblade to sell active wear items, such as T-shirts and mesh shirts, under the Rollerblade and Blade Runner labels. Many of these items are aimed at women, who are more likely to buy outfits and athletic wear for specific activities. And, of course, Rollerblade sells protective gear for skaters-helmets, knee pads, and elbow pads. Sales of these items could add millions of dollars to revenues and help to promote the Rollerblade and Blade Runner names.

But keeping up with the competition is tough. Nike and Reebok are both entering the in-line skating market and both bring hundreds of millions of dollars to support product development and promotion. Both of these well-known brands have strong consumer appeal. Nike has developed a "Reuse-A-Wheel" recycling program in which the substance from used skate wheels is reused to make new athletic courts and playground surfaces. Rossignol plans to market skates with removable wheels that will allow skaters access to areas that are currently closed to them. Competing with well-known firms such as these, and preventing any more slides in its market share, demands that Rollerblade stay in close contact with its market.

Questions for Discussion

1. What subculture, family, reference group, life cycle, or social class influences affect the purchase of in-line skates?

2. According to the Maslow hierarchy, what motives are satisfied by in-line skating? How does learning affect participation in and purchase of in-line skates?

3. Using the four categories of buying behavior identified in the chapter, describe the first-time purchase of in-line skates and a fourth-time purchase of such skates. How will the knowledge base of the consumer change between the first and fourth purchases?

4. How is post-purchase behavior likely to affect the purchasers of fabric skates versus the purchaser of the Synergy skates from Rollerblade?

5. Fabric skates are an innovation in the in-line skating industry. Evaluate these on the basis of relative advantage, compatibility, complexity, divisibility, and communicability. Has Rollerblade made the best response to fabric skates with its soft-shell skate?

6. How might the entry of Reebok and Nike affect Rollerblade's position in the in-line skating industry? How could Rollerblade respond to the marketing efforts of these competitors?

Sources

[1] *Vendors Line Up for In-Line*, Women's Wear Daily, March 20, 1997, p. 11.

[2] *Showscope Q1 '97*, Sporting Goods Business, March 24, 1997, pp. 50-2.

[3] *In-Line Activewear*, Women's Wear Daily, November 2, 1995, p. 18.

[4] Andy Bernstein, *The SGB Interview with Dennis Shafer (President and CEO Rollerblade)*, Sporting Goods Business, June 23, 1997, pp. 42-43.

[5] Alyssa Lustigman, *Shaping Up*, Sporting Goods Business, June 1996, p. 36.

[6] Elif Sinanoglu, *Whiz Past Those $339 In-Line Skates*, Money, March 1995, p. 178

[7] Information from the Rollerblade web site.

DUPONT: SHAPING UP THE WORLD

Imagine how tough it would be to be responsible for marketing a "disappearing" product. That's the challenge faced by a group of marketers at DuPont, a company with a portfolio of brands that, for the most part, reach final consumers only as ingredients in finished products. Teflon non-stick coating, Lycra fibres, Freon refrigerant, Kevlar bullet-resistant fabric, Stainmaster carpet-these well-known DuPont products share the distinction of being used in the manufacture of products that ultimately bear some other company's brand.

Jamie Murray, the person in charge of managing what people think of the overall DuPont brand, doesn't mind marketing products that can't be found on store shelves or ordered from catalogues. "We are the youngest 200 year-old company you will ever meet. We are always out there searching for those needs that we can invent something to satisfy."

The company's slogan, "better things for better living," hints broadly at the variety of needs DuPont has satisfied over the years. When the computer industry required new forms of insulation for smaller and smaller electrical components, or the aerospace program needed stronger material for satellite tethers, or firefighters wanted fire-retardant suits, DuPont researchers headed to the laboratory. The company owns almost 2,000 trademarks and markets them in 200 countries around the world.

The challenges DuPont faces in marketing its ingredient brands are no less daunting than the challenges it faces in inventing them, so the company has developed five key principles to guide its actions. The first is personality management-controlling what the brand stands for and means to consumers. Gary Johnston, national marketing communications manager for nylon furnishings, says that, for DuPont, it's "science, business savvy, and a moral core". The second principle is visibility management, which entails creating awareness and familiarity for the invisible ingredients through integrated marketing communications.

The third is target management, which Johnston says involves "very clearly defining who it is that you need to connect with". For a brand such as DuPont, that includes not only the end consumer, but also the many constituencies in the manufacturing or value chain. The fourth principle is marketing management, which has to do with understanding the dynamics of the marketplace so the company can fashion the best connections with its target. Finally, there is reputation management, which is a proactive approach to helping people understand what the company is and what it is about.

All these principles are evident in DuPont's marketing of Lycra. To connect with consumers worldwide, Lycra management started a global campaign in 1994 to make customers familiar with the Lycra name and icon. To emphasise what the product does, the company used the tagline "Nothing moves like Lycra", which they added to in 1996 with the line "Clothes that move the way you do". As a result, more than 50 percent of consumers recognise the brand name and, more important, ask for garments made with Lycra. And it's rare when customers ask for a fibre by name.

To reach consumers, however, Lycra must be marketed to manufacturers of garments and retailers. This requires careful cultivation on the part of Lycra management. An example is the successful Wool Plus Lycra program initiated in 1995. For this venture, Lycra management teamed with the International Wool Secretariat to produce woven fabrics made with wool and lycra. This union is particularly noteworthy because it is the first time that two fibre groups have joined to promote a product globally. It works because the union provides value to both groups. The venture gives wool a new value-added feature by leveraging recognition of products off the well-known Lycra name. DuPont can market Lycra beyond its traditional markets in areas where it has little expertise. Moreover, because the program was sponsored evenly by the two partners, working together means that each group has to expend fewer funds. As a result, each side gets increased promotional awareness and market visibility for a few dollars.

Understanding the dynamics of the marketplace has led DuPont to invest in research to develop a newer, softer Lycra product. As the baby boomer market ages, it also gains a few pounds, sags a little, and moves up to a larger size despite diets and exercise. Consequently, these consumers are looking for more support, lift, and control in bodywear, undergarments, and active wear. The new product, Lycra Soft or Type 902C, has higher elongation that almost doubles the stretch qualities and gives it a consistent level of pressure for all-over control, and it has significant recovery force-all important characteristics to ageing boomers.

By developing new products such as Lycra Soft, DuPont not only helps its own profit line, but also that of its immediate customers. Firms such as Wacoal Japan, a Kyoto-based innerwear giant, have begun using Lycra Soft in the Far East in a control brief called "Magic Pants". According to Alan Fisher, vice-president of merchandising at the Wacoal America unit, "It's a premium fibre... (and) it certainly has the stretch advantages of all-over fit and function, and less yardage is used. Prettier, more feminine-looking shape wear items can be made."

Firms in the United States are not missing out on this opportunity. Maidenform is already into wear-test trials with it, so U.S. consumers may soon see these products in stores around the country. One store, in particular, where they may find garments containing Lycra Soft is Macy's, which is negotiating for use of the product in garments sold through Federated Stores.

Some manufacturers are even willing to tie their names to that of Lycra. A case in point is Liz Claiborne, a giant in women's clothing. The new line, called Liz and Lycra, includes leggings, pants, turtlenecks, a crewneck, an A-line dress, an A-line wrap skirt, and two jackets. All pieces will have a special Liz and Lycra hangtag.

The decision to launch Liz and Lycra was made based on information from Europe, which showed stretch items increasing in popularity, and on market research in which the company found that women wanted versatility, comfort, and durability in a garment. The products were wear-tested by staff at Claiborne headquarters, who found that Lycra eliminated the bagging which generally occurs at the knees on leggings and stretch pants.

Given these good results, the new line kicked off in Macy's Herald Square in March 1996 with in-store events, following a New York Times ad on the preceding Sunday. The ads and in-store visuals featured American Ballet Theatre principal dancer Julie Kent photographed by Jose Picayo. Thus, the creation of Liz and Lycra benefited not only Liz Claiborne and DuPont, but also Macy's, which is considering adding its own products that include Lycra. Association with the American Ballet Theatre is also a plus for all parties. ABT adds cachet to the Liz, Lycra, and Macy's brands and also creates a positive association between each brand and the ballet-a sort of good citizenship status. The ballet gets promotion at no charge to it.

High standards are required of all the partners with whom DuPont enters into arrangements. "One of the most serious challenges any ingredient brand faces is [that] when your brand becomes very popular and very strong, lots of companies want to use it," says Mary Kopf, brand manager for Kevlar and Nomex. "Unfortunately, not all of those companies have high ethical standards, so you might run into what we call counterfeiters. These are companies who either don't buy any of your product at all, or companies who may use a tiny bit of it, or use it sometimes and other times not. But they label the product as if it contains our ingredient, and what we have to do as responsible trademark owners is make sure that we pursue those counterfeiting situations."

Enforcing the proper use of its ingredient brands is well worth the cost to DuPont, which sees those brands as the source of the company's success during its almost 200-year history.

To enforce the Lycra name, DuPont has a toll-free number in the United States (1-800-64-Lycra) for customers and final consumers to report any suspected infringement or counterfeiting. It also runs campaigns stating that Lycra is trademarked, and its staff continually tests garments for Lycra brand authenticity worldwide. When labeled products that do not contain the Lycra brand are identified, the company takes steps-frequently legal steps.

"Your competition may try to imitate you technically, they may try to imitate you with service, but one thing they can't imitate is your brand," Kopf says. In this case, the appropriate use of the Lycra brand protects not only DuPont, but also Liz Claiborne, the International Wool Secretariat, Macy's, Maidenform, and any of DuPont's hundreds of partners. They all benefit from the value added by the Lycra name.

Questions for Discussion

1. What are the markets for Lycra?

2. How does the "selling-buying" relationship that occurs when Liz Claiborne wants to team up with Lycra differ from that in which a consumer purchases a garment that contains Lycra?

3. What type of buying situation occurs when Liz Claiborne wants to team with DuPont to obtain Lycra for the Liz and Lycra line?

4. Why would Liz Claiborne want to use Lycra rather than some other elastic-type product that might be less expensive?

5. DuPont spends tens of millions of dollars for consumer advertising for Lycra and for tracking down counterfeiters. Does it make sense for the company to spend money advertising to a market that it does not sell to directly? Does it make sense to track down counterfeiters?

Sources

[1] *DuPont Launches Lycra Spandex*, Women's Wear Daily, Jan. 26, 1996, p. 15.

[2] Elizabeth Gladfelter, *Liz Stretches Out*, Wind, March 6, 1996, p. 9.

[3] Michael McNamara, *DuPont, IWS Expanding Wool Plus Lycra Program*, Women's Wear Daily, Oct. 2, 1995, p. 2.

[4] Karyn Monget, *Next Generation of Lycra Targets Ageing Baby Boomers*, Women's Wear Daily, Jan. 29, 1996, p. 6.

MASTER CARD: GOING UPSCALE

Check, cash, or credit card? How many times have you heard that question and replied "credit card" without even thinking about it? When you do think about it, however, credit cards are a relatively new phenomenon. Yet when it comes time to pay, it seems we're more likely to use the credit card (and to have several of them) than checks or cash. Indeed, some writers have even suggested that, in the not so distant future, we will all operate with "plastic money" all the time.

MasterCard had its beginnings in 1966, when a group of banks joined together to form the Interbank Card Association (ICA). The ICA was founded by an association of banks rather than by a single dominant bank. Member committees ran the association by establishing rules for authorisation, clearing, and settlement as well as marketing, security, and legal matters. In 1968, ICA went "global" by forming an association with Banco National in Mexico and later with Eurocard in Europe. Since then, MasterCard has expanded around the world-even into the communist world of the 1980s when it entered the People's Republic of China in 1987 and Russia in 1988. By 1993, China was the second largest country in terms of MasterCard sales volume. Today, MasterCard is affiliated with more than 23,000 financial institutions around the world and has nearly 370 million credit and debit cards in use . These cards are accepted at more than 13 million locations worldwide. Gross dollar volume in 1995 was almost $500 billion. At present, MasterCard offers several global products, including Maestro (the world's first truly online debit program) and Cirrus (the world's largest ATM network). Wherever you are, you can use your MasterCard to pay for goods and services, obtain cash, or debit your checking account directly. MasterCard faces fierce competition from systems such as Visa and American Express, so selling 370 million credit cards requires a lot of ingenuity in finding prospects. To keep ahead of the competition, MasterCard constantly seeks new segments and fashions new product offerings. One segment that MasterCard has targeted with a vengeance is the health care market. To be successful in this market, MasterCard must convince doctors, dentists, and other medical practitioners to accept credit cards. For decades, medical practitioners have complained of difficulties in collecting payments for their services. Few doctors actually want to initiate legal proceedings against non-payers, so credit cards should have a strong value for them. With such cards, the credit card company takes care of collections. Of course, the doctor must pay transaction fees, but these may well be less than the costs associated with fee collections.

There are other reasons why medical practitioners might be interested in accepting credit cards. Many doctors demand immediate payment, which can be difficult for patients when cash flow is tight. In such situations, credit cards are a useful option. A survey by MasterCard found that many would-be patients postpone both routine and emergency visits to the doctor because of financial problems. Most medical practitioners realise, however, that early detection of problems will likely lead to faster and perhaps less expensive "cures". So, the failure of patients to come to the doctor when symptoms first strike often makes the doctor's job more difficult later on. Finally, MasterCard might be especially attractive to Medicare patients needing a medical procedure not covered by Medicare-the patient can still receive treatment even if it means spreading payments out over time. For the patient, MasterCard offers more than just a payment mechanism. It also provides a free Health Care Guide and Planning Kit, which enables consumers to track previous medical expenditures and plan for future ones. MasterCard offers lots of health-related tips, and its Website links cardholders to different types of health care associations. MasterCard holders also receive coupons with savings of up to 60 percent on health and fitness products such as Nordic Track, Jenny Craig, Pearle Vision, Xenejenex health videos, and Solgar Vitamins and Herbs. In addition, MasterCard has ties with services such as SMOKENDERS, the Nutrition Action Health letter, the American Running & Fitness Association, and the American Medical Association.

One of the newest MasterCard health products is a joint offering with Mellon Bank Corporation. These two companies provide a package of depository, payment, and processing services for medical savings accounts (MSAs). Included in the package is a MasterCard Master Money debit card that allows holders to pay for MSA-related medical expenses. MSAs are health plans that combine money-saving, higher-deductible healthcare polices and tax-deferred savings accounts for the self-employed or for people working for companies with 50 or fewer employees. In an MSA system, employers buy high-deductible health insurance policies coupled with tax-deferred medical savings accounts. Employees make pre-tax contributions to their accounts, which can then be used through the Master Money debit card to pay for medical care. Such plans enable employees of participating companies to pay healthcare providers directly for services, quickly and easily.

Another market that MasterCard targets is the sports enthusiast. To reach sports markets worldwide, MasterCard has sponsored World Cup Soccer. One of its newest ventures is the Jordan Grand Prix Formula One team sponsorship. MasterCard sponsors the B&H Jordan Mugen-Honda Formula One team worldwide, and announced expansion of this sponsorship in January 1998. "Expansion of the Jordan Grand Prix Formula One team racing sponsorship provides MasterCard with all the key elements of a successful program: a global sport with a year-round calendar of races and events, a high-performance, competitive team, famous personalities, and countless loyal and passionate fans," says Mava Heffler, senior vice president of Global Promotions and Sponsorships for MasterCard. She continues, "Sports sponsorships are among the most powerful tools MasterCard has to effectively build our brand and our business". MasterCard can tap into the vast emotional affinity that racing fans have for Formula One through Jordan Master Cards, Jordan team licensed merchandise, and cardholder promotions such as the opportunity to drive a Jordan car.

There's another reason why MasterCard wants to expand its sports sponsorships to Formula One racing. Whereas stockcar racing is the darling of the masses of the U.S. population, Formula One racing attracts many well-heeled fans. After decades of building volume by attracting millions of credit-hungry consumers, MasterCard decided recently to go after a different target-the affluent. Although providing credit to the rich might seem like a contradiction (you might think that the affluent don't need credit), the affluent are actually a good target for a credit card company. One of the major benefits of a credit card system is the ability to pay when cash and check would be unacceptable or difficult. The rich need this benefit as much as others-perhaps more. Traditionally, however, you might think of a credit card system as making money from people who incur high interest charges on outstanding balances carried from month to month. So, how could MasterCard improve its revenues by catering to the wealthy, who pay their credit card bills on time? The answer is the 1 to 2 percent interchange fee that credit card companies receive on each transaction made by these big spenders. According to Michael Auriemma, a credit card consultant, the average card user charges $3,000 a year, resulting in interchange fees of $42. Assuming 80 percent of card users carry a balance, averaging $1,800 each, he estimates that a customer paying 16 percent interest would accrue $230 in annual interest charges. By contrast, a wealthy card user may charge $20,000 a year, meaning that, even without interest charges, the bank will earn $280 in interchange fees, in addition to annual fees paid for the cards. To attract these consumers, MasterCard will provide elite cards offering special perks, from 24-hour-a-day concierge services-running errands, arranging travel, booking tickets, and the like-to VIP treatment at concerts and sporting events. Bank America Corp has become the first credit card issuer to launch a World MasterCard. Like cards from rival American Express, the World MasterCard will charge a higher annual fee, which is $75. Not to be outdone, Visa is working on a comparable card.

Targeting the wealthy has another benefit for MasterCard. Many of the millions of MasterCard holders are mired in debt and are failing to pay their credit balances, which results in losses for the banks in the MasterCard system. Furthermore, the ready availability of credit cards from numerous banks has conditioned consumers to shop for no fee and low fee cards-the best rates and rewards programs. These are actions that further reduce the revenue to MasterCard banks. By targeting the wealthy, MasterCard reduces its reliance on more debt-ridden, less loyal consumers. However, in targeting this upscale market, MasterCard pits itself directly against American Express. Is AmEx worried? Gail Wasserman, an American Express spokesperson, claims that AmEx is not overly concerned.

"History has shown that Visa and MasterCard have often come out with cheap imitations of American Express products. They never are quite as good as ours". Some industry observers remain skeptical that MasterCard can succeed with this venture. "No issuer in the world has committed itself to the same level of customer service that American Express has," says David Robertson, president of the Nilson Report, a credit-card research firm in California. He adds, "The crux of the matter is Visa and MasterCard can't control their member banks; and since the members have that flexibility, no matter what the product, it'll be a variation of gold and platinum. Ultimately, it'll all become middlebrow." His comments raise another issue. So many member banks have issued gold and platinum Master Cards that the image, value, and status of such cards have been tarnished in the minds of Americans. In contrast, since its introduction in 1984, the American Express Platinum Card has dominated the market for very affluent card holders. AmEx charges an annual fee of $300 and offers perks such as free upgrades at leading hotels and free companion tickets for customers buying a first- or business-class international ticket on selected airlines. There are only 300,000 to 400,000 platinum AmEx cardholders, compared to the millions of Master Card platinum cardholders. It stands to reason that, if necessary, AmEx will defend its market fiercely and aggressively. And AmEx has experience in serving this market, whereas Master Card does not.

Questions for Discussion

1. What segmentation criteria has MasterCard used in the healthcare, sports, and affluent market segments? What segmentation criteria are implicit in MasterCard's selection of these segments?

2. How does MasterCard differentiate its offerings for each of these target segments? How has MasterCard positioned its offerings?

3. What competitive advantages and disadvantages does MasterCard have with its World MasterCard, targeted to the affluent?

4. In your opinion, will MasterCard's World card be a success? Why or why not? What recommendations would you make for marketing the card?

Sources

[1] Kristie Perry Dolan, *Getting Patients to Pay*, Medical Economics, pp. 48-62.

[2] Stephen E. Frank, *Burned by the Masses, Cards Court the Elite*, Wall Street Journal, November 5, 1997, p. B1

[3] The following Master Card press releases and other information found at the Master Card Web site, February 1998: "Mellon and Master Card Introduce Breakthrough Debit Product as Key to Accessing Medical Savings Accounts;" and "Master Card Expands Popular Jordan Grand Prix Formula One Team Sponsorship into Global Program."

THE RITZ-CARLTON: GOING FOR 100 PERCENT

After Ritz-Carlton won the Malcolm Baldrige National Quality Award in 1992, many people within the company and in the rest of the hospitality industry asked, "Where can Ritz-Carlton go from here?" If you already give the best customer service, how can you improve? What can you do to build stronger relationships with customers?

An ordinary firm might have hung the award on the wall and been content with its status, but not this company. Ritz-Carlton management knows that total quality management is an ongoing process. After all, the hotel chain was only satisfying 97 percent of its customers-that leaves 3 percent room for improvement. Perhaps this much improvement doesn't seem like a difficult task, but when you consider all the changes in employee recruiting and training, empowerment, and managerial planning that Ritz-Carlton had already made, you have to ask "What's left to improve?"

To answer that question, you first need to know what total quality management processes Ritz Carlton already has in place. Total quality management has to permeate every level of an organization, from top management down to the lowest-level employee. It's not enough for managers to say that they believe in quality service; employees must be trained and motivated to provide quality service.

How can a firm build a quality service orientation among employees? It starts with hiring the right employees. In the case of Ritz-Carlton, employees aren't "hired," they are "selected." In an industry notorious for low pay levels and high turnover, many competitors hire people with minimal skills and give them minimal training. The result is poor quality or inconsistent service, low employee morale, and high turnover. At the Ritz-Carlton, employees are carefully selected; for every new employee at an introductory orientation session, ten others applied. Once selected, each employee attends a two-day orientation to learn about the Ritz-Carlton corporate culture, followed by extensive on-the-job training that results in job certification.

To ensure that employees are adequately trained, the Ritz-Carlton routinely tests more than 75 percent of its employees. Employees are tested on two front: (1) their mastery of skills associated with their particular employment and (2) their grasp of knowledge that will qualify them as "quality engineers." Skills testing varies with the job: telephone operators might have their customer calls monitored to ensure that they adhere to standards such as answering the phone by three rings. Housekeepers might be asked about what to do if they encounter a floor spill. When an employee fails the skills test, a company trainer attempts to determine the cause of the problem—the teaching method, the employee's personal difficulty, or something else. The company expects 100 percent compliance with skills testing. If an employee cannot pass the test, then he or she may be assigned to another position before leaving the firm.

To pass the "quality engineer" certification, employees must understand the company's TQM philosophy and credo. To reinforce this knowledge, each Ritz-Carlton hotel has a daily lineup at which employees affirm their commitment to quality. In addition, employees discuss one of the company's twenty basic points of service. All employees must learn the company credo and the three steps of service. The Ritz-Carlton Credo states:

The Ritz-Carlton Hotel is a place where genuine care and comfort of our guests is our highest mission. We pledge to provide the finest personal service and facilities for our guests who will always enjoy a warm, relaxed yet refined ambiance. The Ritz-Carlton experience enlivens the senses, instills well-being, and fulfils even the unexpressed wishes and needs of our guests.

The three steps of service are: (1) a warm and sincere greeting, (2) anticipation and compliance with guest needs, and (3) a fond farewell, using the guest's name if possible.

At the Ritz-Carlton, employees are not servants, they are "ladies and gentlemen serving ladies and gentlemen." This necessitates changes in their demeanour and language. The appropriate way to greet customers is to say "Good morning" or "good afternoon", not "Hi, how's it going." The appropriate way to respond to a request is "Certainly" or "My pleasure" rather than "Sure." According to Mary Anne Ollman-Brigis, corporate director of training at Ritz-Carlton, the purpose of all this training is to make employees feel more comfortable in their jobs, so that they will be more successful. "We certify people to empower them to make decisions," she says. What sorts of decisions can employees make? They can handle any customer complaint on the spot and spend up to $2,000 doing so. And they can demand the immediate assistance of other employees. Twenty minutes later, they should telephone the guest to make sure that the complaint was handled properly. In addition, once employees learn of a particular customer's wants, such as foam pillows or desire for a particular newspaper, that information goes into a 240,000-person database. The customer will automatically get the desired service the next time he or she stays at a Ritz-Carlton. Does such employee empowerment pay? The answer is yes according to Patrick Mene, Vice President of Quality. He expresses this as the 1-10-100 rule: "What costs a dollar to fix today will cost $10 to fix tomorrow and $100 to fix down-stream."

Ritz-Carlton doesn't work just to solve customer problems, it works to avoid them in the first place. Any employee who spots a potential problem in service delivery brings this to management's attention and a solution is found. By eliminating internal complaints generated by employees, Ritz-Carlton avoids external complaints that might come from customers.

Attention to quality extends beyond hotel staff. Top managers meet weekly to review measures of product and service quality, guest satisfaction, market growth and development, and other business indicators. From top management down, Ritz-Carlton's quality management is characterized by detailed planning. To ensure that quality standards are maintained, Ritz-Carlton collects daily reports from each of the 720 work areas in each of the 30 hotels it manages. It tracks measures such as annual guest room preventive-maintenance cycles, percentage of check-ins with no queuing, time spent to achieve industry-best clean-room appearance, and time to service an occupied room. Ritz-Carlton responded to the "What's left to improve?" question in two ways. First, the company aimed at global recognition for its quality efforts. Second, it revolutionised global operations through the implementation of Self-Directed Work Teams (SDWTs). Progress toward the first goal occurred when the Ritz-Carlton, Cancun, won Mexico's National Quality Award, and other Ritz-Carlton hotels won the Australia State and National Customer Service Awards, Hawaii's State Quality Award, and Houston's City Quality Award.

The Self-Directed Work Teams project got off the ground in Tysons Corner in 1993. It proved so successful that it was rolled out in the other 30 Ritz-Carlton Hotels. A SDWT is a group of employees responsible for a complete work process. Such teams are responsible for:

- Sharing various management or leadership functions
- Planning and improving work processes
- Developing team goals and mission
- Scheduling and payroll

- Team performance reviews
- Coaching and training team members
- Ordering and purchasing of supplies and maintenance of inventories

SWDTs have two major benefits: They liberate and unleash the creative potential and entrepreneurial abilities of employees, and they free managers from the day-to-day operational aspects of a hotel or work area. As a result, employees are happier and more satisfied with their jobs and managers are free to provide vision and direction rather than direct supervision.

In the future, the Ritz-Carlton may be able to "sell" its service know-how. Recently, United Airlines enlisted the help of the Ritz-Carlton to train flight attendants to cater to passengers in first class on international flights. Attendants learned to refine skills ranging from pouring champagne (grasp the well on the bottom of the bottle) to gracefully serving from a platter during turbulence (maintain your composure). More important than the skills training, however, may be instilling in employees the attitude that serving the customer is a pleasure.

The president of the Ritz-Carlton chain has set a new goal of 100 percent customer satisfaction and a reduction in defects to just four in every million customer encounters. Eliminating virtually all problems, however, is a costly process that can reduce company profits, and some critics believe that Ritz-Carlton is not sensitive enough to its bottom line. For example, to improve customer satisfaction from 97 percent to 98 percent, some would say, is a marginal improvement that could require a great deal of expense and employee effort for a relatively low dollar return. Besides, how can any firm anticipate all possible problems and eliminate all complaints? Should it even try?

Questions for Discussion

1. Why is it important for Ritz-Carlton to insist that employees not think of themselves as servants, but rather as ladies and gentlemen?

2. In what ways does Ritz-Carlton engage in relationship marketing?

3. Is quality at Ritz-Carlton cost-effective? Even if it costs $2,000 an incident?

4. Should Ritz-Carlton attempt to move toward the president's goal of 100 percent customer satisfaction? Why or why not?

5. How could the Ritz-Carlton credo and principles of customer service be applied to: (a) hair-care salons, (b) banks, (c) medical offices, (d) auto repair garages?

Sources

[1] Patricia A. Galagan, *Putting on the Ritz*, Training and Development, December 1993, p. 41-45.

[2] Margaret Loftus, *Up-Front Care: Touch of Class*, U.S. News and World Report, May 19, 1997, p. 71.

[3] Jenny McCune, *Testing, Testing 1-2-3*, American Management Association Review, January 1996, p. 50-52.

[4] Charles G. Partlow, *How Ritz-Carlton Applies 'TQM'*, The Cornell H.R.A. Quarterly, August 1993.

[5] Numerous company supplied and Internet site materials.

INTEL: INSIDE EVERYTHING?

What's in a name? Ask Dennis Carter and he'll tell you it's the not-so-secret ingredient to his company's success in the computer industry. Carter is vice president and director of sales and marketing for Intel, which became the third most valuable brand in the world by convincing consumers that, when it comes to computers, it's what's inside that counts. Prior to the 1980s, few but the most sophisticated computer users knew what kind of microprocessing chip their machines contained, let alone who made it. Technology had swept through the corporate world and revolutionised business practice, but consumers were only just beginning to see the benefits of having a computer in their homes. The biggest brand names in the industry were not those of component makers, but those of computer manufacturers such as IBM, Apple, and Hewlett-Packard.

All that changed in 1989, when Intel, one of the world's largest makers of semiconductors, took the cover off of what many consumers thought of as a black box and gave them a look around. The company's decision to focus on end users was based on its recognition that the pace of technological change and the rate of sales growth in the consumer market were both accelerating. Intel had experience in talking to the engineers who were the primary buyers in the business-to-business market. But the company realised that, in order to stay ahead of the competition, it had to begin talking to consumers in the mass market.

The Silicon Valley-based firm initiated an advertising campaign to educate users about its 386X chip, which would replace the 286 microprocessor as the industry standard. "From very early on, the technique we've used in our advertising is to take the consumer inside the computer, literally to fly inside the computer, de-mystify it a little bit, show them the technology, the electronics, take them to the microprocessors, show them what it is, and then explain what the microprocessor does-the fact that it may run their software faster or that it [runs] a greater range of software-whatever the particular benefit of that particular processor is," Carter says.

In the process of explaining the benefits of Intel's newer generation microprocessor and how it measured up against the competition, he says the company "accidentally created a brand." Similar success followed with the 486, leading Intel to begin thinking it needed a branding strategy to carry it through subsequent generations. But it felt no sense of urgency until March 1991, when a judge ruled that 386 and 486 were numbers that anyone could use and thus could not be trademarked or branded.

The ruling was a blow because it meant that all the time, money, and energy invested in associating Intel with the 386 and 486 microprocessors could not protect the company from competitors who might use the numerical designations on components with slower speeds or of lower quality. With the chips down, Intel management moved into high gear. Working around the clock on the weekend after the judge's decision, the branding team developed a simple slogan—Intel Inside—which subsequently became a marketing tool not only for Intel, but also for the computer manufacturers who use the company's microprocessors.

Intel initiated a two-pronged push and pull campaign to enlist the support of original equipment manufacturers (OEMs). At the heart of the pull strategy was the need to make it easy for consumers to identify, at the point of purchase, computers that contained Intel microprocessors. Consequently, manufacturers who included the Intel Inside logo on their machines and in their advertising received rebates from the company. Smaller, third-tier OEMs were eager to embrace the program because it helped level the quality playing field among them. But first- and second-tier OEMs were reluctant to get on board. They feared the program would build Intel's equity at the expense of their own. However, they changed their minds and their policies once the logo became more familiar to the public and when retailers told them consumers were asking for it. The Intel Inside campaign made Intel a highly visible and familiar brand name, which is both a source of strength and of weakness. As a weakness, a flaw in the Pentium chip a few years back focused global attention on Intel in a way that would have never happened to low-profile and unknown computer components manufacturers. By branding and advertising its chips, Intel had not only opened computers to consumers, it had also opened itself to criticism and possible sales losses.

But from weakness may come strength. After the Pentium flaw fiasco, "...no one asked me anymore 'Why do you do this? People don't care about the processors.' It is really evident [that] people do care about the processor... it's important emotionally to people," Carter says. Today, Intel is considered one of the most valuable brands in the world-right behind consumer brands such as Coca-Cola and Marlboro. Intel's substantial investment in building the brand name has paid off in brand recognition, requests for the product, and loyalty, which Intel hopes to use as the springboard to inclusion in a variety of other extended and new products.

In early 1997, major computer makers announced their intentions to enter the below $1,000 computer market segment. From once viewing this segment as "Segment Zero," Intel has now moved to make it a top priority. Why? Simply because of volume. Sales in this segment surged from 7 percent of market volume to 25 percent in a single year, and they are expected to grow another 33 percent in 1998. Sales of $1,500 computers are expected to grow from 39 percent of market volume to 50 percent during the next few years. This means that higher-priced PCs with Intel Inside will be a smaller percentage of the market. As the market has moved to lower-priced PCs, Cyrix Corporation, an Intel rival, has marked this territory as its own. To continue to dominate this industry, Intel will have to be inside lower-priced PCs. Doing so, however, will cut Intel's margins from as high as 74 percent to 55 percent, which means reducing chip prices by stripping down the chip.

Should Intel pursue this market vigorously? There's no clear answer. Studies reveal that 40 percent of customers buying the cheaper PCs are buying a computer for the first time. The rest are split between people replacing an old machine and those buying a second or third computer for their children. It's not clear how much the sales of lower-priced PCs are cannibalising sales of higher-priced ones. "We won't really know for two years," says Andy Grove, CEO of Intel. However, IDC analyst Kevin Hause disagrees: "[Cannibalisation is] absolutely happening." To counterbalance the loss of margin on stripped down chips, Intel expects to sell lots of Pentium IIs and the highly promoted 64-bit Merced chip expected in late 1999, both of which are used in workstations and servers. At present, Intel has a large share of the under $25,000 server market but is only a bit player in the market between $25,000 and $250,000. The Merced is Intel's ticket to the high end of the workstation and server market. It was designed with radically different technology that speeds software by running multiple tasks simultaneously. Merced will cost $1,200 or more and could help Intel grab 41 percent of the high-end server market. But the competition there will be tough-Intel will be battling giants such as Sun Microsystems and Hewlett-Packard.

The workstation market could become another cash cow for Intel, because it slip-streams behind Microsoft's Intel-based Windows NT software. Market share in this market is expected to grow from 50 percent to 86 percent by the year 2000 and revenues could total as much as $26 billion, going a long way toward offsetting the lower margins on cheaper chips.

While Intel is going upscale in the workstation and server markets, it may have to go downscale in non-PC markets. One alternative is set-top boxes for televisions. At present, companies such as Hitachi, ARM, and MIPS Technologies crank out processors for this market that cost as little as $15. These companies also dominate the market for hand-held PCs, smart phones, and digital cameras. To compete, Intel might be forced to opt for low price rather than the latest technology. However, Grove doesn't think so-he argues that more is better. For example, Intel envisions new set-top boxes ranging in price from $300 to $500 that will receive TV, offer basic menus, and possibly provide for Net cruising, E-mail, and PC games on more expensive models. For this market, Intel would use Pentium MMX chips, possibly moving to Pentium IIs in 1998. For network computers-stripped down PCs that leave most of the heavy lifting to servers-Intel would use old chips and possibly some Pentium chips.

Why enter these low-end markets? Again, the answer is volume. TVs, VCRs, and CD players are in virtually all homes, whereas computers are likely to penetrate only 60 percent of homes by 2000. "Our business depends on expanding the market," says Ronald J. Whittier, an Intel senior vice-president. "We want to be in living rooms, cars, and appliances."

To help achieve its position in our homes, cars, and appliances, Intel fired up a major advertising campaign in 1997. This campaign features the Bunny People characters, modelled after Intel technicians who manufacture microprocessors. Dancing Bunny People, first seen in ads introducing the Pentium processor with MMX technology, will be travelling the world (in ads) to demonstrate what Pentium II processor-based systems can do for consumers. The Bunny People will take a global road-trip and show up in places such as Intel factories and downtown Hong Kong.

If Whittier and Intel have their way, they will be inside, well, everything. And their one brand will cover everything from smart phones to car computers to home PCs in all price ranges, to massive office systems. Like rabbits, there will be an explosion of Pentium chips. They'll be in everything from low-priced to high-priced products-a much bigger stretch than Intel envisioned when it first developed the Intel Inside logo in 1991.

Questions for Discussion

1. What is the value of the Intel brand? What does it mean to consumers?

2. How will placing its components in the new lower-priced PCs affect the market's perception of Intel? How would placing them in products such as smart phones and set-top boxes affect perceptions? Does it matter whether Intel uses its newest chips or older ones in these applications?

3. What types of markets are purchasing the set-top boxes, smart phones, lower-priced PCs, and workstations and servers? Where is each of these markets in its life cycle? Where are various current Intel chips in their product life cycles?

4. Where is Intel in the new product development process for each market? How could Intel test the effect of using its name in the new smart phones or set-top boxes?

5. What are Intel's advantages and disadvantages relative to competitors such as Cyrix, Hewlett Packard, and SunSystems in each of the markets that buy the various products that may have Intel Inside? Which markets should Intel emphasise.

6. What marketing strategy and mix would you suggest for each market?

Sources

[1] Peter Coffee, *Embedded Chips Deliver Invisible Software*, PC Week, October 13, 1997, p. 45.

[2] Tom Quinlan, *Intel, Digital Seek to Resolve Trademark Battle*, Knight-Ridder/Tribune Business News, October 7, 1997, p. 100

[3] Andy Reinhardt, *Intel*, Business Week, December 22, 1997, pp. 70-77

[4] Materials from the Intel Web site (Intel.c)

WATSON PHARMACEUTICALS: FROM GENERICS TO BRAND NAMES

The high cost of medical care concerns everyone these days, from the President of the United States to the ordinary citizen. In response, medical care firms and practitioners have taken a number of actions to reduce costs. The 1990s witnessed the growth of health care management organisations (HMOs), mergers among hospitals, the growth of for-profit hospitals, and the hiring of managers to run local medical practices. Another way to hold down health care costs is to use generic drugs rather than the proprietary drugs usually specified by doctors. Pharmacists frequently ask purchasers if they would like to have their prescriptions filled with generics, which sell for 20 to 50 percent less than their brand name counterparts. Not only do consumers win with lower prices, the pharmacists also win-generics usually have wider profit margins than branded prescription drugs, so that pharmacists make more selling generics. Where do these generic drugs come from? Some of them are made by well-known pharmaceutical firms, but most of them are made by companies such as Mylan and Watson Pharmaceuticals, which specialise in generic and off-patent proprietary medicines. Why would a firm specialise in generics? The most obvious answer is that lots of consumers want them in order to lower their pharmacy bills. However, the market for less expensive drugs has also grown because many HMOs and insurance firms want to hold down costs. One way to do this is to specify that lower-priced pharmaceuticals be used to fill prescriptions. Given these forces, the market for generics and off-patent pharmaceuticals has grown rapidly. That's why Hoechst Marion Roussel, one of the largest pharmaceutical companies in the world, entered the generics market. It was convinced that the lower-priced segment would explode and wanted to capitalise on the segment's growth.

Another reason for specialising in generics is the lower cost of operations. Major pharmaceutical companies spend hundreds of millions of dollars each year promoting their products—primarily through nationwide sales forces that call on doctors all across the country to convince them to prescribe branded products. Pharmaceutical sales representatives also leave thousands of samples for doctors to dispense. This personal selling effort is backed by lots of advertising in medical and trade journals. All this marketing results in a hefty addition to the cost of branded products.

Watson Pharmaceuticals is typical of many firms that started with limited funding for marketing. By focusing on the generic and off-patent prescription drugs market, they greatly reduced their marketing expenses greatly. These firms engage in limited advertising and sell to distributors and drug chains throughout the country. Their sales forces are more efficient because calls are made not to individual doctors, but to buying agents who may purchase for many pharmacies located in a large geographic area.

Watson not only clamps down on marketing costs, it also minimises research and development costs. Drug manufacturers may take decades to develop a new drug, during which time the firm encounters heavy costs but no revenues. Then, not all drugs developed in their labs become profitable. By selling generics, which are basic versions of drugs developed by other manufacturers, Watson capitalises on existing knowledge to refine "sure winners."

The first generic offered in a product category usually sells for 60 to 70 percent of the branded product's price and captures about 40 to 50 percent of the market. The following, or second wave, generic products have even lower prices and have less of the market open to them. Fifteen percent of customers are likely to remain loyal to the branded product, and many pharmacists are not willing to change from one generic product to another. Most pharmacists would think it foolish to stock two competing generics, so they often buy from only one generic manufacturer per product category. Thus, to obtain market share, the second-wave generic has to have a significantly lower price.

The key for the manufacturer of the first-wave generic is to get to market on time and keep its distributors and chain purchasers happy. Otherwise, buyers might shift to another manufacturer who offers an even cheaper product. Although generics and off-patent products sell for less, the generics firm does not wish to start a price war that will reduce margins too much. To prevent customer defections, Watson must back its products with good service, such as reliable, on-time delivery, and possibly flexible payment terms, such as longer times to pay or bigger discounts for volume purchases.

Another tactic used by Watson is to focus on niches A niche is a market segment-usually a small one-that can be served adequately by one or a few firms. Because the niche is too small to support many firms, it normally presents less competition. "Watson has succeeded historically by rigorously executing its strategy of developing niche products with limited competition and attractive margins," comments Dr. Allen Chao, chairman and chief executive officer of Watson. Watson has strong niche positions in pain relievers, feminine health care, and difficult-to-produce pharmaceuticals.

In September 1996, Watson purchased Oclassen Pharmaceuticals, which specialises in dermatological products. "The addition of Oclassen Pharmaceuticals to Watson's business provides Watson with a developed platform on which to extend its proven strategy into the dermatology market. The market for dermatological pharmaceuticals is highly fragmented and, as such, is perfectly suited to Watson's niche strategy" says Chao.

According to Chao, "Oclassen Pharmaceuticals has been successful with in-licensing compounds, completing development, and bringing these proprietary products through the clinical regulatory process into the market. Oclassen has a sales force of over 60 people specialising in the dermatology market segment. It has an attractive product pipeline that presents near-, medium-, and long-run potential. Oclassen is a key structural element for Watson in building a significant new business segment in an exciting pharmaceutical niche."

Watson went on a buying spree in 1996 and 1997, when, in addition to Oclassen, it purchased Royce Laboratories and the Rugby Group from Hoechst Marion Roussel. Both firms manufacture generic products. According to Chao, "Royce was particularly attractive to us ... as their business complements our existing business. This acquisition fits perfectly with our current strategy of focusing on the development, production, and marketing of difficult-to-produce niche pharmaceuticals."

This focus on niche positioning has been extremely important to Watson because of the price erosion for generic drugs in the United States in 1996 and 1997, caused by wholesalers holding bloated inventories and seeking price reductions. It was pricing problems that drove Hoechst Marion Roussel to sell the Rugby Group. For Watson, purchase of a generic competitor helps shore up its position in the market.

Another way Watson is shoring up its market position is by entering the branded segment of the market. In late 1996, Watson received approval to sell its first brand-name product, Microzide, which is used to treat high blood pressure. The hypertension market in the United States is worth more than $500 million in sales, but market size is not the only reason Watson is pushing Microzide. "Its significance relates to the fact that it's their first branded product," says Steve Gerber, analyst at Oppenheimer & Co. He estimates potential annual sales for Watson in the $10 million to $20 million range. Following on the heels of the Microzide approval, Watson obtained a worldwide licence to distribute Dilacor XR for the next four and a half years.

In October 1997, a subsidiary of Watson Pharmaceuticals, Watson Laboratories, entered an agreement with CoCensys in which Watson Labs acquired the rights to hire approximately 70 sales and marketing personnel employed by CoCensys Pharmaceuticals' Sales and Marketing Division and the rights to two co-promotions agreements. The co-promotions are for Somerset Pharmaceuticals' Eldepryl (R), used for the treatment of Parkinson's disease, and Parke-Davis' Zarontin (R), used for the treatment of pediatric epilepsy. In Chao's view, "As part of our strategy to diversify our revenue base, this acquisition adds an important dimension to Watson's existing sales and marketing capability. This sales force will complement both our existing primary and recently established female health care sales forces, as well as Oclassen's dermatological sales force.... [It will] be a key component in our expansion and diversification program."

With Microzide, Dilacor XR, and other branded products acquired through recent purchases, Watson has decreased its dependence on the price-oriented generic and off-patent markets. In 1993 all of Watson's revenue came from generic products; in 1995 only 86 percent came from generics. As Watson has decreased its dependence on generics, its stock price has risen. In August 1996, before the purchasing spree, Watson's stock price was $44; by August 1997, its stock price had risen to $52.31. The firm's earnings per share also rose rapidly, from about 40 cents a share to 56 cents. Watson's market capitalisation (number of stock shares outstanding divided by stock price) now exceeds that of Mylan, which actually has more prescriptions written on its drugs. Thus, in a sense, Watson has become the "biggest" generic manufacturer without increasing the number of generics and off-patents it sells.

Although the stock market applauds these moves, some analysts are skeptical. Watson's strength is in its ability to perfect formulations developed by others, its attention to cost containment, and its niche strategy. Although the company has acquired sales reps and marketing personnel through deals with Oclassen and CoCensys, it does not have strong marketing skills. Its skill at promoting, selling, and distributing branded products has not been severely tested. Strong firms in the pharmaceuticals industry, such as Parke-Davis, Glaxo, and Hoechst Marion Roussel, have the capital and marketing resources to provide such a test.

Questions for Discussion

1. What internal and external factors affect Watson's pricing?

2. What pricing approach does Watson Pharmaceuticals use? What pricing strategy does it use?

3. What sorts of price adjustments does Watson make? Why are these important?

4. "Watson's product pricing strategy drives its corporate expansion strategy." Is this statement true or false? Why? In your answer, be certain to discuss Watson's recent purchases.

5. In your opinion, is it wise for Watson to enter the branded segment of the market?

Sources

[1] Don Benson, *Investors, Analysts Upbeat on Watson Pharmaceuticals of Corona, California*, Knight-Ridder/Tribune Business News, July 14, 1997, p. 714.

[2] Don Benson, *Watson Pharmaceuticals Deal to Expand Generic Line*, Knight-Ridder/Tribune Business News, September 1, 1997, p. 901.

[3] Julius Karash, *Hoechst Marion to Sell Generic Drug Unit to Watson Pharmaceuticals*, Knight-Ridder/Tribune Business News, August 27, 1997, p. 827.

[4] Don McAuliffe, *California-Based Company Expected to Get Go Ahead for New Drug*, Knight-Ridder/Tribune Business News, October 14, 1996, p. 101.

[5] Don McAuliffe, *Watson Pharmaceuticals Gets Okay to Sell Its First Brand-Name Drug*, Knight-Ridder/Tribune Business News, December 31, 1996, p. 123.

[6] Articles from www.prnewswire.com.

DHL: More Global than Local

Since the early 1970s, DHL has been the leading (or often only) overnight carrier in many markets around the world. Founded in 1969 by Adrian Dalsey, Larry Hillblom, and Robert Lynn (hence, the D, H, and L) to transport letters of credit across the Pacific, DHL expanded rapidly in Asia and Europe (the early 1970s), the Middle East (1976), Latin America (1977), Africa (1978), Eastern Europe (early 1980s), China (1986), and Albania and the Baltic States (1992). Today, DHL has more than 53,000 employees, 209 aircraft, 2,381 stations, 12,203 vehicles, and 32 hubs and subhubs serving more than 675,000 destinations in 227 countries. In one year, it handles 95 million shipments-not bad for a company approaching its thirtieth birthday!

To handle all these shipments, DHL uses a worldwide hub and spoke system. It collects packages, documents, and letters from individual local business offices and sends them to the nearest service centre. The service centre then sends the parcels to a hub that serves a larger geographic area (such as Australia or the Middle East). There, the items are sorted by destination and shipped to service centres in each country, where they are resorted for the last leg of the journey to a local destination.

The Brussels hub is typical. Each night, starting at 10:30 P.M., the first of more than 120,000 documents and packages begin arriving at the hub. As they are unloaded, workers throw them onto $15 million worth of sorting machines, resembling a kind of crazy amusement park ride. Dozens of conveyor belts whisk the parcels away. As many as 400 people sort packages and put them on other belts, hurrying to get them loaded on trucks and airplanes by 3:30 A.M..

In another room, more than 50 people frantically read paperwork in dozens of languages so that all the parcels can clear customs without delay. In-house translators and customs clearance services are among DHL's distinguishing characteristics. Another is that DHL employs its own people to deliver documents and packages abroad; most other carriers hire local agencies. However, DHL does not always use its own airplanes, as FedEx and UPS do. Instead, wherever possible, DHL buys lift capability from international carriers, establishing its own air service only when it must. By doing this, DHL can find flights at all times between locations rather than relying on one or two flights of its own. This gives DHL greater flexibility not only in timing, but also in capacity.

Flexibility is important in serving today's distribution customers. One important form of flexibility is the timing of delivery and pickups. To provide such flexibility, DHL is experimenting with mobile collections. In Dublin, it launched the Super Bus, which follows a set route through the city to pick up and deliver parcels. From the bus, walking couriers deliver and collect shipments from businesses. By using one large bus to replace the multiple trucks or vans that once crisscrossed Dublin's city centre, DHL has reduced congestion. More important, it has improved service through earlier deliveries and later pickups.

DHL follows the same principle in its floating express distribution centre in Amsterdam. The centre, actually a canal boat, follows a set route through Amsterdam's canals, using bicycle couriers to handle parcels. The boat not only relieves congestion and improves service, it also reduces pollution in one of Europe's most crowded cities.

DHL provides another important customer service through DHLNET-a high-speed data network developed jointly by DHL and IBM. When packages first arrive, DHL employees enter shipment information into the network. Each package's airbill receives a unique barcoded number that is scanned into DHL's information network at each stage of its journey. The system provides DHL management with information on routing, delivery times, and volumes.

DHL has also created a system called EasyShip, which lets customers prepare their own shipping documents and maintain databases of their customer addresses in-house. DHL will either install the EasyShip computer and software free of charge in the customer's office or provide software that users can install on their own computer systems. Working with AT&T, DHL has also introduced a comprehensive automated international shipment notification system which lets U.S. shippers alert recipients electronically that a delivery is on its way. Along with other critical shipment information, recipients are given the shipment airbill number for easy tracking.

When preparing a shipment with DHL's shipping software, customers have the option of sending their recipients an e-mail message or a fax describing the shipment's contents and other information. Because the shipment airbill number is included, progress can be traced through DHL's Web site (DHL.com), DHL's GlobalTrackSM Software, or by calling DHL's automated GlobalTrack telephone service. With some e-mail applications, customers can even link directly from the Electronic Shipment Advisory e-mail message to the tracking page on the DHL Website. In some countries, the message is translated automatically from English to the local language. "As DHL is the leader in international air express delivery, Electronic Shipment Advisory is designed with the international shipper in mind, offering 10 language options," says Alan Boehme, director of customer access for DHL Airways.

'Confirming the trend toward the growing importance of information in international and domestic shipping, our customers indicated that there was demand for a system that automatically advises a recipient that a shipment is coming their way," said Patrick Foley, DHL's chairman and chief executive officer. "Shippers can now eliminate the extra phone calls, faxes, and paperwork associated with informing a recipient of an inbound shipment."

In addition to its traditional services, such as overnight documents and parcels delivery, same-day service between locations in the United States and to some foreign countries, and international air freight-DHL also provides third-party logistics services. As corporations downsize and work to trim costs, they have begun to reduce their investments in inventories and warehouses by outsourcing logistics functions. An example is DHL's experience with Japan's Kubota. DHL warehouses spare parts for Kubota computers. When customers call the Kubota service number, they actually reach DHL, which immediately ships needed parts through the DHL system.

Another example is Bendon, Ltd., a New Zealand manufacturer of women's lingerie. In the past, it took 10 days for Bendon to ship goods to Australia. However, through its alliance with DHL, Bendon can now accept Australian orders until 1:00 P.M. for next-morning delivery. By using DHL's information system, Bendon knows that all its shipments have cleared customs, and it receives delivery reports on all shipments. As a result, Bendon can invoice customers more quickly, improving its cash flow and reducing inventories.

More recently, DHL Worldwide Express formalised a multimillion-dollar agreement with Roche Diagnostics, a division of the international healthcare company, F. Hoffman-La Roche Ltd.. DHL will act as Roche's logistics partner, with responsibility for the storage, pick and pack distribution, and inventory management of parts for diagnostic analytical systems. All routine deliveries will be dispatched from the DHL Strategic Parts Center in Hoofddorp, the Netherlands. Consignments will be delivered door-to-door using DHL's air express capabilities. This partnership with DHL will enable Roche Diagnostics to keep fewer spare parts in stockpiles around the world, provide speedier and more reliable response to customer requests, and offer value-added emergency service that will set Roche apart from its competitors in the worldwide diagnostics market.

Although DHL has captured the leading share of the international air express market, it lags behind FedEx and UPS in the United States, with less than 2 percent market share. However comments Patrick Lupo, chairman and CEO of DHL Worldwide Express, "[DHL's share may be less than 2 percent of the intra-U.S. market, but from the United States to a foreign point, DHL's share would be in the 22 percent to 25 percent range. That's a statement about our management focus on export shipments. As the large U.S. couriers are launching expensive fleets of aircraft, they're saddled with high fixed costs. DHL's U.S. position is that it can buy uplift on an as-needed basis to match customer requirements. This gives us a lot of flexibility."

Lupo's comments highlight the heightened competition in the air express business. FedEx, with 30 percent of U.S. overseas shipments, spends millions on advertising and touts its image of speed and reliability. UPS, with only 10 percent of U.S. exports, also spends heavily on advertising that emphasises speed and diversified services to more than 200 international territories. How do these U.S. giants stack up against DHL? When FedEx and UPS announced same-day delivery in 1995, they found that DHL was already providing such a service.

Is DHL worried about the competition? "DHL has always had a very good reputation," says Chairman Foley. "We find that international customers have a proclivity to stay with their service provider much more than in the United States. In the United States, if you mis-ship one shipment out of 400, or even 4,000..., your customer may lose patience and make a change. Internationally, that isn't so. We were the first in the international field, and we service the international field very professionally and efficiently. Because of that, we rarely lose customers."

Another asset is that DHL does not have a single national identity. It is a truly global corporation. "If you look at our main competition, FedEx and UPS, their [international] focus has always been into and out of the United States. That's where they advertise and that's where they specialise. But its a big world and DHL goes everyplace," comments Foley. Perhaps so. Still, some critics wonder if DHL can keep its international market share without more U.S. market share.

Questions for Discussion

1. When DHL acts as the logistics supplier for Kubota, Bendon, and Roche; what type of marketing system does this exemplify? What are the advantages of the partnership for each party?

2. Explain how DHL helps partners Kubota, Bendon and Roche with (a) order processing, (b) warehousing, (c) inventory, and (d) transportation.

3. Explain how DHL helps its other customers with (a) order processing, (b) warehousing, (c) inventory, and (d) transportation.

4. What are DHL's primary competitive advantages and disadvantages in the air express service business? What are the competitive advantages and disadvantages of FedEx and UPS?

5. Why would obtaining a large share of the U.S. market be important to DHL? What actions would you suggest DHL take in order to achieve a larger share?

Sources

[1] Lisa Coleman, *Overnight Isn't Fast Enough*, Brandweek, July 31, 1995, pp. 26-27.

[2] Douglas W Nelms, *Holding Its Own*, Air Transport World, June, 1996, pp. 151-154.

[3] Andrew Tausz, *DHL Is Delivering on Courier Challenges*, Distribution, September 1997, pp. 22.

[4] Mitch Wagner, *Apps Gather Diverse Data from the Web*, Computerworld, April 14, 1997, pp. 61.

[5] Numerous company supplied materials and information from the DHL web site.

STARBUCKS: BREWING A BRAND CONCEPT

To say that Starbucks Corp. has stirred up the coffee industry would be an understatement. In 1987, the Seattle-based company's sales were only $10 million; today, they're $1 billion. Its more than 1,000 stores serve almost 5.5 million customers a week, many of whom visit twice a day, some as often as 18 times a month. Not bad for a company that charges four to five times as much for a cup of coffee as the competition, does not advertise much, and sometimes refuses to give the customer what he or she wants. So what is Starbucks' secret? Howard Schultz, company founder, believes the brand is so strong because it was built from within. "I am concerned about the customers who pay for the coffee, but my primary concern is for the people who serve it," he says. "We built the brand by putting them in a position to win by recognising that we wanted to build a company in which they were not left behind. We want to exceed the expectations every single day of the customer buying coffee at Starbucks. But we could not do that if we didn't first try, every single day, to exceed the expectations of our people."

Starbucks employs 25,000 people, each of whom-even part-timers-receives equity in the company in the form of stock options and comprehensive health care, plus a free pound of coffee each week. The health care plan is so novel that President Clinton invited Schulz to the White House for a private lunch to talk about it. Scott Bedbury, Vice President of Marketing, believes the emphasis on employee welfare is a specific example of a general philosophy toward business at Starbucks.

"I think it's respect for the product. I think Starbucks respects coffee far more than almost any other company in the category. I think it's respect for the employees. And then, finally, respect for customers."

He might add respect for the cities and towns in which the company operates, too. Before opening a new store, Starbucks develops added-value programs that give something back to the local community, such as establishment of a hospice, food bank, or AIDS foundation. On a national level, in 1997 the company inaugurated the Starbucks Foundation, which will provide financial and other support for children in need and children-related causes. These grassroots efforts take the place of more conventional forms of marketing. The company has spent more money on employee training in the last 10 years than it has on advertising. Bedbury says using traditional mass media to communicate to consumers is risky because the credibility of such messages is low to begin with.

"Delivering on a positive experience, face-to-face with someone in a store is probably a hundred times more effective than the best claim you could ever make in a piece of advertising," he says. According to Bedbury, personal interactions are more conducive to building emotional connections with consumers. He says emotional ties are the cornerstones of good brands, and that they require observing some of the conventions of marriage."You have to be honest, you have to be loyal, you have to be committed and demonstrate that you're compassionate. I think a lot of brands have forgotten to make those investments both internally first, in terms of reminding the people who work inside the company of what the brand is all about, and then communicating that to consumers."

Even so, Starbucks rolled out a new television campaign in the spring of 1997. The tagline of the campaign, "Purveyors of coffee, tea ,and sanity," was chosen because of its simple and upscale nature. Starbucks and the ad agency wanted something that evokes the neighbourhood coffeehouse where friends meet to relax and unwind. The image conveyed should be that of a friendly, intimate, neighbourhood sort of place. The advertising campaign uses simple stick figures that are almost crudely drawn, and that do not detract from the focus on the coffee. In these ads, it's the coffee that performs.

Image is crucial to retailers. The wrong image will lose customers and put a store out of business. It would seem that Starbucks with its squeaky clean decor and fresh-faced employees has overcome the bohemian atmosphere and nonconformist connotations of coffeehouses of years past.

Forging ties with consumers doesn't mean always giving them what they want, however. Schultz notes that 40% of the growth in the coffee industry comes from artificially flavoured brews. He points out that, if Starbucks "slapped its name" on such coffees, it could increase its business incrementally by that amount. But the company simply isn't interested in doing such a thing. Instead, says Jerome Conlon, Director of Consumer Insights and Brand Planning, Starbucks will focus on enhancing the complete coffee experience.

Starbucks has the opportunity to become the chief protagonist of coffee culture in the world and to become a lifestyle brand, not just a coffee company. Coffee is a great excuse to bring people together. There are lots of fabulous ways we can do that. We can design new forms of coffeehouses that become centres for cultural activity - whether it be art-related, literature-related, or music-related. We see strong links, historically, between coffee and art, literature, and music.

Whatever the company does to keep business percolating, he says, will involve "surprising and delighting" customers, because that is the key to "keeping the brand glowing in the long run".

Questions for Discussion

1. In terms of service and product line, how would you classify Starbucks?

2. As a corporate chain, what advantages does Starbucks enjoy?

3. What are Starbucks target markets and how has the company tried to appeal to these markets?

4. How has Starbucks positioned itself? Describe all the actions that Starbucks has taken to support its positioning.

Sources

[1] Donna Hood Crecca, *Coffee Klatch*, Restaurants and Institutions, January 15, 1997, pp. 64-68

[2] Robert Goldrich, *Starbucks Chooses Simple Spots for Simple Pleasures*, Shoot, June 20, 1997, pp. 22-23

[3] John Simons, *A Case of the Shakes: as Starbucks Cafes Multiply, So Do the Growing Pains*, U.S. News & World Report, July 14, 1997, pp. 42-45

[4] Richard Turcsik, *Starbucks to Test Lines in Chicago Supermarkets*, Supermarket News, July 14, 1997, p. 38.

GOT MILK?

What would you do if you were in charge of marketing a product that people only noticed when it was all gone? If you were Jeff Manning, you wouldn't be depressed by research indicating that consumers took your product for granted -you'd milk the news for all it was worth. As the executive director of the newly formed California Milk Processing Board (CMPB), Manning faced the challenge of reinvigorating sales of a staple in American households that had been declining steadily in consumption for more than 15 years. In 1993, the year the CMPB was established, per capita consumption of milk was 23 gallons, down from 29 gallons in 1980. In contrast, per capita consumption of soft drinks had increased 80 percent over roughly the same period. "And there was really no reason to believe that it wouldn't continue to go down to some base level of 15 or 18 gallons because you had this incredible influx of, obviously, the sodas, but then the New Age beverages, the Snapples, the isotonics, the Gatorades, and then all of this bottled water stuff," Manning says.

According to a survey by Beverage Industry magazine, 1,805 new beverages were introduced in 1991 alone. However, a consumer research study commissioned in 1992 by the United Dairy Industry Association revealed that the proliferation of beverage alternatives wasn't the only factor behind milk's decline. People also cited milk's lack of portability and flavour variety, the belief that milk is not thirst-quenching or refreshing, and the fact that milk is "forgettable" because of low spending on advertising.

Although these research results were useful, it was a different kind of finding that especially caught the eye of Manning and representatives of the CMPB's advertising agency, Goodby Silverstein and Partners in San Francisco. In the minds of consumers, drinking milk is closely tied to the consumption of other types of food, such as cereal and cookies. This perceived link was important because it opened up a completely new direction for a marketing communications campaign. At the time, the dominant advertising strategy for milk around the world was "Milk is good for you." But, as Manning points out, "The problem is, was, remains, that 92 or 93 percent of the people already believed milk was good for you. So what do you have to say? It's white? It comes in cartons? We had no news whatsoever."

The connection between milk and food gave the CMPB something new and different to talk about, but it was only half the glass. The other half—the truly compelling portion of the story—was based on Goodby Silverstein's insight that the time milk was most important to people was when they ran out. "[Consumers] pour their Cheerios, they slice the banana, and they reach in [the refrigerator for] the carton [of milk]. They bring the carton [out], and it's got about two ounces of backwash from their teenagers from the night before. They're out of milk," Manning says. "Milk suddenly becomes very, very important to them. And nothing else wins. You can't take Snapple and put it on there; you can't take orange juice or tea or coffee. Only milk is important at that moment." To help develop the concept of "milk deprivation," a group of consumers was asked to live without milk for one week. They couldn't have milk in their coffee, in their cereal, with meals or desserts, or in any recipes. After seven days without milk, Manning says, they were "insane" because they realised how much they took the beverage for granted. "I keep saying it's like air. You know, we don't walk around [inhaling], saying 'Whoa, good air.' Take it away for about a minute and see how you feel about air. That's kind of how it is with milk deprivation, because without it you realise, 'I can't live without this product'."

Jeff Goodby, a principal with the advertising agency, believed that the best way to execute the milk deprivation idea was not to lecture consumers about keeping enough of the beverage on hand, but to ask them to think about it and answer the question for themselves. This is how "Got milk?" was born.

The campaign was launched in November 1993 and produced spectacular results, both in terms of the attention it garnered among consumers and its impact on consumption. The Los Angeles Times reported that the ads had a "near-cult following." More important, the number of individuals who reported consuming milk at least "several times a week" jumped from 72 percent at the start of the campaign to 78 percent a year later. The total turnaround in first-year sales volume was $31 million, in contrast to the rest of the country, where consumption continued to decline. This shake-up was accomplished on a budget of only $23 million in a product category where total competitive media spending tops $2 billion annually.

In 1995, the CMPB licensed the hugely successful campaign to the National Dairy Board. Television advertisements depicting people in frustrating situations without milk are the keystone of the integrated marketing communications campaign, which also includes billboards, print ads, sales promotions, joint promotions with major brands, and public relations. One popular "Got milk?" advertisement features Oscar the grouch from Sesame Street looking at a big pile of chocolate chip cookies with a more-than-usually disgruntled look on his face. The slogan "Got milk?" appears above his right shoulder. He's obviously unhappy about no milk.

What's next? The key challenge is, how do you nurture "Got milk?" How do you make "Got milk?" stronger and bigger and more influential in people's lives, which is exactly the challenge for any good advertising campaign? There are lots of ideas on the subject. One would be to change the situations in which people haven't got milk. Instead of situations people might usually encounter, such as no milk to go with cereal in the morning, the campaign could use unusual situations. An example might be an airplane pilot who sees a cart with cookies in the aisle behind him and sends the plane into a nose-dive in order to move the cart his way. Of course with this pilot's luck, a passenger opens a lavatory door and stops the cart. Another possibility might be a couple who meet at the refrigerator in search of milk but are distracted by a steamy romantic encounter. Spots such as these would feature humour and sex-both of which are successfully used to sell products. But do they sell milk? And is sex appropriate to use to sell milk, which heavily targets children?

An alternative would be to use celebrities in embarrassing situations where they've not got milk. Perhaps Seinfeld could have his cereal ready and not find milk in the refrigerator; perhaps Kramer, Elaine, or George stops in, opens the fridge and finds-no milk. Or the friends find cereal but no milk. Such situations use humour but avoid sex.

The present ad campaign encourages consumption of milk, primarily at home, which is where 90 percent of milk is consumed. Another advertising objective might be to encourage consumption of milk away from home. Future ads could feature situations in which milk could be used at work or during leisure activities. Such a campaign is a variant on the "It's not just for breakfast anymore" orange juice campaigns. Advertisers try to create the idea that "milk is not just for home use anymore." Spots might show a family that has stopped at a roadside table to enjoy a cookie break but find they've not got milk. Or workers could stop for lunch and find no milk in their lunchboxes or the office refrigerator.

A final possibility would be to replace the "Got milk?" campaign altogether. After all, it's been running for over five years, and consumers may tire of the slogan. Perhaps the campaign is worn out, especially in California, where consumers have had the opportunity to watch it for even longer. Even Nike has replaced the famous "Just do it" slogan in its television advertising. Knowing when to replace an ad campaign is important-advertisers don't want to bore consumers or risk zapping when ads come on during commercial breaks. Consumers are exposed to hundreds of promotional messages every day, and they learn to screen out ads that are overly familiar, to focus instead on the new and unusual. So, although Manning and associates may view the "Got Milk?" campaign as a brand or product that can be cultivated for decades, they may find that they have been too successful—that everyone knows about "Got milk?" and no longer pays close attention to the message.

Questions for Discussion

1. Why has the "Got Milk?" campaign been so successful?

2. What are the current objectives of the "Got Milk?" campaign? What audiences does the campaign target?

3. Would the proposed ads—featuring either unusual situations or celebrities—fit with the campaign's objectives and the target audience?

4. What are the pros and cons of attempting to stimulate milk usage in situations away from the home?

5. Should the "Got Milk?" campaign be replaced? What information would the CMPB and its agency need to make that decision? How could they get this information?

6. Suppose the CMPB decides to replace the campaign and you are in charge of developing a new theme and slogan. Develop at least two new ideas. Be certain to specify the target audiences, campaign objectives, message themes, and appropriate media to use.

Sources

[1] *Got Milk?-California Fluid Milk Processors Advisory Board*, Adweek, August 5, 1996, p. A6.

[2] *Milk Ads Shaking Up Sales*, Supermarket News, August 12, 1996, p. 39.

[3] Jerry Dryer, *Milk's About Face*, Dairy Foods, Feb. 1997, p. 28.

[4] Donna Hemmila, *Award-Winning 'Got Milk?' Ads Promote Healthy Sales*, Power Marketing, July 18-24, 1997, pp. 4A-5A.

[5] Kathy Tyrer, *Goodby's Got More Milk*, Adweek, March 25, 1996, p. 4.

GE: BRINGING GOOD THINGS TO INDUSTRIAL CUSTOMERS

GE's prowess as a consumer goods manufacturer is well known. After all, who has not purchased a GE lightbulb at some point or used a GE appliance? Less well known is GE's strategic importance in the industrial goods markets. Some of those bulbs that light American homes are also used to light American factories. Some of the parts used in GE appliances are also used to build goods with different brand names or are part of the finished goods of other brand-name manufacturers.

In fact, in terms of sales, the industrial market is more important to GE than the consumer market, not just because of greater total sales volume, but because the industrial accounts are larger. Whereas sales of lightbulbs through a grocery chain might be worth tens of thousands of dollars, sales of parts to a manufacturer—even very small, inexpensive parts—might be worth millions.

So, how do all those GE-made bulbs and parts get to industrial users? GE Supply is a major part of the answer. In the United States alone, GE Supply maintains over 120 sales and distribution locations to sell a full line of electrical products, including distribution equipment, transformers, industrial controls, lamps, lighting, wiring devices, motors, drives, silicones, and renewal parts from GE. With yearly sales of $2 billion, GE Supply is an integral part of the GE Company and a national leader in the electrical distribution industry.

GE Supply offers not just goods and parts, but distribution, inventory, and reordering systems as well. The heart of the GE Supply system is its hub-and-spoke warehousing/distribution system. Hub and spoke, the industry's first "just in time" inventory control system, permits the company to ship direct to customers while reducing costly inventory overhead at customer sites. It is flexible and state-of-the-art, allowing overnight access to a broad range of electrical products for customers. Five hubs-in New York, Texas, California (2), and Illinois-support more than 50 branches.

GE Supply sells more than just parts. It also sells high-value-added services through GE Support Services (GESS). In general, GESS provides tailored distribution solutions and customer support for spare parts and components of industrial products. GESS can advise on inventory (what stocks to maintain) and order/reorder levels that will meet production needs without incurring high inventory costs. It will not only customise a solution for a firm, it will also implement the solution.

Through OASIS (On-site Acquisition and Stock Inventory System), GE Supply can help firms reduce acquisition costs, reduce up-front inventory requirements, minimise shortages and overruns, and feel confident that they will have all the materials they need when they need them. This "just-in-time" inventory system can be handled by a PC with a 486 processor (50 MHz), 8MB RAM, fax modem, scanner, and light pen. It includes a comprehensive bar coding system, automated online reordering, summary billing, and usage reporting. Anyone of GE Supply's specialists will be glad to help a customer install and use this system.

How do customers order from GE Supply? Through Electronic Data Interchange, customers can send or receive electronic requests for quotes, purchase order changes, order status, or invoice and payment. There are two routes for ordering goods. First, there's Quick Link, a Window-based client server procurement system that allows customers to place orders directly into GE Supply's order, ship, and bill system. Customers can also determine the availability of parts and prices. A second route is through Supply Net, a Web-based procurement system that gives full access to the GE Supply system from an Internet browser. It allows customers to place orders directly into the system, and provides inventory availability information and pricing.

In addition to parts and GESS, GE Supply also offers a wide range of customised services to meet customer's energy needs, from facility energy audits and product workshops to access to energy specialists and project financing (through GE Capital, of course). Once the audit has been completed, GE Supply can meet many of the energy-saving lighting and electrical needs indicated by the energy audit. Reducing customers' energy needs can improve cash flow by reducing operating and maintenance costs.

To handle the sales of products and services, GE Supply offers two types of sales arrangements. First, it maintains the Customer Service Center to provide lower-volume customers with a single source of contact and with services from a staff of highly trained professional sales representatives. Accessed through a toll-free number, the Center provides smaller customers with the same products and services as larger customers. Second, GE Supply maintains a national account management program aimed at large, multi-location customers. For firms in this category, GE Supply will appoint a national account program manager, whose function is to ensure consistent, thorough, and efficient service. This arrangement is highly beneficial to both parties: Customers can contact one person for all their needs instead of dealing with multiple sales representatives from each GE division. The arrangement also enables GE Supply to establish ongoing relationships with customer firms. By handling all of a customer's parts and electrical needs, GE Supply can spot opportunities to reduce inventories or change order cycles or sizes in order to save the customer money.

The national account project manager is not alone in servicing customers. Depending on the customer's needs, the project manager will put together a sales team that may consist of technical specialists, such as engineers who are familiar with the customer's type of business; specialists who can help with computerised inventory and ordering systems; and distribution specialists who can determine the most efficient supply sources and routes to get goods to the customer. In addition, the team can call on the marketing, purchasing, and finance resources of other GE divisions.

Building this sort of selling relationship requires top-notch people. "All we can do is bet on the people whom we pick," says General Electric CEO Jack Welch. This is not an empty claim-Welch personally interviews all candidates for the top 500 jobs at GE. With that sort of example of demanding leadership, you can be certain that GE Supply tries to attract the best and brightest people to be customer service and national account project managers.

This is especially true of Kathleen Carroll Mullen, a national account project manager. With her mechanical engineering degree, she has the technical knowledge to understand a customer firm's production process and to determine how to meet its needs. With her aggressive though pleasant personality, and with her personal desire for change and challenge rather than slogging through the day at a desk job, she is ideally suited for a selling position with GE Supply. She knows that she cannot wait for customers to ask for a supplier through the formal Request for Quote (RFQ) process. She must talk to customers regularly, keep up with their operations and anticipate the sorts of products and services they are likely to need as they grow and expand.

Listening is a key requirement of Kathleen's job. By listening, she learns a lot about a customer-who's involved in the purchase decision, what these people are thinking about, what sorts of people they are, and what affects their decisions. Some customers are very rational and may want a hard dollars-and-no-nonsense approach. Others may be more interested in the relationship side of the sale. Good sales representatives know the personalities of the people in customer firms. They customise not only the product and services side of the sale, but also the approach, presentation, and closing side. As Kathleen Mullen says, "You have to know when the customer is ready to close-not when you want to close."

One of GE Supply's bigger recent customers is AlliedSignal, a conglomerate with holdings in the aerospace and automotive products industries, chemicals, fibres, plastics, and advanced materials. It was created by a 1985 merger of the Allied Corporation-a chemical and dye company founded in 1920-and The Signal Companies-a gasoline and oil drilling company in Texas. Through its purchase of Bendix Corporation, Allied entered the automotive products industry and also gained entry to the aerospace industry. Since then, AlliedSignal has further increased the number of automotive products that it sells.

Currently, AlliedSignal's automotive division sells Bendix and Jurid friction materials, FRAM oil/air/transmission/fuel filters, Autolite spark plugs/oxygen sensors/ignition wires, and Garrett turbochargers. It is the world's largest producer of truck brakes and friction materials, the world's leading manufacturer of turbochargers and branded oil/air filters, number two in spark plugs, and a major manufacturer of air bags and seat belt systems.

AlliedSignal is an aggressive company. It has a goal of increasing sales revenues annually by 8 percent by introducing new products, globalisation (manufacturing and selling outside the United States), and buying firms whose product lines enhance those of AlliedSignal. The company is committed to Total Quality Management and has trained all of its executive and line employees in Total Quality Leadership. Currently, it plans a second Total Quality Leadership program in order to provide the very best customer service.

What may be of more interest to Kathleen Mullen is that AlliedSignal has reduced its number of suppliers from 10,000 to 3,000 through its Materials Management program. It gives these preferred suppliers a greater volume of business if they can produce better quality, lower prices, and improved productivity.

AlliedSignal has seven business principles: (1) satisfy customers; (2) maintain the highest level of ethical conduct; (3) maximise the potential of all employees; (4) build efficient and effective work teams; (5) focus on speed of innovation in reducing process and cycle times; (6) focus on innovation and change; and (7) encourage high expectations, set ambitious goals, and meet its financial and other commitments.

Selling to AlliedSignal would be difficult. This would be a demanding customer with high expectations. However, it could also be a very, very lucrative customer. AlliedSignal is looking for partnerships and GE Supply is looking for relationships. It might be a perfect match, but it will take a lot of work and preparation to get this partnership off the ground.

Questions for Discussion

Suppose you were advising Kathleen Carroll Mullen as she prepares for a sales call on the purchasing people at the automotive division of AlliedSignal. How would you advise her on the following questions?

1. How should Kathleen handle the pre-approach step? The approach step?

2. Assume that Kathleen is preparing for the first meeting with AlliedSignal automotive division buyers. What do the AlliedSignal buyers want to hear about in this first meeting? What is Kathleen selling to AlliedSignal's automotive division? What should be her goal at this first meeting? What information should she put into her presentation?

3. How will the character of AlliedSignal affect Kathleen's presentation?

4. Would you advise Kathleen differently if GE Supply were transaction-oriented rather than relationship-oriented?

*This situation of Kathleen Carroll Mullen selling to the automotive division at AlliedSignal is hypothetical and for educational purposes only.

Sources

[1] Anne Fisher, *The World's Most Admired Companies*, Fortune, October 27, 1997, pp. 220-240

[2] Information from the GE and AlliedSignal Web sites (www.ge.com and www.allied.com).

MOUNTAIN TRAVEL SOBEK: ANYWHERE IN THE WORLD

Would you like to trek in Nepal? Raft down rivers in Chile? Walk the Great Wall of China? Inspect icebergs and penguins in the Antarctic-up close? If you answered yes, you're not alone. More than seven million Americans engage in adventure travel annually, making it the fastest growing form of travel (30 percent annual growth). Mountain Travel Sobek (M-T-S) is the premier adventure-travel firm, offering trips to seven continents. It was formed in 1991 when the two most venerable firms in adventure travel, Mountain Travel and Sobek Expeditions, joined operations. Mountain Travel, founded by Leo Le Bon, Allen Steck, and Barry Bishop, specialised in trekking and mountain expeditions. It was the first company to offer treks to Everest Base Camp, walking safaris in East Africa, expeditions to Kilimanjaro in Africa and Mt. Anyemaquen in China, and cross-country ski expeditions to the South Pole.

Sobek Expeditions was founded by two river rafters from Bethesda, Maryland-Richard Bangs and John Yost. Their last fling before entering the working world was a rafting trip on the Awash, a little-known and unrun African river. They recruited clients to pay for the trip and, upon successfully completing the adventure, formed Sobek, named for the Egyptian crocodile god who seemed to have guided them through the croc-infested waters of the Awash. Sobek went on to lead the first descents of 35 rivers around the world, including the Bio-Bio (Chile), Bashkaus (Russia), Blue Nile (Ethiopia), and Tatshenshini (Alaska). During the 1980s, both Mountain Travel and Sobek prospered. Mountain Travel increased its annual departures by 50 percent to 478, and Sobek upped its departures by 70 percent to 415. Annual revenues climbed to more than $7 million for Mountain Travel and to $5 million for Sobek. However, this success disguised deteriorating profitability resulting from the offering of less profitable trips. With the help of Hap Klopp, former owner of North Face, the companies merged. The new company has improved profitability by combining trekking and rafting trips to the same parts of the world and by eliminating 180 money-losing trips to 100 destinations.

What is it like to take an M-T-S trip? If you envision hardship, cold food, and primitive facilities, forget it. Accommodations are actually quite pleasant, with comfortable cabins, spacious tents, and delicious food prepared by local chefs. What sets M-T-S trips apart is the high-quality amenities, staff who are knowledgeable about local conditions and cultures, and the small size of groups, which are limited to 15 or fewer. But all this doesn't come cheaply. Trips through the Northeast passage cost more than $10,000, and safaris in Africa can cost more than $4,500. However, not all M T-S trips are this expensive. A trip to the Galapagos may cost less than $3,000, and kayaking in the Sea of Cortez costs only about

$1,500. Who takes these trips? It's mostly men and women aged 30 to 60. However, the average age of adventure travellers is likely to rise in the future. The population of Americans 55 years old and older will increase from 53 million in 1990 to 75 million by 2010. Older people have greater buying power, more leisure time, and, lately, a greater inclination to explore. Close to 50 percent of Mountain Travel Sobek's business comes from seniors. In "soft" adventure travel, the army jeeps of the past have been replaced by more comfortable Land Rovers and minivans.

Not only is M-T-S an innovator in adventure travel, it is also an innovator in promoting adventure travel. In 1993, the firm offered The Adventure Disc, an interactive photo CD on which you could hear the calls of wildlife, listen to voices of explorers such as Edmund Hillary, look at hundreds of spectacular photos of the world's wonders, and view shots of M-T-S trips. In 1994, the company developed The Traveller, an interactive CD-ROM catalogue for the Macintosh and Windows systems produced by Magellan Systems.

These efforts are dwarfed by M-T-S's award-winning Website (mtsobek.com), which has received substantial praise: "Aims to take the worry-but not the excitement-out of adventure travel" (Magellan Internet Guide); "exceptional presentation and depth of content" (Starting Point); "rich content, high aesthetic merit, and 'techno smartness'" (Net Magazine); "opportunities to make your own unique dreams come true by travelling with us to exotic locations, both online and off" (The Best of Europe Online); "the best home page design there is" (WEB 500).

So, what's on this home page? What is the great design? Why is it "techno smart"? First, the site offers fantastic photos taken by guides and travellers on actual M-T-S trips. It's worth a visit just to see the photos in all their color, variety, and scope. The site offers pictures of cheetahs sleeping in trees, close-ups of lions, millions of penguins, and landscapes that range from dramatic shots of deserts and soaring mountain peaks to hazy views of gardens in bloom. The color, clarity, and appeal of the photos create a longing to be there—to experience the sights, the sounds, and colors of one of these trips. How can you not want to see zebras close up, descend runs of clear river waters splashing through lush countrysides, or glide across the frozen tundra in a dogsled. To see it is to want to be there.

The site is highly interactive. Send one of your friends an electronic postcard, there are dozens to choose from. All you need is your and the recipient's e-mail addresses. Without spending a cent, you can reach out to touch someone and write lots as well. In the journals section, you can read stories of trips written by travellers and guides who have trekked, sailed, driven, or bicycled with M-T-S through the Serengeti desert, the New Guinea rain forest, the Andes mountains, the Pacific ocean, or the mountain passes of the Alps. Imagine hiking in Peru with Don Harrison. Each day we cross a pass of 15 or 16 thousand feet. Each night we make camp at 12 or 13 thousand feet. The hiking is, as Mountain Travel promised, strenuous. But our exertions bear sweet fruit! -the Andean peaks, the crystalline lakes, the waterfalls, the occasional lush green meadow, the sense of achievement and exhilaration that flow from awareness of our growing physical endurance.

Join other travellers on the bulletin board discussing trips already taken and asking questions about trips to come. This is not like talking to your travel agent. These people have paid for and taken M-T-S trips, and you'll get the unvarnished truth from them, usually accompanied by glowing recommendations. If you don't want to ask questions of your own or don't know what to ask, check out the FAQs—frequently asked questions. The answers to any question you might have-whether it's how strenuous a trip is, what clothes to take, what sights you'll see, the value of the trip-are available in one of these two places. Had your appetite whetted? Want to find out what trips are available? Click on "World Map," then on the part of the world you're interested in, and you can access all the trips there. Trips are listed by activities and destinations. If you want to go to Costa Rica, click on Latin America, where you'll find sea kayaking, rafting, and rain forest hikes, all in just one trip to one country. By looking to the left of the trip description, you can find times of departure, the trip rating, types of accommodations, and cost. Note that the trip may include as few as six people-a real plus for many travellers.

Ready to go? Call M-T-S at 1-888-MTSOBEK or use the handy booking service at the Web site. It can't get much easier than that. If you don't care where you go, you can select adventures randomly. If you have specific things you'd like to do on a trip, you can use the custom search. Maybe you're seeking a ten-day trip to see wildlife in Africa or to bicycle around Europe. It's easy to follow the instructions to locate just the trip you want or to see if M-T-S would consider designing and offering a custom trip for you and your friends. Want to know more about the company and what it's up to? You can check the "About Us" section to find a letter from M-T-S President Richard Weiss or read the latest news from M-T-S. If you want to know more about the guides to whom you might be entrusting your well-being, you can read about trip leaders. Finally, if you just don't know much about using Internet sites, you can click on the "Help," and find out how to make the site work for you-no matter how computer literate or illiterate you are.

Obviously, M-T-S has invested a lot in its Website. Beyond the wealth of written information, the abundance of pictures at the site increase the cost. Some might question whether the Website is a wise investment for M-T-S. After all, many travel services haven't found the Internet to be particularly well suited for selling expensive travel plans. Web travel shoppers seem to be more interested in comparing prices. Let's face it-an M-T-S trip isn't cheap, and comparing prices for adventure travel can be difficult. It's all a matter of spirit. You have to want to get out and see places, to experience the culture, to feel the exhilaration that Don Harrison felt at 15,000 feet. Above all, you have to want something out of the ordinary-not just travel, an adventure!

Questions for Discussion

1. Do Mountain Travel Sobek's target markets match the profile of typical Internet users?

2. How does M-T-S "create enough value and excitement to get consumers to come to the site, stay around, and come back again"?

3. How well does M-T-S score on exploiting the opportunities of online marketing to provide benefits to consumers? Compare the benefits offered to consumers by the M-T-S Website to those listed in the chapter.

4. How well is M-T-S using its Website to build relationships with consumers?

5. Compare the use of a Website to catalogues for selling trips. What benefits does each offer to M-T-S? How can they be used together? Is adventure travel the sort of product that should or could be sold successfully over the Internet?

6. Ask five of your friends to visit the M-T-S Website, and get feedback from them. Based on this feedback, assuming that your friends are typical of the adventure trip market, provide an overall evaluation of the M-T-S site. Do the results justify the money and time it costs M-T-S to create and maintain this site?

Sources

[1] *Logging On: Internet Usage Is Widespread*, Travel Weekly, August 12, 1996, pp. 4-5.

[2] *Mountain Travel Sobek Puts Clients in the Musher's Seat*, Travel Weekly, January 20, 1997, p. 55.

[3] James M. Clash, *Survivalists*, Forbes, November 22, 1993, pp. 154-156.

[4] Isae Wada, *Agency Sets Out on Virtual Adventure*, Travel Weekly, November 13, 1995, p 45-46.

[5] Jeffery D. Zbar, *More Than a Cool Bus Ride Needed to Sway Seniors*, Advertising Age, June 27, 1994, pp. 34-37.

[6] Information from the M-T-S Web site.

NIVEA: SOFTENING AND STANDARDISING GLOBAL MARKETS

Just as healthy skin requires the proper pH balance to flourish, a strong global brand must find the right balance between marketing efforts that build consistency in overall worldwide positioning and the need to appeal to specific geographic and cultural markets. Beiersdorf (BDF), the German manufacturer of Nivea skin care products, seems to have mastered that balancing act with all the skill of an Olympic gymnast. Introduced in 1912, Nivea Creme was a unique water-in-oil emulsion, a formulation that set it apart from the fat-only creams available at the time. The brand's positioning also made it distinct from other products on the market: It was a multipurpose cream sold at a price that made it available to the masses, rather than to only the upper-class women who were the competition's target market.

Over the years, Nivea's positioning strategy has remained as simple and steadfast as the now-familiar blue-and-white package. Despite all the technological developments the company has introduced in skin care products, and all the markets it has sold in, Nivea's marketing always focuses on key brand benefits-high quality, reasonable price, straightforward approach, and mild skin care. This commitment to the mainstream market and focus on multipurpose applications means that every product introduced under the Nivea name has to conform to guidelines which ensure that everyone working on the brand around the world knows what it stands for. Nivea's marketing strategy is well stated by Rolf Kunish, chairman of the Beiersdorf Group: "The strategy of concentration on exploiting market potentials and regional growth opportunities is to be continued. The same applies to moves into new market segments and to increased investment in research and development."

Exploiting market potentials means constantly introducing new products that meet current market needs and the needs of newly targeted market segments. One example from the past is Nivea's emphasis on health and active lifestyles as more women went to work in the 1920s. Others include the introduction of sunscreen, skin protection, and tanning products to match the more active, outdoor lifestyles in vogue from the 1960s to today; plus products for every skin type and need. To meet the needs of new market segments, Nivea expanded its product lines to include children and men. All these new products were guided by the Nivea standards: each product must meet a basic need, be simple and uncomplicated, not offer to solve only one specific problem, be a quality leader, and be priced such that consumers perceive a balanced cost-benefit relationship.

BDF's new product strategy was honed in the 1970s when competitive challenges prompted the company to take steps to revitalise the brand. It used a two-pronged approach. First, to counteract perceptions that Nivea had an older, less dynamic image, the company for the first time described specific product benefits in its advertising. Before this, advertising had focused on the variety of settings in which each product could be used. Second, BDF introduced additional products that would leverage the recognition and reputation of the Nivea name in growing segments of the market. These are sub-brands, such as Nivea Shower and Bath, Nivea for Men, Nivea Sun, Nivea Hair Care, Nivea Body, Nivea Visage, and the recently introduced Nivea Baby.

During the 1980s, new products were supported by separate ad campaigns that helped build individual personalities and associations for each sub-brand, while linking them to each other and to Nivea Creme through the use of the word "care" in all headlines. The sub-brands helped establish Nivea as a broad skin and personal care brand, but their success was both pleasing and a problem for BDF. The company worried that the proliferation of products bearing the Nivea name might leave consumers confused about what the brand represented, and that the image of Nivea Creme, the heart of the brand, might be weakened or diluted. After conducting studies, the company embarked on a marketing strategy that would deliver on the concept of the "universality" of Nivea products while reinforcing the image of the brand as a skin care specialist. All ads for the core brand, Nivea Creme, had to incorporate its underlying values of timelessness and agelessness, motherhood and a happy family, honesty and trustworthiness, and the product benefits of mildness and quality. Ads for the sub-brands had to reflect elements of these values as well as those that were uniquely their own.

In 1990 BDF internationalised its brands by creating a worldwide name for each product category and implementing common packaging on a global basis. Moreover, all ads, regardless of the country in which they ran, had to evoke a common emotion, use the same typeface, incorporate the same kinds of people, and use a uniform Nivea logo. The result is a highly standardized approach to global marketing. Rather than focusing on the individual differences among peoples around the globe, the firm focuses on the similarities. After all, as one company official notes, all people have skin and many people have the same needs and ideas. This leads to a direct approach and a high degree of consistency.

When a firm operates in as many markets as BDF, consistency, simplicity, and focus on the same benefits not only create a universal brand image, they also reduce headaches. Many fewer marketing decisions have to be made. Standardized advertising campaigns need be adapted only slightly by translation into the local language. Because the costs can be spread around the globe, it's much less expensive to run a single global campaign rather than many separate regional ones. And marketing control is much simpler and easier with a standardized program. Packaging costs are reduced and product recognition is very high when people encounter the product in other countries and cultural situations.

The second element of the BDF strategy is exploiting regional growth opportunities. Doing so, however, may necessitate some adjustments to the standardized approach. Because Nivea Creme is a European product, its appeal and marketing approach can be very similar in many parts of the globe. The United States, Canada, Latin America, and South America were all populated by European settlers. This produces some commonality in cultural background and light skin type, with the result that many products developed for the German market can be sold in these markets with little or no product or marketing adaptation. A focus on healthy, glowing skin will sell cosmetics in nearly all these markets. Of course, the company might use darker-haired models with more olive complexions in the Latin and South American markets. And it might develop tailored sub-brands and programs for important sub-segments of all these markets. However, as Nivea moves further away from this common European cultural base, its products may be less well suited to the market. This is particularly true in African nations, where a majority of people have much darker skin and may require different sorts of moisturisers and sunscreen products. In between the European and African markets are the Asian markets, which are characterized by yellow and frequently more pale complexions. Although Nivea sells well in some Asian markets, such as Indonesia and Thailand, it sells less well in Japan. The difference in sales is attributable to both market and cultural conditions.

In the past, Japanese markets were strongly protected and there was relatively little competition from non-domestic manufacturers. Unfortunately for Japanese merchants, the resulting high prices provided a strong lure to foreign producers. When BDF first entered the Japanese market, it was highly successful. But as Japanese markets have opened up, competition has increased, price maintenance has been abolished, and prices have fallen. As a result, BDF has reduced the number of products sold there, and focused on the more profitable ones.

There are cultural differences between markets such as Germany, the United States, and Japan. Germany and the United States are classified as "low-context countries," which means that ads should state explicitly what the product will do. Japan, in contrast, is a "high-context" country in which product claims do not need to be stated explicitly. Rather, because Japanese consumers want to form relationships with companies, the company itself should be prominently featured in advertising. If the company is worthy of consideration, then the quality of its products is assumed to be high. Thus, an advertising campaign prepared for Germany requires more than just a little tweaking in order to promote products successfully in Japan.

All these differences argue for more adaptation of Nivea products and marketing to match cultural and market differences outside Germany and the European market. However, as economies develop, they tend to acquire many of the same tastes as developed economies. An example is Russia, where men—especially younger men—are beginning to spend more on cosmetics. They are buying many of the same brands as their Western European counterparts—Gillette, Nivea for Men, Old Spice, and a few designer brands such as Christian Dior, Armani, Boss Lancome, Aramis, Guy Laroche, Gucci, and Paco Rabanne. Price is not the crucial variable in the purchase decision—men are buying based on product characteristics such as fragrance and brand awareness. For companies such as Nivea and Gillette, which are willing to spend on advertising, the market seems quite responsive. The bottom line is the increasing homogenization that argues against customisation of products for specific markets. Speaking of bottom lines, Beiersdorf has done very well with its own. Total sales for Beiersdorf's cosmetics business grew at 5.7 percent in 1996, despite decreased sales of the company's higher priced Labella and Atrix lines and lower sales in Japan. The Nivea line grew by 13.3 percent, far outpacing the more expensive cosmetics and skin care products. However, growth around the world has been uneven. Although BDF's brands experienced double-digit growth in Eastern Europe, Scandinavia, Southern Europe, and South America, sales growth within Germany and some Northern European countries has been much lower due to the difficult economic situation. Nivea held its own in the United States, but grew by 36.3 percent in Mexico. Despite strong growth in Thailand and Indonesia, sales in Asia and Australia fell by 10.4 percent, affected by the downward trend in Japan and China. Compounding the Japanese losses are unfavourable exchange rates between the yen and the mark, which reduced earnings even further. Even so, although the overall global picture for Beiersdorf is quite good, it's still just a little fuzzy in some parts of the world.

Questions for Discussion

1. How do economic, legal, and cultural factors affect the worldwide marketing of Nivea products?

2. Describe Beiersdorf's product and promotion strategies for Nivea. Is BDF engaging in product adaptation, dual adaptation, or something else? What are the arguments for and against this strategy?

3. Would you say that Beiersdorf engages in global rather than international marketing? Explain your answer.

4. Find a Nivea ad and try to adapt it for the Japanese market.

5. From a marketing viewpoint, is the homogenization of global markets good or bad? From a national viewpoint, is this homogenization good or bad?

6. Should Beiersdorf continue with its fairly rigid standardized marketing strategy?

Sources

[1] *Men's Lines Grow in Russia*, Cosmetics International, March 25, 1997, p. 2.

[2] *Beiersdorf Beauty Sales Get a Boost from Nivea*, Womens' Wear Daily, March 1, 1996, p. 11.

[3] *Sales Indicate Global Direction of Beiersdorf*, Cosmetics International, July 10, 1997, p. 12.

[4] *Beiersdorf Increases Profits as Nivea Sees Continued Success*, Cosmetics International, June 25, 1996, pp. 12-14.

[5] Melissa Drier, *Beiersdorf's Growth Bolstered by Nivea*, Women Wear Daily, February 28, 1997, pp. 11.

[6] Information from the Nivea web site (`www.nivea.com`).

Sources:

APPENDIX - B
GLOSSARY

A

✳ **AAA:** American Association of Advertising Agencies.

✳ **ABC:** Audit Bureau of Circulation. An organization that conducts audits of magazine and newspaper circulation numbers.

✳ **Above the Fold:** Material, such as an ad, is appearing above the fold in a broadsheet newspaper. While the meaning has been lost, this term has been carried over into the Internet marketing. In that context it means an ad that appears on the screen when a Web page first appears, without the need for the viewer to scroll down to see it. Because browser screen sizes vary a standard of 800 pixels wide by 600 high is usually assumed (thus, "above the fold" means in the first 600 pixels), however this standard will likely change as higher resolutions become the norm.

✳ **Absorption Pricing:** The setting of a product price such that it includes both the variable cost of making each item plus an appropriate portion of the fixed costs incurred by the company.

✳ **Access:** Access to library materials and services, on one dimension, is represented in the location of physical facilities. Because libraries are travelled—to outlets, marketing location theories can be applied successfully to library sitting. (Wood and Koontz).

✳ **Accordian Insert:** An ad insert that has been folded like an accordion

✳ **Account Executive:** The advertising agency employee who is responsible for maintaining the relationship between the agency and the client.

* **Accountability:** Libraries like private sector businesses are increasingly called upon to make all units accountable for results. Growing funds are needed for technology as opposed to only books. Funders often cut the library budget first, in favour of other agencies such as police and fire or other seemingly, more necessary agencies. Libraries are developing better performance measures within the present day control systems to offer better accountability. (Wood and Koontz).

* **Acculturation:** The process by which people in one culture or subculture learn to understand and adapt to the norms, values, life styles and behaviours of people in another culture or subcultures. For example, acculturation is the process by which a recent immigrant learns the way of life of the new country. Library services and materials facilitate this process.

* **Acquisitions Value:** The users' perception of the relative worth of a product or service to them. Formally defined as the subjectively weighted difference between the most a buyer would be willing to pay for the product or service, less the actual price of the item. Time user must spend to 'acquire' is often used as a surrogate for 'relative worth or price paid,' in library research. For example, a user might be willing to expend drive time and a brief time in the library to check out a best seller, but not wait two weeks for a copy to be returned.

* **Activities, Interests, and Opinions (AIO):** A measurable series of psychographic (as opposed to demographic) variables involving the interests and beliefs of users. Note, because psychographics are usually expensive to gather, yet offer a more precise profile of users, demographic variables are usually relied upon.

* **Adjacency:** A local television commercial spot that is purchased in a time period that usually is adjacent to a network program.

* **Adopter Categories:** Persons or agencies that adopt an innovation are often classified into five groups according to the sequence of their adoption of it. (To illustrate this think of individual use of the Internet within the library, and for an agency, libraries that offer Internet access to the general public. 1) Innovators (first 2-5%); 2) Early adopters (10-15%)' 3) Early majority (next 35%); 4) Late majority (next 35%); 5) Laggards (final 5-10%). This is important when considering how long it may take for the general public to 'adopt' a product or service.

* **Advertising:** Sponsored mass communications. The placement and purchase of announcements and persuasive messages in time or space in any of the mass media by business firms, nonprofit organisations. This has not been a traditional method

for libraries of informing the public, but rather public service announcements, which are placed at no cost, are the norm.

✳ **Advertising Allowance:** Money a manufacturer gives to another member of the distribution channel (wholesaler, distributor, sales representative, affiliate, value added reseller, retailer, etc.) for the purpose of advertising the manufacturer's product, service or brand.

✳ **Advertising Medium:** The collection of all advertising vehicles of a particular type. For example television is an advertising medium, newspapers is another, etc.

✳ **Advertising Speciality:** A product (such as a T-shirt, baseball cap, pen, paper weight, etc.) displaying a logo or other promotional image. Sometimes jocularly (or occasionally disparagingly) referred to as "trinkets and trash." (Synonym: Logo Merchandise.)

✳ **Advertising Substantiation:** A (US) Federal Trade Commission regulatory program that requires advertisements to provide documented support of the claims made in advertisements.

✳ **Advertising Vehicle:** The specific entity into which an advertisement is placed.

✳ **Advertorial:** A print or Web advertisement designed to look like a news story. The television or radio equivalent is known as an "infomercial".

✳ **Advocacy Advertising:** Advertising that promotes a political view, social cause, controversial issue or other point of view rather than a product, service or organization.

✳ **Aggregation:** A concept of market segmentation that assumes that most consumers are alike. A library of the past had an 'opening day' collection of materials that could be found in most towns and cities. Today's libraries are more aware of considering the unique needs of individuals in the market area.

✳ **Attitude:** A person's enduring favourable or unfavourable evaluation, emotional feeling, and action tendencies toward some object or idea.

✳ **Augmented Product:** A product that includes features that go beyond consumer expectations and differences and differentiate the product from competitors.

✳ **Average Cost:** The cost per unit at a given level of production, it is equal to total costs divided by production.

✳ **Back Matter:** (Also called "end matter.") Items placed after the main body of a document. Examples of back matter include appendices and indices.

✳ **Backgrounder:** A document containing background information about a product, company, service or event.

✳ **Banner Ad:** On the Web, a standard advertisement (either static or animated) that normally, although not necessarily, appears near the top of a Web page. The term is generally taken to mean a particular size ad (industry standard: 468 x 60 pixels) rather than placement on the page.

✳ **Barrier to Entry:** A hurdle that a new competitor would have to overcome in order to enter the market for a particular product class. For example, a patent that locks up an entire product class is an extremely high barrier to entry. It can only be overcome if a substitute product can be developed without breaking the patent. Patents aren't the only barriers to entry, requirements for the investment extremely high upfront capital costs or the need for expert skills that are in very short supply would also be barriers to entry. Likewise, if it is a mature market and customers must incur high costs to switch from their existing supplier to a new one, this too would be a high barrier. These are only a few examples of barriers to entry. Others exist.

✳ **Backward Invention:** Reintroducing earlier product forms that can be well adapted to a foreign country's needs.

✳ **Belly Band Advertising:** Advertising that is printed on a band (of any width up to the dimension of the publication) wrapped around a newspaper or magazine. This wrapper is designed such that the reader cannot read the publication until he or she removes the wrapper.

✳ **Basic Product:** What specifically the actual product is.

✳ **Belief:** A descriptive thought that a person holds about something

✳ **Below-the-line:** Below-the-Line Advertising - all advertising communications where no commission is payable, outside the five major media - the press, television, radio, cinema and outdoors; below-the-line includes direct mail, print such as sales literature and catalogues, sponsorship, merchandising, exhibitions, etc. A card inserted into a publication that allows readers to request information from one or more of a group of companies listed on the card.

✳ **Bleed:** Ads, illustrations or photographic images printed so as to run to the edge of the page (after trimming if the page is trimmed).

✳ **Blind Ad:** An advertisement that does not identify the advertiser, but provides a box number for replies.

✳ **Blocking Chart:** A graph of a planned media schedule.

✳ **Blow-In Card:** A printed card "blown" into a publication and, therefore, loose rather than bound to the publication.

✳ **Blue line Proof:** A one-color print typically used as a final check (other than to check colors) of the film that will be used to create a print piece.

✳ **Body Copy:** The main text of any marketing communications vehicle.

✳ **Boilerplate:** Pre-written, standardized copy used whenever a particular marketing communication requirement arises. It may be written to adhere to legal or company standards. It may also be used to eliminate the need for original writing when a specific communication requirement is likely to arise frequently.

✳ **Brand Awareness:** Consumer's ability to identify the brand under different conditions, as reflected by their brand recognition or recall performance.

✳ **Brand Development Index (BDI):** The index of brand sales to category sales.

✳ **Brand Equity:** The added value endowed to products and services.

✳ **Brand Elements:** Those trademarks devices that serve to identify and differentiate the brand such as brand name, logo, or character.

✳ **Brand Line:** All products, original as well as line and category extensions, sold under a particular brand name.

✳ **Brand Mix:** The set of all brands lines that a particular seller makes available to buyers.

✳ **Brand Promise:** The marketer's vision of what the brand must be and do for consumers.

✳ **Branded Entertainment:** Using sports, music, arts, or other entertainment activities to build brand equity.

✳ **Branding:** Endowing products and services with the power of a brand.

✳ **Brick-and-Click:** Existing companies that have added an online site for information and e-commerce.

✳ **Business Market:** All the organization that acquire goods and services used in the production of other products or services that are sold, rented, or supplied to others.

✳ **Call to Action:** A statement, usually at the end of a marketing piece, encouraging the reader/viewer/listener to take the action that is the objective of the piece. This action may be buying the company's product or service, or simply taking the next step in the sales cycle, such as arrange a product demonstration.

✳ **Callout:** A line of text beside, above or below a photograph or illustration. It typically highlights a detail in the graphic, verbalises the analogy implied by the graphic or emphasises the message delivered through the graphic.

✳ **CAN-SPAM Act:** A (United States) law with a number of provisions that restricts the use of unsolicited emailing for commercial purposes. Under this act, there are a number of stipulations that, to avoid breaking the law must be adhered to when sending unsolicited commercial email messages. Fines for any contraventions of this law can be quite severe so you should review the act before undertaking any email marketing campaigns.

✳ **Cannibalisation:** An action, such as the launch of a product that is competitive with or a substitute for another of the same company's products that lessens the revenue of one of a company's products. One reason why a company might undertake an action that cannibalises the sales of one of its products is, "if you don't cannibalise yourself, someone else will do it for you." Multiple similar products with somewhat different features that appeal to different market segments, even if there is some crossover from one segment to segments already addressed by one of the company's other products, are likely to, in total, capture a larger share of the broader market and, possibly, block competitors' entry into the targeted segments.

* **Car Card:** An advertisement placed in public transit (bus, subway, trolley, etc.) A collection of post card size advertisements, each promoting a different product, service, brand, organization or event, distributed as a group. The post card is usually pre-addressed, and often postage-paid, to be mailed back to the advertiser to request more information place an order, register for an event, etc.

* **Card Rate:** The rate for advertising as appears on the media outlet's rate card. Discounts against this rate may be available depending on volume purchased and current supply and demand.

* **Center Spread:** An advertisement appearing as a single printed sheet running across both facing pages at the centre of a publication. This is considered favourable placement both because it is a single, unbroken sheet flowing across two pages and because the publication tends to naturally fall open at the centre spread.

* **Channel Marketing:** Active management of a sales channel from a marketing perspective, with the aim of making that channel attractive, customer friendly and efficient. Meaning: marketing communication, product marketing and e.g. buying incentives.

* **Cheshire Label:** Paper specially designed to allow name and address labels to be mechanically affixed to individual mailing pieces, thus allowing the process to be automated.

* **Classified Advertising:** Print or Web advertising that is classified as to the product or service offered. Classified advertising typically, but not necessarily, contains only text, not graphics.

* **Cleansing:** In direct marketing, the removal or revision of a name and/or its related data on a customer/prospect list. This done to correct errors (although they might not have originally been an error, such as an old address on file after someone moves), remove duplicate entries on the list or improve the quality of the list data in any other way.

* **Click-Through:** This is a Web term. A click-through is counted if a viewer clicks on a Web page ad, thereby triggering the link assigned to it.

* **Click-Through Rate:** The number of times a Web page ad is clicked on as a percentage of the number of times the ad is displayed.

* **Closing Date:** The final date by which artwork, video or audio material must be received by the media outlet for it to appear in the desired issue or time slot.

* **Customer Churn:** High customer defection.

* **Customer Consulting:** Data, information systems, and advice services that the seller offers to buyers.

* **Customer Lifetime Value:** The net present value of the stream of future profits expected over the customer's lifetime purchases.

* **Customer Perceived Value:** The difference between the prospective customers' evaluation of all the benefits and all the costs of an offering and the perceived alternatives.

* **Customer Profitability Analysis:** A means of assessing and ranking customer profitability through accounting techniques such as Activity Based Costing (ABC).

* **Customer Training:** Training the customer's employees to use the vendors' equipment properly and efficiently.

* **Customer Value Analysis:** Report of the company's strengths and weaknesses relative to various competitors.

* **Customerisation:** Combination of operationally driven mass customisation with customised marketing in a way that empowers consumers to design the product and service offering of their choice.

* **Database Marketing:** The extensive use of data stored in electronic databases to better target marketing communications and more finely tune marketing messages for individual prospects at specific points in their lives and buying cycles. The information stored in the databases can come from internal sources (order entry systems, sales lead tracking systems, retail checkout scanners, accounts receivable systems, etc.) or outside sources such as third-party market research databases.

✳ **Decoy:** A name in a mail, telephone or email list placed solely for the purpose of tracking the use of the list to ensure that the list purchaser or renter does not break the sales or rental contract. The decoy person, household or organization either works for the list owner/broker or otherwise agrees to help by reporting any misuse. A similar term, "dummy", is a fictitious name included for this purpose. The process of including decoys or dummies is called "seeding" or "salting".

✳ **De-Dupe:** Eliminate any duplicate ("dupe") listings in a mail, telephone, e-mail list. This is not a trivial exercise since the listings may not be perfect duplicates. For example, one may carry a first initial while another carries full first and middle names; one may contain an old address while another contains the new one; etc.

✳ **Demographics:** Statistics denoting the personal and socioeconomic characteristics of a particular segment of the market. The statistics cover characteristics such as age, gender, income level, nationality, and religion.

✳ **Direct Digital Marketing:** A digital marketing method that provides relevant marketing communications that are addressable to a specific individual with an email address, a mobile phone number or a Web browser cookie. Traditional direct marketing uses an individual's postal address. With the evolution of direct marketing to direct digital marketing, addressability comes in the form of the three primary digital channels. Mailed advertising that is addressed to specific individuals rather than being dropped unaddressed and en masse to a whole geographic area.

✳ **Direct Marketing:** The targeting of marketing communications directly to individuals (typically a large number at a time) rather than through a mass media.

✳ **Discriminatory Pricing:** Despite the unfortunate choice of the term used to describe this practice it is not necessarily unethical or even politically incorrect. It is the practice of charging - or attempting to charge - different prices to different groups of customers, in order to earn the maximum revenue that each segment will bear. Surrogate variables must often be used to discriminate between groups. For example, an airline charges more when customers need flexible, refundable tickets or when they must fly on short notice and on specific dates. The assumption is that the majority of people who require tickets under these conditions are travelling for business reasons and will be willing to spend more for a ticket than someone travelling for pleasure. In other cases group assignment is specific, such as offering student prices under the assumption that students have less disposable income and therefore will be more likely to forgo the purchase if required to pay the full price. Also referred to as "price discrimination".

* **Display Ad:** An ad (typically, but not necessarily, box-shaped) that appears anywhere outside of the classified advertising section of a print publication.

* **Double Truck:** Print advertising that uses any two full side-by-side pages (not necessarily the centre ones, see "centre spread") in a publication.

* **Drive:** A strong internal stimulus impelling action.

* **Drive Time:** A radio term for the morning and evening rush hour time slots. These are considered prime times for radio listeners.

* **Drop amount:** Number of pieces mailed, number of impressions, mail volume contributed.

* **Dual Adaptation:** Adapting both the product and the communications to the local market.

* **Dumping:** Situations in which a company charges either less than its costs or less than it charges in its home market, in order to enter or win a market.

* **Duplicate Elimination:** Eliminate any duplicate listings in a mail, telephone, email list. This is not a trivial exercise since the listings may not be perfect duplicates. For example, one may carry a first initial while another carries full first and middle names; one may contain an old address while another contains the new one; etc.

* **Durability:** A measure of a product's expected operating life under natural of stressful conditions.

* **Early Adopters:** Those who are among the first to buy a new product or service, typically in a new product or service category, when it is launched.

* **E-Business:** The use of electronics means and platforms to conduct a company's business.

* **E-Commerce:** A company or site offers to transact or facilitate the selling of products and services online.

* **E-Purchasing:** Purchases of goods services, and information from various online suppliers.

* **Exchange:** The process of obtaining a desired product from someone by offering something in return.

* **Everyday Low Pricing (EDLP):** In retailing a constant low price with few by offering something in return.

* **Early Majority:** The large portion of the market that tends to adopt a new product or service (typically in a new product or service category) only after it has gained some level of acceptance and credibility in the market.

* **End Matter:** (Also called "back matter") Items placed after the main body of a document. Examples of end matter include appendices and indices.

* **Envelope Stuffer:** An advertising piece included in an envelope used primarily to deliver other business correspondence such as invoices, letters, etc.

* **Eye-Tracking:** An advertising research method that uses technology to track where on any ad a viewer's eyes fall in order to determine what first captures the viewer's attention and on which parts of the ad the reader spends the most time.

* **Expected Profit:** A set of attributes and conditions buyers normally expect when they purchase this product.

* **Experience Curve (Learning Curve):** A decline in the average cost with accumulated production experience.

* **Fact Sheet:** A document containing factual information about a product, service, company or event, without high-pressure sales or flowery language.

* **Fad:** A craze that is unpredictable, short lived, and without social, economic and political significance.

* **Family Brand:** Situation in which the parent brand is already associated with multiple products through brand extensions.

 ❋ **Family of Orientation:** Parents and siblings.

 ❋ **Features:** Things that enhance the basic function of a product.

 ❋ **Fill-In:** Information inserted into a form letter to personalise it. Examples may include the recipient's name, address or information about

 ❋ **Flighting:** The scheduling of advertising over time such that the amount of advertising varies according to a predetermined pattern, usually including some periods without any advertising.

 ❋ **Focus Group Discussion:** A qualitative market research technique. The researcher or research organization assembles a group of individuals who are representative of a target market. A moderator focuses discussions on a series of topics of interest to the research sponsor. If the target market consists of distinct segments, multiple focus groups, each consisting solely of representatives of a single segment, may be assembled to focus on reactions of that segment without the risk of influence by members of other segments.

 ❋ **Forecasting:** The art of anticipating what buyers are likely to do under a given set of conditions.

 ❋ **Form:** The size, shape, or physical structure of a product.

 ❋ **Four Color:** Artwork reproduced in full color.

 ❋ **Fractional Ad:** An ad that occupies less than a full page in a publication.

 ❋ **Freelancer:** A self-employed service provider.

 ❋ **Freestanding Insert:** Marketing literature (such as a brochure) that is delivered with a newspaper as an insert as opposed to being printed as part of the newspaper's regular pages.

 ❋ **Frequency:** The number of times that an individual or household sees a particular marketing message within a given timeframe.

 ❋ **Frequency Programmes (FPs):** Designed to provide rewards to customers who buy frequently and in substantial amounts.

❋ **Friend of a Brand:** The term refers to a particular situation when a brand (say-A) normally promotes another brand (say B) at its own cost; whereas the brand B doesn't show any favour to the company which is promoting it. Brand A which is promoting B is called the friend of B, for example, suppose there is a company which produces noodles especially for kids. Now, suppose they start giving any particular super hero comics or poster with every purchase of their brand. Now what will happen is that kids will go to buy noodles not because they want to have noodles, but because they want to get that poster or comics of that particular super hero. In this way, the noodles brand will get its sales increased and the super hero brand will also have its sale of comics increased. In this way, the super hero brand is not paying anything to the noodles company, but it is getting promoted by that. That is why the noodles company will be called as the friend of the super hero brand.

❋ **Front Matter:** Introductory and organisational material that comes before the main content of a document. Examples of front matter include: title page, table of contents, copyright material, publication data, etc.

❋ **Fulfilment House:** A company to which another company can outsource fulfilment processes, i.e. a company that fulfils orders or literature requests on behalf of another company. Also known as a fulfilment shop.

❋ **Fulfilment Piece:** Any marketing material that is sent in response to a reader, viewer or listener's request for more information.

❋ **Fulfilment Shop:** Also known as a fulfilment house.

❋ **Full Position Ad:** An ad that is surrounded on all sides by non-advertising reading material rather than filling a whole page or being placed next to another ad. Readers are more likely to read full position ads than ads that are isolated from the editorial material.

❋ **Galley Proof:** The "final" copy, used for proofreading purposes, of all of the pages of any material that will be professionally printed. Unless errors are found, the galley proof will appear exactly as the material will be printed in production.

❋ **Galvanometer:** An instrument that measures galvanic skin response—the electrical conductivity of the skin as produced by perspiration—to measure emotional arousal levels. Galvanometers are used in marketing research to measure the reaction to an advertisement by a subject in a study; i.e., does the ad interest/excite the subject.

* **Giveaway:** Promotional item given away to a prospective customer - typically at a trade show, conference or exhibition.

* **Global Formulation:** The process of developing specific goals for the planning period.

* **Global Industry:** An industry in which the strategic position of competitors in major geographic or national marketers are fundamentally affected by their overall global positions.

* **Going Rate Pricing:** Price based largely on competitors price.

* **Gray Marketing:** Branded products diverted from normal or authorised distributors channels in the country of product origin or across international borders.

* **Guerilla Marketing:** Coined by Jay Conrad Levinson, guerilla marketing usually refers to using innovative and aggressive tactics to market on a very small or even non-existent budget.

* **Gutter:** In bound documents, the gutter is the margin space closest to the binding

* **Harvest:** Reduce various costs and hope that sales hold up.

* **Hiatus:** A period of time during which advertising is not run.

* **Hickey:** (If you're not familiar with printing terminology, it's not what you think.) In printing, a spot or imperfection in the printing, due to dirt on the film, flakes in the ink, or any other cause.

* **High-Touch Service:** Customer service that includes a high level of personal (as opposed to automated, machine-based) interaction with customers.

* **High Low Pricing:** Charging higher prices on an everyday basis but then running frequent promotions and special sales.

✳ **Horizontal Publication:** A business publication targeted at individuals who share common interests, responsibilities or positions, regardless of the industry in which they work. An advertising agency that is owned and operated by the advertiser.

✳ **House List:** A mail, telephone or email list compiled and therefore owned by a company rather than being purchased or rented from a third party. (A list bought with a contract that allows unlimited use would, after purchase, become part of the purchaser's house list.)

✳ **House Organ:** A company-published newsletter or magazine.

✳ **Hybrid Channels:** Use of multiple channels of distribution to reach customers in a defined market.

✳ **Image:** The set of beliefs, ideas, and impressions a person holds regarding an object.

✳ **Image Advertising:** Rather than promoting a product or service's specific attributes, image advertising promotes an overall perception of a company, product or service. Image advertising is generally used to position a product relative to the competition. For example, to create an image of it as a luxury product.

✳ **Impression:** On the Web, an impression is counted when an ad is displayed once. If an ad has had 10 impressions that could be 10 times to the same person (likely on different pages of a site) or it could be 10 different people each seeing the ad once – or any combination that totals 10. In other media, an impression is counted when the ad is seen once by one person.

✳ **Industry:** A group of firms that offers a product or class of products that are close substitutes for one another.

✳ **Industrial Advertising:** Advertising of industrial goods and services to manufacturers.

✳ **Infomercial:** A television or radio commercial designed to look like a documentary or news story. The print or Web equivalent is known as an "advertorial".

✳ **Innovation:** Any good, service, or idea that is perceived by some one as new.

✳ **Insertion:** A single placement of an ad in a publication.

✳ **Insertion Order:** An advertiser's authorisation (often through the advertiser's ad agency) for a publisher to run an ad in a specific issue at the agreed upon rate.

✳ **Installation:** The work done to make a product operational in its planned location.

✳ **Institutional Market:** Schools, hospitals, nursing homes, prisons other institutions that must provide goods and services to people in their care.

✳ **Integrated Marketing Communication:** The use of a mix of all appropriate marketing communication disciplines, media and vehicles in a well coordinated campaign to achieve a unified objective or set of objectives.

✳ **Internal Branding:** Activities and processes that help to inform and inspire employees.

✳ **Interstitials:** Advertisements, often with video or animation, that pops up between changes on a website.

✳ **Island Display:** A point-of-purchase display away from competitive products, typically in the middle or at the end of an aisle.

✳ **Joint Demand:** Highly correlated demand for two different products. i.e., demand for Product A tends to increase when demand for Product B increases and demand for Product A tends to decrease when demand for Product B decreases. This occurs when the use of one product requires the use of the second product.

✳ **Joint Venture:** A company in which multiple investors share ownership and control.

✳ **Key Success Factors:** The factors that are a necessary condition for success in a given market. For example in a highly Hispanic market, a library to succeed would have Spanish language materials.

✳ **Knowledge:** Consumers' meanings or beliefs about products, brands, stores, that are stored in memory.

✳ **Laggards:** Those consumers who adopt the product/service as it reaches the end of its life cycle. They usually pay a competitive price for the benefit of waiting.

✳ **Leading:** The amount of space that appears between the lines within a paragraph (as opposed to the space between paragraphs) in a printed document (pronounced "ledding".)

✳ **Learning:** Changes in an individual's behaviour arising from experience.

✳ **Leave-Behind:** Any item that a sales person leaves with the prospective customer after a sales call. The leave-behind is intended to jog the prospect's memory about the sales call and the product or service being sold.

✳ **Letter Shop:** A firm that undertakes the production and mailing of sales letters and other marketing communication vehicles on other organisation's behalf rather than its own.

✳ **Lexicographic Heuristic:** Consumer choosing the best brand on the basis of its perceived most important attribute.

✳ **Life Cycle Cost:** The product's purchase cost plus the discounted cost of maintenance and repair less the discounted salvage value.

✳ **Lifestyle:** A person's pattern of living in the world as expressed in activities, interests and opinions.

✳ **Lifetime Value:** The net present value of all future purchases expected from a customer. ("Net present value" means that future sales are discounted to take into account the fact that a dollar received tomorrow is worth less than a dollar received today.)

✳ **Line Stretching:** A company lengthens its product line beyond its current range.

❋ **List Broker:** A company or individual who sells or rents mail, telephone or email lists. The lists may have been assembled by the broker or, more likely, by a third-party organization that uses the broker as its sales agent.

❋ **List Rental:** Rather than being purchased, mail, telephone and email lists are often rented for one-time use or a limited number of uses. Mailing, calling or emailing people on the list more than the specified number of times is a breach of contract. (If someone on the list responds to the initial campaign, the list renter is then considered to "own" that name and can then conduct unlimited communications with the person or organization.)

❋ **Logo:** A graphic element used to identify a company, product, service, or brand. The logo is typically trademarked to protect it from use by other companies.

❋ **Logo Merchandise:** A product (such as a T-shirt, baseball cap, pen, paper weight, etc.) displaying a logo or other promotional image. Sometimes jocularly (or occasionally disparagingly) referred to as "trinkets and trash." (synonym: advertising speciality.)

❋ **Logotype:** A company or brand name rendered in a specific graphical style and color. This differs from a logo, which is usually an icon representing the company or brand.

❋ **Long-term Memory:** A permanent repository of information.

❋ **Low-Touch Service:** Customer service that includes a low level of personal interaction with customers. This does not necessarily mean that there is little interaction with customers. A high level of interaction may occur through Web-based systems, vending machines or automated kiosks.

❋ **Loyalty:** A commitment to re-buy or re-patronise a preferred product or service.

❋ **Market Demand:** The total volume of a product that would be bought by a defined customer group in a defined geographical area in a defined time period in a defined marketing environment under a defined marketing program.

❋ **Market Forecast:** The market demand corresponding to the level of industry marketing expenditure.

* **Market Opportunity Analysis (MOA):** System used to determine the attractiveness and probability of success.

* **Market Partitioning:** The process of investigating the hierarchy of attributes consumers examine in choosing a brand if they use phased decisions strategies.

* **Market Penetration:** When talking about sales, market penetration is the percentage of customers in a particular market that buy the product/service/brand.

   When talking about the effectiveness of advertising or other promotions, market penetration is the percentage of the customers in a particular market who have been exposed to the company's messages.

* **Market Segment:** A subgroup of the total market defined by one or more characteristics. There are any number of ways to segment the market. Income, age, location, education affiliation to organisations and psychographics are just a few that apply to the consumer market. Common business market segmentation criteria include, among others, industry, company size (which may be defined by any available measure such as revenue, profit, number of employees, etc.) and job classification. Two or more characteristics can be used to define segments more precisely than a single characteristic (e.g., physicians with incomes over $300,000 living in the NYC area), however at some point the segments may become too small to target profitably.

* **Market Share:** The percentage of the total market for a product/service category that has been captured by a particular product/service or by a company that offers multiple products/services in that category. In the latter case, the company may choose to look at share on both an individual product/service basis and on a company-wide basis.

   Share can be calculated either on a unit basis (i.e., if a company sells 1 million units in a total market of 10 million units, it has a 10 percent share) or on a revenue basis (i.e., if a company sells $1 million worth of widgets in a $10 million market, it has a 10% share). Obviously, if a company is able to command a higher price for its product/service than its competitors, it would show a higher market share when calculated on a revenue basis than on a unit basis.

   Market share numbers can vary greatly depending on how the market is defined. For example, a company may have a 1 percent share of the "widget" market, 15 percent of the "sports widget market", 45 percent of the "luxury sports widget market" and 85% of a particular geographically defined luxury sports widget market.

* **Marketer:** Someone who seeks a response (attention, a purchase, a vote, a donation) from another party, called the prospect.

* **Marketing:** All business activities focused on developing, expanding and facilitating the profitable introduction and promotion of a company's products and/or services. Traditionally, this is taken to include the "4Ps" – Product, Price, Promotion and Place.

  - *Product* refers to discovering market requirements and ensuring that those requirements are reflected in the products and/or services offered by the company.
  - *Price* is obvious – determining and setting the most appropriate prices for the products/services.
  - *Promotion* refers to all activities involved in making potential customers aware of the company, its products and services and their benefits – and encouraging them to buy.
  - *Place* is a little less obvious. In addition to determining the best geographic areas to sell in, it also refers to the determination and management of the best "channels" for reaching those markets – direct sales, distributors, resellers, etc.

* **Marketing Audit:** A comprehensive, systematic, independent, and periodic examination of a company's or business unit's marketing environment objectives, strategies and activities.

* **Marketing Channel:** The term marketing channel is often used interchangeably with "sales channel" or "distribution channel", i.e. any individual or company used in making the subject company's products and/or services available to its customers. More specifically, a marketing channel would be any individuals or products through which the subject company conducts its marketing efforts.

* **Marketing Communications:** All strategies, tactics, and activities involved in getting the desired marketing messages to intended target markets, regardless of the media used.

* **Marketing Decision Support System:** A coordinated collection of data, system tools and techniques with supporting software and hardware by which an organisation gathers and interprets relevant information from business and the environment and turns it into a basis for marketing action.

* **Marketing Plan:** A plan – either standalone or a component of a larger business plan – that defines all aspects of the marketing strategy. Areas that the plan should cover include product pricing, promotion, messaging, channel strategies and an analysis of the competitive environment.

* **Markup:** Pricing an item by adding a standard increase to the product's cost.

✳ **Mass Marketing:** The distribution of marketing communications through mass media that, while often offering access to audiences with some common characteristics due to a shared interest in the content of the media vehicle, do not offer the ability to communicate with a specific individual, household or organisation.

✳ **Materials and Parts:** Goods that enter the manufacturer's product completely.

✳ **Mechanical:** Copy and graphics pasted onto a rigid board backing for reproduction by a printer.

✳ **Media Kit:** A package of information distributed by a media outlet to sell its advertising space. The kit typically includes information about the media vehicle, advertising rates, information about the audience it can deliver, mechanical specifications for ads, closing dates, etc.

✳ **Media Plan:** A plan providing clear definitions of the types media, specific media vehicles and media scheduling. The plan may be for a specific campaign or for all campaigns within a year. In addition, it may be a plan for a single product or service or for the whole company or division.

✳ **Media Release:** Information written by an organization and distributed to media outlets with the hope that they will incorporate the information into their news or other services. (The term is often used interchangeably with press release, however a media release implies a wider distribution – to all media outlets – than a press release.)

✳ **Media Selection:** Finding the most cost effective media to deliver the desired number and type of exposures to the target audience.

✳ **Mental Accounting:** The manner by which consumers code, categorise and evaluate financial outcomes of choices.

✳ **Merge/Purge:** A run of a computer application that merges multiple mail or telemarketing lists, possibly reconciling different formats on different lists, and purges any duplicates that either existed erroneously on one of the lists or that were a result of the same person appearing on multiple lists.

✳ **Micro-sales Analysis:** Examination of specific products and territories that fall to produce expected sales.

✳ **Minority Marketing:** Marketing that specifically addresses minority groups (not necessarily visible minorities) within a larger population.

✳ **Mission Statements:** Statements that an organisation develops to share with managers, employees and customers.

✳ **Mixed Bundling:** The seller offers goods both individually and in bundles.

✳ **Multi-channel Marketing:** A single firm uses two or more marketing channels to reach one or more customers segments.

✳ **Multitasking:** Doing two or more things at the same time.

✳ **Mystery Shopper:** Someone who is paid by a company to pose as a regular shopper in order to be exposed to the normal shopping experience in a company's stores and report back to the company on the quality of that experience. Obviously, to form an unbiased view of the normal shopping experience, the people working in the store should not be aware of the mystery shopper's identity or purpose.

Mystery shoppers are typically employed to test the shopping experience at the sponsor's stores, but they could also be used to analyse the shopping experience at competitors' stores.

✳ **Narrowcasting:** The use of broadcast media to target very narrow interests (such as a cable channel dedicated exclusively to trout fishing).

✳ **Nesting:** Embedding one enclosure inside another before inserting it into an envelope.

✳ **Neuromarketing:** The use of brain-mapping technologies, such as functional Magnetic Resonance Imaging (fMRI) and Quantitative Electroencephalography (QEEG), to study brain activity that occurs in response to stimuli such as buying decisions or exposure to advertising images and messaging. This is believed to provide more accurate insight into people's psychological reactions to these stimuli and, hence, their actions in buying situations because:

  – People can't always verbalise their feelings and thoughts in accurate, unambiguous ways.

- People's conscious thoughts are sometimes contrary to their subconscious thoughts and emotions, but those subconscious thoughts and emotions influence their actions.

- Many people lie if they think that expressing their true feelings will make them appear foolish or politically incorrect.

❊ **News Release:** News information written by an organization and distributed to media outlets, with the hope that they will use it as the basis of a written news story. (The term is essentially synonymous with "press release".)

❊ **Non-compensatory Models:** In consumer choice, when consumers do not simultaneously consider all positive and negative attribute considerations in making a decision.

❊ **Non-Price Analysis:** Analysis that encompasses company list price, average discount, promotional spending and co-op advertising to arrive at net price.

❊ **Nonresponse Error:** When doing market research using surveys, some people will be unreachable, such as people without a phone when conducting the survey over the phone, people with only a cell phone when conducting a phone survey in a jurisdiction that does not allow you to call cell phones, or people who are never home during the hours you call. Gregarious people are out more often and, therefore, less reachable. People who are more into modern technologies are probably more highly represented among the group of people who only have cell phones and not landlines (except in developing countries where cell phones are a way of getting around the absence in wired lines).

In addition, some people will simply refuse to answer your survey. The same character traits that led them to refuse to answer your survey may have affected their responses if they had in fact responded.

These groups of nonresponders will be, at best, underrepresented or, possibly, unrepresented in your survey results, meaning the results will not be a reflection of the entire market. This error is known as nonresponse error.

❊ **Objectives:** The desired or needed result to be achieved by a specific time. An objective is more specific than a goal, and one objective can be broken down into a number of specific actions.

✳ **Observation:** A method of data collection in which the situation of interest is watched and the relevant facts, actions and behaviours are recorded. This is an important area of library use which is usually uncounted–what people are actually doing in the library e.g., browsing, using the computer, reading to a child, etc.

✳ **Opinion:** A belief or emotionally neutral cognition the individual holds about some aspect or object in the environment.

✳ **Ordinal Scale:** A measurement in which numbers are assigned to attributes of objects of classes of objects to reflect the order.

✳ **Organisation:** A company's structures, polices and corporate culture.

✳ **Organisational Buying:** The decision-making process by which formal organisations establishes the need for purchased products and services and identify, evaluate and choose among alternative brands and suppliers.

✳ **Output Evaluation:** An objective measure of use performance, such as circulation per capita of a library population, reference transactions per capita, etc.

✳ **Overall Market Share:** The company's sales expressed as a percentage of total market sales.

✳ **Patronage Motives:** The motives that drive an individual/user toward selection of a particular outlet, retailer, or supplier of services.

✳ **Penetrated Market:** Actual set of users actually consuming the product/service (Kotler).

✳ **Per Capita Income:** A nation's or other geographic market's total income divided by the number of persons in its population.

✳ **Perception:** Perception is the cognitive impression that is formed of "reality" which in turn influences the individual's actions and behavior toward that object.

✳ **Personal Income:** The current income received by persons from all sources less contributions for social insurance–e.g., Social Security (US).

❋ **Personal Interview:** A direct, face-to-face conversation between a representative of the research organization (the interviewer) and a respondent or interviewee.

❋ **Personality:** Consistent pattern of responses to the stimuli from both internal and external sources.

❋ **Physical Inventory:** An inventory determined by actual count and evidenced by a listing of quantity, weight, or measure. Number of volumes, periodicals, videos a library owns.

❋ **Place:** In the channels of distribution, the physical facilities point of location (book-mobiles, branches, etc.)

❋ **Point-of-Purchase:** Promotional materials placed at the contact sales point designed to attract user interest or call attention to a special offer, e.g., 'Sign up for Summer Reading Program.'

❋ **Point-of-Sale (PoS):** A data collection system that electronically receives and stores bar code information derived from a sales transaction. This could be the zip codes for library users, facilitating the library in determining geographic market are that users reside in.

❋ **Population:** The totality of cases that conforms to some designated specifications.

❋ **Positioning:** *(see)* Product Positioning

❋ **Potential Market:** Set of users who profess some level of interest in a designed market offer (Kotler).

❋ **Poverty Level:** The poverty level is based solely on money income and updated every year to reflect changes in the consumer price index, used to classify families as being above or below the poverty level.

❋ **Pre-Industrialised Country:** Characteristics: (i) low literacy rates and high percentage of employment in agriculture; (ii) low population density and low degree of urbanisation; (iii) linguistic heterogeneity and a small percentage of working age population; (iv) industrial sectors nonexistent and undeveloped; (v) heavy reliance on foreign sources for all manufacturers and principal engagement in agricultural endeavours.

* **Press Conference:** A convening of media by a person or organization to explain, announce or expand on a particular subject.

* **Price:** The formal ratio that indicates the quantities of money goods or services needed to acquire a given quantity of goods or services. For a library user price may come in the form of time the library users must expend to obtain library materials or services.

* **Private Sector:** Activities outside the public sector that are independent of government control, usually, but not always carried on for a profit.

* **Product:** A bundle of attributes or features, functions, benefits and uses capable of exchange, usually in tangible or intangible forms. The library's products include materials to use, questions answered, story hours, online searching, etc.

* **Product Life Cycle:** The four stages products go through from birth to death: introductory, growth, maturity, and decline.

* **Product Mix:** The full set of products offered by an organization e.g., books, videos, story hours, etc.

* **Product Positioning:** The way users/consumers view competitive brands or types of products. This can be manipulated by the organization/library. The library's video collection, available for free, is competitive with local video stores that charge, if video collections are comparable. If the collections are not, the library is differentiating the video collection from the video store.

* **Promotion Mix:** The various communication techniques such as advertising, personal selling, sales promotion, and public relations/ product publicity available to the marketer to achieve specific goals. A library may use a combination of newspaper editorial, public service announcements (PSAs) on radio and possible television, if no budget is available for advertising.

* **Psychographic Analysis:** A technique that investigates how people live, what interests them, what they like–also called lifestyle analysis or AIO because it relies on a number of statements about a person's activities, interests and opinions.

* **Psychographic Segmentation:** Dividing markets into segments on the basis of consumer life styles.

* **Public Opinion:** The consensus view of a population on a topic.

✻ **Public Policy:** A course of action pursued by the government pertaining to people as a whole on which laws rest.

✻ **Public Relations:** The form of communication management that seeks to make use of publicity and other nonpaid forms of promotion and information to influence feelings, opinions or beliefs about the agency/library and its offerings. This is a traditional form of communication for library management, as paid advertising media is rarely used.

✻ **Public Sector:** Those marketing activities that are a carried out by government agencies for public service rather than for profit.

✻ **Public Service Announcement (PSA):** An advertisement or commercial that is carried by an advertising vehicle at no cost as a public service to its readers, viewers, or listeners. While the no-cost aspect is appealing, a library or other agency utilizing this media quickly realises there is no control on the most effective time of placement.

✻ **Publics:** The groups of people that have an actual or possible interest in or impact on the company's efforts to achieve its goals.

✻ **Purchase Probability Scale:** A scale to measure the probability of a buyer making a particular purchase.

✻ **Pure Bundling:** A firm only offers its products as a bundle.

✻ **Pure-Click:** Companies that have launched a website without any previous existence as a firm.

✻ **Push Strategy:** When the manufacturer uses its sales force and trade promotion money to induce intermediate to carry, promote and sell the product to end users.

✻ **Quality Control** An ongoing analysis of operations, to verify goods or service meet specified standards, or to better answer customer/user complaints. Libraries have been criticised for not employing more quality control standards on library services.

✻ **Quality of Life:** Sometimes measured by income, wealth, safety, recreation and education facilities, education health, aesthetics, leisure time and the like.

❋ **Quantity Discount:** A reduction in price for volume purchases.

❋ **Questionnaire:** A document that is used to guide what questions are to be asked from respondents and in what order, sometimes lists the alternative responses that are acceptable. An excellent research instrument for libraries to assess customer satisfaction on exit interviews.

❋ **Range:** The maximum distance a consumer is ordinarily willing to travel for a good or service; as such it determines the outer limit of a store/library's market area. Research in the library field indicate there is an average two mile limit for a library user to travel to a branch, while for a central library with specialised good, it may widen to even 10 or 15 miles. This research does not allow for the travel limitations imposed by culture, age, or physical handicap, or topographical barriers.

❋ **Reach:** The number of people or households exposed to a particular advertising media or media schedule during a specified time.

❋ **Reference Group:** A group that the individual tends to use as the anchor point for evaluating his/her own beliefs and attitudes. Teenagers influence their peers regarding library use.

❋ **Regression Analysis:** A statistical technique to derive an equation that relates a single, continuous criterion variable to one or more continuous predictor variables.

❋ **Reilly's Law:** A model used in trade area analysis to define the relative ability of two cities to attract users from the area between them.

❋ **Reliability:** A measure of the probability that a product will not malfunction or fail within a specified time period.

❋ **Representativeness Heuristic:** When consumers base their predictions on how representative or similar an outcome is to other examples.

❋ **Respondent:** A person who is asked for information using either written or verbal questioning, typically employing a questionnaire to guide the questioning.

❋ **Risk Analysis:** A method by which possible rates of returns and their probabilities are calculated by obtaining estimates for uncertain variables affecting profitability.

✳ **Roles:** The behavior that is expected of people in standard situations.

✳ **Rural Population:** The part of the total population not classified as urban.

✳ **Salary:** Compensation paid periodically to a person independent of performance (in sales or levels of use stimulated).

✳ **Sample:** The selection of a subset of elements from a larger group of objects.

✳ **Sample Survey:** A cross-sectional study in which the sample is selected to be representative of the target population and in which the emphasis is on the generation of summary statistics such as averages and percentages.

✳ **Scanner:** An electronic device that automatically reads imprinted codes, as the product is pulled across the scanner. The library field is successfully using these for circulation and other use counts.

✳ **Secondary Shopping District:** A cluster of stores outside the central business district that serves a large population within a section or part of a large city.

✳ **Segmentation:** (*see*) Market Segmentation.

✳ **Self-Concept:** The ideas, attitudes, and perceptions people have about themselves.

✳ **Self-Service:** The type of operation in which the customer/user is exposed to merchandise (browsing and self-selection) without assistance, unless customer/user seeks assistance.

✳ **Selling Orientation (Wood):** A company-centred rather than a client-centred approach to conduct of business. This orientation tends to ignore what the customer/user really wants and needs.

✳ **Service(s):** Products such as a bank loan or home security or library loans, that are intangible or at least substantially so.

✳ **Shopping Good:** Goods and products can be classified as convenience, shopping or speciality. A shopping good is one that more time is spent selecting (browsing) than a quick convenience good. Example, a certain type of mystery book.

* **Situation Analysis (SWOT):** An examination of the internal factors of a library to identify strengths and weaknesses, and the external environment to identify opportunities and threats.

* **Slogan:** The verbal or written portion of an advertising message that summarises the main idea in a few memorable words–a tag line.

* **Social Advertising:** The advertising designed to education or motivate target audiences to undertake socially desirable actions.

* **Social Class:** A status hierarchy by which groups and individuals are classified on the basis of esteem and prestige.

* **Social Indicator:** The data and information that facilitate the evaluation of how well a society or institution is doing.

* **Speciality Advertising:** The placement of advertising messages on a wide variety of items of interest to the target markets such as calendars, coffee cups, pens, hats, note paper, TT-shirts, etc. These are widely given out to librarians at professional conferences from vendors. Libraries may use these items as well, but are usually sold in library gift shops.

* **Speciality Good:** A speciality good is one that users/consumers will spend more time searching for, and time travelling to and pay higher for. A library speciality good could be a certain online service or special collection of materials.

* **Stakeholder:** One of a group of publics with which a company must be concerned. Key stakeholders for a library could be users, employees, board members, vendors or other who have a relationship with the library.

* **Store Layout:** The interior layout of the store/library for the ease of user movement through the store to provide maximum exposure of good and attractive display. Retail store layout, is also successfully applicable to library layout.

* **Strategic Market Planning:** The planning process that yields decisions in how a business unit can best compete in the markets it elects to serve. The strategic plan is based upon the totality of the marketing process.

* **Style:** A product's look and feel to the buyer.

* **Sub-Brand:** A new brand combined with an existing brand.

* **Subculture:** The segments within a culture that share distinguishing meanings, values, and patterns of behavior that differ from those of the overall culture. These subcultures are important to recognise in library communities that may serve a disproportionate number, whose information needs may be nontraditional and unique.

* **Subliminal Perception:** A psychological view that suggests that attitudes and behaviours can be changed by stimuli that are not consciously perceived.

* **Super-Segment:** A set of segments sharing some exploitable similarity.

* **Supplies and Business Services:** Short term goods and services that facilitates developing or managing the finished product.

* **Supply Chain Management:** Procuring the right inputs converting them efficiently into finished products and dispatching to the final destinations.

* **Target market:** The particular segment of a total population on which the retailer focuses its merchandising expertise to satisfy that sub market in order to accomplish its profit objectives. Or for the library, a target market might be within the market area served, children 5-8 years old, for summer reading programs, to increase juvenile use and registration.

* **Target Market Identification:** The process of using income, demographic, and life style characteristics of a market and census information for small areas to identify the most favourable locations.

* **Technology:** The purposeful application of scientific knowledge; an environmental force that consists of inventions and innovations from applied scientific and engineering research.

* **Telephone Interview:** A telephone conversation between a representative of the research organization, the interviewer, and a respondent or interviewee.

* **Total Cost:** The sum of the fixed and variable costs for any given level of production.

* **Total Costing:** Deduction the desired profit margin from the price at which a product will sell, given its appeal and competitors prices.

✳ **Total Customer Value:** The perceived monetary value of the bundle of economic, functional and psychological benefits customers expect from a given market offering.

✳ **Tracking Studies:** Collecting information from consumers on a routine basis over time.

✳ **Transaction:** In the case of values between two or more parties. A give X to B and receives Y in return.

✳ **Transfer:** In the case of gifts, subsidies and charitable contributions A gives X to B but does not receive anything tangible in return.

✳ **Two-Part Pricing:** A fixed fee plus a variable usage fee.

✳ **Typing Agreements:** Agreement in which producers of strong brands sell their products to dealers only if dealers purchase related products or services, such as other products in the brand line.

✳ **Underdeveloped Country:** Characteristics: small factories erected to supply batteries, tires, footwear, clothing, building materials and packaged foods; agricultural activity declines and degree of urbanisation increases; available educational effort expands and literacy rises.

✳ **Underprivileged Family:** A family in social class that does not have enough money to purchase the necessities, i.e., shelter, clothing and transportation, appropriate for its class status.

✳ **Unit Control:** The control of stock in terms of merchandise units rather than in terms of dollar value. This is representative of the number of books, magazines, etc of a library collection.

✳ **Unsought Goods:** That consumer does not know about or does not normally think of buying, like smoke detectors.

✳ **Urban Population:** Persons living in places of 2,500 or more inhabitants incorporated as cities, villages, boroughs, or areas designated as such by the US Census, with some exceptions.

❋ **Utility:** The state or quality of being useful. What is the utility of marketing practices to the library field?

❋ **VALS (values and lifestyles):** An acronym standing for values and life styles. VALS is a psychographic segmentation approach developed at Stanford Research Institute International. This data is useful to public and private sector. Unfortunately, the data is still largely expensive, therefore, libraries and other non-profits still widely rely on demographics.

❋ **Value:** The power of any good to command other goods in peaceful and voluntary exchange.

❋ **Values:** The beliefs about the important life goals that consumers are trying to achieve. The important enduring ideals or beliefs that guide behavior within a culture or for a specific person.

❋ **Variety:** The number of different classifications of goods carried in a particular merchandising unit. How many different children's authors are represented in the juvenile collection?

❋ **Vicarious Learning:** The changes in an individuals behavior brought about by observing the actions of others and the consequences of those actions. Research indicates that immigrant adults often learn about the reading land library habit through their children's same experiences at school.

❋ **Viral Marketing:** Using the Internet to create word of mouth effects to support marketing efforts and goals.

❋ **Vision:** A guiding theme that articulates the nature of the business/library and its intentions for the future, based upon how management believes the environment will unfold. A vision is informed, share, competitive and enabling.

❋ **Wants:** The wishes, needs, cravings, demands or desires of human beings.

* **Wealth:** The aggregate of all possessions of economic good owned by a person.

* **Will-Call:** The products ordered by customers/users in advance of the time delivery desired. Books on reserve.

* **Word of Mouth Communication(WOM):** This occurs when people share information about products or promotions with friends–research indicate WOM is more likely to be negative.

* **Workroom:** A service department such as apparel alterations, drapery manufacture, library materials processing.

* **Yield Pricing:** Situation in which companies offer (i) Discounted buy limited early purchases, (ii) Higher priced late purchases and (iii) The lowest rates on unsold inventory just before it expires.

* **Zapping:** The use of a television remote control to switch channels in order to avoid watching commercials.

* **Zero Level Channel:** A manufacturer selling directly to the final customers.

* **Zipping:** Fast-forwarding through commercials when playing back a pre-recorded program on a VCR.

* **ZIP code:** A geographical classification system developed by the U.S. government for mail distribution, a nested numeric range of 5 to 9 numbers.

APPENDIX - C
CURRENCY SYMBOLS

Country and Currency	Currency Code	Graphic Image	Code 2000
America (United States of America), Dollars	USD	$	$
Argentina, Pesos	ARS	$	$
Aruba, Guilders (also called Florins)	AWG	ƒ	ƒ
Australia, Dollars	AUD	$	$
Bahamas, Dollars	BSD	$	$
Barbados, Dollars	BBD	$	$
Belgium, Francs (obsolete)	BEF	₣	₣
Belize, Dollars	BZD	$	$
Bermuda, Dollars	BMD	$	$

Bolivia, Bolivianos	BOB	$	$
Brazil, Reais	BRL	R$	R$
Brazil, Cruzeiros (obsolete)	BRC	₢	₢
Britain (United Kingdom), Pounds	GBP	£	£
Brunei Darussalam, Dollars	BND	$	$
Cambodia, Riels	KHR	៛	
Canada, Dollars	CAD	$	$
Cayman Islands, Dollars	KYD	$	$
Chile, Pesos	CLP	$	$
China, Yuan Renminbi	CNY	元	
Colombia, Pesos	COP	₱	
Costa Rica, Colón	CRC	₡	₡
Cuba, Pesos	CUP	₱	
Cyprus, Pounds	CYP	£	£

Denmark, Kroner	DKK	kr	kr
Dominican Republic, Pesos	DOP	₱	
East Caribbean, Dollars	XCD	$	$
Egypt, Pounds	EGP	£	£
El Salvador, Colón	SVC	₡	₡
England (United Kingdom), Pounds	GBP	£	£
Euro	EUR	€	€
European Currency Unit (obsolete)	XEU	₠	₠
Falkland Islands, Pounds	FKP	£	£
Fiji, Dollars	FJD	$	$
France, Francs (obsolete)	FRF	₣	₣
Gibraltar, Pounds	GIP	£	£
Greece, Drachmae (obsolete)	GRD	Dρ	Dρ
Guernsey, Pounds	GGP	£	£

Guyana, Dollars	GYD	$	$
Holland (Netherlands), Guilders (also called Florins) (obsolete)	NLG	ƒ	*ƒ*
Hong Kong, Dollars (General written use)	HKD	$	$
Hong Kong, Dollars (BOC notes)	HKD	圓	
Hong Kong, Dollars (SCB notes)	HKD	圓	
Hong Kong, Dollars (HSBC notes)	HKD	元	
India, Rupees	INR	₹	₹
Iran, Rials	IRR	﷼	
Ireland, Punt (obsolete)	IEP	£	£
Isle of Man, Pounds	IMP	£	£
Israel, New Shekels	ILS	₪	₪
Italy, Lire (obsolete)	ITL	£	£
Jamaica, Dollars	JMD	$	$
Japan, Yen	JPY	¥	¥

Jersey, Pounds	JEP	£	£
Korea (North), Won	KPW	₩	₩
Korea (South), Won	KRW	₩	₩
Laos, Kips	LAK	₭	₭
Lebanon, Pounds	LBP	£	£
Liberia, Dollars	LRD	$	$
Luxembourg, Francs (obsolete)	LUF	₣	₣
Malta, Liri	MTL	£	£
Mauritius, Rupees	MUR	Rs	Rp
Mexico, Pesos	MXN	$	$
Mongolia, Tugriks	MNT	₮	₮
Namibia, Dollars	NAD	$	$
Nepal, Rupees	NPR	Rs	Rp
Netherlands Antilles, Guilders (also called Florins)	ANG	ƒ	ƒ

Netherlands, Guilders (obsolete)	NLG	ƒ	ƒ
New Zealand, Dollars	NZD	$	$
Nigeria, Nairas	NGN	₦	₦
North Korea, Won	KPW	₩	₩
Oman, Rials	OMR	﷼	
Pakistan, Rupees	PKR	₨	Rp
Peru, Nuevos Soles	PEN	S/.	S/.
Philippines, Pesos	PHP	₱	
Qatar, Rials	QAR	﷼	
Russia, Rubles	RUB	руб	руб
Saint Helena, Pounds	SHP	£	£
Saudi Arabia, Riyals	SAR	﷼	
Seychelles, Rupees	SCR	₨	Rp
Singapore, Dollars	SGD	$	$

Solomon Islands, Dollars	SBD	$	$
South Africa, Rand	ZAR	R	R
South Korea, Won	KRW	₩	₩
Spain, Pesetas (obsolete)	ESP	₧	Pts
Sri Lanka, Rupees	LKR	₨	Rp
Sweden, Kronor	SEK	kr	kr
Suriname, Dollars	SRD	$	$
Syria, Pounds	SYP	£	£
Taiwan, New Dollars	TWD	元	
Thailand, Baht	THB	฿	฿
Trinidad and Tobago, Dollars	TTD	$	$
Turkey, New Lira	TRY	£	£
Turkey, Liras	TRL	£	£
Tuvalu, Dollars	TVD	$	$

United Kingdom, Pounds	GBP	£	£
United States of America, Dollars	USD	$	$
Uruguay, Pesos	UYU	₱	
Vatican City, Lire (obsolete)	VAL	£	£
Vietnam, Dong	VND	đ	đ
Yemen, Rials	YER	ريال	
Zimbabwe, Dollars	ZWD	$	$

Source: http://www.etem.de

INDEX